and Societies

of **AFRICA**

EDITED, WITH A GENERAL INTRODUCTION, COMMENTARIES,
AND NOTES, BY Simon AND Phoebe Ottenberg

RANDOM HOUSE   NEW YORK

AFRICA

Meek

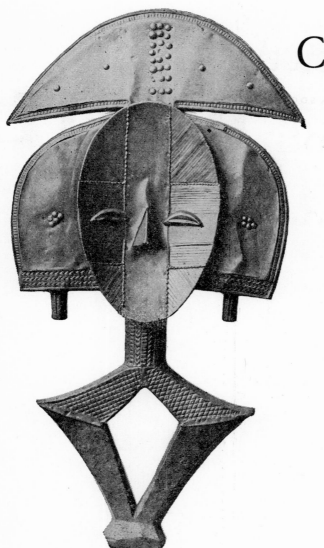

PREFACE

This collection of readings has grown out of our long-standing interest in African anthropology and our desire to fill the need, felt in our teaching experience, for a collection of readings on Africa suitable for use in American colleges and universities. The quality of anthropological writing on Africa is high, and selecting the articles to be included was not easy. We hope that the readings we did choose will constitute a true reflection of the anthropological research that has been done on Africa south of the Sahara and that they will indicate some of the main types of approaches and analyses used in African studies today.

First we wish to acknowledge the kindness of the authors and publishers who have permitted us to reprint their writings. To those who first turned our attention to Africa as an area for anthropological research, particularly Dr. Melville J. Herskovits and Dr. William R. Bascom, we owe a deep debt of gratitude. We wish to thank all those who have given so freely of their ideas and time in discussing the reader, but particularly Dr. Edgar V. Winans. Without the assistance of the Library Committee and of the librarians of the University of Washington, this book would not have been possible. Thanks are also due to Miss Ailsa Currie, Miss Ruth Jones, and other members of the staff and library of the International African Institute who so ably facilitated the handling of many details; to the librarians of the Royal Anthropological Institute for their helpfulness; to Miss Maureen Connors for her contributions to the map indicating the tribes discussed in the reader; and to Dr. Verne F. Ray for technical aid. We are also indebted to Colin M. Turnbull, Morton H. Fried, and Joseph H. Greenberg, for valuable advice. Mr. Charles D. Lieber has been of great help in guiding the preparation of the manuscript, and we wish to thank Mrs. Leonore Crary Hauck for editing the manuscript and seeing it through its final stages.

CONTENTS

3

Social Groupings

4

Authority and Government

5

Values, Religion, and Aesthetics

6

Culture Contact and Change

1

Introduction

AFRICA AND ITS PEOPLES

Since World War II Africa has become one of the major areas of world interest. Every day we read of African nationalism, political agitation, economic development schemes, and military bases in the newspapers, magazines, and books. Race relations in South Africa and uprisings in central Africa have become matters of world-wide concern. We are increasingly conscious of African problems and argue their possible solutions. Yet we often lack the kind of knowledge that it is imperative we should have—knowledge of the traditional way of life of African peoples, their social groupings and culture. African customs and values play an important role in what is happening in the "dark continent" today, yet it is precisely of these that we often have the least accurate information. There is a tendency, even among scholars, to think that because traditional African culture is changing, it is of little scientific importance: since Africa is rapidly becoming westernized, its traditional life need not be studied.

Yet Africa, like India, will probably never become wholly westernized. Its characteristic social patterns, ideologies, and customs are changing and will change in the future, but they will continue to play an important role. Western ideologies are being accepted by Africans, but not without changes in their meanings and content. This book is not primarily concerned with present-day social change in Africa; rather, it focuses on traditional African society and culture in order to give a fuller picture of African life and a better background for understanding the present changes.

Since the early years of European contact, a number of myths have grown up concerning Africa. One of the most unfortunate of these is the belief that it was an area of little change, of static societies, of a kind of cultural stagnation, in the days preceding European colonial rule. The African is thought of as living the same life his ancestors lived many generations before. There is also the implication that since he is not accustomed to change, the process of westernization will necessarily take a very long time. Actually, the entire history of the African continent has been one of change, and in thinking about African cultures we need to have an awareness of the many changes they have undergone. Though these have often been in different directions from those of our own civilization, they are nevertheless significant.

Another myth is that all African cultures are basically alike. While it is true that there are elements common to the social life of many African groups, there are also differences. African societies range from small family groupings to large states and kingdoms, from societies that are almost com-

3

pletely self-sufficient to those with well-developed economic systems and extensive trade, from peoples whose art is crude or virtually nonexistent to those whose work is of the finest quality. Indeed, one of the essential problems facing African nations as they emerge today is that of cultural and linguistic diversity.

What is the extent of our knowledge of African social life? For Egypt and North Africa we have detailed information derived from archaeological research, and a rich historical record going back to pre-Christian times. Travelers, explorers, settlers, and administrators have left us important materials, and valuable Arabic documents exist, though these have not been fully exploited by social scientists. Anthropological research on the social life and culture of the North African has never been extensive. In some ways we know more about the Egyptian in ancient times than we do about his life today. Anthropological knowledge of the Saharan peoples is even scantier.

For Africa south of the Sahara, the main focus of this book, the picture is somewhat different. All we have for some peoples are occasional brief references in government reports or perhaps a short word list or dictionary; for other groups we have good general accounts. Among our best sources from about 1880 to 1930 are the works of missionaries, such as the writings of Junod on the Thonga. Some of the early missionaries, though they had no formal training, were "natural" anthropologists. From the same period come a number of fine reports by government officials, such as the works of Rattray on the Ashanti and of administrators in the German colonies before World War I. These men felt that it was impossible to govern a people without knowing something of their way of life, and they had a scientist's curiosity about cultures different from their own.

Although some African research was also done at this time by anthropologists, most of them focused in other directions—the British on the Pacific and southern Asia, the Americans on the American Indian, while the French did not yet have a strong tradition of field work. Anthropology during this period was developing as a science, and there were few professional workers in the field.

Since 1930 few first-rate anthropological reports on Africa have been written by government officials or missionaries—both of whom have become enmeshed in administrative organization and programs—and explorers' accounts have, on the whole, been replaced by the more trivial records of travelers and tourists. During this time, however, anthropology has grown greatly in the sophistication of its ideas and in the number of its practitioners, and Africa has become one of its main centers of interest. African cultures, unlike those of many American Indian or Pacific Island groups, are still relatively well-functioning wholes, and there have been relatively few barriers to field work on this continent. The last thirty years have seen a great increase in African research, some of which has had a marked effect on anthropological theory. Some anthropologists have also been concerned with practical administrative problems during this time and have been employed by colonial governments to investigate such problems as traditional political organization, land tenure, and urban growth.

British anthropologists particularly have emphasized studies of African kinship and political organization and have developed a strong sociological approach in their anthropological analyses. They have produced a large number of monographs in recent years. The French, working mainly in French West Africa, have emphasized religious beliefs and cosmology. American and Belgian anthropologists have been eclectic, dealing with a broad variety of subjects. In recent years scholars of African birth have increasingly turned their attention to the study of African culture and history, and have published some fine studies. A number of novels with an African setting have also appeared, most of them poor in their representation of traditional life, but a few rich in the kinds of insights into African thought and feeling that are sometimes lacking in the formal anthropological monograph.

This collection of readings is prepared at a time when much research is in progress and when important gaps exist in our knowledge of Africa. It does not undertake to give a complete coverage; rather, its purpose is to provide an introduction to the anthropology of Africa south of the Sahara and to show the range of African social and cultural forms.

TOPOGRAPHY AND PEOPLES

The topography of Africa has been important in determining the location and movement of peoples, and the communication between different groups. The continent consists primarily of a succession of plateaus with elevations roughly from 1,000 to 4,000 feet above sea level. Since these often end abruptly, close to the coast or directly at the shore itself, lowland coastal areas are generally not extensive.

This kind of topography favors large inland water basin areas that feed into long rivers. Two of the largest basins are those of the upper Niger and the Congo. The former feeds the Niger River, some 2,600 miles long, cutting through several climatic areas of West Africa; the latter includes a large interior tropical forest area and drains into the 3,000-mile-long Congo River. There is also a basin in the East African Lakes area and another in the upper Nile region, both of which feed the Nile River. Other major basins include the Chad in the central Sudan, draining into the Shari River and eventually into Lake Chad (which has no outlet), and the Northern Kalahari basin, which drains into the Zambezi River in south central Africa.

All the rivers tend to be sluggish and to overflow their banks. They are also characterized by sudden cataracts or waterfalls at points where the river drops down to a lower level.

Before the coming of Europeans these rivers were fairly important channels of trade and communication (they have not, however, proved profitable for large European ships because of their shallowness and sudden falls). Friction between groups controlling or attempting to control sections of the waterways seems to have been continual in pre-European days although one tribe or group rarely dominated large stretches of water for very long. However, the most important trade routes were over land. African use of rivers for trade increased greatly after European control of the river areas and after the development of ports along the coast.

Although many Africans lived along the rivers, fishing and trading up and down them by canoe, and trading fresh and dried fish into nonriver areas, the traditional African cultures did not seem to focus strongly on the rivers. Nor was there a well-developed lake fishing culture. Extensive lakes are rare in Africa, consisting mainly of Lake Chad, a low swampy body of water, and a series of lakes in East Africa (including Lakes Nyasa, Tanganyika, Albert, and Rudolf) associated with the Great Rift, a broad valley that cuts north to the Red Sea and south to Mozambique. The Rift (which in many places is miles across and in some areas has precipitous sides as high as 2,000 feet) opens like a funnel at its northern extremities into the Red Sea and the Gulf of Aden. For about a thousand years, it has been a route for southward population movement, with groups in some cases spreading out into the surrounding plateau areas as well.

The coastal areas, except in northern Africa, were not settled intensively by Africans in pre-European times; and, indeed, one of the results of culture contact has been the movement of Africans to the developing coastal urban centers. Most of the better agricultural and herding areas were found inland, and fishing along the coast was not highly developed, perhaps because in many parts of coastal Africa the sea bottom drops off so sharply close to shore, that there are few ocean banks where fish are plentiful. Africans south of the Sahara did not evolve boat forms more complex than the wooden canoe, and it was probably the Arabs who introduced the sailing vessel to East Africa many centuries ago.

There are several important mountain ranges, but they have not, on the whole, formed barriers to the communication between peoples. The Atlas Mountains in the northwest, geologically a continuation of the mountains of Spain and the Alps, were never a major obstacle, and today, as in the past, herders and farmers pass through and about them without great difficulty. In East Africa a range of high plateaus, the Ethiopian Highlands, and to the south the East African Highlands, capped by such well-known mountains as Kilimanjaro and Kenya, are geographically not sharply demarcated from the surrounding areas; and though some of the country is rugged, it is no real barrier to the movement of peoples. The mountainous ranges of the Central Sahara—the Tibesti and the Ahaggar —are little-known areas that permit some farming and pastoralism. To this day some of the important north-south trans-Saharan trade routes pass through or near these mountains. The Cameroons range in West Africa was not high or rugged enough to bar contacts across it. The only other important range, the Cape Mountains along the tip of South Africa, was a relatively isolated and underpopulated section until European contact.

The three major desert areas of Africa, which may have been more effective than the mountains in limiting human movement, are sparsely populated. Two of them, however, the Kalahari in southwest Africa, and the Somali Desert along the southern edge of the East Horn (which includes Ethiopia, Eritrea, and the Somali area), never lay in the path of major population movements. The numerous migrations in the section of the Great Rift in the Horn area seem to have passed north and west of the Somali Desert, with peoples filtering into the desert from the "funnel" of the Rift along the coast. The great migrations of Negro Bantu from farther north into South Africa in the past fifteen hundred years or so passed mainly to the east of the Kalahari Desert.

The Sahara, on the other hand, has played a more crucial role in Africa. The people to the north of this desert are strongly influenced by European and Near Eastern cultures; those to the south differ markedly in physical type and cultural forms. However, in the Sahara and in the Sudan to the south we can see these strikingly differing cultures in contact. The Sahara has always been formidable, but there has evidently been trade and contact across it, both in the Nile area and across the Western Sudan, for more than a thousand years. And the barrier itself, which helped to maintain cultural differences to the north and south of it, made the contacts and movements of peoples across it more meaningful when they did occur. Both north and south of the Sahara there has been, probably for thousands of years, much east-west contact and trade in the relatively open country of these two regions.

In short, most Africans live in inland plateau areas in which land resources rather than water resources are paramount, and in which, with the exception of the Sahara, topography has not barred the contact and movement of peoples.

CLIMATE AND CULTURES

Africa shows a relatively close relationship between climatic conditions and cultural groupings, though climate is but one of several factors that have shaped African cultures. The climate for the continent as a whole can be described in terms of a mirror image extending north and south from the equator. The Equatorial Zone of central Africa extends across the continent on both sides of the equator. Its climate is tropical, its rainfall high, averaging 60 or more inches a year, and it has extensive forest areas. To the north and south are bands comprising the Sudanic zones of climate, where the rainfall is less, averaging between 20 and 60 inches, and the country is open, frequently grassland. Next north and south of these are deserts, the Sahara and the Kalahari, respectively; beyond them, in the southernmost parts of the continent and along sections of the northern coast, are zones of mediterranean climate. A characteristic of all these climatic belts is the lack of sharp demarcation between them. Exceptions to the mirror-image concept do occur, such as the presence of the Somali Desert in the East Horn area (which would be Equatorial, if the concept were precise) and the fact that the Kalahari Desert in the southwest does not extend to the east coast as does the Sahara in the north. Nevertheless it is useful in considering the major African zones of climate and their relation to gross differences in cultural forms and productive techniques.

The Equatorial Zone

The Equatorial Zone can be subdivided into three major areas. The first, the Central African, includes the Congo area, northern Angola, and the southern portion of French Equatorial Africa. It has relatively constant high temperatures throughout the year, heavy rainfall, and high humidity. Some of the densest forests in Africa are found here, yet communication along paths (and now also by railways and roads) is possible in most places. The region is predominantly inhabited by agricultural Negro peoples who live in distinct villages or settlements and who have cleared sections of the forest for their farms. Root crops, particularly cassava (manioc), a New World plant introduced into Africa following the discovery of America, but also yam and coco yam (taro), are commonly grown, as well as bananas, plantains, palm fruits, and other fruits. Domestic goats, sheep, chickens, and ducks are kept, though they are not herded and are rarely systematically fed. Their meat provides a small but important portion of the diet. Fish from local rivers and lakes also add to the food supply. Cattle and other large domesticated animals are lacking because of the tsetse fly, which causes sleeping sickness among them and is found in most forested areas and in some open regions of tropical Africa.

Small bands of Pygmy hunters and gatherers are scattered about the Central African area, generally in heavy forests in the west, north, and east. They live in a variety of symbiotic relationships with their Negro agricultural neighbors, trading game, honey, and other products of the forest for those of the agriculturalists. The Pygmies, once more widespread, are clearly dominated by the agriculturalists today. Among the latter the village or local settlement is the basic social and political unit and most of the kin groupings trace descent patrilineally (that is, through the male line). Despite the small population and agricultural surpluses, the region's political structures are well-developed and varied—even to complex states such as the Bakongo, formed by the federation of villages in large areas, with centralized authority and leaders. Systems of courts and other judicial organizations are also present. The area is famous for its art, particularly woodcarving, but craft skills in ironworking and basketry are also important, and a complex system of markets covers most of the region. Secret societies and other types of association groups, frequently organized on a village basis, are also common.

The second subdivision of the Equatorial Zone, the Guinea Coast, bands coastal West Africa from Portuguese Guinea to the Cameroons. At its center in southeastern Ghana and in southern Togoland it thins out to a few miles in depth. Elsewhere it extends inland for more than one hundred miles, gradually merging into the Sudan. Its climate is similar to that of the Central African area, but differs mainly in having two strikingly distinct seasons: a rainy one from June to November, when most of the year's rain falls, and a dry season for the remainder of the year during which a dry dusty wind, the harmattan, blows steadily southward from the Sahara. Some large mangrove swamp areas along the coast are inhabited by small fishing groups, and inland dense forests thin into wooded savanna farther north. The people of the Guinea Coast are Negro in physical type. Their crops and livestock are similar to those of the Central African area, though yams are more important than cassava, and bananas are not grown in large quantities. Hunting or gathering groups are rare, agriculture being the predominant form of productivity in this area, with some fishing.

The general features of culture that characterize the Central African area are also found here. There are large political states, such as those of the Yoruba and Dahomey, though many societies, such as the Kru and the Ibo, are organized on a much smaller scale. Patrilineal kin groupings predominate. The environment, like that of the Congo, seems to permit a wide variety of social and political forms. Craft skills are highly developed, and there is an elaborate system of local and central markets.

The third subdivision of the Equatorial Zone encompasses the East African Highlands and the Ethiopian Highlands. The East African Highlands include most of British East Africa—Kenya, Tanganyika, and the southern portion of Uganda—as well as the Belgian trust territory of Ruanda-Urundi; the Ethiopian Highlands comprise almost all of present-day Ethiopia and parts of Eritrea. The rainfall is moderate in these areas, and seasonal variations in climate are not as marked as along the Guinea Coast. The temperatures are high during the day but drop at night. There are some pockets of tropical forest, such as the Buganda area of Uganda, where plantains and other tropical forest crops are important, but much of the region is grassland, devoted to grain crops and cattle herding. Basic foods are cow's milk prepared in several different ways and various forms of porridges and other prepared grains. Unlike the other two areas of the Equatorial Zone, root crops are relatively unimportant. Small domestic animals are also found, and in the Ethiopian Highlands horses and donkeys are common. There is some fishing in the Lakes area. Some groups in the highlands, such as the Masai of Kenya and Tanganyika, are primarily cattle herders; others, such as the Baganda,[1] are basically agriculturalists; still others, as the Nandi of Kenya, are both. In some cases the choice of productive activity has clearly been determined by geography, while in other cases it has been made in terms of the past interests and experience of a particular group. Cattle, almost everywhere they are found, have an importance in excess of their food value, being used in marriage contracts and to give their owners prestige. Some small groups of hunting and gathering peoples are found scattered about both these highland areas, but they are clearly on the wane today, and have been for some time.

In contrast to the Central African and Guinea Coast areas, these highland regions have been the scene of extensive movements of peoples, particularly pastoral peoples, often with considerable warfare. State systems built on the idea of caste, or on the principle of descent through one line, or on a combination of descent and territorial bonds are common, but smaller societies are also found in which groupings of persons on the basis of age, or of descent, or of both, dominate the social organization. Patrilineal descent groups are most characteristic of both state and non-state societies. Secret societies are almost absent from these areas. Craft skills are less well developed than in the other two regions of the Equatorial Zone, and the market system is simpler. Parts of Ethiopia, however, have wide trade, and are known for metallurgy and cloth weaving. The presence of these skills among Ethiopian groups is undoubtedly related to Ethiopia's proximity to and long history of contact with the Near East. In fact, many of the cultural features that differentiate the peoples of the Ethiopian Highlands from those of the East African Highlands are the result of Ethiopian contacts to the north and east. The Ethiopic Church. the official church of Ethiopia, has developed as a result of early Greek and Near Eastern Coptic influences. Islamic beliefs and practices are dominant among some groups (such as sections of the Galla) in Ethiopia and Eritrea. In the East African Highlands, and indeed throughout the rest of the Equatorial Zone and the areas to the south of it, religion is based on belief in the supernatural power of ancestors and certain forces associated with nature, and magic and witchcraft are frequently found.

The Sudanic Zones

At the next step away from the equator, both to the north and south, lie the Sudanic climate zones. The one in the north, that of the Sudan, stretches from the Atlantic Coast to the Red Sea. It is quite hot during most of the year with moderate rainfall, mainly between May and October. The harmattan is prevalent in the Western Sudan during much of the dry season. The country is savanna, characteristically grassland with low bushes and trees, gradually merging into the Sahara Desert to the north. Grains, cotton, and peanuts are common crops, and shea butter is made from the oil found in the nuts of the shea tree. This is one of the major cattle-herding areas of Africa, though horses, sheep, goats, and other domestic animals are also kept. Some of the Sudanic groups, such as the Mandingo of the Western Sudan, have long records of expansion and movement. Others, such as some of the pastoral Fulani of Nigeria, follow regular cycles of migration between wet- and dry-season grazing areas; still others, such as the Konkomba of Northern Togoland, are sedentary and stress agriculture more than herding. Cattle play as important a role in this area as they do among East African groups.

Culturally the whole zone is transitional between the cultures of Egypt and North Africa on one hand and those of Equatorial Africa on the other. Many groups are Moslem, and through migration and contact have helped to spread Islamic beliefs throughout the region and to the south. However, there are also numerous well-known groups, such as the Mossi, the Nuer, and the Tallensi, who have retained their indigenous religious systems. The societies of the Sudan are mainly patrilineal and vary in size and organization from small autonomous groups to large kingdoms and even empires. The history of some of these states is known, and the region seems to have undergone periods of conquest, state building, and the decline of states, under both cattle-herding and agricultural peoples.

Trade centers, such as Kano and Timbuctoo in the Western Sudan and Sennar on the Blue Nile, have been important for many years, and are the scene of considerable north-south trade, as well as east-west contact. These centers and the associated trade routes have in the past been prizes of warfare, and their conquest has made possible the organization of state systems.

Association groups, such as age grades and secret societies, are absent or undeveloped in the Sudan. Craft skills in weaving and metallurgy are well developed, and woodcarving is found among some groups in this area, particularly in the west. Arabic is read and written in some Moslem groups. The people are primarily Negro or Negroid, though some Caucasoid groups are found in the region.

The Sudanic zone in southern Africa south of the Equatorial Zone, known as the South Central African Zone, is geographically similar to its northern counterpart. It extends almost to the tip of South Africa in the southeast but is narrower in its central and western areas because of the presence of the Kalahari Desert. The temperature remains high most of the year. Rainfall occurs mostly between December and May, flooding much of the lowland and valley regions, but the rest of the year is dry and sunny. As in the Sudan, cattle herding and the farming of grain crops are the chief productive techniques in this grassland climatic zone. Small domestic animals are kept.

Groups in this region have been moving and reorganizing for fifteen hundred years, as Negro pastoralists and agriculturalists have pushed southward from the Congo and East Africa and as states, such as the Bemba of Northern Rhodesia and the Tswana of Bechuanaland, have arisen and absorbed surrounding peoples. Many peoples of the region, such as the Bemba, possess cultural characteristics that are clearly reminiscent of their previous areas. Extending east and west along the more northerly portion of this region is a "matrilineal belt," where many groups trace descent through the female line, and where the local villages and settlements are unstable, tending to break up and re-form after one or two generations. In the western extremes of the South Central African Zone, bordering on the northern Kalahari Desert, are groups such as the Herero, who are primarily cattle herders tracing descent through both male and female lines in a form of reckoning known as double descent. The groups in the south of the zone are generally patrilineal and tend to be organized in large political units or kingdoms. Throughout the zone, association groupings vary considerably in their importance, markets are rare, and crafts, particularly those involving artistic skills, are not so highly developed as among their more northerly neighbors.

The Desert Zones

The desert zones differ considerably from one another. The Sahara (which, despite the impression given by Hollywood, is composed not mostly of sand dunes but of rough earth, gravel, and rocky areas) has almost no precipitation, and its people depend mainly on ground water. The temperature is usually cool in December and January but extremely hot the rest of the year, though the range between day and night temperatures is wide. Many sand and dust storms occur. The culture of the Sahara is mainly an oasis culture; its people grow dates and garden crops, and the camel and horse are the principal domestic animals, though in some areas sheep are grazed. Some of these oases serve fairly large populations and have been permanent settlements for hundreds of years. Trade routes connect these communities, and peoples move freely between them.

On the whole, however, the Sahara is very sparsely populated, much of it uninhabited, though some areas provide sufficient grazing land for use during part of the year. The Tuareg, Berbers, and Arabs, the predominant groups, are almost entirely Moslem, though local rituals and beliefs vary widely. Descent is almost all patrilineal, and male authority is characteristically autocratic and hierarchical. The size of the individual groups is variable, ranging up to several thousand persons in some instances. Only in the eastern Sahara, where the Nile cuts across the desert and farming along its banks is profitable, is there a history, revealed largely by archaeological records, of state formation. Although the Saharan peoples are predominantly Caucasoid, a few important Negro groups, such as the Nubians, who live along the Nile, are found.

The Somali Desert Zone has two monsoon periods, the southwest monsoon from about May to September, and the northeast monsoon from about November to March. The rainfall, which is generally more than in the Sahara Desert, averaging up to 20 inches a year, falls mainly from April to June and October to November. Some rivers flow all year round and numerous wells are found, particularly in the coastal areas.

The northern Somali desert area has regions of thorn growth, and also of grassland suitable for grazing part of the year. Most of the northern groups are herders who migrate seasonally between grazing areas and certain wells. Some sections to the south have sufficient rainfall and fertile enough soil to allow sedentary agriculture, as well as herding. Throughout the Somali zone cattle and camels, the principal domesticated animals, provide milk products which form basic foods. Horses are much prized and were formerly very useful in warfare. Agricultural crops include millet and other grains, and along certain river valleys and in portions of the more fertile southern section, root crops and fruits are grown. The predominant cultural group in this area, the Somali, is composed of independent or semi-independent "tribes," which are characteristically patrilineal and Islamic. The Somali appear to be Caucasoids who have largely replaced earlier Negro hunting and farming groups.

The Kalahari Desert in southwestern Africa averages about 5 to 10 inches of rain a year and becomes progressively sandier and drier toward the Atlantic coast. Much of it is flat grassland, with some bush regions. In many areas the shortage of water becomes acute during part of the year. Small bands of Bushmen, a hunting and gathering people differing in physical type from the Negro peoples of Africa, once inhabited much of the sparser areas, hunting large and small animals and gathering roots, fruits, and berries. A people related to the Bushmen in physical type, the Hottentots, are found in the grassier sections of the Kalahari and along its borders, and formerly lived in the Cape region to the south. They are cattle herders living in somewhat larger groups than the Bushmen.

A third group, the Bergdama, are Negro, though they speak the Hottentot language and live like the Bushmen, by hunting and gathering in small bands in central southwest Africa. Many of the Bushmen, Hottentots, and Bergdama have now disappeared from this desert area. The traditional mode of livelihood and the level of technology are probably as simple in this region as anywhere in Africa, producing little surplus in food or goods.

The Mediterranean Zones

The Mediterranean climatic zones include Northwest Africa and Egypt in the north, and the Cape area and Southeast Africa in the south. Northwest Africa has a mild climate, with moderate rainfall, practically all of it occurring between November and April. Though there is considerable climatic variation between the mountainous inland areas and the lower coastal regions, the summers are generally warm and the rainy seasons cool. Sheep and goats are herded, particularly in the higher regions, and the agriculture resembles that of southern Europe. Wheat, barley, oats, European vegetables, grapes, dates, oranges, figs, and olives are common. The shifting of some groups from valley or lowland farming to highland herding during the year is characteristic of the area. Some evergreen and cedar forests are found.

The indigenous inhabitants, the Berbers, have been successively influenced or dominated by Phoenician, Roman, Jewish, Arabic, and European peoples. They are now heavily Moslemized, and some groups are indistinguishable in culture from the Arabs who live in large numbers in the area, having come from the Arabian Peninsula in a series of migrations that began in the seventh century A.D. Berbers, such as Riffians and Kabyles, tend to stay in the mountainous areas; Arabs dominate many of the coastal villages and towns. But the two groups intermix widely. Several large cities, some of them of considerable antiquity, form one major locus of political and social activity, the other being among the more independent groups of the interior mountains and plateaus.

Both Arabs and Berbers emphasize patrilineal ties. The basic unit for both is the village, a number of villages forming a "tribe." Craft skills are highly developed; certain foods and goods are produced in surplus; and wide differences in wealth and living standards occur. Markets, key features in the social and political structure as well as in everyday life, are found everywhere.

The Egyptian area technically belongs to the Sahara Desert Zone, since the rainfall is sparse and the climate hot. Yet the waters of the lower Nile and Nile Delta make intensive agriculture possible along the river, and make for productive activities and cultural groupings that resemble those of Northwest Africa. The bulk of the population lives in the Nile Valley, the surrounding deserts being sparsely settled (mainly by

Bedouins, nomadic camel-herding Arabic peoples who live in more or less autonomous groups or "tribes"). The majority of Egyptians, however, are Moslem peasants (fellaheen), who live in small towns and villages along the Nile, where they employ complicated irrigation techniques permitting two or three crops a year in the more northerly sections. They grow wheat, barley, maize, rice, cotton, coffee, dates, olives, and many vegetables, and keep small domesticated animals. More than a million Copts, members of a pre-Islamic Christian sect, are also found in Egypt. They too are a peasant people, though in urban areas they tend to form a white-collar class. The Nubians, a Negro agricultural and herding people in the more southerly sections of the Nile area of Egypt and in the Sudan, have had cultural contact with Egyptians for many years but are more properly a desert and Sudanic people.

The large cities such as Cairo and Alexandria dominate the political and social life of the country. Class differences are great, the average fellaheen living in small mud huts and subsisting on such foods as dates, vegetables, and dried fish, the wealthier Egyptian living in larger houses and enjoying abundant meat, fruit, and wine. The Egyptians are known for their highly skilled craft work, particularly in metallurgy and weaving. The area is a focal point for trade—up and down the Nile, along the northern coast of Egypt, and by water with Arabia and Northwest Africa.

The Egyptian area has long influenced African cultures—contributing numerous innovations that spread to other sections of the continent—but precisely how influential it has been is a subject of scholarly debate. Some scholars feel that most of the great advances in African culture and technology diffused from Egypt; others feel that Egypt's importance has been overemphasized without due credit for indigenous developments south of the Sahara. Though the present authors tend to take the latter point of view, the argument will probably not be resolved until we know more about the prehistory of Africa. Egypt, nevertheless, was one of the earliest places in Africa to develop agriculture, to produce African urban centers and states and kingdoms, and to evolve complex technologies. In these and many other cultural characteristics it is clearly linked to Mesopotamia and other regions of the Near East. Egypt and the East Horn form points of contact between the African and Asiatic cultures.

The climate of the Cape area of the southern coast of Africa is similar to that of Northwest Africa, though the rain falls mainly between May and September, which is the cool period. The small independent groups of Hottentot herders who once inhabited the area have disappeared from it in the last few hundred years, leaving evidence of their presence in the mixed European-Hottentot-Negro physical type, the Cape Coloured. The Cape area is now heavily populated by persons of European descent, mainly English and Dutch, who live in urban centers such as Cape

Town. The people of the rural areas surrounding these centers grow crops similar to those of Northwest Africa, and herd cattle and sheep.

The Southeast African region stretches from the Cape area to the Limpopo River along the east coast and consists of a high interior plateau, with relatively flat, dry grassland and bush country, and a subtropical coastal area with richer plant growth and heavier rainfall. Because of the southeast trade winds along the coast, it rains from October to March (in contrast to the rains of the Cape area, which are from May to September) and the temperatures are also high. The remainder of the year is cooler and drier.

The area used to be inhabited by large numbers of cattle-herding and agricultural Bantu Negro people, apparently migrants from farther north at some earlier time who had more recently formed into states such as the Zulu and the Swazi. Other Bantus in the area followed independent patrilineal groupings. It is clear that the Bantu in the Southeastern area are not distinct culturally from those in the South Central African Zone farther to the north and west. Much of the interior plateau region has now been taken over by farmers of European origin, particularly Dutch, and by mining interests. Traditional African cultures have been greatly modified, and Africans either live in reserves (rural areas set aside for African residence by national governments), or work as laborers, mainly in the European urban centers.

Madagascar

There remains only the Island of Madagascar, which poses a number of puzzles to anthropologists. About a thousand miles long, it has a climate that is extremely varied but that can be divided into three major geographical zones. A rugged central plateau is relatively cool, with seasonal rainfall. Here wet rice, grown in terraced fields, is the staple product. In the west and south the plateau slopes to the sea, and in these lower areas the climate is hot and dry and open plains and bush are common. Since the soil is inadequate for agriculture, cattle herding is the main occupation. To the east of the central plateau an escarpment region, with high rainfall and heavy forests, blends into the eastern coastal zone, which is hot and humid. In these eastern sections of the island maize, wet and dry rice, taro, and sweet potatoes are grown.

Throughout the island there is a diversity of cultural groups, from large kingdoms to small tribes. The islanders speak mainly a single Malayo-Polynesian language, Malagasy, and many characteristics of their culture indicate extensive contact with southeast Asia, and possibly Indonesia, in some remote past. Overlaying this is Arabic and Islamic influence dating from about the eighth century. Physically the islanders seem

similar to the African Negro, as far as the usual anthropometric measurements indicate. Little is known about the people's prehistory and early
history—but they are clearly an important, though unexplained, link between southeast Asia and Africa.

POPULATION

The population of Africa is about two hundred million persons. The
exact figure is unknown, since census data are frequently inaccurate or
based on estimates rather than on actual counts. Yet the main features of
African population are clear.

For the continent as a whole the population density averages about 15
per square mile. This is low, compared to many tropical regions of the
world, and famines due to the press of large populations are rare in
Africa, though many Africans do not live much above the subsistence
level. The density varies considerably, however, from place to place.
In the Nile Delta and lower Nile region it averages over 1,000 persons per
square mile. In Sierra Leone, southern Ghana, and southern Nigeria, and
in the Northern Plateau of Nigeria, a density of at least several hundred
persons per square mile is found. The Congo area has never been heavily
populated, averaging about 8 persons per square mile. In Ruanda-
Urunda, however, on the eastern border of the Congo, and in the Lake
Victoria region of East Africa, the density is quite high. The high figure
for the Nile area is undoubtedly related to the extensive irrigation agriculture there, and the high densities along the Guinea Coast may be related to the pull of peoples southward toward the coast as a result of the
European slave trade. However, the variation in Africa's population
density has never been fully explained.

"Underdeveloped" areas commonly have high birth and death rates.
No accurate figures for all of Africa exist, but it is clear from local studies
that infant mortality is extremely high. However, the widened use of
Western medical techniques is lowering the death rate, more rapidly apparently than social and economic changes can effect a lower birth rate.
As a consequence of this, among other factors, the population is growing,
and all areas of Africa must make productive and technological adjustments to this increase.

About five million persons of European orgin or descent live in
Africa. About two and a half million are in the Union of South Africa and
the Rhodesias; a third of a million are in central and eastern Africa, particularly in Kenya, the Congo, and Angola; and about two million more
live in North Africa, mainly in Algeria. It is in these areas of white settlement that the frictions between European and African are strongest,
and that racial and political tensions seem most irreconcilable. In West

Africa, and in the Sudan and desert regions, Europeans are found in smaller numbers. The European has preferred to settle in the less tropical open regions of Africa.

European settlement has also been directly responsible for the rapid development of many cities. Two hundred years ago most of Africa was rural. There were, however, some cities not of European origin (many of which still exist today): the well-known cities of Egypt and North Africa; some in the western Sudan, such as Timbuctoo and Kano, which were already hundreds of years old; others of unknown age in southwestern Nigeria and in the Congo; and Arabic cities that have flourished along the east coast of Africa for centuries. Yet it is in cities, settled by Europeans, and by large numbers of Africans, a characteristic of the present-day population picture, that the new centers of high population density are developing. Today there are in Africa more than fifty urban centers with populations of over 50,000 persons. For example, Johannesburg has a population of about 1,000,000; both Ibadan, in Nigeria, and Cape Town have more than 500,000; and Dakar has over 150,000. Such population concentrations bring new problems in employment and in the production and distribution of food and services that are not yet fully solved.

PHYSICAL TYPES

The general features of the physical types of Africa are known, though few accurate studies and analyses have been made. No precise classification exists; the relationship between the various African physical types is obscure; and the origin of most of them is unknown. In line with a trend in anthropology, research is turning from the measurement and observation of external bodily features to the analysis of genetic factors, particularly those associated with blood types and conditions. Such research, though promising, has been more suggestive than conclusive.

Past classifications of African physical types have included many inaccuracies and misconceptions, fostered not only by travelers and popular writers, but also by scholars. A common error has been to confuse linguistic with racial categories; these do not coincide in Africa and refer to quite different things in the first place. For example, the term "Bantu race" is sometimes employed, although the word *Bantu* actually refers to a linguistic grouping and not to a physical type. Furthermore, the literature on Africa is full of statements such as that the skin color of a certain group shows Mongoloid influence, or the thin straight lips of another indicate Caucasoid features. Single traits such as these are poor indicators of origins and contacts and are as likely to be due to local variation within a population as they are to past contacts. In short, most of our knowledge of African physical types is inaccurate; it is clear that all peoples in Africa are *Homo sapiens,* capable of interbreeding with one another; beyond this all that we can do is to indicate some of the readily observable gross physical differences among Africans and to suggest the direction of current genetic research on African populations.

Numerically, the major physical type in Africa is the Negro, sometimes called the "true" Negro. Although the Negroes are often divided into numerous subcategories, they can be classed together. They are located in the Sudanic Zone south of the Sahara (and even to some extent in that desert), along the Guinea Coast, through central Africa and most of East Africa, and in southeastern Africa and Madagascar. African Negroes have dark pigmentation of the hair, eyes, and skin; woolly hair; broad, flat noses; everted lips; and some prognathism. They vary considerably in height and in many other characteristics.

Scattered about the forest areas of central Africa are small groups of Pygmies, who are essentially Negro in their physical characteristics but differ mainly in height, averaging about 57 inches for males and about 54 inches for females. There is some evidence that the Pygmies were once more widespread in central Africa than they are today, and that they may even have lived on the island of Madagascar. The evolutionary relationship of Pygmy and Negro is unknown, and it has not been established which is earlier in development.

In East Africa, particularly in Ruanda-Urundi, Uganda, and the Eastern Sudan, are found unusually tall, slender, and long-headed Negroes, the Nilotes, who seem to form a distinct subgrouping. Some authors feel that they show Caucasoid features, indicating North African influence, but present evidence suggests that they are simply a localized variant of the Negro. Other Negro groups are also found throughout this Nilotic area.

In North Africa and Egypt, and south into the desert area and the Sudanic climatic zone, most people are of the Caucasoid physical type. Wide variation occurs, and some authorities would distinguish those in the eastern parts of northern Africa from those in the western. However, they generally belong to a Caucasoid subgroup living all along the shores of the Mediterranean with brown hair and eyes, hair ranging from wavy to straight, skin color of light olive to dark brown, fairly thin lips, and high-bridged narrow noses. There is considerable intermixture of Mediterranean Caucasoid and Negro in the Sudan and in Ethiopia and other parts of the East Horn; and some mixture along almost the whole length of the East African coast as well, mainly as a result of Arab-African contact. The Mediterranean Caucasoid population of Africa seems clearly related to the Caucasoid groups of Europe and the Near and Middle East, though its origin, if it had a single origin, is unknown.

In southwest Africa are two groups closely related physically to each other, the Bushmen and the Hottentots, who, despite past efforts of scholars to classify them, are difficult to place within any other major racial typology and must be considered as a distinct physical type. The Bushmen are short—but not as short as the Pygmies—averaging perhaps five feet tall. Their yellow-brown to yellowish skin is wrinkly. Their hair is "peppercorn" in form and dark in color, and they have broad cheekbones, flattish noses, and fairly pointed chins. They also exhibit steatopygia, a condition in which the buttocks are enlarged by fatty deposits. The Hottentots, slightly taller and somewhat more long-headed, are otherwise very similar to the Bushmen in physical type, though differing in culture. The origin of the Bushman-Hottentot physical type is unknown, and its relation with other forms of *Homo sapiens* uncertain. Archaeological and other evidence indicates that it is of considerable antiquity and was once more widespread in southern Africa, possibly even in central Africa, having been driven into its present inhospitable region by Negroes moving into South Africa.

Through intermarriage and interbreeding between Hottentots and European settlers (particularly the Dutch), with some Negro intermixture as well, in the Cape area of South Africa, a mixed physical type has developed. These Cape Coloured are almost all urban dwellers who have lost most elements of Hottentot culture. They now number more than a million and form a distinct population group in South Africa.

There are also East Indians, several hundred thousand in southeast Africa, and smaller numbers in East Africa, who have migrated to Africa chiefly within the past hundred years. They are generally considered by anthropologists to be a distinct subgrouping of the Caucasoid physical type.

The presence of approximately five million Europeans, who are mainly Western European Caucasoid in physical type, has already been mentioned.

Thus the African continent is peopled by three distinct physical types —Negro, Caucasoid, and Bushman-Hottentot—the first two being large in number and the third fairly small. The Negro type subdivides into the "true" Negro, the Pygmy, and the Nilote; the Caucasoid, into a Mediterranean Caucasoid of considerable antiquity in Africa, a Western European Caucasoid of a later period, and an Indian Caucasoid of even more recent date. The Bushman-Hottentot type, of course, has two subgroups representing these two peoples.

It has often been suggested that differences in physical type involve some environmental adaptation, but precisely how has been difficult to explain in terms of the physical characteristics used in traditional racial classifications. For example, dark skin color may be adaptive to hot and relatively humid tropical climates, or tall slender body build to hot desert conditions. Both of these occur in Africa. Yet there are groups of slender Africans who do not live in desert conditions, and Negroes who live in relatively cool highland areas. If such features do represent adaptations they occur very slowly, only after many generations. But because the genetics of such physical features are not fully known it is difficult to understand the exact nature of such adaptations.

The genetic approach to studying African physical types is based on the premise that knowledge about the genetics and hereditary patterns of physical traits will give us insight into the origins, migrations, and contacts of African populations, as well as tell us something about adaptation to specific environments. (For the student of human evolution and human genetics, studies in Africa have other uses as well, which need not concern us.) Those characteristics of African populations about which we know the most genetically are blood types (particularly the ABO series, the Rh factor, and the MN series), certain blood conditions, such as the sickle-cell trait, and some diseases which appear to have a genetic basis. For example, a condition known as sickling of the red blood cells seems to bring about resistance to malaria. (In its severest form it causes death from anemia at an early age.) In Africa this blood condition is found most often in the areas having the highest malaria rates. The hereditary pattern of this condition is known. Here, apparently is a case of environmental adaptation of a physical condition whose genetics is understood. It is hoped that eventually many other physical traits can be similarly analyzed so that a scientific understanding of adaptation in terms of a large number of genetic factors can be made. For example, the distribution in Africa of certain blood types whose genetics is known is leading to an understanding of the possible place of origin of certain African peoples, of their interconnections, and even of the connections between Africans and peoples in Europe and Asia, though the results are still tentative. It is likely that within the next twenty years much of the misunderstandings and even mysticism concerning African physical types will have been cleared up through genetic analysis.

MEANS OF LIVELIHOOD

Hunting and Gathering

The hunting and gathering peoples of Africa represent an environmental adjustment that is found in isolated areas of low population density. They are small population groups with the simplest of technologies, usually owning no more material goods than they can carry on their persons in their migratory search for food, and being directly dependent upon wild plants and animals for their survival. As a general type they are unusual for Africa, for the continent is largely peopled by farming and herding societies.

Various hunting and gathering peoples have made specialized adaptations to their particular environments, sometimes involving, for example, resourceful techniques of finding and preserving water in regions where it is scarce, or ingenious disguises for tracking animals in open country. Some hunting and gathering societies lead self-sufficient, relatively isolated lives in small bands, moving across the countryside in response to the demands and resources of the changing seasons. Others, though they are migratory, live in a more or less symbiotic relationship with nongathering, usually sedentary peoples.

In their desert environment, the Bushmen of the Kalahari are scattered over approximately 60,000 square miles. Their life is oriented around water holes, on which both the people and the game they hunt depend for survival. The largest social group is the band, made up of primary families and numbering from twenty to a hundred persons. Each band has a recognized territory with permanent water holes, near which it gathers in the dry season. In the rainier part of the year families spread out over the band's territory in search of food. They live in temporary shelters that are half-domes of sticks and twigs, thatched with grass.

Each family is economically self-sufficient. Men hunt game, particularly antelopes and ostrich, while women collect plant foods and "slow game" such as tortoises, frogs, and lizards. Here lack of water even more than lack of food is a limiting factor, for it restricts the size of groupings and makes impossible an agricultural or herding economy, with its potentialities for population growth, accumulation of wealth, and development of large-scale social and political institutions. With the encroachment of groups of Bantu-speaking peoples, and later of Europeans, the Bushman population declined, but it is now increasing. However, the way of life for many Bushmen has been greatly altered, although a few isolated groups still live the indigenous life of the desert. Their traditional means of coping with their hostile environment is described in the opening paper of this book, Fourie's "The Bushmen of South West Africa."

A hunting and gathering people who are not completely self-sufficient but live in limited co-operation with other societies are the Pygmies, who live mainly in the tropical forest region of French Equatorial Africa, the Congo, and Ruanda-Urundi. In nomadic bands of a hundred or more, they move to a different camp when the game in one area becomes scarce. Certain Pygmy groups of the Congo make their camps near the villages of Negroes who are sedentary farmers. The two ethnic groups have been described by some authors as living in a symbiotic relationship, the Pygmies serving as hunters for the Negroes, whom they supply with game, honey, and forest products in return for plantains grown by the agriculturalists and iron tools such as knives and projectile points obtained by them in trade. In addition, Pygmy youths attend the initiation schools of the socially dominant Negroes, and there is occasional intermarriage of Negro men and Pygmy women. For some groups the Negro-Pygmy relationship is reported to be an interfamilial one, with hereditary obligations on the part of both the Negro patrons and the Pygmies.

Other hunting and gathering peoples are found in scattered groups in the East African Highlands. The Dorobo or Wandorobo are forest dwellers who live in the upland regions of Kenya and Tanganyika. Those of the Kenya Highlands were already living there at the arrival of the pastoral and agricultural peoples who now dominate the area. Until recently this Dorobo group lived in small isolated settlements inside the dense, high-altitude evergreen forest, their permanent home and wet-weather hunting ground. In dry weather they ranged downward over the bush and grassland plateau country and into the Rift Valley. They had a purely hunting economy, catching large and small game and gathering honey from beehives kept in trees. In the past thirty years or so, since European contact relocated some of them outside the forest, the Dorobo of the Kenya Highlands have taken up limited cultivation and cattle-herding. They exchange skins and honey with the neighboring Nandi, a farming and herding people, in return for such products as iron knives and axes, pottery, and tobacco. Here, however, their relationship differs from that between the Congo Pygmies and Negro cultivators: except for their economic exchange, the Nandi and Dorobo maintain complete independence of each other. Other Dorobo groups carry out limited trade with the agricultural and herding peoples of their areas.

Agriculture

As the listings of crops of the various climatic zones show, African agriculture is divided into two principal traditions: the cultivation of grain crops, in the more temperate areas, and of root crops, in the tropical zones and some of the temperate regions as well. Digging sticks are widely used, but the most important farming implement is the traditional African hoe, made by ironworkers in sizes and styles that vary with different localities. Although the plow has been introduced in some areas, there is no tradition of using draft animals in African agriculture, virtually all of which has traditionally been accomplished by human labor.

Soil is prepared most commonly by the so-called slash-and-burn technique, in which uncultivated land is cleared by cutting and then burning the forest or bush in the section that is to be farmed. Except for the benefit to the soil from the ash left by this method, techniques of fertilization are not generally practiced in African agriculture, though many peoples employ a system of crop rotation.

Agriculture carries with it the tradition of sedentary residence, but local patterns of settlement—scattered homesteads, or dispersed or compact villages and even towns—vary greatly despite a basic similarity of productive techniques. The two best known techniques are shifting cultivation and bush fallowing, both of which have been included under the former term in some of the earlier writing on Africa. Properly speaking, shifting cultivation is a system in which people settle on a piece of land, farm it until the soil is exhausted, and then move on to a new territory. Homesteads or whole villages may thus move periodically, usually for a distance of only a few miles. Bush fallowing, on the other hand, is the practice of leaving a section of previously cultivated land fallow for a number of years in order to restore its fertility. This is accompanied by true sedentary residence, with permanent settlement in one location. Crop rotation, or occasionally fertilization, may be used with either system.

In a farming tradition land is a primary form of wealth—the most important property people possess and the object of many of their chief concerns. Land tenure is a major consideration in economic, social, and political organization; there are many legal controls over land and disputes arising over their infraction. We find also that among the agricultural peoples of Africa religion is deeply concerned with the fertility and success of crops, often in direct association with human fertility and the well-being of social groupings, and that there are often spirits or gods of the principal crops and of the earth itself, as well as of the rains, the rivers, and the springs. The closeness of agricultural peoples to the land and its crops, and their dependence on them for survival, is expressed in two of the papers in this collection, Linton's "Rice, A Malagasy Tradition," and Richards' "The Bemba—Their Country and Diet."

Herding

A large proportion of the peoples of Africa subsist by herding. Many herders also keep sheep and goats, but their chief interest is cattle. Herding is often combined with the cultivation of grains and sometimes vegetable crops. As has been mentioned, cattle-keeping is limited in much of tropical Africa by the presence of the tsetse fly, although a breed of tsetse-resistant dwarf cattle is found in some agricultural areas of the Guinea Coast.

Among the so-called cattle peoples of East and South Africa herds are not only their chief means of subsistence and form of wealth, but are of great importance in their social and religious life. Cattle are owned primarily by groups of kinsmen rather than by individuals, and significant changes in a person's life—for instance, his initiation or marriage—are marked by the exchange of cattle. When a man marries, the cattle given as bride wealth by his kinsmen to those of his wife establish the legal paternity of children she may bear, as well as guaranteeing his responsibility for her welfare. In return, the acceptance of the cattle by the bride's kinsmen signifies a pledge that she will be a good wife and bear children for her husband; should she fail in her marital obligations they must return all or part of the cattle. When, for example, the Nuer of the Eastern Sudan say, "Cattle beget children," they are saying that it is the possession of cattle that makes possible the institution of marriage and the legitimate birth of children—in short, the ordered continuity of the society. To call the children of a lineage "children of the cattle" is, in a literal sense, to acknowledge the role of this property in maintaining the lineage.

As with land and crops among agricultural peoples, so cattle in the religious beliefs and practices of herding peoples are closely bound to social identity and human welfare. In his paper, "The Sacrificial Role of Cattle among the Nuer," Evans-Pritchard gives a detailed account of the place of cattle in Nuer religion and contrasts it with the more mundane, but nevertheless important, aspects of cattle in the Nuer economy.

The importance of the social and ritual relationship between people and cattle has in some cases been brought home to agents of colonial governments when Africans have refused to cooperate—sometimes with unexpected animosity—with proposed conservation programs designed to improve pastoral techniques. Here such measures as the reduction of herds have been interpreted by Africans as unwarranted interference with the social and supernatural orders—to the dismay of all concerned. Similar situations have been reported in the case of agricultural reform programs among farming peoples.

Technology

A wide variety of materials and processes is used in indigenous African technology. In addition to the simpler techniques involved in the manufacture of articles for everyday life, many specialized crafts are found, and the skill and antiquity of some of them are striking. For example, terra cotta heads from the archaeological excavations of the Nok culture of northern Nigeria have tentatively been dated as of shortly before the time of Christ. In western Nigeria, brass work of a quality no longer achieved, made by techniques not known to indigenous craftsmen today, is thought to date from around the fifteenth century.

The processing of materials is particularly noteworthy in West and Central Africa, where abundant native metals, fibers, wood, and ivory made possible the development of a wide range of crafts. Work in iron and other metals for African consumption, and later for sale to Europeans, has occupied many artisans. Carving in wood and ivory is important in the production of religious and artistic objects and, like metalwork, for sale. Weaving, beadwork, and leatherwork are employed for clothing and other objects. Pottery is important in only a few areas.

The extensive development of crafts in these parts of Africa is related to several factors: first, a surplus large enough to free some individuals from the primary tasks of getting a living; following this, economic specialization, sedentary residence allowing an accumulation of material goods, a system of trade and markets, and a means of conveying goods. Although there have long been well-developed systems of trade in parts of Africa, the accessibility of foreign markets and the building of modern transportation systems during the present century have altered the entire economic picture.

Economics

Economic activities have traditionally been organized in African societies in many different ways. The most fundamental of these, the division of labor according to sex, is marked as compared with that in Western society. The prerogatives of one sex to an economic task, such as growing certain crops or dairying, are set by custom and reinforced by prestige and even by supernatural sanctions. For instance, in parts of West Africa, for a woman to climb a palm tree in order to harvest its fruit would not only be a shocking offense to male dignity but might also be thought to bring about the danger of supernatural retribution. In East Africa the conventions surrounding cattle vary from women's being forbidden ever to enter the kraal to the absolute necessity of having women as dairymaids. These attitudes concerning the proper activities of men and women vary from one society to another, but within a given society they are consistent with the social and religious ideology of the people.

There are several other bases for the organization of labor in African societies. Some activities, particularly skilled crafts, are organized along kinship or descent lines. In some societies such as the kingdoms of West Africa gold- or silversmithing and ironworking are the perquisites of certain lineages. Some crafts, such as blacksmithing in certain parts of East Africa, are performed by members of caste groups. Among the Masai there are smith families in each clan who constitute a distinct and inferior caste. They marry among themselves and, instead of herding cattle like their fellow-tribesmen, manufacture iron tools and weapons in return for food and livestock provided by their customers.

Craft associations are found in some African societies. For example, in some of the kingdoms of the Western Sudan skilled artisans such as weavers, glassmakers, woodworkers, metalworkers, builders, and butchers are organized in a guild system, while other craftsmen such as tailors, leatherworkers, and matmakers work individually. To varying degrees, the craft guilds are closed professions with centralized controls and hierarchies of rank and grade.

Patterns of cooperative labor for community tasks or for projects such as housebuilding or those aspects of farming that are difficult for an individual alone to perform are common in African societies. These may be organized in terms of age groups, as when a headman directs the villagers of a certain age category to build or repair a road, or they may be individually arranged, as when a man calls on his friends to help him clear farmland. When cooperative labor is interpreted as a tribute to a person in authority or as a civic duty, no recompense is made, but if it is to help an individual with a project of his own, it is repaid either in feasting when the task is finished or by similar services for the helpers at a later time.

The development of indigenous markets has been greatest in North Africa and in West and Central Africa. Though markets were in some cases introduced by European administrations after the occupation of South and East Africa, there seem to have been few in these areas before Europeans came. In markets and in other types of transactions, forms of exchange traditionally ranged from barter—the exchange of one article for another—to money, with traditional forms of currency such as cowrie shells or metal rods. At present, most indigenous forms of money have been replaced by the official currency of the various countries.

Commodities for sale in African markets, both in the cities and in remote rural areas, include local agricultural and craft products, live animals, meat, and European goods such as cloth, hardware, tinned foods, and kerosene. Traders may be local farmers and housewives who have carried their surplus crops and craft products along bush paths for distances of fifteen miles or more; middlemen who have brought their goods by bicycle, rail, or canoe from the city for resale in the country; or men of wealth and position who own fleets of trucks and employ many workers.

In some market systems, in West Africa, for instance, the markets of neighboring communities meet on successive days of the African week, so that for any individual there is a market offering similar commodities and services within walking distance each day. In some cases the markets within one network share the same price structure; in others prices of given commodities vary according to supply and demand. As in rural Europe, the African markets serve much broader purposes than that of trade: they form recreational, political, and sometimes ritual gathering places; they are centers of communication; and they offer other services such as legal counsel, letter writing, and barbering.

Whatever the place or scale of his trading activities, the present-day

African's fortunes are inextricably bound to the world market—whether he is aware of its existence or not. A drop in the stock market may be reflected within days in a fall of the price of palm oil, cocoa, or cotton, with its resulting threat to the security of the peasant producer. With the infiltration of European goods and ideas to some of the remotest parts of the continent, the economic aspiration level of Africans has generally risen and their dependence on the world maket has increased.

SOCIAL GROUPINGS

In African societies, as in others, the division and grouping of people may be considered under three broad principles: kinship; association, or nonkinship groupings; and residence, or locality. A particularly useful concept in the study of these principles and their operation in social systems is that of the *corporate group,* introduced in studies of social structure by British social anthropologists. The term is used in much the same way as *corporation* in the dictionary sense, that is, a group of persons having an identity, rights, and obligations distinct from those of the individuals who make up the group. A group may be spoken of as corporate if it possesses one or more of the following characteristics: its members (or adult members) come together from time to time to carry out some corporate action; it has a chief or council with the authority to represent the group as a whole; it owns or controls property as a group.[2] The type of corporate group most common in African societies is the descent group, usually in the form of lineages and clans.

Corporate groups play an essential and prominent part in the organization of African societies. Not only is kinship the core of the social structure of most African peoples, but associations such as age classes and grades or groups based on common interests are often corporately organized. It is important to remember that the body of theory that has grown up around the concept of the corporate group in the study of African society is not a purely abstract formulation by the social scientist but that Africans themselves conceive of social relations in terms of group membership, with its duties and privileges and symbols of identity. The aforementioned instance of the role in Nuer marriage of cattle owned by the lineage is an example of this.

Kinship

The three basic kin relationships are those of descent, filiation, and marriage. The first two, which are closely related, are commonly referred to by the term consanguinity, or "blood" ties. As used in anthropology, descent refers to the relationship of a group of persons to a common ancestor or ancestors through a number of generations; filiation denotes the relation between parent and child. Thus, filiation is the fundamental process upon which descent is based: successive links of filiation make up lines of descent. The third type of kin relationship, by marriage, often referred to as affinity, is that between a husband and wife and between a person and his spouse's family—the so-called in-law relationships.

Filiation and descent may be thought of as giving a society continuity through the birth of new members, and affinity as the way of arranging for this. Marriage assures an ordered means of providing parents for potential members of the descent groups. Actually, a fourth type of relationship, fictional kinship ties, such as by adoption or by belief in a common descent from an animal or plant totem, fill in the gaps in descent systems, so to speak, providing heirs or ancestors to replace any missing in the actual kinship system.

In African kinship systems filiation and descent refer to the social relationship between kinsmen rather than the physical relationship in the strict sense. The two are usually identical, but they may not be in cases of adoption, adulterine birth, or proxy parenthood on behalf of a sterile husband or wife. Generally, the man who has paid bride wealth for a child's mother is its legal and social father, regardless of who its genitor may be.

Many forms of descent and affinity are found in African societies. In most societies, descent is unilineal, or reckoned on one side only. Unilineal systems consist of three fundamental types: patrilineal, in which descent is reckoned through males on the father's side; matrilineal, in which it is reckoned through females on the mother's side; and double unilineal descent (also called double descent or dual descent), in which a person traces descent both patrilineally and matrilineally, belonging simultaneously to patrilineal and matrilineal corporate descent groups. This is not to say that in a matrilineal descent system a person is related only to his mother, and not to his father, or vice versa, as has sometimes been thought; two lines of filiation, between mother and child and between father and child, occur simultaneously. In a patrilineal or a matrilineal system, however, the so-called line of descent—that is, the line of filiation in which descent is reckoned—is said to be ascendant and the other line is said to be complementary. In such a descent system a person's relations with both his father's and mother's kin are structured and meaningful, but they differ in nature and content. In double unilineal descent, on the other hand, both lines of filiation can be said to be complementary; that is, they are more or less equally balanced and neither dominates the other.

A system also found in some African societies is that of bilateral descent, in which a person traces descent from *both sides* of his father's and mother's families, as in our own society. This is to be distinguished from double descent, which is traced on the father's and mother's sides, but unilineally on each, that is, it is dominantly matrilineal on the mother's side and patrilineal on the father's.

Patrilineal descent is widely found throughout Africa. Matrilineal descent is found in scattered groups in West Africa and in a wide band—sometimes called the "matrilineal belt"—across central and southern Africa from Angola through the southern Congo and the Rhodesias to Mozambique. Double descent is relatively unusual, found in scattered groups in the Guinea Coast, the Sudan, and in southwestern Africa. Bilateral descent is also unusual for Africa as a whole, occurring in southwest Africa and in some central African groups.

The basic unilineal descent groups are the lineage and the clan. As defined by social anthropologists, a lineage is a unilineal descent group whose members can trace descent to a known ancestor; a clan is a unilineal descent group whose members claim common descent from an original ancestor but are not able to trace all the generational steps between the living members and the founder. The founder may be either human or mythical—sometimes in the form of a totem that is a symbol of the group. A clan is usually larger than a lineage and may or may not be made up of a number of component lineages. Although the size of these descent groups varies greatly in different societies, the membership of lineages usually numbers in the dozens or hundreds, while that of clans may number in the thousands.

Lineages are often spoken of as being of two to seven generations (and occasionally more) in depth from the founding ancestor to the young adult generation, while clans may be ten or more generations in depth, with the actual knowledge of descent ties lost in the earlier generations. What sometimes happens in lineage organization is that there is "telescoping" of the generational links in the system, some of the earlier ancestors being simply dropped out in the memory of the lineage members. In some societies the "creation of man," that is, the birth of the first known lineage ancestor of a tribal group, remains the same number of generations behind the present at any given time, moving forward continually to keep the age of mankind constant rather than having it increase within an absolute context as in our conception.

An important characteristic of African lineages and clans is that their membership includes not only the living but the dead, for death signifies not the end of existence, but rather a change from the corporeal to the noncorporeal. As in the Chinese family, the ancestors are served through the ministrations of the ancestral cult and in many respects maintain a position of authority over the living.

Another characteristic of African descent systems is subdivision of lineages and clans with the passage of time. In lineage segmentation, lineages (and sometimes clans) subdivide according to the model of relationships within the primary or elementary family—a man, wife, and their children—or the polygynous family—a man, two or more wives, and their children. For example, in a patrilineal system the first, second, and third sons of the lineage founder and his wife may become the founders of three lineage segments. Or, if the founder of the lineage is polygynous, the eldest son of each of his wives may become the founder of a segment. In a matrilineal system the founders of lineage segments would be daughters of a single mother. (While they might conceivably have different fathers if the mother had remarried, this fact would be irrelevant in terms of matrilineal descent.)

Within a clan or lineage, segmentation is a continuing process. At any one time there may be as many as four or five levels of segmentation within a unilineal descent group, with subdivisions on each level associated with particular activities and interests. As smaller segments grow with the birth of new members, they in turn divide into new segments. Socially, the activities, functions, and prerogatives of the larger and smaller groups are divided in terms of broader and narrower corporate interests. For instance, sections of farmland might be owned and used individually by lineages of a clan, but blood revenge would be the concern of the clan as a whole.

A related process is the fission of the unilineal descent group, by which lineage or clan segments break off to form new descent groups, often also changing residence. The process of fission prevents a lineage or clan from growing beyond a size consistent with ecological and social feasibility for a given society.

There are two basic types of clan organization. In the first, and most common in Africa, the clan is internally segmented into lineages, whose interrelationships are not always clear but who claim common descent from the clan founder. In the second type the clan is not internally differentiated. Some clans are not corporate in nature, and they may be dispersed and very limited in function.

Thus in African societies there may be either matrilineal or patrilineal lineages and clans; there may be lineages but no clan organization; or there may be clans but no lineages. In many cases, lineages or clans are associated with recognized territories, but in others their membership is dispersed. Dispersal, however, does not necessarily mean the weakening of group functions, for strong ties may be maintained despite the geographic separation of the members.

As a corporate group, a clan or lineage may own the farm and grazing land its members use or the herds they keep. The dwellings and other buildings used by the members may be group property. Religious shrines owned by the group serve the members, are maintained by them, and are a focus for ritual activities. This is true particularly in the case of the ancestral cult. Leadership of the lineage or clan is usually in the hands of the eldest male members. In many African societies in-dividual discipline, and by extension community order, is the responsibil-ity of the leaders of descent groups, who are often also the political leaders. In other words, lineages and clans are groups that have jural, or legal, rights over their members and in relation to one another.

An important characteristic of the corporate nature of lineages and clans is that to an outsider one member represents the entire group. This may be seen clearly in the case of clan revenge for the murder of a member of one clan by a member of another. It is common for a murder to be avenged by the death—or the adoption into the victim's clan—of a member of the killer's clan, without concern for the identity or fate of the actual killer, the matter being interpreted as between clans rather than between individuals.

Most clans and lineages are exogamous, and any sexual relations between members are considered incestuous. Again, however, this varies in different societies and even in different descent groups in the same society.

The members of a unilineal descent group have strong feelings of solidarity and group identity. Members often greet one another by use of the lineage or clan name, and if two members who do not know each other are introduced, as may happen in a large clan, they greet each other with the warmth and enthusiasm of compatriots meeting in a for-eign land.

Membership in a unilineal descent group is expressed in family organization as well as in the interests and activities of the group as a whole. In addition to belonging to an elementary family, most individ-uals belong also to an extended family—a grouping of component ele-mentary families according to the system of descent and marriage resi-dence of a given society. In a patrilineal society in which residence is patrilocal (that is, a man remains in his father's place of residence after marriage and brings his wife to live with him), an extended family might include a grandfather, his sons and grandsons, and all their wives and unmarried children. It might, of course, be much smaller, consisting of a father and sons, or of two or more brothers, and their wives and children. Whatever the composition of the extended family it is a widely found type of domestic grouping having certain common basic char-acteristics: it is usually a residence group, sharing the same com-pound or homestead and led by the senior male member in the domi-nant line of descent. Further, it is the group within which a great many of the face-to-face relations of daily life take place.

In societies having unilineal descent, the group of parent and chil-dren—or even the children alone—in the dominant line of descent may form a minimal segment of a lineage. Thus, within a family a father and his children, or two children of the same father, may be a minimal patrilineal segment, or a mother and children a matrilineal segment, and so on. One of the effects of the unilineal basis of the extended family is the drawing of a sharp line between the interests and activities of the sexes, for in most unilineal societies members who have married into the family remain to some extent always outsiders with little or no part in the affairs of their spouses' lineage. The extent to which this is so depends on the degree of ritual and social incorporation of the in-marrying spouse into the lineage or clan, a highly variable factor in African societies. Fortes has given a valuable summary and analysis of recent studies of unilineal descent in Africa, and of their contribution to the understanding of the basic principles of social organization, in his paper, "The Structure of Unilineal Descent Groups," in this volume.

Concerning the third type of kinship, affinity by marriage, varying forms exist in Africa. What constitutes a marriage is defined in different ways in different societies. In some, a man and woman are considered husband and wife if they have had sexual relations, whether or not the relationship has been sanctioned by the couple's kinsmen or a marriage payment made. In others, bride wealth must be paid in full before establishing the conjugal relationship, and a marriage is not considered completed, or confirmed, until one or more children of the union have been weaned. These examples represent perhaps the extreme types of African marriage, but there are, of course, many other forms. In his paper, "Jie Marriage," in this volume, Gulliver has given an analysis of marriage in a society in Uganda, tracing the steps of the complex and long-drawn-out process and showing how affinal bonds between the kinsmen of a man and woman are established through the union of husband and wife.

Monogamy is found in all African societies, but polygyny, or the marriage of one man and two or more women, is found in most. In the Lele of the Kasai district of the Belgian Congo a specialized form of polyandry, or the marriage of one woman to two or more men, sometimes occurs concurrently with the predominating polygynous marriage, and this may also be true of other societies.

Although polygyny is a distinctive characteristic of African marriage, as far as is known there is no striking inequality in the sex ratio. However, the age of first marriage differs markedly for men and women: women usually marry soon after puberty but men often not until their late twenties or early thirties. Thus, though many men may have several wives at one time, many women are widowed early in life and remarry. There are several possible explanations for the difference in marriage age. In many societies men traditionally devoted their young adulthood to warfare and defense; for example, in parts of East Africa a man could not marry until after he and others of his age class had served an allotted period in a military regiment. In most African societies that require the payment of bride wealth before marriage, the acquisition of the necessary wealth often takes a number of years. But probably the most significant explanation of this age differential is that the combination of polygyny and the early marriage of women affords the maximum exploitation of women's fecundity, a factor that must have been of great importance in terms of group survival in societies having high infant mortality, limited economic surplus, and, often, a tradition of warfare.

The polygynous family is found in societies having all the different types of descent. Marriage residence often follows the dominant line of descent, being patrilocal in patrilineal societies and matrilocal in matrilineal ones. Here again there is much variation. In several matrilineal societies marriage is initially matrilocal while the husband performs obligatory services for his wife's parents, but later he sets up his own household, often in a place of his choosing, and takes his wife with him. In some societies a wife remains with her own family until after she has borne her first child, and then goes to live with her husband and his lineage. In others the place of marriage residence is optional.

One factor seems constant in polygynous marriage: regardless of the location of the household, each co-wife of a husband has her own quarters, either separate houses or rooms within a larger building, in which she and her young children live. The resources and property of co-wives are also usually kept separate. The relations between co-wives are structured in some societies by a set system of ranking in order of marriage, with a position of honor and prestige accorded the first wife; other societies have a strict convention of equality of co-wives. Similarly, the relations between children of co-wives are patterned by their mothers' relative positions in the family. Although jealousy and hostility between co-wives are more marked in some societies than in others, co-wife relations seem to be regarded as a stress point in the social structure of all polygynous societies.

In most African societies there are so-called preferred forms of marriage, that is, one is expected to marry a person standing in a designated kin relationship to him, such as his cross-cousin—the child of his father's sister or of his mother's brother. Other forms of preferred marriage are the sororate, in which if a wife dies or is barren her family supplies her husband with her sister (or cousin) as a wife, and widow inheritance, in which a widow is "inherited" as a wife by her dead husband's brother (this institution is known as the levirate), or by a son of her husband other than her own son. Both the sororate and widow inheritance are based on the idea that the marriage contract is not broken by the death—or by the failure to reproduce—of one of the spouses, and the marital obligation continues throughout the lifetime (or at least the reproductive period) of each. For example, in some patrilineal societies a woman is married not only to her husband, but also in a sense to his lineage; that is, her reproductive powers are permanently transferred to her husband's patrilineal descent group, and if he dies it is still her duty to bear children for the lineage by his brother or son. In matrilineal systems, in which children belong to their mother's, rather than their father's, lineage or clan, this is not true, for the wife's obligation to bear children is to her own descent group rather than to her husband's.

Such arrangements accord with the view universally held in African societies that the goal of marriage is reproduction. The institutions described above also clearly reveal the concept of social relationships in terms of group membership, with the interests of the lineage, for example, being paramount over those of the individual if there should be a conflict between the two. It should not be assumed, however, that a kinship group is, in effect, a strait jacket into which the individual may be forced for the sake of the group, for in almost any situation there are alternative forms of behavior. Young people will not usually be forced to marry cross-cousins if a match is distasteful to them. A widow who does not wish to be "inherited" may in some societies enter into a relationship of so-called widow concubinage with a stranger, any children of the union belonging to the lineage of her late husband and being considered his children. Her obligation to the lineage is thus carried out by a fictional kinship bond, and the interests of the group are served without undue hardship to the individual.

There is wide variation in the stability of marriage in African societies. Since marriage is seen as an alliance between the kin groups of husband and wife as well as a union between individuals, the problem of stability must be considered on two levels: the jural, or legal, aspect, and the conjugal aspect seen in terms of relations between spouses within the psychological-social context. In societies that forbid divorce or make it difficult—as when it is necessary for a wife's kinsmen to return a substantial number of cattle to her husband before she can be freed of her marital ties—a marriage may be spoken of as jurally stable simply because a divorce has not taken place, despite the fact that the husband and wife may no longer be living together.

Traditionally, African marriage seems to have been more stable jurally, and perhaps conjugally, in patrilineal societies than in matrilineal ones. In matrilineal systems there is a basic inconsistency between a man's role as a father, with only limited authority over his children, and as maternal uncle and guardian of his sister's children, with distinct power and influence. In the event of divorce he loses custody of his own children, who are members of their mother's descent group. It is thus much more difficult for a husband to maintain controls over his wife than it is in a patrilineal system, in which he would retain custody over his children if his marriage were dissolved.

Aside from type of descent, other factors seem important in marital stability, both jural and conjugal. One is the degree of social absorption of the in-marrying spouse into the local groupings and activities of the other spouse's community, that is, whether he or she is granted full membership in the group or is considered an outsider. Another is whether a means exists for proxy parenthood on behalf of a sterile husband or wife. This is effected in some societies by a man's calling upon a "seed-raiser" to impregnate his wife, or a woman's paying bride wealth for a co-wife, whose child by their common husband she will consider her own. In societies that have no such arrangements, childlessness is often a recognized grounds for divorce.

Association

The second principle of social grouping, association, is of particular importance in the social structure of some African societies, though it has been less thoroughly studied than kinship and some of its basic classifications are still being worked out. It is paradoxical that in a part of the world where kinship is of such great importance in social organization, nonkinship groupings should also figure importantly in many aspects of people's lives, cutting across kin groups, and uniting members of different families, lineages, and clans in common interests and activities. Membership in associations may be either voluntary or prescribed, and many forms of associations are found.

The type of association of probably the greatest overall importance for Africa is age groupings. These are primarily men's associations. Women's age groupings are also present in some societies, but they tend to be simpler in organization and more limited in function. Although age groupings are widely found, they are of greatest importance in East and Southeast Africa. The organization and working of the age-set system of one East African society is described in Huntingford's paper, "Nandi Age-Sets," in this volume.

Associations based on age are of two types, which have been referred to in past writings by an inconsistent set of terms. In recent attempts to unify the terminology, groups of the first type are called age sets, or sometimes age classes, and those of the second type, age grades. An age set may be called a "vertical" group. It is formed of persons born in the same year or within a designated time and has the same personnel and group identity, signified by a distinctive name, throughout its existence. An age set endures from formation, usually in adolescence, until its members have died. An age grade may be characterized as a "horizontal" category. It consists of an age set, or group of sets, performing specific functions and occupying a particular status during a given period. For instance, we may compare an age set to a group of persons who go through school together. The academic statuses through which they pass—elementary school, secondary school, university—may be compared to age grades, with the group of persons also referred to as an age grade while occupying one of these categories. As in a school, new sets are formed as older ones move upward in the system. Thus an age set may be said to be *in* the warrior grade—or to *be* the warrior grade—at a particular time in its career. An age set has a recognized leader or leaders throughout its existence; leadership in an age grade is usually determined by that in the set or sets occupying the grade at any one time. Within a given society the existence of one type of age association does not necessarily imply the presence of the other, though societies having age grades usually have age sets as well.

The prescribed functions of age grades are related to qualifications of age, training, and experience, and to the particular needs of the social system. A common pattern for East African societies is that of the following broad categories: initiates, youths who have recently been initiated; a warriors' grade of young men in their physical prime, responsible for the defense of the community; one or more grades of mature men who take an important part in government; and old men, the elders. These may be subdivided, and conventions vary concerning the social status of the warrior group, the age of those responsible for government, the relative responsibility and prestige of the men in their declining years, and so on.

Though membership in an age set is associated in some societies with puberty initiations, there is no connection between them in others. In some areas, particularly East Africa, boys acquire membership in an age set at initiation early in adolescence. In others there is no formal initiation, or initiation is into a secret society rather than into an age grouping. In such cases age sets may be organized informally during adolescence or early adulthood, and a set's identity may be officially recognized by the older age sets in a ceremonial which is sometimes referred to as the "initiation" of the set as a whole. In an age grade system, not only is the initiation of a new set ceremonially recognized, but the periodic moving up of sets within the hierarchy is ritually observed.

The prescribed functions of age grades are related to qualifications of age, training, and experience, and to the particular needs of the social system. A common pattern for East African societies is that of the following broad categories: initiates, youths who have recently been initiated; a warriors' grade of young men in their physical prime, responsible for the defense of the community; one or more grades of mature men who take an important part in government; and old men, the elders. These may be subdivided, and conventions vary concerning the social status of the warrior group, the age of those responsible for government, the relative responsibility and prestige of the men in their declining years, and so on.

In addition to the integrative and regulatory functions of systems of age groupings for a society as a whole—such as social training, defense, and government—they also have internal functions for their members irrespective of their relation to outside groups. Between age mates, members of the same age set, there is usually a strong bond, and age sets serve in some respects as mutual aid societies for their members. They support one another in ceremonials such as marriage and other personal rituals, acting in some ways like kin groups. They are corporate groups but differ from descent groups in several ways: they do not usually own property, they are nonperpetuating—they cease to exist with the death of the last member—and they usually lack the religious shrines or cults often associated with descent groups.

The secret society is a type of association of great importance in West Africa and the Congo. Usually a men's group resembling somewhat in organization and ritual the fraternal orders of Western society, it often involves complicated initiation procedures and constitutes a major force in training for adulthood. It may help to maintain social order within a community by enforcing the rules of correct behavior among the population as a whole, and it is often backed by strong religious sanctions. Secret societies are often characterized by the following features: they may own a section of sacred bush associated with initiation, but they do not usually own productive property, they may have guardian or other spirits, there may be a system of ranking and positions of prestige within the society. Though less common than men's, women's secret societies are found in some areas, particularly in Liberia and Sierra Leone. Among the Mende and related peoples of these countries, the role of secret societies is extremely pervasive and includes the canalizing of supernatural power, the structuring of social training and standards of conduct, and even the supervision of various political and economic activities. An account of the working of these societies is given by Little in his paper, "The Role of the Secret Society in Cultural Specialization," which is included in this volume.

Associations for the purpose of cooperative labor and craft work have already been mentioned in the context of economics. Though some such groups are based on kinship, most are based on the association principle. Membership in some work groups, such as those organized for farm work or for building, is usually voluntary—a group of friends and sometimes relatives joining in a common task; and it is often limited in time—for a season or simply for the duration of a project. However, the chain of obligations built up by certain individuals' working for others tends to lead to the later formation of similar groups.

The patterning of craft and professional organizations is more formal than that of cooperative work groups. Craft guilds are similar to those of medieval Europe, with the classifications of apprentice, journeyman, and master, and with a similar type of contract, period of training, and economic and quasi-parental responsibility for the apprentice on the part of the master. Professional organizations found in Africa include societies of medical and religious specialists and of artists, such as drummers or praise singers. These protect the interests of the specialists and help to maintain the standards of the profession as defined by the society. In some cases, particularly those of religious functionaries, they enforce the moral standards of the community and guard against the encroachment of undesirable change, whether from foreign innovations inconsistent with traditional cultural values or from improperly qualified persons, for example, "quacks" seeking personal gain at the expense of the community.

Residence or Locality

The third principle of social grouping, residence or locality, though perhaps not as pervasive in Africa as kinship, is nevertheless an important aspect of the structure of a society and may have a great influence on its basic organization. A number of considerations are involved. First, residence is related to habitat, though it is not necessarily determined by it. The natural surroundings of a people are often more favorable to one method of earning a living than to another, and this in turn is often reflected in patterns of residence. In addition to natural resources, seasonal differences may determine patterns of population movements in response to the needs of people and their domestic animals—as in the case of the transhumance, or seasonal movements, of herding peoples.

Another factor related to residence is the level and type of technology of a people. This constitutes a screen through which they perceive their natural environment, seeing its potentialities or limitations in terms of the techniques they have devised for coping with it. Examples of this may be brought to mind by the mention of the words irrigation, fertilization, or well-digging—techniques whose presence or absence may make very fundamental differences in the residential patterns of a society.

In addition to natural environment and technology, the relations between societies may be an important factor in residence. In a continent with long traditions of population expansion and warfare, defense considerations have influenced the size of social groupings and their choice of locations to settle; and these, of course, have been further influenced by the factors already mentioned. Parts of Africa are inhabited jointly by tribal groups with different types of technology, such as agricultural and hunting, or agricultural and herding, peoples. When certain peoples move in and out of territory inhabited more or less permanently by others, the ownership or control of the land used by both must be agreed upon so as not to encroach upon the rights of either, and such a situation often affects residence, particularly that of the migratory groups. Here also, the factor of warfare was sometimes involved in pre-European times.

Social factors internal to the organization of a society may also be important in determining its type of residence. Although kinship is very often the basis of local groupings—a common pattern being an extended family living together in a homestead or compound, or a lineage forming the basis of a village segment—the principle of association may also strongly influence residence. This seems to be particularly true in parts of East Africa, where a warrior age grade traditionally had to be a mobile unit of defense for a people and their cattle. A South Central African people, the Nyakyusa of southwestern Tanganyika, have quite an unusual system of age villages, the local unit being a group of age mates, their wives, and young children. An age village begins when a group of young herd boys of approximately the same age build huts outside their fathers' village. They sleep in them and spend their spare time there, and gradually, as new boys join, the group of huts assumes the proportions of a village, to which the boys later bring their wives. The village "dies" with the death of the last age-mate founder. The Nyakyusa stress the ideal of good fellowship among age mates, and this concern is backed by supernatural sanctions associating tendencies toward social isolation with witchcraft. Also, they feel strongly that the sex activities of parents and children should be kept separate—thus there is an avoidance taboo that forbids familiarity between a man and his son's wife. Residence in age village facilitates this avoidance pattern as residence in a patrilineal lineage with patrilocal marriage, for instance, could not. The organization and functioning of these villages are described by Monica Wilson in her paper, "Nyakyusa Age-Villages," in this volume.

To illustrate the variation in residence found in Africa, it may be helpful to imagine a continuum from a small, truly nomadic band living on the simplest level of technology to a large, compact sedentary grouping possessing the industrial and scientific techniques of the Western world. Although the latter is present in Africa only as a result of European contact, many positions on the continuum are represented by traditional African societies, as a few examples will indicate.

The Bushmen of the Kalahari Desert, as previously mentioned, are a nomadic hunting and gathering people, each band living in its own recognized territory. Their residential pattern is to congregate during the dry season around a permanent water hole, where both water and game are most likely to be available, and to disperse over the band's territory in search of food during the wetter part of the year.

The various Pygmy hunting groups of the Congo region are nomadic peoples who move about from place to place in search of game and other forest products. They differ from nomadic groups such as the Bushmen, however, since their so-called symbiotic relationship with the sedentary Negro farmers within whose territories they move about makes them part of a system of limited social interdependence and economic exchange unlike the marked self-sufficiency of the Bushmen. Because the rainfall of the forest region in which the Pygmies live is fairly evenly distributed throughout the year, they do not have the pattern of congregation and dispersal in response to seasonal demands, but rather migrate in a body when the supply of game in the band's temporary camp becomes exhausted. Here the factor of technology is important also, for the Pygmies hunt and gather in an area where their Negro neighbors farm successfully. This distinction is, in fact, said to be the basis of the Negroes' feeling of superiority toward the Pygmies, who, they think, have an inferior and backward way of life.

The Pastoral Fulani are a cattle-herding people of the Western Sudan, who derive their subsistence from cattle, sometimes supplemented by a few camels, sheep, or goats. They move about from place to place, living on dairy products and exchanging surpluses for grain in the markets of agricultural peoples of the area. The direction of Pastoral Fulani transhumance is southward in the dry season in search of water and pasture, and northward in the wet season to avoid the attacks of the tsetse fly and of wild animals such as the hyena. The people congregate during the wet season and disperse in the dry season, when the amount of water and pasture in any one location is most limited. Unlike many of the cattle-herding peoples of East Africa, the Fulani do not have permanent places of residence or own the land upon which they keep their herds. Rather, they must obtain water and grazing rights from the acknowledged owners of the land, the sedentary agricultural peoples of the region. Thus their seasonal movements vary from local area to area and from year to year, depending on such factors as the length of the wet and dry seasons, the number of cattle in the area in relation to the resources necessary for their maintenance, and the arrangements with local agricultural peoples, including the availability of markets for the exchange of farm and dairy products. The flexibility of Fulani population movements, and the importance of both environmental and social factors in structuring them, are analyzed in Stenning's "Transhumance, Migratory Drift, Migration: Patterns of Pastoral Fulani Nomadism," included in this volume.

Among the East African herding peoples, the Masai, who live in the grassland area of Kenya and Tanganyika that is transected from north to south by the Rift Valley, practice a limited form of transhumance. They settle near permanent water supplies such as springs, water holes, and wells in the dry season, and in the wet season they move out to temporary waters that form, leaving the pastures near the permanent waters to reestablish themselves. In both seasons they live in kraals (settlements of cattle-herding peoples, including houses and cattle enclosures) of two basic types: that of the elders, including married men, their wives, and children; and that of the warriors, inhabited by the members of the warriors' age grades for the district and their mothers, younger sisters, and sweethearts. The elders' kraal approximates a village in its organization, while the warriors' kraal was in pre-European times the unit of defense. At present the people of both kraals keep cattle, each moving as a group between the wet- and dry-season settlements. The Masai own the land on which they live and graze their herds, but, holding the practice of farming in disdain, must trade with neighboring agricultural peoples for the vegetable products with which they supplement the foods provided by their cattle. For the Masai, the residential division into elders' and warriors' kraals fitted their former status as feared warriors among other tribal groups in the area. The members of the elders' kraal maintained the herds, while the warriors fought and raided neighboring tribes for cattle, thus expanding the holdings of the Masai and increasing their territory. As for ecological factors, the presence of enough water and pasture for their cattle free the Masai of the need for frequent migration, population dispersal, or marked dependence on neighboring peoples, and social factors perhaps play as large a part in determining their residence pattern as ecological considerations.

The Nuer of the Eastern Sudan are a cattle-herding and farming people living in marshes and savannas along the Nile. Although cattle provide their chief means of subsistence, shortage of pasture during the dry season and the presence of such cattle diseases as rinderpest make it necessary for them to supplement their food supply with grain and vegetable crops from their gardens. These needs determine the ecological cycle of Nuer life, their village sites, and the relationships between the various tribal segments into which they are divided. Many of the villages are located on elevated grounds high enough to be free of the wet-season floods; as the rains increase, cattle graze higher and higher on the slopes leading to the villages. Within a village the homesteads are strung out along a ridge, with garden land at the back and grazing land in the front; thus the size of a village depends on the amount of high ground suitable for cultivation. With the coming of the dry season, the youths and girls take the cattle temporarily to small early cattle camps where water is more plentiful, while the older people remain in the villages to harvest millet. After the harvest the cattle are brought back and fed on the millet stalks. As the pastures become exhausted toward the height of the dry season, all the people of the villages leave with cattle for the later dry-season camps along the banks of rivers or on the edges of permanent swamps. There is a short period of wandering between the two periods of stable residence. As pastures become scarcer in the different Nuer villages, the population of the cattle camps increases. With the beginning of the rains the older people return to the villages for sowing, and the rest follow with the cattle a month or two later. The size of the later dry-season camps varies according to the amount of available water and pasture, but on the whole their population tends to be larger than that of the villages. Neighboring villages usually share the same cattle camp, cooperating in the tasks of caring for their cattle that are usually performed separately by the members of each homestead in the village. Thus the transhumance patterns demanded by the environment of Nuerland create an interdependence between the people of different villages that makes impossible the self-sufficient isolation in smaller village units that is found among some neighboring peoples who place greater emphasis on cultivation.

A group whose exceptional type of residence has an important effect on its social organization is the Lozi (Barotse) of Northern Rhodesia. Practicing a mixed economy of gardening, fishing, and cattle herding, most of them live in villages on mounds in the flood plain of the Upper Zambezi. The number of persons who can live on one mound is limited by its size, and during the flood season the Lozi must move from the mounds to settlements on the margin of the plain. They go to stay with kinsmen in other communities, but there is no consistent pattern of migration, so that throughout the year the same people are not in any territorial unit. This pattern is reflected in their bilateral descent system in which there are no lineages or clans and in which specific kinship groups are not associated with particular territories.

Many sedentary peoples are agriculturalists, but some combine farming and herding. They require pasture and water sufficient to avoid the necessity of mass seasonal movements of people and cattle and also land fertile enough to permit successful cultivation. The Nandi of Kenya, to the north of the Masai and with a similar culture in many respects, inhabit an area of abundant water and grassland. They live in homesteads scattered across the countryside, near which they keep their herds of cattle, sheep, and goats and cultivate grain and vegetable crops. The economic unit is the family, made relatively self-sufficient by the presence of sufficient resources to free it of dependence on others for its basic subsistence needs.

Agricultural peoples also have variations in patterns of residence, with implications for their social structure as a whole. As has been mentioned, a group may practice shifting cultivation, moving from one location to another every few years, or they may be truly sedentary, using techniques such as fertilization, crop rotation, or bush fallowing in order to maintain soil fertility. Sedentary agricultural peoples may live in small homesteads dispersed across the countryside, in villages with outlying farmland belonging to the community, or even in cities.

In Northern Rhodesia, the Bemba, an agricultural people of Congo origin, live in villages located as much as sixteen to twenty miles apart. Since the area is one of generally poor soils, they practice shifting cultivation, the villages moving to new farming sites every few years. Land is selected that has a growth of trees suitable for pollarding—cutting off the top branches—and burning the lopped branches to form an ash bed in which seeds are sown. The village develops as a kinship unit when a man with a sufficient following of relatives applies to the chief for, and is granted, permission to set up his own community. The personnel of Bemba villages tends to be variable, with young men moving to their wives' villages at marriage and later taking them away after their obligatory services to their in-laws have been fulfilled, established men setting up new villages, and so on. The practice of moving villages every few years as a part of the agricultural system seems to give impetus to the internal changes in village composition. The Lele of the Belgian Congo also live in villages and practice shifting cultivation. Here also the personnel is changeable, but the villages are compact and coherent social units. The role of kinship and political factors in determining village composition is explored by Douglas in her paper, "The Pattern of Residence among the Lele," in this volume.

Another sedentary agricultural people is the Ibo of southeastern Nigeria, who practice a system of bush fallowing in which plots of land are cultivated for a year or two and then left unused for several years, after which the bush that has grown up is cut down and burned in preparation for another period of cultivation. Residence among various subgroups of the Ibo is of two types. The great majority live in homesteads dispersed across the countryside, with farmland and bush lying between them. The basis of the homestead is the patrilineal extended family, with a group of neighboring homesteads forming the basis of a patrilineage. A larger population group, the village, consists of several contiguous lineages plus the women from other lineages who have married into it. Here the village is not a compact, visible unit, however, for it extends from a central meeting place into the bush, sometimes for a distance of several miles. In contrast, the villages along the eastern periphery of Ibo country are compact in organization, with a central meeting place, which is sometimes also the market. They are divided into wards or quarters and further subdivided into compounds, each having one or more patrilineages as its basis. The farmland of each village extends sometimes for several miles from its borders and is divided into sections which are alternately farmed and lying fallow. For both types of Ibo residence the kinship basis of village organization and the system of bush fallowing are similar in principle, though spatial relationships differ.

Although the Yoruba of western Nigeria are an agricultural people, more than a third of them are city dwellers. The city is a traditional form of residential grouping, early European travelers having estimated populations of close to a hundred thousand for some Yoruba cities over a century ago. Unlike the cities of Western countries and African urban centers that have arisen through European culture contact and industrialization, Yoruba cities were and are culturally homogenous entities. Their principle of organization is similar to that of the villages in which a considerable proportion of the tribal population lives. The different segments are based on patrilineal lineages; in the cities they are organized politically into wards, which are subdivided into precincts, while in small villages the population may consist of a few lineages, or sometimes only one. In both village and city, the individual's orientation is first in terms of his lineage, and after that in terms of the larger grouping. The basis of the Yoruba economy is farming, supplemented by craft production and trade. Belts of farmland surround the cities, extending outward for as much as fifteen miles. Although some persons with farms in the more outlying districts maintain temporary shelters where they may stay for a few days at a time during the height of the agricultural season, they have permanent dwellings in the city and consider it their home. The nature of the Yoruba city, as contrasted with the city defined in the literature of sociology, is discussed in this volume by Bascom in his paper, "Urbanization among the Yoruba."

In parts of Africa, particularly the Western Sudan, trading cities have existed for a thousand years and more. These are characterized by heterogeneous populations that are more unstable in composition than those of the Yoruba, for example. Timbuctoo, on the Niger Bend in French West Africa, was the meeting place of trans-Sahara caravan routes and the river trade to the south. Developing from the eleventh century as a trade center, Timbuctoo grew into a city with a large number of crafts and professions practiced by persons of different ethnic backgrounds, predominantly Arabs from North Africa, Tuareg from nomadic Caucasoid groups in the Sahara, and Songhai, who were Negroid inhabitants of the Niger Bend area. The present-day city is divided into a number of quarters and outlying districts, each identified with certain ethnic groups and their economic activities, such as Arab caravaneers, wholesalers, and retailers, Songhai craftsmen, butchers, barbers, and so on. Unlike the Yoruba agricultural cities, some of which are much larger, Timbuctoo influences, and depends on, quite distant peoples, having a commercial hinterland extending for hundreds of miles in several directions.

Modern commercial, administrative, and industrial cities have developed in many parts of Africa as the result of European contact, particularly along the coast and in areas of rich mineral resources. These are essentially European in their organization and activities, though distinctive patterns of African urban life which represent a blend of European and African cultures are gradually emerging.

* * *

In summary, two generalizations may be made concerning the relationship between the principles of kinship, association, and residence. First, many functions can be performed for a society as a whole by either kin or association groups. For example, among the Konkomba of Northern Togoland, whose social structure is strongly dominated by the principle of patrilineal descent, government is in the hands of patrilineal clans, while in other societies having the same type of descent government may be in the hands of senior age grades. Similarly, certain aspects of child training may in some societies be the function of the family but in others be the prerogative of a secret society.

Second, kinship and association are by definition mutually exclusive: a kinship group cannot be an association, and vice versa. However, the third principle, residence, plays a significant role in the organization of both. In many social systems it may be secondary to kinship in importance, but it still is vital in shaping interpersonal relations within the kin group. In associations, by contrast, the factor of residence may be primary in determining the membership of a particular group—for example, an age set or secret society will draw its members from the persons living in a particular location. Different African societies may, in fact, be characterized by their relative emphasis upon kinship and association and the particular manner in which residence affects their total organization.

POLITICAL ORGANIZATION

The political forms of traditional African cultures range from very small groups with simple leadership to large states with intricately organized systems of government. The diversity of types is striking, and the complexity of the political systems impressive. Anthropologists have yet to work out a well-ordered classification of all African political systems, though considerable attention has been and is being paid to this problem. The complications in analysis, which are many, are compounded by such problems as differentiating the external political relations of a society from its internal political ties. For the external relations in African societies, not only in the days before European contact but also today, are important, and form one basis for the understanding of the nature of political systems.

African political systems are characterized by the interrelations of the factors of kinship, territoriality, and allegiance. In some societies one may be more significant than another, but they all seem to be present to some extent.

In analyzing African political systems one is struck by the important role of kinship. Lineages, and sometimes clans, are often the building blocks of political systems, and they are arranged in a variety of ways to create different types of political structures. Ties of marriage and filiation may also be important, linking unilineal groups politically and providing the basis for positions of leadership. The leader or ruler generally is surrounded by kinsmen who guide and advise him and who take part with him in the political system. The private lives and public activities of leaders are often closely linked and perhaps not as clearly separated as in Western society. Positions of leadership are frequently inherited from a specific relative, or an individual is able to exert authority by virtue of membership in a particular kin group. Thus political and kinship relations are inextricably bound together in many African societies, so that what may be thought of as purely political in social organization and in action may be difficult or impossible to isolate. An example of such a society is the Konkomba of Northern Togoland, in which the clan is the largest political unit. Tait analyzes its organization and functions in the paper, "The Political System of Konkomba," in this volume.

Nevertheless, kinship is not an all-pervasive basis for leadership. Most African societies are flexible enough to allow for particular skills in leadership, such as oratorical talent or the ability to bring about the settlement of disputes, so that individuals who would otherwise have an inferior position within a society or kin group may sometimes find a political role for themselves. Achievement for individuals in the political field is thus possible. For example, in societies in which leadership positions are usually inherited by eldest sons, a younger son may find himself in a leadership role if he has the desired qualities. Or, if a man outside the formal leadership structure is able to acquire wealth, he may be given a political position or he may be able to apply pressure until he obtains one. It is, of course, precisely because such achievements are possible that friction may arise between those who inherit leadership and those who are striving for position through personal qualities. Such conflicts are endemic in Africa.

In addition to kin ties, but perhaps secondary to them in many African societies, are the ties based on territoriality. The political unit almost invariably has a territorial basis in Africa, though its borders may not be clearly defined. Clans or lineages that form political units frequently are residentially based. The political structure of a society having unilineal descent thus may be mirrored in its residential organization. The territorial aspect of traditional African states is almost always very important. Not only is the state a collection of persons who may or may not be related, but it has a territory with which it is identified.

Individuals and groups may in some cases be considered a part of the political system of an African group even if they have no kin ties within it, by virtue of living within the area that the political group controls. Though they rarely wield significant political power or dominate the government, they have roles to play, and there are usually regular techniques of incorporating or assimilating them into the political organization.

Territorial ties are also important since political ties require some contiguity, or some possibility of maintaining social contacts if contiguity is absent. If linked political groups become separated through disputes or ecological pressures, there must be a territorial limit beyond which they cannot be united. Such a limit, of course, would be expected to vary from group to group, depending upon ecology and social organization.

The third basis of political organization, closely related to the second, is the factor of personal attachment of individuals and groups to a political leader or leaders. Political systems incorporate outsiders by this technique. Sometimes such persons or groups are joined to a political group by fictional kin ties, but often they are not. Frequently an incorporated group may maintain considerable political autonomy in internal affairs, its leader becoming, for example, a subchief within a larger political system. These processes of attachment may be forced upon an individual or group as a result of conquest or of seeking protection from another group, or they may be voluntary. Again, groups or individuals within some African societies may shift their allegiance from one headman to another who is considered a more desirable leader. In all of these situations there is generally a kind of contractual agreement between the incorporated individual or group and the ruling group as to their relative rights and obligations. This agreement, which of course is unwritten, sometimes provides land for the individual or group, defines his or its political and social rights vis-à-vis the larger society, and gives the individual or group a clearcut place within it. Such individuals or groups are probably rarely bound as tightly to the political system as the kin groups that dominate it, and they may break away in times of stress. Nevertheless, the factor of personal or group allegiance to those in political control is important in Africa.

Certain other significant features in African political systems should also be mentioned. Ritual and religious beliefs are an integral part of government, and political leaders often have religious functions to carry out for the welfare of the society. Such leaders may have sacred qualities associated with them. Religious sanctions are an important means of social control, and ritual actions may express the solidarity of the group as a political entity. The close relationship between religion and social groups has its expression in the political system as well as in other aspects of the society.

The political group also seems to be characterized by its legalistic emphasis, which is clearly expressed in the many regulations concerned with the rights of the group and of the individual, with the concern over the nature of property such as land, and with contractual relations such as marriage agreements or the exchange of cattle. The judicial aspects are not only very important in the course of government affairs but are often coupled with the executive arm of government. The administrators are often the judges as well. However, African societies are not highly organized for legislative action. Such action does, of course, occur, but the enactment of new legislation is not as important as in Western societies. Specific legislative branches of government are generally absent, new legislation being made by executive action of the leaders as new problems arise or as an outgrowth of legal cases that develop with the changing social scene.

The role of women in the political organization of Africa is in general a limited one, and their primary concerns are productive activities.

While occasionally groups of "Amazons" have been found in African states, such as the specialized female military forces of the ruler of Dahomey in West Africa, the political significance of such groups has been overrated, and their importance in Africa has been vastly overemphasized in some popular writings. Even in African matrilineal systems, such as the Ashanti of Ghana or those found in South Central Africa, women do not dominate politics, though kin ties through females form the basis of much of the political organization and action of the men. But it is clearly the men who control the society and who have the ultimate rights over property. In some indigenous states of southern Africa, the role of the chief's mother or wife may be a very important one, and there are a few instances when a ruler has been a woman, such as among the Lobedu of the Transvaal. Nevertheless, political systems are generally dominated by males regardless of type of kinship ties or of other factors in the political system.

If African political systems are weighed in terms of size and complexity, and the degree to which component units are hierarchically organized and internally differentiated, three very broad types of political groups appear: small scale, middle range, and state. This classification is a modification of ones already in existence[3] and serves here as a point of orientation toward African political systems rather than as an attempt at definitive analysis. It should be understood that the key concept involved here is that of society rather than culture, that is, the organization of social relations through social groupings, rather than the body of customs of a people. For example, in certain kingdoms the political unit and the group of people sharing the culture are the same: there is but one culture and one political system. But frequently in Africa a people, such as the Nuer, who share one culture, are composed of separate and independent political units. There is one Nuer culture but there are many Nuer societies. Our focus is on the societies as political systems.

Small Scale Societies

Small scale societies are composed of groups of from about twenty to several hundred persons, and include the Bushman and the Bergdama bands of southwest Africa, the Pygmy groups of central Africa, and other small groups in East Africa, the Horn, and elsewhere. Such small scale societies are rare in Africa today and have been little studied by systematic field research.

The small scale society is culturally homogeneous and is characterized by face-to-face social relations of a group of kinsmen. It frequently consists of an extended family to which other kinsmen may be attached. Sometimes, the band forms a simple patrilineal clan or lineage, but if so it normally does not segment into smaller clan or lineage segments.

Kin ties through males are clearly important in these small scale societies. The band is usually nomadic within a relatively large area of low population density. Hunting and gathering, and sometimes fishing, are the major productive activities. The level of technology is low, a meager subsistence with little or no surplus is obtained, and there is little specialization of labor other than on the basis of age and sex.

This type of society is simple politically. It has a single leader, frequently the senior kinsman of the group, whose position is sometimes inherited from father to eldest son, though there is flexibility here in terms of individual capabilities. The leader usually helps guide the band in its productive activities, decides when to move and where, and attempts to ease social frictions and to end disputes. Decisions affecting the group are made by the leader in the company of the adult men of the band, who act as an informal council. The leader may carry out ritual duties, though in some cases another man will be responsible for them. Disputes within the band may be settled by self-help rather than by the leader and council, but in any case there is no formal court or judicial system. Disputes with outside groups may be resolved by raiding or through conciliation by the leaders of the groups concerned.

In a small scale society there is no internal political differentiation, since it is composed of families that lack political identity as separate units. Class and caste groups are absent and economic distinctions are rare; there is a strong pattern of sharing food and goods. People of small scale societies in Africa have sometimes, through conquest or capture, become slaves or persons of inferior status in more complex political groupings.

There appear to be at least two basic types of small scale societies in Africa. In the first, exemplified by the Bushmen, among whom this form of political organization has now virtually disappeared, the band was an autonomous political unit. A little trade and considerable intermarriage between bands occurred, but each band was a distinct group roughly similar in organization to other bands. In the second type, exemplified by the Pygmy bands of central Africa, there is a strong economic interdependence between the band and some neighboring larger political entity, particularly in terms of trade in foodstuffs and tools. As has been mentioned, this interrelationship sometimes also involves intermarriage, joint rituals, and other activities carried out by both groups. Such a band is only partly autonomous, and in cases in which the ties with the larger political group are very close, it is possible to think of the smaller group as being in intimate symbiotic relationship with the larger, or even as existing within the larger political system rather than as a separate political grouping. The degree of interdependence between different Pygmy groups and the Negroes with whom they are associated varies. That the symbiosis may sometimes be only skin deep, so to speak—at least from the point of view of the Pygmies—is indicated by Turnbull's article in this volume, "Initiation Among the BaMbuti Pygmies of the Central Ituri."

Middle Range Societies

The middle range society is the most widespread type of political unit in Africa, occurring throughout virtually all parts of the continent. Societies of this type number from several hundred to thousands of persons. A large number of more or less independent middle range societies will make up one cultural grouping, such as the Nuer or the Masai. The economy of these societies is generally based on agriculture, herding, or on a combination of these productive techniques. They vary from being completely sedentary in the case of some of the farming groups to being nomadic in the case of herding groups. Though the population density of the areas in which they live varies, it is generally greater than that of small scale societies.

The levels of technology and of subsistence seem to be clearly higher than in small scale societies, and there is some specialization of labor, particularly of craftsmen and religious officials. Trade is not a necessary condition of middle range societies; some carry out extensive trade while others do not. Social class differentiation on the basis of wealth is greater than in small scale societies but is not marked. In some middle range societies a slave caste or class is found, or a specialized craft group, such as the ironworkers among the Masai, may have special status. Such differentiated status groups usually have few or no political rights.

Middle range societies are as a rule culturally homogeneous. They are autonomous political units existing side by side over considerable areas without strong domination of one society over others. They seem to have a maximum size, based on a combination of ecological and social factors, beyond which they do not grow, but rather split into two or more separate societies.

These autonomous societies are based on a variety of principles of internal organization. As has been mentioned in the discussion of social groupings, some are formed almost entirely on the basis of kin ties, particularly of lineages and clans, while others minimize kin relationships and emphasize residential and association groupings. Still others are based on a mixture of kin, association, and residential groupings.

Not only is there a lack of strong political domination by one society over other like ones in middle range societies, but strong centralization within the society is rare. Rather, it is usually internally differentiated into smaller and smaller segments that have some political functions. For example, a large lineage may form an autonomous society with its own geographic area. It may also be divided into smaller lineage segments each of which has its own localized area and political activities. Or the society may be composed of a number of villages in which each forms a sub-unit of the group, and each village may in turn subdivide for political purposes into wards or compounds. The sub-units at any particular level appear to be roughly similar in size and to possess similar political rights. They may compete against one another for prestige, economic gain, or political influence, but they also unite as part of the larger political unit for certain activities. The type of political action necessary will largely determine what particular sub-units are involved or whether the political entity as a whole will be drawn into action.

The type of leadership within a middle range society will, of course, depend on whether it is organized in lineages, whether age grades are present, and so on. In the middle range society there is frequently a recognizable head or spokesman and a council of advisors, composed of elders, who are the leaders of the smaller segments of the political group. The extent to which authority is centered in the leader or in the council varies from one society to another.

Religious functionaries, whose positions are often inherited, also play important roles in the government of these societies. Sometimes a ritual leader is also the head of a sub-unit of the political group or even of the whole group itself. For example, a clan head may also perform rituals at the clan ancestral shrine. At other times religious officials, such as diviners, may have key roles to play regardless of their secular position in the group.

The judicial aspects of government are much more important in middle range than in small scale societies. This is related to the significance in the former of property, such as land, cattle, and agricultural products. Well-defined legal procedures exist for trying disputes and accusations within the society, and sometimes appeal to a higher judge or court within the group is possible, so there may be some hierarchical arrangement of the judicial system. This is but another representation of the hierarchical nature of the internal organization of the society. Extra-legal devices of social control may exist, though as yet little is known of such mechanisms. Bohannan's account in this volume, "Extra-Processual Events in Tiv Political Institutions," interprets a so-called "anti-witchcraft movement" in central Nigeria as an extra-constitutional device for maintaining order.

External relations between middle range societies are complex and varied, with frequent trade or intermarriage between such political units, and some joining together for common rituals. There are often regular devices for resolving disputes between two autonomous societies, or between members of two societies. This might be by a regularized type of feud or by negotiation between the leaders of the groups concerned. Warfare between two or more societies generally involves killing and the seizure of property, but not geographic expansion or the incorporation of conquered people by the victorious group. In those middle range societies in which age grades are important—and this seems to be particularly true of East African herding societies—the military units are unusually well organized on the basis of the age grades, and cattle raiding is common.

The classification of middle range societies into subtypes is now being explored by anthropologists. There are clearly a number of different kinds organized according to lineages and also another kind, found in South Central Africa, based on kin ties, where local settlements rise and fall with the shifting allegiances of individuals to the leaders of different settlements. One of a large number of kin ties, often matrilineal, is generally used to justify the allegiance. Cunnison has explored this type of shifting relationship in British Central Africa in his paper, "Headmanship and the Ritual of Luapula Villages," included in this volume. In middle range societies in which age sets and grades dominate much of the political system, several subtypes probably exist that are based upon the particular arrangements of these age groupings. Still another type involves a secret society as well as other association groups within the framework of the autonomous political group, but little analysis of the political aspects of African secret societies has yet been made. The answers to many questions, such as the relationship of ecology to political organization, or of the internal and the external aspects of middle range societies, depend upon the analysis and eventual classification of these types of political units.

State Systems

The prevalence of state systems in Africa is not usually realized. There are more than forty indigenous states in Africa, ranging in population size from a few thousand to hundreds of thousands. These states, which in most cases have a fairly high population density for Africa, are generally based on agriculture, or agriculture and herding, and are primarily sedentary. While nomadic cattle herders have played important roles in state formation, such states have usually evolved around groups of non-herders, or the herders themselves have become sedentary.

Technology in African states ranges from that typical of many middle range societies to a somewhat more complex level. This is true also of subsistence. Some states have much wealth and surplus, and trade is important. In others the level of wealth is lower and trade may be virtually absent, though different forms of exchange, such as the payment of tributes to rulers, may be important. But it is clear that the levels of technology and subsistence are not the only factors to be considered in determining the development of states in Africa.

Whatever the subsistence and technological levels, there is almost always specialization of labor in terms of craft skills and also in the administrative and religious spheres. While in middle range and small scale societies, administrators and religious officials also carry out normal work activities, such as farming, in state societies they are often full-time specialists who are dependent on the productive labor of others. The roles of these political and religious functionaries, which together form the framework of the political organization of the state, seem more clearly distinguishable from other aspects of social organization in the state than in middle range or in small scale societies.

A state typically has a small ruling class of nobles, based on a dominant clan, lineage, or grouping of families, or on a special status group or caste. This is, of course, a group with considerable wealth and prestige. A class of commoners usually forms the bulk of the population. Its members are mostly ordinary farmers or herders, though some differences in wealth are found. There may also be a group of slaves—people of inferior status, who may work for the rulers and for the more influential commoners of the state. In some African states professional craft groups occupy a position between the nobility and the commoners. In addition to these groups, which tend to extend through the whole society, others based on ethnic, linguistic, and physical differences are generally found, since the state is usually heterogeneous in composition.

The African state is characterized by considerable centralization of authority within the ruling group, which has a distinct headquarters, sometimes within a city, and may also have another elsewhere. Usually there is an influential chief or king with one or two councils of advisors, but unlike the situation in some middle range societies, the power of the head seems clearly to be much greater than that of the councils. There is an established pattern of inheritance of chieftainship, and since most African kingdoms are patrilineal (the matrilineal Ashanti and Bemba are exceptions), inheritance from the ruler to a specifically designated patrilineal heir (first born son, first son of a specific wife, and so on), is common. In actual fact, however, the close relatives and advisors of the ruler may have a great deal to say as to which particular person within the royal line succeeds the ruler, and personal qualities, as well as power politics, may determine the choice of candidate.

The ruler usually has close relatives and friends, and sometimes influential commoners, as members of his inner advisory council. There may also be another council, made up of representatives of the various sections of the state, which serves more or less as the instrument of public opinion. This council sometimes acts as a check on the ruler if he misuses his authority.

There was formerly great instability in the ruling groups of many African states. Palace intrigues and the assassination of rulers were frequent. Stabilizing devices, such as the sending of ambitious noblemen or relatives of the chief to distant provinces to rule local divisions of the kingdom, or the custom of not announcing the death of a ruler until his successor had been confirmed by the ruling group, checked but did not prevent irregularities. Factionalism usually involved the ruler's sons or brothers, or other close relatives, who were anxious to seize power. Uprisings were rebellions rather than revolutions, for even when they succeeded they did not change the basic form of government, but merely replaced certain persons with others. These rebellions frequently made little difference to the lower levels of government. After European conquest many African chiefs came to be approved and even selected by the European administration to lead the Native Administration in their areas, and much of this intrigue has now disappeared or is no longer as concerned with succession to chieftainship as formerly.

African states are internally segmented into geographic and political subdivisions in complex ways. Districts, subdistricts, villages, or homesteads all relate in some fashion to the central government. Sometimes the leaders of these subgroupings, particularly of the larger ones, are appointed by the ruler of the state; at other times they inherit their positions locally but must be sanctioned by the ruler. If the positions are filled by the ruler he may select members of his own lineage or other kin, so that the whole state is united to the royal family through such ties. Even where leaders are selected locally, the ruler may have royal homesteads led by his kinsmen scattered about the country. These relatives have certain specialized authority: they may receive tribute in goods from persons in their locality, and they may have military barracks attached to the homesteads.

States of this type have sometimes been joined in confederacies under a central ruler. Before British conquest in 1900, the kingdom of Ashanti in southern Ghana was a union of city states in the region of Kumasi, ruled by the *Asante Hene* (King of Ashanti), who sat upon the famed Golden Stool. The member states, known also as territorial divisions, were made up of subdivisions, villages, and lineages all having political functions on the local level. The growth of this kingdom through military conquest at the beginning of the eighteenth century is recounted in this volume in Rattray's "The Ashanti Constitution," in which he traces the development of the kingdom from an earlier group of independent political units.

In many states a voluntary form of contractual arrangement known as clientship is found, through which individuals and social groupings within the state align themselves with a particular subchief who is popular or is considered to be fair, or whose subjects prosper under him. This system of allegiance, which has already been described as a major feature of African political systems, is certainly more characteristic of states than of middle range or small scale societies in Africa. A consequence of client-ship is the movement of populations from one district to another according to the qualities of the particular subchiefs in power at the moment. The renunciation of allegiance to one subchief is not always easy and may be followed by the seizure by the subchief of property belonging to those who are leaving. Yet it occurs. The system also acts as a check on the authority of subchiefs, since autocratic behavior may lead to a decrease in the population of their districts. Clientship seems to exist in some caste organized states as well as in other types.

The state may be internally differentiated into a series of related or unrelated lineage or clan groups, each with a measure of local autonomy. In such cases the powers of the localized groups may be similar to that of the central government, though less extensive. This kind of political organization has been called a segmentary state and occurs, for example, among the Ngoni of Northern Rhodesia and Nyasaland. Or the organization of the state may be based on administrative units made up of residential districts or ethnic divisions in which unilineal organization is politically unimportant outside of the ruling group. Here authority may be highly centralized, with certain rights and duties exclusively held by the central government, as is the case with the Nupe of Nigeria. Again, particularly in East Africa, there are states, such as Ruanda, where the basis of authority is a caste system, with a ruling caste and one or two other caste groups. Maquet discusses this relationship in this volume in his paper, "The Problem of Tutsi Domination." In this case authority is largely held by the upper caste; within this group it is based on unilineal ties. All districts, subdistricts, and smaller units are subject to caste authority and obligations. With respect to the nature of the internal arrangement and the focus of authority, there are also other types of state systems in Africa, but these will indicate something of the range of political types.

African states have complex and hierarchical judicial systems. Almost every level of government has its own court or system of adjudication. Cases may frequently be appealed to higher courts representing a larger administrative unit. In some states certain serious cases, such as murder or witchcraft accusations, can be tried only by the ruler or his representative. The legal system plays an important role in settling disputes between persons from different districts since their case can be brought to the court of the higher administrative unit that includes both districts. Instead of settling disputes between two societies by feud or by conciliation between the leaders, as in middle-range societies, the state has a formal and permanent machinery for settling differences among its segments.

African states have all had periods of conquest and incorporation of other groups, and, unlike many middle range societies, they have often fought to acquire land and to absorb outside peoples, as well as to secure booty. Conquered groups, as has already been indicated, are a characteristic part of African states. They have usually been permitted to keep considerable internal autonomy, becoming administrative regions within the state, but they have sometimes been broken up and their members distributed throughout the state.

The fluidity of African state systems is exemplified in the changing fortunes of the Fort Jameson Ngoni, one of a number of Ngoni groups pushed northward from South Africa by Zulu expansion in the 1820's. Settling permanently some forty or fifty years later in what is now Northern Rhodesia and Nyasaland, they conquered a number of matrilineal peoples and incorporated them in varying degrees into the Ngoni state. With the British conquest of the Ngoni in 1898 and the subsequent establishment of colonial government, both the former conquerors and their captives acquired similar status in relation to Europeans as part of the larger national political system. The reaction of the Ngoni to conquest and their consequent reinterpretation of their position vis-à-vis other peoples is described in this volume in Barnes' paper, "History in a Changing Society."

The expansion and conquest so typical of the growth of African states was made possible by their well-organized military units. All the states appear to have had standing armies and full-time military leaders who were sometimes members of the royal family. Some armies, such as that of the Zulu state, were organized on an age-grade basis, though in other cases kin or residence groups were the unit for the formation of military companies. These armies developed techniques and styles of warfare that were quite sophisticated, though, of course, rarely effective against European firearms. The ruling group of the state kept a close eye on the armed forces, for rebellions led by dissident military units sometimes occurred. Besides their value in conquest, the armies were also effective in maintaining peace between groups within the state and in preventing dissatisfied groups from leaving. These military units have now disappeared, or survive only in attenuated form and carry out mainly ritual activities.

SOCIAL CONTROL AND LAW

Almost all Africans have strong group referents, particularly to unilineal groupings, but also to villages and other types of settlements or to still other groups. Social control and behavior are clearly linked to an individual's sense of reciprocity with the groups to which he belongs. This is certainly more important in Africa than any sense of obligation to laws in the abstract. This group identification, with its social and emotional rewards—and with its difficulties for those who cannot always adjust—is not overriding, but is very important in maintaining order and in guiding individual behavior.

If a person commits a serious crime within a group to which he belongs, strong group action is generally taken through its leaders. This is particularly true in cases of theft or adultery, both of which are almost universally considered extremely serious crimes in Africa. The individual may be fined, ostracized, or even banished from the group, particularly for repetition of theft or of adultery. The killing of a fellow-member of a group, however, is rarely punished by legal means. It is considered an unfortunate or inexplicable happening, sacrifices and other rites are carried out to appease the spirits associated with the group (as is also done in the case of other crimes), and the guilty person frequently loses prestige within the group. In all these cases there is a strong sense of the importance of the group and of maintaining the proper relationship between it and the spirits associated with it.

The stability of the group is further reinforced by the religious beliefs concerning crimes and moral offenses—such as that wrongdoers and other members of the group may be subject to bad luck, sickness, or other misfortunes as a result of such behavior. These mishaps are believed to follow more or less automatically through the agency of the wrongdoer's ancestors or other spirits associated with him or his group. Religious ideology, so closely tied to the groups with which the individual is associated, is thus a deterrent to crime and other inadmissible actions as long as the belief system is maintained. An example of the supernatural basis of a morality system is that of the Nyakyusa, who believe that sin and crime are punished by witchcraft, magic, and retribution on the part of ancestors. Nyakyusa witchcraft is unusual for Africa in having two dimensions: "defensive" witchcraft, in which certain persons having supernatural powers use them to reinforce group ideals, and "aggressive" witchcraft, in which a person commits the criminal act of taking witchcraft into his own hands for selfish motives. Similarly, sorcery may be used both aggressively and defensively. Kinship sins are thought to be punished by misfortune caused by an offended ancestor. In his article in this volume, "An African Morality," Godfrey Wilson outlines the way in which these three types of religious belief reinforce good behavior and punish immorality.

The importance of the social group does not diminish when a member commits a crime outside the group, though the group may act differently than it would in a case involving only its own members. This is in keeping with the idea that to outsiders a person represents his entire group, and that a crime against an outsider will ultimately involve the offender's group in attempts to settle the issue. If a man commits adultery, theft, or murder outside his group, its leaders will usually try to defend and aid him even if they know he is guilty. Similarly, if a crime is committed against a member of the group by an outsider, the victim's group will frequently take the responsibility of seeing that compensation is made. The method of settlement of cases involving members from more than one group varies in terms of the particular political system. If both groups belong to a larger political organization, such as a state, or if they are linked by ritual and political ties of other kinds, a settlement can usually be reached through some discussion or adjudication. If the groups have no direct or indirect political ties at all, the matter may involve a feud, blood revenge, or raiding—or may never be settled at all. Cases involving contractual obligations, such as marriage, between members of different groups within the same political system are usually settled in a court of the larger society. Contractual relations between members of different societies that are not linked politically or otherwise are rarer, and the techniques of settlement less well defined. The breaking of a contract between members of the same group is usually settled within the group, and recourse to an outside judgment is avoided if possible.

To the extent that courts or judges of some kind exist, the law can be said to be present. Legal social control, that is, response to a violation of norms within a society that is backed by the sanctioned use or threat of force, is most characteristic of middle range and of state societies. The form of force may vary: it may be applied to a person himself or to his property. Force may be used to bring about the settlement of a legal case, or the punishment for the guilty party may involve fines, banishment, or death.

The system of courts and adjudication for many matters is clearly prescribed. The most frequent cases appear to be concerned with land or other property, such as cattle, and with divorce, which involves sexual rights and rights over offspring. The methods of trying cases vary greatly in Africa, but there is frequently some sort of court where evidence is presented by the principals, by other witnesses, and sometimes by persons specifically called upon by the judge or judges. Speed of procedure is not as important as presentation of information and discussion, and cases often take a long time. In the absence of written records, verbal recall of similar cases, particularly by elders, may be important. There is an attempt not only to arrive at a settlement but frequently to reconcile the parties concerned so that they can live at peace in the future—an important aspect in societies whose members live in close contact with one another.

In many parts of Africa there is a great admiration for the well-tried case, for the speaker who summarizes a dispute or gives the judgment with clarity, for the elder who is able to cite past cases of significance or quote proverbs to make a legal point. Although sometimes during a case arguments or even fighting may break out, the sessions are usually handled with dignity.

Some cases remain unsettled either because the truthfulness of witnesses is in doubt or because, in the last analysis, the evidence is inconclusive. Resort may then be made to a supernatural technique: trial by poison, swearing innocence to a spirit (if a person who swears becomes ill or dies within a specific period of time he is believed guilty; otherwise he is considered innocent), or consultation of a diviner or an oracle. There is usually no appeal from a decision arrived at by such supernatural techniques, but they are generally used only in more serious or difficult cases.

RELIGION AND WORLD VIEW

In the traditional life of most African societies religion plays a major role in everyday thought and action. As in other societies outside the stream of Western scientific tradition, formal distinctions between theories of natural and supernatural causation are often lacking; and, without the resources of specialized technical and scientific knowledge and written records, supernatural explanations of events receive a relatively greater emphasis than those we think of as "natural" ones. A common example concerns the theories of supernatural causation of death and disease; in Africa, as well as in other parts of the world, it is thought more logical for a person's illness to be caused by the wrath of a spirit or an ancestor than by some invisible substance residing, according to the white man, in the air or water, or carried by a mosquito. The vagaries of members of the spirit world, similar to the observable goings on of the world of humans, provide more understandable answers to the "why" questions of daily life than do obscure foreign explanations in which the connection between cause and effect depends on knowledge not readily available to the African. Thus a scientific "fact," in our society distinguished from a superstition on the basis of methodical, verifiable investigation, may be a "superstition" to an African lacking both the information on which it is based and faith in the system of which it is a part.

The difference in emphasis on natural and supernatural causation between African and Western societies is related to differences in the importance of supernatural sanctions as guiding principles. As we have seen, religion is often an important basis of authority in government and in nonpolitical affairs. Thus the categories of sacred and secular may be quite different in an African society and in one in which, for example, a rigid distinction is made between the provinces of church and state. The relative emphasis laid on supernatural sanctions for behavior will be illustrated in the discussion of types of religious belief in African societies.

Several types of beliefs are found in varying combinations in different parts of Africa. These include belief in spirits, both ancestral and non-ancestral; magic; witchcraft and sorcery; and, of course, the imported religions, Christianity and Islam. Ancestor worship is practiced in a great many African societies. The ancestors are seen as functioning members of the family, lineage, and clan: they are in a position of authority over the living and must be treated with honor and respect. The principle of respect for seniority is extended to the ancestors, for whom death has been not so much a departure from the world of the living as a change of status within the social group. The give and take between the dead and the living is similar to that among the living members of the kin group. The living honor their ancestors by offering them sacrifices and behaving in a way of which they will approve, and in turn are rewarded or punished according to how they have performed their duties. Needless to say, the authority wielded over the living by the dead gives cohesion to the corporate kinship group. It is an actual working system with powers of enforcement rather than the individual matter of the internalized ideals of a distinguished ancestor that has so often served as a guide in our own society. The role of the ancestors as guardians of the living and censors of their conduct in a Northern Rhodesian society is described in this book by Colson in her paper, "Ancestral Spirits among the Plateau Tonga."

The nonancestral spirits in African religious beliefs may be classified as spirits associated with the control of natural phenomena, such as the ground, thunder, or water; spirits concerned with vital functions such as human reproduction and crop fertility; and guardian spirits. One or more of these categories may be present in the religious system of a given society, and within each class there may be a variety of spirits. They may be associated with individuals or with groups. Of course, the total range outlined here will rarely be found within one society, because the predominant interests and concerns of a people are reflected in the number and type of spirits they worship. For example, belief in spirits of thunder and lightning is found in forest areas where frequent electrical storms endanger life, or an agricultural people may believe in a number of spirits concerned with plant fertility, and so on. Group ideals of proper behavior may account for belief in spirits supposed to prevent a person from quarreling or to make him wise or industrious.

The authority of nonancestral spirits is based on the principle of immanent justice, that is, the spirits' response to the actions of humans is an automatic one based on qualities inherent in the deities. Here there is no doubt as to right and wrong, and the spirits, unlike the occasional renegade ancestor who may mistreat his descendants, are not subject to human caprice. A frequent example of the authority of spirits is the oracle, a powerful spirit called upon to determine guilt or innocence in disputes in which the human authorities involved are unable to make a decision.

To summarize the role of nonancestral spirits, the way to the good life, both material and nonmaterial, is aided by spirits that help people cope with the undependability of nature and the fallibility of man. Conversely, spirits, like the ancestors, work to preserve the social order by punishing wrongdoers, causing them misfortune, illness, and death.

As there are different types and functions of spirits, there is also variation in the interrelations between deities in African religious systems. In some there are complex pantheons of gods, headed by a high god who is often the creator, with a number of gods, godlings, and sometimes minor spirits. Kin relationships are often assigned to the members within a pantheon. Deities are designated as gods or spirits acccording to their relative power and, sometimes, whether they have human form or not. A system may include one or both types.

Often the organization of the gods or spirits in a religion parallels that of the human society: pantheons of spirits may be found in hierarchical societies such as some of the kingdoms of West Africa, while in some societies lacking a central government and social classes the spirits are unranked and diffuse. For example, instead of being associated with a formalized body of spirits, each with its set province, a people may have many spirits from which to choose according to individual necessity and preference; some spirits are concerned with general welfare and may be propitiated for varying purposes; others, though they have specialized functions, may in a general way keep a protective eye on an individual or group. One man may align himself with a quite different set of spirits from his neighbor, each being motivated by his personal needs and the experiences of his kinsmen and associates. The spirit world can thus be an "empire" with a formalized power structure or a "democracy" in which the people to some extent at least choose their supernatural authorities.

The people of a society relate to their spirits in varied ways. In the West African kingdoms of Ashanti and Dahomey, there are cults to the pantheons of the earth and sky gods, to which members are admitted by a long and complicated initiation involving the learning of dances and secret rituals associated with the deities. In some societies an individual may form an association with a spirit through being sponsored in a public ceremony by a person, such as an elder kinsman, who has already become affiliated with the spirit. This may occur when a person has a particular need, such as success for his crops or the wish for children, which the spirit can fulfill. In both these cases there is an element of initiation, or confirmation, into the cult of the deity in question. In other cases, such as those in which a spirit is the guardian of a social group, there is no ritual of incorporation of individual members into association with the spirit; rather, this relationship comes automatically with group membership.

The people of African societies are often concerned with questions of their origin and their place in nature, of why certain rituals, such as circumcision, are important to the society, and with ideas of the nature of the individual as a person. The answers to these and related problems of the nature of man and the universe are frequently given in the form of myths in which ancestral spirits, gods, and other nonancestral spirits, play important roles. These spirits are believed to have been involved in the creation of the world, or of the first members of the group, and it is through these myths that the past is understood. Even genealogies of descent groups, often partially fictional, may be myths to explain the present arrangement of the groups: the supposed role of the ancestors in past times is closely related to the present nature of the group.

The degree to which African societies are concerned with the past, with nature, and with concepts of themselves as individuals and as groups varies greatly. Some peoples are relatively indifferent and have little in the way of a mythology. Others, such as the Dogon in the French Sudan, have very elaborate mythologies, and are greatly interested in such problems. Griaule's article, "The Idea of Person among the Dogon," published in this volume, indicates how elaborate these mythologies can become and how valuable they are in shaping the present-day world view of the Dogon.

Belief in a nonspiritual supernatural force, magic, is an important part of religion in many African societies. Magic may be used to promote good or to promote evil: to help and to cure, or to harm. Medicines, often herbal in nature, are used in both types. Charms and amulets are employed to ward off injury and evil. Spells may be uttered as a part of magical procedures to activate the supernatural processes thought to be inherent in the magician's paraphernalia. Magic may be used to manipulate people, as in the case of love potions or harmful medicines. It may be used also to control spirits—a mother may obtain a talisman from a diviner to protect her sick child from the wrath of an ancestor. A person may employ a magical technique himself, or he may seek the services of a diviner to achieve a desired end.

A common practice based on magical techniques is sorcery, which bears some resemblance to witchcraft and has often been confused with it. The distinction between the two that has been made by Evans-Pritchard and followed by other anthropologists working in Africa is that sorcery is the conscious practice of "magic that is illicit or is considered immoral," while witchcraft is a manifestation that is inherent in persons having "a supposed psychic emanation from witchcraft-substance," a harmful material, thought to be present in the bodies of certain persons, that may be diagnosed by oracles in the living and discovered by autopsy in the dead.[4] There have been numerous speculations as to whether the supposed witchcraft substance may be the vermiform appendix, something contained in the small intestine, or some other manifestation, anatomically normal or pathological, but the important consideration from our point of view is how witchcraft beliefs operate in African society.

There are two basic distinctions between witchcraft and sorcery. First, looked at objectively, the process of witchcraft, though it is often described in dramatic detail by persons believing in it, does not actually exist. Belief in it and the effects attributed to it are real enough, but there is no actual evidence for such things as the alleged presence of withcraft-substance in the bodies of supposed witches, statements that witches have familiars in owls or other night animals and leave their sleeping bodies at home while they go on their nefarious rounds, or the idea that the misfortunes or deaths of those said to be bewitched are actually caused by other persons. Sorcery, on the other hand, in which persons use evil magic to harm others, actually exists, though doubtless many false accusations of it are made. Second, witchcraft is said sometimes to be completely involuntary—a person may not suspect that he is himself a witch until an accusation against him has been "proved"—whereas sorcery is voluntary and consciously performed, although it may be instigated by someone other than the sorcerer.

In any one society sorcery or witchcraft, or both, may be found. They may be considered expressions of so-called stress points in the social structure: the relationship between certain kinsmen who are in positions of conflict, such as that of the mother's brother in a matrilineal society and his sister's son, who is his heir and in some matters his rival, or that of jealous co-wives of a polygynous husband, are such stress points. Whether a woman uses a magic potion to "turn her husband's head" from her co-wife or whether a maternal uncle unknowingly bewitches (that is, is accused of bewitching) his nephew who has long waited to inherit his power and wealth, the assumption behind both processes is the same: malice toward a person whose position one would like to occupy oneself, or fear that one's position will be usurped by another. As revealed by the ubiquitous mother-in-law jokes of our own society, any social system has what we might call weak points that are prone to strain in human relations. In his paper in this volume, "Witchcraft in Four African Societies: An Essay in Comparison," Nadel presents an analysis of both sociological and psychological factors in the witchcraft beliefs of two pairs of societies having similar cultures, two in Northern Nigeria and two in the Sudan.

The chief categories of practitioners in traditional African religions are priests, diviners, and rainmakers. Priests are the intermediaries between specific deities and individuals or groups: they serve a particular god or spirit and watch over the behavior and needs of its adherents. A clan or lineage elder may be the priest of its ancestral cult, a secret society may have its priest, or a priest may serve the guardian spirit of a compound or village.

Diviners serve their clients both as doctors and as ascertainers of the unknown. They employ magical techniques to determine what may have caused a misfortune, illness, or death, and they sometimes also call upon spirits to give them the desired knowledge. Magical techniques may involve the throwing of a number of objects such as bones or seeds and reading a message from the patterns in which they fall, or killing a chicken and examining its entrails to obtain the information sought. In some cases diviners also have an extensive knowledge of herbal remedies, which they use in treating illness. Divination is often a highly skilled profession requiring rigorous training over an extended period and the learning of innumerable formulas—according to one authority, the equivalent in time and effort of that needed to obtain a Ph.D. In some societies women diviners serve as midwives, using their herbal knowledge and magical resources in the promotion of conception and the treatment of feminine ailments, as well as presiding over deliveries.

In theory the role of the diviner is to promote the social order, and this is usually true also in practice; but occasionally a "bad" diviner is found who finds it profitable to dispense evil magic despite strong group sanctions to the contrary. This may possibly be an illustration in reverse of the diviner's position as a sort of a hub of the social group, coordinating the human, magical, and spiritual forces of a people in time of need. For it is the fact that evil medicines are usually obtained from a diviner outside the group of which the purchaser is a member that points up the importance of local group loyalty and solidarity. A man who is a "good" diviner for clients of his own group, upholding their social and religious ideology, may feel no such compunction in relation to strangers.

Rainmakers are found in many African societies. Their task is not only to insure sufficient rainfall for the needs of pastures and crops, but also to stop the rain if floods threaten. The persons in which this office is vested are very different in different societies. The rainmaker may be the chief or king, he may be a priest or a professional functionary such as a diviner, or he may be a member of a lineage or clan who serves this purpose for various clients. Rain may be sought by magical techniques or by sacrifices to gods or spirits thought to bring rain or stop it. Rain may be sought at shrines dedicated to this purpose, or a rainmaker may be summoned to an area suffering from drought. As in the case of death and disease, rain is often thought to be a reward for good behavior, and drought (or floods), to be a punishment for evil—either from inside the group or from interference by outsiders.

LANGUAGE

African linguistics is a complex field, and only a few of its major features can be touched on here. Few African languages have been thoroughly studied, except for those spoken north of the Sahara. For many we have only a short word list or a dictionary compiled by a non-linguist. Furthermore, as a result of the many population movements in Africa, the interrelations of languages and language families are difficult to clarify, and scholars disagree about the family groupings of African languages. The classification of Greenberg,[5] which appears to be generally accepted among American anthropologists, will be used here. It is based on the principles of linguistic analysis used in classifying Indo-European languages, though written records have not been as commonly available for Africa.

There are more than eight hundred African languages. Some are spoken by millions; the speakers of others number in the hundreds. A few languages seem to have disappeared completely within the past hundred years, and others, such as ancient Egyptian, have been extinct for generations. Until recently most African languages were unwritten, except for some in North Africa and the Ethiopian area. The lack of writing in many parts of Africa has not prevented the development of traditional political states and of sophisticated theological systems, two elements frequently associated with writing. It has meant, however, a great dependence on oral traditions and oral literature, as well as on skill in public speaking.

If we include Madagascar, there are six major language families represented in Africa, and at least seven other language groups or individual languages that appear to be distinct or are not well enough known to classify with the major families. One major family is the Click languages, spoken by the Bushmen, Hottentots, and Bergdama of southwest Africa and by two small groups in Tanganyika, the Hatsa and the Sandawe. A second is the Niger-Congo family, a large grouping that includes the languages of West, central, and southern Africa, and some parts of East Africa. One of the subgroups of this family is Bantu, which dominates central and southern Africa, and in which the close similarity of languages indicates a relatively recent expansion, possibly from the West African area. A third major family, the Macrosudanic, is found in the Nile-Congo divide, the central Sudan, the upper Nile, and the northern Great Lakes region. In the Macrosudanic area there are also groups speaking languages belonging to other families. The fourth family, the Central Saharan, which stretches over a wide area of the central Sahara Desert, is little known. The fifth, called Afro-Asiatic by Greenberg, is a large family covering North Africa and much of the East Horn area, and extending also into southwest Asia. It includes Berber, Cushitic (a major language group of Ethiopia), the Chad languages spoken to the west of Lake Chad, Semitic (including Arabic), and ancient Egyptian. Finally, the people of Madagascar speak Malagasy, which belongs to the Malayo-Polynesian family, thus indicating some past ties with southeast Asia. It is possible that some of these African language families may be related to one another, but this has not as yet been established.

Trade languages are common in Africa and are used not only in economic exchanges but also for a variety of political and social purposes in contacts between speakers of different languages. None of these are artificial or mixed languages, but, have all spread from a particular linguistic grouping. Swahili, a Bantu language, is spoken by small African groups along the coast of Kenya and Tanganyika. After it was adopted by Arab slave traders along the East African coast as far south as Madagascar it became a common trade language throughout much of East Africa, and some Arabic elements were incorporated in it. Galla has been a widely known tongue of Ethiopia and the surrounding areas, and Hausa and Fulani are widely spoken in the Western Sudan and parts of the Guinea Coast. Trade languages are common elsewhere in Africa, their presence indicating that contact and trade between peoples speaking diverse languages have probably not been severely handicapped by linguistic differences.

Western contact has led to the introduction of European languages and to their use by national governments in many parts of Africa. Various forms of pidgin have appeared as a result of this linguistic contact. Most Africans still speak their traditional languages which, with the exception of a few languages with a small number of speakers, do not show signs of disappearing. Some trade languages, such as Hausa and Swahili, are regularly used by Europeans in communicating with Africans. Orthographies have been developed for the major African languages, and for some there is now a vigorous vernacular literature.

AESTHETICS

The aesthetic life of the African is a rich one. It is rarely set off from other aspects of everyday existence; rather, it is intimately bound up with social behavior and religious life. Of the major forms of art the best known and most characteristic are woodcarving, folklore, music, and the dance. Other art forms are relatively unimportant in Africa, particularly south of the Sahara. Pottery and basketry are usually simple and utilitarian. However, terra cotta heads and figures of some antiquity have recently been found in West Africa. Though cloth is made from cotton and from bark, it is not usually woven or printed in decorative patterns. Ironworking is important throughout the continent. but it is mainly restricted to the manufacturing of hoes, blades, and other tools. Nevertheless, outstanding work in bronze and gold has been produced by West African metallurgists. Aside from some very fine rock paintings of humans and animals formerly made by Bushmen in South Africa (though they are no longer made today), the art of painting on flat surfaces is not highly developed in Africa. The great traditions of aesthetic creation are in folklore, carving, music, and the dance.

Two papers in this volume, Fagg's "The Study of African Art" and Herskovits' "Negro Folklore," are summary accounts of these branches of aesthetics and the studies that have been made in them. For music a valuable summary has been made by Merriam.[6] Other studies of these fields are listed in the Bibliography at the back of this volume. African aesthetic life exhibits a great deal of variation from society to society, and within a single society. Highly localized traditions are found within small groups, sometimes within families. Because of this it is sometimes difficult to generalize adequately on African aesthetics as a whole. But there is also much borrowing of ideas and techniques from one group to another.

Innovation also occurs frequently, particularly in verbal art. Topical songs, so common in Africa, may be based on old rhythms and melodies, but with their texts composed for specific occasions they are essentially creative commentaries on the present social scene. Wise sayings soon become proverbs. Innovation or change in tales and other forms of narrative is common. Though recorded chiefly in the study of verbal art, innovation is also present in other aesthetic forms, though it may not seem so striking. It does not seem to occur as a result of a specific effort to be different, but rather as an adjustment to particular situations, through artistic play, or as an outgrowth of the development of a particular art form.

In examining the relationship of aesthetics to social relations and to social groupings in Africa we find that aesthetics is associated with a variety of social controls. When an African dons a mask and performs certain dances or sings about people or events, he is no longer acting as a person but as a being or spirit. In this role he often has freedom for comments on social relations and for actions that, if made unmasked, would produce social frictions or hostilities. By their very difference, the actions of masked dancers serve to make clearer the desired qualities of everyday behavior. Again, topical songs, explanatory tales, or tales with a moral, help to point the way to expected and proper conduct in the society. These are all techniques of informal social control involving aesthetic devices.

The use of proverbs and sayings in court cases has already been mentioned. The court itself frequently has an element of drama in it, and persons unconnected with a case may go to watch and listen out of general interest. After the case is decided it may be discussed for many days in the community. The qualities of the speakers and the judges in court cases clearly have an aesthetic element that may influence the decision of the court.

Social control through religious beliefs and practices is also expressed in aesthetic forms. For instance, carvings are used to represent spirits or are thought to house the spirits. People act toward the carvings as if they were spirits—the carvings symbolize the spirits in visible form and become identified with them—so that the sacredness of spirits and carvings are bound together. Again, diviners sometimes make use of proverbs and other forms of folklore in arriving at a decision or giving advice. The interpretation of the folklore form becomes the key to the client's understanding of what action is to be taken.

But it would be a mistake to think that social control is the only area with which aesthetics is associated in Africa. There is an element of pleasure, of humor, of physical release in African aesthetics that relates to psychological and bodily needs. This aspect of aesthetics has never been explored to any great extent in Africa. What, precisely, is the pleasure in taking part in, or in watching, an African dance? What makes one thing humorous, another fearful? How do Africans themselves perceive beauty, the shape and the form of a mask? These are difficult questions to answer, but they are important for the understanding of African culture.

The role of the artist is not the same in all African societies. In some cases, notably in states, as has already been indicated, the artist is a full-time specialist who makes his living by art. In many other societies an artist is a farmer, herder, etc., as well, and while the aesthetic forms produced by a carver, for instance, may be important to the society, the artist does not have unusual wealth, prestige, or authority by virtue of his aesthetic talents. In some cases the role of the artist is inherited within a family or descent line; in other cases it is attained without such kin ties.

Carving is almost universally the work of men in Africa. Folklore, music, and the dance are probably more characteristically male than female activities, particularly those aspects that are directly associated with religious and legal controls. Nevertheless, women do a great deal of dancing and singing and employ various forms of folklore in a number of different situations.

PREHISTORY AND HISTORY

To the people of the Western world, Africa has always been the "Dark Continent," a static society relatively isolated from the rest of the world until recent years, and with little social or cultural development of its own. These views have been reinforced by ignorance of African prehistory and history.

In reality, however, Africa was changing profoundly even in the remotest past, as a result of internal forces as well as of contact with non-African peoples. Knowledge of these changes can provide a perspective on present-day African culture and social change.

There is sound evidence that in Africa, particularly South Africa, early forms of man were probably developing as early as a million years ago. The exact relationship of these *Australopithecinae,* or South African Man-Apes, as they have been called, to the major lines in human evolution is still being analyzed. Nevertheless, the fossil evidence from southern and eastern Africa indicates change, diversification, and development of proto-human types, showing that several physical forms of early man developed over long periods of time in Africa. The relationships of these early fossils to present-day African physical types are not clear, if indeed any direct relationships do exist.

There is also evidence of a social and cultural development in Africa during the Paleolithic period (from about a million years ago until about ten thousand years ago), largely parallel to that in Europe. Hunting and gathering peoples, and later fishing societies as well, populated both areas in small, relatively isolated groups. Their stone tools, which show increasing complexity and diversification with time, follow remarkably similar stages of development in Africa and in Europe, with some notable exceptions: for example, the early stone tools made of pebbles and found in South and East Africa seem to be absent from Europe, and some of the stone tools of the Congo seem to reflect a localized specialization. What was once thought to be a characteristically European pattern of development in material culture during prehistoric times is now believed to have been more widespread. The exact origin of specific tool types, whether in Europe or Africa, is not known in many cases, but the resemblances suggest long-range contacts between the two continents. Taken together, the physical and cultural evidence from the Paleolithic period in Africa indicates that the continent probably had a significant place in man's early physical and social development.

Agriculture and the domestication of animals, which developed on a large scale in the Near East (including Egypt as well as the Tigris-Euphrates region of Mesopotamia) from about 8000 B.C., were to have important consequences for Africa as a whole. Recent research indicates that some of the innovations for which this Near Eastern area is famous may not have developed in the Fertile Crescent itself, but around it, including northeastern Africa. There is some evidence, for example, that certain grains domesticated in the Ethiopian Highlands spread from there to the Near East.

There is no doubt, though, that from this area of Afro-Asiatic contact many Near Eastern techniques of production and, regardless of their specific point of origin, many material items diffused throughout large sections of Africa. The spread of agriculture, herding, and the use of iron all from the Near East into Africa was probably gradual over many centuries, and was undoubtedly related to major population movements. A similar situation occurred in Europe, but in Africa the exact course of these diffusions and the precise contributions of the Near Eastern cultures to local indigenous developments are little known, mainly because of the paucity of archaeological records for Africa. Neolithic influences undoubtedly also reached Africa from southeast Asia by way of Madagascar, but this is even less well understood than the developments in Africa itself.

By A.D. 1000 agriculture and herding were apparently widespread in Africa and hunting and gathering groups, diminishing in size and importance, were being pushed into less fertile areas. There is evidence, for example, that the Bushmen, once more widespread in southern and central Africa, were pushed into southwest Africa by the movement into their area from the north of Bantu-speaking Africans possessing agriculture, herding, and a superior technology. This southward movement, which must have started more than fifteen hundred years ago, was still continuing at the time of the early European settlements in South Africa during the seventeenth century. In the process some Bantu groups formed complex political groupings. States, such as the Swazi and the Bemba, conquered and absorbed some groups and dispersed others, even creating a northward countermovement in southeast Africa of Bantu-speaking peoples fleeing political control. The states arose by dominating land and people rather than by controlling trade or markets, which were unimportant in the area. Much movement, fighting, splitting, and absorption of groups seems to have occurred in central and southern Africa in the past fifteen hundred years—a sort of Neolithic expansion that took its own unique form in these regions.

In another movement, African herding people, some of them Nilotic, made their way generally, though not invariably, southward into predominantly agricultural tribal areas around the Rift and the Great Lakes. Though the time of origin is unknown, this movement was still in progress in the nineteenth century when European travelers entered the area and had certainly been going on for hundreds of years. The herding groups frequently conquered, absorbed, or dominated the farming tribes, and some adopted agriculture as well. In some cases states arose, some of which, such as Ruanda, have caste groups based on the conquerors and the indigenous inhabitants, with considerable elaboration of political ritual and symbolism. In many other cases the groups, such as the Masai, remained nearer to what was probably their original type of social system, segmented patrilineal clans. This general movement had profound effects on the cultures of the whole East African area.

Farther to the northeast, Cushitic-speaking, predominantly herding peoples from what is now British Somaliland and northern Somalia moved deep into Ethiopia and into southern Somalia over a considerable period of time. By the twelfth century or even earlier, one of these groups, the Galla, was apparently pushed southward by expanding Somali peoples living in the same area. The Galla moved south to the Lake Rudolf area, and in the sixteenth century expanded northward into Ethiopia; the Somali spread into the southern areas of the East Horn. Moslem Arab traders also entered the Horn area at various times and formed some settlements. Indigenous African groups, including Bantu-speaking hunters and agriculturalists, were absorbed or were pushed south into Kenya, leaving only small groups, particularly noticeable today in some Somali regions.

In addition to internal movements, populations and cultures from outside the continent have also influenced African history. One migration of peoples, originating in the Neolithic period and enhanced by the technological developments that followed, was the expansion of Arabic and other Asiatic peoples down the east coast of Africa. By the time of Christ, peoples from the Arabian Peninsula were trading along the coast, taking advantage of the monsoons, which blow northeast for approximately six months of the year and southwest the other six months. There is evidence that even at this time they had small settlements along the east coast. Their political power, trade, and the numbers and size of their settlements along the coast gradually increased until their dominance and control of the Indian Ocean was destroyed by the Portuguese in the early part of the sixteenth century. But Portuguese power soon declined, and peoples from Oman, in southeastern Arabia, revived Arab domination for a period between the middle of the seventeenth and the end of the nineteenth centuries. After this the influence of the Arabs weakened as a result of European control of the coast. Nevertheless, Arabic peoples today dominate many of the coastal settlements and some of the trade from Madagascar and Mozambique to Arabia. Persians, Indians, and even Chinese also took part in trade along the east coast at times. For well over a thousand years this area has been part of the complicated network of economic and political relations among the peoples bordering the Indian Ocean.

The early Arabic groups along this coast were, of course, pre-Moslem, but by the end of the seventh century they were followed by Moslem Arabs who were either fleeing troubles in Arabia or interested in dominating the East African trade. These Arabs settled in fair numbers along the coast and on offshore islands such as Zanzibar. They had few settlements inland, mainly small trading posts. Swahili, a local Bantu language, was Arabicized and became the *lingua franca* of the coastal area. Arab political confederacies and states rose and fell, sometimes linked with southern Arabia and sometimes independent of that region. The Arabs traveled into the interior, up the Zambezi River, overland to Lakes Nyasa and Tanganyika, and even into the Congo area, in search of slaves, ivory, and gold. Large caravans of slaves carried the ivory to the coast, where both slaves and goods were traded to Arabia, Persia, India, and Egypt, with the result that African peoples were, and still are, found throughout the Indian Ocean and Near East area. Some slaves were kept to work the plantations of cloves and other food products that the Arabs established along the coast.

The impact of this whole movement is difficult to estimate. Large numbers of Africans were taken from the East African area and this must have deeply affected the remaining population. Some goods of non-African origin, such as guns, were introduced. Some African groups cooperated willingly in the slave trade and benefited in wealth and goods, but other groups either took no part or resisted the Arabs. In general, Arabic culture did not spread inland and there was little Moslemization of the interior. Along the coast Arab-African intermarriage was common, with some African groups virtually disappearing as a result of marriage or conquest.

Moslem Arabic influences swept over North Africa from Arabia, dominating Egyptian life, and gradually, despite bitter resistance, controlling many of the Berber and Tuareg groups farther to the west. There were two main periods of westward movement. The first, in the second half of the seventh century, following the death of Mohammed, was only partly religious in nature, since economic and social gains were also important incentives for some Arabs. This movement destroyed Byzantine control in Egypt and led to the domination, not always secure, of most North African cities by Moslem Arabs. The second movement, during the eleventh century, was the invasion of North Africa by Bedouin Arabs from Arabia. More rural in orientation than the earlier invaders, they sacked cities and overran large areas, and formed the basis of the present-day Arab population of much of North Africa. From the time of the first invasion there is a long history of the development of Arab states in North Africa, states sometimes linked closely to Arabia, sometimes independent, and sometimes fighting among themselves. North Africa clearly became Arabic and Moslem in culture, despite the presence of indigenous Berber populations of considerable size, and retained cultural ties with the Near East from the seventh century onward.

The coming of Moslem Arabs to North Africa was to lead to an eventual linking of their culture with that of the peoples of the Western Sudan. While the historical record is incomplete, large states were evidently developing in the Western Sudan at the time of the early Arabic expansion in North Africa. One of the earliest known is Ghana (or Gana), from which the present country of Ghana has taken its name, which existed from about the fourth century to the eleventh, and which at one time apparently extended from Senegal to the middle Niger. From the tenth century, such states rose and fell at various points between Lake Chad and the Atlantic Ocean. They dominated trade routes across the Sahara as well as the major cities in the Western Sudan, which were also market centers, and some of them controlled the valuable gold fields in the western part of this area. Beginning with the eleventh century, Arabic and North African influences began to make themselves felt through the Moslemization of the region and the repeated attempts to control the Sudan and the trans-Saharan trade. However, the population remained basically non-Arabic and there was never the successful pattern of Arab settlement that occurred in North Africa. The building of states continued until, at the conquest of the Sudan by European powers in the second half of the nineteenth century, there were a number of Fulani empires, largely Moslemized, in the Sudan. Since then, the trans-Saharan trade has changed in terms of the kinds of goods involved, but it still continues. Moslem and Arabic influences, particularly the former, are probably still growing, but not all Sudanic groups have by any means been converted.

In the southern regions of the Western Sudan and in the tropical forest areas of the Guinea Coast, a series of states, such as Ashanti (Asante) and Dahomey, arose at different times from about the fifteenth century on, perhaps as a result of contact with the Sudan. Whether there were states in this region at an earlier time is not known. These political systems changed from an inland to a more coastal orientation as a result of the European and American slave trade, which was flourishing by the eighteenth century. Expanding to the coast, they dominated the slave trade routes from the interior, the markets, and the sale of slaves to Europeans and Americans along the coast. They were also important during the second half of the nineteenth century when slave trading gave way to other forms of trade, and they played important roles during the period of European exploration and domination of the whole area. There were many nonstate groups, such as the Ibo, in this area, who were also involved in the slave trade. The rise and fall of kingdoms before and after European contact and their relation to the nonstate societies of West Africa are outlined in this volume in Forde's paper, "The Cultural Map of West Africa: Successive Adaptations to Tropical Forests and Grasslands."

We have indicated some of the major developments in African prehistory and history. Many others could be touched upon: the influence of Greece, Rome, Persia, and Turkey, in North Africa; the ties of Madagascar with southeast Asia; the development of large-scale indigenous political groupings in the Congo; the influence of Asiatic and American native food plants on African diet and productive resources. As our knowledge of Africa's past grows, it becomes clearer that the continent has gone through many radical social and political changes and has been far from static in its internal development or in its sensitivity or reactions to external influences.

THE PRESENT

The modern period of culture contact with the Western world is actually a continuation of earlier periods of change and ferment rather than a sharp break with the past, though the particular social and cultural developments and the forms of action differ. The history of these contacts has been quite fully recorded and discussed in a variety of publications.

Four major periods of contact are evident. The first, from about 1600 to 1850, was the time of European exploration of the coastal areas of Africa and the immediate hinterland. It was also the period of the slave trade, when European and American ships took millions of Africans from the region between Senegal and Angola in the west and from sections of the east coast as well. Africans in the coastal areas cooperated in this trade, and slaves came from many miles inland as well as from along the coast. The second period, from approximately 1850 to 1900, saw the exploration of most of the interior of Africa and its partitioning and domination by European powers. The third period, from 1900 to the end of World War II, was that of colonial rule, when the African countries were administered by various forms of indirect rule and when the development of natural resources began to tie the continent to the world economic market. The final period, from the end of World War II to the present, has seen the rise of nationalist movements and the development of political organizations patterned after those of the Western world. It is the time of independence for African countries. During this postwar period there have been serious attempts in African countries to develop self-sufficient economies and to balance the extraction of raw materials with industrial development.

From the point of view of the anthropologist these four major periods are extremely important. Many researchers have devoted their full attention to the nature of the social changes taking place, rather than exclusively dealing with the more traditional aspects of African culture. The great variety of reactions to European contact in Africa, ranging from violent opposition to acquiescence or willing acceptance on the part of different African groups—and even of the same group at different periods—makes generalization difficult. For example, the people of the Mau Mau movement, the Kikuyu of Kenya, have been very receptive to European contact as well as (at least some of them) violently anti-European. Nevertheless, it is possible to indicate a few general trends of change that are characteristic of much of Africa today.

Perhaps the earliest fundamental change in social relations among Africans resulted from the cessation of warfare, and the decline in intertribal tensions of the more violent kind, after European conquest and control of Africa. Traditional hostilities between African groups gave way, and widespread freedom of movement without fear of seizure became possible. Frictions between tribes and groups continue today in the form of competition to obtain favorable political and economic positions, but the older isolation has disappeared and the world view of Africans has enlarged to include greater distances and more varied peoples and cultures.

A second factor, which became significant early in the colonial period and is becoming more and more so, is the shift from localized self-sufficient economies to cash economies, with greater dependence on trade and the specialization of labor and skills. True, before European contact African cultures were rarely completely self-sufficient, and trade was important in many areas, but the present-day emphasis is increasingly on production of raw materials for the commercial market, generally for export, using the money gained in exchange to purchase necessities as well as luxuries. The use of money, while it existed in some parts of pre-colonial Africa, is more widespread, due to the development of export and mining economies, the increase in wage labor, and specialization. The level of prosperity of Africans is becoming associated more with world economic conditions and less with localized factors. Goods of the industrial world are in great demand, and those produced by local craft play a smaller and smaller role in the economies. There is an increasing commitment to purchasing industrial products, as well as to supplying raw materials for foreign trade. The greater physical mobility permitted by the cessation of warfare and other frictions has facilitated the economic expansion that is now integrating Africa into the world market.

The growth of cities in Africa is closely related to increasing physical mobility and economic change. While some indigenous cities existed, it is probably safe to say that before extensive European contact Africa was predominantly rural in outlook and that one of the most striking changes has been the increasing urbanization of the continent. With the current growth of cities south of the Sahara, there are virtually no areas of Africa except the desert regions where the process of urbanization is not occurring.

Urbanization in Africa is characterized by the emergence of class systems, most strikingly at the moment, perhaps, of a middle class. With the growth of cities, the emphasis on cash economies, on more impersonal economic transactions, traditional kin obligations break down in favor of other kinds of social relations. While tribalism does not disappear —in fact, urban life sometimes leads to an increase in tribal frictions— the city does tend to be a place where custom and culture mingle until pan-urban cultural forms develop. The urban environment and living conditions of Africans from a number of tribes living in a large city in South Africa are described in Hellmann's paper, "Life in a Johannesburg Slum Yard," in this volume.

Modern African cities have existed long enough so that first- and second-generation city-born Africans are often found. It is in these people that we see the greatest change from the rural life. They have an interest in their country relatives, but they generally prefer to live in the city. They visit their rural cousins but find their lives strange, and they are ashamed or upset by some aspects of rural culture. While those who first moved to the city frequently felt free to go back and forth between city and country, their descendants view the world more and more as urbanites. The stereotypes of the country bumpkin, of the "bush cousin," appear, as well as that of the "wickedness" of the city.

The relationship between the city and its hinterland is also changing. Before European conquest, the rural areas, even those with large-scale political systems, were essentially self-sufficient, with a great deal of local political control and relatively well-integrated systems of local belief and ideology. True, there were periods of conquest, centralized authority, and the imposition of external political, economic, and ideological controls, but in the long run there was a great deal of local autonomy in African communities regardless of type of government. Today we find that this autonomy and the isolation of the rural areas are giving way more and more to dependence on the city. Decision making is being carried out in the urban centers, and political power is leaving the countryside. The rural areas depend on the sale of goods to the city and look more and more to the city for professional services and material things. Urban values, often in conflict with rural ones, become important in the rural areas, even if they are not always acceptable to farming, herding, and fishing people. Whether one characterizes this transition as that from primitive to peasant life, as some anthropologists have done, or not, it is clear that the great change occurring in the rural areas is related to the development of urban life. We can expect these changes to continue as urban centers grow larger, new cities develop, and urban influences spread more and more to rural areas. Eventually it is likely that, as in the United States, much of rural life will disappear, urban culture and custom coming to exist in the countryside as well as in the cities. McCall's paper, "Dynamics of Urbanization in Africa," included in this volume, summarizes the major developments in the urbanization process.

Many anthropologists who have carried out field research in Africa have commented on the Africans' interest in traditional politics and law. Whether Africa is really different from other areas in this respect is diffi- cult to say. Certainly, however, political movements, nationalism, and political change are characteristic of the continent today. The new politi- cal activities tend to be led by city dwellers, who accept urban existence as their way of life. The cities are becoming the focus of many political movements, though rural areas may play decisive roles in political action at certain times.

The widening perception of space and of people is nowhere more clearly seen than in political action. The more or less arbitrary boun- daries of the colonial territories have provided the framework for modern political action by Africans. The pattern of political growth has varied. Characteristically, however, small localized political associations, "im- provement" clubs, economic groups, or other associations have de- veloped into political parties on a tribal basis, each tribe evolving its own political machine, with its own ideology and sense of self-enhancement for the tribe. This has sometimes occurred in tribal groups which had little or no tribal identity before European contact. For example, the Ibo of southeastern Nigeria were composed of more than two hundred rela- tively autonomous groups without a common name. Today Ibo are very conscious of their tribal identity and are the main force behind one of the major Nigerian political parties.

The presence of tribal political organizations has in some countries led to serious internal disputes, so that national issues have become fo- cused on tribal interests. Tribalism has become a kind of regionalism, since tribes frequently represent solid territorial areas with their own char- acteristic cultures and economies. Today there is a growing tendency for these tribal and regional groupings to cooperate, even sometimes to merge, in the larger identity of the nation or state, but the process is a slow one.

Beyond this we see the beginnings of a pan-African political iden- tity, of attempts at cooperation in political and economic matters between the rising nations of Africa. Even further, we see African countries taking part in the United Nations and other international organiza- tions. The shift from the local group to the tribe and region, to the nation, to Africa, to the world, has implied a very rapid reorganization of political activities and also of concepts of the nature of political function- ing and resources.

In this situation of expanding horizons the role of the traditional po- litical leader becomes less important. In the early days of colonial rule the traditional leaders—or those the colonial governments thought were, or ought to be, the leaders—became the focus of indirect rule, the keepers of the peace, the arbiters of disputes. As economic and social changes occurred these leaders have been caught between the demands of Western values and the traditions of their indigenous cultures. Fallers' paper, "The Predicament of the Modern African Chief: An Instance from Uganda," in this volume, focuses attention on this very problem. With the rise of political parties and national governments, many traditional leaders have been or are being by-passed. Some have become ritual figureheads with no real authority; others have joined political parties, or even founded them, in which case they have tended to be conservative and to rely more on tradition than do many of the emerging nationalistic political leaders, who would have had less important roles, if any, in traditional political structures.

The rapidly shifting political scene is associated with the rise of charismatic leaders—persons whose political appeal is based more on their particular personality characteristics, and individual way of acting, than on the authority of their political office. They often begin their leadership activities with little political organization behind them and build as they go along, until parties become firmly established and their basic structure and lines of authority clearly delineated. Present-day African leaders live in a swiftly-changing period in which, except in South Africa, they have more and more come to replace Europeans in government. Constitutions and local governments are rapidly replaced by new constitutions and new forms of local control as nations approach independence. Leaders of the developing political parties find their way into government positions through constitutional means, political pressures, and other techniques. Their roles are often uncertain, untested, and without the authority of established traditions of office. In such situations charismatic qualities play a very important part.

As African countries become independent, and their mode of government more permanent, we find that the formal government positions become more precisely defined, that a sense of tradition in political action develops, and that the importance of an office increases and the uniqueness of the individual holding it declines somewhat. Personality factors in leadership, though still important, become encased in more formalized political roles.

Most of what has been said concerning political organization and leadership is not true of South Africa. Here a caste system, seemingly more rigid every day, forbids Africans political participation, limits their economic development, and has created a sense of racial separation and differentiation that has few parallels in the world today. In this volume, Kuper's paper, "The Uniform of Color in Swaziland," focuses on one aspect of the problem of race relations—the perception of Africans by whites and of whites by Africans. The general patterns of change occurring almost everywhere else in Africa exist also to some extent for the African in South Africa, but in attenuated form, with severe limits that in other parts of Africa are unknown or rare. Yet it is among the whites in South Africa that there has been the greatest development of industrialization and of Western modes of living found anywhere on the continent. We are seeing a situation in which Africans outside South Africa, farther from immediate contact with the Western world, are approaching the standards of Western life found among the whites of South Africa more rapidly than are the Africans in South Africa itself. It is impossible to predict the future course of social change in South Africa except in the light of increasing pressure by the indigenous inhabitants toward opportunities for westernization, and of increasing pressures upon South Africa by Africans from without.

If we move from the broad social picture to the narrower one of smaller social groupings and interpersonal ties, we arrive at further exciting changes that are ultimately related to the broader trends. For one, the importance of the obligations of kinship, of the place of the lineage and larger family groupings in African society, is decreasing. Physical and social mobility and the emphasis on individual enterprise are destroying the place of larger kin groups in African life. This is particularly noticeable in cities but it is true in the rural areas as well. The functions of the larger family groups, of lineages and clans, are being taken over by association groups or are disappearing. Respect for seniority and beliefs in the efficacy of the ancestors are losing ground. The monogamous and the small polygynous families emerge more clearly as the basic kin units. Bilateral ties extending from these units replace ties in which family life was partially submerged in the web of lineage and clan obligations. The family becomes the basic economic unit. Parents are less concerned over land and property, arranged marriages, and the birth of grandchildren to guarantee the continuation of the line of descent, and more over education for their children and the children's rise in economic and social class position. The rivalry for prestige among individuals, formerly eclipsed in the greater competition between large-scale relationship groups, now stands out more and more as a focal point in the life of the African.

Kinship ties are replaced with those of social interests, work activities, and economic level. Association groupings, which in traditional society are based largely on age or on initiation into some secret or semisecret organization, become based on tribal identity, welfare needs, political interests, Christian belief, social compatibility, and so on. These new forms of association groupings play an important role in the adjustment of individuals to changing conditions, particularly in the cities.

It has sometimes been said that westernization and urbanization increase the emphasis on voluntary contractual relations between individuals at the expense of the more personal social roles of traditional culture. This may be true to some extent in Africa, but one is struck rather with the notion that social ties are still very personal and binding and that purely impersonal contractual relations are rare, though highly personalized human interrelationships are now based less on kinship and descent than on other kinds of ties.

Some social scientists have argued that the cessation of warfare and the economic changes following European contact have led to a noticeable rise in the status of women in Africa. The term "status" is an ambiguous one, having meaning mainly in terms of some referent. It is true that in precontact times women, as well as men, were more restricted to local areas, that danger of seizure limited their mobility, and that their economic opportunities were sometimes meager. Within this framework, their personal influence and place in society varied greatly from group to group, and certainly from person to person. The cessation of hostilities and the opportunities for trade have increased their freedom to move about, to take an active part in trade and other phases of the developing economy, and to increase their economic resources. However, it is frequently difficult to estimate whether they are more or less influential in society at large.

One cannot discuss the subject of cultural and social change in Africa without some reference to religion. Two great "world" religions, Islam and Christianity, are proselytizing in Africa today. In some areas there is no contest between them: Islam dominates North Africa, and most of southern and central Africa is subject to Christian influence. In the region between the Sahara in the north and the Congo and East African Highlands in the south, both religions are active in gaining converts.

Islam has relied largely on African proselytizers to spread its beliefs to members of their own society. It allows for considerable variation in interpreting dogma and for the incorporation of local religious beliefs in spirits and magic within the total theology. As customarily presented to Africans, it permits polygynous marriage with a maximum of four wives. These and other features, in which cultural differences are minimized, have probably added to its attractiveness. It has the disadvantage, in the eyes of some, that its Koranic schooling and some of its theology do not prepare one for the Western world, for Western forms of government, as much as Christianity does at the present time. Islam is spreading south quite rapidly in some sections of the Sudan and in the area south of this broad zone, though some groups holding traditional religious beliefs have resisted it very strongly. Greenberg's paper, "Some Aspects of Negro-Mohammedan Culture-Contact among the Hausa," in this volume, examines the influence of Islam among a Northern Nigerian people.

Part of the appeal of Christianity lies in its close association with Western culture. Mission schools—and until recently much of the educational system in colonial areas was in missionary hands—inculcate not only fundamental Christian beliefs, but also Western modes of thought and values. For the present-day African, education is the avenue to positions within the rapidly developing economic and political system. Christianity is thus closely linked with the prestige of the Western world.

Furthermore, Christian theology, with its emphasis on a single God or on a few significant figures, is appealing to some Africans, though the precise reasons why this is so are sometimes obscure. Christianity has the disadvantage that it does not, in its more rigid forms, allow for African beliefs and practices, and that it tends to negate many aspects of African life, from the payment of bride wealth to the place of traditional artistic forms such as ceremonial dancing and drumming. Some Africans find Christian ritual colorless and are perplexed by the lack of visible emotion. For Africans who are critical of colonial policy, of the white man's attitudes toward race relations, there is a tendency to feel that missionaries are the hypocritical handmaidens of colonial governments. Finally, there is the evident failure, until very recently, of Christian missions to develop a large and active group of African clergymen and other religious officials. Schapera's paper in this volume, "Christianity and the Tswana," surveys and evaluates the impact of Christianity among a people living in the Bechuanaland Protectorate in South Africa.

Despite the problems raised by Christianity and Islam, both have had considerable success in Africa. Probably the average African has little sense of competition between them. If he lives in a local area that is becoming Islamicized, he is likely to become a Moslem. If he lives near a Christian mission, he is more likely to become a Christian. There is often no serious local friction between the two faiths. It is more in the context of Africa as a whole, and of political movements in certain African countries, such as Nigeria, that one can see the two religions in competition, the one oriented toward the west, the other either with a local orientation or with some feeling of ties with North Africa and Egypt.

Traditional African religious beliefs and rituals are changing, but they are by no means totally disappearing. They are being modified partly as a result of the pressure of Islam and Christianity, but also as a result of the general social changes such as those outlined above. As lineages, clans, and other large-scale kin groupings decrease in importance, so would we expect beliefs in their extensions into the spirit world, the ancestors, to wane. Once the force of the kin or descent group declines, its religious associations have less meaning. Again, of what value to the urbanite are beliefs in the spirits of the earth, of the growth of crops, of the weather? Further, traditional religious beliefs were means of controlling interpersonal relations, of preventing theft, adultery, and other crimes. Not that secular techniques of dealing with these are absent from the framework of traditional society, but that the religious component of social control, whereby wrongdoing is thought to bring misfortune to the person concerned and those close to him, is a strong one. With the growing emphasis on the secularization of legal life, with the development of the police and the secular judicial systems of the Western world, there is less and less emphasis on religious forces as means of social control.

Even though some of the specific features of African religion and ritual are disappearing in the areas of most intensive European contact, certain aspects survive and seem well integrated into the changing social scene. Separatist churches that have broken away from European-controlled Christian organizations are common in Africa, particularly in South Africa. They reflect resentment over European control and over the stricter forms of Christian dogma, while at the same time allowing practices that Africans still find meaningful—traditional music, dancing, and ritual. Belief in personal spirits that are thought to protect and guide the individual is important in some areas and is sometimes fused with Christian belief. Witch-finding cults, modifications of traditional witchcraft beliefs, are sweeping areas of West, central, and East Africa, and are now found even in groups which had little or no belief in witches in pre-contact times. Whether these movements express social discontent and maladjustment, as some claim, or whether they have other causes, they are clearly a part, albeit a perplexing part, of Africa today. Magical techniques have adjusted to modern times, so that a clerk in an office can use magic to make his superiors appreciate his work more, or to help him find other employment. Patent medicines, those magical devices of Western civilization, are commonly found in stores and markets and are sold in large quantities. In Moslem areas, as has been indicated, conversion to Islam has allowed for the well-integrated retention of numerous traditional practices and ideologies. The spirit and force of African religion has adjusted, at least in some important respects, to the changing social scene.

NOTES

[1] I.e., the people of Buganda. According to the system of prefixes in Bantu languages, the prefix Bu- denotes a political entity, Ba- is the plural form indicating the people, and Mu- is the singular form denoting one person.

[2] Radcliffe-Brown, A. R., "Introduction," in Radcliffe-Brown, A. R., and Forde, D. (eds.), *African Systems of Kinship and Marriage,* London: Oxford University Press for the International African Institute, 1950, p. 41.

[3] See particularly, Fortes, M., and Evans-Pritchard, E. E. (eds.), *African Political Systems,* London: Oxford University Press for the International African Institute, 1940; Brown, Paula, "Patterns of Authority in West Africa," *Africa,* 1951, *21,* 261-278; Schapera, I., *Government and Politics in Tribal Societies,* London: Watts, 1956; Middleton, John, and Tait, David, *Tribes without Rulers,* London: Routledge and Kegan Paul, 1958; Kaberry, Phyllis,

"Primitive States," *British Journal of Sociology,* 1957, *8,* 224-234.

[4] Evans-Pritchard, E. E., *Witchcraft, Oracles and Magic among the Azande,* London: Oxford University Press, 1937, pp. 9, 10.

[5] Greenberg, Joseph, *Studies in African Linguistic Classification,* New Haven: Compass Press, 1955.

[6] Merriam, Alan P., "African Music," in Bascom, William R., and Herskovits, Melville J. (eds.), *Continuity and Change in African Cultures,* Chicago: University of Chicago Press, 1959, pp. 49-86.

2

People and Environment

THE BUSHMEN
OF SOUTH WEST AFRICA[*]

L. Fourie

In the harsh environment of the Kalahari Desert the life of the Bushmen is oriented around the constant struggle for food. Until recent years completely dependent on the resources of their natural environment, Bushman bands wandered from one waterhole to another in their search for game and wild plant foods. The different bands which together form a "tribe" speak a common language but otherwise have no shared activities or social solidarity. It is the band that is the landowning group and whose members share the toils and rewards of daily life. Through their intimate knowledge of their environment the Bushmen have managed to subsist in a region where without resourceful techniques, such as caching water in ostrich shells, or obtaining subterranean water by digging a hole in the sand and sucking it through a reed with a grass filter in the bottom, they could not survive. Also, in addition to using various weapons, snares, and poisons of their own fashioning, the men of some Bushman groups disguise themselves in the feathers of an ostrich, carrying a long stick with the end curved like a head, and imitating the movements of the bird in order to come within shooting range of a flock. The delicacy of this balance between man and nature is expressed in the social and religious setting of the food quest, in which the strict patterns of sharing and the supernatural precautions surrounding the hunt are thought to insure the food supply.

SOCIAL ORGANIZATION

The Family Group

Each of the language groups into which the Bushmen have been classified consists of several main subdivisions. Though for the sake of convenience the latter will be referred to as "tribes" in this report, there is no evidence

---

[*] Reprinted from *The Native Tribes of South West Africa,* Cape Town: Cape Times Limited, 1928, pp. 84-103, by permission of the Legislative Assembly of South West Africa.

of any tribal organization among them. The various so-called tribes bear distinctive names, mostly of Bushmen or Hottentot origin, the significance of which is in most instances no longer known. Judging by the practice which still exists among the Bushmen they are in all probability descriptive either of the territory occupied by certain groups or of some physical or other characteristic of such territory or groups. Each tribe is composed of a number of family groups [bands] all of whom claim relationship to each other through a common tribal ancestor. Thus, for example, according to the traditions of the ‡Ao-//ēin all the groups constituting that tribe descended from a "first big ‡Ao-//ēin Bushman." A similar belief likewise exists among other tribes. Nothing in the nature of a central authority whose decisions are binding on all members of the tribe is met with among them, nor is collective action taken in the interests of the tribe as a whole. Each family group forms an independent unit by itself, possessing its own group area and authority over and specific rights within such area only. In relation to other groups it is collectively responsible for the actions of each of its members. When differences arise they are confined to the groups concerned and not participated in by the rest of the tribe. On occasion, however, a weak group will seek and sometimes obtain assistance from a stronger one, but such alliances are never of a binding or permanent nature. . . . The more widely separated groups of the tribe have no personal knowledge of or direct personal contact with each other and generally live in such superstitious fear and dread of each other that the members of one will not undertake journeys into the territory of another, even when accompanied by Europeans. The group areas are separated from each other by neutral zones into which nobody will venture except during the course of visits. These zones are usually formed by belts of trees, open flats, water courses, etc. Territorial boundaries are observed in a most scrupulous manner even by closely related groups who are living on the most friendly terms with each other. Each family is inseparably united to its habitat and has a superstitious dread of any locality but its own. The result is that even the members of completely disorganized groups are loth to seek employment outside the boundaries of their ancestral territory.

At the head of each group is a big man or chief. Though usually considered to be a chief in name only and without any authority over the members of the group, he in fact does exercise considerable influence in the life of the community because in him are vested certain functions, the performance of which are of vital importance to the wel-

---

[The symbols used to represent the click sounds of Bushman language are:
// = lateral click, something like a "k" sound forced off the side of the tongue
‡ = alveolar or palatal click
! = frontal click, like our "tsk, tsk" sound
/ = like !, but held before release]

fare of his people. The family area with its food and water supply, as well as the fire, are all looked upon as belonging to him. . . . Marriage in the group being exogamous and patrilocal, the rest of the group consists of male relatives of the chief with their wives and families. The whole group lives in a common werft or encampment which is laid out on a definite plan. The huts of the married families are placed about 15 to 20 feet apart and arranged in the form of an irregular circle 60 to 80 yards in diameter. Among the *Hei-//om* the hut of the chief is always placed in the east, facing, but at some distance away from, the others. In the Kalahari it may occupy any part of the circle. At or near the middle of the werft is situated a large tree which is reserved as the meeting place for the men and for ceremonial and other purposes. Among some tribes women are entirely forbidden to approach it or to join the men when gathered underneath it. Within the circle adolescent young girls and boys are accommodated in separate huts some distance away from each other. Among the more primitive groups the boys are not provided with a hut, but sleep under the tree in the center. Mature nubile young women either remain in the young girls' hut or occupy huts next to those of their parents, but inside the circle. Old widows and widowers, as also visitors, live outside the circle of the married people. The dancing place is situated within the circle.

Huts vary considerably in size and shape among the various tribes. In its most primitive form the hut is four to five feet in height and of a very simple design, consisting merely of a semicircular shelter of branches planted into the ground and covered with grass. Hut-making is the work of women, and a husband does not interfere with his wife's building operations. When it becomes necessary to desert an old camp and establish a new one the site for the latter is selected by the chief, who deposits his household and other effects on the place on which his own hut is to be erected. After the other members have done likewise he proceeds to light a new fire by means of firesticks. Brands from the fire of the old werft may not be used for this purpose. From the fire kindled by him each family then lights its own, after which the women may begin with the building of the huts.

In each group area the permanent encampment is situated in the vicinity of the main water supply. When the area is of considerable extent the group, however, moves about from one place to another according to the season and the distribution of the rainfall upon which it is mainly dependent for its food supply. . . .

Family Life

Each family within the group occupies its own hut. Children sleep with their parents until they are strong enough to go about by themselves, when the boys join the others under the tree and the girls take up residence in the hut for unmarried girls.

The women rise early, light the fire and prepare the food for the morning meal which usually consists of veldkos [wild plant foods]. After having eaten, the men go out visiting or hunting or engage in some other occupation such as preparing skins, weapons, etc. The women accompany each other in search of veldkos and go out soon after the men have left. When food is obtainable at no great distance they are usually back in camp towards midday. When they have to go far they may not reach home until late in the afternoon. Wood is collected on their way back. Immediately after their return they proceed to prepare food, the younger married women and young girls in the meantime fetching water. The food is ready by the time the men arrive in the evening and the latter are able to partake of it without delay.

There is a sharp division of labor between the men and women of the group. The former do the hunting and snaring of game, prepare the weapons, skins for clothing, snares, firesticks, pipes, etc., and occasionally assist the women in fetching wood and water. The women build the huts, collect veldkos and prepare the food, make the fire and keep it going, gather wood, fetch water and manufacture ostrich eggshell beads for ornaments, etc. The latter are also responsible for keeping the camp clean.

Infants and young children accompany their mothers on their daily excursions in search of food until they are old enough to look after themselves. From that time onward the mothers take practically no share in their education which, in the case of girls, is entrusted entirely to an old woman who lives in the hut with the young girls, and in the case of boys, to their fathers.

Little girls, while still with their mothers, are taught to love and respect the old woman and to seek her company of their own accord. After taking up residence with her they accompany her daily into the veld and thus gradually come to learn from her all the duties which will ultimately devolve upon them. Boys sleep under the tree in the center of the camp at night or in a hut specially set apart for them. Each morning they accompany their fathers into the veld. At first they are given little bows and wooden arrows with which to amuse themselves. Towards the eighth or ninth year each is provided by his father with a proper bow and three arrows which, however, are not poisoned. With these he is allowed to shoot hares, guinea fowl and other birds, wild cats, small buck, etc. After killing his first steenbuck or duiker he is given a few poisoned arrows and later, when he has become proficient in the use of these, he is taught to stalk and shoot big game. By the time he reaches the age of puberty he has, as a rule, gained a very good knowledge of veld craft. . . .

ECONOMIC CONDITIONS

Food Supply, Etc.

The source of the food supply varies very considerably in different localities. In some it is derived mainly from the vegetable, in others from the animal, kingdom. The Kalahari and northern parts of the territory are rich in both plant and animal life and the Bushmen inhabiting those parts consequently have a fairly well-balanced dietary. In the central and southern Kalahari the most important among the vegetable foods are the *tsamma* (citrullus vulgaris), öintjes (cyperis edulis Dtr.) and //*nōun* (Bauhinea esculenta). As one proceeds northwards various fruit-bearing trees appear, *e.g.*, the wild fig, palm, omungete nut, wild orange, omuandi, omuve, etc. In addition to the above numerous varieties of edible roots, bulbs, tubers, berries, etc., appear in great profusion during and after the rainy season. . . .

Among insects, locusts, ants, scorpions, young bees and honey are greatly relished. Frogs, lizards, snakes, etc., are also eaten. In fact, all living animals are eaten with the exception of the mole and the hyena, the former because its winter larder of öintjes forms a valuable and easily obtainable addition to the supplies of the Bushmen and the latter because it eats human corpses.

The methods used in the pursuit of game vary according to the season, the year being divided into a cold, dry season (winter), a hot, dry season (spring and early summer), a small, rainy season (September and October) and a big, rainy season (January to April). Snaring is resorted to only during the dry season in the case of such animals as guinea-fowl, bustard, aardvark, ostrich and small game. Pitfalls are not made use of except for hare and springhare as too much work is entailed in making them. Springhare and snakes are also caught by means of a long barbed stick which is passed into the burrows, the animal being transfixed and then dug out. During the big rainy season when the ground is sodden with moisture small buck such as duiker and stembuck are run down on foot and killed with a knob kirri. This method is not applicable to small game during the dry season owing to the difficulty in following the spoor. In the hot weather, however, young buck are easily caught in this manner as the hot sand causes the hoofs to come off. The gemsbuck does not tire easily. It is run down, therefore, only during the big rainy season when the soft ground impedes its progress and causes it to be caught comparatively easily. All other varieties of big game are run down in the hot, dry season. After a herd of game has been located one or more men give chase at a steady trot. The animal is pursued relentlessly until it is exhausted and brought at bay, when it is killed with assegaai.

Bow and poisoned arrows are used all the year round. These weapons differ considerably in character in various localities. The Kalahari bow is small compared with that used by the *!Kũng* of the Oschimpolo-veld, and *Hei-//om* of the Etosha Pan region; the arrow consists of a reed shaft, bone foreshaft and bone or iron tip, whereas the latter use arrows with feathered wooden shafts and iron tips only. The poison also varies in different localities. In southern Namaqualand it is constituted of a mixture of plant juice (euphorbia), snake poison, scorpions and spiders; in the southern and central Kalahari only insect poison is used, and further north and northwest only plant poison.

All tribes observe certain customary practices in connection with the hunting of animals with bow and arrow. These vary considerably among the different tribes. The following is an account of the practice as met with among the *Hei-//om*. After an animal has been shot it is followed by the hunter until it expires or until nightfall when he returns to the *//gāus* (camp). The following morning the whole community takes part in the search for the carcass, as the previous day's tracks had in all probability been effaced during the night by other animals. The searchers spread out on a wide front and keep a very sharp lookout for the presence of vultures. After the carcass has been found it is skinned by the men. The belly is then opened and the entrails removed and cleaned. Bags are made from the stomach and into these the blood is collected. The animal is next cut up and, after this has been done, the liver is roasted and eaten by the men. The skin, if suitable for the purpose, is cut into sandals, bowstrings, etc., on the spot. The meat is then removed to the *//gāus* by the men who may occasionally be assisted by the women. On arrival at the *//gāus* all the meat is laid on the ground under the *!heis* [the large tree in the middle of the camp] either on sticks which were used in carrying it or on branches. The *gei-khoib* (chief) now comes forward and if he finds that the *|hei-|ais* [fire under the tree, regarded as essential to the welfare of the community] has gone out he returns to his hut, brings fire and wood and relights it. If he is absent when the meat is brought in he is immediately sent for, the meat in the meantime being hung on the *!heis*. . . . After having kindled the fire the *gei-khoib* instructs one of the men—the one who has shot the animal is excluded from doing any work—to open the bones and collect the marrow. The blood and the marrow are placed on the fire in separate pots and at the same time some of the meat for the men is also cooked. As soon as the latter is ready for eating the *gei-khoib* removes a piece from the pot and "tastes" (tsã-tsã) it. This is done by holding it between the teeth and fingers and cutting off and eating a morsel or two. The meat is now safe for the members of his group to eat. The cooked meat is then pounded with a stone, teased between the fingers and thrown into the pot containing the blood. The melted marrow is next stirred into the mixture of blood and meat. The resulting dish is known as ǂḳoms.

All meat killed with bow and arrow is *soxa* [taboo] and may not be partaken of until it has been tasted by the *gei-ḳhoib*. The liver, however, is eaten by the men immediately after the animal has been cut up and is thus excluded from the scope of the *soxa* as far as men are concerned, but to the women it is *soxa*. All parts of the animal are eaten, but certain categories of people may eat only certain prescribed portions of the animal, the rest of the meat being *soxa* to them. For example, the wife of the man who killed the animal is entitled to the superficial covering of meat and fat of the hind quarters, the entrails and the trotters (*ǂei-ti*). Her portion is known as the *ǂnoe-di* and is the only meat which may be partaken of by women. . . . If women partake of any other meat than the *ǂnoe-di,* the poison of the arrow will not act when an animal has been shot.

* * *

[Strict rules for the sharing of meat by the man who shot the animal and by other members of the camp are observed lest the poisons weaken and refuse to act in the future.]

Any want of success in the chase is generally attributed to some chance incident. For example, a man, who has had bad luck in hunting while his wife had her periods, will not hunt again when she is in that condition nor will she eat any of the *ǂnoe-di* at such times. The meat of an animal killed by a dog may not be eaten by women or by any men whose wives are menstruating. This prohibition is to prevent bad luck befalling the dog in the pursuit of game. . . .

Soxa applies only to meat killed with bow and arrow and as far as is known at present this practice exists among the *Xom-ḳhoin,* /*Koma-ḳhoin* and *Go-gara-ḳhoin.* Among these groups the meat of the following animals is *soxa,* namely, steinbuck, duiker, springbuck, hartebeest, gemsbuck, kudu, wildebeest and giraffe. The eland, which is a comparatively rare visitor to the parts occupied by these groups is not killed at all by the *Xom-ḳhoin* who believe that harm will befall any person who eats its meat. In other words the *Xom-ḳhoin* consider the eland to be absolute *soxa.* Among other groups the man who shoots an eland must, on returning to the //*gāus,* sleep under the !*heis* as intercourse with his wife will prevent the poison from killing the animal. The same applies to a person who shoots a giraffe.

The implements and utensils which are used in the collection and preparation of food are very few in number. Vegetable food is dug up with a sharpened stick, 2 to 5 feet in length. Öintjes, //*ñoun* and other similar plant foods are roasted in hot ashes covered with cinders. Ants (Bushman rice) are dealt with in a similar manner and then recovered again by means of a sieve of grass matting. Locusts are either roasted or boiled. Frogs, etc., are sometimes roasted over the fire on a wooden spit (braaistok) stuck into the ground. Birds, snakes, small antelope, etc., are prepared by placing them in a hollow made in the ashes with a flat paddle-shaped wooden scoop and covering them over with live coals. The meat of larger animals is either cooked or roasted. Among the tame partly disorganized groups any sort of receptacle such as a paraffin tin serves for cooking purposes. The more primitive groups use clay pots bartered from the neighboring Bantu. Roasted plant food is eaten whole or in the form of soup or porridge after being pounded up in a wooden mortar or on a stone and mixed with boiled blood.

Food is eaten direct from the pot or from bowls made of wood or the hide of big game. Many groups nowadays make wooden spoons. Generally, however, either the hands or tortoise-shell spoons are used in eating.

Every part of an animal is eaten or made use of for some purpose or another. Nothing is allowed to go to waste except by those groups which, through possessing dogs, find it comparatively easy to kill game. The camps of the latter are generally littered with bones, etc., whereas among the wild Bushmen even the bones are broken up and eaten. In the case of small antelope when for any reason the skin is not suitable for other purposes it is roasted with the animal and eaten. Small skins are used for karosses [skin cloaks], food and tobacco pouches, quivers, loincloths, etc. From the skins of big game on the other hand sandals, blankets and, among certain groups, bows, quivers and bowstrings, are made. The /Nu-// ẽin and // Aikwe are more expert in preparing skins than the ‡Ao-//ẽin and other tribes living to the north. Articles made by the former form an important medium of exchange. The sinew is used for making bowstrings, for reinforcing bows and arrow-shafts, and as thread for sewing skins. From it also is made the string of the nets in which the Kalahari groups carry their belongings. In the Kalahari the foreshaft and tips of arrows are made from the long bones of the ostrich and various kinds of big game. Bones are also made into knives, awls, pipes, etc. The horns are manufactured into spoons, whistles, small quivers for carrying arrow-tips during the rainy seasons, implements for stripping the fibre required for snares, artificial leeches, etc. The stomach of large animals when not required for food is fashioned into bags for collecting the blood and for carrying water. Ostrich eggshells are used for carrying and storing water and for the manufacture of the eggshell beads which at the present time form the most important article of barter among the /Nu//ẽin, Kaukau Bushmen and Hei-//om. Among the most northerly groups on the other hand arrow poison and red ochre, obtained from the wood of the *omuva* tree, are the principal media of exchange.

FOR FURTHER READING

Schapera, Isaac, *The Khoisan Peoples of South Africa,* London: Routledge, 1930. A compilation of earlier writings on the Bushmen, Hottentots, and Bergdama; a basic reference on the Bushmen.

Bleek, D. F., *The Naron, a Bushman Tribe of the Central Kalahari,* Cambridge: Cambridge University Press, 1928. An anthropological report on one of the best-known Bushman groups.

Schapera, Isaac, "A Survey of the Bushman Question," *Race Relations,* 1939, 6, 68-83. A general paper on the Bushmen.

Tobias, Philip V., "On the Survival of the Bushman," *Africa,* 1956, 26, 174-86. The report of recent evidence that the decline of the Bushman population has stopped and they are now increasing in numbers.

Thomas, Elizabeth Marshall, *The Harmless People,* New York: Knopf, 1959. A nontechnical report on present-day life among the Bushmen, illustrated with excellent photographs.

THE BEMBA—THEIR COUNTRY
AND DIET*

Audrey I. Richards

Living in undulating tree-covered plateau country that is well watered but has generally poor soils, the Bemba traditionally have practiced a type of shifting cultivation typical of many South Central African peoples. As in other areas where the distribution of rainfall in marked wet and dry seasons permits only one crop a year, the food supply of the Bemba alternates between periods of dearth and plenty. Although they are organized politically in a kingdom with well-defined class differences, these are not expressed in the type and quantity of food consumed, for in Bemba tradition wealth is defined not in terms of land or of cattle but of the amount of service a person can command. A chief owns land in theory and exacts tribute from those who farm it; in turn, he is supposed to use his supernatural powers over the prosperity of the land and the welfare of his subjects in carrying out the economic rituals on which their food production depends. Thus a person accumulates wealth by acquiring food to give to his followers. Both political and kin relationships are symbolized by the giving and receiving of food, which, being scarce for all Bemba at times and representing power and prestige in their minds, is of great emotional importance to them. As a herding people may seem to the outsider to be obsessed with cattle, or of a landowning agricultural group with its land, the interests of the Bemba center around food, and this may be seen not only in their feelings concerning generosity and hospitality but also in their perception of their natural environment.

Although Bemba economic conditions had been altered considerably from those of pre-European times by the 1930's, when the research on which this selection is based was done, and have changed even more since, this paper, and the larger work of which it forms a part, remains an important contribution to the study of African diet and its significance in human relations.

---

* Adapted from *Land, Labour and Diet in Northern Rhodesia,* London: Oxford University Press for the International African Institute, 1939, Chapters 1, 2, and 3, by permission of the publisher, the author and the International African Institute.

THE PEOPLE AND THEIR COUNTRY

Origin

The Bemba are the largest and most highly organized tribe in North-Eastern Rhodesia.[1] They are a warrior people of Congo origin which apparently invaded their present territory at the end of the seventeenth or the beginning of the eighteenth century. Moving eastwards from the banks of the Kasai, they eventually reached the great Luapula river which forms the western boundary of this part of Northern Rhodesia. They passed north of the Bangweolu swamps, according to most traditions, travelled up the Chambesi in a northeasterly direction, and finally established their Paramount chief, the Citimukulu, in the center of this Tanganyika plateau not far from the present Government station of Kasama. From this point they gradually expanded, pushing back earlier immigrants of the same origin. . . . Hence numbers of scattered tribelets came to acknowledge the rule of the Citimukulu and paid him tribute, and groups of his chosen followers were settled in the outlying districts to exact these dues. His power seems to have been still further consolidated by the arrival of Arab traders in the middle of the nineteenth century, since they brought him guns, of which he kept complete possession, in return for ivory and slaves. In fact before the coming of the white man at the end of the century it seems that the Citimukulu held sway over the whole of the district between the four great lakes, Tanganyika, Nyasa, Bangweolu, and Mweru, and south into the present Lala and Lamba country. With the establishment of the British South Africa Company at Kasama in 1899 the military conquests of the Bemba suddenly ceased. The Citimukulus of today rule over their own territory only. It stretches from 29° west to 32.5° east and from 9° north to 12° south, and covers the whole of the administrative district of Kasama and most of those of Mpika, Chinsali, and Luwingu, an area rather larger than that of Ireland. It includes much of the Bisa and Lungu territory occupied during the last century and now predominantly inhabited by them, and the Bemba are still regarded as the dominant tribe in the district by members of other groups.

* * *

[The Bemba, originally an offshoot of the great Luba tribe, and neighboring tribes such as the Bisa, Lunda, Lamba, Kaonde, and others, are all predominantly agricultural peoples of Congo origin who are closely akin and have a matrilineal descent system and a common body of custom, as distinguished from other tribes of Northern Rhodesia that have been dominated by the invasion of predominantly patrilineal herding peoples from the south and from the cattle-owning tribes of the area.]

Mode of Life

As regards their general mode of living and economic activities the Bemba are, broadly speaking, typical of the Central Bantu. . . . [They] live in small communities, the average village consisting of 30 to 50 huts, while that of the present Citimukulu numbers 150, and in the old days chiefs' villages reached higher figures still.[2] Each village is a kinship unit under the rule of a headman who is appointed by the chief of the district and responsible to him. It changes in composition from time to time, as well as shifting from site to site. The settlements are widely scattered and the density of the population never reaches a greater figure than 3.9 per square mile.[3] This system of local grouping resembles that of the kindred peoples of North-Eastern Rhodesia, but is in marked contrast to that of the Eastern Bantu tribes such as the Ganda, Chagga, &c, who live in isolated homesteads, from the smaller family kraals composed of a man, his wife, and his sons common in South Africa, or the larger Bantu settlements numbering as many as 10,000 inhabitants found, for instance, in Bechuanaland.

The Bemba have already been described as an agricultural people, though, like most of the Bantu, they are fond of hunting and fishing and rely on the bush for many of the wild plants and fruits used for food. Their chiefs used formerly to capture cattle from the surrounding tribes, and kept these sporadically, but the Bemba lack entirely the pastoral tradition. Only a third of the Province is free from [tsetse] fly, and today neither chiefs nor commoners own more than a few goats or sheep, and occasional cattle in urban areas. The people are shifting cultivators, that is to say, they clear a fresh strip of the bush each year to make their gardens, and when the forest land round their villages has all been used (four or five years) they move to a fresh site a few miles away, build themselves new huts, and start cultivating again. This general type of agriculture is practiced over most of Northern Rhodesia, the Belgian Congo, large parts of Nyasaland, Tanganyika, and the less highly developed areas of Uganda and Kenya, everywhere giving place to fixed cultivation of an elementary type with the introduction of European cash crops, shortage of land, or urban development. But a recent intensive study of native agricultural methods in one area—North-Western Rhodesia—shows that the term "shifting cultivator" can cover the greatest variety of methods of utilizing bush land.[4] The Bemba cultivate by clearing the undergrowth, pollarding the trees over a strip of bush, and burning the branches and brushwood so obtained on a small space in the center of the cleared patch to make an ash-fertilized bed on which the seeds are sown broadcast without further hoeing. In subsequent years the gardens are dug up into mounds on which other crops are grown. This method, known from the earliest days of the British occupation as the *citemene* system after the native name for a cut garden, is practiced all over this part of North-Eastern Rhodesia, and by some of the Lamba-Kaonde and Lunda-Luba peoples on the northern plateau of North-Western Rhodesia. It is reckoned as one of the most primitive forms of bush cultivation, everywhere associated with poor soil. The Bemba show great ingenuity in the alternation of crops and the use of the fertile soil of old village sites, yet as a whole their cultivation is much less complex than that of a number of the neighboring tribes. . . .

The aboriginal crops in this part of the country seem to be finger millet, Kaffir corn, bulrush millet, Kaffir beans, Livingstone potatoes, and numerous cucurbits—pumpkins, edible gourds, cucumbers, melons, etc. Groundnuts, maize, cassava, sweet potatoes and yams, all grown widely in Central Africa, are of New World origin, apparently introduced by the Portuguese in the seventeenth century. Bemba tradition confirms this classification. They declare that their first ancestor, Citi Muluba, travelled from the Luba country carrying in his hair the seeds of Kaffir corn, finger millet, Kaffir beans, cow peas, pumpkins, and the small wrinkled cucumbers known as *amankolobwe*. Their most important economic rites center round the cultivation of Kaffir corn, now less often grown, quick-growing finger millet, cow pea, Livingstone potato, pumpkin, maize, and *amankolobwe,* and the ritual associated with any particular crop has often been reckoned as an index of its age.[5] Bemba maintain that they have grown maize and groundnuts "for a long time," that sweet potatoes were introduced by Swahili traders in the reign of a chief who lived at the end of the nineteenth century, while the Bisa, the neighboring tribe to the west, taught them how to grow cassava.

Of all these crops their staple is the finger millet, a coarse tufted grass about 3 feet high bearing fine grain of the size of birdseed on five or six radiating fingerlike spikes.[6] This is a hardy plant specially suited to poor soils, but its distribution in Central Africa seems to show that Kaffir corn is grown in preference wherever the soil makes this possible, and that it has been ousted from its position as a staple crop by cassava and maize in all the more fertile environments. . . . In many other parts of Africa the finger millet is now cultivated entirely for the purpose of brewing beer, for which it seems specially suited, and is grown in this way in Southern Rhodesia, Tanganyika, the Congo, Uganda, and Kenya. Thus in their almost entire reliance on finger millet the Bemba are now in rather an unusual position as regards the composition of their diet. They grow less Kaffir corn than before because of the lack of suitable soil and the labor to protect it from birds. It is sometimes described as a chief's crop on the latter account. Maize gives a poor yield in this district, and sweet potatoes and cassava have only been grown widely during the recent locust raids in response to direct Government pressure.

Material Culture and Economic Organization

The material equipment of the Bemba is of the simplest. It consists of four implements, (a) a wedge-shaped axe blade (*isembe,* plur. *amasembe*) forged locally, fixed into a wooden haft, and used to clear the bush, to cut poles for fencing, hut-building, and simple furniture such as beds or storing racks, to hollow out tree-trunks for canoes, to fashion logs into drums, stools or mortars, or to hammer out bark-cloth; (b) a hoe (*ulukasu,* plur. *amakasu*), the only instrument used exclusively for cultivation, formerly traded from the Lungu and other more skilled iron-workers to the west and now bought at European stores; (c) a spear (*ilifumo,* plur. *amafumo*) forged locally and used for war, hunting, fishing, and protection against wild beasts; (d) a bow (*ubuta,* plur. *amata*) formerly used in war and hunting and important as a family heirloom, but rarely made nowadays.[7] All these implements are of the simplest kind, neither carved nor ornamented, and all arts and crafts are extremely poorly developed in this district compared to the contiguous areas. Iron-work, which reached such a high perfection among peoples like the Shongo, Kuba, and Luba, and is practiced to a greater or less degree among the Kaonde, hardly exists among the Bemba. . . .

The economic organization of the Bemba is not a complex one. The strongest ambition of the old Bemba chiefs seems to have been the conquest of territory and the exaction of tribute from the surrounding tribes rather than the accumulation of material goods. Wealth among the Southern Bantu consisted in herds of cattle, which marked a man's status, enabled him to marry, to pay his fines, to make offerings to his chief or ancestral spirits, and to carry out all his kinship obligations, but the Bemba had few material possessions that could be accumulated as capital or used as any form of currency. Ivory tusks were the monopoly of the chiefs of each district and used for display, or traded for Arab goods, such as bales of cloth or guns, with which faithful warriors and subjects were rewarded. Beyond this the wealth of a Bemba chief consisted in the amount of service he could command as agricultural labor or military force, and the number of slaves, whether of his own tribe or conquered peoples, he possessed. Marriage contracts and most other kinship obligations were fulfilled by the giving of service, not goods, and enslavement was often enforced in lieu of a fine. No organized system of barter or exchange existed. Salt and hoes seem occasionally to have been traded, but regular markets which are a prominent feature of tribal life among the Eastern Bantu, and in such Congo tribes as the Shongo and Kongo, were quite unknown among the Bemba. We are dealing with a warrior people in which the whole economic system was dominated by the political relationship of subject and chief, and the organization of labor founded on it.

* * *

[The present economic position of Bembaland is that of a labor reserve, where large numbers of adult men must leave annually to look for work. The agricultural system is deprived both of manpower and traditional incentives to work.]

Social Structure

It is impossible to describe in detail the tribal structure of the Bemba, either as a preface to this special study, or from a comparative point of view. There are, however, certain main principles of their social organization which are absolutely fundamental to an understanding of all their organized activities and forms of cooperation, and give the direction to their interests. Of these the dominant institution of the Bemba is their highly complex political system and the particularly autocratic character of the chieftainship on which it is based. Allegiance to a common Paramount—the Citimukulu—is the main tie uniting the members of a tribe that is scattered very thinly over a wide area. It determines their local grouping, and is the basis of the traditional pride of this warrior people and its distinction from neighboring tribes. On a man's relationship to his chief depends his residence, his use of land, the economic group he works with, the way in which his food is distributed, the religious and magic beliefs that sustain him in his work, and his social ambitions.

* * *

The power of the chief rests ultimately on his people's belief in his supernatural powers over the prosperity of the land and the welfare of his individual subjects. By his inheritance of the guardian spirits (*umupashi*, plur. *imipashi*) of the line of dead chiefs, and his possession of the sacred relics (*babenye*) of the tribe, he has power of approach to the tribal deities and he is responsible for the economic rites on which the food production of these people is thought to depend.

Besides their supernatural powers the chiefs formerly based their apparently unchallenged authority on the physical force they could exert. They controlled and armed their warriors, and had power of life or death over their subjects, whom they could kill, enslave, or sell, and in the case of women, bestow in marriage. Their legal system gave them the right to mutilate those who offended them, and it put them in supreme charge of the poison (*mwafi*) ordeal. The land theoretically belonged to them, and they exacted tribute in labor and kind from those who cultivated it, and maintained monopolies over ivory and salt. No Bemba could reach a high social status or obtain economic privileges unless related to the royal family or a personal favorite with them. Thus it is impossible to study land tenure, leadership in economic enterprises, incentives to agricultural labor, the distribution of land and goods, or exchange, without bearing the political system of this tribe in mind. Linton has recently used the word "Orientation" to describe for comparative purposes the chief focus of the interests and social institutions of any particular people under review. In this sense military ambition under an autocratic chieftainship is the orientation of the Bemba tribe.[8]

It is obvious that chiefs of this type who relied on the use of military force, tribute labor, and slavery for their supremacy, but did not accumulate material possessions or possess any valuable economic resources in their territory, are in a particularly poor position at the present day. The Bemba chief receives a small subsidy from the Government—£60 a year in the case of the Paramount chief and less for the territorial chiefs —and therefore earns annually about the same amount as a clerk. Rich African rulers such as the Nigerian emirs, the Barotse king, or some of the South-African potentates, do not exist in this area, and hence one of the important practical problems to discuss is the effect of this poverty of the Bemba chiefs on an economic system which is as closely linked with the political organization as is theirs. . . .

THE BEMBA DIET

All Bemba individuals can be reckoned as eating, roughly speaking, the same type and quantity of food. Class distinctions practically do not exist in this respect. Chiefs certainly have a much more regular supply of food than commoners and drink very much more beer. In fact they often subsist entirely on the latter to the complete exclusion of solids. Their wives, children, and courtiers also eat on the average more than the ordinary family, so much so that natives describe especially lavish hospitality as "housekeeping after the fashion of the capital" (*umusango wa ku musumba*). But the difference is one of certainty of supply rather than of greatly increased consumption per day, and a small class of individuals only are affected. Otherwise the rich man and his poorer neighbors eat very much the same throughout the year.

Sex distinctions are not marked either. The man gets a larger share of meat or any favorite relish, but there are no foods specially tabooed to women, and I do not think the inequality is any greater than that common in many working households in this country. Age distinctions in diet are not pronounced. Young boys between 10 and 16 are probably the worst-fed section of the community since they have to forage for themselves and have no regular portion allotted to them, but even then the difference is not a striking one. Geographical variations in the food supply certainly exist, but they are limited chiefly to differences in the amount of meat and fish consumed and not to the staple food. Therefore for all general purposes the following account may be taken as applying to the population as a whole.

Variations from Hunger to Plenty

The most pronounced feature of this dietary is its alternation between hunger and plenty, a characteristic common to African peoples in areas where the distribution of rain allows only one season of cultivation a year, and where one staple crop is relied upon. In this territory the existence of a definite scarcity is noticed at once by the most casual observer. The Bemba constantly talk about 'hunger months' as distinguished from food months. At the end of the rainy season they regularly expect a shortage, whether it is severe or not. When the scarcity becomes marked the whole appearance of village life is changed. For adults meals are reduced from two to one a day, and beer is rarely if ever brewed. Children who seem to munch extras all day long in the plentiful season (April to October) are reduced to a single dish late in the day. In one bad year I saw cases of elderly people who ate nothing during the course of a day, and though this is not common, most adult natives can remember occasions when they went two days without food, and "sat in the hut and drank water and took snuff."

These extreme cases of hunger are admittedly rare, but it is a fact that when the supply of the staple millet is at an end, the Bemba are reduced to foods with a much lower nutritive value. The millet, of which, as we shall see, their diet is mainly composed, lasts on an average for nine months of the year only (April to November or December). Chiefs reckon to make their supply last till the new harvest and even later. In a good year some commoners would be able to do so, but I should doubt if this number ever reached more than half of the villagers in any one settlement. When the staple food runs low, the only other cultivated crops available in the scarce season are edible gourds, which are largely composed of water, and small quantities of maize. Otherwise the natives rely on the bush, which provides fungi and caterpillars during these months.[9]

Thus the existence of a pronounced hunger season can be established without making any elaborate quantitative investigation. It is correlated with changes in the social life of the people which are equally marked. All activity is reduced to a minimum when food is short, and in a specially bad year garden work tends to be skimped. . . .

Other activities are also affected. There is little or no dancing in the hunger months, partly owing to the absence of beer.[10] Few journeys are planned, and the children tend to play listlessly. Usually more good-tempered than the average English baby, they whimper at the slightest provocation. I found it difficult to get informants to concentrate for more than short periods at this time of the year.

The physical effects of a seasonal shortage of food on the health of a people and the growth rate of their children has not yet been investigated, but from a sociological point of view there are other effects to be considered besides the lowering of energy due to actual under-feeding which the natives themselves recognize and describe. . . . In a society in which people regularly expect to be hungry annually, and in which traditions and proverbs accustom them to expect such a period of privation, their whole attitude towards economic effort is affected. In some primitive tribes it is considered shameful for an individual or a whole community to go hungry.[11] It is something unexpected, and to be resisted with energy. Among the Bemba scarcity is within the ordinary run of experience, and accepted as such. This fact has a subtle but very powerful effect on their ideas of wealth and their incentives to work.

Composition of the Diet

The Bemba diet is in a sense a simple one since it is composed very largely of one cereal food—the finger millet already described. The bulk of each meal consists of a porridge made of this flour, and the subsidiary foods, meat or vegetable, are eaten with it in small quantities only (about half a pound of the latter to five pounds of the former). For their nutrition the Bemba depend almost entirely on the amount of millet they are able to get, and the seasonal variations from hunger to plenty consist in effect of the shortage or absence of this particular grain.[12]

As a staple food, finger millet has a high nutritive value compared to other cereals used in this area. It is far superior to cassava in protein, fat, and mineral salts, and to the white millet of East Africa both in fat and minerals. Though inferior to maize in protein and fat, it is only very slightly so, and is again superior in minerals (iron, calcium, and phosphorus). On the other hand, as has been pointed out, the supply of millet as produced by the Bemba only lasts some nine months of the year, whereas the cassava roots remain in the garden beds throughout the year and are used a little at a time as wanted, so that people like the Bisa, who live on this crop, have a regular diet throughout the year. Sweet potatoes also can be eaten at most seasons, except during the rainy months. Millet has a further drawback in that it is used for beer as well as for porridge, and though the former evidently provides a valuable source of vitamin B contained in the germinating grain, yet it is an extravagant way of using the supplies, and the Bemba are in a worse position than peoples who grow a separate cereal for the purpose of brewing.

Their next most valuable foodstuffs are the pulses, groundnuts, groundbeans, Kaffir beans, cowpeas, &c., commonly grown by most of these Bantu peoples. These are a valuable source of protein and fat, groundnuts being particularly rich in the latter, and this adds to their importance in a diet in which fats of all kinds are very deficient. In fact, Trapnell suggests that the nutritive value of most of these simple cereal diets of Northern Rhodesia depends largely on the amount of the subsidiary pulses grown in addition to the main cereal crop.[13] In the case of the Bemba this supply of pulses seems to be far from adequate. The store of dried beans and peas lasts only a few months of the year.

* * *

[Bemba obtain animal proteins from fish, game, and insects. Green leaves, fruits, gourds, and mushrooms are available during some months of the year.]

As far as it is possible to speak of the composition of the diet as a whole, generalizations based on figures collected in three villages at different seasons of the year show that the average calorie intake is 1,706 per man value per day, i.e. just over half that which is considered adequate in England and America. The fat is only an eighth as much as is usually eaten on our mixed diets. The intakes of calcium and phosphorus compare very favorably with those in England and America. Salt is exceedingly deficient at all seasons of the year.

* * *

[Here follow a discussion and a table showing the comparative amounts of various foodstuffs and total caloric value of the daily diet of Bemba villages, of a minimum ration scale laid down by Government for industrial workers, and of a Rhodesian mining company.]

Seasonal Changes in Diet

It is obvious, however, that the seasonal changes are so marked in this area, as in most other African tribes, that such figures of "average" daily intake do not represent the actual situation at all. In effect the people have a harvest season from May to September in which millet, beer, green food, groundnuts, pulses are plentiful, and meat in some areas, and the diet is therefore ample and probably varied. This is followed by a dry season (October-November) in which millet and beer are still available but green vegetables scarce or nonexistent. The wild fruits are much liked, but only last about a month or six weeks. Meat and fish are obtainable in these months also, but only in certain districts. At the beginning of the rains, November and December, the diet changes. Millet is already beginning to be short, and mushrooms and caterpillars are the main standby as additional relishes. In the late rains millet is practically nonobtainable, and gourds and occasional maize-cobs are often the only available foods. Thus the diet changes completely in composition from one season to another[14]—a characteristic feature of primitive societies, of which the effects have not yet been investigated. Such essential constituents as are provided by the green vegetables, fruit, meat, and fish, are only available for short periods of the year.

To conclude, it can be said that most constituents considered essential to a balanced dietary are present in the Bemba environment, with the important exceptions of sufficient animal protein, fat, and salt. There is an absolute shortage of millet reckoned either by the figures of the amount available annually or from the obvious seasonal scarcity, and the natives' reliance on this one staple makes this lack a dangerous one. The most valuable accessory foods such as the pulses only last part of the year, and the supply of green vegetables is limited to a few months. Milk is never obtainable. Except in the case of meat and milk these deficiencies appear to be due to difficulties of production, storing, and exchange rather than to any particular environmental defects. . . .

NATIVE VIEWS ON FOOD

Food as a Center of Interest

Food and beer are without doubt the most exciting and interesting topics of native conversation, with the exception of money, in areas affected by white contact. Any one who can follow the ordinary gossip of a Bemba village will be struck at once by the endless talk shouted from hut to hut as to what is about to be eaten, what has already been eaten, and what lies in store for the future, and this with an animation and a wealth of detail which would be thought quite unusual in this country. It is, of course, natural in an area where the supply is never constant from day to day that the daily meal should be a subject of vivid interest. For those who are accustomed to buy food ready prepared, it is difficult to realize the emotional attitudes to foodstuffs among peoples who are directly dependent on their environment for their diet. Most of their food the Bemba grow, and hence they view their fields and gardens concretely in terms of their future prospects of food and drink. These they constantly discuss. I timed two old women talking over an hour on the single topic of the probable order of ripening of the pumpkins in three gardens, and the way in which they were likely to be distributed. The question evidently dominated their imagination. I have visited millet fields, near harvest time, and heard the owner exclaim ecstatically, "Just look at all that beer!" Foods collected from the bush, animal or vegetable, are perhaps of even greater interest because of the element of luck in their discovery. A sudden find of caterpillars or mushrooms, or a fish caught by hand in the reeds of a swamp, will be discussed all over the village that night.

The European notices, too, that the natives tend to describe their actual environment and the passage of the seasons in terms of the dietetic changes associated with them. They talk of different parts of the country according to their food deficiencies as "where they only eat pumpkin leaves," i.e. where game is short and the people have to rely on vegetable relishes. They refer to a visit to a village on a big river as, "He has gone to eat fish with So-and-So." The fortunes of each district are discussed year by year and villages described as "with hunger" (*pa nsala*) or the converse, "with beer" (*pa bwalua*), i.e. with so much grain that they can make beer frequently. The seasonal changes in food, and the stages in its production, give their names to the periods of the year. While a definite calendar of moons exists . . . the Bemba more often time events as having taken place "in the hunger months," i.e. the last months of the rains when the millet supply is low; or "when we were eating mushrooms," "when the *mupundu* fruit was ripe," and "when we were reaping, sowing," etc., and the ages of babies are usually reckoned by dating their births in this manner.

The position of the Bemba traveller, dependent as he is on the hazards of hospitality, provides a further element of uncertainty. The correct greeting to one who has returned from a journey is *Mwalyeni bwino,* "Have you eaten well?" To which the courteous reply is *Kulila mulelya,* "Provided you have eaten well yourself," or *E Mukwai kufipwishya,* "Yes, sir, I eat everything up completely," or else *Fia kwa cilime bafipwa kano wa kulapo nganda,* "It would have been impossible to finish up all the crops unless you had built a house alongside," i.e. it was so plentiful. There is a regular form of magic used to ensure a guest's arrival before a meal has been finished and not after. A knot tied in the grass with the right formula repeated will secure this result, and I found my staff even performed this rite on my own behalf if at all doubtful as to my reception on a visit to unknown English hosts.

Besides this direct interest in the food he is going to eat in the day, or the beer he may have the luck to come in time for, the secondary values acquired by food give it an added emotional interest to the Bemba. It must be remembered that there is no other way of accumulating wealth in this area except by acquiring sufficient food to feed many followers. The giving or receipt of food is a part of most economic transactions, and many come to represent a number of human relationships whether between different kinsmen or between subject and chief. For this reason the whole question of handling or dividing food acquires tremendous emotional significance for the native, and discussions of personalities or legal relationships tend to be ultimately expressed in this idiom. To speak of a chief is to mention before the end of the conversation his reputation for generosity or meanness in the giving of porridge and beer. To describe an attitude to any particular kinsman leads almost invariably to a comment, for instance, on the food in his granary, the number of relatives he supports, the share of meat he has asked for, or the amount of beer he contributed at the marriage of his daughter or the visit of an elder. In daily life the women, whether at work in the kitchen or sitting gossiping on their verandas at night, exchange interminable criticisms as to the way in which some particular dish of food has been divided, or the distribution of the four or five gourds of beer made at a brew. These casual observations of native life are significant. For us it requires a real effort of imagination to visualize a state of society in which food matters so much and from so many points of view, but this effort is necessary if we are to understand the emotional background of Bemba ideas as to diet.

NOTES

[The starred items are recommended as further readings.]

[1] J. Moffat Thomson gives the following figures for the biggest tribes of NE. Rhodesia: Bemba 114,274, Cewa 78,400, Ngoni 53,991, and none of the other tribal groups number more than 30,000. N. Rhodesian Government "Memorandum on the native tribes and tribal areas of N. Rhodesia," 1934.

[2] Here as in other parts of Africa the establishment of European rule and the prevention of war has led to a far greater dispersion of the people than was possible in the old days when they tended to group themselves under the protection of their chiefs in large stockaded villages. At the present day the Bemba villages divide and subdivide as often as possible within the limits of the Government minimum of ten adult males.

[3] [Here and elsewhere footnotes, and sometimes passages of text, showing variation among Bemba subgroups and comparisons with neighboring tribes have been omitted.]

[4] *The Soils, Vegetation and Agricultural Systems of N.W. Rhodesia*, Report of the Ecological Survey by C. G. Trapnell & J. N. Clothier, 1937. (Subsequently referred to as Report of the Ecological Survey.)

[5] Junod, *Life of a South African Tribe*, 1927, vol. i, p. 395.

[6] *Eleusine corecana*. . . .

[7] Small wedge-shaped razors, reaping knives, and flat 8-inch needles for threading mats form additional implements.

[8] Cf. R. Linton, *The Study of Man*, 1936.

[9] In one of the villages observed in February 1934, one family lived six days on gourds, while in another a woman who was nursing a baby fed herself and three children on mushrooms only for two days. At a third village in April of the same year, one family lived on wild spinach only for five days.

[10] No ceremonies such as initiation rites or the founding of a village are carried out in the last moon of the rains, *Kutumpu* (March), probably for this reason. But it is also interesting that the people give ill health and bad luck as reasons for not holding ceremonies in this month. They say: "March is an unlucky month. Look how many people fall ill at that moon."

[11] Cf. Malinowski's account of the Trobriand islanders, who consider hunger shameful and give all their efforts to displaying food and producing it in excess. *Coral Gardens and their Magic,* 1935, vol. i, p. 227; *Argonauts of the W. Pacific,* 1922, p. 109.

[12] Dr. Widdowson calculates that the Bemba gets 75 per cent. of his calories from this carbohydrate food, and about 5 per cent. from fat, whereas we get 40-50 per cent. from carbohydrates and 30-40 per cent. from fat. Cf. [A. I. Richards and E. M. Widdowson, "A Dietary Study in Northern Rhodesia,"] *Africa,* vol. ix, no. 2, 1936.

[13] Report to the Diet Committee of the N.R. Government, 1937.

[14] [A chart showing seasonal changes in the food supply of the Bemba has here been omitted.]

FOR FURTHER READING

Richards, Audrey I., "The Bemba of North-eastern Rhodesia," in Colson, Elizabeth, and Gluckman, Max (eds.), *Seven Tribes of British Central Africa,* London: Oxford University Press on behalf of the Rhodes-Livingstone Institute, 1951, pp. 164-93. A general paper on the Bemba.

Richards, Audrey I., "The Political System of the Bemba of Northern Rhodesia," in Fortes, M., and Evans-Pritchard, E. E. (eds.), *African Political Systems,* London: Oxford University Press for the International African Institute, 1940, pp. 83-120. An account of Bemba government.

For comparison with the agricultural system of a people in the Eastern Sudan, see de Schlippe, Pierre, *Shifting Agriculture in Africa: The Zande System of Agriculture,* London: Routledge, 1956.

RICE, A MALAGASY TRADITION*

Recorded by Ralph Linton[1]

*This account is a translation of a native text by a Merina of the central
plateau region, Imerina, of Madagascar. The Merina practice wet rice
cultivation using more complex techniques of terracing, irrigation, and
fertilization than do most African farming societies. However, the place
of agriculture in their life is similar to that of many African peoples. Here
the intimate relation between the growth of crops and religion is seen in
the role of the diviner in determining a propitious day for planting and
of the sorcerer in keeping hail and locusts away. Most important, though,
are the ancestors, who have the power over the success or failure of the
harvest. The Merina's involvement with their staple crop is seen also in
their contention that the Malagasy cannot live without rice and in the
statement "We do not eat the foreigner's bread . . . for it does not fill us
up."*

We believe that Madagascar was the original home of rice. Although we
know that our ancestors came to this island after a long voyage across
the sea there is no story of their bringing it with them or of its having
been introduced by strangers. Rice was known to the Kimo and
Vazimba.[2] We have a saying "Aza mana totovarim-bazimba," "It accom-
plishes nothing to pound rice in the fashion of the Vazimba," for they
pounded their rice clumsily, two people working together and striking
their pestles into the mortar at the same time. Rice that grows poorly
and among weeds, as though it were wild, is still called "rice of the
Vazimba." According to the traditions of the ancestors rice was first found
growing wild. The Vazimba gathered the seeds as they did those of other
wild plants, crushed them, and roasted them in earthen pots. They found
that rice was the best and most strengthening of all foods, and since then
it has been the principal food of all the Malagasy. It is the treasure of
Madagascar and we have a saying "Varying Andriaminitra," "Rice is a
god." For this reason it was formerly forbidden to feed it to pigs or to
sell it to foreigners unless it had first been cooked, so that they could not
carry it away and plant it in other lands.

All the Malagasy call rice "vary," "seed of the water," but there are

* Reprinted from *American Anthropologist*, 1927, 29, 654-60, by permission of *American Anthropologist* and Chicago Natural History Museum.

more than seventy kinds, each of which has its name. It is cultivated everywhere except in the high mountains and in a few places where the soil is too poor. The tribes of the east coast have a variety which they plant on hillsides. They cut and burn the brush and plant the seeds among the ashes one by one, making holes for them with a pointed stick. New brush must be allowed to grow between crops, and for this reason they have to move their villages every three or four years. They have another kind of rice which they plant in the heads of valleys, where small springs make the soil moist, and still another which they plant in the swamps. These give good crops in the hot lowlands but are not good on the high plateau.

Our ancestors knew more about rice growing than any of the other tribes. They understood all about soils, fertilizers, and the preparation of the fields. The best soil is clay with lime and a little sand. Pure clay is too hard and stays too wet, while if there is too much sand the rice will not bear well. Unless the field is new and rich in humus, or there is plenty of volcanic ash in the ground, fertilizer has to be used. The best is the half rotted straw from the cattle pits. Ashes from the fireplace must be spread on the seed beds and our ancestors also covered them with the sweepings from their dwellings. They kept the sheep and chickens in their houses, so these sweepings were good fertilizer. If nothing better can be gotten the fields are covered with green lily leaves which are dug in when the field is cultivated.

The seed beds are usually made on hillsides, one above the other. They are surrounded by little walls of earth which keep in the water and also serve as paths when the fields are flooded. The preparation of the beds takes a long time. First little canals are dug across them to dry them thoroughly. Then the earth is cut out in square clods, like bricks, and these are piled up to dry and air. When they are quite dry they are broken and mixed with manure and the beds are leveled and flooded ready for the planting. The fields are prepared in the same way, although the clods are not cut so carefully, and at the last cattle are driven back and forth over the flooded field to make the mud smooth and soft. The digging is done with a long heavy spade. His spade is a matter of pride to every farmer. The blade is polished and the handle is of valuable wood oiled and polished. A man will sometimes pay as much for his spade as he can earn in two weeks. An old spade that has been tried will bring more money in the market than a new one, for the foreigners' iron is not as good as our own.

Formerly rich people's fields were worked by their slaves. Poor people gathered together and worked all the fields belonging to the family one after the other. The man whose fields were worked that day made a big feast for everybody in the evening. There was no hired labor as there is nowadays.

The seed for the first crop is sown in April or May, that for the second crop in September. The blooming of the Ambiaty is a signal for the planting of the second crop, but it stays in bloom about a week and families who could afford it would consult a diviner to find which day was most propitious. Rice will still sprout after several years, but it is best to use that from the last harvest. Ripe grains that are very dry are selected and stored in earthen jars. When planting time comes the seed rice is soaked in water for three days, until it sprouts, and is then sown broadcast on the flooded seed beds. Our ancestors never sowed the last handful of seed rice. They carried it home and put it in the northeast corner of the house, where the family charm was kept and the offerings to the ancestors were placed. The man who was carrying it had to go home by the shortest road and could not turn aside for anything. If he did the harvest would fail.

As soon as the seed has sprouted well the water is drawn off and the seed bed is covered with manure. A few days later the water is let in in the morning but drawn off at night. This is kept up for two or three weeks, after which the water is left on the bed until the young rice is ready for transplanting. This is women's work. They uproot the plants, tie them in bundles, and carry them to the fields, where they plant them again in the soft mud, pressing them in with their fingers.

The rice has many enemies. While it is still in the seed beds it is eaten by rats and mice if the beds are dry, and by wild ducks if they are wet. We build clay pillars at the corners of the seed beds, whitening them with earth and putting hats of dried banana bark on them. The birds think these are people and are frightened away. After the rice has been transplanted it may be choked by weeds, or its roots may be eaten away by an insect called Fano, or a swarm of locusts may descend upon it. The locusts are the worst of all and when the farmers see them coming they make big fires so that the fields are covered with smoke. In former times almost every village had a sorcerer who claimed to be able to keep the locusts away. When a swarm was seen he went out of the village, usually climbing a hill, and stood there without saying anything. As long as he remained standing the locusts would not settle on the rice fields. Every one injured and insulted him, for this was part of the charm. The sorcerer's power over the locusts was inherited from his ancestors. The same sorcerer made charms against the hail. When the storm began he would go out naked except for a loin cloth. He carried a rice pestle with which he beat the wind and rain. Afterwards he leaned the pestle against the wall of the house, close to the southeast corner. He also carried a small round pebble, like a hailstone, in his mouth, and it was believed that in this way he kept the hail in his power. While the rice was growing it was forbidden for the people to eat peanuts or to burn green plants at the fire in the house. If locusts came or hail fell the sorcerers would claim that it was because these rules had been broken.

When the rice is ripe its leaves turn yellow and its heads bend toward the ground. When it is just beginning to ripen it is said to "mampandainga zaza," that is, "to make the children lie to their parents." The children see that it is turning yellow and run home shouting that it is ripe and ready to cut. When the sun is high it is hard for any one to tell whether the rice is really ripe. To be quite sure one must look at the fields early in the morning or just at sunset. The men reap the grain with straight knives that have teeth along the edge, like saws. The women and children tie it into sheaves and carry it to the threshing floor. There it is left lying in the sun for a week or more, until it is quite dry. There is a threshing floor in every village. It is a level place with a hard clay floor and a low clay wall around it. In the center there is a low stone pillar. When the rice is dry a man takes the sheaves one by one and beats them against the stone so that the grains fall out of the head. Sometimes several men work at this, but then there is always danger of their striking each other in the face. In the Tanala country five or six men thresh at once and we have a saying that when you see three Tanala together one of them is sure to be a one-eyed man. The women gather the grain and chaff in baskets which they hold above their heads and pour out slowly, so that the wind carries the chaff away.

When the rice has been threshed and winnowed it is stored in the granary. Our ancestors had four kinds of granaries. One sort was a little wooden house on posts. The posts were made very smooth and had broad wooden collars around them to keep out the rats. Another sort was built in the southeast corner of the house, like a square room. The only opening was a hole in the top and one climbed up to it with a ladder and then dropped down inside. Another kind was made of mud and stood fifteen or sixteen feet high. It was shaped like a beehive and there was a little door on one side just below the top. The commonest kind was a pit dug in the hard clay soil. It was small at the mouth but large enough below for a person to stand up and walk about in. Our ancestors sometimes put witches and other bad people in these pits and poured boiling water on them.

The rice is taken from the granary a little at a time, as it is needed. The women pound it in wooden mortars with long heavy pestles. After pounding it is winnowed. The first pounding takes off the husk and it is then red rice, the food of poor people. At the second pounding the red layer comes off, leaving it white, and that is what the rich eat. To make some dishes the grain is crushed to coarse meal. For breakfast we have Sosoa, whole rice boiled with a great deal of water. This is also given to sick people. For dinner we have Ampangoro, rice boiled until the water is all gone. We also make rice dumplings, doing up the meal in pieces of banana leaf and boiling it. We call these Betrosa, because one takes off the banana leaf before eating it, just as in old days a creditor would take away the cloths of a debtor who could not pay. When the dumplings are long they are called Fatinzaza, "body of an infant." The rice is also roasted and crushed. This is called Lango, and was the food of the ancestors. It is eaten at the harvest ceremony and is a good food to take on journeys. Poor people eat boiled greens with their rice while the rich have meat or fish. At a meal the wife always serves the rice and the husband the meat and gravy.

All parts of the rice are useful to us. There is little wood here in Imerina and we use the chaff and broken straw for fuel. The better straw is used to bed the cattle and to thatch poor people's houses. When I was a young man straw could be gotten for almost nothing, but now people ask insane prices for it. The price of rice, too, rises every year. This may be good for the rich people and the rice merchants, but the lives of the poor are getting harder all the time. We Malagasy can not live without rice. We do not eat the foreigners' bread even when we can afford it, for it does not fill us up.

In the old days every family held a ceremony of thanksgiving when its rice had been gathered and stored. The following things were gathered for use in the ceremony: Three times three perfect heads of rice, a sprig of the Sodifana plant and another of the Tatamo plant, a little basket used for measuring rice, and some fish of the sort called Toho. The rice was an offering. The Sodifana plant will live even when uprooted and laid in the sun, and the Tatamo plant will come up time after time when you think it has been destroyed; together they symbolized the persistence of the family. The rice measure was a symbol of wealth and prosperity. The Toho fish symbolized continuation, for that is another meaning of its name. When all was ready the family gathered in the northeast corner of the house, which was the sacred place. It was sacred because the dead were always laid out there and their spirits lingered there even after the bodies had been buried. We used to believe that our ancestors were still alive and had great power. They were like gods to us.

The father of the family acted as priest. He put the heads of rice under the roof in the corner and prayed: "Oh Creator God, thou who hast made us and art the source of our existence, we present ourselves before thee to offer thee these chosen heads of rice. But thou art not alone, Creator God. Our ancestors are with thee and have also become Gods. This offering is for all of you." At the end of this prayer all the family cried "Hahasoa! Hahasatva! May this bring us good things and well being."

The wife had prepared some of the new rice in the form of Lango (roasted and crushed) and had boiled some of it with water. She had also boiled the Toho fish. The Lango was placed before the family first and the father prayed: "Oh Creator God, we make this prayer about Lango, the first food of our ancestors, and thank thee before all. We pray that the first taste may bring us happiness and prosperity, well-being for the children and their parents during the day and the night, during the weeks, the months, and all the years that follow each other. May the earth provide us abundant food. May our ancestors also guard us." The whole family then cried "Hahasoa! Hahasatva!" as before. After this day they ate a little of the Lango, picking it up with their right hands, for it was forbidden to touch it with a spoon.

When the boiled rice and Toho fish were brought, the father prayed again: "We are about to eat the rice cooked with water. The water is the source of our existence. Oh God who has made all and knows all, hear my prayers. I pray first with the Sodifana plant. Keep us from death and let us live with well-being and affection for a thousand years. I pray now with the Tatamo plant. Preserve our family. Do not let it be uprooted by jealousy or evil ways of life. I pray now with the rice measure. May our house be kept in good order and may no trouble approach us. Let wealth enter our home. I pray now with the Toho. It lives in the water that we drink and we will eat it with the first rice. Let our health and strength be continued." The whole family responded as before. It was forbidden to eat the new rice until this ceremony had been held.

NOTES

[1] Capt. Marshall Field Expedition to Madagascar. By permission of Field Museum of Natural History, Chicago.

[2] The Kimo, "rich people," and Vazimba, "dwellers in caves," are frequently mentioned in Hova traditions as the first inhabitants of the island. They were conquered and absorbed by the Hova, but their tombs are still held sacred.

FOR FURTHER READING

Linton, Ralph, "The Culture Areas of Madagascar," *American Anthropologist*, 1928, 30, 363-90. Types of culture in relation to geographical setting.

Linton, Ralph, *The Tanala, a Hill Tribe of Madagascar*, Chicago: Field Museum of Natural History, Anthropological Series, 22, 1933. Ethnography of a Malagasy people living southeast of the Merina.

Paulme, Denise, *Les gens du riz: kissi de Haute-Guinée française*, Paris: Plon, 1954. A study of a people who practice rice cultivation in Guinea.

Richards, Audrey I., *Land, Labour and Diet in Northern Rhodesia*, London: Oxford University Press for the International African Institute, 1939. A study of Bemba nutrition with much material on agriculture and its place in the people's life. Parts of this book are included in Richards' reading in this volume.

THE CULTURAL MAP OF WEST AFRICA: SUCCESSIVE ADAPTATIONS TO TROPICAL FORESTS AND GRASSLANDS*

Daryll Forde

Much of the anthropological writing on Africa in the past twenty-five years has been concentrated on ethnographic or social structural studies of specific societies, or of certain institutions found within a single society. Before this time, broad sweeping surveys of geographic areas or of the whole continent were made, but most of them were based on inadequate data. Today however, the growing body of information gathered by anthropologists, linguists, historians, archaeologists, and biologists makes broad syntheses of areas of Africa possible, if only to help indicate the gaps in our knowledge. Forde's paper is such a synthesis. The area about which he has written is one that has undergone so much change and development that it is difficult to estimate the relative influence of different cultural traditions in molding the life of the people. Many important group migrations obviously took place in West Africa, though it is frequently impossible to trace these in detail. But the broad outlines of cultural contact and of ecological adjustment emerge clearly from Forde's analysis.

Beyond the desert lands of the Western Sahara, and some 1500 miles distant from the Mediterranean coastlands of North Africa are the basins of the lower Senegal and middle Niger rivers and of Lake Chad. From their northern margins and extending southward for nearly a thousand miles again to the Guinea coast which faces the Atlantic to the south is a segment of tropical Africa that has long stood out in Western minds. Vague stories of its torrid heat and its black peoples reached the Roman World. Medieval traders in the Mediterranean heard of its resources and

* Reprinted with the author's revision from *Transactions of the New York Academy of Sciences*, 1953, Series 2, Vol. 15, No. 6, pp. 206-19, by permission of the author and publisher.

obtained some of the products through the Arabs of North Africa and in the 16th century, with the Age of Discovery, it was brought earlier and more clearly within the knowledge of the West than any other part of trans-Saharan Africa.

This knowledge came from two very different sources and concerned quite distinct parts of this great tract of country between the desert and sea. On the one hand there were the chronicles of medieval Arab travelers, teachers, merchants and adventurers who had, from the 10th century, made the journey of many weeks across the deserts to reach the savanna lands of the western Sudan. On the other hand European merchant adventurers were now making regular sea voyages past Cape Verde, round the western bulge of Africa to establish trading posts where the rain forests of the south came down to the shore on the surf-beaten Guinea coast.

Although European acquaintance with this area goes back a long way, detailed knowledge of its conditions and resources of its peoples and their ways of life is very recent and still sadly incomplete. It was not until the end of last century that western penetration of the interior for pacification and the extension of commerce began. Indeed, we owe a great debt to a generation of scholars of that time, most of them French and British administrators, among whom there still existed the direct and personal interest in the character and traditions of the people they governed and a sense of obligation, as an important part of their public duty, to record and study what they could concerning the peoples among whom they worked. Although the pace of linguistic, ethnographic and historical research has in recent years quickened again in this as in other parts of Africa, the sources for their study are being carried away ever more rapidly by the tide of Westernization. This is happening, moreover, at a time when our knowledge in all these fields, and the insight it could afford to those responsible for administration and developement in increasingly complex circumstances, remains fragmentary and often unmeaningful to all but a few specialists. This must be my excuse for attempting, from such fragmentary knowledge, to portray the broad features of the cultural map of West Africa and the forces that appear to have affected its delineation.

The older documents of Arab and European travelers; linguistic studies, which for many of the hundreds of West African languages are forced to rely on nothing more than incomplete wordlists recorded by amateurs; preliminary ethnographic surveys of a few regions and a handful of intensive professional studies of the cultures and social systems of particular peoples; these are the materials with which, in our present state of ignorance, any such attempt must be made. But obviously tentative and oversimplified as any such sketch must be, it has its uses in affording those with interest in the peoples of West Africa, whether general or specialized, scientific or practical, a provisional frame of reference against which the wider significance of their more special concerns can be viewed. It will also, I hope, point to the fact that more adequate resources, in research funds and trained specialists, are urgently needed for cultural studies in this important area; that given these there is every promise that the provisional and incomplete outline which it is possible to give today may be developed into a considerable body of systematic knowledge concerning the complex phases and conditions of cultural development in West Africa.

Between Dakar on Cape Verde in the west and Lake Chad nearly 3000 miles away to the east there extends south of the Sahara the belt of wooded grasslands nearly a thousand miles deep at its widest, which is generally known as the Western Sudan. At their most characteristic these tropical savannas are fittingly described as orchard bush, covered as they are with waist high grass during the summer rains and closely studded with low trees. Towards the north in the latitude of the lower Senegal river, the bend of the middle Niger and Lake Chad, the vegetation dwindles, trees are sparser and more and more replaced by thorn bushes while the grass cover is low, thin and shortlived, and gives way to the stretches of bare rock and sand that constitute so much of the Sahara desert. On its southern margin the grass and woodland of the savanna become taller and more dense. The country is seamed by belts of forest along flooded river valleys. It merges insensibly southward into a belt of country some two hundred miles deep behind the Guinea coast which, but for the interference of man, would be almost continuous forest.

This gradation of climate and vegetation from the humid forest belt along the coast, which may be drenched in a hundred inches of rain over eight or nine months of the year, to the desert margin nearly a thousand miles away to the north, where there is only a brief flush of short grass during two or three months of showers and storms each year, gives a belt-like character to the West African environment. Although their extent may be modified and even interrupted locally by special features of the terrain, the successive zones of rain forest, open woodland, grass and scrub characteristically succeed one another from south to north as one moves from the coast to the Sahara. Equally significant from the point of view of the spread of different patterns of human settlement and cultural adaptation, each zone extends laterally for enormous distances from east to west and continues still further eastward across Africa. It will be clear that in West Africa there have always been marked contrasts between these zones in the opportunities they have afforded for human movement and settlement, for cultural elaboration and diffusion.[1]

These distinctive life zones of West Africa severally link it to adjacent regions of Africa. The forest belt continues without interruption eastwards across the northern part of the Congo basin; the orchard bush and scublands in the western Sudan also extend eastwards beyond Lake Chad across the continent to the valley of the Nile and the Ethiopian highlands. Finally there is no sharp line at which the Sahara begins, for within that desertic region, thanks to elevated massifs and raised water tables there are tracts, like the Aïr and the Hoggar massifs and parts of the Atlantic coast zone, where seasonal herbage and opportunities for primitive irrigation and herding have sustained human settlement and movement throughout the centuries.

Beyond the desert to the north lie the Mediterranean lands of North Africa that lay on the western flank of the ancient civilizations of the Near East, were afterwards developed and organized on a large scale by the Romans and, later still in the first millennium A.D., became the western lands, the Mahgreb, of the Mohammedan Arab world. The Sahara was, as we shall see, no complete barrier between tropical West Africa and North Africa in Ancient or Medieval times. Despite its size and aridity it included a number of tracts that were permanently settled, wider areas over which seasonal pasture was available and lines of water holes along which caravans could water men and beasts. It was thus a hurdle and filter that restricted and selected the kinds of human movement and cultural forces that could penetrate and the sort of influence they could exert on the established populations.

With the opening of the Western Age of Discovery at the end of the 15th century, the Sahara was outflanked by sea. The exploring navigators were followed by sea traders along the southern coasts of West Africa, and the first great stretch of well watered tropical African coast became dotted with the trading posts of European merchant adventurers. The surf-beaten beaches that had so long presented an ultimate frontier to settlement for the peoples of the forests of West Africa were breached and direct contact was established with the expanding mercantile civilization of the west. Western knowledge of this region was no longer confined to classical allusions to a land of Pactolus and to translations of Arab chronicles concerning strange empires beyond the desert. The lure of gold, ivory and slaves brought traders from all parts of Western Europe to the fever-stricken lagoons which later became ports of entry to the interior and, with the opening of this century, the bases from which a new and contemporary phase of cultural change is sweeping over West Africa.

The fact that the peoples of West Africa are predominantly negroid in racial type is the first general indication that their oldest cultural traditions are, with those of the rest of trans-Saharan Africa, likely to be distinct from those of the Mediterranean and European world. And this is confirmed by the character and distribution of languages, those unwitting and perduring indicators of a substantial element in the cultural traditions of peoples. Very few of the hundred or more languages of West

Africa have been studied in detail, but it is already clear that except in the north-east between the Niger and Lake Chad, all the known forms of speech of both the forest and the savanna zones belong ultimately to a single great group of languages, commonly known as the Western Sudanic family.[2] To this group belong linguistically all the West African peoples south of a line running from the west coast at about the Senegal river along the parallel 15° N. to cut across the great bend of the Niger and curve south below Lake Chad. There are indications, too, that further study will link them in a still wider grouping to include the Bantu forms of speech that are spread so widely over central and southern Africa. Ultimately then, despite great local differences, which betoken centuries of separation of different regions and considerable extraneous influences, the forest and savanna zones have elements of a common tradition that one would expect to find expressed in other archaic features of their culture (see FIGURE 1).

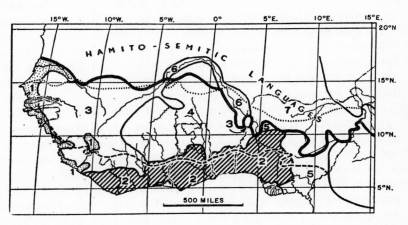

FIGURE 1. *Distribution of major language groups in West Africa (generalized). Smaller groups are omitted.*

1. Western Sudanic Group *West Atlantic*
2. *Kwa-Kru*
3. *Mande*
4. *Gur (Voltaic)*

5. Benue-Cross and Bantu Groups
6. Songhai Group (unclassified)
7. Chado-Hamitic Group

—————— Northern limit of Western Sudanic Languages
– – – – Northern margin of Dense Forest
. . . . . . Northern margin of Savanna

There is, however, as has been mentioned, a notable exception in the country east of the middle Niger where Chadic languages of the Hamito-

Semitic family that form part of a widespread group extending over the Western Sahara and North Africa have spread deeply into the savanna belt. Still further east in the country close to Lake Chad the languages belong to a distinctive Central Saharan group. Human movements from the north in this area, it would appear, have not been confined only to small bodies of people but to have been sufficiently great and pervasive to displace the Western Sudanic tongues that probably preceded them.[3]

Within the Western Sudanic language area there are further points of distribution, that are significant for the early peopling of West Africa. In the difficult and, for landsmen, inaccessible mangrove swamps of the coastal lagoons of the Ivory Coast and the Niger delta there are small populations whose languages are very distinctive and divergent from the more widespread linguistic groups that surround them. These comparatively isolated fishing peoples in their remote situations may, like other isolated and divergent groups, such as those found in the hills of Togoland, be survivors of once more widely spread linguistic stocks—the equivalent of such linguistic survivals as Erse and Gaelic on the Atlantic fringes of Europe—and it is unfortunate that so far no close study of these remnant peoples has been made. But the greater part of the forest belt of West Africa over a distance of a thousand miles from central Liberia to beyond the lower Niger in Nigeria is occupied by peoples speaking a series of related languages to which the general name Kwa, the common root for "people," has been given. Although the actual forms of speech differ greatly over this area and distinct tongues, unintelligible to outsiders may be confined in places to a few thousand people, there are underlying similarities in vocabulary and structure that indicate their derivation from a common ancient speech and point to an early cultural continuum over much of the forest belt, it suggests the proliferation through it of communities derived from a single stock at an early but unknown date. It points, too, to the obstacles which the forest imposed on penetration by later peoples. That such penetrations occurred, and with profound effects, is clear. They would appear, however, not to have been mass migrations but confined to small if dominant groups which despite great cultural influence were absorbed linguistically by the local populations. Even where, as among the Yoruba-speaking peoples of Southwest Nigeria or the Akan of the southern Gold and Ivory coasts, more complex cultures marked by high technical skills and ritually elaborate state organizations of northern provenience were established, the ancient forest tongues persisted.

In the far west of the forest belt, however, northerners penetrated in large numbers, establishing warrior chiefdoms, as among the Mende of Sierra Leone, which carried Mande languages from the western Sudan right down to the coast. At the eastern end, the forest and adjacent savanna of the Cross and Benue river basins appear to belong to another series of forest tongues. These congeries of little studied class languages may, it is claimed, prove to have diverged from one or more closely related stocks from which the Bantu languages of the Congo basin and beyond also derive. Thus there is no sharp linguistic frontier in the forest zone between West and Central Africa.

In the savanna belt linguistic groupings and their distributions suggest a different cultural situation, one of large scale prolonged movements of culturally dominant populations over great tracts of country. Except in the northeast towards Chad the languages are again all West Sudanic, showing ultimate derivation from the same stock as the forest tongues, but, it would appear, long separated from these. We should look therefore for an early phase of separation of the forest and savanna zones into distinct cultural spheres within each of which there was more internal interconnection than there was interchange between one zone and the other.

Secondly it is to be noted that the West Sudanic languages in the savanna zone do not fall predominantly into a single major subgroup but are divided into a number of divergent stocks each, broadly speaking, occupying a compact block of country extending across the zone from the desert to the forest margin. In the west along the Atlantic there is an area of internally strongly differentiated languages—the West Atlantic group—suggestive of the early entry and proliferation of a number of comparatively self contained populations. That the area they once occupied has been reduced and interrupted by later migrations and cultural influences from the East is shown by the many islands of West Atlantic speech persisting to the East where the widespread group of Mande languages predominate over the upper basins of the Senegal and Niger rivers. The Mande speaking peoples (such as the Mandingka and the Bambara of Senegal and French Sudan; and the Mende of Sierra Leone and Western Liberia) share a tradition of centralized military organization under strong chiefs. They were still expanding in the west and south when European pacification began. Moreover, the general distribution of the Mande tongues corresponds broadly to the sphere of influence of a vigorous civilization that, according to the Arab chronicles, was already flourishing early in the Christian era in this part of the Western Sudan.

East of the area of the Mande languages there is another body of peoples occupying nearly all of the great tract of savanna country south of the Niger bend who speak various languages of the Gur or Voltaic group. These peoples vary greatly in complexity of culture and scale of social organization for, as we shall see, they were situated on the flanks of powerful early kingdoms lying to the west and north and while the more remote remained isolated in small independent communities others, like the Mossi, while retaining their old languages became organized in military chiefdoms after the model of their dominant neighbors.

East again we enter the area of a distinct language family, an area of Chadic speech occupying much of what is now Northern Nigeria and the French territory that flanks it to the north. Most of this area was early organized into a number of strong chiefdoms which by their traditions and their continuing commercial and other connections were linked to the oasis peoples of the Western Sahara.

Thus the linguistic distributions in West Africa suggest several important underlying features of cultural development. First, since apart from the Saharan extensions into the savanna around Lake Chad, all the languages of West Africa appear to be ultimately derived from a common stock, one would expect to find significant elements of a common early tradition in the cultures of all West African peoples. Little systematic enquiry has so far been given to this question but there are many indications that underlying the great regional and tribal differences in the elaboration of cult and cosmological ideas there is a very widespread substratum of basic ideas that persists in the rituals, myths and folk tales of West African peoples.

On the other hand the tendency of linguistic frontiers to correspond with the savanna-forest margin suggests an early and important cultural differentiation between these two zones. In the savanna, where until recently the human movement over considerable distances was so much easier than in the forest we find that a series of distinct subgroups have expanded over compact areas. The resulting marked differentiation of the major linguistic stocks in the savanna belt would appear at first sight to conflict with the fact that the country is so much more open and so more favorable to human movements under primitive conditions but here it is to be noted that the several major stocks are not confined to small areas or populations. The savanna zone is far wider than the forest and the area over which the Mande languages for example, are spoken is at least as great as that covered by those of the Kwa group in the forest zone. It is to be noted also that there are far flung outliers of Mande speech as far east as Nigeria. What appears to be significant is the emergence of a number of distinct foci of linguistic differentiation in this wide, deep zone which severally expanded transversely across the savanna as also, at a presumably later date, did the intrusive Hamito-Semitic stocks in the east. This configuration of language groupings is of particular interest in connection with what we know of the early political framework of the Western Sudan, where a series of elaborate political systems such as the Gana and Mande empires and their succession states and offshoots in the west, the Dja, Songhai and Mossi Kingdoms in the center and the Hausa states in the east appear to have maintained their structural identities over the centuries. We reach the provisional conclusion that the grasslands of the Western Sudan covered too vast an area and was too open to distinct external influences on too long a front for it to retain or to have imposed on it by migration or conquest any complete linguistic or cultural homogeneity. At the same time the more open character of this country made it possible for expanding ruling groups to maintain partial unity, linguistic, cultural and political, over very extensive areas.

When we turn to consider the indigenous modes of subsistence of the known peoples of West Africa we again find a general, though by no means complete, dichotomy between the forest and the savanna peoples.[4] If we abstract from the cultures and social systems of the forest peoples those elements which appear to have developed following maritime contact with the west, including new food plants such as maize and cassava, and if we also exclude, for the moment, certain more complex societies of the forest zone that afford evidence of northern origins, the broad features are as follows: The forest peoples were and are cultivators depending basically on root crops, yams (*Dioscorea*) and cocoyams (*Colocasia esculenta*), and fruits, especially varieties of the cultivated banana (*Musa* spp.). These are supplemented by a variety of legumes and supplies from cultivated or protected bushes and trees notably the oil and raphia palms, pepper bushes and the cola tree. Stock-raising, hunting and trapping, although much reduced recently, was prominent in the traditional economy but livestock was and is confined to small numbers of goats, fowl, and pigs attached to the household.[5] Their fabrics were confined to pandanus and raphia matting and bark cloth and they had no true loom. Iron tools were generally available but often only through trade since the centers of ore-smelting as distinct from the smithing of iron bars were comparatively few. With iron tools they had well developed wood working crafts serving both utilitarian, ritual and esthetic ends with such products as stools, slit gongs, large assembly houses, statuary and masks. Pottery was generally available but it, too, was often traded at considerable distances from specialized centers of surplus production.

The older cultivated food staples of the West African forest belt are also found throughout the great forested areas of central Africa to the east. They undoubtedly reached West Africa from that direction for they are not African plants by origin. The yam (*Dioscorea alata*) and the cocoyam (= Taro, *Colocasia esculenta*), the banana and the plantains (*Musa*) were all, the botanical evidence indicates, first domesticated in an archaic planting area in southern Asia extending from the Bay of Bengal to Indochina where agriculture was based not on the sowing of cereals but on vegetative reproduction of food plants from cuttings. The domestic forest goat and the fowl, too, which are ubiquitous in the Guinea-Congo region, were ultimately derived from South Asia. These domesticated plants and animals appear to be part of an ancient craft complex which included matting with pandanus and palm fibers and the beating of bark cloth. The period and the route by which it reached tropical Africa remains unknown but the biological evidence makes it clear that the basic plants and animals concerned are exotic there. The Guinea forest peoples appear, however, to have made an important addition to the assemblage in developing two African yams—the white and yellow Guinea yams (*Dioscorea rotundata* and *cayensis*) as cultivated plants.[6]

One outstanding exception to the general pattern of indigenous cultivation in the forest belt is very significant. In the west from the Gambia to Western Liberia, rice, grown both dry and in swamps is a staple crop. None of the early European reports suggested that it was a recent introduction and it was not recorded from anywhere further East at the time of European discovery. Its presence in the west is, therefore, more satisfactorily explained by the fact that rice had long been an important riverain crop on the middle Niger whence, like the southward spread of Mande languages it reached the forest peoples.

As far as they can be judged, from those existing forest peoples who have remained outside the spheres of the more complex state organization of northern origin or of later developments in response to European commerce, the older patterns of social organization in the forest belt, while variable, were all small in scale and rooted in local ties of kinship. The local community, rarely exceeding a few thousand persons and often only a few hundred strong, was virtually autonomous, with its own organization into groups of kinsfolk and its own system of authority. It had external contacts with similar neighboring groups, intercourse that was sufficient to maintain general similarity of speech, custom and social organization. Beliefs, skills and social innovations could spread widely from one to another and a sense of cultural unity maintained among a considerable number of communities. Their interrelations were not regulated from above, they took the form of chains of friendships and alliances, liable to be broken by feuds and intermittent hostilities. A lineage system (patrilineal, matrilineal, or even dual) whereby kinsmen in one line of descent maintained solidarity for both internal organization of their own group and for external cooperation and competition with similar groups, appear everywhere to have provided the first order of grouping within a locality. Among some peoples the lineage principle was more widely extended to embrace a series of local communities conceived and organized as a body of kin, segmented into ultimately related groups. Elsewhere, and associated with peoples living in larger compact settlements comparatively isolated geographically and socially from one another, a village organization, with territorial, age-set and status-associations, is superimposed on the system of kin groups of more restricted significance. Nowhere, except where the extraneous influence of invading minorities is both traditionally asserted and intrinsically probable, were politically centralized states with an administrative and territorial system of government established. The relations between lineage or small clan-organized tribes or between autonomous village communities were those of give and take in trade and intermarriage, punctuated by differences settled through arbitration, feud or warfare.[7]

The savanna peoples show an overall contrast with those of the forest in their subsistence patterns. But it is also apparent that beyond the general contrast in type of cultivation there is great internal variation in technical development. The peoples of the Western Sudan are predominantly grain cultivators as compared with the root and fruit growing forest peoples. But the intensity and technical efficiency of their agriculture ranges widely. Some, like many plateau peoples of Northern Nigeria and perhaps of the Cameroons knew, until recently, only an inferior small grain, *Digitaria*. Others, like the pagan peoples of much of the Northern territories of the Gold Coast, although they cultivated varieties of millet which are widespread and ancient food plants in Africa, merely scratched the soil with light hoes and dibbled in their seed to secure a catch crop. But other savanna peoples such as the Hausa of Northern Nigeria, the Bambara and Mandingka of the French Sudan have a much more advanced agriculture practicing deep hoeing and ridge cultivation for their millets and irrigation for special crops. The level of agricultural production whether per head or by area appears to be in general considerably higher and can provide a surplus to maintain specialists in craft, ritual or government. It is only in connection with this more advanced agriculture that cotton is generally grown and true looms are used to provide cotton cloth. Associated with it, too, is the long established tending of livestock either by the people themselves, as in Senegal among the Wolof and Serer, or by specialized pastoralists living in symbiotic relations with the cultivators as do the pastoral Fula among the Bambara in Sudan or among the Hausa in Northern Nigeria.

The various millets, a botanically heterogeneous assemblage of small-seed cereals, which have so long provided the food staples of the West African savanna zone, belong to an agricultural tradition that is quite distinct from that of the root and fruit crops of the forest. Their distribution in Africa and beyond make it quite clear that seed cultivation in the West African grasslands was not historically derived from forest cultivation or vice versa. The genetical and distributional studies of Vavilov and others have also shown that the flanks of the Ethiopian highlands in Northeast Africa must have been an early center for the development of several varieties of cultivated millets and that Guinea corn (*Sorghum vulgare*), *Pennisetum spicatum*, and Eleusine (*E. corocana*) were probably first cultivated there. Thus the early development of agriculture in the Western Sudan must, like that of the forest cultivation, be derived from the east but by a different route.

Although the two traditions were later, following on subsequent interpenetrations, combined on the forest margins they appear to have been originally separate. Agriculture must have spread separately among the early populations of the two zones. And since, as we have seen, the speech families of the forest and the savanna are derived from an ultimate common stock, their early linguistic divergence into distinct forest belt and savanna groups may well have been associated with the introduction of these two distinct patterns of cultivation and the independent growths and westward expansions of populations that they made possible. This question is one that deserves close attention linguistically, ethnographically and archeologically, for data from these three fields may in combination make it possible to learn a great deal concerning the character and antecedents of the first agricultural peoples in West Africa.

But the agricultural patterns of the Western Sudan have also gone through several phases of development as more advanced techniques and additional crops and associated crafts were developed in some areas. Among some of the savanna peoples, as we have seen, there persists a more primitive economy with a less productive agriculture, lacking textiles and other specialized crafts and often dependent on sporadic trade for iron. When we consider the social organization of such peoples we find it broadly similar in character to that of the forest peoples in the high degree of autonomy of small local communities and the importance of extended kin groups for the organization of social relations within and between them.

The more advanced and productive agricultural systems and the elaboration of specialized crafts in cloth and metal, on the other hand, are associated with a different social order. Such peoples whether Mandingka in the West or Hausa and Kanuri in the East are organized in states, which although they vary greatly in size, have basic features of social organization in common, namely the centralization of authority in a ruler with his councilors and subchiefs drawn from an aristocracy of birth; an elaborate etiquette of obeisance, expressive of ranking and subordination of classes in the social order; the collecting of tax and tribute to maintain the central organs of government and its agents. The more primitively organized peoples referred to above have persisted only in areas which have not been dominated and incorporated in these states and one of the processes of incorporation was very apparent when Europeans first penetrated and began to administer the various territories in the Western Sudan. The kin-organized tribes on the periphery of the centralized states were the slave-raiding reservoirs of the former. Only those in the more remote and difficult country remained unmolested.

For many centuries Islam has been the religion of the barbaric states of the Western Sudan. But the records of the Arab Moslem chroniclers, who visited the Western Sudan in medieval times, themselves confirm the later ethnographic evidence that, however great the importance of Islam in reorganizing various Sudanic kingdoms at different periods, their fundamental ideas and customs concerning political rule and other social relations are much older than the introduction of Islam and that elements of older royal rituals and social codes have everywhere persisted in varying degrees.

What, in broad terms, do we know of the formation and the technical and social basis of these ancient chiefdoms and empires? The earliest contemporary records are those of Arab Moslems who crossed the western Sahara, on an already well established trade route from Sigilmassa, then the great desert port of what is now Morocco, to the Senegal. Ibn Haukel in the 10th century A.D. and El Bekir in the 11th century recorded vivid and often detailed impressions of an empire then extending over many thousands of square miles from the upper Senegal to the Upper Niger and southward over the highland country to the forest margins (see FIGURE 2).

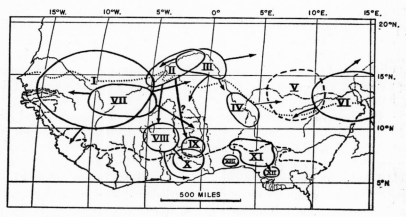

FIGURE 2. *The orbits of early State systems of West Africa.*

I. Ghana (4th C.? to 11th C. A.D.) and Mande (11th C. to 17th C. A.D.)

II. Dja (? to 10th C. A.D.)

III. Songhai (9th C. to 16th C. A.D.)

IV. Kebbi (13th C.? to 18th C. A.D.)

V. Hausa States (10th C.? to 19th C. A.D.)

VI. Bornu (10th C.? to 19th C. A.D.)

VII. Bambara (17th C. to 19th C. A.D.)

VIII. Kumbu-Bona (Akan) (12th C.? to 16th C. A.D.)

IX. Bono (Akan) (12th C.? to 17th C. A.D.)

X. Asante (Akan) (18th C. to 19th C. A.D.)

XI. Yoruba (? to 19th C. A.D.)

XII. Benin (14th C.? to 19th C. A.D.)

XIII. Dahomey (Fon) (17th C. to 19th C. A.D.)

The then ruling dynasty of this empire of Gana or Ganata not only claimed an ancestry of several centuries but also succeeded to a still older Kingdom founded by "white" men from the north. Gana of the 10th century was controlled from a great city, the royal capital. The kingship was a sacred institution and the ruler himself hedged by an elaborated ritual and regarded as possessed of supernatural powers. The state organization with the aid of a standing army controlled a vast area, collecting tribute in kind from the towns and villages of its provinces and its dependent chiefdoms, imposing customs dues on trade and exercising a royal monopoly on the gold production from the auriferous gravels of the southern hill country which appears to have been all-important in promoting and maintaining the trans-Saharan trade with North Africa. Although we have only tantalizing glimpses of the elaborate court ceremonial and religious ideas of Gana it was clearly not a Moslem state. Moslems from North Africa were tolerated as merchants but they had their own quarters and were not incorporated into the society.

It was not until late in the 11th century that the first recorded attempt at Islamic domination took place with the Almoravid conquest of part of Gana by Moslem Berbers. Although the Almoravids did not succeed in establishing their own rule, Islam, continually reinforced we may presume by traffic along the western trans-Saharan trade route, was henceforth powerful in this part of the Western Sudan. The rulers of Mali or Mande, formerly a subordinate chiefdom southwest of Gana, adopted Islam in the 11th century on their rise to power and secured a fluctuating but growing control of much of the former territory of the empire of Gana. Ibn Khaldoun's account of his stay in the capital of Mali, when it was at its zenith in the early part of the 14th century, portrays a state system with a sacred ruler, essentially similar in its main features to Gana, deriving its revenues, directly or indirectly, from the tribute of thousands of peasant villages, grouped in provinces or subordinate chiefdoms. Mali maintained regular commerical, diplomatic and scholarly relations with North Africa and many of its kings made the pilgrimage to Mecca before it dwindled to a petty chiefdom in the 17th century with the rise of new centers of power on the middle Niger to the east.[8]

Although contemporary records do not carry us so far back in the country to the east of the empires Gana and Mali, there is much indirect evidence of the early establishment of pre-Islamic Kingdoms in the country of the Niger bend and further east across the northern savanna from the Niger to Lake Chad. As both of these regions were in later times in contact with North Africa across the Sahara by other caravan routes and since, as we have seen, part of it became an area of Hamitic speech it is likely that infiltration of these parts of the western Sudan by northerners also began early in the first millennium A.D. when the camel appears to have been first introduced from the east and established as the beast of burden in North Africa. Although they cannot yet be confirmed by archeological or ethnographic evidence, it is significant that the traditions of the older states of this wide zone all independently assert, as did those of Gana, that their founders were "white" Berber speaking peoples from the North. This holds for the Kingdom of Dja on the Niger bend which was disrupted and succeeded by the Songhai at the end of the first millenium A.D. when, significantly enough, the latter adopted Islam as the state religion. There are similar traditions in the later and mutilated chronicles of the Hausa states such as that of Kano which ascribed its original rulers to invaders from the Saharan oases of Aïr long the home of Hamitic speaking Berber peoples. Similarly the foundation of Kanem, the forerunner of the latter-day chiefdom of Bornu, was attributed by medieval Arab chronicles to invaders from Tibesti in the central Sahara.

The widespread conversion to Islam of the rulers of the many chiefdoms and empires of the Western Sudan that began around 1000 A.D., and the strengthening of cultural and commerical links across the Sahara with which this was associated, had widespread effects on the social systems and political forms, not least in assisting the rise to power of new centers and ruling groups. But it is clear that the impact of Islamic traders and teachers and later military forces from North Africa were not responsible for the first development of more productive crafts and agriculture, the specialization of occupations, the emergence of ruling aristocracies, of political centralization and administrative government. All these go back to a more remote period. Considerable chiefdoms had already been established early in the first millennium A.D. in the Western Sudan and the more successful expanded to form considerable empires.

On the other hand this cultural and political development, whereby wide territories and large populations were organized and specialized crafts in metals, textiles and building developed, was clearly not a spontaneous development from small self-subsistent communities of primitive cultivators whose descendants survive in those parts of the Western Sudan, such as the south of Senegal, much of the Northern territories of the Gold Coast and the "middle belt" of Nigeria which were never brought effectively within the orbit of the chiefdoms. To explain the emergence of the more complex cultures and political systems of the Sudan we have to seek the sources of their more elaborate crafts such as lost-wax casting in bronze and brass, filigree work in silver and gold, cotton weaving on narrow and broad looms, the construction of vaults and arches in adobe building; their possession of superior transport in the use of camels, horses and donkeys, and not least important their elaborate systems of belief in which the authority of king and chief is derived from their supernatural powers as the incarnation of gods.[9]

Fragmentary and little studied as is our knowledge of the rituals and cosmogonies of these early states and of their latter day successors it is clear that they belong to a tradition that is quite distinct from those of the clan-ancestor and earth cults of the kin-bound pagan communities. It has long been obvious too that many features of this tradition have close parallels in the beliefs and rituals of the ancient civilizations of the Levant. There the more advanced crafts found in the Western Sudan have a history extending back to the second millenium B.C. Since the Western Sudan is but the western segment of a habitable savanna belt extending east to the upper Nile and the Ethiopian highlands one might have expected that this would have provided a main route of cultural diffusion to the western lands south of the Sahara, more particularly since there were early chiefdoms and empires to the east between the Nile and Lake Chad as in Darfur and among the Baguirmi. But, up to the present, only meager and late indications have been found of cultural contacts with the old Nubian civilizations of the middle Nile. Such clues as we have point rather to indirect and intermittent traffic and incursions from North Africa into the Western Sudan by way of the oases of the Central and Western Sahara, and many of the recurrent elements have close parallels in the ancient civilizations of the Mediterranean and the Levant. How far back these trans-Saharan incursions go we do not know for our knowledge of the later prehistoric cultures of northern Africa is meager in the extreme. But it is clear that by the first millennium A.D. there were already considerable states strung out over the Western Sudan, that they traced their foundation to Hamitic speaking non-negroid invaders coming by way of the Saharan routes and oases.

The period of this development suggests the crucial importance of the introduction of the camel into North Africa which took place early in the first millenium and provided for the first time a riding animal and a beast of burden that could carry large bodies of men and goods across the waterless stretches of the desert.

Underlying the large scale organization and the widespread transport and exchange of goods in these early states of the Western Sudan was the possession not only of the camel, of key importance in more arid zones, but also of the horse and donkey. The horse, ultimately derived from S.W. Asia, was vitally important as a political and military instrument, for it made possible the concentration of military force at short notice against foot-bound peasantries, rapid communication of orders from capital to province, and the penetration of uncontrolled areas for slave raiding. Displays of horse riding on ceremonial occasions, the mounting with elaborate trappings of the chief and his emissaries which remain so characteristic today among all these peoples from the Mandingka to Bornu, are not meaningless ostentations, they remain symbols of authority expressed in what was once the key to power over this vast region.

The donkey as an economical beast of burden which could carry the loads of grain, raw materials and craft products from field to granary and market and from village to town and capital, afforded a great advance on human porterage. It may have been first domesticated in northeastern Africa but was not introduced into the Western Sudan until long after the first expansion of agriculture there.

It is with the more elaborately organized states too that the more advanced agriculture, the growing of cotton and the weaving of textiles is found. Voluminous tailored clothing in a Northern style, varying in elaboration and decoration according to rank contrasts strongly with the nudity of the pagan primitives outside the states.

Attention must also be called, in even the briefest survey, to the fact that a distinctive pastoral people is also widespread through the Western Sudan from Senegal to the Cameroons. Living for the most part in small scattered communities this cattle keeping people, the nomadic Fula, are linguistically and racially distinctive. The main patterns of their culture and social life appear to be essentially the same over this vast range except where some groups have, from the 16th century onwards, dominated and later merged with the surrounding populations. Such Fula chiefdoms are known from the Lower Senegal river and the Futa Jallon highlands in the west to Northern Nigeria and the Cameroons. But the initial spread of the Fula peoples was not one of conquest. It was a much older dispersion of unobtrusive migrant cattle people living on the outskirts of the areas closely settled by cultivating peoples. Although often economically linked to these by an exchange of cattle for farm products they did not merge with them.

In language the Fula belong to one of the more northerly stocks of the West Atlantic group and have spread from the region of the Lower Senegal river. Their extensive and peaceful proliferation over the vast area extending eastwards for some 3000 miles must, as the closeness of their dialects shows, be comparatively recent but it appears to have been largely accomplished by the 15th century and may have long preceded the Islamicization of the Western Sudan. For the pastoral Fula have remained pagans and until the 18th century they actively resisted the encroachment of Islam, organizing opposition to it in many areas. The conditions that permitted these pastoral groups to expand so quickly and rapidly and to maintain their separate cultural identity are to be sought in the comparative stability and large scale organization of the early empires of the Western Sudan. It would appear that these migrant pastoralists were not only valued for their contributions to the economy but that their independence and freedom of movement was protected. Islam did not easily reach them and it was only when, in a remarkable *volte face* that some groups, beginning in the west in the late 17th century embraced Islam with fanaticism, that there developed the later Fula empires with which the French and British had to contend when they first sought to pacify and administer parts of the Western Sudan.

The essential features of the higher civilization of the Western Sudan, as it existed on the eve of Islamic penetration and persisted little changed under an Islamic veneer until the end of the 19th century, are even now only slowly being transformed under the impact of the railway and the truck, export crops and trade goods, European control and western administration.

This brief summary must not be taken to suggest that there was any sudden and wholesale imposition of an alien culture from across the Sahara. As in any other complex culture, there are all the marks of an amalgam built up over a long period, some of its elements in the ritual as much as in the technical sphere may be archaic, others late increments established in the Moslem period. Its particular configuration in any region varied considerably no doubt through time. Some features were more widely diffused than others. The dogmas of divine chieftainship with its attendant rituals could reach peoples like the Jukun of the southern savanna in Nigeria unaccompanied by substantial advances in crafts or new techniques of political control by a ruling class. Cotton growing and the loom could spread from the great states to surrounding peoples who knew nothing of divine chiefs or tribute to the state treasury. It was a slowly built cultural complex strongly established in some areas the elements of which spread unevenly over surrounding areas in the Western Sudan according to the vicissitudes of geography, cultural resources and human endeavor.

Incomplete as was the dispersion of these developments through the savanna belt of West Africa they were not confined to it. For the tropical rain forests to the south did not prove a complete barrier and at a number of points they penetrated deeply into it introducing new religious doctrines, sacred chieftainship, weaving and brass-working which were amalgamated in various ways with the archaic economy and social systems of this zone. But these introductions do not appear to have been effected by wholesale movements of population, for it is only exceptionally, as in the case of the Mende warrior chiefdoms of Sierra Leone, that northern language stocks have displaced the Kwa and other languages of the forest belt. Even where there have been profound modifications of social structure and great advances in craft and art one must look rather to the intrusion of small bodies of northerners who achieved dominance among preexisting populations building up societies from which in turn others hived off to incorporate further groups in societies of similar pattern. Thus the Akan speaking peoples of the Gold Coast and the Ivory Coast belong linguistically to the Kwa group but, as the records of early travelers confirm, were already organized in chiefdoms with an elaborate state ritual, highly developed crafts and capable of confederation into considerable states. And the Akan everywhere ascribe their origins, which does not necessarily mean the source of most of their populations, but that of their social system and sacred symbols, to a process of expansion and hiving off of state after state from ever farther to the north.

In southwestern Nigeria a series of chiefdoms also clearly deriving their impetus from some, at present unknown, northern focus developed among the Yoruba speaking peoples. Some were integrated prior to the 19th century under the powerful hegemony of Oyo, others proliferated more or less independently on the flanks to spread west into Dahomey and east among the Edo speaking peoples and the western Ibo as far as the Niger. To the north of the Yoruba on the edge of the savanna were other chiefdoms among the Nupe, Igala and other peoples that had existed long before the southward incursions of Moslem Fula who had, in the early 19th century, usurped control over the Hausa chiefdoms to the north.[10]

In addition to the development of major chiefdoms and the rise of centers of advanced crafts and elaborate art and ritual symbolism among such peoples as the Akan and the Yoruba, elements of this more complex civilization were introduced piecemeal over the centuries among other peoples so that its pale reflection is found in small epigonal communities. It is as far a cry from the 17th century capital of the King and Queen Mother of Bono, with its mile long avenues, elaborate court ritual and wealth of gold and silver ornaments to the petty chieflets of the Ewe in Togoland as it was from the court of the Alafin of Oyo, before the Fulani raiders disrupted his empire, to the priest chief of Nri among the Northern Ibo. But all belong to the same ferment that was still spreading through the West African forest zone when Europeans first appeared on the surf-beaten coast to introduce new and powerful cultural forces.

The techniques and skills, whether in craft or social organization, that are characteristic of the main centers of cultural development in the forest belt, as among the Akan and the Yoruba, present a remarkable contrast to those of autonomous village communities remote from such centers. Cotton is grown for weaving; the high status of chief or official is marked by the wearing of long robes and elaborate head gear; precious metals and stones are elaborately fabricated for decoration; the technique of casting bronze and brass is elaborated for ceremonial objects; man power is organized to build elaborate courts and to raise armies for conquest and defense, towns are protected by encircling ditches and walls and defended gates. Despite the hazards of infection in the tsetse-ridden bush and forest, the Yoruba succeeded in rearing horses for use by chiefs and officials, in ceremonials and not least in war. Although the diffusion of some crafts and customs to some surrounding peoples produced cultural gradations of many kinds, the technically elaborate culture and the centralized social systems of such peoples contrast strongly again with those of such forest peoples as the southern Ibo of Nigeria or the tribes of the western Ivory Coast and Liberia to whom such things remained quite unknown.

The establishment of European trading posts along the Guinea coast introduced not so much new knowledge as opportunities to acquire a few vitally important supplies which in some regions profoundly affected indigenous political relations in the hinterland. Of the western goods the traders offered the most portentous were muskets and gunpowder. These, combined with the European demand for slaves, put a premium on militarization. Slavery and slave raiding was almost certainly established on a considerable scale in the larger states of the forest belt. Slave raiding and trading now became the means whereby the new instruments of dominance and empire could be obtained. But the coast had hitherto offered little attraction to the rulers of the larger chiefdoms. These had looked northward to traffic with the Sudan. Thus old Oyo, the capital of the paramount chiefdom among the Yoruba down to the 18th century was 200 miles inland as were Bono and Bona the largest and wealthiest chiefdoms of the Akan in the 16th century and those to which the lesser states nearer the coast traced their origins. Unexpected opportunities were offered to leaders among the coastal peoples to build up trading empires. Where a state system already existed as among the coastal Akan this provided the framework within which, with increasing militarization of organization, they sought to obtain slaves by raiding and to defend local monopolies over the supplies of guns and powder that offered so unexpected a means to wealth and power. In the same way petty coastal chiefdoms among the Yoruba rose to influence in the new traffic with the interior. But the inland states were also driving for direct access to the European trading posts and control of routes through the forest. It was in this way that, after many vicissitudes between warring states, the minor and recent Akan state of Kumasi broke the power of its great neighbors Denkyera to the south and Bono to the north and by overawing others, created and dominated the confederacy of Ashanti in the 18th and 19th centuries.[11] So, too, a succession of rulers of a petty state among the Fon were able from small beginnings at Abomey to build up one of the most remarkable chiefdoms of the forest belt. Dahomey, with its combination of elaborate state ritual that combined traditional features of sacred chiefship with military leadership, political despotism, complex business administration of plantations, trade and markets, and its organization of slave raiding and warfare, was a response to the unique opportunities that European trade provided. The story of the rise of the Kingdom of Benin in the forests west of the Niger follows a similar pattern. In nearly all cases these strong chiefdoms of the forest belt resisted by force later European attempts to penetrate and control the interior and their power could only be broken by war.

Where the coastal peoples were, at the time of European contact, still dispersed in small communities and out of range of inland states, they responded by developments consistent with their earlier social systems. Local kin groups built up bodies of slave dependents to man trading and war canoes and monopolize rivers and creeks that gave access to their neighbors and opportunities for raiding and trading. In this way, for example, the coastal Ibibio built up at the mouth of the Calabar river and in the Delta of the Niger, settlements controlled by rival bodies of kinsfolk which organized the traffic in slaves and later in palm oil with the hulks of the Europeans moored alongside. So grew up the wealthy "Houses" of Calabar in the 18th and 19th century and the shortlived commercial dominance of Jaja at Bonny at the end of the last century. From such trading centers the impact of commerce on the coast spread back to the interior. Participation in the trade in slaves and later oil provided a means of securing guns and powder, of raiding instead of being raided, promoting the rise of petty war leaders with their personal followings and their new patterns of prestige at the expense of the traditional authority of the elders of lineages and the priests of the local shrines.

But direct European influence did not begin to penetrate into the forest belt until the end of the 19th century and the grasslands were almost completely cut off from it except in the far west where they extended to the sea in Senegal. Thus the missionary and educational influences, the beginnings of western literacy and the participation in overseas commerce which began to be significant on the coast from the middle of the nineteenth century remained insignificant in the western Sudan until after the first world war. This immense contrast between the coast and the grassland interior of West Africa in the period over which western ways and resources became gradually more familiar and acceptable is often forgotten in appraisals of the economic and political situation in West Africa today.

The old cultural forms and social systems of West Africa are now being eroded and superseded at an ever-increasing rate as its peoples are, often at their own vigorous insistence, being incorporated economically and ideologically into the modern world and are being reorganized domestically and politically along Western lines. In relation to the pace of cultural and social transformation that is taking place today the amount of research into the traditional patterns of life has been and still is pitifully small. Those who recognize that a deeper understanding of the cultural history of man, and of the processes underlying the variety of socio-cultural patterns, depends in large measure in record-

ing and analyzing as fully as possible, with the tools of modern anthropology, the ways of life of non-Western peoples; those who recognize
that knowledge of the background and past of a people is a powerful aid
to constructive cooperation with them, should also understand that unless
far more resources are devoted to training and financing field research
and comparative study of these West African peoples over the next
twenty-five years the opportunity will be forever lost. For, unlike the
biologist who can still count on finding many older forms of life surviving for investigation, the anthropologist is only too clearly aware that
the socio-cultural plasticity of Man is such that an ancient cultural pattern
or a social system can disappear virtually without trace over a few
generations.

This has been in part my reason for attempting in a brief space
the overbold task of sketching, from woefully incomplete knowledge,
what seem to me to be some of the outstanding phases of the cultural
development of West Africa and to suggest the ways in which the broad
factors in the natural environment combined with a succession of external stimuli and local responses have contributed to the complexity
and variety of the cultural map of West Africa. That I have oversimplified I know; that I have entertained historical connections or adaptive
relations which cannot be substantiated on present knowledge I recognize. But a useful purpose in the field of scholarship and cultural understanding will have been served if I have been able to point to some of
the probabilities and possibilities in this field and to show that these are
a challenge to more intensive and systematic inquiry while there is yet
time to study the native cultures of West Africa that have survived
into the modern world.

NOTES

[Starred items are recommended as further readings.]

[1] Richard-Molard. 1949. *Afrique Occidentale Française*. Paris.

[2] [The linguistic classification employed here and in Figure 1 differs
somewhat from Greenberg's, which has
been used in the introduction to the
readings. Forde's Hamito-Semitic family
is the Afro-Asiatic family in Greenberg's
classification, and his Western Sudanic,
Benue-Cross, and Bantu groups are all
included in Greenberg's Niger-Congo
family. Songhai remains the same in both
classifications.]

[3] Westermann, D., & M. A. Bryan.
1952. *Handbook of African Languages*.
Part 2. Languages of West Africa. International African Institute.

Greenberg, J. 1949. "Studies in African
linguistic classification." Southwestern J.
Anthropology, 5:79.

[4] Archeological research in West Africa has not advanced sufficiently to attempt any comprehensive regional or
culture-sequence interpretations, or to
yield much evidence concerning pre-
agricultural peoples. It must be recog-

nized, however, that the ancestors of the present language stocks may well have been first introduced by foraging and hunting peoples before the introduction of crops.

5 It is only in limited areas that dwarf cattle, ultimately of northern origin, are reared.

6 See Burkhill, L. H. 1951. "The rise and decline of the greater yam in the service of man." The Adv. Sci. 7:443 et seq. For a general account of the early development of Old World tropical agriculture in South Asia and references to the literature see C. O. Sauer, "Agricultural Origins and Dispersals." Bowman

Memorial Lectures, Series Two, 1952. Am. Geog. Soc.

*7 Brown, P. 1951. "Patterns of authority in West Africa." Africa. 21:261.

* 8 Bovill, E. W. 1933. Caravans of the Old Sahara. London.

* 9 Greenberg, J. "Negro Kingdoms of the Sudan." Trans. N. Y. Acad. Sci. 11 (4): 126-135.

10 Forde, D. 1951. The Yoruba-Speaking Peoples of S.W. Nigeria. Ethnographic Survey of Africa, Western Africa Part 4. London.

11 [See Rattray's "The Ashanti Constitution," pp. 303-11, below.]

FOR FURTHER READING

Bovill, E. W., The Golden Trade of the Moors, London: Oxford University Press, 1958. A revised version of his Caravans of the Old Sahara, cited above by Forde. It views the history of the Sudan from the point of view of North Africa.

Hogben, S. J., The Muhammadan Emirates of Nigeria, London: Oxford University Press, 1930; Delafosse, M., Haut-Sénégal-Niger, Paris: Larose, 1912, 3 vols.; Meek, C. K., A Sudanese Kingdom: An Ethnographical Study of the Jukun-speaking Peoples of Nigeria, London: Kegan Paul, 1931; Urvoy, Y., Histoire de l'empire du Bornou, Dakar: Institut Français d'Afrique Noire, Mémoire, 7, 1949; Urvoy, Y., Histoire des populations du Soudan central, Paris: Comité d'Études Historiques et Scientif-

iques de l'Afrique Occidentale Française, Série A, 5, 1936. Useful specialized studies of particular areas or kingdoms in the Western Sudan.

Fage, J. D., Introduction to the History of West Africa, Cambridge: Cambridge University Press, 1955. Fage covers the early history of West Africa, though he does not make full use of anthropological materials.

Murdock, George Peter, Africa, Its Peoples and Their Culture History, New York: McGraw-Hill, 1959. A broad interpretation of cultural movements and contacts of African peoples.

TRANSHUMANCE, MIGRATORY DRIFT, MIGRATION: PATTERNS OF PASTORAL FULANI NOMADISM[*][1]

Derrick J. Stenning

The pastoral Fulani, who are widely distributed over many parts of the Western Sudan, are characterized by three different types of population movement. Transhumance is the regular shifting of people and herds from one locality to another in response to the seasonal demands. Migratory drift is a gradual displacement of the transhumance routes that results eventually in a completely new geographic setting for a particular group. Migration is a dramatic shift in transhumance patterns for a specific cause, either an ecological catastrophe such as an epidemic of cattle disease or a social upheaval taking the form of an intolerable political or ideological conflict. Although both ecological and social factors may be operative in all three types of movement, the first two are primarily responses to ecological conditions and the third, to socio-political circumstances.

In his account of the population movements of pastoral Fulani in Northern Nigeria, Stenning illustrates the interplay between seasonal changes in locality and social factors of relations among tribes and those within the family, lineage, and clan. The mutual interdependence of the Fulani and their cattle is such that each is necessary to the survival of the other. Whereas the needs of the cattle are constant, those of the people are adjusted to the demands of the changing seasons: in the dry season, when maintenance of the herds is most difficult, cattle take priority; the wet season, when herding is easier, is the time of social congregation, celebration, and ritual.

The Fulani are an important African population, numbering perhaps seven millions, widely distributed in the Western Sudan from Senegambia in the West to French Equatorial Africa in the East, with their main

---

* Reprinted from *Journal of the Royal Anthropological Institute*, 1957, 87, 57-73, by permission of the author and publisher.

concentration in Senegambia, Upper Niger, Northern Nigeria, and the British and French Cameroons (FIGURE 1).

They are known as Fula in Gambia and Sierra Leone; Fellah by the Arabs of the Western Sudan; Fellaata by the Kanuri and other peoples of the Chad Basin; Peuls by the French; and Fulbe in the German literature. Their own term for themselves is Fulbe (sing. Pullo) and their language Fulfulde. The British in Nigeria use the Hausa term Fulani, and this will be used here, since the information on which this paper was based was obtained in Northern Nigeria.[2]

In Nigeria, the Fulani may be divided sociologically into four categories. First, the ruling dynasties of most of the Northern Nigerian Emirates, established during the Holy War of 1804-30 (Hogben 1930). Second, the settled Fulani, who fill a range of occupations in Northern Nigerian society—court officials, judges, scribes, entrepreneurs, farmers, and so on. Third, the semisedentary Fulani, who are primarily farmers, but who maintain herds of cattle for which pasture has to be sought at a distance. Fourthly, the Pastoral Fulani (often called Bororo in the literature) who depend completely on their herds of zebu cattle for subsistence, and whose lives are tuned to continuous transhumance, migratory drift, and periodic migration. This last element of the Fulani population, and the various kinds of movement which it practices, are the subject of this paper. The observations of which it mainly consists are based upon field data obtained among the Wodaabe and Wewedbe of West Bornu; the Wewedbe of Pankshin Division, Plateau Province; and the Wewedbe of South Katsina. These are three areas which exhibit significant geographical and historical variations (FIGURE 1).

It is pertinent to give first a brief account of the major forms of social grouping in Pastoral Fulani society. The basic residential and economic unit is the family, moving its few domestic belongings on pack animals with the herd whenever it is moved to new pastures. The family consists of a man, his wife or wives, and dependent children. It is sometimes augmented by other dependents—hirelings and, formerly, slaves; aged parents of the male household head; and some others. Ownership of the herd is vested in the male household head. He has full rights of slaughter, sale, and deployment of cattle in the herd, and is responsible for its fertility by rational as well as magical means. His sons are his herdboys, and they receive cattle from their father's herd with which to start their own herds on marriage. There is no bride-wealth in first marriages, and no bride-wealth in the form of cattle in subsequent marriages. The household head's wife or wives have milking rights in all or a part of the herd. Assisted by unmarried daughters, they prepare dairy products for home consumption, but more particularly for sale or exchange against cereal or root foods, which they acquire in village or hamlet markets. Meat is eaten only on ceremonial and ritual occasions, and beasts are sold only where an overriding need for cash occurs, principally to pay tax. The Pastoral Fulani family may be regarded as a herd-owning, milk-selling enterprise. It has a great deal of economic independence, which is fostered by geographical conditions. Ideally, it exhibits a balance between the fertility of the household head and his wife or wives, which provides the herd with those who minister to its needs. Households, based on the family, range from the theoretical minimum to fifteen members. Ten cattle per household member is a mean found to obtain in samples studied in all three areas.

The agnatic lineage group is formed by the common relationship, through males, of a number of household heads to a common male ancestor three to five generations past, and is named after him. A typical agnatic lineage group might consist of five to twenty household heads and their families, or some twenty-five to one hundred persons. The major function of this group, in the present context, is to ensure the smooth establishment and continuity of families. For first, and sometimes subsequent marriages by betrothal, the agnatic lineage group is endogamous. Household heads make loans or gifts of cattle to a member of their agnatic lineage group when the latter's herd is inadequate in some way for the support of his family. When a member's labor force is inadequate for the care of his herd, he can rely on temporary help from members of his agnatic lineage group. On the death of a household head, a member of his agnatic lineage group will inherit his widow, act as guardian for his dependent children, attend to their betrothals, and administer the herd for their benefit until they marry. Although dispersed most of the year, when its constituent families pursue their own interests, the agnatic lineage group makes a common camp in the wet season. Its political function now emerges; it has a leader, chosen by his fellow household heads on criteria of age, descent, prosperity, and pastoral skill. The leader (*ardo,* vb. *arta,* "lead") represents the agnatic lineage group before whatever political authority stands above him, and transmits the commands of that authority to his followers.

The clan is a cluster of agnatic lineage groups, the link between which is the putative agnatic relationship of their respective ancestors. The clan is endogamous for first and some subsequent marriages. It is a unit of pastoral cooperation. Widow inheritance and its consequences occur within it. But it has no formal political functions, and is only in a very loose sense coresidential in the wet season. Formerly the clan was in some areas a congregation which joined in the performance of increase rituals for cattle, and fertility rites and *rites de passage* for humans. The Pax Britannica and conversion to Islam have done much to reduce the cohesion of the clan.

The tribe is a vague cultural entity, distinguished as the widest social grouping to which Pastoral Fulani see themselves as belonging traditionally. A tribe is believed to favor a particular strain of cattle; to use a certain range of cattle calls; to practice a common basic decoration of milk calabashes; to circulate a common repertoire of songs; to favor a particular feminine coiffure; to practice a common cycle of puberty ceremonies; and to speak a subdialect.

None of these forms of social grouping had, or has, any *de jure* rights to ownership of pasture, water, or cattle tracks enforceable either by the sanctions of Pastoral Fulani society, or those of the alien political entities within which the Pastoral Fulani move. The nomadic movements of Pastoral Fulani are a constant adjustment to the changing demands of the natural habitat and the fluctuating pressure of the social environment. Field analysis establishes, by different techniques, three forms of movement, each of which has a specific term in Fulfulde. Transhumance, defined as "regular seasonal movements," is translated *kodol* (vb. *hoda* "to come round, like the seasons"). There are a number of terms for more specific types of movement within its scope, such as:

ruuma	to spend the wet season
banga or *wurtoya*	to move towards dry season pastures
woossoya	to move about in a limited area
cheedoya	to spend the dry season
tijjoya	to move towards wet season pastures
fabbita	to postpone movement.

Migratory drift, defined as "the gradual displacement of transhumance orbits," is rendered in Fulfulde *eggol* (vb. *egga,* "to wander"). Migration, defined as "the assumption of new transhumance orbits by a sudden and often lengthy movement," is translated *perol* (vb. *fera,* "to flee").

TRANSHUMANCE

To understand transhumance one must have a picture of the habitat in which Pastoral Fulani are found. West Africa may be divided into a number of lateral zones. From south to north these are labelled the Mangrove, Guinea Forest, Guinea Savanna, Sudan Savanna, Sahel, and Desert zones. From south to north, again, these zones show a progressive decrease in the mean annual rainfall, a progressive increase in the number of dry months per year, a progressive instability of rainfall incidence, a progressive decrease in average humidity, and a progressive deterioration of the climax vegetation (Buchanan & Pugh 1955).

The zone of West Africa in which the economic strains of zebu cattle may be kept is generally stated to be the Savanna Zone, a belt of more or less open woodland or orchard bush, interspersed with grassland. In Nigeria, this is a transitional zone between the Guinea Forest, which lies south of the 7° North parallel of latitude approximately, and the Sahel, or thorn scrub fringe of the Sahara Desert, north of the 15° North parallel of latitude approximately (FIG. 1). In neither of these two zones is the keeping of zebu cattle practicable. In the Sahel, grass cover is intermittent; this is predominantly the zone of the goat, and, where it shades into the desert, of the camel. In the Guinea Forest, the climax vegetation is too thick for successful pasturage, although small herds of dwarf cattle may be kept.

The Savanna zone itself is divisible into two. The southernmost of these divisions, the Guinea Savanna, has a heavier type of woodland, with many varieties of tree which are not fire-resistant. It coincides strikingly with the mean annual rainfall belt of 45-60 inches. The more northerly division, the Sudan Savanna, is a zone of lighter woodland, with a greater proportion of fire-resistant trees. It coincides with the 30-45 inch rainfall belt (FIGURE 1).

This description of the Savanna, the cattle keeping zone, is however something of a simplification. For much of the Savanna is infested with certain varieties of tsetse fly, the carriers of human sleeping sickness and bovine trypanosomiasis. For convenience in this paper, these will be called simply bush tsetse and riverain tsetse. The activities of tsetse, in so far as they affect cattle, are associated with seasonal changes in temperature, humidity, and vegetation cover (Nash 1948). These changes also affect the availability of pasture and water to cattle.

Seasonal changes are brought about by the alternate action of the dry northeast monsoon from the Sahara, the Harmattan, which brings the dry season; and the moist south-west monsoon from the Gulf of Guinea, which brings the wet season. The dry season starts earliest in the north of the Savanna zone, in September or October, and lasts longest there, till April or May. The wet season comes to the southern part of the Savanna zone in March or April, and lasts longest there, till September or October. With the onset of the dry season, the northern part of the Savanna zone begins to partake of the desert conditions prevalent to the north. Standing water is evaporated and herbage is dried by the sun. As dry season conditions extend southwards, they begin to affect the zone in which tsetse are prevalent. Riverain tsetse are greatly affected by this desiccation, and retreat along watercourses, or are isolated in patches of standing water. Bush tsetse retreat to thickets in underpopulated stretches of bush, where game is likely to be found. As the wet season in its turn moves progressively northward, vegetation again recovers, pools of standing water again appear, and water flows along the river and stream beds. Both bush tsetse and riverain tsetse again attain their maximum distribution. In Nigeria, this accounts for all but a small northern proportion of the Savanna zone.

These seasonal changes also have their effects upon the zebu cattle

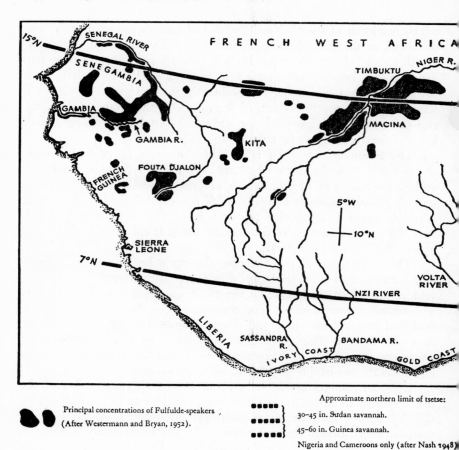

Principal concentrations of Fulfulde-speakers ,
(After Westermann and Bryan, 1952).

Approximate northern limit of tsetse:
30–45 in. Sudan savannah.
45–60 in. Guinea savannah.
Nigeria and Cameroons only (after Nash 1948)

FIGURE 1. *Distribution of Fulani in relation*

of the Pastoral Fulani. At the height of the wet season, the bulk of the cattle in Nigeria are concentrated in the fly-free zone, which extends across the northern parts of Sokoto, Katsina, Kano and Bornu Provinces. There are also concentrations of cattle in this season in areas which belong to the tsetse belt by virtue of their latitude, but are fly-free because of their altitude. These are the Jos Plateau, and the Cameroons and Bamenda highlands (FIGURE 1).

When the dry season begins, it is the northernmost herds, in French West Africa, which first experience shortages of pasture. Although cattle are watered from wells, only reduced holdings can be maintained, and there is a southward movement of herds in search of pasture. These conditions progressively affect areas further south, from which tsetse has itself retreated, and the cattle population spreads into pasture lands

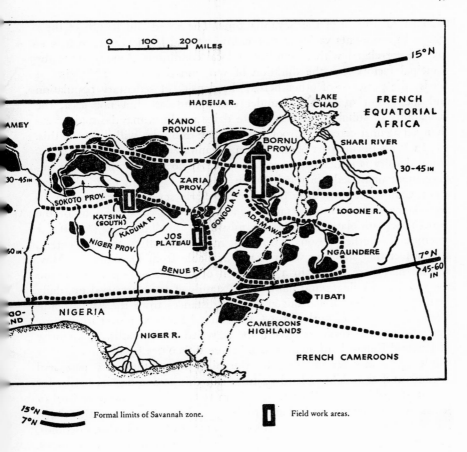

to the Savannah Zone of West Africa.

from which a major hazard has been removed. Under certain conditions this cession is not maintained. When the instability of rainfall in this region manifests itself in an undue prolongation of the dry season, herds may impinge, for fodder, upon areas to which bush tsetse has retreated, or may be forced to water at streams or at water holes in stream beds where riverain tsetse is prevalent. It is likely that the incidence of trypanosomiasis in zebu herds may be correlated primarily with conditions such as these. It should be noted, further, that Pastoral Fulani are well aware, so far as their own practical purposes go, of the relation between tsetse fly infestation and trypanosomiasis.

This regular seasonal movement of cattle, southward in the dry season in response to shortages of pasture and water, northward in the wet season to avoid tsetse, is a consistent pattern of transhumance among the Pastoral Fulani of the Savanna zone. The speed and length of these seasonal movements varies from area to area and from year to year, and may be correlated with a number of local conditions. Among these the principal factors are: the duration of wet and dry seasons; the size of herds; the presence of other herds; the density of sedentary population and the extent of farmland under crops; and last, but not least, the availability of suitable markets where dairy products may be sold or exchanged against cereal and root foods. Some examples will illustrate this.

In West Bornu, part of the Sudan Savanna zone, the sedentary population density is under 20 per square mile. At no time of the year is impingement upon sedentary cultivation a serious factor in pastoral movement. Camps are moved, in principle, regularly seven times a month, in accordance with an interpretation of a lunar cycle, at all seasons of the year. There are elaborate rules for missing a "loading day" (baire) for ceremonial or other reasons. This great mobility is offset, to some extent, by the fact that standing water is not available from December to May, so that herds are bound to a succession of dry season wells, mostly in the vicinity of villages and hamlets. As stands of grass are used up, daily herding has to be carried out at greater distances from the water point, often into pockets of bush tsetse. Camps may be moved nearer to pasture, but now greater distances have to be travelled to the wells. A minority of Pastoral Fulani herd-owners avoid these difficulties by moving further south in the dry season into the Biu hills, where there are perennial streams and abundant upland pasture. But this course has its perils, for the basalt gullies may never be free from tsetse, and a delicate control of herds while grazing may have to be practiced. In 1951-2, the mean length of the transhumance orbits of some two hundred households, practicing both techniques of dry season deployment, was sixty miles. The term "transhumance orbit" refers to the straight-line distance between the most northerly wet season camp and the most southerly dry season camp. The yearly orbital distance travelled in transhumance is thus approximately twice the transhumance orbit. These measurements are the most convenient for comparison of different areas. Clearly, the Pastoral Fulani do not move in a straight line from sojourn to sojourn, so that the "transhumance track" is invariably considerably greater than the orbital distance covered. These distances, also, do not include the daily grazing distances covered by cattle to and from pasture and wells.

In a Guinea Savanna area in South Katsina, by contrast, the wet season area of the Pastoral Fulani population studied supports a sedentary population of 150 per square mile. This density extends into the northern part of their dry season area in Gwari division of Zaria Province, but decreases as the southern part of the dry season area in Niger Province is approached. Farmland is a constant factor in pastoral movement in this area. Wet season quarters are taken up in June, and only limited areas are open for grazing without fear of trespass. Movement out of the wet season area is not made until October, when the guinea corn harvest has been taken in. Thereafter much of the southward movement of the Pastoral Fulani of this area is on to guinea-corn farms as they are cleared; the pastoralists are paid by the Gwari farmers for manuring their land. The southward path of the South Katsina Fulani lies along the innumerable streams (from which they water their herds) leading into the Kaduna River and thence to the Niger. Their constant preoccupation is with riverain tsetse in the dry season. Nevertheless, this form of movement brings them into continuous proximity to suitable markets. The mean length of the transhumance orbits of some forty households was calculated at a hundred and eighty miles.

The habitat in which the Pastoral Fulani live enjoins upon them a seasonal movement north and south. But there is a further characteristic of transhumance. Although the dry season denies the most northerly part of the Savanna zone to them, the fly-free Savanna is open still to a reduced holding of cattle, while at the same time a much larger area is opened up—the area from which the tsetse has for the most part retreated. This dry season area is exploitable only on the condition that maximum mobility is maintained for taking advantage of diminishing reserves of pasture and water. These general conditions suggest that the wet season sees a congregation of Pastoral Fulani while the dry season promotes a dispersal.

* * *

[In West Bornu, wet season concentrations are largely specific by tribe and clan in a locality, and number up to five agnatic lineage groups including fifty or sixty households; dry season dispersal into groups of one or two households involves intertribal congregation at dry season wells and markets.]

This characteristic rhythm of dispersal and concentration of Pastoral Fulani imposes striking seasonal contrasts on their social life. In the hot dry season, herding is arduous; grazing may take the herd up to ten miles from the camp, since tracts of burnt-out country may have to be traversed. A conscientious herd owner sees that his cattle graze from dawn to dusk, and often into the night. He may also have to make lengthy reconnaissances to find suitable pasture. Watering cattle, too, may be hard work. In many areas, well-digging was formerly the work of slaves, and Pastoral Fulani take hardly to it. A Bornu herdsman was calculated to raise and lower his watering calabash fifteen feet more than four hundred times a day to water his herd of fifty head. Owing to increase in temperature, increases in distance travelled to and from pasture, poorer quality of pasture, and fewer lactations, the milk yield of herds is lowered. The household diet may have to be supplemented by berries and wild plants. Stock may have to be sold to pay for grain. These daily tasks disperse household members, already isolated from others of their agnatic lineage group. The dry season is a time of unremitting labor, unrelieved for the most part by those gatherings which give zest to social life.

In the cool wet season, by contrast, herding is easy, although sometimes uncomfortable in the rain. Cattle are pastured at very short distances from camp, watered at convenient pools of standing water, and brought back replete to the vicinity of the corrals in midafternoon. Milk yield rises, until there is a considerable surplus to be devoted to the feasts which the congregation of clansmen make possible. Puberty ceremonies are carried out. Betrothals are contracted and solemnized. The various stages of induction into married life are enacted. Communal cattle fertility rites are performed. Allegiance to chiefs and leaders is demonstrated. Fealty to Emirs, and the commitments of the Pastoral Fulani community to the British Administration are embodied in the assessment and remittance of cattle tax. The wet season is a time of concentrated ritual and ceremonial activity.

Pastoral Fulani transhumance is carried out in response to the special conditions of the West African Savanna habitat. For the herdowner it involves a detailed knowledge of specific tracts of country; their characteristic pasture and terrain; their endowment of standing, running, or well water; the incidence of tsetse, ticks, and biting flies. A herdowner must also have a clear picture of the movements of other Pastoral Fulani whose herds may compete for pasture or water, or bring disease. He must also maintain contact with his clansmen, so that he may discharge his obligations and exercise his rights. In addition he must be aware of the sedentary populations through which he passes; the extent of their farmland, the suitability of their markets, the friendship or animosity of their chiefs. All this intelligence is not assembled merely by deploying the herd on which the subsistence of one's household depends. The day to day tasks of herding, its tactics if you will, are left to boys and young men. A herdowner concerns himself with a wider scene, with the strategy of herd deployment. Whenever possible he visits markets where news is exchanged; he visits kinsmen; and before each move is made he attends a camp council, in which all this evidence is sifted by interminable discussion, before each herdowner decides which course he will follow. Social obligations play their part in keeping herdowners and their families together, but it is the demands of the herd which regulate primarily a herdowner's decision, and it is generally recognized that this overrides other considerations. Pastoral Fulani transhumance does not consist of random wanderings. Rather the reverse; it consists of a conservative exploitation of a known habitat, involving continuous and careful appraisal of environmental and social demands which are not necessarily in harmony.

MIGRATORY DRIFT

Most of the details of transhumance can be seen and experienced by a field worker in the course of the yearly cycle of the seasons. But data on migratory drift cannot be gathered by direct observation and experience, since this second form of movement is a gradual displacement of customary transhumance tracks and orbits, resulting eventually in a completely new orbit, often in different surroundings in which many factors in the total environmental situation have altered. Evidence of migratory drift becomes available in the life histories of herdowners, who describe their seasonal movements in the past, and who may yet have wives drawn from tribes beside which they no longer pasture. Corroborative evidence arises in genealogical enquiry, when the seasonal movements, at crucial periods in their lives, of agnatic and affinal kinsmen in ascending generations are recounted. Indeed the timing of events in the past is done in the first instance with reference to the seasonal location of vital persons concerned.

From this sort of evidence, and from what is observable in the decisions affecting current seasonal movements, migratory drift may be analyzed more fully. Clearly a number of variations in existing transhumance tracks are possible. The northern or southern ends of the track may be extended. The northern or southern ends may be displaced. The middle of the track may be displaced. As life histories of individual herdowners show, these extensions and displacements occur time and again, and in successive years, owing to the operation of factors affecting transhumance. Both prolongation of the wet season and heavy rainfall in a wet season of the expected length may extend a track northward. Conversely a long dry season may extend it southward. The incidence of bovine disease (not only trypanosomiasis, but rinderpest and bovine pleuropneumonia) may cause wide detours in the southward or northward movement. The extension of farmland, the cutting of a new road, the opening or development of a market, may attract or repel Pastoral Fulani at any point in their northward or southward track.

Migratory drift may be said to have occurred when a stated range of seasonal grazing grounds has given way piecemeal to a completely new range. This may occur within the lifetime of a herdowner, or within two or more generations, depending upon the urgency of the environmental factors involved.

In the minor changes in transhumance which may or may not result in migratory drift, it must be recalled that there are no formal rights of possession of pasture, water, or cattle paths to be lost or gained. Vacua created by them are adjusted by the advent of new users, either pastoral or agricultural. It may be asserted that overgrazing is a short term phenomenon, obviated almost automatically by alterations in transhumance tracks. This assertion applies to the Savanna; it cannot be maintained for highland areas such as Jos, Bamenda, and the Cameroons.

A classic case of migratory drift can be reported from the southeastern part of the Jos Plateau in Pankshin Division (FIGURE 2). It is given here in some detail, since migratory drift, usually somewhat vague and tentative, has here been, as it were, telescoped, owing to abnormal conditions. The Jos Plateau is high (4000 feet), well watered, and fly-free, rising out of the surrounding Guinea Savanna. In the 'eighties and 'nineties of the last century a clan of Pastoral Fulani, the Butanko'en, pastured in the wet season in the vicinity of Bauchi. In the dry season, they moved up the rivers flowing from the Plateau to Chad, and spent the height of the dry season round Lere, at the foot of what is now called the Plateau. By 1900, when the British arrived in Bauchi, elements of the Butanko'en had extended their dry season movements to Gindiri. Southwestwards beyond the Lere and Gindiri country, which was the limit of the jurisdiction of the Emir of Bauchi, and is today crossed by its boundary, the Fulani could not proceed. The Pastoral Fulani sent out scouts westwards and southwards up the branches of the Lere river, but the rich pastures which these reconnaissances revealed were denied them by the intransigence of the well-armed and mounted Sura pagans. Secure in their rocky hamlets, neither negotiation nor successful war could be made with them. The entry of the Butanko'en, and others, to the Plateau had to await the pacification of this and neighboring pagan tribes by the British Administration. Their first punitive expedition in these parts was made from the north in 1904 and was followed in the following year by a column from Bauchi itself. The final pacification of the Sura tribe was achieved in 1908 when they were defeated near Panyam. These operations opened up to the Pastoral Fulani a range of unrivalled highland pasture which they had coveted for some years, and they proceeded to make their way on to the Plateau.

The migratory drift which followed has been one in which dry season pastures are found, after a period, to be suitable for wet season grazing. It involves a lengthening of the dry season end of the transhumance track, followed by a retraction of the wet season extremity. . . .

By 1925-30 the High Plateau watershed in Pankshin Division was both wet and dry season pasture for the Butanko'en and other groups. This migratory drift was accomplished by tentative extensions of transhumance tracks into areas in which friendly relations had to be established with sedentary pagans. So far, migratory drift was promoted

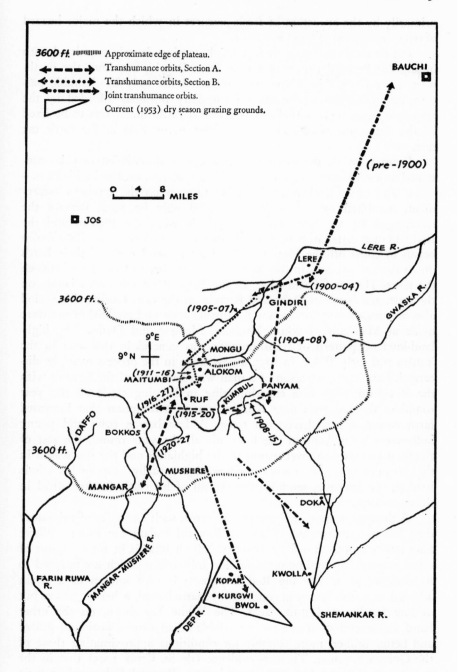

FIGURE 2. *Migratory Drift, Butanko'en (Wewedbe) Pankshin Division, Plateau Province.*

primarily by the attraction of fresh pastures in which the major hazard of tsetse infestation was not apparent.

But by now the High Plateau was becoming densely populated with immigrant Pastoral Fulani, not only from Bauchi, but from the north-western or Zaria side. These were attracted not only by desirable pasture, but by the profitable market for dairy products afforded by the tin-mining camps. Eventually, a wet season cattle quota was to be fixed by the Administration, and buttressed by an increase in the cattle tax rate.

From now on, the migratory drift of the Butanko'en may be construed as a response to pressure of cattle population on the highland pastures. The forward elements found themselves on the southern escarpment, inhabited by pagan tribes pacified only by 1934. Beyond the escarpment lay the fly-infested Savanna between the Plateau and the River Benue. After overtures to the escarpment pagans, the Butanko'en began to come off the Plateau, or at least to send parts of their herds down to the lowlands, in the dry season. They began to pasture between the rivers Dep and Shemankar, in the Kopar-Kurgwi-Bwol triangle on the west, and between Doka and Kwolla on the east. During this period also, wet season pasture was sought further west and establishments were made at Maitumbi, Bokkos, Mushere, Mangar and Daffo. The high-land-lowland pattern of transhumance was general in this area in the 'forties and early 'fifties. In 1953, a new stage in the process could be discerned. One herdowner, son of a man who had entered the Plateau with the Pax Britannica, was experimenting in keeping cattle all the year round in the lowlands near Kurgwi, on an assumption that increased farm clearance had driven out tsetse. A few barren cows and young bulls were being kept in the lowlands all the year round, the rest of the herd spending the wet season in the highlands and the dry season in the Savanna. This herdowner anticipated eventually keeping his whole herd in the Savanna, sending some or all of his cattle further afield in the dry season.

Although perhaps in less extreme forms, such examples of migratory drift are a commonplace wherever Pastoral Fulani are found. Where long association with a local variant of the habitat is in force, strains of cattle are built up by line breeding and inbreeding which are adapted to its characteristics. The big Red Longhorn is well known as a strain adapted to Sudan Savanna conditions—coarse-boned, a hardy grazer, but of low fertility and milk yield. The White Longhorn, on the other hand, has a reputation as a more tractable beast, a more fastidious grazer and better milker, more suitable for conditions approximating those of the Guinea Savanna. There is evidence (de St. Croix 1945) that in the transition to changed conditions of habitat, Pastoral Fulani adapt their herds by crossbreeding with strains long accustomed to that area. This may be done by purchasing selected beasts, but more commonly by cattle exchanges between herdowners of different provenance.

MIGRATION

We come finally to the third form of movement practiced by Pastoral Fulani. Again, a period of fieldwork would not normally afford direct evidence of this form of movement, which is a dramatic shift to different transhumance orbits without the piecemeal abandoning of pastures which characterizes migratory drift. Evidence of migration is obtained in the recounting of tribal history.

It has been apparent in the discussion of transhumance and migratory drift that these occur in fine response to environmental conditions, principal among which are purely ecological factors. The precipitate quality apparent in accounts of migration must be matched—if we are to attribute migration to these causes also—by catastrophic changes of an ecological nature. It may happen that this is indeed the case. The widespread ravages of the rinderpest which swept what is now Northern Nigeria in 1887-91 must have caused extensive dislocations in the territorial grouping of Pastoral Fulani. Some evidence of this is apparent in all three areas studied. To take only one example, before the epidemic the Dayi of West Bornu pastured along the river Gana between Mugrum and Gumuk on the southern borders of Bedde. During 1887-91, many herdowners retired whence they had come, to grazing grounds near Gayawa south of Katagum. Here, it appears, they were unable to escape the epidemic, lost the major portion of their cattle, and were forced to farm until their herds could be established once more, when they returned to West Bornu. The famine of 1913 in Bornu is a possible cause of much of the exodus of Wodaabe herds southwards to Adamawa, although other factors operated at this time, and the exact nature of the movements involved was not discernible in field enquiry.

But in Fulfulde the term *perol* ("flight" or "migration") is not used principally to refer to movement in response to ecological factors. It is used to refer to flight from intolerable conditions of a political or ideological nature. It is significant that the archetype of *perol* is the Hejira of Muhammad. It is also used to refer to gatherings of the supporters of Shehu dan Fodio, who initiated the coups by which many of the Hausa states passed into the hands of Fulani between 1804 and 1830. Clearly, in discussing migration, attention should be fixed upon the territorial and political environment in which Pastoral Fulani find themselves. In the mass of sedentary populations among whom they are disseminated, they are a minority, and a particularly elusive one, because of their lack of ownership of land. But although they do not own land, Pastoral Fulani use it, and are aware that at least recognition of their use must be secured from political authorities in whom title of ownership is vested. It is, as we shall see, the demands of certain aspects of this relationship which may cause migration. Both in pre-Protectorate times and at the present day, Pastoral Fulani impinge in their seasonal movements upon two main types of political system in which territorial rights are vested. These are: firstly, acephalous societies, called Pagan in Northern Nigeria, and secondly, Muslim States.

In pre-Protectorate times, and to some extent today, the right to pasture in Pagan tribal territory was secured in several ways. In many areas, the Pastoral Fulani appointed functionaries whose duty it was, on behalf of the leaders of agnatic descent groups, to herald the approach of the herds and to give gifts of milk and butter or of bulls for slaughter, to the Pagans in whose territory pasture was sought. Cattle might be corralled on fallow land shortly to come into cultivation. These arrangements set in train a further relationship of mutual advantage—the women's trade in dairy produce against grain and root foods. The relationship of Pagan and Fulani was a symbiotic one of simple economic reciprocity between face-to-face units of comparable scale and organization. This relatively informal relationship continues in a modified form today.

Where, however, such small-scale sedentary communities were parts of Muslim states, there were superimposed upon these mutual services other relationships of a more sophisticated kind. In so far as the central authority of the state reacted upon the village populations, it did so proportionately upon the pastoralists also. Fulani rendered tribute in kind, often known as "grass-payment," either direct to an Emir or to his local representative. In some areas they furnished bowmen, and later, horsemen, when the Emir waged war nearby. In return they received a degree of protection, but more particularly material benefits such as slaves and horses. Finally, as Muslims, they were liable to render compulsory alms. The incidence of these relationships between Pastoral Fulani and the Muslim State varied in proportion to the degree of control exercised by the State over the area in which the Pastoral Fulani sought pasture.

Pastoral Fulani never speak of "flight" from a Pagan area. They do not think of their relationship with Pagan communities in terms of their own subordination. It seems that in pre-Protectorate times, active relations of this sort were not governed by the use of force. Only where the Fulani were acting on behalf of an Emirate to which they owed allegiance, or were viewed by Pagans in this light, was there room for misinterpretation. The whole relationship was initiated by the pastoralists, often by the leaders of agnatic descent groups through their special agents. Once extricated from situations of friction which undoubtedly arose, there were no claims which the Pagans could, or might be disposed to, pursue. These arrangements arose in a situation in which mutual benefit was immediately apparent. They were transitory, often involving quite short sojourns at particular junctures in the seasonal cycle, and were brought to an end for the time being by the onward move of the Pastoral Fulani in search of new pasture.

In the Muslim states, conditions were different. The greater area covered by a single authority or delegates of it might include the complete transhumance orbits of whole clans of Pastoral Fulani. Islamized Pastoral Fulani held themselves to be members of the Muslim community of the Emirate, and, during the nineteenth century, considered themselves to be of the same ethnic group as the ruling houses of the Fulani-Hausa states taken over or newly formed in the Holy War of 1804-30. Their legitimate pastoral interests were more profitably pursued in the less densely populated periphery of an Emirate. This was often a no man's land, control of which varied with the military fortunes of the State. When the State was weak, it was prudent for the Pastoral Fulani to transfer a semblance of allegiance to a neighbor State. When the State was strong, it extended military operations, often in the form of slave raids, to its nominal and often ill-defined boundaries (Urvoy 1949). These disturbances both affected the availability of pasture and markets, and brought the machinery of tribute collection closer to the Pastoral Fulani. On the other hand, some material benefits became available to them, particularly when intransigent Pagan areas were brought under control, and as we have suggested, the Pastoral Fulani sometimes became involved in these military excursions. But for the most part, they ran counter to essential pastoral interests. When State inactivity of this sort bore too heavily upon them, the Pastoral Fulani sought safety in flight.

The establishment of the British Protectorate had its effects upon these political relations. Symbiosis of pastoralist and Pagan agriculturalist still goes on. But since District Administration has been instituted in Pagan areas, bringing with it the assessment and collection of cattle tax, entry of Pastoral Fulani into these areas, particularly in the wet season, is not nowadays accompanied by such extensive gifts by way of peaceful overture. In the Muslim States, where Indirect Rule was almost immediately practicable, compulsory alms were turned into a statutory tax payable at a standard cash rate on each head of cattle. Collection was regularized, and penal sanctions for nonpayment were instituted and effectively implemented. This does not mean that under certain circumstances, evasion is not widespread. In other respects, too, the effects of Indirect Rule on State administration have increased the liability of Pastoral Fulani before Muslim and statutory law. Death duties, and the regulations of the Forestry and Veterinary Departments are the principal matters, besides cattle tax, in which State organization runs counter to Pastoral Fulani interests as they see them. Moreover, improvement in communications, and the proliferation of executive and judicial authorities in the Divisional and District organization, make the sanctions more readily applicable. Conversely, the Pastoral Fulani believe that the duties which they have towards the State are not matched by their rights in it, in terms of the betterment of their pastoral interests. Although rarely constituting more than five per cent of the Provincial population, Pastoral Fulani contribute from six to twenty-five per cent of Provincial revenue (Shaw & Colville 1950). It has been calculated that for every three shillings contributed in cattle tax, the Pastoral Fulani receive no more than fivepence in services, including charges for basic administration. Understandably, they have until recently been regarded mainly as a fiscal asset. Just as understandably, when Pastoral Fulani feel that their interests have suffered at the hands of the State—as in over-zealous collection of cattle tax, quarantine regulations and the like— they take the one retaliatory measure which the present form of their social organization affords them. This is movement beyond the borders of the administrative unit, be it Province, Division, or District, in which they have allegedly been hardly used.

In fleeing from a political unit which is uncongenial to them, Pastoral Fulani violate the principles of transhumance at their peril. Thus it appears that migration is never undertaken into country of which they have no knowledge, at least by reliable report. Fresh pastures are broached by the piecemeal operation of migratory drift. Where the political situation is inimical, Pastoral Fulani do not add to their hazards by deploying their herds in untried areas. Thus migration of a given Pastoral Fulani population for political reasons is either a recoil upon areas in which the tribe has previously pastured, or an advance into an area into which elements have already moved. This is not to deny the fact that migratory movements necessitate a degree of hardship for the groups making them which is not encountered in the normal process of transhumance. Forced marches are made, often out of season, so that wet season pastures are abandoned early, or dry season pastures utilized for longer than is customary. It is to be expected that herds suffer from this treatment, and the families dependent upon them no less. It is in situations such as this that methods of obtaining intelligence are exercised to the utmost, and the duplicity for which Pastoral Fulani are noted has full scope.

* * *

[The present-day political context of migratory movements is summarized in the protest of the Wodaabe of West Bornu in 1944 against deflation in livestock prices, a heavy cattle tax, and a local disturbance with the Native Administration, in which over a hundred households made an unauthorized forced march outside the jurisdiction of Bornu Emirate.]

CONCLUSION

These three types of movement account for the current wide distribution of Pastoral Fulani (and in part for other categories of Fulani) in the Western Sudan. They have been going on for perhaps eight centuries. The origin of the Fulani, and at what point they arose as a coherent population of the Western Sudan, is a matter of considerable ethnological debate (Tauxier 1937) which cannot be discussed here. It must be mentioned that, physically the Fulani are of non-Negroid stock. Although again, the classification of their language presents problems, current work (Westerman & Bryan 1952) allies it most closely with the Atlantic group of languages, such as Serer and Wolof; vocabulary content varies greatly in all areas in which Fulani are found.

There is no doubt, on both ethnological and sociological evidence, that the gross movement of Fulani has been from west to east within the zebu cattle-keeping zone of the Savanna belt of the Western Sudan. The natural conditions of this zone, in which there are few topographical barriers, has facilitated the cumulative process of migratory drift and migration. These movements continue in the Protectorate era, and have not been prevented by Administrations, whose interest in the Pastoral Fulani has until recently been fiscal. This interest has in the main coincided with that of the Fulani in so far as it relies on the continued maintenance or expansion of herds which transhumance and migratory drift make possible. It is likely that the era of European administration in West Africa has seen an increase in the gross movement of Pastoral Fulani, and therefore of their distribution. The expansion of sedentary populations in this period has probably promoted settlement of Fulani on a semisedentary basis, but has driven purely pastoral elements further afield. Pacification has also opened new areas for pastoral exploitation. In the last fifty years, Pastoral Fulani have moved into areas hitherto denied them. This is especially noticeable at the eastern end of the zone in which Pastoral Fulani are found: in French and British Cameroons, French Equatorial Africa, and what was until recently the Anglo-Egyptian Sudan.

The broad outlines of this ethnic movement, which is still in progress, have been appreciated by Europeans scholars for over a century. More recently, detailed knowledge of the ecological characteristics of the zone in which they have taken place has become available. This paper is intended as a contribution to the study of Pastoral Fulani nomadism from a more intimate point of view, by referring to certain of the small, mobile, relatively autonomous groups whose pursuit of pastoral interests account for it in a large measure. Three types of movement have been put forward and defined, on the basis of observation, enquiry, and linguistic usage. It is to be hoped that further detailed analysis and comparison will produce further refinements of our knowledge of Pastoral Fulani nomadism.

NOTES

1 The substance of this paper was read at an Ordinary Meeting of the Institute, March 1956.

2 I carried out field work in Northern Nigeria in 1951-3 as a Travelling Scholar of the Worshipful Company of Goldsmiths, with the further assistance of a Colonial Development and Welfare Grant administered by the Government of Nigeria. I gratefully acknowledge the generosity of these bodies and the kindness of their representatives. Also, I am indebted to Professor Meyer Fortes for his encouragement and guidance.

REFERENCES

[Starred items are recommended as further readings.]

* Buchanan, K. M., & Pugh, J. C. 1955. *Land and People in Nigeria; the Human Geography of Nigeria and Its Environmental Background*. Chap. 17. London.

St. Croix, F. W. de 1945. *The Fulani of Northern Nigeria*, p. 25. Lagos.

* Hogben, S. J. 1930. *The Muhammadan Emirates of Nigeria*, pp. 68-190. Oxford.

Nash, T. A. M. 1948. *Tsetse Flies in British West Africa*, pp. 8-19. London.

Shaw, T., & Colville, G. 1950. *Report of the Nigerian Livestock Mission*, p. 44. London.

Tauxier, L. 1937. *Moeurs et Histoire des Peuls*, pp. 14-115. Paris.

Urvoy, Y. 1949. Histoire de l'Empire du Bornou. *Memoires de l'Institut Français de l'Afrique Noire*. No. 7, pp. 17-130. Paris.

Westermann, D., & Bryan, M. A. 1952. *Languages of West Africa*. (Handbk. of Afr. Languages, Pt. 2) pp. 11-30. London.

FOR FURTHER READING

Stenning, Derrick J., "Household Viability among the Pastoral Fulani," in Goody, Jack (ed.), *The Developmental Cycle in Domestic Groups,* Cambridge: Cambridge University Press, Cambridge Papers in Social Anthropology, *1,* 1958, pp. 92-119. A study of changes in size and composition of the family in relation to its cycle of growth and dissolution and environmental conditions.

Stenning, Derrick J., *Savannah Nomads,* London: Oxford University Press, 1959. The history and present-day life of the Wodaabe pastoral Fulani of Northern Nigeria.

Hopen, C. Edward, *The Pastoral Fulbe Family in Gwandu,* London: Oxford University Press, 1958. The report of a related study of a Northern Nigerian Fulani group.

For comparison with the life of East African cattle herding peoples, see Gulliver, P. H., *The Family Herds,* London: Routledge and Kegan Paul, 1955, the report of a survey of the Jie and Turkana; and Evans-Pritchard, E. E., *The Nuer,* Oxford: Clarendon Press, 1940.

3
Social Groupings

THE STRUCTURE OF UNILINEAL
DESCENT GROUPS*

Meyer Fortes[1]

The unilineal descent group is probably the most significant social unit in Africa. This paper represents a summing up of our knowledge of this type of descent in Africa by an anthropologist whose own research among the Tallensi of Northern Ghana was one of several pioneer studies in delineating the structure of this kind of group. The emphasis of much of the research on descent groups has been on structure, that is, on the underlying form of social groupings and social relations, rather than on the particular cultural context in which these find expression. It is largely a nonhistorical approach, but it is concerned with how a people's own view of time—of past generations—is related to their social structure, and how the segments of a society split or join or otherwise change in regular or cyclical fashion through time.

Anthropologists from all countries are now taking the concepts of descent evolved in African studies mainly by the British and applying them to societies in India, South America, New Guinea, and elsewhere. As a result, some of these ideas on descent are being broadened or modified, and the contributions developed through research in one continent are beginning to find their place within the anthropological world on a wider basis.

As is well known, Africa has loomed large in British field research in the past twenty-five years. It is, indeed, largely due to the impact of ethnographic data from Africa that British anthropologists are now giving so much attention to social organization, in the widest sense of that term. In this paper what I shall try to do is to sum up some positive contributions that seem to me to have come out of the study of African social organization. I want to add this. British anthropologists are well aware that their range of interests seems narrow in comparison with the wide and adventurous sweep of American anthropology. This has been due to no small extent to lack of numbers and there are signs that a change

---

* Reprinted from *American Anthropologist*, 1953, 55, 17-41, by permission of the author and *American Anthropologist*.

163

is on the way with the increase in the number of professional anthropologists since the end of the war. At the same time, I believe that the loss in diversity is amply balanced by the gains we have derived from concentration on a limited set of problems.[2]

Social anthropology has undoubtedly made great progress in the past twenty years. I would give pride of place to the accumulation of ethnographic data obtained by trained observers. It means, curiously enough, that there is going to be more scope than ever for the "armchair" scholar in framing and testing hypotheses with the help of reliable and detailed information. For Africa the advance from the stage of primitive anecdotage to that of scientific description has been almost spectacular; and most of it has taken place since 1930, as can be judged by comparing what we know today with the state of African ethnography as described by Dr. Edwin Smith in 1935. Mainly through Malinowski's influence we now have a respectable series of descriptive monographs on specific institutional complexes in particular African societies. Studies like Evans-Pritchard's on Zande witchcraft (1937), Schapera's on Tswana law (1937) and Richards' on Bemba economy (1939), to cite only three outstanding prewar examples, typify the advance made since 1930. They are significant not only for their wealth of carefully documented detail but also for the evidence they give of the validity of the thesis, now so commonplace, that the customs and institutions of a people can only be properly understood in relation to one another and to the "culture as a whole." They show also what a powerful method of ethnographic discovery intensive field work on "functionalist" lines can be.

The field work of the past two decades has brought into clearer focus the characteristics of African societies which distinguish them from the classical simple societies of, say, Australia, Melanesia or North America; and the mark of this is easily seen in the thought and interests of Africanists. One of these is the relatively great size, in terms both of territorial spread and of numbers, of many ethnographic units in Africa as compared with the classical simple societies. There are few truly isolated societies in Africa. Communication takes place over wide geographical regions; and movements of groups over long stretches of time, exactly like those that are known from our own history, have spread languages, beliefs, customs, craft and food producing techniques, and the network of trade and government, over large areas with big populations. A tribe of ten thousand Tswana, two hundred thousand Bemba or half a million Ashanti cannot run their social life on exactly the same pattern as an Australian horde, which is, after all, basically a domestic group. In Africa one comes up against economics where in Australia or parts of North America one meets only housekeeping; one is confronted with government where in societies of smaller scale one

meets social control; with organized warfare, with complex legal institutions, with elaborate forms of public worship and systems of belief
comparable to the philosophical and theological systems of literate civilizations. Even before its subjugation by Europe, Africa boasted big and
wealthy towns. Certainly there was knowledge of all this before professional anthropologists began to work in Africa. But it was patchy
and on the whole superficial. In particular, it lacked the explicit conceptualization and integral presentation that mark the kind of monograph I have mentioned. That a belief in witchcraft occurred in many
African cultures was known long ago. But the precise nature of the belief, and how it was related to the notion of causation, the rules of moral
conduct, the practice of divination and the art of healing to form with
them a coherent ideology for daily living, was not understood till Evans-
Pritchard's book appeared. It was known, from the works of nineteenth
century travellers and administrators, that many African societies had
forms of government similar to what political philosophers call the
State. But there was little or no accurate information about the constitutional laws, the structure of administration, the machinery of justice,
the sanctions of rank, the getting and spending of public revenues, and
so forth, in any African state before Rattray's important studies in Ashanti
in the twenties (Rattray, 1929 and later). Rattray's description of African
state structure has now been superseded. We have a pretty good idea of
how a monarchy was kept in power not only by ritual constraints and
prerogatives, as in the case of the Divine Kingship of the Shilluk (see
Evans-Pritchard, 1948) but also by means of shrewd secular sanctions
and institutions such as the control of public revenues and armed forces
in Dahomey, described by Herskovits (1938); or the manipulation of a
rank and class based administration as in Nupe (Nadel, 1942); or by
means of both ritual and secular institutions as has been so vividly described for the Swazi by Dr. Hilda Kuper (1947).

Of course, African customs and institutions often have significant
resemblances to those of the simpler peoples of other continents. Indeed
it is just these resemblances that make the distinctive features of African
ethnology stand out in proper theoretical perspective. Take the customs
of avoidance between affines or between successive generations, known
from many parts of the world. We are apt to think of them, even with
reference to such characteristically African cultures as those of the
Southern Bantu (cf. Hunter, 1936) as expressing specific interpersonal
relationships. It is the more striking to find among the Nyakyusa (Wilson, 1951) that the whole scheme of local organization in age villages
turns on such avoidances. Moreover we can, in this case, see sharply and
writ large, how the avoidance between father-in-law and daughter-in-
law is an aspect of the tension between successive generations in a patrilineal kinship system.

Implicit and sometimes explicit comparison of African cultures with those of other areas is important in the recent history of field research in Africa. Seligman's pioneering researches in the Sudan were done against the background of his experiences in New Guinea and among the Veddas (cf. C. G. and B. Z. Seligman, 1932). More important, though, is the fact that the main theoretical influence behind the field work of British anthropologists in Africa in the middle twenties and the thirties was that of Malinowski. Now Malinowski's "functional" theory is ordered to the concept of *culture,* essentially in a sense derived from Tylor and Frazer, and his empirical model was always the Trobrianders. It has taken twenty years for the Trobrianders to be placed in a proper comparative perspective in British social anthropology.

It is not, I think, a gross distortion to say that Malinowski thought of culture fundamentally in terms of a utilitarian philosophy. The individual using his culture to satisfy universal needs by attaining culturally defined ends is central to his ethnographic work. It is in the real events of social life, in situations of work, ceremony, dance, dispute, that he saw the interconnection of all aspects of culture. And this approach, crystallized in his formula for the institution—the group, the universal need, the material basis, the legal or mythical charter—has proved to be of the greatest value for the empirical task of field observation. Methodologically, it might be described as a form of clinical study. The net of enquiry is spread to bring in everything that actually happens in the context of observation. The assumption is that everything in a people's culture is meaningful, functional, in the here-and-now of its social existence. This is the cardinal precept for the anthropological study of a living culture. It is the basis of the rigorous observation and comprehensive binding together of detail that marks good ethnographic field work of today. However we may now regard Malinowski's theories we cannot deny him credit for showing us how intensive field work can and must be done. That is, I believe, one of the major contributions made by social anthropology to the social sciences, though it can probably only be satisfactorily used in homogeneous and relatively stable societies or sections of societies.

What I am concerned with in these remarks is the local history of British social anthropology. We all know that Malinowski's functionalism was part of a wider movement; but this is not my subject. The point I am leading up to is this. Malinowski had no sense for social organization, though paradoxically enough his most valuable specific hypotheses fall within the frame of reference of social organization. This applies, for instance to his restatement of the Durkheimian hypothesis of the function of myth as the "charter" of an institution, to his remarkable analysis of the configuration of social relations in the matrilineal family, and to his development of the concept of reciprocity. But he had no real understanding of kinship or political organization. Thus he never overlooked an opportunity of pouring scorn on what he called "kinship algebra," as I can vouch for from personal experience. This prejudice prevented him from completing his often promised book on kinship. It is beautifully documented in the *Sexual Life of Savages* (p. 447). Kinship is to him primarily a tissue of culturally conditioned emotional attitudes. So he is puzzled by the extension of the term for "father" to the father's sister's son: and being quite unable to think in what we should now call structural terms, he commits the appalling methodological solecism of attributing it to an anomaly of language. Malinowski was reacting against the preoccupation with terminologies and with conjectural reconstructions of extinct marriage rules which was so widespread in the early years of this century. It is a measure of the progress made since 1929 that no one today coming across so obvious a case of a Choctaw type lineage terminology would make Malinowski's blunder.

Malinowski's bias is the more instructive because of the debt we owe to his genius. It is reflected in the field work directly inspired by him. We see this in what I regard as the most outstanding contribution to African ethnography we have as yet had, Evans-Pritchard's Zande book (1937). It is notable that he refers only incidentally and casually to the way witchcraft and oracles are tied up with Zande political organization. Firth's study of Tikopia kinship (1937) is an exception for its grasp of the theory of social organization; but he still held the view that social organization is an aspect of culture of the same modality as the others usually enumerated by Malinowski. I mention these two books because they mark important steps in the advance of both ethnography and theory; and I am not suggesting that they follow a wrong track. What I want to stress is that they follow the track which leads to "culture" as the global concept subsuming everything that goes on in social life. A serious limitation to this point of view is that it is bound to treat everything in social life as of equal weight, all aspects as of equal significance. There is no way of establishing an order of priority where all institutions are interdependent, except by criteria that cannot be used in a synchronic study; and synchronic study is the *sine qua non* of functional research. There is, for instance, the criterion of viability over a stretch of time which enables us to say that parliamentary government is a more vital institution in the British Commonwealth than slavery because it has outlived the latter; or that, for the same reason, matrilineal kinship is more significant among the coastal Akan of the Gold Coast than the worship of their pagan gods. Such a criterion, for what it is worth, is not applicable in the absence of historical documents. It is arguable, of course, that this is a false problem, that in fact all the customs and institutions of a society at a given time *are* of equal weight. But it is not scientifically satisfying to accept this assumption without more ado. If our colleagues in human biology had been content with such an assumption in the nature-nurture problem they would have given up their studies of twins and so left the science of human heredity lacking in some of its most critical data. For human society and culture the problem has hitherto been posed and dogmatically answered by the various brands of determinists. Or at the other extreme it has been implied and subtly evaded by the hypostatization of patterns, geniuses and styles. But the problem remains wide open and Malinowski, in common with all who think in terms of a global concept of culture, had no answer to it.

Social anthropology has made some advance on this position since the thirties. Most social anthropologists would now agree that we cannot, for analytical purposes, deal exhaustively with our ethnographic observations in a single frame of reference. We can regard these observations as facts of custom—as standardized ways of doing, knowing, thinking, and feeling—universally obligatory and valued in a given group of people at a given time. But we can also regard them as facts of social organization or social structure. We then seek to relate them to one another by a scheme of conceptual operations different from that of the previous frame of reference. We see custom as symbolizing or expressing social relations —that is, the ties and cleavages by which persons and groups are bound to one another or divided from one another in the activities of social life. In this sense social structure is not an aspect of culture but the entire culture of a given people handled in a special frame of theory. Lastly, we can consider ethnographic facts in terms of a socio-psychological or bio-psychological frame of reference, seeking relevant connections between them as they come into action in the whole or a part of an individual life process, or more widely, as they represent general human aptitudes and dispositions. And no doubt as our subject develops other special techniques and procedures will emerge for handling the data. No one denies the close connection between the different conceptual frames I have mentioned. By distinguishing them we recognize that different modes of abstraction calling for somewhat different emphases in field enquiry are open to us. What I am saying is commonplace today. It was not so in the middle thirties and this was a source of theoretical weakness as Bateson pointed out (1937).

British anthropologists owe their realization of this methodological distinction both to ethnographic discoveries of recent years and to the catalytic influence exercised on their thought by Radcliffe-Brown since his return to England from Chicago in 1937. But the distinction had of course long been implicit in the work of earlier ethnologists. We need only think of the contrast between Lewis Morgan, whose idiom of thought was in terms of a social system, and Tylor, who thought in terms of custom and often had recourse to psychological hypotheses. Rivers (1914) whose own work and influence in England contributed significantly to the development of the idea of social structure, saw this. So did Lowie whose *Primitive Society* (1921) is, I suppose, the first attempt at a systematic analysis of what we should now call the principles of social structure in primitive society. What he brought out was the very obvious but fundamental fact that closely similar, if not identical, forms of social relationship occur in widely separate societies and are expressed in varied custom.

By social organization or social structure, terms which they used interchangeably, Rivers and Lowie meant primarily the kinship, political and legal institutions of primitive peoples. And these, in fact, are the institutions with which British anthropologists are mainly concerned when they write about social structure. The advantage of this term, as opposed to the more usual term "social organization" is that it draws attention to the interconnection and interdependence, within a single system of all the different classes of social relations found within a given society. This leads to questions being asked about the nature of these interconnections and the forces behind the system as a whole.

What I want to stress is that the spur to the current interest in structural studies in Britain comes in equal measure from field experience, especially in Africa, and theory. Anybody who has tried to understand African religious beliefs and practices in the field knows, for example, that one cannot get far without a very thorough knowledge of the kinship and political organization. These studies have thus given new content to the familiar postulate that a living culture is an integrated unity of some sort. We can see more clearly than twenty years ago that this is due not to metaphysical qualities mysteriously diffused through it but to the function of customs and institutions in expressing, marking and maintaining social relations between persons and groups. It is this which underlies the consistencies between the customs and institutions of a people that are commonly emphasized. A unit must, by definition, have a boundary. A culture, certainly in most of Africa, and I venture to believe in many other areas too (as indeed Wissler long ago stressed), has no clear-cut boundaries. But a group of people bound together within a single social structure have a boundary, though not necessarily one that coincides with a physical boundary or is impenetrable. I would suggest that a culture is a unity in so far as it is tied to a bounded social structure. In this sense I would agree that the social structure is the foundation of the whole social life of any *continuing* society. Here again Rivers showed great insight when he stated (1911) that the social structure is the feature of a people's social life which is most resistant to change. It is certainly a striking fact that the family and kinship institutions of a continuing society in Africa display remarkable persistence in the face of big changes in everyday

habits, in ritual customs and belief, and even in major economic and social goals. The Tswana (cf. Schapera, 1940 and 1950) are a good instance. But we must be careful. There is also plenty of evidence from
emigrant groups, such as Chinese, East Indians and particularly the Negro populations of the New World (cf. Herskovits, 1948, p. 542 ff.) of
the retention of religious and aesthetic customs in the face of radical
changes in structural arrangements. This is a warning against thinking of
culture and social structure as mutually exclusive. The social structure of
a group does not exist without the customary norms and activities which
work through it. We might safely conclude that where structure persists
there must be some persistence of corresponding custom and where custom survives there must be some structural basis for this. But I think it
would be agreed that though the customs of any continuing and stable
society tend to be consistent because they are tied to a coherent social
structure, yet there are important factors of autonomy in custom. This
has often been pointed out ever since the facts of diffusion became
known. The part played by dispositional and psychogenetic factors in the
content and action of custom is now being clarified. A house is not reducible to its foundations and custom is not reducible simply to a manifestation of social structure.

The recent trend in British social anthropology springs, as I have
said, primarily from field experience. Evans-Pritchard's description of
Nuer lineage organization (1933-35), Firth's account of Tikopia kinship
(1937) and Forde's analysis of clan and kin relations among the Yakö
(1938-39) are the important ethnographic landmarks. A prominent feature
in all three is the attention given to the part played by descent rules and
institutions in social organization, and the recognition that they belong as
much to the sphere of political organization as to that of kinship. Following this lead, other students have been making intensive studies of the
role of descent principles in African societies where unilineal descent
groups often constitute the genealogical basis of social relations. Good
ethnography is both a continuous test of existing hypotheses and continuously creative of theory and technique; and this is happening so rapidly just at present that one can hardly keep pace with it. The younger research workers to whose unpublished material I shall be referring are
developing structural analysis into a very effective technique and applying it not only in Africa but also in India, New Guinea and Indonesia.

Seen against the background I have sketched, there is no doubt that
big gains have been made in the study of social structure since the nineteen-twenties. This is well illustrated in recent investigations of unilineal
descent groups, both in Africa and elsewhere (cf. Eggan, 1950; Gough,
1950) but I will deal mainly with the African data. We are now in a position to formulate a number of connected generalizations about the structure of the unilineal descent group, and its place in the total social system

which could not have been stated twenty years ago. It is moreover important to note that they seem to hold for both patrilineal and matrilineal groups. Some of the conditions governing the emergence of such descent groups have recently been discussed by Forde (1947). He makes the interesting suggestion that poverty of habitat and of productive technology tend to inhibit the development of unilineal descent groups by limiting the scale and stability of settlement. Taking this in association with Lowie's hypothesis of 1921 (Lowie, 1921, p. 149) that the establishment of the principle of unilateral descent is mainly due to the transmission of property rights and the mode of residence after marriage, we have two sides of an hypothesis that deserves much further testing. The ground has been well cleared for this by Murdock (1949). For it does seem that unilineal descent groups are not of significance among peoples who live in small groups, depend on a rudimentary technology, and have little durable property. On the other hand, there is evidence that they break down when a modern economic framework with occupational differentiation linked to a wide range of specialized skills, to productive capital and to monetary media of exchange is introduced (Spoehr, 1947; Eggan, 1950; Gough, 1950). Where these groups are most in evidence is in the middle range of relatively homogeneous, pre-capitalistic economies in which there is some degree of technological sophistication and value is attached to rights in durable property. They may be pastoral economies like the Nuer (Evans-Pritchard, 1940) and the Beduin (Peters, 1951), or agricultural economies like those of the Yakö (Forde, 1938, 1950), the Tallensi (Fortes, 1945, 1949) and the Gusii (Mayer, 1949)—or if we look outside Africa, the Tikopia (Firth, 1937) and the Hopi (Eggan, 1950) and many other peoples. The Nayar of South India, classically a test case of kinship theories, are of particular interest in this connection, as a recent intensive field study by Dr. E. J. Miller and Dr. E. K. Gough shows. Though the total economy of South India was even formerly a very complex one, the Nayar themselves traditionally formed a caste of very limited occupational range. It is only during the past hundred years or so that they have gradually entered other occupations than soldiering and passive landlordism. And with this change has come the breakdown previously mentioned in their rigid matrilineal lineage organization. This does not imply that unilineal descent groups are either historically or functionally the product of economic and property institutions alone. Other factors are undoubtedly involved. There is the example of the Hausa of Northern Nigeria, for instance, who have a rural economy of the same type as that of the Tallensi, though technically more elaborate, and well developed property concepts; but they have no unilineal descent groups. The socially significant genealogical grouping among them is of the cognatic type based on the equal recognition of kin ties on both sides, as among the Lozi and other Central African tribes (Dry,

1950; Colson and Gluckman, 1951). Nor can the Hausa arrangement be ascribed to the local influence of Islam since the Cyrenaican Beduin have sharply defined patrilineal lineages (Peters, 1951).

I have lingered a little on this problem to bring home a point which I have already referred to. It is the problem of assigning an order of relative weight to the various factors involved in culture and in social organization, or alternatively of devising methods for describing and analyzing a configuration of factors so as to show precisely how they interact with one another. Much as we have learned from intensive field work in relation to this task, we shall learn even more, I believe, from such studies of local variations within a uniform culture region as Radcliffe-Brown's (1930), Schapera's (in Radcliffe-Brown and Forde, 1950) and Eggan's (1950).

The most important feature of unilineal descent groups in Africa brought into focus by recent field research is their corporate organization. When we speak of these groups as corporate units we do so in the sense given to the term "corporation" long ago by Maine in his classical analysis of testamentary succession in early law (Maine, 1866). We are reminded also of Max Weber's sociological analysis of the corporate group as a general type of social formation (Weber, 1947), for in many important particulars these African descent groups conform to Weber's definition. British anthropologists now regularly use the term *lineage* for these descent groups. This helps both to stress the significance of descent in their structure and to distinguish them from wider often dispersed divisions of society ordered to the notion of common—but not demonstrable and often mythological—ancestry for which we find it useful to reserve the label *clan*.

The guiding ideas in the analysis of African lineage organization have come mainly from Radcliffe-Brown's formulation of the structural principles found in all kinship systems (cf. Radcliffe-Brown, 1950). I am sure I am not alone in regarding these as among the most important generalizations as yet reached in the study of social structure. Lineage organization shows very clearly how these principles work together in mutual dependence, so that varying weight of one or the other in relation to variations in the wider context of social structure gives rise to variant arrangements on the basis of the same broad ground plan.

A lineage is a corporate group from the outside, that is in relation to other defined groups and associations. It might be described as a single legal personality—"one person" as the Ashanti put it (Fortes, 1950). Thus the way a lineage system works depends on the kind of legal institutions found in the society; and this, we know, is a function of its political organization. Much fruitful work has resulted from following up this line of thought. As far as Africa is concerned there is increasing evidence to suggest that lineage organization is most developed in what Evans-

Pritchard and I (1940), taking a hint from Durkheim, called segmentary societies. This has been found to hold for the Tiv of Nigeria (P. J. Bohannan, 1951), for the Gusii (Mayer, 1949) and other East and South African peoples, and for the Cyrenaican Beduin (Peters, 1951), in addition to the peoples discussed in *African Political Systems*. In societies of this type the lineage is not only a corporate unit in the legal or jural sense but is also the primary political association. Thus the individual has no legal or political status except as a member of a lineage; or to put it in another way, all legal and political relations in the society take place in the context of the lineage system.

But lineage grouping is not restricted to segmentary societies. It is the basis of local organization and of political institutions also in societies like the Ashanti (Fortes, 1950; Busia, 1951) and the Yoruba (Forde, 1951) which have national government centered in kingship, administrative machinery and courts of law. But the primary emphasis, in these societies, is on the legal aspect of the lineage. The political structure of these societies was always unstable and this was due in considerable degree to internal rivalries arising out of the divisions between lineages; that is perhaps why they remained federal in constitution. In Ashanti, for instance, this is epitomized in the fact that citizenship is, in the first place, local not national, is determined by lineage membership by birth and is mediated through the lineage organization. The more centralized the political system the greater the tendency seems to be for the corporate strength of descent groups to be reduced or for such corporate groups to be nonexistent. Legal and political status are conferred by allegiance to the State not by descent, though rank and property may still be vested in descent lines. The Nupe (Nadel, 1942), the Zulu (Gluckman in Fortes and Evans-Pritchard, 1940), the Hausa (Dry, 1950), and other state organizations exemplify this in different ways. There is, in these societies, a clearer structural differentiation between the field of domestic relations based on kinship and descent and the field of political relations, than in segmentary societies.

However, where the lineage is found as a corporate group all the members of a lineage are to outsiders jurally equal and represent the lineage when they exercise legal and political rights and duties in relation to society at large. This is what underlies so-called collective responsibility in blood vengeance and self-help as among the Nuer (Evans-Pritchard, 1940) and the Beduin (Peters, 1951).

Maine's aphorism that corporations never die draws attention to an important characteristic of the lineage, its continuity, or rather its presumed perpetuity in time. Where the lineage concept is highly developed, the lineage is thought to exist as a perpetual corporation as long as any of its members survive. This means, of course, not merely perpetual physical existence ensured by the replacement of departed members. It means perpetual structural existence, in a stable and homogeneous society; that is, the perpetual exercise of defined rights, duties, office and social tasks vested in the lineage as a corporate unit. The point is obvious but needs recalling as it throws light on a widespread custom. We often find, in Africa and elsewhere, that a person or descent group is attached to a patrilineal lineage through a female member of the lineage. Then if there is a danger that rights and offices vested in the lineage may lapse through the extinction of the true line of descent, the attached line may by some jural fiction be permitted to assume them. Or again, rather than let property or office go to another lineage by default of proper succession within the owning lineage, a slave may be allowed to succeed. In short, the aim is to preserve the existing scheme of social relations as far as possible. As I shall mention presently, this idea is developed most explicitly among some Central African peoples.

But what marks a lineage out and maintains its identity in the face of the continuous replacement by death and birth of its members is the fact that it emerges most precisely in a complementary relationship with or in opposition to like units. This was first precisely shown for the Nuer by Evans-Pritchard and I was able to confirm the analysis among the Tallensi (Fortes, 1949). It is characteristic of all segmentary societies in Africa so far described, almost by definition. A recent and most interesting case is that of the Tiv of Northern Nigeria (P. J. Bohannan, 1951). This people were, until the arrival of the British, extending their territory rapidly by moving forward *en masse* as their land became exhausted. Among them the maximal lineages are identified by their relative *positions* in the total deployment of all the lineages and they maintain these positions by pushing against one another as they all move slowly forward.

The presumed perpetuity of the lineage is what lineage genealogies conceptualize. If there is one thing all recent investigations are agreed upon it is that lineage genealogies are not historically accurate. But they can be understood if they are seen to be the conceptualization of the existing lineage structure viewed as continuing through time and therefore projected backward as pseudo-history. The most striking proof of this comes from Cyrenaica. The Beduin there have tribal genealogies going back no more than the fourteen generations or thereabouts which we so commonly find among African Negro peoples; but as Peters points out, historical records show that they have lived in Cyrenaica apparently in much the same way as now for a much longer time than the four to five hundred years implied in their genealogies. Dr. P. J. and Dr. L. Bohannan have actually observed the Tiv at public moots rearranging their lineage genealogies to bring them into line with changes in the existing pattern of legal and political relations within and between lineages. A genealogy is, in fact, what Malinowski called a legal charter and not an historical record.

A society made up of corporate lineages is in danger of splitting into rival lineage factions. How is this counteracted in the interests of wider political unity? One way is to extend the lineage framework to the widest range within which sanctions exist for preventing conflicts and disputes from ending in feud or warfare. The political unit is thought of then as the most inclusive, or maximal, lineage to which a person can belong, and it may be conceptualized as embracing the whole tribal unit. This happens among the Gusii (Mayer, 1949) as well as among the Nuer, the Tiv and the Beduin; but with the last three the tribe is not the widest field within which sanctions against feud and war prevail. A major lineage segment of the tribe is the *de facto* political unit by this definition.

Another way, widespread in West Africa but often associated with the previously mentioned structural arrangement, is for the common interest of the political community to be asserted periodically, as against the private interests of the component lineages, through religious institutions and sanctions. I found this to be the case among the Tallensi (Fortes, 1940) and the same principle applies to the Yakö (Forde, 1950 (b)) and the Ibo (Forde and Jones, 1950). I believe it will be shown to hold for many peoples of the Western Sudan among whom ancestor worship and the veneration of the earth are the basis of religious custom. The politically integrative functions of ritual institutions have been described for many parts of the world. What recent African ethnography adds is detailed descriptive data from which further insight into the symbolism used and into the reasons why political authority tends to be invested with ritual meaning and expression can be gained. A notable instance is Dr. Kuper's (1947) account of the Swazi kingship.

As the Swazi data indicate, ritual institutions are also used to support political authority and to affirm the highest common interests in African societies with more complex political structures than those of segmentary societies. This has long been known, ever since the Divine Kingship of the Shilluk (cf. Evans-Pritchard, 1948) brought inspiration to Sir James Frazer. But these ritual institutions do not free the individual to have friendly and cooperative relations with other individuals irrespective of allegiance to corporate groups. If such relations were impossible in a society it could hardly avoid splitting into antagonistic fractions in spite of public ritual sanctions, or else it would be in a chronic state of factional conflict under the surface. It is not surprising therefore to find that great value is attached to widely spreading bonds of personal kinship, as among the Tallensi (Fortes, 1949). The recent field studies I have quoted all confirm the tremendous importance of the web of kinship as a counterweight to the tendency of unilineal descent grouping to harden social barriers. Or to put it slightly differently, it seems that where the unilineal descent group is rigorously structured within the total social system there we are likely to find kinship used to define and sanction a personal field of social relations for each individual. I will come back to this point in a moment. A further point to which I will refer again is this. We are learning from considerations such as those I have just mentioned, to think of social structure in terms of levels of organization in the manner first explictly followed in the presentation of field data by Warner (1937). We can investigate the total social structure of a given community at the level of local organization, at that of kinship, at the level of corporate group structure and government, and at that of ritual institutions. We see these levels are related to different collective interests, which are perhaps connected in some sort of hierarchy. And one of the problems of analysis and exposition is to perceive and state the fact that all levels of structure are simultaneously involved in every social relationship and activity. This restatement of what is commonly meant by the concept of integration has the advantage of suggesting how the different modes of social relationship distinguished in any society are interlocked with one another. It helps to make clear also how certain basic principles of social organization can be generalized throughout the whole structure of a primitive society, as for instance the segmentary principle among the Nuer and the Tallensi.

This way of thinking about the problem of social integration has been useful in recent studies of African political organization. Study of the unilineal descent group as a part of a total social system means in fact studying its functions in the widest framework of social structure, that of the political organization. A common and perhaps general feature of political organization in Africa is that it is built up in a series of layers, so to speak, so arranged that the principle of checks and balances is necessarily mobilized in political activities. The idea is used in a variety of ways but what it comes to in general is that the members of the society are distributed in different, nonidentical schemes of allegiance and mutual dependence in relation to administrative, juridical and ritual institutions. It would take too long to enumerate all the peoples for whom we now have sufficient data to show this in detail. But the Lozi of Northern Rhodesia (Gluckman, 1951) are of such particular theoretical interest in this connection that a word must be said about them. The corporate descent group is not found among them. Instead their political organization is based on what Maine called the corporation sole. This is a title carrying political office backed by ritual sanctions and symbols to which subjects, lands, jurisdiction, and representative status, belong. But every adult is bound to a number of titles for different legal and social purposes in such a way that what is one allegiance group with respect to one title is split up with reference to other titles. Thus the only all-inclusive allegiance is that of all the nation to the kingship, which is identified with the State and the country as a whole. A social structure of such a kind,

knit together moreover by a widely ramifying network of bilateral kinship ties between persons, is well fortified against internal disruption. It
should be added that the notion of the "corporation sole" is found among
many Central African peoples. It appears, in fact, to be a jural institution
of the same generality in any of these societies as corporate groups are in
others, since it is significant at all levels of social structure. A good example is the Bemba (cf. Richards, 1936, 1940b) among whom it is seen in
the custom of "positional inheritance" of status, rank, political office and
ritual duty, as I will explain later.

What is the main methodological contribution of these studies? In
my view it is the approach from the angle of political organization to
what are traditionally thought of as kinship groups and institutions that
has been specially fruitful. By regarding lineages and statuses from the
point of view of the total social system and not from that of an hypothetical EGO we realize that consanguinity and affinity, real or putative, are
not sufficient in themselves to bring about these structural arrangements.
We see that descent is fundamentally a jural concept as Radcliffe-Brown
argued in one of his most important papers (1935); we see its significance, as the connecting link between the external, that is political and
legal, aspect of what we have called unilineal descent groups, and the internal or domestic aspect. It is in the latter context that kinship carries
maximum weight, first, as the source of title to membership of the
groups or to specific jural status, with all that this means in rights over
and toward persons and property, and second as the basis of the social
relations among the persons who are identified with one another in the
corporate group. In theory, membership of a corporate legal or political
group need not stem from kinship, as Weber has made clear. In primitive
society, however, if it is not based on kinship it seems generally to presume some formal procedure of incorporation with ritual initiation. So-
called secret societies in West Africa seem to be corporate organizations of
this nature. Why descent rather than locality or some other principle
forms the basis of these corporate groups is a question that needs more
study. It will be remembered that Radcliffe-Brown (1935) related succession rules to the need for unequivocal discrimination of rights *in rem*
and *in personam*. Perhaps it is most closely connected with the fact that
rights over the reproductive powers of women are easily regulated by a
descent group system. But I believe that something deeper than this is
involved; for in a homogeneous society there is nothing which could so
precisely and incontrovertibly fix one's place in society as one's parent-
age.

Looking at it from without, we ignore the internal structure of the
unilineal group. But African lineages are not monolithic units; and
knowledge of their internal differentiation has been much advanced by
the researches I have mentioned. The dynamic character of lineage struc-

ture can be seen most easily in the balance that is reached between its external relations and its internal structure. Ideally, in most lineage-based societies the lineage tends to be thought of as a perpetual unit, expanding like a balloon but never growing new parts. In fact, of course, as Forde (1938) and Evans-Pritchard (1940) have so clearly shown, fission and accretion are processes inherent in lineage structure. However, it is a common experience to find an informant who refuses to admit that his lineage or even his branch of a greater lineage did not at one time exist. Myth and legend, believed, naturally, to be true history, are quickly cited to prove the contrary. But investigation shows that the stretch of time, or rather of duration, with which perpetuity is equated varies according to the count of generations needed to conceptualize the internal structure of the lineage and link it on to an absolute, usually mythological origin for the whole social system in a first founder.

This is connected with the fact that an African lineage is never, according to our present knowledge, internally undifferentiated. It is always segmented and is in process of continuous further segmentation at any given time. Among some of the peoples I have mentioned (e.g. the Tallensi and probably the Ibo) the internal segmentation of a lineage is quite rigorous and the process of further segmentation has an almost mechanical precision. The general rule is that every segment is, in form, a replica of every other segment and of the whole lineage. But the segments are, as a rule, hierarchically organized by fixed steps of greater and greater inclusiveness, each step being defined by genealogical reference. It is perhaps hardly necessary to mention again that when we talk of lineage structure we are really concerned, from a particular analytical angle, with the organization of jural, economic, and ritual activities. The point here is that lineage segmentation corresponds to gradation in the institutional norms and activities in which the total lineage organization is actualized. So we find that the greater the time depth that is attributed to the lineage system as a whole, the more elaborate is its internal segmentation. As I have already mentioned, lineage systems in Africa, when most elaborate, seem to have a maximal time depth of around fourteen putative generations. More common though is a count of five or six generations of named ancestors between living adults and quasi-mythological founder. We can as yet only guess at the conditions that lie behind these limits of genealogical depth in lineage structure. The facts themselves are nevertheless of great comparative interest. As I have previously remarked, these genealogies obviously do not represent a true record of all the ancestors of a group. To explain this by the limitations and fallibility of oral tradition is merely to evade the problem. In structural terms the answer seems to lie in the spread or span (Fortes, 1945) of internal segmentation of the lineage, and this apparently has inherent limits. As I interpret the evidence we have, these limits are set by the condition of stability in the social structure which it is one of the chief functions of lineage systems to maintain. The segmentary spread found in a given lineage system is that which makes for maximum stability; and in a stable social system it is kept at a particular spread by continual internal adjustments which are conceptualized by clipping, patching and tele-scoping genealogies to fit. Just what the optimum spread of lineage seg-mentation in a particular society tends to be depends persumably on extra-lineage factors of political and economic organization of the kind referred to by Forde (1947).

It is when we consider the lineage from within that kinship becomes decisive. For lineage segmentation follows a model laid down in the pa-rental family. It is indeed generally thought of as the perpetuation, through the rule of the jural unity of the descent line and of the sibling group (cf. Radcliffe-Brown, 1951), of the social relations that constitute the parental family. So we find a lineage segment conceptualized as a sibling group in symmetrical relationship with segments of a like order. It will be a paternal sibling group where descent is patrilineal and a ma-ternal one where it is matrilineal. Progressive orders of inclusiveness are formulated as a succession of generations; and the actual process of seg-mentation is seen as the equivalent of the division between siblings in the parental family. With this goes the use of kinship terminology and the application of kinship norms in the regulation of intralineage affairs.

As a corporate group, a lineage exhibits a structure of authority, and it is obvious from what I have said why this is aligned with the genera-tion ladder. We find, as a general rule, that not only the lineage but also every segment of it has a head, by succession or election, who manages its affairs with the advice of his comembers. He may not have legal sanc-tions by means of which to enforce his authority in internal affairs; but he holds his position by consent of all his fellow members, and he is backed by moral sanctions commonly couched in religious concepts. He is the trustee for the whole group of the property and other productive re-sources vested in it. He has a decisive jural role also in the disposal of rights over the fertility of the women in the group. He is likely to be the representative of the whole group in political and legal relations with other groups, with political authorities, and in communal ritual. The ef-fect may be to make him put the interests of his lineage above those of the community if there is conflict with the latter. This is quite clearly rec-ognized by some peoples. Among the Ashanti for instance, every chief-ship is vested in a matrilineal lineage. But once a chief has been installed his constitutional position is defined as holding an office that belongs to the whole community not to any one lineage. The man is, ideally, so merged in the office that he virtually ceases to be a member of his line-age, which always has an independent head for its corporate affairs (cf. Busia, 1951).

Thus lineage segmentation as a process in time links the lineage with the parental family; for it is through the family that the lineage (and therefore the society) is replenished by successive generations; and it is on the basis of the ties and cleavages between husband and wife, between polygynous wives, between siblings, and between generations that growth and segmentation take place in the lineage. Study of this process has added much to our understanding of well known aspects of family and kinship structure.

I suppose that we all now take it for granted that filiation—by contrast with descent—is universally bilateral. But we have also been taught, perhaps most graphically by Malinowski, that this does not imply equality of social weighting for the two sides of kin connection. Correctly stated, the rule should read that filiation is always complementary, unless the husband in a matrilineal society (like the Nayar) or the wife in a partrilineal society, as perhaps in ancient Rome, is given no parental status or is legally severed from his or her kin. The latter is the usual situation of a slave spouse in Africa.

Complementary filiation appears to be the principal mechanism by which segmentation in the lineage is brought about. This is very clear in patrilineal descent groups, and has been found to hold for societies as far apart as the Tallensi in West Africa and the Gusii in East africa. What is a single lineage in relation to a male founder is divided into segments of a lower order by reference to their respective female founders on the model of the division of a polygynous family into separate matricentral "houses." In matrilineal lineage systems, however, the position is different. Segmentation does not follow the lines of different paternal origin, for obvious reasons; it follows the lines of differentiation between sisters. There is a connection between this and the weakness in law and in sentiment of the marriage tie in matrilineal societies, though it is usual for political and legal power to be vested in men as Kroeber (1938) and others have remarked. More study of this problem is needed.

Since the bilateral family is the focal element in the web of kinship, complementary filiation provides the essential link between a sibling group and the kin of the parent who does not determine descent. So a sibling group is not merely differentiated within a lineage but is further distinguished by reference to its kin ties outside the corporate unit. This structural device allows of degrees of individuation depending on the extent to which filiation on the noncorporate side is elaborated. The [patrilineal] Tiv, for example, recognize five degrees of matrilateral filiation by which a sibling group is linked with lineages other than its own. These and other ties of a similar nature arising out of marriage exchanges result in a complex scheme of individuation for distinguishing both sibling groups and persons within a single lineage (L. Bohannan, 1951). This, of course, is not unique and has long been recognized, as everyone familiar with Australian kinship systems knows. Its more general significance can be brought out however by an example. A Tiv may claim to be living with a particular group of relatives for purely personal reasons of convenience or affection. Investigation shows that he has in fact made a choice of where to live within a strictly limited range of nonlineage kin. What purports to be a voluntary act freely motivated in fact presupposes a structural scheme of individuation. This is one of the instances which show how it is possible and feasible to move from the structural frame of reference to another, here that of the social psychologist, without confusing data and aims.

Most far-reaching in its effects on lineage structure is the use of the rule of complementary filiation to build double unilineal systems and some striking instances of this are found in Africa. One of the most developed systems of this type is that of the Yakö; and Forde's excellent analysis of how this works (Forde, 1950) shows that it is much more than a device for classifying kin. It is a principle of social organization that enters into all social relations and is expressed in all important institutions. There is the division of property, for instance, into the kind that is tied to the patrilineal lineage and the kind that passes to matrilineal kin. The division is between fixed and, in theory, perpetual productive resources, in this case farm land, with which goes residence rights, on the one hand, and, on the other, movable and consumable property like livestock and cash. There is a similar polarity in religious cult and in the political office and authority linked with cult, the legally somewhat weaker matrilineal line being ritually somewhat stronger than the patrilineal line. This balance between ritual and secular control is extended to the fertility of the women. An analogous double descent system has been described for some Nuba Hill tribes by Nadel (1950) and its occurrence among the Herero is now classical in ethnology. The arrangement works the other way round, too, in Africa, as among the Ashanti, though in their case the balance is far more heavily weighted on the side of the matrilineal lineage than on that of the jurally inferior and noncorporate paternal line.

These and other instances lead to the generalization that complementary filiation is not merely a constant element in the pattern of family relationships but comes into action at all levels of social structure in African societies. It appears that there is a tendency for interests, rights and loyalties to be divided on broadly complementary lines, into those that have the sanction of law or other public institutions for the enforcement of good conduct, and those that rely on religion, morality, conscience and sentiment for due observance. Where corporate descent groups exist the former seem to be generally tied to the descent group, the latter to the complementary line of filiation.

If we ask where this principle of social structure springs from we must look to the tensions inherent in the structure of the parental family. These tensions are the result of the direction given to individual lives by the total social structure but they also provide the models for the working of that structure. We now have plenty of evidence to show how the tensions that seem normally to arise between spouses, between successive generations and between siblings find expression in custom and belief. In a homogeneous society they are apt to be generalized over wide areas of the social structure. They then evoke controls like the Nyakyusa separation of successive generations of males in age villages that are built into the total social structure by the device of handing over political power to each successive generation as it reaches maturity (Wilson, 1951). Or this problem may be dealt with on the level of ritual and moral symbolism by separating parent and first born child of the same sex by taboos that eliminate open rivalry, as among the Tallensi, the Nuer, the Hausa and other peoples.

Thus by viewing the descent group as a continuing process through time we see how it binds the parental family, its growing point, by a series of steps into the widest framework of social structure. This enables us to visualize a social system as an integrated unity at a given time and over a stretch of time in relation to the process of social reproduction and in a more rigorous way than does a global concept of culture.

I do want to make clear, though, that we do not think of a lineage as being just a collection of people held together by the accident of birth. A descent group is an arrangement of persons that serves the attainment of legitimate social and personal ends. These include the gaining of a livelihood, the setting up of a family and the preservation of health and well-being as among the most important. I have several times remarked on the connection generally found between lineage structure and the ownership of the most valued productive property of the society, whether it be land or cattle or even the monopoly of a craft like blacksmithing. It is of great interest, for instance, to find Dr. Richards attributing the absence of a lineage organization among the Bemba to their lack of heritable right in land or livestock (Richards, 1950). A similar connection is found between lineage organization and the control over reproductive resources and relations as is evident from the common occurrence of exogamy as a criterion of lineage differentiation. And since citizenship is derived from lineage membership and legal status depends on it, political and religious office of necessity vests in lineages. We must expect to find and we do find that the most important religious and magical concepts and institutions of a lineage based society are tied into the lineage structure serving both as the necessary symbolical representation of the social system and as its regulating values. This is a complicated subject about which much more needs to be known. Cults of gods and of ancestors, beliefs of a

A Hausa hunter of Nigeria, wearing, around his neck and in his cap, amulets containing verses of the Koran.

Top: A Bushman father teaches his son to hunt in the Kalahari Desert of South Africa.

Bottom: In the Kalahari Desert, a small band of Bushmen starts out on the day's hunt.

Opposite: A Tiv girl, of Benue Province, in Nigeria, with the characteristic elaborate geometrical design tattooed around the navel.

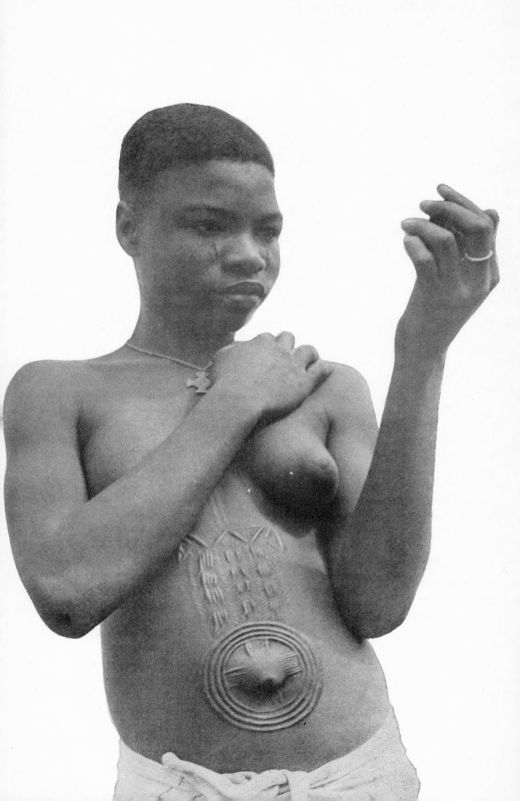

Above: Girls of the Xhosa people of South Africa use white clay and ochre for make-up.

Below: Swazi girls of South Africa bleach their hair with carbolic soap.

Top: Fulani youngsters at the Kano Festival, Northern Nigeria

Bottom: At a Zulu wedding ceremony in South Africa the bride hands her
groom the traditional spear.

British Information Services

SATOUR

A Fulani girl brings in milk for sale at the dairy in Zaria, Nigeria.

Above: The country people bring their products to be sold at the cotton market, in the Uele district of the Belgian Congo.

Below: Typical African market scene, in British Togoland

Left: A Yoruba woodcarver at work on a ceremonial staff for the river goddess *Yewa*

Right: A Pygmy of Poko in Uele, Belgian Congo, in conversation with a Balele Negro.

Opposite: Pygmy women help an old Negro prepare food, in the Belgian Congo.

Opposite, top: Women before their compound in a village in Togoland. Each family compound can have as many as twenty houses, all connected by a mud wall.

Opposite, bottom: A house at Kano, Nigeria, where the façades of even simple homes are elaborately decorated.

Below: Nomads of the Sahara Desert, their belongings piled high on their camels.

Embassy,
d Information

A Moslem school at Usumbura, Ruanda-Urundi

totemic nature, and purely magical customs and practices, some or all are associated with lineage organization among the peoples previously quoted. What appears to happen is that every significant structural differentiation has its specific ritual symbolism, so that one can, as it were, read off from the scheme of ritual differentiation the pattern of structural differentiation and the configuration of norms of conduct that goes with it. There is, to put it simply, a segmentation of ritual allegiance corresponding to the segmentation of genealogical grouping. Locality, filiation, descent, individuation, are thus symbolized.

Reference to locality reminds us of Kroeber's careful argument of 1938 in favor of the priority of the local relationships of residence over those of descent in determining the line that is legally superior. A lineage cannot easily act as a corporate group if its members can never get together for the conduct of their affairs. It is not surprising therefore to find that the lineage in African societies is generally locally anchored; but it is not necessarily territorially compact or exclusive. A compact nucleus may be enough to act as the local center for a group that is widely dispersed. I think it would be agreed that lineage and locality are independently variable and how they interact depends on other factors in the social structure. As I interpret the evidence, local ties are of secondary significance, *pace* Kroeber, for local ties do not appear to give rise to structural bonds in and of themselves. There must be common political or kinship or economic or ritual interests for structural bonds to emerge. Again spatial dispersion does not immediately put an end to lineage ties or to the ramifying kin ties found in cognatic systems like that of the Lozi. For legal status, property, office and cult act centripetally to hold dispersed lineages together and to bind scattered kindred. This is important in the dynamic pattern of lineage organization for it contains within itself the springs of disintegration, at the corporate level in the rule of segmentation, at the individual level in the rule of complementary filiation.

As I have suggested before, it seems that corporate descent groups can exist only in more or less homogeneous societies. Just what we mean by a homogeneous society is still rather vague though we all use the term lavishly. The working definition I make use of is that a homogeneous society is ideally one in which any person in the sense given to this term by Radcliffe-Brown in his recent (1950) essay, can be substituted for any other person of the same category without bringing about changes in the social structure. This implies that any two persons of the same category have the same body of customary usages and beliefs. I relate this tentative definition to the rule of sibling equivalence, so that I would say that, considered with respect to their achievable life histories, in a homogeneous society all men are brothers and all women sisters.

Societies based on unilineal descent groups are not the best in which to see what the notion of social substitutability means. For that it is better to consider societies in which descent still takes primacy over all other criteria of association and classification of persons in the regulation of social life but does not serve as the constitutive principle of corporate group organization. Central Africa provides some admirable instances (cf. Richards, 1950; Colson and Gluckman, 1951). Among the Bemba, the Tonga, the Lozi and many of their neighbors, as I have already remarked, the social structure must be thought of as a system of interconnected politico-legal statuses symbolized and sanctioned by ritual and not as a collection of people organized in self-perpetuating descent units. The stability of the society over time is preserved by perpetuating the status system. Thus when a person dies his status is kept alive by being taken up by an heir; and this heir is selected on the basis of descent rules. At any given time an individual may be the holder of a cluster of statuses; but these may be distributed among several persons on his death in a manner analogous to the widespread African custom by which a man's inherited estate goes to his lineage heir and his self-acquired property to his personal heir. Ideally, therefore, the network of statuses remains stable and perpetual though their holders come and go. Ritual symbols define and sanction the key positions in the system. What it represents, in fact, is the generalization throughout a whole society of the notion of the corporation sole as tied to descent but not to a corporate group. Descent and filiation have the function of selecting individuals for social positions and roles—in other words, for the exercise of particular rights and obligations—just as in cross cousin marriage they serve to select ego's spouse.

The concept of the "person" as an assemblage of statuses has been the starting point of some interesting enquiries. A generalization of long standing is that a married person always has two mutually antagonistic kinship statuses, that of spouse and parent in one family context and that of child and sibling in another (cf. Warner, 1937). This is very conspicuous in an exogamous lineage system; and the tensions resulting from this condition, connected as they are with the rule of complementary filiation, have wide consequences. A common rule of social structure reflected in avoidance customs is that these two statuses must not be confounded. Furthermore, each status can be regarded as a compound of separable rights and obligations. Thus a problem that has to be solved in every matrilineal society is how to reconcile the rights over a woman's procreative powers (rights *in genetricem* as Laura Bohannan has called them in her paper of 1949) which remain vested in her brother or her lineage, with those over her domestic and sexual services (rights *in uxorem,* cf. L. Bohannan, *loc. cit.*) which pass to her husband. Among the Yao of Nyassaland, as Dr. Clyde Mitchell has shown (1950), this problem underlies the process of lineage segmentation. Brothers struggle against one another (or sisters' sons against mothers' brothers) for the control of their sisters' procreative powers and this leads to fission in the minimal lineage. It is of great significance that such a split is commonly precipitated by accusations of witchcraft against the brother from whose control the sisters are withdrawn. By contrast, where rights over a woman's child-bearing powers are held by her husband's patrilineal lineage the conflicts related to this critical interest occur between the wives of a lineage segment; and among the Zulu and Xhosa speaking tribes of South Africa these lead to witchcraft accusations between co-wives (cf. Hunter, 1936). As Laura Bohannan's paper shows, many widespread customs and institutions connected with marriage and parenthood, such as the levirate and the sororate, wife-taking by women, exchange marriage as practiced by the Tiv, and ghost marriage as found among the Nuer (Evans-Pritchard, 1951) have structural significance not hitherto appreciated if they are regarded from the point of view I have indicated.

But one thing must be emphasized. This method of analysis does not explain why in one society certain kinds of interpersonal conflict are socially projected in witchcraft beliefs whereas in another they may be projected in terms of a belief in punitive spirits. It makes clear why a funeral ceremony is necessary and why it is organized in a particular way in the interest of maintaining a stable and coherent social system. It does not explain why the ritual performed in the funeral ceremonies of one people uses materials, ideas and dramatizations of a different kind from those used by another people. In short, it brings us nearer than we were thirty years ago to understanding the machinery by which norms are made effective, not only in a particular primitive society but in a type of primitive society. It does not explain how the norms come to be what they in fact are in a particular society.

In this connection, however, it is worth drawing attention to certain norms that have long been recognized to have a critical value in social organization. Marriage regulations, incest prohibitions and the laws of homicide and warfare are the most important. Analysis of lineage structure has revealed an aspect of these norms which is of great theoretical interest. It is now fairly evident that these are not absolute rules of conduct which men are apt to break through an outburst of unruly instinct or rebellious self-assertion, as has commonly been thought. They are *relatively* obligatory in accordance with the structural relations of the parties. The Beduin of Cyrenaica regard homicide within the minimal agnatic lineage, even under extreme provocation, as a grave sin, whereas slaying a member of a different tribal segment is an admirable deed of valor. The Tallensi consider sex relations with a near sister of the same lineage as incest but tacitly ignore the act if the parties are very distant lineage kin. Among the Tiv, the Nuer, the Gusii and other tribes the lineage range within which the rule of exogamy holds is variable and can be changed by a ceremony that makes formally prohibited marriages legitimate and so brings marriage prohibitions into line with changes in the segmentary structure of the lineage. In this way previously exogamous units are split into intermarrying units. In all the societies mentioned, and others as well, an act of self-help that leads to negotiations if the parties belong to closely related lineages might lead to war if they are members of independent—though not necessarily geographically far apart—lineages. Such observations are indications of the flexibility of primitive social structures. They give a clue to the way in which internal adjustments are made from time to time in those structures, either in response to changing pressures from without or through the momentum of their own development. They suggest how such societies can remain stable in the long run without being rigid. But this verges on speculation.

The contributions to African ethnography mentioned in this paper are only a small and arbitrary selection from a truly vast amount of new work that is now going on in several countries. My aim has been to suggest how this work links up with a theoretical approach that is much in evidence among British social anthropologists. It is perhaps needless to add that this approach is also being actively applied by American, French, Belgian and Dutch anthropologists concerned with the problems of social organization. What I wish to convey by the example of current studies of unilineal descent group structure is that we have, in my belief, got to a point where a number of connected generalizations of wide validity can be made about this type of social group. This is an advance I associate with the structural frame of reference. I wish to suggest that this frame of reference gives us procedures of investigation and analysis by which a social system can be apprehended as a unity made of parts and processes that are linked to one another by a limited number of principles of wide validity in homogeneous and relatively stable societies. It has enabled us to set up hypotheses about the nature of these principles that have the merit of being related directly to the ethnographic material now so abundantly at hand and of being susceptible of testing by further field observation. It cannot be denied, I think, that we have here a number of positive contributions of real importance to social science.

NOTES

[1] *Editorial note:* This paper was presented by Professor Fortes at the Symposium on the "Positive Contributions of Social Anthropology," held at the 50th annual meetings of the American Anthropological Association in Chicago, November 15-17, 1951. Professor Fortes' participation in the symposium was made possible by the generosity of the Wenner-Gren Foundation for Anthropological Research, Inc.

[2] This was written before I saw the discussion between Dr. Murdock and Professor Firth on the limitations of

British social anthropology in the Octo-
ber-December 1951 number (Vol. 53, No.
4, Pt. 1) of the *American Anthropologist*.

[3] In the bibliography that follows, references marked by [a dagger] are cited
by permission of the author.

BIBLIOGRAPHY

[Starred items are recommended as further readings.]

Bateson, G., 1937, *Naven*.

* Bohannan, Laura, 1949, Dahomean
Marriage: a revaluation. *Africa*, 19. 4.

———, 1951, *A Comparative Study of
Social Differentiation in Primitive Society*. (D.Phil. thesis, University of Oxford.)†

Bohannan, P. J., 1951, *Political and
Economic Aspects of Land Tenure and
Settlement Patterns among the Tiv of
Central Nigeria*. (D.Phil. thesis, Univer-
sity of Oxford.)†

* Busia, K. A., 1951, *The Position of
the Chief in the Modern Political System
of Ashanti*.

Dry, P. D. L., 1950, *The Social Structure of a Hausa Village*. (B.Sc. thesis,
University of Oxford.)†

Eggan, F., 1937, Cheyenne and Ara-
paho Kinship Systems, in *Social Organisation of North American Tribes*.

———, 1950, *Social Organization of
the Western Pueblos*.

Evans-Pritchard, E. E., 1933-35, The
Nuer: tribe and clan. *Sudan Notes and
Records*, Volume XVI, Part 1, Volume
XVII, Part 1, Volume XVIII, Part 1.

———, 1937, *Witchcraft, Oracles and
Magic among the Azande*.

*———, 1940 (a), *The Nuer*.

———, 1940 (b), The Political System of the Nuer, in *African Political
Systems*.

———, 1948, *The Divine Kingship of
the Shilluk of the Nilotic Sudan*. Frazer
Lecture.

———, 1951, *Kinship and Marriage
among the Nuer*.

Firth, R., 1937, *We, the Tikopia*.

*Forde, C. Daryll, 1938, Fission and
Accretion in the Patrilineal Clans of a
Semi-Bantu Community. *Journal of the
Royal Anthropological Institute*, Vol-
ume 68.

*———, 1939, Kinship in Umor:
Double Unilateral Organization in a
Semi-Bantu Society, *American Anthro-
pol*. Volume 41.

———, 1947, The Anthropological
Approach in Social Science, in *The Advancement of Science*, Volume IV.

*———, 1950 (a), Double Descent
among the Yakö, in Radcliffe-Brown and
Forde, 1950.

———, 1950 (b), "Ward Organisation among the Yakö" *Africa*, 20. 4.

———, 1951, The Yoruba Speaking
Peoples of South-Western Nigeria. *Ethnographic Survey of Africa*. Pt. IV.

Forde, C. Daryll and G. I. Jones, 1950,
The Ibo and Ibibio-Speaking Peoples of
South Eastern Nigeria, *Ethnographic
Survey of Africa, Western Africa, Part
III*.

* Fortes, M., 1945, *The Dynamics of
Clanship among the Tallensi*.

*———, 1949, *The Web of Kinship
among the Tallensi*.

*———, 1949, Time and Social Struc-
ture: an Ashanti Case Study, in *Social
Structure: studies presented to A. R.
Radcliffe-Brown*, Ed. by. M. Fortes.

———, 1950, Kinship and Marriage
among the Ashanti, in Radcliffe-Brown
and Forde, 1950.

* Fortes, M., and E. E. Evans-Pritchard 1940 (edit.) *African Political Systems*.

Gluckman, M., 1950, Kinship and Marriage among the Lozi of Northern Rhodesia and the Zulu of Natal, in Radcliffe-Brown and Forde, 1950.

*———, 1951, The Lozi of Barotse-
land in North Western Rhodesia, in
Seven Tribes of British Central Africa,
edited by E. Colson and M. Gluckman.

Gough, E. K., 1950, *Kinship among
the Nayar of the Malabar Coast of India*.
(D.Phil. thesis, University of Cambridge.)†

Herskovits, M. J., 1938, *Dahomey*.

——, 1948, *Man and His Works*.

Hunter, Monica, 1936, *Reaction to Conquest*.

Kroeber, A. L., 1938, Basic and Secondary Patterns of Social Structure. *Journal of the Royal Anthropological Institute*, Volume 68.

Kuper, Hilda, 1947, *An African Aristocracy*.

——, 1950, Kinship among the Swazi, in Radcliffe-Brown and Forde, 1950.

Lowie, R., 1921, *Primitive Society*.

Malinowski, B., 1929, *The Sexual Life of Savages*.

Maine, Sir Henry, 1866, *Ancient Law*.

* Mayer, P., 1949, The Lineage Principle in Gusii Society. *International African Institute, Memorandum XXIV*.

Mitchell, J. Clyde, 1950, *Social Organisation of the Yao of Southern Nyasaland*. (D.Phil. thesis, University of Oxford.)†

*——, 1951, The Yao of Southern Nyasaland, in *Seven Tribes of British Central Africa*, edited by E. Colson and M. Gluckman.

Murdock, G. P., 1949, *Social Structure*.

Nadel, S. F., 1942, *A Black Byzantium*.

*——, 1950, Dual Descent in the Nuba Hills, in Radcliffe-Brown and Forde, 1950.

Peters, E. L., 1951, *The Sociology of the Beduin of Cyrenaica*. (D.Phil. thesis, University of Oxford.)†

Radcliffe-Brown, A. R., 1930-31, "Social Organisation of Australian Tribes," *Oceania*, 1.

*——, 1935, Patrilineal and Matrilineal Succession. *Iowa Law Review*, Vol. XX. 2.

*——, 1950, Introduction to *African Systems of Kinship and Marriage*.

* Radcliffe-Brown, A. R., and C. Daryll Forde (edit.), 1950, *African Systems of Kinship and Marriage*.

Rattray, R. S., 1929, *Ashanti Law and Constitution*.

* Richards, A. I., 1936, Mother Right in Central Africa, in *Essays presented to C. G. Seligman*.

——, 1939, *Land, Labour and Diet in Northern Rhodesia*.

——, 1940 (a), Bemba Marriage and Modern Economic Conditions, *Rhodes-Livingstone Institute Papers No. 3*.

*——, 1940 (b), The Political System of the Bemba, in *African Political Systems*.

——, 1950, Some Types of Family Structure among the Central Bantu, in Radcliffe-Brown and Forde, 1950.

Rivers, W. H. R., 1911, Presidential address, *British Association for the Advancement of Science*, Section H.

——, 1914, *Kinship and Social Organisation*.

Schapera, I., 1940, *Married Life in an African Tribe*.

*——, 1950, Kinship and Marriage among the Tswana, in Radcliffe-Brown and Forde, 1950.

Seligman, C. G. and B. Z. Seligman, 1932, *Pagan Tribes of the Nilotic Sudan*.

Smith, E. W., 1935, Africa: what do we know of it? *Journal of the Royal Anthropological Institute*, Volume 65.

Spoehr, A., 1947, Changing Kinship Systems. *Anthropological Series, Chicago Natural History Museum*, Vol. 33, No. 4.

——, 1950, Observations on the Study of Kinship. *American Anthropologist*, Vol. 52.

Warner, W. L., 1937, *A Black Civilization*.

Weber, Max, 1947, *The Theory of Social and Economic Organisation*, translated by A. R. Hudson and Talcott Parsons.

* Wilson, Monica, 1950, Nyakyusa Kinship, in Radcliffe-Brown and Forde, 1950.

——, 1951 (a), Nyakyusa Age-Villages, *Journal of the Royal Anthropological Institute*, Vol. 79. [See pp. 227-36, below.]

——, 1951 (b), *Good Company: A Study of Nyakyusa Age Villages*.

FOR FURTHER READING

Of the unpublished material on Africa mentioned by Fortes some of the work of the Bohannans and of Mitchell has appeared. Bohannan, Laura, "A Genealogical Charter," *Africa*, 1952, *22*, 301-15; Bohannan, Paul, "The Migration and Expansion of the Tiv," *Africa*, 1954, *24*, 2-16; Bohannan, Paul, *Tiv Farm and Settlement*, London: H.M.S.O., Great Britain Colonial Office, Colonial Research Studies, *15*, 1954; Mitchell, J. C., *The Yao Village*, Manchester: Manchester University Press, 1956.

Other useful studies of unilineal groups in middle-range societies include: Tait, David, "The Political System of Konkomba," *Africa*, 1953, *23*, 213-23, reprinted in this volume; and Middleton, John, and Tait, David (eds.), *Tribes without Rulers*, London: Routledge & Kegan Paul, 1958.

Three studies which discuss the role of unilineal groupings in state societies are: Cunnison, Ian, "History and Genealogies in a Conquest State," *American Anthropologist*, 1957, *59*, 20-31; Barnes, J. A., *Politics in a Changing Society*, London: Oxford University Press for the Rhodes-Livingstone Institute, 1954; and Southall, Aiden W., *Alur Society: A Study in Processes and Types of Domination*, Cambridge: Heffer, 1956. The first is concerned with the Luapula of Northern Rhodesia and the Belgian Congo, the second with the Ngoni of Northern Rhodesia and Nyasaland, and the third with peoples found in Western Uganda and the Belgian Congo.

Smith, M. G., "Segmentary Lineage Systems," *Journal of the Royal Anthropological Institute*, 1956, *86*, 39-80; Fried, Morton H., "The Classification of Corporate Unilineal Descent Groups," *Journal of the Royal Anthropological Institute*, 1957, *87*, 1-29. Two recent evaluations of unilineal descent theory.

JIE MARRIAGE*

P. H. Gulliver

*In his account of marriage among the Jie of Uganda, Gulliver outlines the
steps by which a marriage is established and confirmed, giving their social significance to the principals and to others. In a woman's transition
from unmarried girl to full-wife and in the accompanying rituals, the
basic principles of African marriage are expressed. First, marriage is a
contract between kin groups, here signified by the fact that a man does
not seriously embark upon marriage until his kinsmen have approved
his choice. Second, a change in marital status is signified by the transfer
of property (or services)—in the case of the Jie, cattle belonging to the
man's agnatic kin group. Third, in addition to kinsmen, other intimate
associates of those involved express their approval of the match. Here,
the age mates of the bride's father give their sanction to the marriage and
perform a ritual to promote its success; in other societies the age mates
of the husband or wife may conduct mock ordeals through which the
bride or bridegroom must win acceptance. Fourth, the goal of marriage
is procreation. Among the Jie this is expressed in the various fertility
rituals and, perhaps more significantly, in the fact that it is only through
the birth of children and their survival through infancy that a marriage is
confirmed. Fifth, the in-marrying spouse may be ritually incorporated
into the husband or wife's residence group. This occurs among the Jie
when the wife, with her two or more children, goes to live permanently
at her husband's homestead. Finally, avoidances between a spouse and a
parent-in-law may be lifted following the ritual of incorporation. The
marriage being a fait accompli at last, suspicions of the "newcomer" may
be laid at rest. Despite the great variation in the forms of African marriage and the complexity of the steps involved, these principles are almost
everywhere found in elaborated or attenuated form.*

For the Jie[1] marriage is not just the act of making a girl the wife of a certain man, but is a lengthy process (beginning with formal preparation
for the wedding) the effects of which are to found and establish the legal,
social and spiritual elements of the marital union between the man and
the woman, to ensure and maintain the fertility of the wife and the wel-

* Reprinted from *African Affairs, Journal of the Royal African Society*, 1953, 52,
149-55, by permission of the author and the Royal African Society.

fare of her children, and to produce and strengthen the vital affinal relationships.

For a young man the process of marriage (*akotan*) begins at the time when normal courting of the girls resolves into an established liaison between him and a particular girl. For an older man, active courtship is often neglected in a more dispassionate search for a suitable girl to make a good wife, and whose father and brothers will make satisfactory affines. Whether he is a young or middle-aged man however, his mother and/or his wives have the final word regarding the girl's suitability, and in fact they may themselves select the girl from a number of otherwise eligible ones. At the same time a man does not embark seriously upon marriage preliminaries until it is agreed that sufficient livestock are available for the bridewealth. This matter concerns the man's father and the latter's full-brothers, or, if they are dead, his own full-brothers for herds and flocks are corporately owned by sets of full-brothers ("houses"). Thus before the marriage process is set in motion the adult close kin of the prospective suitor will be aware of and have expressed at least preliminary approval of the affair.

In the case of a younger man, at least, the girl will almost certainly have given her approval to the man. In cases where a man has older full-brothers, and when therefore his opportunity for marriage is delayed, he often already has a permanent mistress by whom he has children. Only very rarely is such a mistress not married at the first opportunity. Occasionally a girl is seized by the man and his age-mates and taken off to his homestead,[2] but this seems only to occur where she herself is willing to accept the man but her close kinsmen have opposed the courtship even before the question of a formal suit has been raised. However, whether the girl be an established mistress or whether she has been seized and taken to the man's home, formal suit must be made in exactly the same way as for other unmarried girls.

The stages of the marriage process are as follows:—

1. *Apudor:* "asking for a girl in marriage."

The first formal approach to the girl's parents by representatives of the suitor. The suit is made by the man's close agnatic kinsmen, and is conventionally repeated two or three times before the father gives (or finally withholds) his preliminary approval.

2. *Atukokin ngitunga:* "assembling the people."

1) The suitor and his father inform their kinsmen and seek their approval.

2) The girl's father informs his kinsmen and the girl's maternal kinsmen and seeks their approval. Bridewealth requirements are drawn up.

3. *Atuk ebelai:* "the assembly of the stick."

The two groups of people meet together at the homestead of the girl's father. Formal approval of the suit is now declared by both sides, and the suitor is given his "wedding stick." [3] The bridewealth demands are formally stated, but they are not discussed at this stage.

4. The collecting of the bridewealth by the suitor.

5. *Akimuj*: "food."

The suitor brings gifts of food to the girl's parents and initiates discussions about the actual size, composition and distribution of the bridewealth. A long series of mutual adjustments is begun and is carried on through semiformal meetings until agreement is reached.

6. *Akiram ngatuk*: "driving the cattle."

This is the formal and public handing-over of the bridewealth animals. It takes place in the large cattle kraal of the suitor's homestead. Each recipient gets his share at this time.

7. *Akimumwar*: "ceremonial dancing."

This occurs later in the same day when the transfer of the stock is finished. It is held at the homestead of the bride's father and marks the public affirmation of the acceptance of the bridewealth and thus of the marriage union. The bride's father's share of the bridewealth is ceremonially "allowed" to be driven into his kraal by the suitor and his kinsmen and friends, and a good deal of skirmishing and mock fighting occurs. After the *akimumwar*, beer, milk and other food is supplied for the benefit of the groom's people.

8. *Akimar*: "the counting."

This occurs on the following day at the homestead of the bride's father. A final reckoning of bridewealth is agreed on by both sides. Some stock may remain for payment, but the bulk has actually changed hands. Each kinsman of the bride states what share he has received and his satisfaction with the transaction.

The girl is now a "bride-wife" (*nateran*), but she remains at her father's homestead. Cohabitation may now begin, although usually it has tacitly been allowed by the girl's father and brothers since the conclusion of *apudor* (stage 1).

9. *Lobwo*: ceremony.

This occurs some months later at the homestead of the bride's father. It is partly a family ceremony marking the marriage of a daughter, and partly an age-set ceremony when the age-mates of her father make public approval of the union and, together with the bride's clanfolk, they perform ritual to promote its success.

Following *lobwo*, the bride visits her husband at his homestead for the first time. She returns to her father's homestead after a few days.

10. *Loburia*: ceremony.

This takes place at the ritual grove of the settlement in which the husband lives. It is a clan and settlement ceremony to further the success and fertility of the union. It is initiated by the husband who provides an ox for the feast. On this occasion great emphasis is laid upon the bearing and rearing of children.

11. *Emong lolamanit nakai:* "the ox of suckling in the hut."

This is carried out in the central kraal of the homestead of the bride-wife's father at the time of the birth of the first child. Her father provides an ox for ritual slaughter, the hide of which is given to the mother as a sleeping mat.[4] The ceremony signifies the pleasure of the father and his kinsfolk at this successful progress of the union, and it attempts to ensure its further success and fertility.

12. *Ediakwokwo:* "the child."

The corresponding ceremony at the homestead of the new father. Porridge, milk and beer are provided for the older men and women of the husband's clan who assemble to bless the event.

13. *Emethek:* "the sheep."

The bride-wife brings the baby to her husband's homestead after she has recovered from her confinement. A sheep is killed and its skin is taken for the baby-carrying sling. A small feast is held and the baby is ceremonially named by an old woman of the clan. The skull of this sheep is kept by the father, and later it will be put over the doorway of the mother's hut (when she comes to live there). The skull is thought to protect the children of the woman throughout their childhood.

The birth of a second child calls for little formal ceremony other than its naming at its father's homestead.

14. *Lomari:* "the going out."

When the bride-wife has borne at least two children and reared them to the walking stage, she is ready to go and live at her husband's homestead. *Lomari* is held at her father's homestead before she goes. There is a big ceremonial feast for her kinsfolk and men of her father's settlement. Her husband and his agnates attend but only drink beer on the periphery. Her father and her kinsmen signify their approval of her impending departure and reiterate, in ritual prayer, their desire for her fertility and happiness.

The bride-wife can now go to live in her husband's homestead, where a yard and huts and granary baskets have been prepared for her by her husband and co-wives. Her father sends her off with one or two cattle and some goats to take to her husband. It is said conventionally that this is done to ensure that there will be a supply of milk for the woman and her children, for her husband's herd is supposed to have been exhausted by the provision of the bridewealth: and in fact it often is so.

After *lomari* the avoidance taboo between the man and wife's mother is lifted.

15. *Lokidor:* "the gate of the cattle kraal."

After the woman has lived for some time with her husband (even up to a year or more) she and her children are ritually incorporated into the man's clan, and give up their former affiliation to her father's clan, entirely and permanently. The ritual ox must be supplied by her father who thus gives approval of this last act of marriage. Entreaties are made to the High God for the marriage union, for her continued fertility and for the welfare of all the children of the union. The event occurs in the central cattle kraal of the husband's homestead, and eventually she is ceremonially led through the cattle gate and thus into the homestead.

Following *lokidor* the woman has become a "full-wife" (*aberu*) and a full member of her husband's clan. She has, that is, full ritual status in this clan and full legal status in her husband's house and extended family.

Of 48 bridewealth transactions recorded in Jieland, the average number of stock transferred was 50 cattle and 129 sheep and goats. No other type of wealth is used to make up a payment. About half of these animals are provided by the herd of the groom, and the remainder are collected by him from his agnatic and maternal kin, his affines and bond-friends. Upwards of 40 people contribute in this way, from the distant kinsmen who give a goat to the half-brother who may give three or four cattle. These animals are transferred directly to each of the bride's agnatic and maternal kinsmen, about one half being taken by her father (or her full-brothers if he is dead). At least about three quarters of the total number of animals are handed over before the actual wedding (stage 7), and the remainder (if any) are usually given within a few weeks.[5]

The stages of the process as given above are those followed by the majority of the Jie. The actual details of ritual performance are determined by the clan affiliation of the husband or bride's father as the case may be. Variations according to clan membership are not great and have no effect on the general pattern of the total process. A very few clans prescribe one or two extra stages for their members, but these again do not much alter the common pattern. As may be seen, many of the stages involve public participation. Under the Jie ritual system a man is dependent upon the assistance of all his clansmen and of members of other clans which form the total settlement. Sometimes the man's whole district becomes involved, and at one ceremony (stage 9) his age-set also.[6]

It will be seen from the above synopsis that for the Jie marriage consists of a series of discussions followed by essential ritual performances. Discussion relates chiefly to the size and distribution of the bridewealth, and these should be completed and most of the animals handed over before the ritual stages begin. The ceremonial dancing (stage 7) is but the first of a series of events through which the girl advances to the full status of wife. Some of the ceremonies are small, relatively trivial affairs; some involve large numbers of people, much ritual and feasting and dancing: but they all fit into one process which would be dangerously incomplete without any one of them. The whole success of the marriage depends upon them all. Only with their successful conclusion does the woman become a "full-wife"; until then she is but a "bride-wife."

I am aware that in a general way many or all of these elements of Jie marriage are commonly found amongst other simpler peoples, and that the general intent is similarly known elsewhere. Nevertheless it is felt necessary to point out that the Jie themselves specifically conceive of marriage as a train of successive stages, each one of which expresses a new or developed part in the total process of marital union and the welding of affinal ties. Carried out in the traditional order and manner, the whole process itself comes to have a mystical efficacy of its own in the minds of the participants.

For the Jie marriage means not only the social and sexual union of a man and a woman, but also the establishment of affinal bonds. Thus this marriage process, *akotan,* can, from one point of view, be resolved into two interwoven processes. One is the development from unmarried girl (*apethe*), to bride, to bride-wife (*nateran*), to mother, to full-wife (*aberu*). Only with the final incorporation of the woman and her first two children into her husband's clan will Jie say, "*Adowun akotan daang* —the marriage is completely finished."

Secondly there is the gradual binding together of the husband with his wife's father and full-brothers, and to a lesser extent the close agnatic kin of each. In Jieland close affinal relations are of very real and great importance; the husbands of a man's sisters and daughters, and the fathers and full-brothers of his wives are amongst his closest friends and most important practical supporters throughout life. Great pains are almost invariably taken to maintain these ties.

It should be noted that the list of stages of the marriage process has been given by numerous informants; it is what the people themselves conceive of as marriage. Whilst analytically, of course, it is possible to determine and isolate certain elements such as marriage preliminaries, bridewealth discussions and transfer, ritual establishment of the marital union, ceremonial cooperation between affines leading to the product of full affinal ties, yet for the Jie there is but a single continuum, a steady process whereby the two principal elements are together brought to a successful conclusion.

By the time the process is completed the union and the surrounding affinal bonds have normally been firmly established, emotional adjustments effected and the woman has an assured, unequivocal status in her new family. The total process can scarcely take less than five years since at least two children must be reared to the walking stage, and a wife usually lives at her husband's home for some time, after she finally leaves her father's home, before she is made a full-wife. In many cases the period is longer, up to as much as eight years in all. Ceremonies may be held up by a death in either group, by shortage of animals for ritual slaughter, and even by the unwillingness of the woman to leave her father's homestead where she may be a vital economic asset owing to her mother's old age or the absence of sisters or of brothers' wives.

As already mentioned, the purely legal aspect of marriage is initially established by the handing over of the bridewealth and marked by the subsequent ceremonial dance. By the transfer of the animals in the name of the groom to the kin of the bride a girl becomes a wife, although not yet a "full-wife" as that term is understood by the Jie. As one Jie put it to me, "You know a woman is married if stock have been given. How do you know a bride-wife if there are no cattle?" Sometimes, when recording genealogies, I have been uncertain whether some woman is married or not, and invariably my query was answered in the form: "Stock have been given. She is a wife." Conversely in the case of an established mistress, for whom perhaps one or two cattle have already been given as a sign of betrothal and an earnest of goodwill, I have been told, "She has not yet eaten the stock; there has not been *akimumwar*," (i.e. bridewealth has not been given yet nor has the public affirmation been given at the ceremonial dance).

In a legal marriage union the man has sexual monopoly over his wife[7] and authority over her children. These children become members of his agnatic line. He also has the right to the economic assistance of his wife as dairy maid, gardener and housewife. The failure of the wife to maintain these responsibilities is regarded as a serious breach of the tacit marriage contract and union. On the reverse side, the wife gains the opportunity to bear legitimate children and the rights of support and protection from her husband. She and her children obtain definite rights in his herds which in this pastoral society are of the utmost importance.

Nevertheless this transfer of bridewealth is but one stage of the whole marriage process, though a critical stage in the eyes of all people. The marriage can only be established by the due performance of the ceremonial and ritual acts. The transfer of stock is itself not connected only with the legal aspects of the union, for it also provides the basis of affinal bonds. Where so large a number of animals have changed hands, most important and permanent relationships have been begun by that very fact, and almost independently of the marriage. In Jie conceptions all significant interpersonal relationships rest upon connections through livestock. Yet here again the proper establishment of affinal ties depends upon the subsequent ceremonial stages.

The later ceremonial stages cannot be carried out unless the bridewealth has been transferred first; but Jie say that unless the later stages are carried out the transfer of livestock is insufficient to produce a proper and lasting marriage union or normal affinal ties. During the process the woman cannot be regarded as fully married; she is in an interim period of becoming married.

NOTES

[1] The Jie tribe inhabit part of the Karamoja District of northeast Uganda, and number about 18,000. Cf. my paper, "The Karamajong Cluster," *Africa*, xxii, Jan. 1952.

[2] The girl is taken secretly by the men with a great pretence of force on their part and reluctance on hers. Nevertheless a girl would not be so dealt with and kept against her adamant opposition. If discovered in the act of seizure by her kinsmen there is usually a fight; otherwise the accomplished deed is accepted philosophically.

[3] This is an ordinary fighting stick which the prospective husband carries with him thenceforth as the symbol of the acceptance of his suit. He must show it to every man to whom he goes to beg contributions to his bridewealth.

[4] This is the only occasion when a sacrificial animal is skinned and its hide put to practical use. Normally the meat is cooked and eaten with the hide attached. This departure from the normal tends to give the affair an added significance.

[5] An account of Jie bridewealth, together with examples, is to be published later in a full-scale analysis of stock ownership.

[6] Some account of the Jie ritual system is given in my paper, "The age organization of the Jie tribe." [*Journal of the Royal Anthropological Institute*, lxxxiii, July 1955, 147-68.]

[7] Adultery was traditionally reckoned as grave a crime as homicide, involving the death of the man concerned or a compensation payment equal to that for murder. Modern native courts award very heavy compensation and still reflect the common outlook here.

FOR FURTHER READING

Gulliver, P. H., *The Family Herds*, London: Routledge and Kegan Paul, 1955. The report of a general study of the Jie and a related tribe, the Turkana.

Marriage among the Jie is similar in many respects to Nuer marriage, which has been studied by E. E. Evans-Pritchard in *Kinship and Marriage among the Nuer*, London: Oxford University Press, 1951, and "A Note on Affinity Relationships among the Nuer," *Man*, 1948, *48*, 3-5.

Radcliffe-Brown, A. R., and Forde, Daryll (eds.), *African Systems of Kinship and Marriage*, London: Oxford University Press for the International African Institute, 1950. The introduction by Radcliffe-Brown and the component papers give a broad survey of marriage in relation to the social structure of a number of African societies.

Richards, Audrey I., *Bemba Marriage and Present Economic Conditions*, Cape Town: Oxford University Press for the Rhodes-Livingstone Institute, Rhodes-Livingstone Papers, 4, 1940. The relation between marriage and family organization in a matrilineal society under conditions of culture change.

Colson, Elizabeth, *Marriage and the Family among the Plateau Tonga of Northern Rhodesia*, Manchester: Manchester University Press, 1958. A comprehensive report on the social and economic factors of Tonga marriage and family life.

Bohannan, Laura, "Dahomean Marriage: A Revaluation," *Africa*, 1949, *19*,

273-87. An analysis of marriage in Dahomey from the standpoint of the rights and obligations of the kin groups of the persons involved.

Schapera, Isaac, *Married Life in an African Tribe,* London: Faber and Faber, 1940. An account of marriage among the Tswana of Bechuanaland.

Barnes, J. A., *Marriage in a Changing Society,* Cape Town: Oxford University Press for the Rhodes-Livingstone Institute, Rhodes-Livingstone Papers, 20, 1951. The effects of culture change on marriage among the Fort Jameson Ngoni.

THE ROLE OF THE SECRET SOCIETY IN CULTURAL SPECIALIZATION[*][1]

K. L. Little

The social structure and the functions of African secret societies have not commanded as much attention from anthropologists or been as well studied as have kinship and descent groupings. Yet in those areas where they exist, particularly the Guinea Coast and the Congo, they are a very important part of the social life of the African. Little's discussion of Mende secret societies carefully delineates their functions, which in peoples lacking these societies are served through other means, such as through age grades. It is interesting to note that the comradeship among boys who are initiated into the secret society together is similar to that of boys who form an age set in other parts of Africa. Note also how the initiation ordeals and the training among the Mende resemble those discussed in Turnbull's paper, included in this volume, on the Pygmies, who have no secret societies.

Among the Mende and the peoples associated with them in Sierra Leone and Liberia, the sanctions on behavior in nearly every sphere of the common life derive largely from secret societies. These societies are, principally, the Poro, the men's society, concerned primarily with initiation of young boys; the Sande, concerned with women's affairs in nearly every aspect; the Humoi[2] concerned with the regulation of sexual conduct within the community in general; and the Njayei, concerned with the cure of certain mental conditions, propagation of agricultural fertility, etc. The Wunde, concerned largely with military training, is popular among the Kpa (western) Mende, but appears to owe its origin mainly to the Timne neighbors of the latter. The above societies are not exclusive to the Mende, but are shared widely, with the exception of the Wunde, among adjacent peoples, such as the Sherbro, the Krim, the Gola, etc., whose cultural affinities to the Mende are very close.

In terms of their institutional personnel and apparatus of hereditary officials, masked spirits,[3] rituals, etc., the secret societies are an embodi-

* Reprinted from *American Anthropologist*, 1949, *51*, 199-212, by permission of the author and *American Anthropologist*.

ment of and a means of canalizing supernatural power. Collectively, they provide an institutional structure which bears certain similarities to the medieval church in Europe, but with one or two important differences. Like the medieval church, they lay down various rules of conduct, proscribe certain forms of behavior, and are the sole agency capable of remitting certain sins. On the other hand, both their control over supernatural power and their regulation of lay conduct and behavior is, to some extent, departmental, and even a matter of specialization. That is to say, particular fields of the cultural life and their regulation tend to fall within the exclusive province of specific societies. The combined effect, however, is to produce a general pattern of life influenced very largely by secret society activity and function.

The extent to which this cultural arbitration and specialization obtains can be studied best by reviewing the various roles which secret societies perform in the secular life. These can be summarized under four main headings, viz.:

A. General education, in the sense of social and vocational training and indoctrination of social attitudes.
B. Regulation of sexual conduct.
C. Supervision of political and economic affairs.
D. Operation of various social services, ranging from medical treatment to forms of entertainment and recreation.

A. GENERAL EDUCATION

Every secret society provides, in its initiation rites, a certain amount of social knowledge and instruction which, in essence, is neither esoteric nor specific to the particular society. But the initiation, or "bush" schools[4] of the Poro and Sande[5] societies are, without doubt, the educational example *par excellence,* and are formally recognized as such within the community itself. Their ostensible object is to turn immature boys and girls into fully fledged members of the adult community. Their aim is, also, to convert the individual into a man or a woman or, more accurately, as the term given to a Poro initiate—*so hini* (one entitled to procreate) implies, into a male, or female.

In both Poro and Sande school, the psychological effect is secured by a combination of symbolical and practical means. The Poro boy is "swallowed" by the spirit when he enters the bush, and the marks made on his back signify the spirit's teeth. At the end of his time, he is delivered by the spirit and reborn.[6] Obedience to the rules of the society and, by implication, to the social regulations of the outside community, is stressed in various impressive ways which commence with entry into the bush. The process of initiation, after the marks have been cut on the boys' backs, include three separate ceremonies, known respectively as *ndehitie, kpowa-mbei,* and *kpia.* These mean respectively "quite fit"; "nonmembers rice"; and the "pulling," i.e., ending of the session. Contributions of food provided by the parents are brought forward, i.e., rice, fowl, and one bottle of palm wine per head. A fowl is seized, its head placed on a large stone and severed by another stone. It is then thrown to the members. All the fowl are killed in a similar way. While the head is being severed, a Poro official says a ritual word to which the boys give the appropriate reply. This is repeated over each fowl in turn, and the ceremony is a warning to the boys to expect the same kind of treatment, if they divulge any Poro secrets to nonmembers. The food is then cooked and a communal feast is held.

Throughout the session, every opportunity is taken to enhance the mysterious and terrifying characteristics of the Poro spirit itself in the minds of the initiates. The boys learn their lessons in this atmosphere, and are made to feel at the same time that they are absorbing something of the spirit's own qualities. Through connection with the spirit, they have intercourse with the supernatural world, and hence with a special source of power which carries the stamp of validity. A thing is true, therefore, because it has been learned in Poro.

In the final ceremony, the boys are lined up in the *palehu,* the most sacred part of the Poro bush. Moss and thread are wound round their toes, so that they are all tied together in a continuous chain. The officiating member, a woman known as the *Mabole,* invokes the spirits of the society on their behalf. She prays that each new member may be as strongly attached to the society as the thread and moss which now bind them together. The ancestors are called in order of seniority, beginning with the oldest and finishing with the one who has died most recently. Thus:

> Father Siaffa, let it reach to you; let it reach to Kanga; let it reach (literally, be laid down) to the head, the Great One. This is what *Leve* (an old name for God) brought down (showed us to do) long ago. These children, whom we are "pulling" from Poro today, let nothing harm them; let them not fall from palm trees; make their bodies strong; give them wisdom to look after their children; let them hold themselves in a good way; let them show themselves to be men.

It is on the psychological basis of these ceremonies and ritual warnings that the social training of the boys is effected by the elders and senior members of the society. To a large extent, the social life of the Poro bush approximates the social life of the larger community. In essence, the boys learn their roles as men in a miniature world of their own.[7]

As a practical example of their training, the boys are allowed no modern equipment. Their material requirements, including part of their food, must be provided by themselves. They start by lighting a fire when darkness falls. For the first night special songs are sung and no one is allowed to sleep. The next morning, the work is apportioned, after the boys have been sorted out in groups of the same size and age. They are expected to bear hardship without complaint, and to grow accustomed to it. They sleep at night on a bed of sticks under covering clothes which have been soaked in water, and they remain out of doors if it rains. The singing and drumming lasts until one or two o'clock in the morning, and the boys are awakened again at dawn. They are expected to get up and sing any time they are called.

The training may also include a certain amount of native law and custom exemplified by the holding of mock courts and trials in which the boys enact the roles of their elders. Boys who can afford to stay for a length of time learn about native crafts, as well as the ordinary duties of a grown man, such as "brushing" a farm and other agricultural operations, cleaning roads, etc. Individual specialists at making raffia clothes, basketry, nets, etc., sometimes give their services in the bush. Bridge-building, the making and setting of traps for animals and fish are also taught. The boys also learn drumming and to sing the special Poro songs. They practice somersaults and acrobatics.

In the case of the Sande girls, training is on complementary lines and is also symbolical. The girls are instructed as to their attitude towards their husbands, other men, and their fellow-wives. There is some training in homecraft, sex matters, the care of children, and the various duties a housewife is expected to perform.

A general and important feature resulting from both Poro and Sande schools is the sense of comradeship imparted. Initiates obtain a feeling of participating in a national institution. The common bonds of the society unite men with men, and women with women, as fellow members over a very wide area, and to an extent which transcends all barriers of family, clan, tribe, and religion. It is this corporate sense arising largely out of the memory of experiences shared at an impressionable age which is mainly responsible for the extra cultural significance of Poro and Sande. It is something, quite apart from a person's social status and position, upon which he or she can draw at any time for mental and moral reassurance.

B. REGULATION OF SEXUAL CONDUCT

With respect to sexual conduct, the part of the Humoi society is as important as that of Poro and Sande is over social behavior and etiquette in general. The head of the Humoi is a woman, and the senior positions in it are held by hereditary right by members of certain families. Outsiders are also initiated in certain circumstances, such as sickness.

The rules of the Humoi constitute, to all intents and purposes, the rules of marriage and mating. Sexual relationships are governed primarily by these rather than by the idea of consanguinity, which enters into the matter almost as a secondary effect. Breach of certain of these laws is known as *simongama* and necessitates the fining and washing of the offending parties.[8] The nearest European equivalent of *simongama* is incest.

It goes without saying that *simongama* is a particularly heinous offense. In general terms, it is *simongama* for a man to have sexual relations with any close relatives on the patrilineal side; with any descendants of the same mother as his own, irrespective of the paternity of such descendants; and with any close relatives of his existing wives. By special dispensation of the Humoi, he may, in some cases, have relations with and marry his wife's sister, after his wife has died. Generally, marriage with father's brother's daughter is regarded as a social evil, and no children are expected to result from the union.[9] Specifically, Humoi regulations prohibit relations on the part of a man with the following categories of person, viz.:

(a) His own mother, or maternal grandmother.

(b) His own daughter, or granddaughter.

(c) His own sister, or half-sister.

(d) His paternal and maternal aunts.

(e) The daughter of his brother and sister, and the daughters of his brother's and sister's children.

(f) His wife's sister, and any immediate descendants of his wife's sister.

(g) The descendants of his wife's brother, while that wife is alive.

(h) The daughter of his wife's father's brother.

(i) The sister, or any close relative, of any woman with whom he has had relations at any time, so long as that woman is alive.

(j) Any woman, irrespective of relationship, with whom his brother, or half-brother, has had relations.

(k) Any woman, irrespective of his relationship to her, who has suckled him.

In addition to restriction on marriage between certain categories of person, the rules of the Humoi prohibit specific kinds of sexual behavior for the community as a whole. It is forbidden to have sexual intercourse with a girl under the age of puberty,[10] or with any person, irrespective of age and social and biological relationship, in the bush at any time, during the day or night. It is also forbidden to have intercourse with any woman who is nursing a child, or with any woman who is pregnant. Other sexual offenses are for a brother to sit on his sister's bed, or a sister on her brother's bed. A man may not shake hands with his mother-in-law or with the mother of any woman with whom he has had sexual relations. A wife may not visit her parents on the same night after intercourse.

There are, also, a number of Humoi rules in regard to sexual hygiene. For example, it is an offense for a woman to speak to, or to remain in the presence of any of her own relatives as well as of members of the family of the man with whom she has had intercourse until she has washed in the morning. If she comes into physical contact in this way with a female relative on either side, the offense amounts to *simongama,* and is dealt with as such. The implication is that the sexual act itself is extended by her action to proscribed relatives and affinals of the man. All women who have had sexual intercourse during the night are required to wash before preparing food the next day.[11]

Breaches of these laws and regulations, whether deliberate or not, are regarded, in the case of *simongama,* as a serious injury to the relatives of the persons concerned, as well as against the Humoi-society itself. It is believed that sickness and disaster will befall all concerned, and the guilty party must make compensation to the woman's family, as well as to the Humoi. The offense has also to be expiated in a ritual way. *Simongama* is regarded as particularly atrocious and disgraceful when notable persons, such as a chief, are involved, and if such an occasion arises, the authorities try to settle it as secretly as possible by means of a tribunal of neighboring chiefs.

C. SUPERVISION OF POLITICAL AND ECONOMIC AFFAIRS

In the political field, the Poro exercises an overriding influence which is both direct and indirect. In the old days, it supplied the mystical quality of authority which is apparently lacking in the purely secular figure of the Mende chief.[12] It is interesting that in the adjoining Timne country, where the chief is hedged with various supernatural associations, the Poro as an institution is less significant, or is absent. In Mendeland, on the other hand, the connection between the Poro and political authority has always been very strong, and the two mutually reinforce each other. This is shown ritually by the fact that the *Gbeni,* the principal spirit of the society, which comes out in public only on the most important type of civil occasion, makes its appearance on the death or coronation of a chief or of a subchief. On the former occasion, the *Gbeni* proceeds to the dead man's grave and bows over it. It has to be bought off by a sum of money from the deceased's family. When a chief is dying, he is taken into the bush for medical treatment, and his death is subsequently announced from the roof of his house by an official of the society.

It goes almost without saying that no person can hope to occupy any political office in the chiefdom without being a Poro member. The chief himself is the society's official patron in all matters external to its secret business. He is expected to uphold Poro interests whenever they come into conflict with the views of Moslems as well as of the British Administration. In recognition of this, and of his position as chief, the society makes him a customary present whenever it holds a session. Traditionally, he is also entitled, like other big men, to the services of the young initiates in working his rice farm.

In the old days, the Poro also acted as an arbitrator in chiefdom disputes, and is said to have been effective enough to end them by sending an armed band of its officials, masked as spirits, against the contending party which ignored its ruling.[13] The Mende Hut Tax Rising of 1898, it is worth remembering, was largely organized and finally set in motion in Mende country by the Poro war-sign—a burned palm leaf—which was passed on from chief to chief and from country to country. The warriors taking part wore the Poro palm leaf token wound round neck and wrist. Prior to the British Administration, the Poro promulgated general laws, regulated trading practices, and was without much doubt the main means by which a uniform system of government and a uniform set of customs was possible throughout a large number of isolated and remotely scattered communities. One way by which common action was taken on such a wide scale was by placing the whole country under Poro oath, before the actual object of the oath was known. After this, everyone was bound to adhere to whatever plans had been decided upon by the senior members in the inner bush.

The Poro helped to conserve the dignity of secular rule by decreeing that disputes affecting important members of the community should be heard *in camera* by a Poro tribunal, the identity of whose president remained secret. This practice is still followed, to some extent, today. No chief, and this point is equally significant today as in former times, could be appointed without Poro approval, and the society had, inevitably, a major voice in his nomination. Nowadays, chiefs are "elected" under the supervision of an administrative officer; but in a large number of cases, if not in most, the matter is settled in advance by swearing members of the electoral body, i.e., the tribal authority, on medicine in the Poro bush. In the old days, given Poro support, it is doubtful if there was any limit to autocratic rule on the part of a chief. It is probable that individual chiefs, like Nyagua of Panguma, who held sway over a local hegemony of chiefdoms, owed most of their success to the use they were able to make of Poro organization. On the other hand, the Poro could be an equally powerful check on rulers who attempted to usurp their position.

In economic affairs, the Poro sign, a spiral of ferns, is used to regulate farming and other practices. It is supposed to bring death or sickness to anyone who disregards it. The sign is also used to ban the use of fishing grounds at certain seasons and the collection of palm fruit, so that the cultivation of necessary food crops should not be interfered with. Formerly, the society also fixed the prices for various commodities and the rate at which certain services, for example, a day's load-carrying.

should be performed. G. W. Brown reported quite recently that the Poro operates its own currency, and still regulates trading practices in parts of Liberia.[14]

D. OPERATION OF MEDICAL AND OTHER SOCIAL SERVICES

From the point of view of social psychology, the medical role of the secret societies is the logical complement to their prohibitive and restrictive function in social and other fields. Since most illness and disease is held to be the result of some ritual infraction or breach of society rules, the proper body to effect the cure is the society against which the sick person has offended, and which possesses the appropriate antidote.

Generally, the course of treatment involves a number of separate stages. The first step is to consult a soothsayer. He has a bag of stones, each of which represents one of the various ills from which humanity suffers. In the course of manipulating his stones, the soothsayer asks his patient if he remembers having broken such and such a rule or done such and such an act. He tries to get the patient to confess some great or small misdemeanor which might be interpreted as a concrete offense against known rules and regulations. If the patient denies any such offense, he is told that he is lying or has forgotten the matter. Finally, the soothsayer informs him of the particular society against which he has transgressed and tells him that the only way to obtain a cure is to make full confession to them.

The person reports himself accordingly, and the next step is for him to be ritually washed by the society concerned, or to be made a member of it and formally initiated. The decision rests on the nature of his offense and the rules of the given society. Sociologically, the reason for initiation is fairly obvious. Through the offense the individual has committed, e.g., trespassing on society bush or coming into physical contact with any of the secret paraphernalia, he is considered to have acquired a measure of the society's own special power. The surest way of preventing his divulging what he has learned to outsiders is to place him under the same oaths and obligations as are incumbent upon members of the society themselves. This also obviates the possibility of his making unauthorized use of society secrets and of setting himself up among the public as an unofficial practitioner. Once initiated, however, the fame of any medical work he does redounds to the credit of the society as a whole rather than to him as an individual person.

There are a number of physical and physiological complaints which fall specifically within the province of certain societies. Barrenness, for example, is usually put down to the woman concerned having trespassed on the sacred bush of the Poro. Whether she did so knowingly or unknowingly is irrelevant. The only possible remedy lies with the Poro, and initiation is obligatory. The woman is escorted into the bush by a young boy known as *ngegba* (*nge gba*—I am different). On their arrival, the spirits of the society are invoked and asked to release the woman from the curse they laid upon her and to pass it on to the boy. Such a woman is then called *bolemui*, from *Mabole*, the senior woman official of the Poro, who is herself responsible for making the invocation. Both the *bolemui* and the *ngegba* are given only elementary instruction and a few cuts on the back.

Illnesses of various kinds in the case of a man may be traced to his having intruded in the Sande bush during the period of the girls' initiation. He may be able to obtain a cure by paying a fine to the society and being washed by them. A really serious illness may be attributed to the person concerned, or to someone closely connected with him, having committed *simongama* which, as already explained, constitutes the most serious breach of Humoi laws.

An advanced grade of the Humoi also specializes in medical as well as ritual washing and is known as *Kpekili* (literally, the heart of the razor) on account of the razor used in the ceremony. The upper part of the patient's tongue is scratched with a razor or needle to wipe away all impurity.

Insanity, and other forms of mental complaint, are put down to breaches of the rules of the Njayei society. They result from the sufferer having trespassed on Njayei bush, or from his having seen the dead body of an important member of the society before it was ritually purified. In such cases, the only way a person can be cured is by initiation, unless he is already a Humoi member. In that case, he undergoes treatment without initiation into the Njayei. There are reciprocal arrangements between the two societies, and the terms brother and sister are used reciprocally between members of the respective societies.

Membership of the Njayei, like that of the Humoi, is hereditary. Its members meet in a round house with distinctively speckled walls. A person is also initiated if he dreams of the Njayei medicine. In addition, the society supplies medicines for fertility purposes in connection with farming, and certain Njayei ingredients have the property of increasing a person's self-confidence and general personality. For example, a candidate in a chiefdom "election" who has the benefit of them, will so impress the authorities concerned, that they will be bound to acknowledge the priority of his claim to the chieftainship over that of all the other claimants.

Most forms of therapy include the prescription of special medicines compounded mainly out of certain kinds of herbs and leaves whose remedial value is of a purely physical, as opposed to psychological character. These are applied in ways which vary from ritual sprinkling of the body, to their external application as poultices and internal consumption as drinks. The Humoi, in particular, makes a prolific use of these materials, and for this reason the leader of the society is known as "leaf person." The bush sacred to the Humoi serves as a kind of hospital in this respect, and small children may be taken there for treatment.

Though medical work is virtually the prerogative of the secret societies, particularly the Humoi and Njayei, there are one or two exceptions which, however, do not detract from the effect of the general rule. There is, for example, the Kpa society which anyone can join. The function of the Kpa is confined to the treatment of minor complaints, such as eye trouble, toothache, etc. In many villages, there are certain stones, known as *kpa-gotu,* and it is here that the *Kpa-bla,* or Kpa people, carry on their work. A man may apprentice himself by applying to the leader of the Kpa, and after learning the use of herbs and medicines, he returns home and sets up his own hospital and dispensary.

Rules of health and hygiene, as illustrated above in the example of the Humoi, are implicit in the prohibitions of various secret societies. A further instance is in the ceremonies performed by the Sande on occasions of abortion, birth, and death in childbirth.[15]

Secret society medicines are also used forensically, and sometimes unofficially, when it is necessary to extract the truth from a witness, or other persons, over an important matter. The *Bongoi* section of the Humoi have a specific role in the latter respect. Society medicines are also used, quite apart from society purposes as such, to bind a person or a group of persons, on oath, to a particular undertaking. An example of this has already been cited in the case of swearing members of a chiefdom electoral body on Poro medicine.[16]

In addition to their spirits which inspire awe, most of the secret societies have one or more ancillary spirits whose function is largely of a purely secular kind. It is to provide amusement and entertainment. Usually, their appearance in public is associated with and signalizes some important institutional activity or event, such as the death or coronation of a Paramount Chief. On the latter occasion, the advent of the *Gbeni,* the sacred spirit of the Poro, to announce the chief's demise, is followed by other Poro spirits, such as the *Ngafagoti,* the *Yavei,* the *Gobai,* etc. The latter remain out dancing after the *Gbeni* has retired to the bush. The individual impersonating the spirit wears a wooden mask and a cape of raffia and straw which is extensive enough to cover his entire body because it is absolutely essential that no part of the person is revealed. The spirit, escorted by a number of attendants and followers, usually visits every big man in the town and squats in various grotesque poses in front of his house. It then proceeds to parade about the town attracting spectators and causing amusement wherever it goes. Bystanders with a position of social standing to maintain hand over a "dash" of money to the spirit's followers.

The performance of these "amusing spirits," as they are popularly termed, is mainly a matter of miming and mimicry; but in the case of the Sande spirit, the entertainment is on more elaborate lines. It is a great honor to impersonate the Sande spirit and one which is reserved for higher grades in the society. Additional to the carved wooden mask, which is dyed a deep black and is the effigy of a human face, an outer garment is worn. This is densely covered with hanging strips of wood fibre sewn on a foundation of black cloth. Black stockings are worn, and tiny bells hang from some of the strings of the dress. The spirit carries a small whip of stiff grass and is accompanied by an attendant or interpreter. Communication with the latter is made by signs with the whip, and the interpreter explains the spirit's meaning to the onlookers.

The Sande spirit has a special dance which she performs as a *pas de seule* to the beating of a *sangbe* (drum) by a male drummer. Her attendant keeps a careful watch while she dances in order to adjust any disarray in dress that might give away the spirit's human identity. One of the most disastrous things that could happen would be for the mask to fall off when nonmembers, or those of a lower grade, are about. The consequences would be serious for the spirit would be bound to take revenge. Secrecy is increased further by giving the spirit some personal name which is either charming or which suggests a virtue, so that the real name of the impersonator goes unmentioned.

The Sande spirit comes out for the purpose of celebrating some important event, such as the visit of a neighboring Paramount Chief. The style of the dance includes a darting and skipping movement taken almost at the run like the preliminary strides of an expert ice-skater on the rink. There are side to side inclinations of the shoulders and head—the head being turned in an opposite direction to the shoulders—and complicated turns and pirouetting on the balls of the feet. While waiting to dance, the spirit feigns restlessness, scatters the crowd around her, and has to be pacified by the attendant. The dance itself takes place in the chief's compound in the midst of a large gathering of townsfolk and visitors, and the entertainment usually includes special exhibitions of dancing of an even more spirited and acrobatic kind than the spirit's own costume allows. If the occasion is a particularly important one, women singers provide additional musical accompaniment with their *segbura* (calabash rattles), and there may be one or two male drummers. The dance is started by the leading singer—*nguole nje* (singing mother) shaking her rattle and intoning the opening verses of a song. This is taken up by her fellow singers and they reply in chorus. The drummers then join in.

These special exhibitions are performed by a picked group of younger Sande initiates. They dance as a group or in individual turns, and, on finishing, the solo dancer is greeted with enthusiasm by the older women. The dancing costume in this case consists of bunches of palm leaf fibre suspended by bangles round the arms and legs, and knicker-bockers of native or European cloth. The practice of "dashing" the dancers with money after each turn is an important part of the institution, and one of the ways in which a person wins and retains social prestige in Mende society. The donor walks into the full view of the assembly to hand over his contribution. Alternatively, the dancing girl drops her head-tie onto the lap of some important spectator and he is expected to return it with money.

CONCLUSION

It follows from the institutional significance and penetration of secret societies, that they are today the main repository of the traditional ways of life in Sierra Leone. This is particularly evident in the case of the Poro which, as an organization, is almost unique in the rapidly changing conditions of native life in offering active resistance to new habits and customs. One indication of this, already cited, is the fact that boys entering the bush are still forbidden anything European in the way of clothes and equipment.

The resilience of the Poro is also shown by the way it has survived opposition from outside, partly by Government ordinance. As early as 1897, the Poro Ordinance forbade the placing of Poro signs on palm trees. It was asserted that the chiefs were using the society's emblem to hold up trade, sometimes in their own interests or in the case of a dispute with their people. Orthodox Islam has also been against the Poro to the extent of forbidding Moslems to become members of it or of any other secret society. But the prohibition is regarded very rarely except, perhaps, by immigrant people, such as the Mandinka, who are already well Islamicized.

Disapproval on the part of the Christian Missions is less strong than it used to be, partly because the social function of the Poro is better known and appreciated than formerly. The Missions generally place no prohibition on their members and teachers belonging to Poro, but expect them to discountenance and not to take part in any of its rituals. Neither Christianity nor Islam appears to have had much direct effect, however, on the Poro's status. On the other hand, indirectly, the acquisition of European ideas and ideals in Mission schools has led not only to a disbelief in Poro sanctions, but to a more fundamental weakening of its prestige on the more general grounds on which most native institutions have suffered by comparison with western ones.

Not surprisingly, the real strength of the Poro and of other secret societies lies nowadays in the attitude of the older members and of the "big men" of native society in general. Most of the latter are not literate and their interests are vested deeply in the older order and in maintaining traditional controls over it. They are well aware of the institutional basis of their own position and are on continuous watch over it. In consequence, Poro and other society secrets are still guarded very jealously; discussion of society matters, and Poro ones in particular, even when superficial, with a nonmember and especially a European, is regarded as a serious offense on the part of a nonliterate man and as an act of disloyalty on the part of a literate person. Nevertheless, a certain amount of compromise with the newer circumstances has been inevitable. Nowadays, in the case of the Poro, for example, boys attending a European school are initiated after only a few nights spent in the bush. In other cases, they still remain for several weeks.

It is indicative of the depth of the cultural roots of the Poro that, unlike the women leaders of the Sande, the Poro elders are hostile to compromises in a more positive direction, in terms of modernizing their own school. In the case of the Sande, the Government has carried out some experimentation with initiation schools as a medium for modern methods in hygiene, etc., which the girls are expected to pass on when they return home. The work has been under the supervision of an African medical officer who does not, of course, himself enter the society bush. Even so, it has been met, on the whole, by considerable opposition from the men as interference in women's business. Ostensibly, the hostility of the older men to this, as well as to the idea of using the Poro in a similar way, has a purely institutional basis. Their objection is that European methods are quite alien to the indigenous function of secret society activities which, in terms of the bush school, are to be regarded as symbolical rather than utilitarian.

It is not the older men alone who prevent adjustment of the secret societies to present-day conditions. For those members of the younger generation of Protectorate people who are imbued with a desire to emulate western standards, social status has to be sought elsewhere. It is to be found largely in social acceptance by the westernized Creole of the Colony[17] to whom native institutions and secret societies, in particular, rank as symbols of primitiveness. For the ordinary literate Mende man, and less so for the ordinary literate Mende woman, society affiliation constitutes one of the few remaining ties with tribal life. But it is a bond which he has decreasing interest in maintaining.

NOTES

[1] This paper is based on material gained in the course of field work carried out in the Sierra Leone Protectorate, in 1944-46, under the auspices of the Wyse Studentship in Social Anthropology at Trinity College, Cambridge, and of the Colonial Social Science Research Council.

[2] {The phonetic spellings and tonal designations of Mende words given in

this article have here been omitted.] The term "Poro" itself is anglicized from *Poo*. Other Mende terms such as Sande Njayei, etc., are in general use among English speakers and are not italicized as foreign words for this reason.

[3] "Spirits" is a direct translation of the Mende term used, which is *ngafanga*. It is as well to note, however, that *ngafanga* is a generic concept which includes ancestral spirits and spirits of the bush. Its specific connotation is denoted by the context in which it is employed.

[4] *See* Watkins, 1943, for a comparative note on the social purpose and curricula of the bush school among the Vai, Krim, Gola, and other peoples of Sierra Leone and Liberia.

[5] Sande is the Mende term for the women's secret society. It is known among the Timne as the Bundu.

[6] *See* Westermann, 1921, for description of this *rite de passage*.

[7] As Watkins (*op. cit.*) points out, training of the initiates is tested out in the "laboratory" of bush school life. Although the bush school is conducted in a special environment, i.e. one which is differentiated from the general social milieu, the degree of artificiality is not so great as it often is under the conditions of formal education among peoples of European and American cultures.

[8] Washing involves a fairly elaborate ceremony which is performed by a special branch of the Humoi, known as the *simongama-bla*, i.e., "the people who specialize in incest." The offending parties are seated on a mat on the ground and tied together by thread. The officiating member, a woman, invites them to confess their misdemeanors. Grains of rice are placed on their heads and the palms of their hands, and a fowl is brought. If it pecks away the rice, it is a sign that they are freed of their sin. They are sprinkled with a special medicine, concocted out of leaves and water. They then spring up, breaking the thread binding them, and go down to the river to bathe.

[9] Nevertheless, this kind of marriage is practiced fairly often by members of chiefly families in order to maintain property and position.

[10] There is, however, one important qualification in this respect. To have intercourse with an uninitiated girl, i.e., one who has not passed through Sande, is an offense against the latter society and should be expiated through its medium.

[11] Another rule of the Humoi, which has no obvious connection with sex, is that cold ashes in the hearth should be swept away before preparing food, and that stale food or drink should never be used. The latter rule is going out of observance with the adoption of European dietary customs.

[12] Little, 1947.

[13] Harley, 1941. Harley provides an important structural analysis of the Poro in an area where, apparently, various institutional activities of the society still retain much of their old vigor.

[14] Brown, 1937.

[15] In the case of a stillbirth, the women of the town go out into the bush under the direction of a senior official of the Sande and collect herbs. Returning, they sprinkle all the houses in the town with this lustral medicine. This must be done before further procreation can proceed with success.

[16] Other important medicines used forensically, such as the *Toma* and *Tilei*, are the property of private hereditary owners and have no connection with the secret societies.

[17] For a discussion of the sociological implications of this point see Little, 1948. "Creole" is the term by which African descendants of the original settlers of Freetown and the Colony of Sierra Leone, as distinct from the Protectorate, are known. The "better off" class of Creoles have always emulated a European way of life.

BIBLIOGRAPHY

[Starred items are recommended as further readings.]

* Brown, G. W., 1937, The Poro in Modern Business. *Man,* No. 3, Jan.

* Harley, G. W., 1941, Notes on the Poro in Liberia. *Peabody Museum Papers,* Vol. *19,* No. 2.

* Little, K. L., 1947, Mende Political Institutions in Transition. *Africa* (Jour. of the Int. Inst. of Af. Lang. and Cult.), Vol. XVII, No. 1.

*———, 1948, Social Change and Social Class in the Sierra Leone Protectorate. *Amer. J. Soc.,* July.

Watkins, Mark Hanna, 1943, The West African Bush School. *Amer. J. Soc.,* Vol. *43,* pp. 666-674.

Westermann, D., 1921, *Die Kpelle.* Göttingen.

FOR FURTHER READING

Little, Kenneth L., "The Poro Society as an Arbiter of Culture: A Note on Cultural Inter-penetration," *African Studies,* 1948, *7,* 1-15; and Little, Kenneth L., *The Mende of Sierra Leone,* London: Routledge & Kegan Paul, 1951. These studies provide further data on the secret society and on the Mende in general.

Harley, George W., *Masks as Agents of Social Control in Northeast Liberia,* Cambridge: Harvard University, Peabody Museum Papers, 32, 2, 1950. Includes an account of the use of masks in secret society functions.

Schwab, George, *Tribes of the Liberian Hinterland,* Cambridge: Harvard University, Peabody Museum Papers, 31, 1947. Contains useful data on secret societies.

Bittermieux, L., *La société secrète des Bakhimba au Mayombe,* Brussels: Institut Royal Colonial Belge, Classe des sciences morales et politiques, Mémoires, Collection in-8°, 5, 3, 1936. An ethnographic description of a Congo secret society.

NANDI AGE-SETS*

G. W. B. Huntingford

This paper is an example of one of the ways in which African societies are organized on the basis of age. Among the Nandi, males are grouped in four broad categories: small boys, initiates, warriors (the "set in power"), and old men. This classification determines the rules of behavior between persons of different relative ages and formerly served the all-important function of providing a military force. Persons of the same age category move up into a new grade approximately every fifteen years, but there is an overlap in the warrior grade during the second half of the period, when the eldest members of the next younger group take over the more ardous duties from the older warriors, who retain their status officially even though their physical vigor may have declined. This is apparently a smoothly functioning age grading system in which there is little of the hostility between retiring warriors and their successors that has been reported for some African societies. •

The Nandi system may be compared with those of two Nuba hill peoples, described in Nadel's paper on witchcraft in this volume. Nadel's study explores the psychological factors of the relation between physical and "social" age in shaping the two peoples' social roles and self-perception. A marked discrepancy between physical and social age in one of the Nuba societies produces a premature "old age," with resentment between older and younger men and frequent accusations of witchcraft, while in the other, in which there is a more realistic correspondence between the two types of age, witchcraft is absent.

I

Every male in the tribe belongs from birth to an age-set, *ipinda,* of which there are seven. These sets are closely connected with circumcision, and in their operation they cut across all departments of tribal life, as their functions are both military and political, and in addition they have considerable effect on behavior and relations between people in the *tiliet.*[1] They are therefore of primary importance, and an understanding of how

---

* Reprinted from *The Nandi of Kenya: Tribal Control in a Pastoral Society,* London: Routledge and Kegan Paul, 1953, Chapter 3, by permission of the author and the publisher.

they work is essential. The subject is one of some difficulty, and before attempting to study it in detail it will be as well to give a summary of the system.

First, I state briefly the working of the system as I understand it from my information and observations. There are, as already noted, seven sets, and at any given time one of these is that of the warriors, two are those of boys, and four are sets of old men. The warrior set is referred to as "the set in power," because during its period of office it is responsible for all military operations, and has in addition certain privileges; it is in power for a period of about fifteen years, at the end of which it retires, and the set next below it, which during this period has been circumcised, takes its place as the set of warriors in power, the retiring warriors becoming elders. During the second half of the period, however, there has been an overlap, for the eldest of the newly circumcised men have taken over the more arduous duties from the older warriors in power, so that for part of the fifteen-year period there are actually two warrior sets, though only the senior of them is said to be in power. At the end of the period, when the warriors in power retire, the recently circumcised set becomes the set in power, and at the same time the set of the oldest men, who by that time are all dead, passes out of existence as an old men's set and its name is transferred to the set of the small boys, the most junior set. The sets thus work in a recurring cycle, and the names appear again and again. This is what actually happened during the last thirty years.

I assume that the length of fifteen years was the same in pre-European days for several reasons: (a) Nandi authorities like Arap Sambai have told me so; (b) men of the Kimnyike set have told me that their set went to circumcision shortly before the Europeans came, an event which took place in 1896, so that if the Kimnyike circumcision began in 1895, it takes the fifteen-year period back at least to this date; and (c) fifteen years is a workable period, whereas anything shorter (e.g. seven and a half years) is not, i.e. when a man's son belongs to the set next but one below his own.

The length of the intervals is determined by the flowering of a bush which marks the beginning of the period during which the boys are circumcised, and the end of the warriors' period of power is calculated from this. As the bush flowers at intervals of about seven or eight years, alternate flowerings are taken to fix the circumcision, and the lengths of the sets may vary a little in consequence.[2] The following terms are used by the Nandi with reference to circumcision: *tum* = circumcision; *awendi tum* = I am going to circumcision; *kiyat tum* = the circumcision is opened; *kiker tum* = the circumcision is closed.

* * *

[Here follows a discussion of circumcision festivals reported as taking place at seven-and-a-half-year intervals in A. C. Hollis, *The Nandi, Their Language and Folk-Lore,* Oxford, 1909.]

We may now examine in detail the working of the sets. The central fact is that there are seven sets with fixed names working in a recurring cycle. The members of a set are those who are circumcised during the same circumcision period (*tum*), though, unlike the Masai system, a boy is born into a set and in that set he remains all his life. Age-sets must be distinguished from age-grades, the latter being, as the term implies, stages through which a person passes between birth and death, and though in some tribes considerable importance is attached to the passing from one grade to another (as among the AKamba), the transition from grade to grade among the Nandi is effected through circumcision and the *saket ap eito* [ceremony marking change-over of age-sets]. Thus, men pass from the grade of *ngetet,* boy, to that of *murenet,*[3] warrior, through the circumcision; and from the grade of *murenet* to that of *poiyot,* old man, by means of the *saket ap eito.* When the *saket* is not held in the year in which it becomes due, the transition from warrior to old man is automatic. Women, who have no age-sets, go through the grades of *tipik,* girls, and *osotik* or *chepiosok,* married women, the transition from one grade to the other taking place at marriage.

Inner circle = 1923   Outer circle = 1938

Diagram to illustrate the cyclic working of sets

The seven age-sets in their order of seniority from 1938 are:

7. Kipkoiimet: oldest men.
6. Kaplelach.
5. Kimnyike.
4. Nyongi: youngest of the old men.
} Four sets of elders.
3. Maina: warriors in power.
2. Juma: young men whose circumcision closed in 1945, and who now overlap with the Maina as warriors.
1. Sawe: small boys who will be circumcised at the next *tum*.

Each set is subdivided into four permanent associating groups called *mat,* which remain constant in each set at all times. The word *mat* (plur. *mostinwek*) means "fire," and the term is derived from "the fire that roars in the seclusion huts (*menjet*) of those who are being circumcised, and those who share such a hut are of the same *mat*." These four groups are:

1. Chonginiot, plur. Chonginiek, "ostrich feathers."
2. Kipalkonyot, plur. Kipalkongek, "we dig out the eyes."
} Senior group.
3. Tetekatindet, plur. Tetekatik, "those who are greeted 'tete.' " [4]
4. Kiptoiyot, plur. Kiptoiinik, "the bull calves."
} Junior group.

All four groups, with the same four names, occur in each age-set. Nowadays, when warfare is no longer possible, the two junior *mostinwek* in each set are combined into one group and called either Tetekatik or Kiptoiinik indifferently, and the number of *mostinwek* has come to be regarded as three instead of four.[5]

The principle of the age-set system is that at any given time, one set is that of the warriors in power, the other sets being therefore those of the small boys (one), initiates (one), and old men (four). The chief apparent difficulty in the working of the system is that between the end of the circumcision and the *saket* there is a period of eight years. If the newly initiated men had to wait till the *saket* before they became warriors, they would then be faced with another period of fifteen years before they could retire: a man who was twenty when the circumcision closed would therefore be twenty-eight when he became a warrior, and forty-three by the time he was due to retire, and thus too old to be an active warrior. The difficulty, however, is got over in the following way. As soon as the circumcision is closed, the eldest of the newly initiated men become warriors, and take over the less responsible part of the official warriors' duties, thus allowing the eldest of the warriors in power to relax and lead a quiet life; during the eight years between the closing of the circumcision and the *saket* there is an overlap, and there are then actually two warrior sets in existence. When the fifteen-year period ends with the *saket,* the overlap ends also, for the new warrior set takes over completely. At the same time, the set of the oldest old men goes out, its name going round to the bottom as the name of the set of the small boys, while the set below that of the new warriors becomes the initiates' set. There is no problem as to what to do with the very old men, because by the time the change-over takes place they are all dead, as was undoubtedly the case in 1938, when all the old men of Sawe had been dead for some years, and the Nandi said that this was what always happened.

* * *

Since the sets and their names are fixed, it is generally possible to tell in advance the set to which a man's eldest son will belong: this is normally, though not invariably, the set next but one below that of the father. . . . Younger sons often belong to the age-set next but two below that of the father, if owing to the interval between births they are too young to be circumcised with the elder sons; and even an eldest son may belong to the age next but two below his father's. Irregular descent of the first kind may be illustrated by the following example:

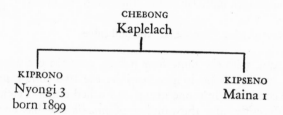

CHEBONG
Kaplelach

KIPRONO
Nyongi 3
born 1899

KIPSENO
Maina 1

The date of Kiprono's birth can be determined, because he was a year old when the government moved from Kipture to Kaptumo. This took place in 1900, so we may give the year of his birth as 1899. The Nyongi circumcision opened at the beginning of 1912, and since Kiprono is Nyongi 3, he was probably circumcised about 1914 (at the age of 15, being about 16 when the circumcision closed). His brother Kipseno, however, is Maina 1. I could not fix the year of his birth, but he missed the 1912 circumcision and had to wait till 1926, because boys are not as a rule circumcised if they are under 12; and assuming he was born in 1904 he would be only 11 when the Nyongi circumcision closed, but not more than 22 when the next circumcision opened, an age at which other Nandi are known to have been circumcised.

The case of an eldest son belonging to the set next but two below his father's—the second kind of irregular descent—is illustrated by Kipchumba arap Ruto, the son of a Kaplelach 2. Kipchumba was born in

1905, and when the Nyongi circumcision closed was therefore only 10 years old. Although he should normally have been a Nyongi, he was his father's third child, having two sisters older than himself. This factor delayed his circumcision, and accounts for his being a Maina.

The age-sets regulate circumcision, because all the boys of a set are circumcised during the same period, and consequently the period itself, and the time for opening the circumcision, are both determined by the same means. The important event is the opening of the circumcision, and this is fixed by the flowering of a bush called *Setiot (Mimulopsis* sp.).[6] At the end of a circumcision period, three age-sets are principally concerned with the approaching new order of the sets, the existing warrior set, the incoming warrior set, and the set of the boys who are about to be circumcised. At the end of 1938 these were:

Nyongi, who were about to become elders;
Maina, who were about to become the warrior set;
Juma, whose circumcision was about to begin.

When the end of a period draws near, watch is kept by the incoming set —in 1938 it was the Maina—for the flowering of the *setiot*. No special watchers are appointed, but the Chonginiek of the incoming warriors take on the duty, and when they see that it has flowered, they tell the Chonginiek of the outgoing warriors that it has done so.

All the proceedings connected with circumcision are done on a *pororiet*[7] basis, and so when the flowering has been reported a meeting is held in each *pororiet,* and from the Chonginiek of the incoming warriors two representatives are chosen, men who have previously been selected as *kiptaienik* or commanders of a *sirityet* (military section). These two then choose two heifer calves from among the cattle belonging to men of their own set. Since they are performing an official duty, they need not themselves provide calves, and the owners of the calves they choose have no right to refuse, for the animals are intended as a gift for the *orkoiyot*.[8] The fathers of the boys whose circumcision is due to be opened have meanwhile been brewing beer, and when it is ready, boys are chosen from the Chonginiek to present it to the *orkoiyot*. These offerings are made to the *orkoiyot* because his permission is necessary before the circumcision may be opened. To hand over these gifts, a man is chosen to represent the *orkoiyot* from among the Chonginiek of the incoming warriors, and is known for the time being as *orkoiyot nepo ipinda,* "the *orkoiyot* of the age-set." Before the Juma circumcision was authorized in 1940 a man named Arap Kimngetich was chosen by the *pororiet* of Tepingot as its *orkoiyot nepo ipinda.* A time and place having been fixed upon, the *orkoiyot nepo ipinda* meets the two section commanders and the representatives of the set to be circumcised, who bring with them the calves and the beer. The *orkoiyot nepo ipinda* conducts them to the chief *orkoiyot*, whose permission is being sought, and tells him that the people of such and such a *pororiet* have brought two calves and much beer, and ask his permission for the circumcision to be opened, since the *setiot* has flowered (*amu kakoyei setiot*). The *orkoiyot* answers, *Ingeyat tum, si kopa lakok tum,* "let the circumcision be opened, that the children may be circumcised." When this has been done, the ceremony called *Kikule kwet,* "we bleed the goat," is held in each *pororiet,* and the circumcision may begin.

Since these things are done on a *pororiet* basis, the proceedings are repeated by each *pororiet,* and the wealth of the *orkoiyot* is thereby much increased. There are twenty-four *pororiet* groups,[9] so he gains forty-eight calves, and a great deal of beer, which is divided among the elders of his *koret.*

The ceremony called *Kikule kwet* is also held separately in each *pororiet* area. It is a gathering of the people of the *pororiet* and lasts for one day. Much beer is drunk by the older men, and goats are killed and eaten by the boys whose circumcision is about to begin. These gatherings are not quite representative of the whole tribe, for the Moi clan do not take part in them, having an analogous festival of their own called *Kiireku leget,* "we take off the belt," which is similar to the *Kikule kwet,* and has the same object—the achievement of an auspicious beginning of the momentous event which will shortly change the boys into men and full members of the tribe.

In addition to the official gifts of beer from the *pororiet* to the *orkoiyot,* beer is given to him privately; fathers of prospective candidates brew beer and combine in sending pots of it to him. The state of the Talai[10] elders at the beginning of a circumcision period therefore can easily be imagined: every beer-pot and drinking tube will be in use, and there will be much staggering homewards in the evenings of old men supporting each other on unsteady legs.

After the *Kikule kwet* there used to be an interval of about three months before the circumcision actually started in the Reserve, as in 1926, when the *Kikule kwet* was held in June, and the circumcision began in October. But this interval was shorter in 1940, the Nandi said.

II

It may be thought that fifteen years is too long to be the effective length of an age-set, and it is therefore necessary to consider this question in some detail. The facts are that (1) the length is approximimately fifteen years, and (2) the warriors in power retain their status officially throughout this period. This is made possible by the overlap already mentioned, which allows the senior warriors to be warriors in name while their duties are performed by the eldest of the newly circumcised age-set before the actual change-over of sets takes place. There are thus in effect two warrior sets during the second half of each fifteen-year period.

* * *

[Here follows an account of the history of Nandi age-sets since about 1895.]

The actual process of dividing the warrior's duties is as follows: the elder men of the set which has just been circumcised become warriors as soon as their circumcision has closed, and they gradually take the places of the official warriors till those of the senior set who are still leading an active life (i.e. the Kiptoiinik), give it up and retire when the *saket* arrives, the new warriors then taking over completely. This relinquishment of active duties by the senior warriors is both tacit and voluntary; the younger warriors in power get promotion, and the newly fledged warriors can start their fighting life without waiting for several years till the *saket*. I have come across no evidence whatever to suggest the hostility which Peristiany says used to occur among the Kipsikis between those due for retirement and those who were to succeed them. (*Kipsigis,* pp. 31, 32.)

The ceremony which marks the change-over, and emphasizes the formal retirement of the outgoing warrior set, is called, as already mentioned, the *saket ap eito,* "the slaughter of the bullock," because it is centered round the killing of a white bullock. This ceremony has not been held, however, since the establishment of the British Administration, and we have therefore no actual record of it, for although it was authorized in 1923, the occasion was used to stage a rising which failed, and the *saket* itself was not held. But it seems, from the description given by Hollis (p. 12), and from what I have been told, to have been arranged as follows:

1. All adult males of the incoming and outgoing age-sets assembled at an appointed place by order of the *orkoiyot.* This is how the rising of 1923 was to have started; and although the Nandi obeyed the *orkoiyot's* order, I am sure that many of them were really ignorant of what was intended.

2. The incoming warriors provide a white bullock, *eito,* which is killed (*sach,* "slaughter">*saket*) in the presence of the *orkoiyot.* In 1923 the bullock had been chosen, but was not killed.

3. The meat is eaten by old men of the senior age-sets, who are present as well as the warriors, and the incoming warriors make small rings of the hide and each puts one on a finger of his right hand.

4. Near the *orkoiyot* is a stool covered with cow dung mixed with fruit of the *lapotwet* plant (*solanum campylacanthum*).

5. The old men and the outgoing warriors stand up, while the incoming warriors sit on the ground.

6. The retiring warriors remove their clothes and put on old men's fur cloaks.

7. The *orkoiyot* tells the new warriors that they are now the *murenik ap Nandi,* "the Nandi warriors," and that it is their duty to do all they can for the advancement of the tribe (by acquiring cattle), and for its protection.

8. Everybody then goes home, and no one may sleep by the wayside. The ceremony was usually followed by a series of raids.

III

Since the tribe is stratified into age-categories which tend to affect behavior, the age-set system is a disciplinary factor of some importance; in fact, as far as behavior is concerned, it cuts across the ordinary kinship rules to a certain extent. The function of the age-sets is twofold. In the first place, they provide the tribe with a source of man power of the right age for military purposes; and secondly, the stratification thus produced affects the normal behavior rules because each set is subordinate, both in theory and in fact, to the set senior to it, though the practical effect of this seniority is felt most forcibly in the three lowest sets, those of the warriors, initiates, and small boys, between all of whom a great gulf is fixed. Behavior between sets, and the rights and privileges of the warrior set are carefully and jealously guarded, and any attempt on the part of the younger people to infringe them is sternly dealt with. In sexual matters the warriors have rights which are accorded to no other set. The uncircumcised are not supposed to indulge in sexual intercourse at all, while members of the warrior set are allowed free sexual license: they may have sweethearts and may marry when the circumcision has closed. The periods during which the fullest sexual rights are allowed [also] overlap: just as active participation in military affairs overlaps, so do the sexual rights.

The warrior set is allowed unrestricted access to the uninitiated girls, and the normal practice is for each man to have his own sweetheart, *mureret,* who is regarded as his and not accessible to others. Any girl who has no lover, *sandet,* is fair game for a roving warrior, and dare not refuse him, even if she wanted to. The result of this, of course, is that Nandi girls are seldom virgins when they go to be initiated, and one who is a virgin has the operation of clitoridectomy performed upon her while sitting on a stool, whence she is called *Chemngecheriat* (from *ngecher,* "stool"); other girls sit on the ground for the operation. A man does not marry his *mureret,* but after his marriage he often continues to associate with her, even after she herself has been married. Towards the end of the fifteen-year period the warriors who are officially to retire cease running after girls; and once the change-over has taken place, they must give it up altogether and confine their attentions to their wives. An old man who solicits the favors of unmarried girls is unmercifully ridiculed, and soon has to stop. Uncircumcised boys, on the other hand, are beaten if the warriors catch them trying to "steal girls"; but whereas a girl will quickly tell about an old man who is after her, she will often accept illicit attentions from well-grown boys who are nearing the time for circumcision, if it is possible to do so without being caught; for although it is the boy who will be punished if found out, the girl will be made to feel that she has not done the right thing.

Age-mates regard themselves as equals, and address each other as *ipindannyo,* "my age-set." Members of the same *mat* allow each other access to their wives; a Chonginiot, for example, who when on a journey puts up for a night in the hut of another Chonginiot of the same age-set, will be offered his host's wife, and if he accepts her, the host will sleep in his *sikiroinet*[11] or in a neighbor's hut. There is no suggestion of any mystical kinship between age-mates.

Relations between the overlapping sets are complicated by seniority: (*a*) On the one hand we have the younger warriors of the set in power who may be somewhat jealous of the usurpation of their rights by the newly circumcised juniors, although this usurpation is quite in order since it is allowed by custom; this feeling is not one of hostility and is of short duration; and the two sets soon settle down in friendliness. (*b*) On the other hand the older members of the set in power are often afraid of the young men of the junior set, who being younger are mostly stronger physically than the seniors. In 1934 a certain Arap Kamwero was employed by me as a maize guard, and one day refused to help a fellow-guard, a Maina, to arrest a man who was caught stealing maize, on the grounds that he was a Nyongi, while the thief, Arap Korir, was a Maina and might retaliate by beating him up. In the subsequent enquiry into Arap Kamwero's action, it was emphasized that it was not customary for elder Nyongi to lay hands on Maina (i.e. for an elder member of the set in power to touch a member of the junior overlapping set), and that in the circumstances he could hardly have done otherwise. I was more impressed by this than I might have been, because Arap Kamwero was disliked by most of the Nandi on the place, and nobody would have troubled to make up a story for the sole purpose of defending him. (A little later, to everybody's amusement, and I fancy to the delight of some, Arap Kamwero himself was caught stealing maize, and paid a short visit to "King George's hotel.")

We must now see how the age-set stratification affects the rules of kinship. We have already noted the facts that (*a*) a man's eldest son normally belongs to the set next but one below his own, and (*b*) younger sons may belong to the set next but two below it; these may be termed (*a*) regular, and (*b*) irregular age-descent, as in the following genealogy:

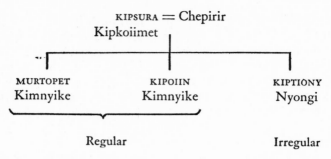

I have said that age-sets tend to cut across the ordinary kinship rules. A man's relatives who are particularly affected in this way are all those whom he calls *tupchet,* that is, his own brothers and his father's brother's sons; and, to a lesser extent, his mother's brother's and father's sister's sons, who are *mama.* These may be of the same age-set as his own, or they may be senior or junior to it, though in many cases he will be of the same age-set as they. In other East African societies both pastoral and agricultural where there are no age-sets, younger boys are generally at the beck and call of the young men and even of the older boys; and so long as they are un-initiated are regarded as vastly inferior by the initiated. Boys have to behave respectfully and unobtrusively in the presence of the men, run errands, and generally make themselves useful when required. Certain duties normally fall to their lot which warriors do not perform unless no boys are available. Among these are the herding of goats and sheep, scaring birds from the growing crops, and odd jobs about the homestead. In the perform-ance of these duties boys take a more or less equal share, though an elder brother will leave as much as he can to a younger. All this is the same in those East African societies which have age-sets. But where brothers belong to two different age-sets (i.e. when there is irregular age-descent), the distinction is sharper when the elder brother has been cir-cumcised. Here the difference of *ipinda* comes out in full; the elder will assert his superiority in every possible way, and the younger is made to feel that he is indeed inferior. Not only must he run errands for his brother, but he will have to listen to him boasting about his cattle, his *ḳamari,*[12] and the herd he will one day possess; he must watch him going with girls, and indulging in a *mureret* of his own. He may—almost cer-tainly will—have to sleep in the *siḳiroinet* while his brother sleeps there with a girl, and will not dare to "steal" her while he is asleep, for she might give him away. By virtue of his age-set seniority the elder will say to the younger while the latter is still uncircumcised: "You are a child, I am a man." In fact, he has to suffer to the full the miseries of a despised junior, and the most he can do to alleviate them is to go away as often as possible, to stay with somebody, or if old enough, to work on a farm though of course in the old days the latter remedy was not available).

Feelings of bitterness may be engendered for a time; but when his turn comes to be circumcised, he soon, in most cases, realizes that no harm has been done to him, and that what he has had to put up with is what many others have been through and survived. This effect of the age-set system is a strong factor in discipline, for it must be obeyed and there is no appeal against it. To it is due, in part, the success of the military discipline which enables a section to make a raid and return with plunder.

Where classificatory brothers, like father's brother's sons, are concerned, the position of a junior is not quite so bad, for he is not in continual contact with them; and it makes little difference whether his mother's brother's sons are of his own or another set, since his relations with them are in any case circumscribed by the mother's brother's status: he is not supposed to sleep in their huts, and they should be avoided rather than sought out. The possibility that he might have a classificatory father (*kwan*) in the person of a brother of his father belonging to a set junior to his own, does not arise, for such a person can belong only to an age-set senior to his own:

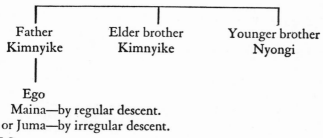

Father
Kimnyike

Elder brother
Kimnyike

Younger brother
Nyongi

Ego
Maina—by regular descent.
or Juma—by irregular descent.

NOTES

[Starred items are recommended as further readings.]

1 [Term used to denote all persons who are bound to a man by descent and marriage and who call each other by relationship terms.]

2 The fifteen-year reckoning may be used for dating events before 1896. Though absolute accuracy cannot be claimed, it furnishes a system of approximate dating for historical traditions which mention age-sets by name, and is something more than a mere guess. E.g. a tradition says that the Juma set was beaten by the Masai, but that the Sawe got the better of them. This story refers to the destruction of the Uasin Gishu Masai, which we know happened not very many years before 1883. It cannot therefore refer to a previous cycle (i.e.

to the eighteenth century), and a date in the middle of the nineteenth century is reasonable because it fits in with what little we do know. I may add that Peristiany considers the fifteen-year interval more reasonable than other estimates. ([Peristiany, J. G., *The Social Institutions of the Kipsigis,** London: Routledge, 1939], p. 31.)

3 *Murenet* = "one who is cut," < *mur,* "cut."

4 From *tete,* a form of greeting, and *ikat,* "greet."

5 A man's *mat* is indicated in the following pages by a number after his age-set: thus, Maina 1 = Chonginiot of Maina; Maina 2 = Kipalkonyot of Maina; Maina 3 = Kiptoiyot (or Tete

katindet) of Maina; and similarly with the other sets.

[6] A specimen of this bush, which belongs to the order Acanthaceae, was identified by Mr. H. M. Gardner, late Conservator of Forests, Kenya, who was good enough to give me the following information: "Certain species of *Mimulopsis* only flower at long intervals, and then gregariously, and die. *Mimulopsis Thomsonii* is said by the Kikuyu to flower in seven or nine years, but I do not think the period is absolutely constant" (Letter dated 16 December 1938). *Setiot* does not grow everywhere in Nandi, and the only place where I have actually seen it is in the forest along the banks of the Pire north of Sangalo. It does, however, grow in some other parts of Nandi.

[7] [Plur. *pororosiek;* land division forming basis of Nandi military regiment.]

[8] [Ritual expert; a diviner and rain-maker who sanctions war and the planting of crops and is thought to have powers of witchcraft.]

[9] I.e. fifteen *pororosiek,* five of which have branches separated from the original area; each branch for public purposes counts as a *pororiet,* so that we have Kapchepkendi, and Kakipoch with four branches each, Tepingot, Kakiptalam, and Kaptumoiis with two each, and ten single *pororiet* areas, which gives a total of twenty-four *pororiet* groups.

[10] [A clan whose men are believed to have powers of witchcraft and who use the threat of bewitching others as a means of terrorizing them.]

[11] [Bachelors' hut of a homestead, where boys and unmarried men sleep.]

[12] An ox with horns of a special shape. See [G. W. B. Huntingford,] *Nandi Work and Culture** [London: H.M.S.O., Colonial Research Studies, 4, 1950], p. 38.

FOR FURTHER READING

Peristiany, J. G., "The Age-Set System of the Pastoral Pokot," *Africa,* 1951, *21,* 188-206. The organization of age-sets of a people in the same geographic area as the Nandi.

Eisenstadt, S. N., "African Age Groups: A Comparative Study," *Africa,* 1954, *24,* 100-112. A general paper comparing the age grouping systems of African societies. Contains a useful bibliography.

Monica Wilson's "Nyakyusa Age-Villages" and Nadel's "Witchcraft in Four Africa Societies: An Essay in Comparison," both in this volume, discuss various features found in some African age-grading systems.

NYAKYUSA AGE-VILLAGES [*][1]

Monica Wilson

Nyakyusa age-villages, with their lifelong separation of generations in different localities, may at first glance seem to represent an extreme in African systems of age grouping. However, the Nyakyusa lack the formalized means, such as circumcision or initiation, that in some African societies structure behavior between groups of different ages. There are only three broad age categories among males: young men and boys, the ruling generation responsible for administration and defense, and old men, who are retired from administrative duties but still perform ritual functions. Rather than moving to and from warriors' barracks or kraals, as among East and South African peoples, Nyakyusa age-sets dwell together from their inception until death and the members bring their wives to their villages to live with them. This arrangement is an expression of two facets of Nyakyusa morality—the necessity for avoidance between fathers and daughters-in-law and the need for close cooperation and friendship among equals. These are backed by supernatural sanctions, discussed in Godfrey Wilson's paper in this volume.

The village is the landholding group. While this is common enough in African societies in which residence units have a kinship basis, it is unusual for groups based on age. Continuity within the larger society is maintained not by inheritance, but rather through the handing down once in each generation of administrative and military leadership from the older to the younger generation and the rearrangement of territorial divisions within the chiefdom to make room for the expanding younger villages. Although Nyakyusa social organization may appear to stress the bonds of association and residence at the expense of those of kinship, kin ties and obligations are also very strong and play an important role in the formation of age-villages.

The Nyakyusa age-village system is a peculiar one. The local unit consists not of a group of kinsmen, as it does in most parts of the world, but of a group of age-mates with their wives and young children. It therefore

* Reprinted with the author's revision from *Journal of the Royal Anthropological Institute*, 1949, 79, 21-25, by permission of the author and publisher.

has some intrinsic interest and its peculiarity raises many theoretical problems.

The Nyakyusa are a Bantu-speaking people living in the Great Rift Valley at the north end of Lake Nyasa. They are cattle owners and cultivators, with elaborate techniques of green manuring and rotation, and unlike most of their neighbors they practice fixed, not shifting cultivation. Well fed and vigorous, they have been an expanding population in a relatively empty country, and at the present time they, together with the contiguous and culturally similar Ngonde people, and small groups absorbed by them, probably number about a quarter of a million. The census returns are far from exact.

The Nyakyusa long remained isolated from the outside world, for their valley is cut off by high mountains and the stormy waters of the north end of the Lake. They were scarcely touched by the slave trade and Europeans first visited the country in 1878, though the Ngonde, whose country is more accessible, had long traded with the Arabs.

Traditionally, the Nyakyusa were divided up into a number of small independent chiefdoms, numbering anything from about 100 to 3,000 married men. They developed no centralized political authority before the coming of the Europeans. The related Ngonde, on the other hand, had a paramount chief, the Kyungu. The reason for the difference in development between these groups turns on their relations with the outside world. The people of Ngonde were sending ivory to the coast and receiving cloth and guns in exchange long before Europeans came to their country. The priest of the main sacred grove of the country controlled this trade, and through his control developed far-reaching secular power, whereas a similar priest among the Nyakyusa developed no such secular power, for they had no trade with the outside world. The Nyakyusa center of worship, Lubaga, was much more inaccessible than Mbande, that of the Ngonde. A similar tendency towards centralization as trade with the coast developed can be traced among some of the neighboring groups also.

The Nyakyusa are patrilineal and patrilocal. Members of agnatic lineages of a depth of three or four generations are bound together by their common interest in the cattle which circulate within and between lineages, and by the supposed mystical interdependence of kin, but kinsmen do not live together. A village consists of a group of age-mates with their wives and young children, while the men of one lineage are scattered through the chiefdom, and may even be in different chiefdoms. Polygyny is the ideal of every pagan, and is achieved by a substantial proportion of the men over 45. In a conservative part of the country nearly a third of the adult men had more than one wife. This is made possible by a gap of ten years or more in the average marriage age of men and women. Except in some wealthy Christian families, men rarely marry before 25, and commonly not until nearer 30, while the girls are betrothed about eight, and go finally to their husbands when they reach puberty. There is an elaborate puberty-marriage ritual for girls, very similar to that of the Bemba, but no circumcision or initiation of men.

Marriage is prohibited between the descendants of a common grandfather, and much disliked between descendants of a common great-grandfather, but there are no clans, or defined exogamous groups.

The age-village starts when a number of herd-boys, about 10 or 11 years old, build together at the edge of their fathers' village. They have been practicing building huts for some time, as small boys in other cultures do also, but when they reach the age of 10 or 11 they actually go to live in their huts, sleeping and spending their spare time in them, though still going to their mothers' huts for meals. A boy should not and does not eat alone, but a group of friends eat together, visiting the mother of each member of their gang in turn. This system is regarded not only as being congenial to small boys (as with us) but also as moral. For the Nyakyusa eating with age-mates is a corner stone of morality, and a boy who comes home alone often to eat is severely scolded.

Moving out of the parent village to sleep is directly connected by the Nyakyusa with decency. They say that a growing boy should not be aware of the sex activities of his parents, *and therefore* he must not sleep at home, even in a separate hut, but in a different village all together. As they put it, "the night is full of lewd talk" and that is all right between equals, but not before people of another generation. Their idea of "mixed company" is not male and female, but fathers and sons.

A boys' village starts quite small, with, perhaps, not more than ten or a dozen members, but it grows as young boys from the fathers' village, or from other men's villages in the neighborhood, become old enough to join it. When the original members are fifteen or sixteen years old the village is usually closed to any further ten-year-olds, who must then start a new village on their own. Conditions vary with the density of population in the neighborhood and other factors, but generally the age-span within a village is not more than about five years, and a village numbers between 20 and 50 members.

The boys who thus establish a village continue to live together through life. When they marry they bring their wives to the village and, when the last of them die, the village dies. As their sons grow up they move out to build villages of their own. Daughters often move out, too, marrying men in other villages, but they may and quite often do marry an age-mate of their father and remain in the village. A village (*ikipanga*) consists of a group of male contemporaries with their dependants, not in a site, and it retains its identity no matter how often it moves.

The men of a village are all of an age and bound together by a common life shared from early youth, but the women in any village are of diverse age and experience. As we have already seen, men usually marry as their first wives girls about ten years younger than themselves, but not all the men of a village marry at the same time, and as they grow older they continue to marry young girls as junior wives. Often the junior wife is a niece—a brother's daughter—of the senior. Moreover, wives are inherited from elder brothers and fathers, so that a man may have some wives older than himself and others who are very much younger.

Once in each generation there is a great ritual at which administrative power and military leadership are handed over by the older generation to the younger. At this ritual there is a new deal in land. The men of the retiring generation move to one side to make room for the expanding villages of the younger generation, but it is not simply a transfer of land from one village of fathers to one of sons; the boundaries within the chiefdom are all redrawn, and the old men move even when there is unoccupied land available for their sons. The only lands excluded from the new deal are the very valuable fields made in the craters of extinct volcanoes, and these are inherited, like cattle, within lineages.

At this ritual, which is called *ubusoka,* "the coming out," each village of young men is formally established on its own land, one of its members is appointed as headman, and its relative status in the hierarchy of villages in the chiefdom is demonstrated. At the same time the two senior sons of the retiring chief are recognized as chiefs, and the old chief's country divided between them. The division does not become absolute until the old man's death, but he was expected to die very soon after the "coming out," and if he did not do so from natural causes he was probably strangled. The Nyakyusa theory is that he died from "the chilling breath" of his people who loved his sons rather than him. The fact that old chiefs do not now die off as they used to do is one of the political problems of the country; power tends to remain in the hands of the older generation much longer than before a European administration was established.

Although chiefdoms were thus divided each generation, they did not necessarily become smaller, because the Nyakyusa were expanding, spreading out in a sparsely inhabited land, and also the conquest and absorption of one small chiefdom by another was constantly going on.

The allocation of land and the selection of a headman for each village of young men is made by the retiring chief, and the headmen of the villages of his generation, who are his advisers and against whose advice he dare not act, since they are believed to have a mystical power over him. Village headmen are always commoners. Sons of chiefs and sons of village headmen of the previous generation are not eligible, for, the Nyakyusa say, if a son of a headman were chosen each generation he would become a chief. The headmen are the leaders of the people, the *commons,* and a contrast is constantly being made between chiefs (*abanyafyale*), on the one hand, and commoners (*amafumu*) on the other. The village headmen are the *amafumu par excellence:* that is, the "great commoners."

At any one time there are three age-grades: that of the old men who are retired from administration but whose leaders have certain ritual functions to perform; that of the ruling generation which is responsible for defense and administration; and that of the young men and boys who have not yet "come out," but who fight when necessary under the leadership of men of their fathers' generation, though in their own age units.

Within each grade are a varying number of villages each composed of near contemporaries. The ages of the men in each grade vary, of course, with the date of the last "coming out" ceremony. Just before such a ceremony the old retired men will all be over 65, while the ruling generation includes those between about 35 and 65; just after such a ceremony everyone over 35 is retired, and those from about 10 to 35 are in office. The youngest members of a generation taking office have at first very little share in public life, but individuals may gain power later, through inheriting the position of an older brother.

The age grouping is somewhat modified by the system of inheritance, under which a man's heir, who is his next younger full brother or, under certain circumstances, a half brother, or his senior son, may take over his homestead and his social personality. An heir, though he be much younger than other men of the village, is treated as one of themselves. Were all heirs to move into the homesteads of their elder brothers and fathers, villages would continue indefinitely, but in fact they do not. Very often the heir chooses to remain in his own village, a member of his own age-set. An heir must move if he succeeds to the office of village headman or priest of the chiefdom, for acceptance of such office is an obligation. It is possible also that movement by inheritance is more common from the junior villages of an age-grade to senior villages of the same grade, than to villages of another grade, but of this I am not certain. Our information on the conditions determining the heir's choice to move or not move is inadequate.

In theory only villages of three generations survive, and we found on analyzing all the villages of the chiefdom we knew best that this was very nearly true in practice. Only one village of the great-grandfathers' generation survived, and it had only eleven members.

The village, then, is the landholding group, its members dividing among themselves the land allocated to their village at the "coming out." The homesteads, each surrounded with bananas, are built compactly in a group, while the main fields are all together on the fringes of the village. Beyond the fields lies the common pasture land. Families each work their own fields and control their own produce, but in cultivating certain crops they must keep in step with their neighbors. Failure to do so is thought to reduce the yield for everyone. Neighbors' cattle are herded together—to herd one's cattle alone is a proud and boastful thing to do—and in any major undertaking such as housebuilding, both neighbors and relatives from other villages cooperate. Traditionally, fellow villagers had certain responsibilities for each other's *torts;* they fought as a group in war and in defense against big game; and they formed and still form a defensive unit against the supposed attacks of witches.

Above all, the village is the group within which "the good life," as the Nyakyusa conceive it, is possible. The good life consists in *ukwangala,* that is, enjoyment of the company of one's equals. The good man is one who is urbane and sociable, a fine debater, a witty raconteur, one who entertains, sharing with his fellows whatever good food or drink he may have, for *ukwangala* requires *ifyakwangalela* . . . the wherewithal for the enjoyment of good company, that is, food and beer. Conversation is held to be the school of law, of logic, and of manners; therefore a man must not keep aloof, or live like a hermit apart in the bush, and he must live with contemporaries rather than kinsmen, since easy communication is limited between men of different generations by the respect required of juniors for their seniors. As for *ukwangala* with women, that is impossible. Women are fit for love-making, not for friendship.

Good fellowship in the village is not merely a pious ideal but a virtue with which at least outward conformity is enforced by fear of witchcraft. The man who does not *ukwangala* but is morose and solitary, or brusque in his manner, or who eats alone, grudging his neighbors a share in the food and beer his wives prepare for him, and one who neglects to provide feasts on certain recognized occasions, is likely either to be accused of practicing witchcraft, or to think himself the victim of it. Witches, the Nyakyusa say, act primarily from the lust for food; they gnaw men inside to assuage their hunger for meat, and steal the milk of cows. But they do not attack indiscriminately; they select as victims those against whom they have a grudge. Moreover, the village, as a group, is believed to defend itself against witchcraft, but only the virtuous are protected. Evildoers are said to be left to the witches, or directly punished by their fellows through a power closely akin to the power of witchcraft.

Witchcraft (*ubulosi*), the Nyakyusa think, is something innate and tangible; it consists in pythons—several of them—in the bellies of men, which are discoverable at an autopsy. Certain individuals are born with it and exercise it for their own nefarious ends. Other individuals have a power called *amanga* which is also innate though not visible at an autopsy, and which is used in defense against witchcraft and to punish wrongdoers. Our Nyakyusa friends made no consistent distinction between the nature of the two types of power, but they were quite clear about the differences in use: witchcraft is used illegally and immorally by individuals, while the power of defense is used to protect the village, or falls upon wrongdoers as the chilling "breath of men," and it is exercised by the village as a whole, under the leadership of the headman. Everyone is agreed that sickness results both from witchcraft and from "the breath of men," but the interpretation of a particular case often varies with the viewpoint of the individual. The sufferer will speak angrily of "the witches," while other people tell one that he neglected to kill a cow when his wife died, or he failed to share some beer which came from his in-laws, or swore at his father, and the neighbors were angry. It is the murmuring of neighbors which brings the "chilling breath" that causes paralysis, or recurrent fever, or some other ill. Public opinion in the village is thus believed to be mystically effective. The disapproval of neighbors spells ill-health.

The first question I asked myself when I began to reflect on this peculiar system was "why age-villages?" Why should the Nyakyusa social structure differ so profoundly from that of any other African people of whom we have evidence? We know far too little about the history of Africa and, I think, will always know too little to offer an answer in such terms as I have offered for the development of a centralized chieftainship in Ngonde and not among the Nyakyusa. According to their own traditions, the chiefs of the Nyakyusa came down in a series of migrations from the Livingstone mountains to the East, about ten generations ago. They found in the valley a people who had not yet discovered the use of fire, but who ate their food raw, and by virtue of their great gift to the aborigines, fire, the invaders became chiefs. (It is a myth which is common enough in Africa.) Some say that the invaders also brought the first cattle. The Kinga who still live on the Livingstone mountains also acknowledge kinship with the Nyakyusa and share with them in a common sacrifice to a supposed common ancestor; but culturally the Kinga are totally different from the Nyakyusa. They live in kinship villages, not age-villages, and have no elaborate age organization, so far as we could discover. The Nyakyusa themselves have no idea whether age-villages came in with the chiefs or were indigenous to the valley, or developed after the conquest. Their myth of origin is not fixed in time, but postulates an invention to meet a social necessity. Once, they say, a certain chief looked upon his son's wife and saw that she was beautiful and said, "she is fit to be a queen (*umwehe*)," and took her; and men thought that very bad and said that henceforth fathers-in-law should never see their daughters-in-law lest they be tempted to commit incest with them, *and so* fathers and sons live in different villages, for if they lived in the same village father-in-law and daughter-in-law would always be seeing one another. In short, the Nyakyusa say that they live in age-villages in order to avoid incest between father-in-law and daughter-in-law.

This myth points us to other questions which we can answer and which, I think, take us further in the understanding of society than any purely chronological answer to my original question, "why age-villages?" I asked myself next: "how does the Nyakyusa system of age-villages really differ from the age organizations of other African people?" and: "what other peculiarities of Nyakyusa society are there which may be connected with age-villages?"

Division of functions between successive generations is, of course, common enough. The great "coming out" ritual of the Nyakyusa, with the transfer of power from one generation to another, is in no way unique, but is typical of many East African peoples, the Nyakyusa form being particularly close to that of the Chaga, who have the same combination of chieftainship and age-organization, and among whom also the functions of defense and administration are undertaken by the same, the ruling generation.

The peculiarity of the Nyakyusa organization consists in the fact that men of an age-set continue to live together in one village after marriage, bringing their wives to the village of the age-set. Warrior villages or barracks exist (or existed) among the Masai, the Zulu, and the Swazi. The cattle posts of the Tswana and Pedi, and the club houses of the Kipisigis and Kikuyu also provided social centers and sleeping quarters for age-sets as yet unmarried, but so far as we know only the Nyakyusa bring their wives to the living quarters of the age-set. Masai, Zulu, Swazi, Tswana and Pedi all establish their wives in the villages of agnatic kin. (I say as far as we know, for another age-village organization may well turn up elsewhere in Africa.) It is possible also that the Nyakyusa are the only people who forbid a grown son to sleep in his father's homestead at any time. The Zulu, Swazi, Tswana and Pedi all permit warriors to sleep at home when not on duty in barracks or cattle post. Of the Masai practice I am uncertain.

This life-long territorial segregation of the generations is, as we have seen, connected by the Nyakyusa themselves with decency in sex life. For them morality consists first in the separation of the sexual activities of successive generations, and, secondly, in close friendship and cooperation with equals. The feeling that the sex activities of parents and children should be kept quite separate is, of course, very common—perhaps universal. We can see it in our own society, and it appears in one form or another in most, if not all, the East and Central African groups of which we have knowledge. Adolescent children sleep apart from their parents; avoidance taboos limit familiarity between father and daughter-in-law, and so on. The Nyakyusa peculiarity lies in the extreme to which this separation is pushed.

Why should they go to such extremes? I have no complete answer to this question but one or two points are relevant. First, the Nyakyusa have no male circumcision or initiation, no formal recognition of the sexual maturity of males; therefore, any young man past puberty is a potential

mate for a woman of his own age. Where circumcision is customary no
male who has not yet been initiated is regarded as adult and a grown
woman scorns him as a mate even in extramarital relations. Therefore,
among the Nyakyusa grown sons are potential lovers of their fathers'
junior wives, some of whom will be of their own age or younger;
whereas among the Chaga and other East African groups who practice
circumcision they are not acceptable to women until they have been initiated. Secondly, the marriage age of men is late and that of girls very
young, so that there are many bachelors and very few girls available to
them. At the same time the polygyny rate is high and most polygynists
are middle-aged or elderly, so there are many young wives of polygynists
who are bored with their aging husbands. Thirdly, the Nyakyusa permit the inheritance of a father's widow by his sons, a practice regarded as
improper by certain other peoples who practice the levirate. A son is required to treat all his father's wives as mothers while his father and fathers' full brothers are alive, and sex relations with a father's wife are
treated as a heinous offense, but after the death of the father and his full
brothers these same women become wives of their former "sons," with the
limitation that a man cannot inherit his own mother or her kinswoman.
It is scarcely surprising, therefore, that the seduction of the young wives of
an aging father is a common theme for scandal, and that a father's jealous
fears are matched by those of his son.

I argue that there is a connection between the existence of age-villages
and the fear of incest between step-son and step-mother on the one hand,
and between father-in-law and daughter-in-law on the other, and suggest that certain features of the Nyakyusa social system facilitate incest
of the first type, and so increase fear of incest of the second type. Fathers drive their adolescent sons out of their village lest they make love
to their mothers, and the sons reciprocate, insisting that when they do
marry they should continue to live apart lest their fathers seduce their
wives. The incest theme elaborated in one fashion among people organized in clans, and practicing clan exogamy, and in another among people
practicing brother-sister avoidance, finds yet a different expression in age-
villages, of which the overt purpose is the separation of sons and
mothers, of fathers-in-law and daughters-in-law.

The constant emphasis on the importance of *ukwangala*—good fellowship with contemporaries—is both an expression and a condition of
the age-village organization. Kinship bonds are strong; wealth in cattle
depends upon cooperation with kinsmen and good health is believed to
be dependent on such cooperation also; but the good life, as the Nyakyusa define it, can only be achieved in the age-village which cuts across
kinship connections. The fear of witchcraft and "the breath of men"
compels generosity and conformity with public opinion in the village and
creates a sense of mutual dependence between neighbors. It is my con-

tention that the peculiar form of witch beliefs among the Nyakyusa, with the emphasis on lust for meat as a main incentive to witchcraft, the belief in the defensive power of the village headman and other men in the village, and the fear of "the breath of men," an innate power exercised by a village group to punish a member who has done wrong, is directly related to the age-village organization.

NOTE

[1] The material on which this paper is based was collected by my late husband, Godfrey Wilson, and myself, between 1934 and 1938. He was then a Fellow of the Rockefeller Foundation and I of the International African Institute.—M. W.

FOR FURTHER READING

Wilson, Godfrey, "The Nyakyusa of South-western Tanganyika," in Colson, Elizabeth, and Gluckman, Max (eds.), *Seven Tribes of British Central Africa,* London: Oxford University Press on behalf of the Rhodes-Livingstone Institute, 1951, pp. 253-91. A general paper on Nyakyusa environmental setting and social and political organization.

Three books by Monica Wilson deal also with age-villages: *Good Company: A Study of Nyakyusa Age-Villages,* London: Oxford University Press for the International African Institute, 1951; *Rituals of Kinship among the Nyakyusa,* London: Oxford University Press for the International African Institute, 1957; *Communal Rituals of the Nyakyusa,* London: Oxford University Press for the International African Institute, 1959.

Other references on social groupings based on age categories are given in the suggested further readings for Huntingford's paper, "Nandi Age-Sets," pp. 214-26 above.

THE PATTERN OF RESIDENCE AMONG THE LELE [*][1]

Mary Douglas

The Lele of the Kasai district live in villages scattered over an area of low population density. Their dispersed matrilineal clans are loosely organized and lack internal differentiation and a well-developed system of authority. In the eyes of the Lele, a village is a cluster of local sections of matrilineal clans, with a constant movement of population between villages because of marriage or following alleged sorcery. The instability of village populations is increased by the practice of shifting cultivation.

In her analysis of Lele village structure, Douglas examines the common types of motivation for migration, such as rights in land or affiliation with a strong leader, and finds them insignificant, the answer lying, rather, in an unusual combination of a system of blood debts for sorcery and various types of rights over women. Here, in her description of a clan section as a "woman-owning corporation," we have another example of corporately held rights that are more commonly found in terms of resources such as land or livestock. Yet when the problem is stated in terms of the grouping of kinsmen so as to exploit their common "property," a seemingly bizarre form of social organization becomes meaningful.

The total population of the Lele is about 26,000. For the most part they live in a clearly demarcated region, bounded on the east and north by the river Kasai, and on the west by the Loange. It is about 180 kilometers long from north to south and about 100 kilometers in the broadest part. The density is now about 3.5 to the square kilometer,[2] but a large proportion of the present population consists of Luba, Cokwe, and other tribesmen of relatively recent entry into the area. Fifty years ago, when the Lele were the main inhabitants, the density cannot have been more than two to the square kilometer.

The district includes three autonomous Lele chiefdoms, each under the rule of member of the same chiefly clan. The doyen of these chief-

* Reprinted from *Zaïre, revue congolaise*, 1957, *11*, 819-43, by permission of the author and publisher.

doms, and the most highly organized politically, is the Kumb Ngomam-bulu, situated between the Lumbundji and the Kasai Rivers. West of it is the Kumb Yamba, and south of these the Kumb Shet. I worked mainly in the western chiefdom, and what I have to say must be taken to apply to the western Lele.

The percentage of foreign tribesmen in the western chiefdom is much less than in the east and south. It has a population of about 10,000 Lele, living in 56 compact villages. The average population per village is 190; the average male population about 50. In practice the size of villages ranges between 10 to 130 men. In spite of low density and a changing population, the Lele villages are coherent and compact units. It is interesting to ask what factors combine to bring their members together, where they come from, and why they stay together and cooperate as effectively as they do.

RECRUITMENT OF YOUNG MEN TO VILLAGES

Lele are born into matrilineal clans. As they practice virilocal marriage there is a constant tendency towards dispersal of clan members. This is partially offset by a movement of young men away from their natal villages towards one of the villages where others of their own clan reside. A young man deciding to leave the village where he was born is theoretically free to go anywhere he likes. His choice is not determined by specific rights to inherit or succeed. There will be several villages where fellow-clansmen of his reside. Which of them he joins depends on personal factors such as the quality of the reciprocal relations he has built up with them in the past. It is important to emphasize this freedom of choice, or rather the lack of specific determinants of residence, because it has several effects on relations within the village.

Any village wishes to expand its membership, for size gives it a competitive advantage in inter-village politics. Every clan section living in a village wishes also to increase its numbers, as size is an advantage in interclan politics. Furthermore, since each village is liable to lose its rising generation of men to other villages, if it should fail to recruit young men, the balance of generations would be threatened.

This possibility is openly recognized. Bystanders urge disputants to compose their differences, lest quarrelsomeness give the village a bad name and keep away young men who might be thinking of joining it. Leaving aside the wish for continuity, one can see that a village of old men is obviously not viable.

It follows that it is to the general interest that newcomers should be welcomed, even canvassed, from all quarters. A distantly related clansman who is regarded as a prospective recruit to the local clan section is not made aware of any difference in his status in the clan compared with clansfellows more closely related to the actual residents. It is re-garded as an offense against clan solidarity to discriminate between clan members on any basis other than age and sex. All senior men are sup-posed to have an equal and like authority over all junior clansmen. The lack of internal differentiation makes for very weak exercise of authority within local clan sections. Equal status for all comers may be a good re-cruiting platform, but it is a poor principle of administration. Not sur-prisingly, the optimum size from the point of view of preserving clan solidarity is very low; as soon as the local clan section numbers more than five or six men, dissensions spoil its unity and factions emerge. There is conflict between the anxiety to recruit members from all direc-tions in which the clan has dispersed (which seems to involve readi-ness to accord equal status regardless of origin), and the practical need for internal differentiation and delegation of authority as soon as the clan section reaches sizeable proportions. The resulting weakness of the authority structure within the clan has far-reaching effects on Lele social organization.[3] To this discussion of population movements, it is relevant to emphasize the ease of securing a welcome in almost any village.

MOVEMENTS OF MEN

Lele say that ideally a man should stay in his father's village, marry a wife there, and support the old man in his last years. The claims that a man can make on his sons are better defined and therefore more easily enforced, than the claims he can make on his sisters' sons. Father-to-son is an entirely individual relationship of superordination of one man over a limited number of junior men. It contrasts with the mother's brother to sister's son relation which is diffuse and ill-defined. A man would be foolish to hope for support in his dotage from his sister's sons, for his claim on their services is no stronger than that of any other of his senior clans-fellows. Therefore, although the Lele clans are based upon matrilineal descent, the father-son relationship is immensely important. It is personal, does not extend to the father's brothers, and ends with the father's death.

When his father dies a man is not only free of obligation to remain in that village, but is likely to feel unwanted there. Fear that the sor-cery which is presumed to have killed his father will be directed against himself is likely to drive him away. The claims of the natal village would generally, in the pre-European days when the age of marriage for men was 35-40, end in this way soon after adolescence. Occasionally a man and his father did not remain on good terms until the end of the latter's lifetime and the son would leave the village earlier.

In any case, there is a well-established tendency for men to leave their natal village sometime before middle age. This can be demonstrated by examining in any village the age-distribution of men born in the village compared with those born away. It is a striking fact that from ¾ to two-thirds of the men of the two senior age-sets (i.e. over 50 years old) in any village, had been born elsewhere than in the village where they were now the most influential and responsible minority. The table below illustrates this trend for the village of Ngoie as I found it in 1949.[4] There, in the over-fifty age groups, only 4 men in a total of 25, that is 16%, were living in the village in which they had been born.

		Born in village	Born away
Total male population, 73	aged 20-30	19 (26 %)	2 (2.7%)
	aged 30-50	8 (10.9%)	19 (26 %)
	aged 50 plus	4 (5.5%)	21 (28.7%)
	Total	31	42

These figures simply illustrate the mobility of the male population, and do not demonstrate the tendency to seek out fellow clansmen and to settle down with them. [In] the distribution of men of different ages through the component clans of a village . . . the general trend is for the two senior-age-groups to be concentrated in 3 or 4 clans and the middle and junior sets to spread through a much wider range of clan membership.[5] The juniors, born in the village by virilocal marriages, can be expected, at some stage after the age of 20, to go away in order to live with their senior clansmen elsewhere.

* * *

The village of Ngoie is a particularly clear example of this general trend: there 23 of the 25 oldest men belong to two clans; the thirteen men of the middle age set include 9 from these 2 clans and 4 from 4 different clans. In other words, the 2 senior age sets, although mostly recruited from different villages, are nearly clan-homogeneous, while the junior sets are clan-heterogeneous. For such a general pattern of age and clan composition to be apparent, there must presumably be forces at work which send young men away from their natal villages and draw them to other villages where small groups of their elder clansmen have in similar circumstances come to reside.

The fact that there is a fairly constant representation of older men of certain clans in each village shows that the process is not a haphazard moving around, but a general reshuffle of the male population which produces, among men of middle age, a settlement pattern more in accordance with clan affiliation.

It is worth recalling the pattern of residence of the tribes of the

Lower Congo, the Mayombe and Kongo, where marriage is also virilocal and succession matrilineal. Here the custom is to send children, at the age of 10, to their maternal uncles, the boys to live with them and eventually to suceed to status and palmgroves, and the girls to be married under the maternal uncle's auspices. This system produces a much higher degree of consistency between residence and clan affiliation than the Lele system, for evidently at one time the local corporate male matrilineage was the core of the village.[6] The Lele pattern bears only a faint, imperfect resemblance to this. About three-quarters of Lele men go, at some time or another, to live with their clansmen in one village or another where they may be found, but the movements of women follow different principles altogether.

MOVEMENTS OF WOMEN

Lele say that a woman has no village. This signifies that it is possible for a woman never to reside in and never to have close ties with the village which is the focus of return of her clansfellows. She is born in her father's village, where her mother came at marriage, and she goes to live in her husband's village. She may perhaps never live, except in elderly widowhood, in the village where her mother's brothers, and sons and daughter's sons tend to congregate.[7] In this sense a woman is never a member of a village in the same way as a man, but a woman does not consider that she has no village. Childhood associations and the strongest ties of affection bind her to the village where she was born, and marriage does not break the tie. At each pregnancy her mother comes to help her, and after the birth of each child she goes back with her mother to receive care in her own natal village. If later her child dies, she goes back there to mourn, for six months or more. If she can arrange that a daughter of hers marries a man of that village, she makes no secret of the pleasure it will give her to go there as his mother-in-law, helping at the delivery of her daughter's children, and looking after them in infancy.

The rule of preferred marriage favors this interest of women to see their daughters married to men in their own natal villages, for the man who has a high claim to marry a girl is her own mother's father. Theoretically he can take his daughter's daughter and marry her himself. In practice he usually uses this privilege of a grandfather to allocate his daughter's daughter to any man who may be identified with himself, that is to one of his brothers, or to one of his sister's daughter's sons. The privilege is accorded as an act of gratitude by his wife's clan for his fathering children for them. For him it is a means of extending his influence in his own clan. Thus it is an important factor in producing the

movement of young men away from their natal villages, as the allocation of a wife is one of the primary interests which they pursue when
they join their maternal clansmen, as I shall show later.

This preferred marriage of a girl into her mother's father's clan is
also a factor, though not always a very effective one, in producing a regular movement of women between the village of birth, and the village of
their mother's birth. If no other factors intervened to disturb the pattern
of residence set up in this way, the movements of men and women
could be diagrammatically represented thus:

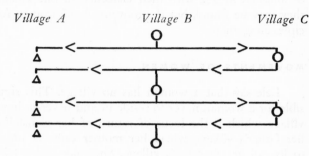

Village A *Village B* *Village C*

In this scheme the residence of matrilineal descendants of one
woman are shown. Women who are born in village B marry and have
their children in village C where their mothers were born; and women
born in village C marry and have their children in village B. Men,
whether born in B or C, go to reside in village A, the village in which
their own senior clansmen have been congregating for generations past.
This pattern would only hold good if marriages were very stable, and if
no other influences affected the marriages of girls. It seems to be valid
for roughly three-quarters of the male population, and for considerably
less of the women, since numerous other influences affect the disposal
of a woman in marriage. A woman may be paid in blood compensation,
or be abducted, or run away. Or again, a woman whose husband is sick,
may follow him in his peregrinations for medical treatment or escaping
from sorcery, and her children may be reared in several different villages.

MOVEMENT DUE TO ILLNESS

The reaction to illness and misfortune accounts for many individual changes of residence. Most illness is supposed to be caused by sorcery,
and if it fails to yield to treatment, it is best cured by moving out of the
range of the suspected sorcerer.

Since sorcery is held to have a strictly local influence, a man who
falls ill is advised to move; if he is living with his clansmen, he escapes
back to the village of his father; if he has not yet left that village, the sick-

ness provides a powerful incentive to go off and join his fellow clansmen. In every case, the commiseration of friends from other villages is invariably expressed as dark warnings that he may die if he stays where he is, and as invitations to recover and enjoy good health in their village. Illness of distant kinsfolk is a normal occasion for canvassing new recruits to a village. Prolonged illness or an epidemic in a village is always regarded as bad for recruitment. People tend to watch their own and their children's health and to attribute any deterioration to a lack of goodwill in the village of actual residence. An intelligent person is supposed to know which villages suit his health and which do not. There is nothing mysterious or undefined in a man's idea of a "good village" for himself,[8] for it is based directly on his estimate of the goodwill he can draw on, and the record of good health he has enjoyed there.

The normal movements following sickness are between father's and clansmen's village, and it remains within these bounds unless the illness becomes chronic. Then it may be varied with experiments in living with affines, or with the mother's father's village, or with other groups of clansmen in more distant parts. Sorcery beliefs themselves set limits to these movements. A sick man will be chary of arriving amongst clansmen to whom he is himself personally unknown, and where he has no powerful friend. The old sorcerers of each clan are thought of as running up debts, with sorcerers of other clans, in their bargaining and counterbargaining. They are believed to hesitate to sacrifice their favorite nephews, and the arrival of a sickly and almost unknown clansman may give them just the occasion they have been seeking, for polishing off old scores. For this reason man naturally likes to be sure of his welcome before he goes to join a distant clansman.

FIELDS OF INTERMARRIAGE

I have shown that the majority of men are born away from the village in which they finally settle. Most of them do not come from very far away. It follows that women do not go to be married in very distant villages. Each village lies in a kind of "field of intermarriage," whose area restricts more than anything else the total range of movement open to individuals changing their residence for one reason or another.

Distance, far or near, is not a simple matter of geography and the field of intermarriage has social as well as physical boundaries. Lele villages are grouped in "families": every village acknowledges two, three or more brother villages which have split off like itself from a parent village. The process of shifting cultivation may have set them very far apart, but they continue to recall their common origin and to make it the basis of political alliance. Thus the Lele have a variant form of the "perpetual relationship" which has been described in other parts of Central

Africa.[9] Theirs is a political association of villages which is described in the kinship idiom. Brother villages do not attack each other; give each other military succor, ritual aid, and arrange other advantages so that their common origin may be an effective basis of cooperation. For any one village, its field of intermarriage includes the other members of its "family" of related villages, together with one or two other villages in close proximity with which alliances have been long established. Villages of rival clusters only intermarry as a rule when a woman has been paid over in blood compensation, from one to the other, and often these marriages, if ill will exists, fail to give rise to the return of a bride, back and forth in each generation (which is the normal procedure consistent with the preferred marriage of a girl into her mother's father's clan described above).

As considerations of geographical proximity affect it to some degree, the field of intermarriage tends to be slightly different for each village in a given "family." [10] . . . the field of intermarriage for South Homb . . . includes Bushongo, which has long been a neighbor, and also Mbombe, far to the south. It excludes markedly the two neighboring but rival villages of Hanga. If we take the three Homb villages together with Bushongo, we find that 74% of the adult men and women of South Homb were born in one of these four villages. Bushongo does not intermarry with any other of the Homb "family" of villages, nor with Mbombe, but it does so regularly with the Hanga and Bwawa "families." Mbombe, in addition to nearby villages, has an old series of marriage exchanges with the other villages, of the Mbombe "family" 90 kilometers to the north. North Homb has scarcely any intermarriage with its nearest neighbors, the Kabamba villages, but intermarries with the Mikope villages, and Yundu to the north, as well as with other Homb villages.

To some extent the social and geographical factors which created these fields of intermarriage are now blurred by administrative action. The Kabamba villages used to be near the Lumbunji, North Homb was near the Loange, and they had different spheres of intercourse. But it is significant that 20 years of geographical proximity since they were brought near the road in 1935 have done nothing to end the social isolation of the Kabamba villages from North Homb. Hanga was also presumably further away from South Homb than it is now, but near enough for the two villages to share a common history of mutual raiding and counterraiding long before the European occupation, and still they do not intermarry. We can conclude that the pattern of intermarriage in the past was much the same as today, except that in the past a greater physical distance separated those villages which preserve the custom of not intermarrying.

The main movements of population took place, as they still do, within limits prescribed partly by alliances with brother villages, and with some other villages whom the hazards of shifting brought so near that it was prudent to conclude alliances with them. When Simpson and Torday recorded that the Lele seemed not to know the path to the nearest village to their own, and armed as if for war when obliged to carry loads thither,[11] they show that even fifty years ago the nearest villages were not necessarily the friendliest to each other.

FACTORS INFLUENCING MOVEMENTS

I have now shown that each village sets up a kind of "field of force," to attract young men from other villages within a limited social and geographical range. The attraction is deliberately exercised, and the constant propaganda against other villages and in favor of one's own creates part of the political atmosphere and provides some motivation for the moves.

NEGATIVE ROLE OF HEADMAN

Men do not join a village because of their kinship with the headman. His office is not strictly hereditary, although it is often vested in one or two clans. It is an honorary position, held by the oldest man of the village. No ritual, administrative, judicial or political duties are expected of him, except to act occasionally as a spokesman in external relations on the rare occasions when no special functionary is *ex officio* deputed to represent the village. He is no more than titular head of the village. Men of his own clan may claim to have joined the village because of their relationship to the village headman, but more often a more vigorous and younger man of the clan will be named, for the headman is in no sense pivotal to village organization in the manner of so many tribes of Rhodesia and Nyasaland.[12] The size of a village does not wax and wane with the administrative ability of its current headman, nor tend to disintegrate at his death. Most people living in the village would be able to find some appropriate kinship term with which to address the headman, but only his immediate family and sisters' sons could trace direct kinship links to him.

A poor memory and lack of interest in genealogical relations is characteristic of Lele kinship attitudes, and is undoubtedly consistent with the settlement pattern of dispersal and recongregation described above. Few adults can name even their matrilineal relatives in the span of 3 ascending generations. There is the convention that it is unmannerly to enquire too closely into the antecedents of kinsfolk and clansmen, and polite to accept kinship terms of address at their face value. My attempts to produce a genealogical chart of relationships within a village were frustrated at each attempt, and when occasionally I found a well-informed man or woman, much embarrassment would follow my too tenacious uncovering of inconsistencies and confusions in their statements. The one inescapable impression was a negative one: if the personality of the headman played any role in recruiting men to the village it would have emerged, but it did not.

Direct questions gave me no general clue to the motives of men who had joined the village I knew best. Some had come to escape from sorcery; others to escape from accusations of sorcery; some came as children when their widowed mothers brought them to live under the protection of a maternal uncle; others came to join their sister. There seemed to be no general pattern underlying their behavior. As often happens, undirected gossip was more instructive than systematic questioning. I found that a number of men took pride in having caused younger men, not always of their own clan, to join the village. "When I came, he followed me," is the usual phrase. Or, "I told him to build here, and I gave him a wife to put in his house." Or a man recounting his life history will generally mention enclaves of his fellow clansmen in other villages whom he visited, and who pressed him to settle with them. "Stay, build your house here, and we will give you a wife." The allocation of a wife as an inducement to settle is something I shall have more to write about later. The positive impression which emerges from a study of individual case histories is that a man who changes his residence thinks of joining, not so much a village as a local section of a clan in that village. Most usually it will be his own clan, but he may be accepted in the village as a son or grandchild of one of its local clan sections. In other words, it is important to realize that the Lele do not think of the village as an unstructured collection of kinsfolk, but as a whole whose component units are local sections of matrilineal clans.

FOUNDING CLANS

The next point of interest is the permanence of a local clan section's association with the village in which it is found. The first enquiry about the clan composition of a village is almost always answered by the names of two, three or four clans, but later investigation always reveals the long established presence of men of several other clans. Certain clans are supposed to have been represented in the village since its foundation. They are called *malunji mahin* or *mbanjabola*, "ground clans," which I translate roughly as founding clans. Their members have a higher status in the village than stranger clans of later origin, but it is hard to point out definite advantages which this superior status confers.

The distinction between original clans and strangers is commonly made the basis of social distinctions in this region. Among the Kele, on the right bank of the Kasai, the descendants of the original clans in a village, the *mimbangata*, have privileges and political duties ascribed to them (e.g. election of the village head, rights to parts of game killed), from which descendants of strangers are excluded.

Among the Lele the pattern is slightly different. I have said that the post of village headman is not hereditary, but is based on seniority in years. In practice the choice is limited to the oldest men of the founding clans of the village, one clan often having some precedence over the others. Other privileges and responsibilities are reserved to members of founding clans. For example, each of the four corner huts of a village should be occupied by a man of a founding clan. The corner huts have ceremonial significance. When the Chief visits the village, he should be carried in procession to each of the four corner huts and receive a tribute of raffia cloth from the occupants. The same procedure is followed when an animal symbolizing chiefship is killed. The carcass, slung on a pole should be carried round to each corner hut, and the hunter rewarded by a gift of raffia cloth. Similarly, in the cult of the pangolin, the dead pangolin is carried round the village, with halts and songs at each corner hut. More important than this ceremonial privilege, membership of the pangolin cult,[13] is reserved exclusively to men who are themselves members of founding clans of the village, and who have married a wife from a founding clan, and have begotten two children by that wife.

It is difficult to assess the power of these privileges as incentives drawing young men to live where their own clan is associated with the foundation of a village. No one would normally calculate on his chance of becoming village headman, since that honor tends to be bestowed at a nearly senile stage, when personal ambition is dimmed by anxiety over gradual loss of physical functions. Nor is a young man likely to think it an inducement that he may be a candidate for the pangolin cult in one village and not in another. The highly ambivalent attitude to cult officials, because of their alleged powers of sorcery, often makes it difficult to recruit candidates for initiation. As for the privilege of inhabiting a corner house, this is more a responsibility than a pleasure. It is thought to be a particularly vulnerable position for attack by outside sorcerers, and if the occupant is a member of a founding clan he can rely on more support from cult officials in his own clan in counteracting the danger to the village.

The fact that membership of the founding clans offers young men certain roles which they can play in one village and not in another has to be discounted as a serious motive for moving to the village founded by one's clansmen. Much more attractive is the expectation of protection from kinsmen in influential roles, and also the excitement and interest of living near the hub of village affairs, instead of always at the periphery as one is likely to be in a village in which one's own clan is a stranger. There is some prestige to be derived merely from being a responsible member of the community. I heard a sick woman, whose sister in the next village was persuading her to go there, emphatically declare that, if it cost her her life, she would never leave the village where she was *"mwanambanj"* child of the foundation.

Under their haphazard system of recruitment, it is inevitable that the time-honored association of its founding clans with a village was sometimes broken. When this happened the connection tended to be forgotten, and so no affront to their sense of local continuity was brought by its absence from the village. It was difficult to hear of such cases, and I only recorded one.

Lele believe that evil might befall a village which lost its association with its founding clans. I knew three cases of villages which acted deliberately to keep at least one representative of a founding clan which was in danger of disappearing from the village population. In one case, Ngoie, the post of village spokesman, generally elective, was turned into a semihereditary post, and a man of the clan in question imported to fill it. In the other, South Homb, a young man of Bulomani clan had to be persuaded to stay in the village, away from his other senior clansmen, and though he already had two wives, a third was found for him as an inducement to stay. In such cases, the young man acquires much more prestige than his age-mates, and his interest in accepting the invitation is obvious. More usually the attempt to keep up the membership of a founding clan in a village is made by establishing a woman, not a man, there. In the third case I noted, the Ndong clan of South Homb was dying out there three generations ago, but a marriage was arranged between the mother's mother of the present clan elder, and a man of the Lubello clan, and the Ndong descended from her are now a well-established clan section in the village. . . .

It is rare for one of the founding clans to constitute a majority of the village population, but the sum of all the founding clans does usually outnumber the members of other stranger clans living there.

NUMBER OF FOUNDING CLANS REPRESENTED BY ADULT MALES IN A VILLAGE, AND PROPORTION OF FOUNDING CLANS TO TOTAL MALE POPULATION

Village	Total Males	No. of founding clans	No. of other clans repres. by adult males	Men of each founding clan	Total
N. Kabamba	25	3	2	6, 5, 9	20 (80%)
S. Kabamba	30	3	6	4, 5, 13	22 (73%)
N. Homb	43	3	8	9, 16, 4	29 (67%)
M. Homb	29	3	3	9, 6, 8	23 (79%)
S. Homb	35	4	3	11, 9, 4, 2	26 (74%)

There is no exact correlation between the scatter of founding clans through the villages, and the political grouping of the villages. One village, which honors a certain clan as one of its founders, may harbor a tradition of enmity with another village which also honors the same founding clan. The convention is that if fighting should break out between the two villages, men of the same clan try not to kill each other, and if by mischance they should recognize a fellow clansman in a fallen enemy, they refrain from mutilating his body. A clan may be known by one name in one family of villages, and by another in a rival family, though for clan members this does not disguise their mutual obligations. For example, the Lumbunji clan, a founding clan in both Middle Homb and in Kabamba, was known in Kabamba as the Lembe clan; the Bwenga clan, founding clan in South Homb, was founding clan under the name of Kom in Mbombe. . . .[14]

LOCAL CLAN SECTIONS NOT THE UNITS OF PRODUCTION

The whole discussion so far has underlined the importance of local sections of matrilineal clans as component parts of the villages. One should ask therefore what roles the individual expects to be able to play through his membership of his local clan section. Certain negative conclusions can be stated at the outset.

Lele economy is deeply influenced by the lack of fixed productive capital. Throughout their economy it is true to say that a man's labor has more value than any fixed assets he may have title to. Territorial rights are vested in villages, and an individual's right to use land is based on his residence in a village. New forest land is cleared every year for the maize crop, and it is not so much allocated to individuals but chosen in a very informal way. Lele are not conscious of land shortage, and disputes about land do not occur. The only exceptions are the fishing ponds of women, which tend to be passed down from mother to daughter, or granddaughter, but as these have a very indirect influence on the building up of the corporate male clan sections, they need not be further considered here. Entitlement to material goods (land or houses or anything else), cannot be taken to explain the congregation of local clan sections in a village.

In this the Lele contrast with the tribes of the Lower Congo, whose settlement pattern theirs resembles. The Kongo and Mayombe live on more fertile land, at a greater density of population, have a more diversified economy, and exploit the eliais palm.[15] In consequence they have two kinds of fixed capital assets which the Lele have not: land, and oil palm groves. It is not difficult to understand the return of young Kongo clansmen to their ancestral village as a response to economic pressure. Lele exploit the raffia palm just as intensively as the Kongo were reported to be exploiting the oil palm in the 1580's.[16] But there is a crucial difference in the effects on the economy of the two types of cultivation. The raffia palm is cultivated for its fronds, fibres and sap for wine, but not for its fruit. Drawing wine kills the palm, and under the Lele system the average life of a cultivated raffia palm should be only about five years. Once it has fruited it is too late to draw wine from it, and the palm is valueless. The same might be true of the oil palm if it were cultivated for wine, but if it is cultivated for oil it may be yielding for up to 100 years.[17] There is no need to press further here the difference between the economy of the Lele and that of the lower Congo tribes. It suffices to emphasize that economic factors which account for the settlement pattern among the lower Congo tribes cannot be used as an explanation of a fairly similar pattern among the Lele. There are fixed capital assets in the Lower Congo region which are absent in the Lele economy.

In some economies the development of unilineal descent groups may be accounted for by the need for a large permanent unit of cooperation for subsistence.[18] Among the Lele this does not account for the cohesion of the local clan section. Men's activities are hunting, exploiting the raffia palm, heavy annual clearing of forest for maize, oil-nut gathering, house-building, and preparing tools and weapons for all these. The clan section provides the cooperating unit for none of these activities. The communal hunt is organized on an all-village basis, and all other hunting is individual.[19] Raffia palms are planted, owned and exploited by individuals. For forest-clearing and house-building and repairing a man relies on the help of age-mates and affines more than for fellow-clansmen, and for his other tasks he works alone. The clan section is not a labor unit.

For certain staple commodities it is also true that it is not either a consuming unit. A man clears a field for each of his wives, and she stores the crops in her granary. When she cooks she sends separate baskets for her husband and sons, for each to share with his age-mates. Only if one of her clansmen, or one of her husband's clansmen is temporarily wifeless will she send food to them individually. Unmarried men pool the contributions of their mothers to eat together with their age-mates. Palm-wine, when drawn, is carried every evening to a meeting place outside the village, where all the men, young and old, can go without special invitation, to have a drink and gossip. Then the drawers of wine carry it into the village and further distribution follows individual lines of kinship on the same pattern as the distribution of meat: wife, in-laws, father and father's sister are as important as matrilineal kinsfolk.

ADVANTAGES OF CLAN MEMBERSHIP

There are, however, certain facilities which clansmen are supposed to accord to each other. A diviner is bound to give free consultation and medical treatment to his own clansmen. This is a material benefit, but not so important as to account for the interest men have in residing near their own clansmen.

A man who has to raise a large sum of raffia cloth to pay for fees or fines, can ask for contributions from fellow clansmen on a reciprocal basis. This is theoretically much more important than anything discussed so far as an incentive to congregating together. Large sums of 50 to 100 raffia cloths can be quickly raised in a big local clan section, but conversely, the more numerous the clansmen, the more frequent such general levies are likely to be, and an individual may be better off in a smaller section. Furthermore, in a large clan section, the fissiparous tendencies are given fuller rein by the weakness of the authority structure. A man living in a large clan section at any given time is likely to be so embroiled in factional disputes that he is able to count on financial assistance from only a small proportion of his coresident clan-fellows. For this reason men often say that they prefer to live with a smaller section of their clan. As raffia cloths can also be raised on the strength of paternal and affinal relationships, the need for help in raising large sums of raffia cloth does not explain the cohesion of clansmen. However, the possibility of easy credit is not to be neglected as a factor contributing to the congregation of clansmen together.

More effective than these interests, is the expectation of obtaining a wife through the good offices of a senior clansman. The local clan section can be regarded as a woman-owning corporation, in which clan-members have nominally equal rights in the allocation of wives. The women, who may be described as constituting a common heritage of the local clan-section, are the wives and widows of members; their daughters' daughters (in accordance with the rule of preferred marriage); women acquired as payment for blood compensation, and female matrilineal descendants of the latter.

Much swopping of wives back and forth between living members of a given clan takes place. Widows are inherited by the local clan-section as a whole, and allocated to individual men by general consent, on a combination of the principles of seniority and need, and respect for the widow's wishes, and for incest regulations. Daughter's daughters of clansmen are similarly allocated, but it is a common cause of dispute whether the girl's mother's father, or the senior men of the clan-section, should have the final vote in bestowing her. According to the institution of *bukolomo,* responsibility for any death must be settled by transfer of rights over a woman and all her matrilineal progeny. The clansmen of the victim become owners in a system of clientship, whose chief advantages to themselves are that they can use their rights over the females of another clan to consolidate their own local descent groups. They can attract young men by the promise of wives, and they need not divert the marriages of their own clanswomen but can use their rights over female clients, to settle their own blood debts.

The effect of this institution is very far-reaching and can only be outlined here. It gives young men scattered in their villages of birth a lively interest in joining the main sections of their clans. Any man at any time is liable to be accused of sorcery and charged with a blood debt. His father can do nothing to settle it for him, as it is regarded as a matter concerning the clan of the victim and the clan of the accused. If the accused is not living under the protection of his senior clansmen he can neither rebut the charge, nor settle the debt by transferring rights over a female client of his clan. He may have to stand by, helpless, while his sister is taken by force in compensation. If this happens, a large part of his own future autonomy as a maternal uncle and clan section elder is threatened. His sister's sons will be born into clientage. If his maternal uncles will negotiate with his accusers, they may query the whole charge against him, by consulting their own oracles, or they may bring up ancient, half-buried countercharges against his accusers; they may even be prepared to rouse the whole village to fight if the quarrel ranges them on lines of hereditary rivalry. If they do none of these things, he can at least expect them to negotiate the transfer of rights over one of their client women to settle the matter. Such negotiations provide the whole context of interclan politics, and it is in this context that sheer numbers is ultimately an advantage to each local clan section. The small clan section, living in isolation from its fellow clansmen, is likely to be intimidated and cheated in dealings with its rivals; all its women will be taken into clientship, its men born to roles of undistinguished dependence, because in the long run such disputes are settled by force.

In the rivalry of the generations a balance is struck, since in the context of interclan relations, young and old are mutually dependent. The young have to accept their own delayed maturity and the hegemony of the old men, because they cannot act without them in interclan disputes. The old do not refuse to help the young men, because in interclan disputes they cannot be effective without the advantage of numbers, and they want the young men to take up residence with them.

The *bukolomo* system of blood compensation is probably the most important reason for the growth of the local clan sections. But it is only one of the institutions which make it true to say that the clan section is essentially a corporation holding rights in women. Inheritance of widows and rights to daughter's daughters also contribute to this effect. Sociologically speaking, the clan section owns jointly a stock of rights over marriageable women of other clans, and these rights constitute an enduring heritage which, in the development of unilineal descent groups among the Lele plays a role very comparable with the role of a common heritage in land or livestock in other communities.

NOTES

[Starred items are recommended as further readings.]

¹ The Lele inhabit the Kasai district of the Belgian Congo, in the region between the Kasai and Loange rivers. My fieldwork among them was undertaken in 1949-1950 and for a few months in 1953, under the auspices of the International African Institute and of I.R.S.A.C. [l'Institut pour la Recherche Scientifique en Afrique Central].

² The density is taken from P. Gourou, *Atlas général du Congo belge*. In miles it must be 63 at the broadest point by 112 in length, and a present density of 8.9 persons to the square mile.

³ See article prepared for publication on "Age Status among the Lele."

⁴ [A graph based on this table has here been omitted.]

⁵ [A table showing the age-clan composition of the male population of seven villages has here been omitted.]

⁶ Van Wing, *Etudes Bakongo*, 1921, p. 121-263. See also C. M. U. White, "Factors in the Social Organisation of the Luvale," *African Studies*, xiv, 3, 1955; and V. W. Turner, "Spatial Separation of Generations in Ndembu Villages," * *Africa*, xxv, 2, 1955, for descriptions of village structures composed of a core of matrilineally related males whose assembly sometime after boyhood counteracts the dispersing effect of virilocal marriage. These villages are smaller than the Lele type, and are built round a single matrilineal core, instead of several.

⁷ See White, *op. cit.*, for a similar account of the residence of Luvale women.

⁸ Compare I. Cunnison, "Headmanship and the Ritual of Luapula Villages," * *Africa*, xxvi, 1956. [See also pp. 284-302, below.]

⁹ I. Cunnison, *Kinship and Local Organisation in the Luapula Valley*, Communications of the Rhodes-Livingstone Institute, No. 5, 1950, and also C. Mitchell, *The Yao Village*,* 1956, p. 122.

¹⁰ [A sketch map showing this field has here been omitted.]

¹¹ Hilton Simpson, *Lands and Peoples of the Kasai*, 1911, p. 332.

¹² M. Gluckman & al., "The Village Headman in British Central Africa," * *Africa*, xix, 2, April 1949, pp. 89-106.

¹³ M. Douglas, "Animals in Lele Religious Symbolism," *Africa*, xxvii, 1, 1957.

¹⁴ [A table showing the distribution of founding clans in three rival village families has here been omitted.]

¹⁵ Compare Van Wing, *op. cit.*, p. 98 sv., and also P. Gourou, *Atlas Général du Congo belge*.

¹⁶ J. Cuvelier et J. Jadin, *L'ancien Congo d'après les Archives romaines*, 1954, p. 116.

¹⁷ A. H. Unwin, *West African Forests and Forestry*, p. 241.

¹⁸ See Daryll Forde, "The Anthropological Approach in Social Science," *Advancement of Science*, iv, 15, 1947. Also P. M. Worsley, "The Kinship System of the Tallensi," in *Journal of the Royal Anthropological Institute*, Vol. 86, I, 1956.

¹⁹ The fact that the group of males, linked by matrilineal descent, forms a cooperating unit for hunting is the basis of Turner's explanation (*op. cit.*) for the composition of Ndembe villages, but this explanation does not apply to the larger and more complex villages of the Lele.

FOR FURTHER READING

Two other works by the same author deal with factors relating to village residence among the Lele: Douglas, Mary, "The Lele of Kasai," in Forde, Daryll (ed.), *African Worlds: Studies in the Cosmological Ideas and Social Values of*

African Peoples, London: Oxford University Press for the International African Institute, 1954, pp. 1-26. A paper giving Lele cultural setting and world view.

Tew [Douglas], Mary, "A Form of Polyandry among the Lele of Kasai,"

Africa, 1951, *21,* 1-12. An account of a system in which women captured by a village or sent to it in settlement for an offense live in polyandrous relationships with groups of co-husbands who are members of the same age sets.

URBANIZATION AMONG THE YORUBA*

William Bascom

The Yoruba are a patrilineal agricultural people who were formerly divided into a number of independent states or kingdoms, and who possess many religious cult groups and craft organizations. They are unusual in that their indigenous culture is essentially an urban one. However, Yoruba cities do not adequately fit the usual concepts of urban groupings, and the reasons for their development in southwestern Nigeria are not thoroughly understood. Bascom uses a definition of the city formulated by Louis Wirth, a well-known American sociologist who pioneered in studies of American cities, as a foil against which to present his own data on Yoruba urban centers.

Wirth has defined a city as "a relatively large, dense, and permanent settlement of socially heterogeneous individuals." [1] His final criterion is not clearly defined; and, in the absence of specific standards which can be applied cross-culturally, it is difficult to distinguish between heterogeneity and homogeneity. Miner has recently commented on "the lack of any concise benchmark from which to appraise the degree of homogeneity" [2] in his study of Timbuctoo, although he concludes that "Timbuctoo is a city. It has a stable population of over six thousand persons, living in a community roughly a square mile in area and patterning their lives after three distinct cultural heritages. The size, density, and heterogeneity of the city are all evident." [3] Miner admittedly rests his case for heterogeneity on the ethnic diversity of the Songhai, Tuareg, and Arabs who inhabit it, but neither he nor Wirth suggests that ethnic diversity is essential to the definition of the city. Many Western cities include groups of different racial, linguistic, and cultural backgrounds, but this can be regarded as a secondary feature of the process of urbanization and a basis for distinguishing cosmopolitan from noncosmopolitan cities.

The shortcomings of Wirth's criterion of social heterogeneity are suggested by the equivocal conclusions of those who have attempted to ap-

---

* Reprinted from *American Journal of Sociology*, 1955, 60, 446-54, copyright 1955 by the University of Chicago, by permission of the author and publisher.

ply it to traditional African communities. Miner describes Timbuctoo as a "primitive city" and its inhabitants as a "city-folk." Schwab, in a study of a Yoruba city, concludes that "if Oshogbo was viewed on the level of form, it was an urban community; if viewed in terms of social organization and process, it was folk." [4] If the concepts of "folk" and "urban" are useful, it should at least be possible to distinguish be. tween them.

Contrasted to Timbuctoo's 6,000 inhabitants, the Yoruba have six cities of more than 100,000, including Ibadan, the largest Negro city in Africa (Table 1). Only Lagos, which is both the principal port and the capital of Nigeria, is ethnically heterogeneous and follows the familiar African pattern of the growth of cities at mining and trading centers, ports, and colonial administrative headquarters.

Nine out of the ten largest cities in Nigeria in 1931 were Yoruba, excepting only Kano, with 97,031 inhabitants. In these nine cities of over 45,000 lived 901,262, or 28.4 per cent, of the 3,166,164 Yoruba recorded in the *Census of Nigeria, 1931,* while 1,077,691, or 34 per cent, lived in sixteen cities of over 20,000 (including, in addition to those listed in Table 1, Ijebu-Ode, 27,909; Ikirun, 23,874; Ikire, 20,920; and Ondo, 20,859). In addition, there were 27 other Yoruba centers with populations between 10,000 and 19,999; 55 with populations between 5,000 and 9,999; and 180 with populations between 2,000 and 4,999. [5]

Taking the average populations of the last three groups as 15,000, 7,500, and 3,500 and counting only the 77 per cent of the population of Lagos who were Yoruba, we arrive at the distribution of urban Yoruba in 1931 given in Table 2. For comparison, the figures for European and North American countries cited by Davis and Casis are included, and, following these authors, the index of urbanization has been computed as the average of the previous four columns. [6] The estimated index of urbanization of Yoruba cities falls between that of the United States and Canada, and the distribution of population in urban centers is remarkably similar to that in France.

Official figures on population density are lacking except for Lagos Island (25,000 in 1901, 50,000 in 1921, 58,000 in 1931, and 87,000 in 1950; in 1950 the three wards of Lagos Island had densities of 67,000, 111,000, and 141,000 per square mile). It has been possible to calculate approximate densities for three other cities, using 1931 census figures and official maps [7] for that period. Abeokuta's area is calculated roughly as 8 square miles, giving a density of 5,720; Oyo's area is about 3½ square miles, giving a density of 13,914; Ogbomosho's area is calculated, probably more accurately than the others, at 2 square miles, giving a density of 43,372 per square mile. Because of the higher ratio of inhabitants per room and per square foot and the greater compactness of the traditional Yoruba housing, the size of the older Yoruba cities is easily underestimated by

TABLE I

YORUBA CITIES WITH POPULATIONS OVER 40,000*

	1952 (Census)	1931 (Census)	1931 (Non-natives)	1921 (Census)	1911 (Census)	Estimates by Millson (1890)	Bowen (1856)	Tucker (1853)
Ibadan	459,196	387,133	226	238,094	175,000	200,000	70,000	60,000
Lagos	267,407	126,108	1,443	99,690	73,766	....	20,000	......
Ogbomosho.	139,535	86,744	0	84,860	80,000	60,000	25,000	45,000
Oshogbo...	122,698	49,599	31	51,418	59,821	35,000– 40,000	......	......
Ife	110,790	24,170	5	22,184	36,231	....	......	......
Iwo	100,006	57,191	4	53,588	60,000	60,000	20,000	......
Abeokuta ..	84,451	45,763	66	28,941	51,255	....	60,000	80,000
Oyo	72,133	48,733	19	40,356	45,438	40,000	25,000	......
Ilesha	72,029	21,892	7	....	....	....	......	......
Iseyin	49,680	36,805	0	28,601	33,362	40,000– 60,000	20,000	70,000
Ede	44,808	52,392	0	48,360	26,577	30,000– 40,000	20,000	......
Ilorin	41,000	47,412	27	38,668	36,342	....	70,000	......

* Other estimates, not included above, are as follows: Ogbomosho: 50,000 (1860, Campbell); Abeokuta: 45,000 (1842, Freeman), 50,000 (1843, Townsend), 100,000 (1852, Irving), twice the usual figures of 60,000–100,000 (1855, Consul Campbell), 80,000 (1858, Bowen), 100,000 (1874, Chause and Holley); Iseyin: 20,000 (1860, Campbell); Ilorin: 100,000 (1858, Bowen). The 1952 figures were kindly made available by the Nigerian government in advance of publication.

outsiders. Abeokuta, for example, appears much larger than Ogbomosho, which is actually something like half again as large and eight times as dense.

The permanency of Yoruba cities is partially documented in Table 1. Bowen's estimates of a century ago are conservative but incomplete; he

TABLE 2

PERCENTAGE OF YORUBA IN CITIES BY SIZE CLASS

	Over 2,000	Over 5,000	Over 10,000	Over 25,000	Over 100,000	Index of Urbanization
Yoruba (1931).....	78.8	58.9	45.9	29.6	15.3	37.4
Great Britain (1931)	....	81.7	73.6	63.1	45.2	65.9
Germany (1939)....	....	57.4	51.7	43.5	31.8	46.1
United States (1940)	....	52.7	47.6	40.1	28.8	42.3
Canada (1941)	....	43.0	38.5	32.7	23.0	34.3
France (1936)......	....	41.7	37.5	29.8	16.0	31.2
Sweden (1935)	....	37.1	33.4	27.0	17.5	28.7
Greece (1937)......	....	33.1	29.8	23.1	14.8	25.2
Poland (1931)......	....	22.8	20.5	15.8	10.7	17.4

visited Ogbomosho but does not estimate its size, and he states: "The eastern parts of Yoruba, and the countries of Ifeh (Ife); Iiesha (Ilesha), Igbona (Igbomina), and Effong (Effon-Alaive) have not been visited by the missionaries. We are assured that there are many large towns in that region."[8] The interior of Yoruba country was first reached in 1825 by Clapperton and Lander, who visited Katunga (Old Oyo) and other large cities, some of which were obliterated before Bowen's arrival in 1849. The wars of the last century destroyed or reduced many Yoruba cities and resulted in a very considerable depopulation of the entire area.

Earlier historical materials can be found in the accounts of Benin, to the east, and Dahomey, to the west, which indicate that both were subject to some measure of political control by Yoruba cities as early as 200-500 years ago. When the Portuguese explorer d'Aveiro first visited the city of Benin in 1485, it was learned that the sanction of the Ogane, a powerful king in the interior, was required when the king of Benin was crowned; the Ogane has been identified by Talbot as the King of Ife. In 1505-8 Pereira mentions "a very large city called Geebuu," which is unquestionably Ijebu-Ode. In 1668 Dapper mentions the kingdom of Oedebo, and D'Anville's map of 1729 locates Oudobo in the region of the province and city of Ondo. Dapper also mentions the kingdom of Ulkami, which Talbot identifies as Old Oyo; Old Oyo may also be referred to in Bosman's account of the invasion of Arder in Dahomey in 1698. Old Oyo was certainly an important and powerful center by 1724, if not earlier, and was able to collect annual tribute from Dahomey for almost a century (1747-1837). Between 1830 and 1841 Old Oyo was evacuated and the present city of Oyo was founded.

Urbanization can therefore be considered a traditional Yoruba pattern and not the outgrowth of European acculturation. It cannot be explained in terms of the development of colonial administrative centers, ports, mines, or industry. The real basis of the Yoruba economy is, and was, farming. Yet the farmers are city dwellers, and the city is not really a "nonfarm area" as we view it. A belt of peripheral farms which are visited regularly surrounds the city, extending as much as fifteen miles or more outside it. Families whose farms are more distant may have farm huts, where they spend several days at a time during the height of the farming activity, but they maintain a residence in the city and regard it as their real home. Some Yoruba, of course, live on farms or in very small villages.

Nearly all Yoruba engage in farming, but the production of many other goods is specialized. Weaving, dyeing, ironworking, brasscasting, woodcarving, ivorycarving, calabash-carving, beadworking, and leatherworking, as well as drumming, divining, the compounding of charms and medicines, and certain other activities, are crafts, whose techniques are known only to a small group of specialists. These specialists, who are organized into guilds, supply all other members of the community with their particular goods and services. Formerly these occupations tended to be more hereditary within the clan or lineage, but the apprenticeship system provided a method by which individuals from outside the kinship unit could be taught a craft. Specialization, however, was only on a craft basis and never reached the extent to which it is found in industrialized societies with the adaptation of labor to the machine.

Trading in local produce within the community is a necessary outgrowth of craft specialization, and both intercommunity and intertribal trade are apparently traditional. The Landers met one hundred wives of the king of Old Oyo trading for him at "Jadoo," north of Ilaro and "Egga." Clapperton and Lander met Hausa and Nupe caravans at "Coosoo" and "Jaguta" between Shaki and Old Oyo and at Kiama, north of Yoruba country, who traded with Yoruba and Dahomeans, with Gonja, Ashantee, and Accra in the Gold Coast, and with Bornu in northeastern Nigeria. In at least Ife, Abeokuta, and Ijebu-Ode, guilds of male traders held monopolies on imported goods from other Yoruba towns and from Europe, buying them in wholesale lots and letting them out to women traders for retail in the markets. Tolls levied on all trade, which provided an important source of income for Yoruba chiefs and kings, are mentioned by Lander on his first visit to Old Oyo. These, and the monopolies on imported goods held by the guilds of male traders, were actively opposed and eventually broken by the British in their efforts to extend trade in Nigeria. The desire to control trade routes to the sea and insure a supply of European imports, including arms, and an outlet for slaves led Ibadan, Abeokuta, and other inland cities to attack coastal enemy towns and defend those of their allies.

Trading is the third basis of the Yoruba economy, and the size and importance of Yoruba markets impress the visitor today as they did the early explorers. Retail trade in the markets is primarily in the hands of women, who also tend to specialize in yams, corn, chickens, cloth, and other commodities, as they become successful, and who are organized into guilds. Trade does not involve a simple exchange of goods between the producer and the consumer but is carried on by middlemen whose role and motivation are similar to those in our own society. In the simplest case a trader buys from the producer and sells at a higher price for a monetary profit; but in some cases goods are sold and resold through a chain of middlemen which has so many links that it becomes difficult to distinguish between wholesaler and retailer. True money in the form of the cowrie shell was used by the Yoruba probably even before European contact, and early European officials received their pay in cowries. Barbot (1732) mentions that "cauries" or "boejies" were being imported from the Maldive Islands in the East Indies as ballast, "no other people in the universe putting such a value on them as the Guineans," but their use as money at Benin is mentioned as early as 1589. Some Yoruba traditions speak of the institution of barter, but others suggest that cowrie shells were used as money before even the Portuguese arrived and that the pecuniary economy of the Yoruba is of long standing. To say the least, it is difficult to imagine how the European traders would have hit upon cowrie shells as an importable commodity which the Africans would accept in exchange for goods if the shells had not been already known and valued. One may conclude that the traditional Yoruba pattern of trade involved large markets, true middlemen, and true money.

The earliest available evidence indicates an important and well-developed trade between Yoruba cities and with other tribes but does not suggest that these cities developed as trading centers of the type represented by Timbuctoo, Kano, and other Sudanese cities. Under British rule, trade in European goods has increased tremendously, and as has trade in local produce, owing to the development of new occupations such as those of clerk, carpenter, and mechanic and to the increasing amounts of farm land devoted to cocoa. The typical pre-British markets, however, excluding those which specialized in the buying and selling of slaves, dealt mainly with local produce rather than with goods from abroad, from other tribes, or from other Yoruba cities. In other words, trade was based upon specialization within the city rather than the city itself being based upon trade growing out of extensive regional or tribal specialization.

It is important to distinguish between industrial and nonindustrial cities. Industrialization, where it has occurred, has produced a kind and degree of specialization that are unknown in nonindustrialized societies. Industrialization has given rise to urbanization in Western societies, but this is not to say that it is its prerequisite or its only cause. On this point, Wirth has stated specifically: "It is particularly important to call attention to the danger of confusing urbanism with industrialism and modern capitalism. The rise of cities in the modern world is undoubtedly not independent of modern power-driven machine technology, mass production, and capitalistic enterprise. But different as the cities of earier epochs may have been by virtue of their development in a preindustrial and precapitalistic order from the great cities of today, they were, nevertheless, cities."[9]

The Yoruba cities were nonindustrial and lacked the degree of specialization based upon the machine. Nevertheless, the craft form of specialization made each individual economically dependent upon the society as a whole. The weaver depended upon the blacksmith for tools and upon the farmer, the hunter, and the trader for his food; the blacksmith depended upon others for his food and upon the weaver for his clothes; the farmer depended upon the hunter and the trader for his meat, the smith for his cutlass and hoe, and the weaver for his clothing.

Each of these, moreover, had to rely upon the diviner, the herbalist, the priest, the drummer, the potter, the woodcarver, and other specialists for goods and services which they could not provide for themselves.

Aside from craft specialization, the Yoruba cities were heterogeneous only in terms of their social stratification and their social and political segmentation. Nine social strata can be distinguished in the Yoruba city of Ife. Oversimplifying for the sake of brevity, the five lowest strata, comprising perhaps 95 per cent of the population, may be described as positions which are ascribed on the basis of clan or lineage, while the four highest strata are primarily achieved, although often only within specified clans or lineages.[10] The patrilineal lineage or clan is basic to Yoruba society, rural or urban. The large cities are composed of many such segments based on kinship, organized politically into permanent, clearly defined wards or "quarters" and precincts or subquarters, while the small villages may contain only a few or even only a single lineage. In Ife heads of each lineage constitute the precinct council, one of their number serving as its chief. Precinct chiefs constitute the ward council, headed by a ward chief. The five ward chiefs and three other city chiefs represent the interests of the townspeople and with eight chiefs chosen from the palace retinue, serve as the king's council and in former times served as a chief tribunal. The king, whose position is hereditary within the related lineages of the royal clan, is responsible for the affairs of the capital and of the outlying towns and villages within the kingdom.

Within the lineage, individual relationships are dependent upon such circumstances as seniority, sex, wealth, personal qualities, and status as slave, pawn, or free; but between lineages individual relationships are dependent upon the relative rank of the lineage.[11] The individual counts for little except as a member of the lineage. Further, in Wirth's words, "interests are made effective through representation." [12] Representation or delegation is clearly illustrated in the system of lineage heads, precinct councils and precinct chiefs, ward councils and ward chiefs, city council with its city chiefs, representatives of the palace officials, and the king himself.

The city is a secondary group, while the lineage is primary. Wirth says: "The contacts of the city may indeed be face to face, but they are nevertheless impersonal, superficial, transitory and segmental." All these characteristics are exemplified in Yoruba market transactions. As in our own urban communities, one may have regular customers with whom relations are not impersonal, but one also must deal with casual customers of whom one must always beware in either buying or selling. Miner notes the cheating of a gullible buyer or seller in Timbuctoo. Among the Yoruba the principle of *caveat emptor* is also well established, as is illustrated by an edict of the king of Ife prohibiting the "hawking" or peddling of palm wine through the streets so as to restrict the possibility of its being watered down. Furthermore, the counterfeiting of government currency was so perfected by one Yoruba subgroup that counterfeit coins became known throughout Nigeria as "Ijebu money." Another new kind of cheating was made possible by the "money doubling" machines of the early thirties. Into these Westernized gadgets the up-country dupe would put shillings and pounds in increasing amounts and have double value returned, until he became greedy for the big kill and put in all the cash he could; at this point the operator explained that the machine had stuck and would take overnight to digest such a large amount, and skipped out of town under the cover of darkness.

Wirth emphasizes that urbanization refers to a distinctive mode of life. This is evident among the Yoruba in clothing, food habits, manners, and attitudes toward each other of even the non-Europeanized city dweller and the people from the small village, the rural farm area, and the hinterland. The city dwellers ridicule the unsophisticated "bush" people; their attitudes, as expressed in conversation and proverbs,[13] closely parallel our concepts of "rube" or "hick." The attitudes of the rural Yoruba toward the city dweller also seem to resemble those in our society. On the other hand, the anomie stressed by Durkheim and later sociologists does not seem to be apparent, unless it is to be found among the rural Yoruba who find themselves in the city. Since the lineage is the residential unit and involves reciprocal social and economic obligations, the city dweller need not feel lonely or insecure. Competitiveness is strong, and economic failure can lead to frustration or suicide but not to starvation.

There is no evidence that the old pattern of city life tended to weaken the lineage, or produce the increased mobility, instability, and insecurity which Wirth suggests are the results of heterogeneity. To the extent that the lineage has been weakened, the causes have been other conditions, such as the increased ease of travel with the ending of warfare and the development of Western forms of transportation, the introduction of a valuable permanent crop in cocoa, the superimposition of British control and European ethics over the traditional Yoruba authorities and mores, and the emphasis on the individual in the teaching of Christian missions, which have affected the Yoruba over the last fifty to a hundred years.[14] All these things are today producing changes in Yoruba cities similar to those in the newer African cities, and to the Western cities of which Wirth speaks; kinship bonds, traditionally a basic element in the structure of the city, are weakening.

Wirth states that "the bonds of kinship, of neighborliness, and the sentiments arising out of living together for generations under a common folk tradition are likely to be absent or, at best, relatively weak in an aggregate the members of which have such diverse origins and backgrounds. Under such circumstances competition and formal contro' mechanisms furnish the substitutes for the bonds of solidarity that are relied upon to hold a folk society together." This statement is undoubtedly true of the cosmopolitan cities in the United States and perhaps elsewhere, but in the Yoruba cities the bonds of kinship and living together which unite the lineage were strong, and the elements of competition and formal control mechanisms were not developed as *substitutes* for kinship control mechanisms but, rather, as mechanisms of control on a supra-kinship, secondary level, transcending the primary groups, such as lineages, which were very much alive and functional.

Although Wirth dismisses forms of political organization as an arbitrary and therefore unsatisfactory criterion for urbanism, the presence or absence of a formalized city government which exercises authority over neighboring primary groups and incorporates them into a community seems, on the contrary, no less arbitrary and certainly far less subjective than social heterogeneity. When coupled with size, density, and permanency, formalized community government would seem to be a useful criterion of urbanism for cross-cultural comparisons. It is this factor which differentiates the urban Yoruba from the Ibo of eastern Nigeria, whose total population is comparable and whose over-all population densities are about double[15] but the growth of whose cities has been recent. We do not know why the Yoruba developed cities and city government while the Ibo did not, but city life is definitely a part of the Yoruba tradition.

Some Yoruba cities, such as Oyo, Ife, Ilesha, Ijebu-Ode, Ondo and Ketu, were metropolitan in that, as capitals, they served as centers of the entire kingdom and can be considered metropolitan. The capital city maintained regular communication with the outlying towns over which they ruled, and representatives of the king were stationed in them. Taxes of several kinds were collected throughout the kingdom and brought to the capital for the king. Death sentences had to be referred to the capital, where executions were performed and where each case could be reviewed by the king's court. Other large cities, such as Iseyin, Ogbomosho, and Ibadan, were not metropolitan except as they served as centers of trade or warfare, but these also had formalized city government. Each was ruled by a "town" chief (*bale*) under the authority of the king (*oba*), who lived elsewhere and to whom allegiance was owed. Ibadan became so powerful as a military center that it achieved a measure of independence from Oyo and could command the allegiance of many surrounding towns, but its ruler is still a *bale,* not an *oba*.

Ethnically the Yoruba cities were homogeneous. With the end of the wars of the last century, individuals from the Hausa, Ibo, Jekri, and other cultural and linguistic groups have settled in them, but in relatively small numbers except for Lagos. One may assume that in earlier times the non-Yoruba consisted mainly of slaves and transient traders.

The wars of the last century flooded some cities with refugees, including those from other Yoruba kingdoms and subcultures; but one may also assume that even on the level of subcultural and dialectical variation Yoruba cities were previously noncosmopolitan.

Despite the absence of industrialization and ethnic heterogeneity and despite the continued importance of kinship units, the Yoruba had cities even before European penetration. They had cities because they had large, dense, permanent communities whose inhabitants were economically independent, socially stratified, and politically unified. These cities were based on farming, craft specialization, and trading. Only Lagos represents the common type of recent growth of African cities as ports, mining and trading centers, and colonial administrative headquarters. Some Yoruba cities were metropolitan, serving as capitals and centers of the Yoruba kingdoms; others were nonmetropolitan. Some were founded as defensive or predatory centers during the wars of the last century; others undoubtedly existed when the Portuguese arrived and before the beginning of the slave wars. Although the cause of their growth is still not fully known, they were definitely a part of the traditional Yoruba pattern, providing permanent residences for farmers and markets for trade within, as well as beyond, the city's boundaries.

It is difficult to decide whether or not the Yoruba cities were heterogeneous in Wirth's sense, because social heterogeneity is not clearly defined. At best, it is a relative criterion which is difficult to apply cross-culturally. Perhaps the answer may be to define it in terms of specialization to the extent that each individual is economically dependent on the production and the special skills of the other members of his community. It is necessary at least to distinguish between industrial and nonindustrial cities and between cosmopolitan and noncosmopolitan cities. It is also suggested that the existence of a formalized government which exercises authority over the primary groups and incorporates them into a political community may be more useful than heterogeneity when applied cross-culturally, since it is less subjective. It is hoped that these points may broaden the concept of urbanization so that it is less dependent upon the historical conditions of Western urbanization and so that it can be applied more profitably to the study of the urban centers of India and Southeast Asia.

NOTES

[Starred items are recommended as further readings.]

*[1] L. Wirth, "Urbanism as a Way of Life," *American Journal of Sociology,* XLIV (1938), 8.

[2] H. Miner, *The Primitive City of Timbuctoo* (Princeton: Princeton University Press, for the American Philosophical Society, 1953), p. 268.

[3] *Ibid.,* p. 267.

[4] W. Schwab, "Urbanization and Acculturation" (MS).

5 There were also 7,338 communities with populations under 2,000.

6 K. Davis and A. Casis, "Urbanization in Latin America," *Milbank Memorial Fund Quarterly*, XXIV (1946), 186-207.

7 Abeokuta: Scale 1:12,500; drawn and reproduced by Land and Survey Department, Lagos, 1947; surveyed in 1930. Oyo: 300/723/3–50; scale 1:12,500; drawn and reproduced by Land and Survey Department, Lagos. Ogbomosho Town: 300/684/1.50; scale 400 feet to 1 inch; surveyed in 1938 and reproduced by Land and Survey Department, Lagos, 1939; reprinted in 1950.

8 The principal historical sources are listed in the Bibliography.

9 Wirth, *op. cit.*, pp. 7-8.

* 10 W. Bascom, "Social Status, Wealth and Individual Differences among the Yoruba," *American Anthropologist*, LIII (1951), 490-505.

* 11 *Ibid.;* W. Bascom, "The Principle of Seniority in the Social Structure of the Yoruba," *American Anthropologist,* XLIV (1942), 37-46.

12 Wirth, *op. cit.,* p. 14.

13 E.g., "They don't call a man a man; they don't call a human a human; therefore the farm people [*ara oko*] wear a breechclout to town," meaning that they do not have enough respect for others to dress properly in public.

14 The effects of these factors cannot be analyzed here. They are touched on partially in W. Bascom, "African Culture and the Missionary," *Civilisations* (Brussels), III (1953), 491-504.

15 Population densities in 1931 for the Yoruba provinces in Southern Nigeria run as follows: Ondo, 56; Abeokuta, 74; Oyo, 94; Ijebu, 125; and the Colony, 153; for the Ibo provinces: Ogoja, 94; Owerri, 268; and Onitsha, 306. In 1931 the Ibo numbered 3,184,585, as against 3,166,164 Yoruba in Nigeria.

BIBLIOGRAPHY

Adams, J. *Remarks on the Country Extending from Cape Palmas to the River Congo.* London: G. & B. W. Whittaker, 1823.

Adams, J. *Sketches Taken during Ten Voyages to Africa, between Years 1786 and 1800.* London: Hurst, Robinson & Co., 1821.

Barbot, J. *A Description of the Coasts of North and South Guinea.* London (no publisher listed), 1732.

Barros, João de. *Ásia de João de Barros: Dos feitos que os portugueses fizeram no descobrimento e conquista dos mares e terras do Oriente.* 4 vols. 6th ed. Lisboa: Divisão de Publicações e Biblioteca, Agência Geral das Colónias, Ministério das Colónias, República Portuguesa, 1945. First published in 1553. Extracts translated in G. R. Crone, *The Voyages of Cadamosto and Other Documents on Western Africa in the Second Half of the Fifteenth Century.* London: Hakluyt Society, 1937.

Bosman, W. *A New and Accurate Description of Guinea.* 2d ed. London: J. Knapton, D. Midwinter, B. Lintot, G. Strahan, J. Round, and E. Bell, 1721. First published in 1705.

Bowen, T. J. *Central Africa: Adventures and Missionary Labors in Several Countries in the Interior of Africa, from 1849 to 1856.* Charleston, S. C.: Southern Baptist Publication Society, 1857.

Bowen, T. J. *Grammar and Dictionary of the Yoruba Language.* ("Smithsonian Contributions to Knowledge," Vol. X.) Washington: Smithsonian Institution, 1858.

Burton, R. F. *A Mission to Gelele, King of Dahomey.* 2 vols. London: Tylston & Edwards, 1893.

Campbell, R. *A Pilgrimage to My Motherland: An Account of a Journey among the Egbas and Yorubas of Central Africa in 1859-1860.* London: W. J. Johnson, 1860.

Census of Nigeria, 1931, 6 vols. London: Crown Agents for the Colonies for the Government of Nigeria, 1932-33.

Chause, H., and Holley. "Voyage dans le Yoruba," *Les Missions catholiques,* Vol. XVII (1885), Nos. 814-21.

Clapperton, H. *Journal of a Second Expedition into the Interior of Africa, from the Bight of Benin to Soccatoo.* Philadelphia: Carey, Lea & Carey, 1829.

Dalzell, A. *The History of Dahomey, an Inland Kingdom of Africa.* London: For the author, by T. Spilsbury, 1793.

Dapper, O. *Umständliche und eigentliche Beschreibung von Africa.* Amsterdam: Jacob von Meurs, 1670. First published in Flemish in 1668.

Dunglas, E. "La première attaque des Dahoméens contre Abéokuta (3 mars 1851)," *Études dahoméennes,* I (1948), 7-19.

Foa, E. *Le Dahomey.* Paris: A. Hennuyer, 1895.

Hermon-Hodge, H. B. *Gazetteer of Ilorin Province.* London: George Allen & Unwin, 1929.

* Herskovits, M. J. *Dahomey: An Ancient West African Kingdom.* 2 vols. New York: J. J. Augustin, 1938.

Hinderer, A. *Seventeen Years in the Yoruba Country.* London: Religious Tract Society, n.d. First published *ca.* 1872.

Labat, (J. B.) *Voyage du Chevalier des Marchais en Guinée, isles voisines, et à Cayenne, fait en 1725, 1726 & 1727.* 4 vols. Amsterdam: La Compagnie, 1731.

Lander, R. *Records of Captain Clapperton's Last Expedition to Africa.* 2 vols. London: Henry Colburn & Richard Bentley, 1830.

Lander, R. and J. *Journal of an Expedition To Explore the Course and Ter-* *mination of the Niger.* New York: Harper & Bros., 1854. First published in 1832.

Meek, C. K. *The Northern Tribes of Nigeria.* 2 vols. London: Oxford University Press, 1925.

Millson, A. W. "The Yoruba Country, West Africa," *Proceedings of the Royal Geographical Society,* Vol. XIII (2d ser.) (1891).

Norris, R. *Memoirs of the Reign of Bossa Ahadee, King of Dahomey.* London: W. Lowndes, 1789.

Pereira, Duarte Pachecho. *Esmeraldo de situ orbis.* Translated and edited by G. H. T. Kimble. London: Hakluyt Society, 1937. First published in 1892. Written in two parts in 1505 and 1507-8.

Population Census of Lagos, 1950. Kaduna: Government Printer, 1951.

Schön, J. F., and Crowther, S. A. *Journals of the Rev. James Frederick Schön and Mr. Samuel Crowther, Who, with the Sanction of Her Majesty's Government, Accompanied the Expedition up the Niger in 1841, in Behalf of the Church Missionary Society.* London: Hatchard & Son, Nisbet & Co., Seeleys, 1842.

Snelgrave, W. *A New Account of Some Parts of Guinea, and the Slave Trade.* London: James, John & Paul Knapton, 1734.

* Talbot, P. A. *The Peoples of Southern Nigeria.* 4 vols. London: Oxford University Press, 1926.

Tucker, Miss. *Abbeokuta; or, Sunrise within the Tropics: An Outline of the Origin and Progress of the Yoruba Mission.* London: James Nisbet & Co., 1853.

FOR FURTHER READING

Bascom, William R., "Les premiers fondements historiques de l'urbanisme yoruba," *Présence Africaine* (Paris) No. 23, New Series, Dec.-Jan., 1959, pp. 22-40; Bascom, William R., "Urbanism as a Traditional African Pattern," in *Urbanism in West Africa* (Kenneth Little, ed.), *The Sociological Review* (University College of North Staffordshire, Keele), New Series, Vol. 7, No. 1, July, 1959, pp. 29-43.

Schwab, William B., "Kinship and Lineage among the Yoruba," *Africa,* 1955, 25, 352-74; Schwab, William B., "La croissance et les conflits de religion dans une communauté yoruba moderne," *Zaïre,* 1952, 6, 829-35; and Schwab, William B., "An Experiment in Methodology in a West African Urban Community," *Human Organization*, 1954, *13*, 13-19. These papers provide a great deal of useful data on Oshogbo, a Yoruba community of more than 100,000 persons.

Lloyd, P. C., "The Yoruba Lineage," *Africa*, 1955, *25*, 235-51. Includes a discussion of the political aspects of the lineage and its operation in the urban setting.

For contrast with the cities of the Sudan, see not only Miner's study mentioned by Bascom, but also Monteil, Charles Victor, *Une cité soudanaise, Djénné, métropole du delta central du Niger*, Paris: Société d'éditions géographiques, maritimes et coloniales, 1932.

Weber, Max, *The City*, translated and edited by Don Martindale and Gertrud Neuwirth, Glencoe, Illinois: The Free Press, 1958. An analysis of ancient and medieval cities of Europe and Asia which has direct relevance for the study of traditional African cities.

4

Authority and Government

THE POLITICAL SYSTEM OF KONKOMBA*

David Tait

Tait's study of the Konkomba illustrates how unilineal groupings can form the basis of both the political and social organization of a society. This kind of social system, with its heavy emphasis on descent ties, is characteristic of the northern parts of Togoland and Ghana. The processes of internal segmentation within the clan and of the fission of subgroups from it to form new clans are typical, however, of many areas of Africa. Within the basic political unit (the patrilineal clan), the political structure and the social organization seem almost to be fused, and it is difficult to separate that which is purely political from other types of social action. It is interesting to note that the ecology, in terms of the level of technological skill possessed by the Konkomba, tends to prevent the development of political units larger than the clan, and that relations between clans are essentially nonpolitical.

The Konkomba live in Northern Togoland in both French and British Mandated Territory and principally about the banks of the Oti River, a tributary of the Volta. Their country lies between 9° and 9° 50′ N. and 0° and 0° 50′ E. The total population is about 45,000. Their language is one of the Gurma group of the Voltaic family. The great majority of them live on a grassland plain that lies between the low hills of eastern Dagomba and the Kotokoli hills. The plain is very low-lying and conditions are severe, alternating between considerable desiccation and severe flooding. The compounds are grouped in small hamlets of a dozen or so straggling along low ridges in the plain; in the wet season communication between hamlets is very difficult.

Konkomba are grain farmers, their principal crop being sorghum or millet, but they also grow yams. The grain is grown on farms close to the compounds, the yams on farms farther out in the bush. Konkomba also keep cattle but they devote little attention to them; the cattle are herded by small boys and girls between the ages of about 10 and 14. Mar-

* Reprinted from *Africa*, 1953, 23, 213-23, by permission of the International African Institute (author's copyright reserved).

riage payments are made in corn and services, not in cattle, though cattle are sometimes used to buy wives from the Kabire, their neighbors to the east.

The most important unit of the social and political system may be called a "clan," and a clan occupies the only precisely known territorial unit, which may be termed a "district": thus when the word "clan" is used it implies a known stretch of territory; and conversely a "district" implies an occupying "clan." Clans are grouped in tribes, the criteria of which will be considered later. Tribal areas can be plotted, each area being the totality of its component districts. A district is a stretch of land of up to 25 square miles which is occupied by a body of clansmen and their dependents, seldom numbering more than about 250 souls. It includes ridges of grain lands and bush areas in which the yam-farms lie and over which wood is gathered. Districts also include stretches of flood plain which are under water for several months of the year and are, in consequence, of no agricultural use. Many clans have fishing rights over stretches of the Oti or its tributaries and all have hunting rights over their own districts.

The clan is commonly segmented into two major agnatic lineages, though in some few cases three and four major lineages to a clan are found. The major lineage, itself segmented, is conceived as a genealogical structure of some five generations' depth and between any two members of a major lineage agnatic kinship can be precisely stated. The major lineage is commonly, though not invariably, segmented into two minor lineages themselves segmented. At the head of each lineage there is an Elder, the oldest man of the lineage, and the senior of the two or more heads of major lineages can be thought of as the clan Elder.

There is no Konkomba term, in the form of an abstract noun, which denotes exclusively the term "lineage," but the word *onibaa* can, in one of its applications, be so used. This word is an abbreviation of the phrase *"Ti je onibaa;* we are (the children of) one man." Also used with reference to the lineage are the terms *odzabaa,* another way of saying "one man," and *mfum mbaa,* "once." The term *onibaa* (one man) is applied to the group that consists literally of the children of one man. It is also applied to the minor lineage—a structure some 3-4 generations in depth; to the major lineage, and to the clan itself, all these being long-enduring, though not permanent, structures. The clan, then, is also conceived as a descent group, as the descendants of some remote, now lost, ancestor, even though the common descent of the clan's component lineages cannot be formulated genealogically.

Each district contains a number of shrines within its boundaries. Of these the most important, in all senses, is the land shrine; it is the principal shrine of the land cult and of the ancestor cult; it is an indispensable symbol of the autonomous clan and district.

Lineage fission is an almost continuous process in this society and results from population increase and land exhaustion. There is intra-district fission when a group of kinsmen separate from their fellows to settle at a fresh point within the boundaries of their natal district. If such a group of kinsmen, commonly brothers, settle in the unoccupied bush of Konkombaland, there is extra-district fission. When extra-district fission is taking place a diviner is always consulted to discover, for the outgoing kinsmen, the land and other shrines in the area they propose to occupy. The discovery of the shrine brings into being a new district and a new clan. Though the new clan is at first only a small group, it will in time grow and segment to form a segmented clan of segmented lineages of the usual Konkomba pattern.

The two component major lineages of some clans are in contraposition. By contraposition of lineages is meant a division of ritual roles between them whereby they are respectively distinguished as the "Owner of the Land's People" and the "Elder's People." The senior man of the "Owner of the Land's People" is the *Otindaa,* the Owner of the Land, while the senior man of the "Elder's People" is the *Onekpel* or Elder. The apical ancestor of the "Owner of the Land" is described as "he who first came here" while the apical ancestor of the "Elder's People" is "he who helped the one who first came here."

The Owner of the Land (*Otindaa*) is the guardian of the shrines held by a contrapuntal clan, but at some of these shrines the Elder (*Onekpel*) performs the actual sacrifices. There is thus a division of ritual roles between them and the *Otindaa* is ritually superior to the *Onekpel.* It is tempting to argue that the *Onekpel* is, in recompense, politically superior to the *Otindaa,* and this may, indeed, be so. But contraposition of lineages is rare in Konkomba; I know of only six such clans at present (out of over a hundred) and in all six the "Elder" happens to be older than the "Owner of the Land." It may be, then, that what I take to be a slight seniority of political authority in the Elder is no more than a conformity to the Konkomba rule that in any situation the senior person present exercises authority. It is safer, on present evidence, to think of these two elders as dividing only ritual duties and to treat the older man as the politically superior Elder in contrapuntal no less than in dual clans.

Contraposition of major lineages comes about, I believe, when a major lineage grows and segments. When a major lineage segments to form two units of like order, and the hamlets in which the members of the lineages live are separated on the ground, then members of the two new major lineages may marry each other. But when a major lineage segments to form two lineages of like order and the members of each lineage live either in a single hamlet or in two closely neighboring hamlets, then no intermarriage takes place and the lineages go into contraposition. The major lineage itself is invariably exogamous; the clan is an exogamous unit when it consists of only one major lineage or of two contraposed major lineages.

Thus there are variations in the forms of clans as they are found at a given point in time. But the alternate patterns of dual and contrapuntal clans, as I have outlined them, may be conceived as the ideal patterns to which all known clans approximate. The form of any one clan varies slightly through time, as does the size of the district it occupies. When the population increases beyond a certain point fission takes place, and it may happen that a neighboring clan has land to spare and gives some to its neighbor in need. In time that clan too may require fresh land and be able to spread at the expense of a third neighbor. District boundaries are thus not fixed and immutable, but advancing or receding.

The clan in its district is an economic, a ritual, and a legal unit. It is an economic unit in farming, herding, hunting, and fishing. Indeed, clans are all but self-supporting and probably were so until the introduction of weaving and the arrival of Moshi weavers. There have always been markets in Konkombaland, but some of them are now growing rapidly. In these larger markets grain, yams, and livestock are sold by Konkomba producers to visiting traders; Konkomba buy cloth, hoe-blades, and so on. The clan is an economic unit in that it is a productive unit. Within the clan a system of reciprocal assistance in farm work operates. Though assistance may be given to any fellow clansman the system is primarily applied within the minor lineage. While land is clearly apportioned between the major lineages of a clan there is no similar division of hunting and fishing rights, which are exercised over all clan lands and waters by any clan member.

As a ritual unit the clan is seen in operation in the principal dry-season rite of "They pour to the Land." This is primarily a sowing rite though it takes place long before the planting season. It is an offering to the land on behalf of the clan and all segments of a clan are represented at it. The clan is not, however, an indivisible ritual unit since the harvest rites are performed in the separate compounds and not as a communal rite. Yet the compound heads do not carry out their household rites at random; men of a minor lineage offer their sacrifices on the same day or over a very few days once the head of the minor lineage gives them the word to do so. In these rites, the major rites of the agricultural year, the clan may be seen as a ritual unit, but a unit composed of parts.

The clan, under its ritual and moral heads, the lineage Elders, is also a unit of social control. Within its limits there is compulsory settlement of disputes without recourse to force.[1] Outside clan limits there is no necessary arbitration, no settlement of disputes by other than forcible means or the threat of retaliation. When some breach of standards has occurred to interrupt communication within a clan and to disturb the steady running of the parts, then countervailing action has to be taken by individuals and groups to restore communication. Such jural activities are: ostracism of a neighbor, insistence on repayment after theft, payment of compensation after destruction of crops and, on occasion, even physical restraint of a fellow clansman. The Elder's role in social control is to insist on the observance of customary standards. He has no power to enforce a decision but he can pronounce what is the proper, the customary procedure on all occasions. His power to do so arises from his relation to the land, of which he is guardian, and from his relation to the ancestors, for he is the closest to them. His power is therefore ritual and moral, not judicial. Homicide among fellow clansmen seems not to occur. Were a man to kill his fellow clansman, Konkomba say, he would die. God will not suffer to live one who has killed his brother and there is no ritual or medicinal protection for the fratricide.

The clan is an autonomous unit of social control in that there is no authority superior to the Elder to impose a solution on recalcitrant members. Within the clan there is no organized force which can be employed to ensure acquiesence, no coercion other than the ritual and moral power of the Elder and the diffuse sanction of kinsmen's disapproval.

Just as there are disapproved actions within clans which are dealt with by jural activities, so between clans of one tribe there are disputes and offenses which are dealt with by means of warlike activities which may be called "feud," the term "war" being reserved for permanent hostility and sporadic fighting between tribes.

Radcliffe-Brown, in his Introduction to *African Political Systems,* said that "in dealing with political systems . . . we are dealing with law on the one hand and with war on the other." In the Konkomba system the clan, as an autonomous unit of social control, is the largest unit within which either feud or war is impossible. It is, therefore, the major unit of the political system, for it is a morally conscious body within which there is a sense of moral obligation towards fellow clansmen and a sense of loyalty to a territory. Moral control within the clan boundaries, but not beyond them, and force or the threat of force outside, but not within, clan boundaries, make the clan the political unit of Konkomba.

Within the clan the authority of the Elder is unchallenged, but no Elder can acquire authority outside his own clan. Nor can any other person acquire political power on other than a clan scale. Diviners may build up a reputation over a wide area, but this confers no political authority. There is no council of Elders of any form on a higher level than the clan. Fusion of clans takes place only in intertribal war and there is no fusion intermediate between the fusion of lineages in clans and the fusion of clans in tribal fighting.

Just as the vertical segmentation of a Konkomba clan is simple, so is its horizontal segmentation. The groups of age-mates which segment the clan into fifteen strata have a relation to the political system only because they lay out the clan members in an order of seniority and juniority and so define who is senior in any situation. Authority is always exercised by the senior person present; the marking out of the age-mates is a device whereby authority is assigned to persons, for aggregates of age-mates are not corporate bodies.

There is, however, another group with corporate functions: the group known as the "Young Men." All the unmarried men of a clan between the ages of 18 and about 40 belong to this association. It has two important corporate functions in the political system. First, it is the group that carries on feud on behalf of the clan as a whole. Secondly, it dances as a group at burials of neighboring clan elders. It is therefore important in relations of amity and hostility between clans. In so far as the lineage segmentation in this society may be said to divide clan members, the "Young Men" may be said to unite them. The centrifugal effect of lineage segmentation is counteracted by the centripetal effect of the "Young Men's" association, in which diversity of lineage status is lost in equality of status as a warrior and dancer.

I now consider the relations between clans of one tribe. Here there are four kinds of positive, enduring relation. Of these, the most important is the reciprocal, dyadic, ritual relation between clans that are *mantotib* to each other. To be *mantotib* means that the clans give each other assistance on ritual occasions. At any rite, even a private rite to redeem a vow, a representative of the *mantotib* clan must be present.

However, as with many Konkomba concepts, that of *mantotib* is not a simple one. Segments of a clan, the two or more major lineages that together form a clan, are also spoken of as *mantotib* to each other. Especially do women, many of whom have married into clans distant from their own clans, need the ritual assistance of their clanswomen. A clan-sister giving ritual assistance is spoken of as *manto* to the woman she assists. It might almost be supposed that the term *manto* is translatable by the phrase "clansfellow in a ritual context."

A second linkage between clans is the parental/filial relation. When extra-district fission leads to the growth of a new clan not far distant from the original clan, a ritual link between them survives long after any precise genealogical connection is recalled. This relation, too, is occasionally spoken of as *"mantotib."* But it seems to me to be somewhat different in kind. Whereas a *mantotib* clan, in the full sense of the term, gives assistance on all ritual occasions and must be present before the rite can begin, clans that are parental/filial clans to each other give assistance only in burials. The Elders simply send a cloth to the burial, to be used to cover the body as it is carried to the grave. Should the clans be so far distant that the giving of this service would be likely to delay the burial, then the two clans simply inform each other of deaths in the clan. At distances of more than 12-15 miles the link between parental/ filial clans seems not to survive as carrying any reciprocal ritual duties, and the descent of the one from the other clan is only a memory.

This link between parent and offspring clan is nontransitive. That is, though a first clan and its offshoot preserve the link, between the first clan and a third that is an offshoot of the second there is no link. The nontransitivity of the parental/filial relation in the ecological conditions of Konkombaland seems to be one of the principal factors which inhibit the growth of large units.

It is tempting to attribute the origin of the relation between *mantotib* to this parental/filial relation. Yet the *mantotib* relation is always dyadic, while a clan may have a number of filial clans. I know, in fact, of only one instance in which the parental/filial and *mantotib* relations overlap. This overlap may have come about after a shift in the relation. Since whole clans sometimes leave their district to settle elsewhere a clan is sometimes left without any *mantotib*. In two cases where this happened a new link was formed between the clan that was left and another clan.

A third link between clans is one I call "kith." Clans that are kith to each other are invariably close neighbors and commonly contiguous. There is no noun in Konkomba of which kith is a translation, but Konkomba do use the phrase "We know them." To "know people" does not necessarily imply reciprocal rights and duties but the relation does operate in many contexts. For example, one does not try to drive so hard a bargain with "someone one knows" as one does with a stranger. A man working a ferry takes "one he knows" over for nothing; he charges another Konkomba 3*d*. and a Moshi 1*s*. The relations out of which kithship grows are the many ties of affinal kinship, of friendship, and love affairs that arise between clans that lie in close juxtaposition. Though the link between *mantotib* may arise from the parental/filial relation between clans, I prefer to think of the *mantotib* relation as one between a clan and the closest of its kith. Kithship is best seen in the major sacrifice to the land when kith clans are invited to share in each other's rites. A distinction is then made by Konkomba between *mantotib* and kith; the *mantotib* must be present at the rite while the kith come for beer.

These three links—the dyadic, ritual relation of *mantotib*, the relation of parent/offshoot clans, and the manifold relation of kithship—help to link clan with clan. They are long-enduring relations between structures, but although long enduring through time they are of narrow extension in space.

Between clans of the same tribe there is one other positive link namely, that they all accept the rite called "They bury the fight" whereby a feud may be ended. Between clans of one tribe, this rite, which is a symbolic burying of arrows, can end a feud after years of fighting. Between clans of different tribes fighting is endless.

Feud commonly breaks out in quarrels over women or after en croachment by men of one clan on another's hunting or fishing rights. Konkomba practice the betrothal of infant girls to young men in their early 20s who then give Bride Services and Bride Corn to their fathers-in-law until the girl is about 18. Thus no man marries a wife, as opposed to inheriting a widow, until the age of about 40. During this long celibacy men carry on love affairs with the nubile girls and the young married women. It is said that, in the past, men sought to discover and to kill the lovers of their betrothed wives. Today this is not often done; but should a man discover the lover of a wife who has come to his compound (there is nothing that can properly be called a wedding ceremony), then he will try to kill the lover. A lover caught *in flagrante delicto* is lucky if he escapes with nothing worse than a severe wound. Should the husband kill the lover, then feud is likely to develop between their clans.

Again, though no clan has the exclusive right to hunt its lands or to fish its waters, but shares them with its kith, each clan has exclusive rights to burn the grass on its lands and to begin the fishing of its waters. Bush hunting is done by firing the grass to drive the game; fishing is done when rivers and lakes are low. Thus, both pursuits are carried out over a very short period of the year and, once the bush is fired and the lakes are fished, they can be neither hunted nor fished again for a year. To fire another clan's bush or to fish its waters is seriously to deprive that clan of food and the income from smoked meats. Such encroachments lead to severe fighting in which a dozen or more may be killed and, should losses on one or the other side be disproportionate, the fighting is likely to continue in feud, for the losing side will seek revenge later.

Whereas fighting over land and water rights involves all or most clan members from the beginning, fighting over women spreads gradually to involve many clan members. A man who is killed by his mistress' husband should, in the first instance, be revenged by one who is a son of the same mother. But the fighting is likely to spread to men of the dead man's household, thence to men of his minor lineage and so to his major lineage and clan. From the first homicide a feud may very well develop and continue for many years until one side or the other, weary of the long fighting, asks a neutral clan to suggest to their foes that they "bury the fight."

The links between clans outlined above have, in addition to their positive aspect of reciprocal duties, a negative aspect in feud, for between clans so linked feud may be obviated or mitigated. Between *mantotib* it is said that feud is forbidden and I know of no instance of feud between *mantotib*. In one case a man of one clan actually caught a man of his *mantotib* with his wife and did not kill him. On the other hand, I have heard a man threaten to kill another man who was not only his *manto* but also his mother's brother. However, he was unarmed at the time.

Similarly, clans in the parental/filial relation do not resort to feud. They are not *dejaa* (clansmen) to each other but the ritual and genealogical connexions between them seem to prohibit feud and homicide. On the other hand, two clans descended from the same clan carried on, some thirty years ago, a feud that is widely recalled in Konkombaland to this day. The fighting, which was very severe, was described in the district notes by the District Commissioner at the time. Though clans in the parental/filial relation do not carry on feuds against each other, they do not come to each other's help should either be involved in feud.

Feud between kith is not impossible but it is improbable. After a homicide involving kith clans there is the possibility of ritual action by the Elders to protect the land. After a killing, the Elders of the dead man's clan prevent their Young Men from marching out to avenge their brother's death until such time as the Elders of the killer's clan offer sacrifice. A fowl and a goat are offered to the Land Shrine of the dead man's clan and, once the sacrifice is made, no retaliation can be carried out.

Thus, though Konkomba say of the killing of a man of another clan that "it does not matter" or "it is nothing," these three positive links between nearby clans in fact operate to prevent feud or to diminish its severity. There is, however, no religious sanction on killing a man of another clan and the homicide has two means of protection available to him. The Young Men sleep together in one room. In this room there is a ritual symbol called *Dzambuna* and a medicine-horn called *igi*. The homicide sleeps with these beside him to protect him against the ghost of the man he has killed.

Yet these ritual links are not sufficient to create a new grouping at a higher level of the structure. Clans linked in these relations are not thereby made into a corporate body of greater scale than the clan. The clan, though linked to four or five other clans, remains the largest corporate unit of the system.

The clans do, however, form tribes. A Konkomba tribe may be defined by five criteria. Each tribe has a name; each is a territorial unit in that the tribal territory is the totality of the districts of the tribe's component clans. Clans of the same tribe can stand as *mantotib* and kith to each other. Clans of the same tribe assist each other in intertribal fighting. In addition, the men of many, though not all, tribes can be distinguished by their face marks. I do not know how many Konkomba tribes there are though I have visited members of a dozen different tribes; the largest number about 6,000 and the smaller about 2,000 members.

Tribes are not corporate bodies in that there are no tribal elders, no chiefs, and no ritual leaders whose powers extend over all the clans of a tribe. There is no seniority and juniority of clans within a tribal framework. It is only in intertribal fighting that tribal unity can be seen in action and that any man of a tribe may stand as its representative.

In tribal war there is no calling out of regiments to fight in a battle line until one or other side yields. It is a permanent state of hostility that intermittently breaks out in small fights. This hostility is not even markedly apparent but is to be seen in the attitude of reserve, the tendency to stand a little apart, displayed by members of one tribe visiting a market of another tribe. After an outbreak of war, this reserve hardens into wariness because any small infringement by either side will lead to a recrudescence of fighting. Outbreaks of tribal war are now rare, but it is clear that when a fresh outbreak occurs, it is explicitly connected with the preceding outbreak. In 1951 two men of the Bemokpem tribe and one man of the Betshabob tribe were killed in a fight between men of the two tribes, and this fight was expressly linked with a fight in 1950 in which one Bemokpem man was killed. Further, no one is in doubt that the Bemokpem will soon try again, for they have lost three men to one in these two fights. In the first of the two fights a man of the Bemwatiak clan of the Betshabob tribe killed a man of Lagea. In the second, men of an unknown Bemokpem clan attacked men of the Bekujom clan of the Betshabob tribe. That is, the Bemokpem sought their revenge not necessarily on the clan of the man who killed their tribesman but on any Betshabob when opportunity offered.

The tribe is therefore a fusion of clans to form a structure of higher order than the clan and between these tribal structures there are permanent relations of hostility. Fusion of segments in this society thus runs as follows: minor lineages fuse for corporate action as a major lineage, major lineages fuse in clans and clans fuse in tribes. The fusion of minor and major lineages in clans occurs in many contexts—of economic, ritual and jural activities—and they form political units which are units of social control. Clans, though they assist each other ritually, unite only in intertribal war.

The political system is, so far, a fairly simple one, but the most difficult question is still to be asked: "Why is there no fusion of tribes into a people?" Konkomba do, very occasionally, speak of "all Konkomba." But there is no evidence that the tribes were ever thought of as segments that could come together in opposition to a structure of higher order than the tribe. All the available evidence concerning the Dagomba invasions suggests that the Dagomba were able to pick off the Konkomba tribe by tribe or even clan by clan. The invasion of the Dagomba from the north and west, part of the spread of the Mole-Dagbane-speaking peoples, took place perhaps in the early sixteenth century and expelled many Konkomba from the areas they then held to their present riverain sites. There is no evidence of concerted opposition to the Dagomba invaders and even clans who today live side by side have no tradition of common defense against Dagomba. Contiguity at present is, however, no indication that the neighbor clans settled side by side after the Dagomba expelled them, for mobility on the ground is high.

It is, therefore, not easy to say what is the conception of the Konkomba people themselves. Clearly, it is not a political concept, in the sense of a unit in a system of social control. There are a number of tribes —at least twelve—who think of themselves as Bekpokpam inhabiting Kekpokpam and speaking Lekpokpam. But there are neighboring peoples, of whom little or nothing is yet known, who, though similar in culture, social organization, and language, yet do not think of themselves as Bekpokpam but as, for example, Tshiemba, better known as Basare. The Basare, along with the Kabire and Gurma, are closely akin to the Konkomba and the four are distinguishable only by variations in language and culture. These names do not denote political units which could wage war with each other. War between one Konkomba tribe and a Basare tribe would not engage other Konkomba or Basare tribes.

As far as our present knowledge goes, therefore, all we can say of the aggregate of peoples who speak the Gurma languages is this: the political system is one of relations between very small units, the clans, within which the use of force and retaliation is forbidden, and between which relations are either potentially or perennially hostile. These relations of hostility are mitigated by a system of dyadic, ritual relations between clans which in effect group the autonomous clans into tribes.

It may be that, in the end, the distinction between these four peoples will be a number of concurrent differences in culture. The only criterion ever suggested to me of a common bond between all Konkomba is their taboo on eating snake; Basare, perhaps, have a similar taboo on eating dog. It may be that many small cultural differences are thus summated and expressed in a difference of taboo.

Over a wide area stretching over the entire Oti plain and on to the low hills surrounding it we find these four peoples, much alike in culture and social organization. The total population cannot even be guessed at. This population is not a political unit, nor is each of the four peoples composing it a political unit. But it forms, as it were, a field within which political units are found, each unit having its own range of relations. The unit within which order is maintained by peaceable means is the clan and each clan stands in relations of potential hostility to all but a few of the other clans of the region. These relations of hostility are not all of equal strength. From any one central clan relations with neighboring clans are for the most part friendly. Beyond these neighbors lie clans with which feud is possible and beyond these lie clans of different tribes with which the tribe of the clan we started with is always potentially at war. But beyond these tribes lie yet others with which our first clan has no known relation. Intertribal war is not such that any one Konkomba tribe is perennially at war with all the other tribes. In fact, few men know even the names of more than perhaps six tribes in all, including their own. The Betshabob fight bitterly with their neighbors the Bemokpem but few of them even know of the Benandem who lie beyond the Bemokpem to the south. That is to say that even the relation of unending hostility does not, in this system, extend widely in space.

Though relations of hostility between tribes exist, the likelihood of particular outbreaks of fighting is diminished, on the plane of relations between individuals, by ties of affinal, and especially matrilateral, kinship. The ties between a man and his mother's clan are effective in two ways. First, he is linked to all the men of his mother's major lineage and, in lesser degree, to men of other major lineages of her clan, in a joking relationship. This joking relation between men who address each other as mother's brother prohibits bloodshed between them. Such a link is primarily between one man and a lineage but, since a widow is inherited within the span of the minor lineage, the relation is extended in both of its terms. It is, however, one that endures only during the life span of individuals. More important, perhaps, though not longer enduring, is the relation between men whose mothers came from the same clan. They call each other *nabo*, literally, mother child. This is a positive relation of obligatory friendliness though it carries with it no other responsibilities or duties. Those who are *nabo* to each other must be friendly when they meet; that is, they may not quarrel and should try to keep each other out of quarrels with other persons. In view of the wide dispersal in space of the women of a clan who have married out of it, it follows that any person's *nabo* are equally widely dispersed and provide a man with points of friendship in otherwise hostile places. This is the most widely extended in space of all positive relations between individuals since women may marry anywhere—into other clans, tribes, and even peoples. It is, of course, the case that the frequency of these links diminishes with distance since most women marry within a radius of 12 miles of their natal hamlets. But the *nabo* relation too, like the relation between structures already discussed, operates most strongly where it is most needed; that is, among clans not widely separated from each other.

All relations between groups, in this system, spread but narrowly in space and, in comparison with other societies, the groups which stand in these relations are tiny. A clan seldom numbers more than 250 souls: the largest districts do not have an extension of more than 25 square miles. Konkomba techniques of production for livelihood are low. This low level of production, the high degree of local self-subsistence, and the difficult habitat together inhibit the growth of large units. Konkomba inhabit a plain broken by the courses of many streams that may, in the wet season, be half a mile wide; in the dry season the plain is a dust-bowl and in the wet season a swamp. The largest compact hamlets do not count a population of more than 200, and many clans are dispersed in as many as eight small hamlets scattered about the district. It is only in the hills on the periphery of the plain that larger groupings are found and there clan segmentation tends to be more complex than the dual and contrapuntal segmentation I have spoken of. Even there, however, not more than four major lineages to a clan have, so far, been discovered.

In conformity with the narrow range of political relations are the scale of land and ancestor cults. The land shrine refers only to the small unit which is a district and the ancestor cult stretches briefly back through only five generations in time.

The ecology is such that only small, unilineal groupings can be developed. From this seems to follow the narrow range of relations between clans, and from the nature of those relations follows the failure of tribes to fuse into a people in opposition to other peoples. Despite long pressure and periodic raiding by the Dagomba and Mamprussi no fusion of tribes has taken place among the Gurma-speaking peoples.

NOTE

[1] I do not speak of "law" since I judge it advisable to confine that term to the usage of Radcliffe-Brown and Seagle, in which "law" is prescriptive, normative and publicly sanctioned. Though there undoubtedly exist, in Konkomba, both moral obligations to achieve standards of behavior and sanctions on breaches of those standards, the standards themselves were not laid down by a legislature, are not interpreted by a judiciary and are not enforced by an executive. Consequently, I speak not of law but of jural activities and a system of social control.

FOR FURTHER READING

Further information on Konkomba political organization is to be found in Tait, David, "Territorial Pattern and Lineage System of Konkomba," in Middleton, John, and Tait, David (eds.), *Tribes without Rulers,* London: Routledge & Kegan Paul, 1958, pp. 167-202. This book is an analytical study of six societies in which unilineal descent groups play varying roles in the political structure.

Background information on the Konkomba can be found in Tait, David, "History and Social Organization," *Transactions of the Gold Coast and Togoland Historical Society,* 1955, *1,* 193-110; and in Tait, David, "The Family,

Household and Minor Lineage of the Konkomba," *Africa,* 1956, *26,* 219-49, 332-42.

Fortes, Meyer, *The Dynamics of Clanship among the Tallensi,* London: Oxford University Press for the International African Institute, 1945. A detailed analysis of the system of unilineal descent among a people in northern Ghana who have a political organization similar to that of the Konkomba.

Evans-Pritchard, E. E., *The Nuer,* London: Oxford University Press, 1940. A careful study of the ecological and political aspects of a Nilotic people having patrilineal descent groupings.

HEADMANSHIP AND THE RITUAL
OF LUAPULA VILLAGES*

Ian Cunnison

Many of the peoples of South Central Africa are matrilineal and live in villages that shift in personnel, and in some cases in location. Cunnison's paper shows how leadership and village organization function in one part of this region. In the introduction to this reader we stressed the close ties between secular and ritual activities among African leaders, and this is clearly the case in the Luapula Valley. Again, clientship was discussed, and Maquet's paper on the Ruanda indicates how it functions in a state society permeated with caste. Among the Luapula people there is no formal clientship in the sense of an economic contract, but the continual shifting of personnel from village to village seeking a "good" village, and the efforts of village heads to maintain a contented following, indicate similarities with the more formal pattern of clientship of the Ruanda. It should also be noted that although matrilineal ties form the focus of the village organization in the Luapula Valley, there is no simple correspondence whereby one matrilineal descent group alone forms one village. The village membership is much more complex. The correspondence of a clan or lineage with a residential area is perhaps more common in patrilineal societies, and is certainly exemplified by the Konkomba, described by Tait in this reader.

This article is intended primarily as a contribution to the study of the village headman in British Central Africa.[1] While most reports from the area have paid attention to the headman's structural position, this has been specifically considered by Gluckman, Barnes, and Mitchell in "The Village Headman in British Central Africa" (*Africa*, xix, no. 2, 1949) and, more recently, by Mitchell in his forthcoming analysis of *The Yao Village*.[2] The closely related question of the values attached to village life has received attention notably from Prof. M. Wilson in *Good Company*.[3]

Whatever form these societies take, the headman plays a key role in them. In acephalous societies the village headman was the head of the

---

* Reprinted from *Africa*, 1956, 26, 2-16, by permission of the International African Institute (author's copyright reserved).

smallest and perhaps the only political group and was *ex officio* an important political personage. In societies with chiefs, the headman represents his chief to the people of the village. In both types the headman is a political representative of the group of more or less closely related kinsmen clustered around him in his village. Thus his person is a link between domestic and political life. He has to play his part with skill. His loyalty towards his kinsmen should not affect his loyalty towards his chief.

His own standing and power are directly linked to the standing and power of other headmen. If his followers leave him, they can do so only by going to another headman whose following thus increases at his expense, for they know no form of residence other than residence in villages. Gluckman (op. cit., p. 93) wrote: "We see the political systems of these people as being rooted in the self-assertion of villages, the smallest corporate units, against one another."

The political balance of village against village on the Luapula is maintained by the freedom which people have, and which they exploit, to go and live in whatever village suits them best. They move from one headman to another until they find a village which, in their own experience, is healthy, harmonious, free from sorcery and premature death, and where they prosper. These are the main values of village life on the Luapula, and it is the headman who is held ultimately responsible for the state of his village in respect of these qualities.

I hope that the account of Luapula village ritual in this article will show that a headman, to be successful, must be more than a good kinsman and mediator in domestic matters, and more than a good politician: he must also be ritually efficient. It will be shown that a headman's political role—one headman among a number of competing equals—which previous studies have emphasized, is vividly expressed and even clarified in village ritual. The ritual also exhibits those values in good village life which have been described by Wilson for the Nyakyusa. Beyond this the ritual emphasizes points of fission apparent in the structure of Luapula villages.

The Luapula River flows out of Lake Bangweulu, turns north and flows into Lake Mweru, thus forming the boundary between Northern Rhodesia and the Belgian Congo. Kazembe is the Paramount chief over the east bank of the Lower Luapula Valley. The villages and their gardens are situated along the road which runs from one end of the valley to the other, a short distance from the edge of the Luapula swamps. On this road are long stretches where village follows village in an unbroken line. These villages are of various tribes. When Kazembe, of the Lunda, arrived there over 200 years ago from Mwata Yamvwa's country in the west, he found a number of villages already in position. Since his domination of the area groups of people have come in from all directions, although mainly from the Chishinga, Lungu, Tabwa, Bemba, Aushi, and Mukulo tribes of North-eastern Rhodesia. Once arrived, they formed villages. Few established villages die out. A village is known by the name of its founder and, on his death, his position is inherited in the female line. The successor takes not only the headmanship but also the name, the relationships, the wives, and some material object, such as the belt, of the deceased. Villages move occasionally but not very often; and even if they do their name and identity remain the same.

New villages are formed either when a man achieves a number of followers and applies to the chief for permission to form a village; or else when a band of immigrants comes to the country and likewise applies. The present rate of formation of new villages in the country is on an average between three and four a year.

Villages vary greatly in size; some consist of a mere handful of houses, but the majority comprise between twenty and forty. A small village is composed of some of the matrilineal kinsmen of the headman, and this remains the nucleus of the village however much it grows. In this paper I do no more than summarize the evidence I have on village composition. The headman always has with him some relatives of his own matrilineage (*cikota*). The rest of the village is made up of groups whose leaders have some relationship—perhaps very slight—with the headman. Such a group, whose members usually build near each other to form a distinct section (*citente*) of the village, is composed mainly of members of the matrilineage of the man who came to follow the headman. Leaders of village sections are generally followed only by their closest matrilineal kin, but headmen are followed by people with remote kinship links.

In the Luapula Valley are representatives of over twenty tribes and more than forty clans which cut across tribal divisions. Headmanship is an office, but the office belongs neither to tribe nor to clan: it is vested in the matrilineage, the *cikota*. This is the largest section of a clan which cooperates for any purpose and it is kept by genealogical fiction at a span of about seven generations. It is the exogamous unit. It is composed of the descendants of a group of clansmen who immigrated to the Luapula together. If a headman—or anyone for that matter—should die, his place must be taken by someone junior within his *cikota*. Thus the headmanship remains in the matrilineage, and the matrilineage is said to "own" the village, even though only a small part of the matrilineage may actually reside there. The matrilineage is widely dispersed up and down the valley. There are no strict rules of residence; in marriage, after two or three years in the village of his bride's mother, a man is free to move where he will, and the choice may be determined by factors other than kinship. Thus not only may there be members of more than one *cikota* in a village; there may also be representatives of different clans and tribes.

The headman (*mwinemushi,* "owner of the village") is not necessarily the senior member of his matrilineage. Its head is usually the man who is the latest successor of the person who led the group of clansmen from their ancestral home outside the valley. He may be of any age, as also may the village headman, and it is very likely nowadays that a young headman may be chosen in order to deal energetically with tasks imposed upon him by the Administration. His appointment must have the approval of his chief, and, if he is young, he has the additional task of running the village to the satisfaction of his matrilineage elders who may be living elsewhere. Once in office the headman is usually secure until his death, unless in his old age he hands over to a successor. He can be ousted by the chief, or by elders of his matrilineage, but not by other members of the village, whose only hold upon him is that they can leave him and go elsewhere. These comparative strangers in the village are living in a place which belongs to a matrilineage other than their own, and they have no strong tie, even of honor, to keep them in it. The general picture, then, is of a village composed of the headman and a nucleus of the matrilineage which "owns" it, surrounded by members of other, stranger matrilineages, who are free to move in and out as they like.

Villages used to be built very close to the swamp edge in a tangle of trees. There are still a few like this, but the majority have now moved back about half a mile to line the valley road. Houses are built nowadays mainly of sun-dried brick in streets—one street lining the main road, with others at right angles to it leading towards the swamp. A village has no obvious center—no village rest-house, no general meeting place for the discussion of village affairs, for conversation, or for eating. The headman's house, although for convenience it is generally near the middle of the village, is not necessarily situated there, and it is impossible to tell the headman's house from any other. The whole area enclosed by the houses is kept in a swept condition. What is not village is gardens or bush (respectively *mushi, mabala, mpanga*), and even land adjoining the village is "bush" if it is uncultivated.

To form a village a man with followers applies to the chief of one of the seven chiefdoms into which Kazembe's country is divided. A man may, without permission, move with a group of followers to form a cluster alongside his parent village, but in the eyes of the chief this is not a new village, for it does not involve the allocation of new land for habitation. If a man wants to be recognized as a headman by the chief and the Administration he must apply to be "written" (*kulembwa*) as a headman and to have his followers tax-listed in his name; and this requires a minimum of ten taxpayers among his followers. The modern word for "to become a headman" is *kulembwa*. If the village is to be set upon new ground, this ground is allocated by the chief.

There is no objection to moving to another chiefdom inside the country. There is, moreover, much movement between Rhodesia and the Belgian Congo, where the valley peoples are of the same origin and, until European administration, were all under Kazembe. The chiefs welcome strangers to their lands and each chief is anxious that his chiefdom should be thronged with people. In this way not only can he command more tribute and boast that he is a popular chief but he is also more likely to have his own pay increased, for this to some extent depends on the number of followers he has. But to the people, what makes their community a village is not the fact that it is written as such in the Administration books. It is the existence of the *nshipa,* the ritual foundation of the village.

THE RITUAL

In the village ritual there are two main elements which are made effective by a third. The first is the *nshipa,* which I do not translate; the second is the *lukunku* or *musashi,* the calabash; and the third is the *nongo,* the marriage pot of the headman's chief wife, which is used for purification after intercourse. When a man succeeds to the headmanship this pot becomes the *nongo ya mushi,* the village pot.

Together these things are believed to protect the village inhabitants from mystical dangers on the occasion of a death or the birth of a stillborn child within the village, or if a member of the village kills or finds dead in the bush a man, lion, leopard, or striped weasel. They are believed to keep wild animals and sorcerers out of the village and to attract and retain inhabitants.

The *nshipa* is installed at the first formation of a village, or again if the village moves its site even a short distance. It is referred to as *ciito ca bantu,* an instrument for calling people to the village. With it are usually associated antisorcery medicines, *miti ya kucingililo mushi.*

If the village has been moved and the *nshipa* is to be changed the old one is first dug up and thrown into a river. The headman and the magician whom he has summoned together cut a young *mutaba* tree (*ficus* sp.).[4] While doing this they loosen their belts. At night, when the people are still talking in their houses, the headman and his wife sit naked in front of their house, the magician with them. A piece of wood, the *nshipa,* is hollowed out and the magician inserts medicines and charms. The charms include one from the honey guide bird. A duiker horn is forced into the wood and more medicines are put into the horn. A hole is dug knee-deep. The headman's wife grasps his arm as he plants the sapling in the hole. A cock is killed, and the heart placed in the hole. The headman and his wife sit facing each other, the headman to the west. He places the *nshipa* between his legs and, seated, edges them forward to the hole. Together he and his wife fill up the hole with loose soil which they stamp down with a medicated stick. They then sleep together and, in the morning, wash ritually in the wife's marriage pot. The *nshipa* is thereby made effective. The wife then cooks mush in the pot, and the meal, with the cock as relish, is shared with the magician. The tree alone remains as evidence of the *nshipa,* which itself is never seen by the villagers. On the death of the headman the *nshipa* momentarily "dies," but is renewed automatically (*kupilibuka,* "it turns over") on the installation of the next headman.

The *calabash* is a small hollowed and dried cucurbit containing medicines and charms, which is kept in the roof of the headman's house. It is used for the purification of villagers as need arises. The calabash "dies" on the death of a headman and cannot be revived. To install it, the headman calls a magician versed in village medicines, usually himself a headman. The magician brings two calabashes with him—the one of his own village, and a new one. He brings appropriate medicines of plants and wood powder and charms of elephant, lion, and scaly anteater, and he and the headman together, by night, put them into the new calabash which, along with the magician's calabash, they hang on a forked stick over a discarded pot containing more medicines and charms. At sunrise the women of the village sweep out their hearths and take the ashes to a cross-paths to the west of the village. The magician buries the ashes under the old pot, washes the women's hands and feet in medicated water, giving them some of this water with which to replaster their hearths. Back in the village the magician lights a fire, using grass from a mole's nest as tinder, and the women take new fire from it. The magician then splits in two one seed each of groundnut, groundbean, lentil, pumpkin, cucumber, sorghum, and finger-millet. One half, "for the year that is past," he thows on to the cross-paths, and the other half, "for the year that is coming," he puts into the headman's calabash. Finally he instructs the headman about tabus, such as bringing firewood into the village from an ant hill. This ends the magician's work, for which he is paid perhaps £2. Next night, when the headman and his wife sleep together and wash in the wife's marriage pot, the calabash is made effective. To use the calabash for purification, the headman smears the face, neck, and hands of the contaminated person with oil which he has poured over the medicines in the calabash.

Nongo, the word for "village pot," is connected with the idea of chieftainship of any rank. One of the phrases meaning "to open up a piece of country" is *kuteke nongo mu calo,* literally "to put the pot on the fire in the country." This same word *kuteka* means both "to put a pot on the fire" and "to rule." This pot makes the *nshipa* and calabash effective when the headman and his wife wash in it after ritual intercourse, and it is their regular washing in it which maintains these elements in an effective state.

Two other rites are practiced in many villages, though they are not regarded as so important. One is "marking out a trail" (*kukomo lukomo*), and is usually performed shortly after the formation of a village, or on a move to a new village site. The headman cuts pegs of wood and medicates them. He makes a wide sweep round the village site, hammering pegs into the ground at intervals. It is said that should the *nshipa* be a good one, the village will expand to this boundary. It is also said that wild animals and sorcerers would fear to cross the line into the village.

The other rite is "standing in the smoke of medicine" (*konto muti*). The headman builds a fire with medicines inside the village and calls the people to come and warm themselves. The smoke is supposed to spread to every nook and cranny of the village and make it safe from sorcerers and wild animals. The people who stand in the smoke are thus protected even outside the village and need never fear should they be benighted in the bush.

There are some minor differences in the charms and medicines used, but, for commoner villages at any rate, the main rites are the same.

PURPOSE OF THE RITES

The rites, taken together, are held to have certain beneficial effects on the village. Both headmen and villagers require the ritual for the protection it affords against the very real danger of wild animals (lions and leopards) and the ever-present fear of sorcery.[5] They believe also that it helps to ensure harmony in village life. The headman wants the ritual in order to attract and retain villagers by the known safety and good living of his village. If a man comes across a *mupamba,* an evil omen such as the dead lion, &c., mentioned above, it is incumbent on him for his own safety to be purified before speaking or eating. He depends upon village medicines for this purification. If he has killed a lion or found a dead one, he comes silently to his village, with his fists clenched on a level with his shoulders, imitating claws; the headman sees him and knows at once what this means, and takes appropriate action. General purification must also be made when a death occurs in the village.

If the rites are effective, the result should be absence of premature deaths in the village; for these arise either from sorcery or from some moral lapse due to lack of harmony in the village. It should be noted that all these rites are concerned with the persons of the villagers: the headman takes no steps ritually to prosper the fishing or agricultural activities of his villagers. But if one inquires which rites are directed towards which ends the answers are confused. Some say that the *nshipa* is purely to attract inhabitants, others that it is also directed against sorcery. Certain elements have a clearer meaning to everyone. It is generally agreed that the honey guide charm is used to attract villagers in the same way as the bird itself attracts men to something good—a beehive. If the headman should draw firewood from an ant hill this would attract the wild animals which sleep upon ant hills. The grass from the mole's nest with which new fire is kindled should make the village safe in the same way as the underground safety of the mole's nest protects the mole against its enemies. The uses of other charms have various interpretations. The scaly anteater, for instance, is said to be powerful since it has to be brought from faraway Tanganyika; again, its power is supposed to derive from its name, *nkaka,* which makes it *kukaka fyonse*—tie everything up, put village affairs in order.

The *nshipa* is regarded as the foundation of the village in that there is no village (*mushi*) without *nshipa,* and no *nshipa* without village and headman. The village, and village medicines, are held by the Luapula peoples to be necessary to all societies. They note with interest acts they have seen Europeans perform, like "laying the foundation stone" and "cutting the first sod" on mission stations; and they thought that the weather gauge at Kawambwa, which the District Commissioner looked at each day, was the equivalent of the *nshipa* for the Government station.

Village medicines are still important in spite of the advance of Christianity, for belief in sorcery dies hard on the Luapula. Nevertheless there are headmen with long schooling in Christianity who fear the reproof of missionaries if they should lend themselves to such things. They realize, however, that if they neglected their medicines their villages would break up. A Christian headman will appoint a young pagan brother and his wife to be ritual heads of the village while he himself deals with the secular aspects of headmanship.

The *nshipa* is closely connected with a certain place. Significantly it is buried in the ground. We noted that if the village moves, even so short a way that the new and old sites overlap, a new *nshipa* is required. After such a move it is quite common for a few of the old people to remain in their houses on the old site outside the new swept area. In this case peripheral houses remain outside the effective sphere of the new *nshipa.* Their occupants do not have its protection, and a death in one of these houses does not contaminate the rest of the village. If, during an interregnum between headmen, a man becomes seriously ill he is moved out of the village, since at such a time there is no one to purify the villagers. It is considered safe if he is moved to a house on the old site. Thus the *nshipa* is connected with those householders who form the heart of the village, where the area is swept, where no grass or gardens intervene, and where houses are contiguous. If a villager dies elsewhere the village need not be purified, even if the body is brought to the village for burial;

it is dying within the sphere of the *nshipa* which contaminates the village.

THE HEADMAN AND OTHER HEADMEN

We consider the ritual first with reference to intervillage or inter-headmen relationships. There are 322 villages between Johnston Falls in the south and the northern border of Kazembe's country, each of them under a headman who has as much right as his neighbor to attract people to his own village. These villages are politically equal under the seven chiefs, and people move as they like from one village to another. A local saying claims that "commoners move where they will, only chiefs remain in one place." This is as true for headmen as for chiefs. Taken at any point of time the composition of a village is ephemeral. Not only individual householders but whole sections move in and out of villages. The people who move about are seeking a village which suits them and where they will prosper. The actual moves are easily made: the crop is cassava, which creates no storage problems; and the main industry is fishing, and fishermen are free to fish where they like. Moreover, there is a ready market in houses.

Although the swamps and the bush are dotted with temporary encampments for fishing, hunting, or other purposes, a man must have a permanent abode in some village. He has to be registered somewhere and may not go and settle *permanently* by himself in the bush. Nor may he go out and "put the pot on the fire" anywhere without the permission of the chief of the area, for the allocation of land for such purposes is one of the most important functions of Luapula chieftainship, and the whole policy of settling the country is in the chiefs' hands. Now that the chief cooperates with the British Administration he has to abide by the ten taxpayer rule and does not allow less than this number to form a village.

Advantages accrue from living in villages and people are blind to any advantages that might accrue from not living in them. What the people require is to live in safety, health, harmony, and prosperity. They must live somewhere in order to have a base for their activities. Politically this place is defined as a village. They can choose what place they want provided it is a place recognized by their chief, through the existence of a headman, for people to live in permanently. In some places they may live badly, their children may die, they may be ill, they may quarrel with their neighbors and become involved in cases. In another place they may live well, their children flourish, and the life of the village may be found harmonious. If they live badly—even if fellow villagers are content with their lot—they want to change their residence and they seek a village where they think they will live well. At the same time they do not want to live as complete strangers in a village and so they look for a "good" village in which there is someone who is related to them in some way.

Although they seek a good place it is only indirectly that the place is good or bad. A place can become "rotten"—and this is the most frequent reason why villages move a short distance. The expression is *kubola*, "to rot"; and *cibolya*, from the same stem, is the word for a deserted village site. But the radical cause of the rottenness of a village, why there are many deaths, diseases, and other misfortunes caused by sorcery, is believed to be the failure of the *nshipa*, for it should create conditions in a village which attract outsiders rather than repel them.

If children die young in a family it is because of sorcery directed against the family. It is always held that the sorcerer is in the same or a nearby village, since the sorcerer, in practice, must go in person to the house of his victim by night. Nevertheless, if the *nshipa* were working properly the sorcery, wherever it came from, would be rendered ineffective. Temporary moves may be made to another village in case of sickness to try out the influence of a different *nshipa*.

The popularity of a headman, and hence the size of his village, is directly related to the harmony and health of his villagers, as well as to his practical ability in settling disputes. That is to say, his popularity depends on factors which to the European mind remain beyond his control; but to the Luapula peoples the harmony and health of a village depend as much upon ritual efficiency as upon just administration and the maintenance of hygiene. In point of fact the headman in the village is an adjudicator only within his own matrilineage. Other family disputes are generally not within his jurisdiction, and in any case he has no formal judicial powers. Although his personality undoubtedly influences the cohesion of villagers, the blame for disharmony is eventually attributed to his working of the ritual. The people know well that a headman can succeed or fail according to his diligence or carelessness about the ritual. So if misfortunes of any kind make people move from a village the headman is indirectly blamed for them and suffers punishment for his presumed inefficiency in seeing his people drift away.

Now of course every headman is in the same position. Each tries to keep his villagers and to attract other adherents. A big village is the sign of a successful headman. Although headmen deny that they try to attract people from other villages, they yet claim that *other* headmen have medicine—*bwanga bwe tuta*—which they can sprinkle in rival villages to attract inhabitants to their own. Headmen therefore seek to guard against this by attention to mystical as well as practical affairs. Indeed, they have been taught at their installation that "subjects are like grass seed, they fall aside" and "subjects are like grease, they melt away." [6]

In this situation headmen have only one resource: they turn to magicians (*ng'anga*). Knowledge of village medicines is in the hands of very few magicians, and six out of the eight whom I knew were themselves headmen of old-established villages. Occasionally medicines may be handed down from a headman to a known successor, but magicians are the only advisers in the matter. Some magicians have long connections with particular villages, but there is no rigid tie between headman and magician, and a headman can change his magician if he wants to. Thus headmen compete against each other with the same or similar medicines—often indeed with the medicines of the same magician.

The choice of magician seems to depend largely upon the type of calabash which he sells, for some are easier to work than others when a purification is necessary. One type requires that the headman and his wife should have ritual intercourse before it is used on any occasion. Another type requires a special kind of oil which is difficult to procure. Others are more simple. One, the "cock," which is much in favor, purifies a village automatically after a death when the first cock crows on the following morning. It is only if things are going wrong that headmen discuss the merits of different magicians. Some headmen suspect that magicians may be bribed by other headmen to give them bad medicines.

No headman admits that his own medicine is *bwanga* (sorcery) for doing other headmen down. Headmen insist that theirs are good medicines (*muti*), designed to secure the harmony of their own villages But they view other headmen as enemies and potential sorcerers. Nevertheless, commoners who know the ritual for the installation of the *nshipa* describe it as a *positive act of sorcery*. The reason is quite straightforward. To go outside naked at night is at all times to be avoided: it is to proclaim oneself a sorcerer, for *bufwiti*, the commonest kind of sorcery, requires that a man go naked at night to the house of his victim. A commoner who was with me when I was hearing a description of the *nshipa* rites exclaimed as the account proceeded: "But this is bewitching the country!" Charges of sorcery against rival headmen are seldom specific. I came across only one. The matter was informally discussed before Kazembe, who played down the charge and said it was obviously the fault of the "offended" headman, who could not keep his people in order.

Commoner villages all have medicines of the same general type. The few commoner villages whose headmen are also ritual "owners of the land" have different kinds of medicine, and there are special medicines for villages of chiefs and sons of the Kazembes, and for the capital of Kazembe itself. Chiefs are also headmen and their villages are larger (supposedly because their medicines are more powerful). They tend to despise the medicines of commoner villages, and do not fear the rivalry of commoner headmen. Thus commoner villages are seen to be ritually similar and in opposition to each other. The ritual implies both protection against the inroads of other headmen, in the medicines for the harmony of the village, and attacks on other headmen, in the honey guide charm. But headmen of commoner villages are not ritually in a position to attack chiefly villages, because these have special medicines which are more powerful, and which no magician would dare give to a commoner headman for fear of losing the favor of the chief.

HEADMEN AND VILLAGERS

In kinship matters the headman has direct authority only over the affairs of his own immediate matrilineage in the village—and even here he may be overridden by older men or even by matrilineage elders from outside the village. The other sections of the village apply on kinship matters to their own matrilineage elders. In the practical matters of headmanship the headman also has to listen to all the elders of the village— the *bacilolo*—to whatever section they may belong. An analogy often noted with the position of the newly appointed headman is that of the girl at puberty, unable to answer back, in a position only to listen to the rules propounded by her elders. But in the matter of ritual the headman is truly head from the start. He alone is responsible. Shortly after the new Kasebula was installed he went round the village shouting an announcement to the effect that he was now headman and if anyone else wanted to shout against sorcerers (*kubile mbila*) they must first bring the matter to him and he would do it. This is a custom whereby, if it is obvious that a sorcerer is at work, the headman goes round at night, keeping strictly within his own village, shouting: "You sorcerer, this is no way to behave, you had better stop, we know who you are."

In addition to formal village ritual headmen in general are held to know many medicines both good and bad. *Bushing'anga* and *bukulu bwa mushi*—knowledge of medicines and headmanship—are more or less synonymous terms. People believe, in fact, that all headmen are sorcerers. This is simply part of a wider belief that success in any sphere cannot be achieved without the aid of bad medicines. Outstandingly successful fishermen, for instance, have killed off their relatives one by one and used their spirits to help drive fish into the nets. People with exceptional crops of cassava have managed, by setting medicines in their gardens, to attract roots from their neighbors. Such is the nature of the system that there are many candidates for all positions of headmanship and chieftainship; and it is widely believed that the successful candidate succeeds only because others are afraid to put themselves forward lest, out of jealousy, he should later use sorcery to kill them. Likewise when a man succeeds to an office it is thought that he continues to live only because he has exceptionally powerful medicines to counteract the sorcery of jealous rivals who would be constantly out for his blood.

It is also said that the stronger medicines—good and bad—are known only to chiefs and headmen: medicines for warding off lightning or thunderbolts, or for sending these things, and the like. Of the dozens of recipes for medicines which I copied out of boys' notebooks there was only one village medicine, written by a boy who was himself the son of a headman. Otherwise the medicines were mostly of the types known to adults, consisting of panaceas for physical strength, sexual prowess, and popularity. Children know well that their own medicines are tame affairs. They know also that headmen have the real stuff; and it is this that prompted the remark I heard so often from children: "All headmen are bad."

Thus the headman's relationship to his villagers has a basis in his strong mystical prestige. Villagers are temporarily—while they are living under a certain headman—at the mercy of his medicines; they depend on him completely for protection against mystical dangers; at the same time he is feared because of the knowledge of powerful medicines which is held to be the stock-in-trade of his calling.

THE HEADMAN AND HIS MATRILINEAGE

The headmanship belongs to the headman's matrilineage. Villagers who do not belong to this matrilineage are not necessarily consulted about succession. The headman is chosen out of many dispersed members of the matrilineage for the position of special rank within it; for there is seldom more than one such political office in each lineage, and, of course, there are matrilineages without a headmanship or village to their name. Even if his name is senior, the headman himself may be a young man who has inherited it and so he may have to listen with respect to elders who are strictly his "juniors." Some of these relationships are made clear in the actions which follow the death of a headman or his wife.

When a headman's wife dies the village is left without its pot, which was her private property. It still belongs to her matrilineage and they remove it from the village. Thus the calabash "dies" and the village is said to "become cold" and "die." The headman's wife's family will be persuaded to find a successor to the dead woman as soon as possible, even before the normal *tobolola* payments, made by a surviving spouse, have been handed over to them. In the interim a magician is called to purify the village, and a brother or other clansman of the headman is appointed to look after the ritual side until a new wife is found. This caretaker (for whom there is no special title) sleeps with his own wife and they purify themselves in their marriage pot, to which special medicines have been added for the occasion. He is given the calabash to look after, which his wife's pot, now temporarily the village pot, has once more made effective. When the headman's new wife arrives, the caretaker and his wife are sent out of the village while the process of the wife's succession goes on. On the night when the headman has intercourse with his new wife for the first time, the other villagers are not allowed to have intercourse, the sanction being misfortune to the whole village. In the morning the villagers, including the children of the headman, leave the village and stand outside the boundaries while the new wife's pot is put on the fire, the headman gripping the pot and his wife gripping the headman's arm. The calabash is now effective again for use by the headman. Strictly it is only those who would normally have sexual intercourse at the time who are obliged to leave the village bounds, but in practice everyone gets out, including the young and the old. The pot is placed on the fire in front of witnesses—old people, if possible, of the headman's matrilineage, who have come, if necessary, from outside the village. Later a meal is cooked in the new village pot and is shared by the headman, his wife, and the witnesses from the matrilineage.

On the death of a headman both the *nshipa* and the calabash become ineffective. The calabash is thrown away into a river. The village is purified by a magician as before. This puts an end to the tabus on cooking food (strictly, of placing pots on fires) and on sexual intercourse within the village which are imposed at any death. But it is still important that no one else should die in the village, because there is no calabash for purification. The elders of the matrilineage are called in to arrange the whole succession. They appoint a caretaker who is ideally the son of the dead headman, and therefore of the clan of the headman's wife. It is wrong to appoint a man of the headman's matrilineage, since it may be difficult to persuade him to yield his position when the time comes for the succession of the selected heir. The succession takes place in a house other than that of the previous headman, with the caretaker and his wife away from the village as before and the villagers outside the village bounds.

In this ritual we see the distinction made between the headman's matrilineage and the other vaguely related groups. It is the headman's matrilineage that is in control of the ritual, even if it means coming from outside the village to control it. They alone are in the village as witnesses when the pot is placed on the fire, and they alone, with the headman and his wife, eat the meal cooked in the pot. Again, when the headman's wife dies the ritual is handed over to a fellow clansman of the headman. The other members of the village partake only in a negative way in the ritual. By abstaining from intercourse and getting out of the village they leave the ground clear for the effective "warming" of the village and the medicines by the headman and his wife supported by his matrilineage elders.

THE HEADMAN AND HIS WIFE

The headman's wife and her matrilineage are in a very special position, for they can make or break the village. The ritual depends upon her as much as upon the headman. It is their marital relationship that makes the village ritual effective. Without this relationship there can be no village so long as ritual is its mainstay. On his wife's death the headman is dependent upon her matrilineage for a successor, and if they do not send one the headman may not remarry (for fear of a disease (*cito*) which strikes any widower or widow who has intercourse during the time between the death of the spouse and the installation of the successor); and thus he is unable to work the ritual. The other role of the wife's matrilineage is to provide a caretaker after the headman's death. This appointment is made by the elders of the headman's matrilineage and is made quite explicitly for the reason that the person appointed must not be in a position later to usurp the headmanship. This is an important point when it is remembered that the headman's sons, of his wife's clan, generally live in the village with their father in order to have some of the reflected glory of headmanship. Here, then, is revealed the high importance of the wife's matrilineage, and at the same time the fact that it is ineligible for headmanship is emphasized.

To inquire why the headman's wife enjoys the important role she does is outside the scope of this paper since it would involve a discussion of symbolism in all ranks of chieftainship. Briefly, where a man's position implies mystical care of land and people he can effect this only through his marital relationship. And the chief wife is identified in speech with her husband: *mwadi e mwata* ("the queen is the king") is a phrase often heard in connection with Kazembe and his first wife. The mystical dangers from dead lions can only be annulled by "owners of the land," and then only after intercourse with their wives; and both spouses have to step on a lion-skin to purify it and the country. A man can rule his country only when it is "hot," and it can be made "hot" only in this manner. Village headmanship is a minor form of this mystical control over land and people, but it contains the same elements as higher chieftainship and its working is in the same general form.

THE VILLAGERS AMONG THEMSELVES

We consider finally the question of the village as a unit. We pointed out that villages were stable, in that a village of one name endures although it may change its site. But the population is continually fluctuating, and the only permanence about this aspect of it is the fact that it always has a man of the same matrilineage as headman, and that he is always surrounded in the village by some of his matri-kin.

We have already pointed to the difference between the matrilineage which owns the village and the members of the other sections which compose it. This particular dichotomy was well illustrated in practice in the village of Kasebula. There was a fairly clear line of demarcation between the houses of the headman's matrilineage at the south end of the village and the others at the north end. Only the house of the headman himself was in a kind of enclave among the stranger groups. Moreover, when the villagers dispersed to fishing camps, those from the south went to one place and those from the north went to another. I lived in the south end, and found it difficult to persuade people from the other end to visit me much. It is not easy to say how general is this physical division. In the only other village in which I lived for any length of time this split was not so marked. In some villages there is another differentiating feature: a special graveyard, in the deserted village site, is reserved for members of the headman's matrilineage who die in the village, while other people are buried in the bush or among the gardens.

Only occasionally does a village unite for economic activities, and some villages never do so. If a channel is to be dug or deepened between the main swamp waters and the village canoe-park, this is done by the village as a team. If the village is situated in part of the country where bush-pigs ravage the gardens, villagers unite in digging a deep ditch, inside which they all cultivate. In marriage, the instructors and go-betweens of bride and groom are found from members of all sections of the village. For children the village is nearly always the play unit.

Politically it is by the village that a man identifies himself: he carries the name of his village about with him on his identity card. All dealings between villagers and chiefs go by way of the headman, who likewise has to publish announcements by his chief to the villagers. If the chief requires tribute of cassava or of labor, this is done on a village basis, and the amount of tribute is assessed according to the population and the age of the village.

The unity of villagers under the headman is revealed in the ritual. It is notable first of all that the village ritual emanating from the headman works impartially: all the inhabitants, kinsmen and strangers alike, have to stand or fall equally by the village medicines. The headman cannot—and does not want to—discriminate through these against any one section. The young headman—to give the political counterpart of this—is told at his installation the names of all important elders in the village, and warned that if he does not do well, these people will not tolerate him and will leave him.

Residence in a village imposes certain obligations upon villagers while they are living in it. They cannot refuse tax or tribute; they have to recognize the headman as their political superior, and as a sort of policeman who can report them for keeping dirty houses, for rowdiness, or for undue drunkenness. Likewise a man when he comes to a village binds himself to observe the ritual tabus and prescriptions imposed on the village on certain occasions. He willingly does this; for what he seeks in a village are those things which are ensured by the proper working of village medicines. His cooperation and the cooperation of all his fellows is required on the ritual plane for the harmony of the village to be sustained.

If a man dies in the village it is not incumbent on a resident to attend the mourning unless he is a close kinsman. Yet ritually the death affects everyone, for all have to take part in the observation of tabus and all have to be cleansed of the death. Again, if a new headman is installed it is not essential for everyone to attend and lecture the new man on headmanship although this is the custom; but ritually all must partake by leaving the bounds when the pot is put on the fire. They are forced into corporate action by virtue of their residence, and the sanction against neglect is misfortune to the village as a whole.

In village ritual the things that are ritualized are marital intercourse, fires, and cooking: things which are especially associated with the household of a man and his wife. Thus, from the point of view of the ritual, the married households appear as equal units in the composition of the village. Youths and old people are to a great extent excluded from the ritual. The emphasis is on the village as a collection of domestic units based on marital relationships and symbolized by their essential elements, sex and fire: elements which themselves are closely linked in symbolic association. It is, of course, these homes that are the basis of any village and the most satisfactory self-sufficient units. Old people and young people, in order to live well, must attach themselves in some way to this kind of unit, whether by being born into it or by being associated with it through some link of sentiment. Each of these households is independent in that it is at liberty to leave the village and settle elsewhere, but during its residence it is bound to other like units by equal participation in a common ritual.

CONCLUSION

If we take as given the fact that people require protection against mystical forces, it remains to be considered why, in Luapula society, the village and headmanship are so important in this respect, for, as we have seen, it is by virtue of residence in a village and under a headman that a man is protected. A man residing temporarily away from a village in a fishing or hunting camp, where there is no headman, must take his own measures for protection if he requires it. One can at present do no more than suggest that the reason should be sought in the essential nature of Luapula society, made up as it is of dispersed matrilineages, where the residential pattern is the village composed of only slightly related groups. Land and water are plentiful and rights in them are not vested in villages, clans, or lineages. Thus although the headman has a position of authority, he does not enjoy a multiplex authority in his relationships with the stranger sections under him. Towards them the headman is political head only. He takes no part in the discussion of their kinship matters; villagers are not bound to him for the provision of garden land and fishing rights. In the old days the ancestral worship of the headman did not bring blessing upon the stranger groups living under him. The stranger groups, for their part, have no voice in the choice or removal of a headman and can express their dissatisfaction only by leaving the village. Thus the headman lacks the natural authority which dependence upon him for kinship, economic, and religious matters would entail. It is only politically that his authority is effective; and this, in a village of one or two hundred inhabitants, is not extensive. There is little to it apart from the fact that a man follows a particular headman to build and live in his village, to be written in his books, to pay tax and tribute labor with others under him.

Those, then, who seek a place to live have no strong links of kinship or of economic or religious interest to guide them. Political allegiance is irrespective of these interests. People no doubt go where they have some kinship connection, but there always remains a choice. It is this situation in which the ritual condition of the village as a unit has point. It is because the economic, kinship, and religious bonds among villagers are weak that the village as a unit is emphatically ritualized.

What is visible at this level of political life is the movement of people from village to village. Each man in his own experience sees that a village is bad, so he leaves, or good, so he stays. To Europeans the goodness or badness of a village depends not upon the ritual but upon things like chance and personality; and a village is big because these intangibles have created conditions in which people can live together without discord. We see the ritual as an unnecessary adjunct to which is wrongly ascribed the state of the village. But whether the matter is approached African or European fashion, the drive behind the moves which distribute people among various headmen is the search for those virtues which the village, the smallest political unit, ought to have.

NOTES

[Starred items are recommended as further readings.]

[1] Field work on which this paper is based was undertaken during 1948-51 for the Rhodes-Livingstone Institute. This article has been read and criticized in the course of preparation by most officers of the Institute, to whom I am grateful for comments. Fuller accounts of village composition, and of the historical build-up of the country, may be found in my *Kinship and Local Organisation on the Luapula,** Communications from the Rhodes-Livingstone Institute no. 5; and *History on the Luapula,* Rhodes-Livingstone Paper no. 21.

[2] [Mitchell, J. C., *The Yao Village,** Manchester: Manchester University Press, 1956.]

[3] *Good Company: A Study of Nyakyusa Age-Villages,** London, 1951. It is clear that the nearby Bemba have village

ritual that presents some analogies (cf. Richards, *Land, Labour and Diet in Northern Rhodesia,** 1952, p. 238). The fullest comparable material is in Junod's account of the Thonga, *The Life of a South African Tribe,** 1927, vol. i, pp. 288 ff.

4 This tree was formerly used for making bark-cloth. It gives the best shade of any tree on the Luapula. It is the "royal" tree of the Lunda, who were told, when they left Mwata Yamvwa's capital in the west, to plant it wherever they might conquer.

5 Generally speaking, animals met in the bush are thought to be natural phenomena, but man-eating lions which enter villages, and even attack houses, are sent by sorcerers.

6 *Abantu ntongwe shilewila lubali; abantu nga majuta baleitika.*

FOR FURTHER READING

Colson, Elizabeth, and Gluckman, Max (eds.), *Seven Tribes of British Central Africa,* London: Oxford University Press on behalf of the Rhodes-Livingstone Institute, 1951. The best compilation of the social organization and culture of the South Central Africa peoples.

Cunnison, Ian, "History and Genealogies in a Conquest State," *American Anthropologist,* 1957, 59, 20-31. A concise discussion of the Luapula Valley from the point of view of the descent groups in the larger political organization of the state. A related article by Cunnison is "Perpetual Kinship: a Political Institution of the Luapula Peoples," *Human Problems in British Central Africa,* 1956, 20, 28-48.

THE ASHANTI CONSTITUTION*

Robert S. Rattray

The basis of Ashanti political organization is kinship. The matrilineal lineage is a political unit whose elected headman represents it on the council of the division, or chiefdom. The chief is, in turn, chosen from a particular lineage by the heads of other lineages. In the decentralized system each unit manages its own affairs under its own leaders, and issues affecting the whole chiefdom are decided by the council of lineage heads. Though lineages are grouped in clans, the clan is not a political unit.

An important factor in the maintenance of social order is the ancestors' concern for the prosperity and well-being of the community. Each lineage has a stool, the shrine of the ancestors, upon which the lineage head gives offerings for the group's welfare. Just as each lineage is protected by its ancestors, so the dead rulers—that is, the ancestors of the royal lineage—guard and protect the whole chiefdom. The Ashanti chief is not only a civil ruler, but, as the one who sits on the stool of the ancestors, he is the symbol of the identity and continuity of the chiefdom.

The powerful Ashanti Confederacy was formed following the Battle of Feyiase toward the end of the seventeenth century and lasted until defeated by the British in 1896. The chief of the Kumasi territorial division became the Asante Hene, *King of Ashanti, and the famed Golden Stool was created as the religious symbol of the unity of the Confederacy. The component chiefdoms were held together both by allegiance to the stool and by the military power of the conquest state.*

In his book, Ashanti Law and Constitution, *Rattray hypothesizes the development of the kingdom of Ashanti from an early time in which the extended family was the center of the social system. The position and power of the subchief, chief, and of the* Asante Hene *himself are, he contends, modeled on the simple pattern of the family head, or "house father." In the society composed of a grouping of homesteads, each family head was the only law binding his group. In the course of time various family groups came to look to the head of one particular family in important matters, and gradually a number of territorial di-*

————————
* Reprinted from *Ashanti Law and Constitution*, London: Oxford University Press on behalf of the International African Institute, 1929, Chapters 9 and 10, by permission of the Oxford University Press.

visions or "tribes" grew up under different independent heads who were often rivals. The tribe was a unit made up of many families belonging to several different clans and regarded by the central authority as a single territorial entity.

THE PERIOD IMMEDIATELY PRECEDING THE BATTLE OF FEYIASE[1]

The community was now a tribe under one chosen patriarch and his sister or mother, i.e. under a Chief and Queen Mother, and governed by them, assisted by the more important heads of the lesser groups, who were at first known simply as the *Mpanyimfo,* i.e. the Elders. Many such communities had grown up in widely separated areas. Each of these lived in its own great settlement, and was independent of all the rest, and subsisted by hunting and fishing in the forests surrounding its township, which it came to consider as belonging to the tribe. The custom administered was still the custom of the individual family groups; the interference of the chief with internal family affairs was possibly very slight, and his authority in most matters only nominal.

As the tribal settlements grew too large to support all the tribe, members of certain kindred groups broke away and wandered farther afield in search of new hunting-grounds. This was the history of the founding of such settlements as Kokofu, Juaben, and Kumasi. Migrations on a larger scale also took place, and whole settlements decamped *en masse* and settled in new areas, e.g. the Mampon, who originally had come from Adanse, the Nsuta and Kumawu, who had traveled from Santemanso. The pressure in some cases may possibly have been due to other causes than lack of food. It is suggestive that Ashanti migration, which had originally almost certainly been from north-northwest to south, now tended to flow back from south to north. It is safe, I think, to hazard the opinion that, about the seventeenth century, more powerful and better armed and organized tribes south of Ashanti had begun to press upon their northern neighbors. Be that as it may, towards the end of the seventeenth century, we know that Ashanti proper was subject to a southern state called Denkyira, and that tribute was demanded and paid to it by the various Ashanti divisions.

These territorial groupings were, as we have remarked, quite independent of each other. Even at this period, some halfdozen of such territorial units had assumed sufficient size and importance to cause them to be known locally as the *Amanto,* i.e. group of *Aman* or tribes. These were Assumegya, Juaben, Kumawu, Kumasi, Mampon, and Offinsu. Nsuta, Kokofu, and Bekwai, though in existence, were still comparatively unimportant. About this time, gunpowder and guns began to be known and used in Ashanti, and to supplant the sword (*afona*) and shield (*'kyem*), and their introduction marked the advent of a revolution in Ashanti internal affairs.

Nominally, as we have remarked, under Denkyira, but wholly independent of each other, these larger tribes began to undertake warlike expeditions upon lesser divisions. The experience gained in local forays was the training for the greater campaign about to come. Their intercourse with, and subjection to, a tribe in touch with the littoral, and thus with Europeans, must have had a considerable educative effect. The value of gold became known; the barbaric pomp and splendor of the Southern Kingdom would have become known also and imitated. Osai Tutu is reported to have served at the court to Ntim Gyakari, the King of Denkyira. The priest Anotche (*Komfo* Anotche),[2] the maker of modern Ashanti, had certainly traveled south and had possibly visited the coast.

This is but a short *résumé* of Ashanti traditional history of this period, a fuller account of which will be found in the historical chapters of *Ashanti Law and Constitution*,[3] but it serves to indicate how the ground was prepared for the struggle which was now beginning, and to explain how the Ashanti, who, possibly one hundred years before these events, were in a state not far removed from neolithic culture, came to be able to unite and to overthrow a powerful well-organized state such as Denkyira.

The part taken in these events by the priest Anotche cannot be overestimated. . . . With a true insight into the psychology of the people with whom he had to deal, he realized that the only way to unite independent and mutually jealous factions was by playing upon their superstitious beliefs. He achieved this difficult task; Ntim Gyakari was defeated at Feyiase, near Kumasi, on the Lake Road, and Ashanti entered upon the post-Feyiase period with which we are here mostly concerned. In that period, the constitution as we now find it was finally evolved. This new constitution was, however, only an elaboration of that which had preceded it. The family had expanded into the clan, both had merged into the tribe, now the tribes were to merge into the nation under a King; but the King stood in the same relation to the great *Amanhene* [paramount chiefs; sing. *Omanhene*] as they had previously stood to their subchiefs, as subchiefs to village headmen, as village headmen to the family heads, and as the family heads to their respective households.

THE FEYIASE AND POST-FEYIASE PERIOD

The amalgamation of the hitherto independent Territorial Divisions into a single fighting unit with which to meet the Denkyira invasion necessitated the organization of these divisions on a new military basis.

Mention has not hitherto been made of any warlike dispositions in the early days when the family organization held the field. The reason is this. Ashanti traditional history everywhere records a time when wars were unknown, and serious disputes between groups, which could not be settled by discussion or arbitration or the handing over of the member who had been responsible for the quarrel, were decided, not by an armed conflict between the whole of the rival groups, but by a kind of "ordeal by battle" between the leaders of the hostile factions. The weapons used were sword (*afona*) and shield (*'kyem*), and the fight was seldom a combat *à outrance*. This method of settling disputes did not possibly survive the growth of the family and clan into the tribe, for, as has already been noted, we hear at a later date of warlike expeditions of tribe against tribe, which postulates the subsequent growth of military formations. Whatever the process of evolution was, the germ of such an organization was already in existence in each tribe. It was necessary, however, for Osai Tutu, the Chief of the Kumasi Territorial Division, to unite the various independent divisions under some system of unity of command. He therefore appointed the head of one territorial division as generalissimo, another as leader of the right wing, a third as leader of the left wing, and so on. The military organization of the Ashanti has been examined in greater detail;[4] here it is sufficient to note that these commanders not only gave orders to their own immediate subjects, but, for this national effort, became leaders of other divisional Chiefs and of their subjects, over whom they had not formerly exercised any control. This point is of importance. After the fight at Feyiase, the making of the Golden Stool, and the acknowledgment of the Territorial Division of Kumasi as the head of a kind of Confederacy, we enter upon a phase where the parallel to feudalism, as known in Europe, appears to me to be very striking. In a previous examination of "Ashanti Land Tenure and Alienation,"[5] I had already drawn attention to this coincidence. At least one of my learned legal friends had quizzed me for straining to find such an analogy. I was interested therefore to find the following (some time after that chapter was written) in Sir Henry Maine's classic, *Ancient Law:* "Feudalism, I have repeatedly asserted, was a compound of archaic barbarian usage with Roman Law; no other explanation of it is tenable, or even intelligible. The earliest social forms of the feudal period differ in little from the ordinary association in which the men of primitive civilization are everywhere seen united."

Osai Tutu, Chief of the Territorial Division at Kumasi, and hitherto holding a position similar to that of any of the surrounding chiefs (Mampon, Kumawu, Offinsu, Juaben, Assumegya), now became more than a *primus inter pares,* which at most he may already have been: he became *Asante Hene* (King of Ashanti). He succeeded to a tribal organization which he strove to form into a state. The Territorial Divisions of many tribes became a kingdom, the men of many tribes became its citizens; the oath of allegiance superseded the kindred tie which had hitherto alone "conferred the privilege to command obedience and alone imposed the obligation to obey commands." A silent and unnoticed revolution took place with regard to land tenure which was in conformity with the main characteristic of feudalism. A kind of multiple proprietorship arose. The King became the superior owner of all land, i.e. soil, in the kingdom, but this claim coexisted with many grades of inferior ownership right down a descending scale until the inferior property of the family landholder was reached.[6] There were other analogies of the feudal system. Like William I, after Hastings, Osai Tutu found himself surrounded by a number of powerful lords, and a host of notables in his own territorial division at Kumasi, who demanded recognition for their services. Mampon was made Chief of the "Silver Stool." Kumawu and Assumegya were accorded certain privileges. An interesting development now arose. The Stools of Bekwai, Kokofu, and Nsuta had hitherto been of small importance. Bekwai at this period "had only thirty guns." Upon these Stools, however, sat members of the *Oyoko* clan, to which Osai Tutu himself belonged. These Chiefs thus became "brothers" (in the classificatory sense) of the King of Ashanti (*Asante Hene*), and they rose quickly to power. Their position *vis-à-vis* such Stools as Mampon, Kumawu, and Assumegya was, however, always clearly defined, and it is only since British occupation that they came to be classed as *Amanhene*. Juaben, on the other hand, seemed, independently of its royal blood-connection, to have been already of some importance, in its own right.

I have referred to the *Mpanyimfo*, that group of Elders who helped and guided a Chief in the administration of his Stool. They were the successors of the senior members of the kindred group who had always acted as advisers of the "house-father," Some of these *Mpanyimfo* may possibly already have borne distinct titles. Almost certainly we had the *Gyase Hene* [major-domo of a chief's palace], and possibly also the *Okyeame* or Spokesman. After Feyiase, we have the inauguration of a whole series of new and high-sounding titles to designate these "Elders." In this manner, among others, were created the titles of *Ko'ntiri Hene, Akwamu Hene, Benkum* and *Nifa Hene, Ankobea, Twafo, Kyidom, Adonten,* and so on. All these were titles having reference to a military organization, and the title holders were the leaders of their particular units in the event of war, while in peace they continued their original functions as the advisers of the Chief. Every Territorial Division now became organized on similar lines. Each had its own army in which every adult male had to serve. Each army was so organized that it could take the field as a separate self-contained unit, with advance guard, flanks, main body, and rear guard. In a national campaign, however, the whole of such a force ceased to function in this manner, and automatically became a part of the national army. In addition to these military functionaries, an official came to be appointed, whose particular designation varied according to the Stool to which he was attached, but whose generic title was *Abusua Hene* (Clan Chief).[7] His special duty was to look after the members of the royal clan belonging to the particular kindred group from which the Chief and Queen Mother were selected. At Kumasi, for example, he would be the *Oyoko Hene,* at Mampon the *Beretuo Hene,* and so on. A whole host of minor officials also came to be created in addition to the officers already enumerated. All will be considered in greater detail when the *personnel* of a typical Ashanti Territorial Division comes up for examination. These appointments were held directly from the Head-Chief, and were, with a few exceptions, in the hands of members of certain Stools tracing descent through the female line. Each of these office holders took an oath of allegiance to his Chief and held office subject to his own good behavior and proven loyalty. They formed an intimate body who were always in closest touch with the Chief as his Councillors, and advisers and commanders in war. As a Chief's wealth and power increased, so they, as his immediate associates, came to have a growing prestige.

One result of the appointment of an *Asante Hene* was that each independent Divisional Head-Chief (later to be given the title of *Omanhene*) took an oath of allegiance to the King at Kumasi, and henceforth nominally held his Stool and land subject to the King's good pleasure.

I have already hazarded the opinion that the subjects who now comprised the citizens of a Territorial Division once lived in large settlements. Offshoots from various kindred groups again formed isolated villages, and the inhabitants of these, for protection and administrative purposes, now came under the direct control of their original family head, who had now possibly become one of the Head-Chief's *Mpanyimfo.* These *Mpanyimfo* now claimed similar allegiance from the scattered members of their family and came directly to rule over certain outlying villages founded by their subjects, who thus came to serve the Head-Chief *indirectly* through them, exactly as they in turn served the *Asante Hene* (King) indirectly through their chief.

We have thus a Territorial Division comprising a capital town in which resided a Head-Chief, who ruled directly over its inhabitants, but also ruled indirectly over outlying villages which owned as their direct head, not the Chief, but one of the Chief's *Mpanyimfo* (Elders).

There still remain other important units in a Territorial Division under a Head-Chief. In the neighborhood of the headquarters of the *Amanto* resided Chiefs only slightly less important and less powerful than those whose names figure more largely in historical traditions. These lesser Stools possessed an organization identical with those of the greater

Divisions, and were originally no doubt independent of them. One after another, however, they came to acknowledge the superiority of the greater Divisional Chief, either accepting the condition of vassalage peacefully and voluntarily, or being forced into a position of dependence by arms. Hence it is that we find, besides those villages under the Head-Chief's *Mpanyimfo*, one (or more) Divisional units, of only slightly lesser importance than the Head-Chief's Division now included within the boundaries of the greater Territorial Unit, owing allegiance through its chief to the paramount Chief of the Head Division.

These Chiefs of Divisions within a Division were known as the *Birempon* of the Head-Chief, just as the latter in turn became *Birempon* when compared with the *Asante Hene.*

The status of these lesser *Birempon* of a Divisional Head-Chief was wholly different from that of the latter's *Mpanyimfo* or *Nsafohene*. Each had his own court, courtiers, and war organization, built upon exactly similar lines to that of his superior. This distinction in the relative positions of *Birempon* and of the *Nsafohene* of the Head Divisional Chief is important for a correct understanding of the Ashanti constitution.

I have now outlined the various units which comprised a typical Territorial Division under a Paramount Chief. Its center was the Stool of the individual now known as *Omanhene*. He, along with the Queen Mother and his *Mpanyimfo,* resided in a town which was recognized as the capital of his Division. In that Division there were many other lesser towns and villages, and, nominally, all these appeared to be under the Head-Chief in equal degree. Again, of the many thousand individuals who resided in the Division, all might, in an equal measure appear to be his subjects. On closer scrutiny, however, it will be found that this is not the case.

I will take first the case of the towns and villages.

(*a*) A town might come directly under the Head-Chief for administrative purposes, as e.g. the capital where he resided.

(*b*) It might be a town over which the Head-Chief had only indirect control, i.e. it might be one which belonged to one of his Elders, or to some one under that *Opanyini* [elder]. In such cases the Head-Chief had not any direct dealings with its inhabitants except through their own immediate Chief. E.g. *A* is an *Omanhene;* he has an Elder (*Safohene* or *'Panyini*) *B,* who had founded a village *X,* where *B* either resided in person as Chief, or had placed *D* as a village headman, directly responsible to himself, *B.* If *A,* the Paramount Chief, wished to give an order affecting the village *X,* he would do so through *B,* who in turn, if someone else were in charge of his village, would pass the instructions on to *D,* who would see to it that the villagers of *X* obeyed, but would resent either *A* or *B* giving these orders directly to the people in the village, whom *D* considered *his* immediate subjects. If it were an order affecting an individual, let us suppose the slave of a slave, the headman would pass it through the "house-father," who would give the order to the slave's master, who would inform his slave, who would finally take the necessary action.

(*c*) Again, within the greater Division there might be many towns under the Divisional Chief's *Birempon;* all orders affecting such would be given by the Head-Chief through that *Birempon,* who would then pass them on through his *Safohene* in the manner described.

With regard to the individuals who comprised the inhabitants of the Division, all these, from the greatest of the *Birempon* down to the last bought *odonko* (slave), were comprehensively grouped under the term *nkoa*[8] (subjects), but the actual authority of the Head Divisional Chief over them varied considerably.

The Head-Stool possessed direct control over (*a*) the *Birempon,* (*b*) its own *Nsafohene,* but only an indirect control over the subjects of these, and a still more indirect control over persons who, although resident within the Division, were in fact subjects of another independent Territorial Unit.[9] These might embrace two classes of individuals; (*a*) strangers, passing through or only temporarily resident in the Division, or (*b*) residents who were subjects (*nkoa*) of another wholly independent state. The latter would include women who had gone to reside with husbands who were subjects of our Chief, and all the children of such, down the female line, theoretically, for ever.

The whole position, I think, thus becomes comparatively clear. The small state was ever confronted with the kindred organization which was always insidiously undermining its authority by placing certain persons outside its jurisdiction. It could only hold its own, therefore, by throwing out an ever-widening circle to embrace those loyalties which were lost to it owing to the workings of the old tribal organization which had survived everywhere.

Carelessness in making a distinction between these various grades of towns, villages, and subjects, resulting in neglect to pass an order through the correct official channel, was a frequent cause of disputes in olden times, *and a knowledge of these conditions, which still exist today, is essential to sound government and to the successful and smooth running of the Native Administration.*

Two facts now stand out clearly; first, that decentralization was the dominant feature of the Ashanti Constitution, and, secondly, that the old family, clan, and tribal organization survived in the new *régime,* which was ever striving to make territorial considerations, and not the incident of kinship, the basis of State control.

NOTES

[1] About A.D. 1700.
[2] See [*Ashanti Law and Constitution.*] Chapter XXIV.
[3] See Chapters XVI et seq.
[4] See [*ibid.,*] Chapter XV.
[5] See *Ashanti,* Chapter XXI.
[6] See [*Ashanti Law and Constitution,*]

Chapter XXXIII.
[7] See also [*ibid.*], Chapter VIII.
[8] See [*ibid.,*] Chapter V.
[9] The status of such persons within the Division in which he resides does not, however, imply the right to claim complete extra-territoriality.

FOR FURTHER READING

Other works by Rattray on the Ashanti are *Ashanti,* Oxford: Clarendon Press, 1923, a general ethnography, and *Religion and Art in Ashanti,* Oxford: Clarendon Press, 1927.

Smith, Edwin W., *The Golden Stool,* London: Holborn Publishing House, 1927, 3rd ed. A history of the wars between the British and the Ashanti during the nineteenth century and the role of the Golden Stool.

There are a number of modern works on the Ashanti: Busia, K. A., "The Ashanti," in Forde, Daryll (ed.), *African Worlds: Studies in the Cosmological Ideas and Social Values of African Peoples,* London: Oxford University Press for the International African Institute, 1954, pp. 190-209. A paper on Ashanti religion and world view. Busia, K. A., *The Position of the Chief in the Modern Political System of Ashanti,* London: Oxford University Press for the International African Institute, 1951. A study of Ashanti government under conditions of colonial rule. Apter, David E., *The Gold Coast in Transition,* Princeton: Princeton University Press, 1955. A general study of the process of transition from tribal dependency to parliamentary democracy; contains material on the Ashanti and their recent political development.

Lystad, Robert, *The Ashanti: A Proud People,* New Brunswick, N. J.: Rutgers University Press, 1958. A nontechnical work on the contemporary Ashanti.

THE PROBLEM OF TUTSI DOMINATION[*][1]

J. J. Maquet

Ruanda, a kingdom in Ruanda-Urundi, has a population of nearly two million persons within an area of about 9,500 square miles. Its organization is based on a caste system within which there are three main groups. The ruling caste, the Tutsi (Batutsi), are the wealthiest and own most of the cattle in the kingdom. They are Nilotic in physical type and comprise about 10 per cent of the population. The intermediate caste, the Hutu (Bahutu), are agriculturalists who also care for the Tutsi's cattle through the institution of clientship. The Hutu, who form 85 per cent of the population, are Negro in physical type. The lower caste, the Twa (Batwa), are hunters and pottery makers, comprising about 5 per cent of the population. They are pygmy-like in physical type, though they are taller than true Pygmies. They are not discussed in Maquet's paper since they are not significant in the Ruanda political system. It seems likely that the Twa or a similar people were the original inhabitants of the area and were dominated by the Hutu agriculturalists. The Hutu, in turn, are known to have been conquered by the Tutsi, who probably came from the north. All the Ruanda speak the same language today.

This article, a brief summary of some of the salient features of the Ruanda political system, illustrates how caste functions despite apparent contradictions. Even though the Tutsi form a strongly dominating upper caste, a clear balance of control between them and the Hutu keeps the caste organization in operation. The system of clientship, which is also common in noncaste states in Africa, plays an important role in maintaining this balance of authority.

Ruanda at the beginning of this century could be characterized as a caste society if by that is meant a collectivity composed of several hierarchical groups, each predominantly endogamous, with its own traditional occupations, and made up almost exclusively of individuals born of parents

* Reprinted in translation from "Le problème de la domination Tutsi," *Zaïre, revue congolaise*, 1952, 6, 1011-16, by permission of the author and publisher. Translated by Kenneth Shaw.

themselves belonging to the group. The two principal castes were the Hutu agriculturalists and the Tutsi herders. The latter enjoyed a dominant position that permitted them to exploit the farmers in the sense that they obtained a proportionately greater quantity of consumption goods without furnishing the counterpart in labor.

How had they succeeded in maintaining this system of domination that fifty years ago appeared quite stable? Two categories of factors are significant in this respect: first, external circumstances in regard to the social system that were actually beyond Tutsi control; then, the social organization through which the noble caste had assured its superiority. This article is principally devoted to the social factors, but we must first very briefly indicate what elements of the physical, biological, and cultural environment were important from the point of view of Tutsi supremacy. However, not all were favorable to it, as we shall presently see.

The demographic proportion between the two castes and their physical characteristics certainly constituted factors favorable to domination. It seems indeed that the proportion of Tutsi in relation to the total population never varied greatly from 10 per cent. This is extremely important. If the Tutsi had, for example, constituted 50 per cent of the population, the Hutu would never have been able to supply them the labor force and products of the soil necessary to assure them a comfortable existence. Also, the different physical appearances included in the stereotype of each caste have been cleverly exploited by the Tutsi. They have used their slender figure and their light skin in order to affirm the idea of a natural superiority over the Hutu, who are of ordinary stature and with coarse features.

Three other external factors seem rather to have constituted obstacles that the Tutsi had to overcome. The orographic configuration of the country (hills with abrupt slopes, a mountainous range separating the Congo basin from that of the Nile) were not favorable to the rapid communication necessary to a centralized government. Then, the agricultural surplus was very limited. This resulted from the poverty of the soil, the irregularity of rainfall, and the methods of cultivation. A centralized government needs a large body of officials and warriors whose subsistence must be assured. Finally, with the very important exception of cattle, the material culture of the Tutsi did not present essential differences from that of the Hutu. By "essential differences" we mean that Tutsi equipment did not include elements like gunpowder, the combustion engine, or electricity, which when they are exclusively possessed by a group suffice to assure it an easy domination.

The problem that the Tutsi had to solve within the limits imposed by this framework can be formulated in three questions: how to maintain a caste system while safeguarding the cohesion of the total collectivity, how to exploit and at the same time to protect the inferior group, how to establish a centralized and absolute government while delegating power to some subordinate authorities.

To begin with let us consider the first of these three apparent contradictions: caste society and social cohesion. For the members of the dominant hereditary group to be able to keep their privileges, the instruments of prestige and power must remain under their exclusive control. In Ruanda social power and prestige rest on the effective disposition of the cattle that the Tutsi invaders brought with them in the past. The distribution of the livestock was made almost exclusively through *ubuhake,* an institution of clientship by which an individual inferior in prestige and wealth offered his services to another, who in return gave him the usufruct of one or several cows. Through this institution, which could be called feudal, the Tutsi retained the final control over all Ruanda cattle. The Tutsi lord, by reserving for himself the ownership without usufruct of the cows he granted to his client, could always take them back again.

Another condition necessary for the maintenance of the superiority of a caste is that its members should enjoy, if possible without effort, a higher standard of living than the common people. Once more the institution of clientship permitted Tutsi possessing a few head of cattle to live well without having to participate manually in the process of production.

For a caste to keep its identity it is necessary for its *esprit de corps* to be preserved and for its traditions to be transmitted from one generation to another. These functions were fulfilled by the military structure. Young Tutsi, and they exclusively, spent several years at the court of the king or of an important chief in military companies where, in addition to training in the use of weapons, they received the full education of young noblemen.

In order that the dogma of innate superiority of the noble caste should not be questioned, it is necessary to prevent the degradation of any member of the race of noblemen. Clientship was an institutionalized way of avoiding such a disgrace. The Tutsi who was threatened with loss of class through impoverishment became the client of another who was wealthier. In return for his counsel and his presence as a courtier, he received several cows which he gave in turn to Hutu clients; this allowed him to live according to his rank.

But if a caste puts too much stress on the characteristics that make it a socially self-contained group—if it isolates itself within the collectivity of which it is but one element—the cohesion of that society can be destroyed. Consequently, powerful factors of solidarity are necessary in order to counterbalance the tendency toward disintegration that exists in any caste structure.

It is again the institution of clientship that most effectively fulfills this function of social integration. Through it a great many Hutu shared in the social power of the superior class by identifying themselves with a protector, a member of the dominant group. They obtained the use of several cows symbolizing the system of pastoral aristocratic values, and they entered into a system of relations through which agricultural and pastoral products were distributed to the whole of the population. The personal tie with a member of the privileged caste and the access to the possession, even though uncertain, of cattle seem to have been essential from the point of view of national solidarity.

Another unifying factor was the plurality of the social structures with which every Nyarwanda was affiliated. Almost every individual participated in three hierarchies and was thus bound to his rulers, and especially to the king, by more than one channel by virtue of dwelling on a certain hill. The Nyarwanda was subject to a territorial chief who was charged with collecting duties and payment in kind from the subjects and with transmitting them to the king through the intermediary of several officials. In the second place, each Nyarwanda formed part of an army. Only the Tutsi were warriors, but the other members of the army were liable to the military chief for certain payments in labor and in kind. They received from the latter certain advantages such as the usufruct of livestock. Finally, the feudal structure integrated almost every individual in a network of loyalty relations such that the person occupying the superior position in one of these relations occupied at the same time the inferior position in another (the great chiefs were in reality vassals of the king).

A third integrating factor was the ideology developed about the institution of monarchy. The *mwami* was regarded not only as the king of the Tutsi but of all Nyarwanda. His divine origin separated him from men and conferred upon him an authority that the mass of his subjects would not dream of doubting. In Ruanda, as in many cultures, the king was a divine and paternal figure. This association helped create a feeling among the inhabitants of the country of belonging to an entirety that offered certain analogies to the family.

The second apparent contradiction sets off the necessity of the exploitation of the Hutu against that of their protection. The dilemma of all conquerors establishing themselves firmly in a new territory is whether they themselves will extract the natural wealth of the country or whether they will do it through the natives. The Tutsi have solved this problem by choosing the second alternative. Various tributes have been imposed on the Hutu: forced labor and contributions in products of the soil. The governors obtained them through the channels of the administrative and military structures, the ordinary Tutsi through the system of clientship. When a group has imposed itself as firmly as the Tutsi its problem is not so much to exploit as to limit exploitation so that the tribute payer neither flees the country nor dies. It is therefore necessary to protect him against excessive assessments and against individual exactions.

The universality and the organization of the obligations contributed to keeping the assessment level bearable, for they assured sufficient and regular revenues to the rulers. Protection against the exactions of avaricious chiefs and lords was assured first of all by the existence of traditionally accepted rules. These rules were not so precise or so severely sanctioned as in Western fiscal law, but they nevertheless established standards beyond which public opinion felt that abuse began. When a lord appeared to be too demanding of his clients he no longer found new ones, and those he had would try to leave him.

This leads us to mention another protection more effective than customary law: the possibility for every man of some capability of assuring himself a defender and a protector. This possibility resulted from the plural character of the political structure. When one has but a single superior, all must be obtained from him and there is no appeal. In a plural system there are several immediate superiors who are approximately equal in rank and are interdependent. It is then possible to obtain the support (or even complicity) of one chief while resisting another.

The third apparent contradiction, which contrasts the necessities of a centralized and absolute power with the dangers of delegation of power to subordinate local authorities, was felt particularly strongly in a feudal and mountainous country. Clientship creates personal ties of fidelity between the client and his lord, but this loyalty does not extend beyond the lord. One obeys his lord because he is his lord and not because he is a representative of the king. Now all the local Tutsi chiefs had clients. The mountainous nature of the country, by rendering communications difficult, also favored the formation of local, independent lordships. Moreover, in a nonliterate culture, to administer the country and to collect the taxes in an efficient manner required that the subject and the authority should know each other personally. Since the population was about 1,700,000 persons, it was indeed necessary to delegate power.

Despite these difficulties the Tutsi governors of the Ruanda were able to prevent the fragmentation of the political unity of their country. The ritual and divine character of royalty did certainly contribute to the chiefs' submission, but, we think, to a very limited degree. History tells us that when a *mwami* appeared weak one or another great chief did not hesitate to revolt and to assassinate him even though he was divine. Besides the strength of armies, the most effective mechanism of submission to the central power seems to have been the multiplicity of chiefs independent of one another. Not only were there chiefs of the same rank belonging to different hierarchies and ruling the same individuals, but in the same administrative structure there were two chiefs who had the same territorial jurisdiction: one who was concerned with food revenues, the other with taxes on livestock. Such a situation successfully maintained distrust, hostility, and jealousy among the chiefs. Thus any one of them was quick to warn the *mwami* if one of his colleagues was plotting treason. Moreover, the inevitable conflicts of jurisdiction permitted the superior authority to meddle in quarrels and to inflame them.

It is in this way that the political organization of the Ruanda, constituted by the administrative, military, and feudal structures, allowed the Tutsi to keep alive the society of Ruanda while profitably monopolizing social, political, and economic power.

NOTE

[1] Paper presented at the International Congress of Anthropological and Eth- nological Sciences in Vienna, September 1-8, 1952.

FOR FURTHER READING

Maquet, Jacques J., *Le système des Relations sociales dans le Ruanda ancien,* Tervuren: Musée Royal du Congo Belge, Annales, Sciences de l'Homme, Série in 8°, Ethnologie, 1, 1954. The basic work on Ruanda political organization.

Maquet, Jacques J., *Ruanda; essai photographique sur une société africaine en transition,* Brussels: Elsevier, 1957; Maquet, J. J., "The Kingdom of Ruanda," in Forde, Daryll (ed.), *African Worlds: Studies in the Cosmological Ideas and Social Values of African Peo-*

ples, London: Oxford University Press for the International African Institute, 1954, pp. 164-89. Both contain valuable background material on the Ruanda.

Oberg, K., "The Kingdom of Ankole in Uganda," in Fortes, M., and Evans-Pritchard, E. E. (eds.), *African Political Systems,* London: Oxford University Press for the International African Institute, 1940, pp. 121-62. A brief description of a state system based on two caste groups.

HISTORY IN A CHANGING SOCIETY[*][1]

J. A. Barnes

The Fort Jameson Ngoni, of whom Barnes writes in this article, are the descendants of one of a number of Ngoni groups that fled from the expanding Zulu nation in Natal in the 1820's. They migrated and raided northward, settling in their present location on the eastern border of Northern Rhodesia at Fort Jameson and over into Nyasaland in the 1860's and 1870's. As they moved north they grew in size and power despite the fission of some of their groups. Following their defeat by the British in 1898, a colonial administration was established. They number about 85,000 today. The Ngoni possessed a patrilineal segmentary state that has persisted to this day in modified form. Their political organization is quite unlike that of many of their neighbors, such as the Cewa, who are mainly matrilineal peoples lacking as highly centralized a form of government. The Ngoni consider their neighbors inferior and formerly conquered and incorporated some of them.

Barnes' paper is a bridge between the study of political relations and folklore. In the widest sense much of the "history" of the Ngoni is legend and myth. There is undoubtedly much truth in it, but the Ngoni use history in terms of the current social scene to explain the nature of their internal and external relations, and sometimes as a basis for action. Legends, myths, and historical facts are retained, changed, or forgotten in terms of the present-day Ngoni view of the world. This is probably characteristic of most African political systems, if not of all political systems everywhere. The article is particularly interesting because in the case of the Ngoni there is sufficient recorded information to check much of the verbal history.

In nonliterate societies there is, strictly speaking, no history; for there are no documents, and history, in the sense of historiography, is essentially

* Reprinted from *Human Problems in British Central Africa*, 1951, *11*, 1-9, by permission of the author and The Rhodes-Livingstone Institute. Also published as "The Perception of History in a Plural Society: A Study of a Ngoni Group in Northern Rhodesia," *Human Relations*, 1951, *4*, 295-303.

318

the study of contemporary documents. There are only legends, by which to a greater or less degree present conditions are related to or explained by alleged former conditions.[2] In fully literate societies with a well-documented past legends take different forms and it is often difficult to distinguish legend from history. In modern societies many socially significant legends relate to the immediate past rather than to antiquity. It is of interest therefore to examine what kinds of legend are current in societies shifting from nonliteracy to literacy and to what extent they have a history.

In many Western cultures the earliest surviving documents are chronicles or codes of law. At an early stage writing was employed to record fact of wide interest rather than things of significance only to a few. When Africans first become literate they employ their skill in writing letters to one another. Only later do individuals begin to write essays, histories and novels and so develop a vernacular literature. They learn to write in an environment already containing a great quantity of vernacular printed matter issuing from European-controlled sources. The spatial separation of kinsfolk and friends brought about by labor migration makes letter-writing worth while and the ephemeral nature of these pencil-written documents is no disadvantage. It requires greater resources than most individuals and Native Authorities can muster to produce a family or tribal chronicle in permanent form.

The Fort Jameson Ngoni[3] are at this stage of transition. Many men and some women can read, if not write, and we can no longer call the tribe nonliterate. Yet a society of this kind behaves in many ways as if it were nonliterate. In particular, information about the past is transmitted orally and laws and customs are not committed to writing. In this paper I shall discuss some of the ways in which this information is manipulated. I shall distinguish between tales of fighting, relating to the period 1821-98, which we may regard as tribal legends of origin; beliefs about customary behavior relating to the same period; private legends which serve to explain the form of relations between present-day groups; and lastly, history proper, in documents describing contemporary events, if such exist.

Early travellers all speak of the various Ngoni groups as fierce warrior tribes interested only in destruction and plunder. With the spread of European control Ngoni raids ceased. Today in villages inhabited mainly by women and children, with scraggy animals and eroded gardens, the traveller looking for signs of a military tradition sees only khaki greatcoats and battledress. Among the Fort Jameson group, if not elsewhere, the great cowhide shields, and the regiments which carried them, have disappeared. Yet the battles of the past are still remembered and are called to mind in songs sung at drunken parties, in tales told to children and, importunately, to sympathetic strangers. Many of these songs are in the old Ngoni language, now largely forgotten, and singers cannot give any precise meaning to the songs they sing. They are the relics of the past learned parrot-fashion; and in the context in which they are sung they do not require any specific reference. In our own culture we do not need to know who were the April rainers before we can sing "Green grow the rashes, O." Prose tales, however, are in ordinary speech and describe military exploits of people known to the speaker, or preparations for raiding ordered by the Paramount Chief and carried out by his lieutenants. The most frequently recounted battle of all is the fight between Ngoni and British troops in 1898. Many men and women are still alive who remember the fighting or even took part in it. The cataclysmic changes which followed the Ngoni defeat and the unusual weapons used combine to make the battle memorable. It is the only admitted defeat, for all other tales tell only of victory. The Ngoni defeated the Bemba, Wisa, Cewa, Kunda, and so on.

We know from contemporary travelers' accounts that though, on the whole, the Ngoni were successful against their neighbors, their run of successes was not unbroken. There is evidence that on occasion even the Cewa raided the Ngoni and took captives. We may regard the form taken by these legends as due in part to the process found in most cultures by which victories are remembered and defeats forgotten. But the distortion introduced is not only the elimination of defeat. The administration and the missions have, in general, encouraged cooperation between tribes and have treated all tribes as equals. They have emphasized the values of peace rather than of war, and have condemned pagan rites. In the light of this teaching legends have been modified to conform to modern values. The barbarity of the raids has been minimized and the good qualities of the old military discipline have been extolled. Sometimes men say that the old armies never fought but only danced, or that people from other tribes were not captured but all joined the Ngoni of their own free will (as in fact some did). It is said that there was never any ancestor-worship; the names of the Paramount Chief's ancestors were merely mentioned in prayers "as King George is mentioned now." This process by which the Ngoni conquerors of yesterday are made to look like the European conquerors of today is no new phenomenon. The Ngoni identified themselves with Europeans rather than with their matrilineal neighbors even before the European conquest. Wiese, himself the main agent of their defeat, wrote "They are very proud, looking down on all the other tribes with contempt, and think they show great courtesy whenever they assure the European traveller that the Whites may be related to them." [4] Another traveller, arriving from the south in 1896, relates how he ran into an armed patrol on the outskirts of Ngoni country. His own carriers ran away but he called out to the patrol that he was a friend of the Paramount Chief, speaking in

Zulu. He then heard them saying "He is an Ngoni and a white man."[5] My own informants told me that the old Ngoni language was closer to English than to Nyanja.

This reinterpretation of the past in the light of the present has not produced a consistent picture of a proto-European society. The inconsistencies of the present remain and are reflected in the ambivalent attitude adopted to the past. Although in one context people recall that everything was well ordered and peaceful in the past, in other contexts they dwell on the unlimited power of the Paramount Chief and the fierceness of his warriors. An aristocratic man once said to me at a beer party, "If this was the old days I would kill all these Cewa drinking here." Yet the general impression which people usually try to convey is of a disciplined, proud, and successful people.

This picture is accepted not only by Ngoni themselves but also by Europeans. For us it is one part of the good old days when Africans still smiled and were nature's gentlemen. Our picture of the Ngoni contains fewer concessions to contemporary White values, for the very distinction between Whites now and Blacks then increases the attractiveness of the picture. Ancestor worship and polygyny are not unwelcome in a Black Arcadia.

Ngoni nowadays compare themselves with their European and Indian neighbors and envy their apparent power and wealth. They seek to rationalize their own relative failure in terms of their past. It is in this connection that the defeat of 1898 is important. Although they claim to have conquered all their African neighbors, Ngoni do not claim success over the British. Instead, defeat at the hands of the British is cited in explanation of every present-day failure and of every departure from traditional practice. Ngoni say "If we had not been defeated we would not have lost our land and we would not now go hungry"; and "If we had not been defeated the tribes would not have been mixed up and we could follow our customs properly," and so on. In the past, captives taken by the Ngoni were rapidly indoctrinated with Ngoni ways and themselves became proud Ngoni; Ngoni complain that now, although captured by Europeans, they never become Europeans.

The general legends of the past from which these notions are derived are common knowledge. In the main they are passed on orally and are maintained by the teaching of tribal history in schools, the appeals to old military traditions when recruiting for the Northern Rhodesia Regiment, the conversations of planters comparing one tribe with another as laborers, by the reports of administrators, and by the writings of ethnologists.

The link between the Ngoni of today and their illustrious forbears is also symbolized in the office of the Paramount Chief. He bears the name of his warrior great-grandfather, and the formal aspects of his relationship to his people are explained by reference to his ancestors' achievements. He cannot attend funerals or take part in some of his own marriage ceremonies because "he has already conquered all others"; he cannot be expected to walk through the bush with the District Officer because "he has already conquered the whole world." He basks in his great-grandfather's invincibility, for in this context the defeat of 1898 is forgotten. The relationship between the Paramount Chief and his eleven minor chiefs is partly determined by the distribution of power in different branches of the royal lineage before European conquest, and the division of the country into these minor chiefdoms is a visible reminder of that distribution.

Associated with these tales of military exploits and royal power are myths about former customs. Ngoni say that in the old days they used to hunt, or marry, or build villages, in a particular way and that now they do differently. Frequently when I asked what happened in such-and-such a situation I would be told what my informant thought would have happened before 1898 rather than what he had seen happen now. Thus if we ask what payments do Ngoni make in marriage we are told that there are two payments, "snuff-box" and bridewealth, consisting of one or more beasts. Further inquiry reveals that these payments are now made only infrequently and that the period referred to is before 1898. More detailed investigation suggests that in many pre-1898 marriages they were not made and that when they were made they did not always consist of beasts. Ngoni do not deny these facts but they do deny their relevance. To them, the distinctively Ngoni way of marrying is with these two payments and it is this process alone which merits the vernacular adjective—cingoni. They regret that people no longer marry in this way and blame the Europeans for it; but it remains part of the distinctive cultural heritage of the tribe.

As we might expect, notions of this kind do not provide sanctioned standards of conduct nor ideal patterns towards which Ngoni strive. They may be used to explain or justify a state of affairs, as we have seen, but they do not directly determine action. An individual who departs from traditional custom, in these terms, is not necessarily censured. Indeed, men who are knowledgeable about the glorious past do not follow traditional ways any more than do less well-informed people. According to tradition the Ngoni are a virilocal people yet if a man goes to live with his wife's relatives his own kinsfolk cannot force him to return by appeal to this virilocal tradition. Traditionally a man avoids his mother-in-law. Yet I once saw an aristocratic man, a great authority on traditional history, on leave from work sitting on a verandah chatting with his mother-in-law. I said to him, "I thought a man should avoid his mother-in-law." He laughed and replied, "Yes, so he should. This behavior is disgusting and as soon as I come to live here permanently I shall see that customs are properly followed."

In certain situations the Fort Jameson Ngoni appear as a tribe in contrast to other tribes. The tribe is an administrative unit, with its own chiefs, its own area and sometimes its own District Officer. Representatives from each tribe in the region sit together to form the Native Urban Court and the Provincial Advisory Council. The Ngoni representatives on these bodies tend to present distinctively Ngoni views to contrast with the views of their colleagues. Thus there may be a discussion on wills. There is an Ngoni view, a Cewa view, and so on. The Ngoni representative repeats the old story about bridewealth, virilocal residence, the rights of the eldest son, and these are recorded as being the Ngoni custom in the matter. Even when discussing such an apparently modern issue as wills, the tendency is to go back to this mythical past. It is in terms of this past, in reality as well as in myth, that Ngoni are different from their neighbors. In the present, as contrasted with Europeans, Ngoni and Cewa are much the same. Ngoni pay bridewealth in the same way as the English eat roast beef. It is a national characteristic, but one located in the minds of men rather than observable in their actions or their aspirations. Instead of the scarifications and totemic observances which distinguish their neighbors Ngoni express their tribal identity by having distinctive customs which, conveniently, need not be followed.

In the Native Urban Court a similar process appears to operate, but here, unlike at the Advisory Council, there is a greater need to come to grips with real situations which require action, and tribal distinctiveness is tempered with practical reality. In the purely Ngoni Native Courts appeals are made to traditional practice in a different way. The courts are required by the Administration to follow tribal custom and people know that the courts are bound in this way. In fact, however, the courts have continually to deal with new situations and to make decisions which are unprecedented. This is done under the guise of drawing attention to some good Ngoni custom which has been neglected. Thus for example a man came to court saying that he was always quarrelling with his wife and that he wished to divorce her. The bench granted the divorce and awarded the woman 30s. damages. The litigant protested. The junior member of the bench, a man aged about 25 years, said, "Don't you know, it has always been the custom in this court to award 30s. damages against men who divorce their wives." Yet this was a comparatively recent practice and the litigant's protest seemed, to me, to be quite justified. The young man had been on the bench only about eighteen months. Even without Administrative stimulus, deliberate acts of legislation are not unknown among the Ngoni, but they require considerable discussion and probably a tribal meeting. It is easier, particularly for a court member as junior as the man in question, to appeal to the unwritten corpus of tribal custom when introducing a new rule. An analogous process in our own society is perhaps concealed under the fiction that judges do not make law. Ngoni do not quote specific precedents in court; and in this undocumented environment new decisions, if they are not soon challenged, become part of what has always been the custom since time immemorial.

We may then summarize by saying that their common store of notions about the past provides Ngoni with a means of distinguishing themselves from similar groups at a time when the cultural distinctions between these groups are in fact becoming less and less. In the courts, appeals to the value of traditional custom are made to gain acceptance for new rulings, while in ordinary life breaches of custom are widespread and are not censured.

When we consider legends associated with particular groups within the tribe the picture is rather different. Separate groups in the population remember, and sometimes act in the light of, particular incidents in the past which link them to other similar groups. Thus village A is linked with village B because of some incident in the past when the erstwhile leader of A captured the leader of B, or because at one time the leaders of A and B were brothers. These incidents, and the present intergroup relations with which they are associated, are not known universally but only by the groups concerned and by those near them. Yet in many ways these incidents are of greater practical significance than the more widely-known tribal history. The relationships to which they give rise, or rather such of those relationships as have persisted, are remembered at funerals, in the formal exchanges of beer, and in the settlement of quarrels. There are at first glance no sanctions to maintain relationships of this kind and indeed the very separate existence of two villages A and B may be due to a quarrel followed by a split. But although, for example, when an old woman dies in A there is no way of directly forcing a messenger to carry the news to B, there is in fact a great deal of social pressure on both groups to keep alive the connection between them. This arises from the general responsibility placed on everyone to preserve the peace, that is, to preserve the existing social order intact. If there are quarrels in a village the headman is blamed by the chief for not controlling his people well.

All disputes are best settled out of court, even if they must be referred to court later on. Therefore a quarrel in village A brings to light all the alliances and cleavages which link A with other villages and differentiate it from them. The headman of A appeals to B for support, invoking the historical incident linking them, and hopes to settle affairs in his village with the authority of B's approval behind him. For if the headman of B is a potential ally he is also a potential rival, and the dissident section in A may themselves invoke their link with B and transfer their allegiance to him. Thus although the details of the relationship between A and B, and the historical incident connected with it, may not be widely known there is considerable external pressure on them to maintain their relationship. Connections of this kind, mainly between villages but also between chiefdoms, play a large part in contemporary Ngoni life. Men walk twenty miles to a funeral and women carry pots of beer all day in response to ties of this kind.

Thus we see on the one hand that tribal legends are widely known, relate to pre-conquest times, and do not directly influence conduct; and on the other that legends associated with intergroup relations are known only by the groups concerned, may relate to either before or after 1898, and do directly influence action. Why is there this difference? We may regard the former legends as of significance mainly in external relations and the latter in internal. Within the tribe, and more particularly within the minor chiefdom, intergroup relations are still largely determined by Ngoni themselves, however much they may have altered in form and content since 1898 and however much Ngoni are part of a wider system. Movement between villages is only slightly controlled by the Administration; and in quarrelling, in marriage and adultery, beer-drinking, and hoeing, Ngoni men and women choose their own allies and enemies. Incidents in reality give rise to intergroup relations and are subsequently invoked to maintain them. History is written not in books but in the names of groups and in the remembered connections between them, and as these connections gradually change so local legendary history is gradually rewritten.

In external relations the Ngoni never act as a tribe except within the framework of European-controlled institutions. As yet no myth or origin is needed to explain the fact that Ngoni and Cewa representatives sit together on the Provincial Council save that the Administration put them there. The world of external relations is one of cultural heterogeneity and comparative adequate documentation. In this field legends have only a limited social function. They differentiate tribe X from tribe Y but do not relate them to each other.

Lastly we must consider Ngoni history proper. There have been many alleged accounts of Ngoni history published in Europe and South Africa, but these seem to have had little influence on the Fort Jameson Ngoni. Recently several histories have appeared in the vernacular and tribal history is now a subject taught in the primary schools. All these are based on the recollections of old Ngoni men and women more than on contemporary documents, of which there are very few. We must therefore regard them as written legends rather than proper histories. Differences between one version and another are sometimes related to the different political affiliations of those providing the information.[6] The period from 1821 to 1898 is treated in detail and the remaining fifty years dismissed in a few lines. It seems likely therefore that in time the tribal legend will be ossified, or that at least there will be one version widely known. Yet the vernacular texts are written in the school language (Nyanja) which is not yet the ordinary village speech (Nsenga), and are learned largely parrot-fashion, sometimes even with unintelligible words included. It remains to be seen how much of what is learned under these conditions is carried over into life outside the classroom.

With the increasing documentation of modern life we might well hope that the period of legend alone will end and Ngoni history proper will begin. Unfortunately this is not so. Although it is fairly easy to find out from contemporary documents what went on in tribal affairs from 1890 to 1898, with the imposition of British rule a curtain descended. Official reports grew shorter and shorter with the years for there was less and less to record. Towards the end of the British South Africa Company's rule the published information on Ngoni life was little more than the annual statement, covering the whole of Northern Rhodesia, that "the conduct of the natives has been satisfactory." From the beginning of the Colonial Office control in 1924 reports have lengthened, but these have dealt with the history not of the Ngoni tribe but of the Eastern Province and of Northern Rhodesia. These larger regions have become the significant units of government, not individual tribes and chiefdoms. The Fort Jameson Ngoni have become more and more closely integrated with the wider society and less and less have any history of their own. When the Ngoni were making history they lacked means to record it; now that means are available they have no history to record.

Thus we see that in this transitional society internal and external relations, as well as the level of technical skill, influence both the way in which people relate themselves to their past and also the timing and content of their written history.

NOTES

[1] Read at the Birmingham meeting of the British Association for the Advancement of Science, Section H, 1st September 1950. This article appeared also under the title, "The Perception of History in a Plural Society: A Study of a Ngoni Group in Northern Rhodesia," in *Human Relations*, 1951, 4, 295-303.

[2] Cf. Evans-Pritchard, "Marett lecture," p. 121.

[3] I worked among these people during 1946-9 while on the staff of the Rhodes-Livingstone Institute.

[4] Wiese, "Geschichte," pp. 200f.

[5] Later, when he had satisfactorily answered questions on Zululand geography, Mpezeni said of him, "He is a chief . . . he is an Angoni, one of us." Deare, "Slave raiders," pp. 19 and 25.

[6] Read and Winterbottom have pointed out that informants from Northern Nyasaland assert that their Paramount

Chief is the heir of Zwangendaba, while those from Fort Jameson say that their Chief is the heir. Cf. Read, "Tradition and prestige," p. 467 and Winterbottom, "Outline histories," p. 17.

REFERENCES

[Starred items are recommended as further readings.]

"A Durban Man." Deare, Major George Russel. "Eighteen months with the last of the slave raiders," *Natal Weekend Advertiser*, 6 April–11 May 1929. (Page reference to typescript in Central African Archives.)

* Evans-Pritchard, E. E., "Social anthropology: Past and Present—The Marett lecture, 1950," *Man*, 1 (1950), 198.

* Read, Margaret, "Tradition and prestige among the Ngoni," *Africa*, ix (1936), pp. 453-484.

Wiese, Carl, "Beiträge zur Geschichte der Zulu im Norden des Zambesi, namentlich der Angoni," *Zeitschrift für Ethnologie*, xxxii (1900), pp. 181-201.

Winterbottom, J. M., "Outline histories of two Northern Rhodesian tribes," *Rhodes-Livingstone Journal*, IX (1950), pp. 14-25.

FOR FURTHER READING

Barnes, J. A., *Politics in a Changing Society: A Political History of the Fort Jameson Ngoni*, London: Oxford University Press for the Rhodes-Livingstone Institute, 1954. A detailed account.

Barnes, J. A., "The Fort Jameson Ngoni," in Colson, Elizabeth, and Gluckman, Max (eds.), *Seven Tribes of British Central Africa*, London: Oxford University Press for the Rhodes-Livingstone Institute, 1951, pp. 194-252. A general survey of this group, with a useful bibliography.

Cunnison, Ian, *History on the Luapula: An Essay on the Historical Notions of a Central African Tribe*, London: Oxford University Press for the Rhodes-Livingstone Institute, Rhodes-Livingstone Papers No. 21, 1951. A complementary and more detailed study than Barnes' article.

Lloyd, P. C., "Yoruba Myths—a Sociologist's Interpretation" *Odù*, 1955, 2, 20-28. Yoruba myths as the charter for the political system.

Smith, M. G., "The Social Functions and Meaning of Hausa Praise-singing," *Africa*, 1957, 27, 26-45. Praise-singing related to social control and as an expression of the social and cultural values of the Hausa.

EXTRA-PROCESSUAL EVENTS IN TIV POLITICAL INSTITUTIONS[*][1]

Paul Bohannan

One of the difficulties the anthropologist faces in field research on political organization is to determine what is considered to be accepted or institutionalized power—that is, authority—and what is considered to be above and beyond institutionalized political force—that is, what Bohannan here calls simply power. There is a tendency among anthropologists to overlook the latter or to consider it exceptional or unusual. As a result all political force in a society may be considered to be institutionalized, no matter how unusual it may seem, because it occurs within the society—in short, if it occurs it is normal. Bohannan's paper is particularly valuable because it is one of the few attempts to delineate the two concepts of authority and power using African ethnographic data, and because it leads us to further thought as to the relationship of power and authority in other societies and even in situations of social change. An interesting comparison might be made with some of the southeastern Bantu states where a king who became a tyrant was likely to be overthrown and replaced by another king from the same line, the rebellion unifying the state and restoring a balance of authority between king and people, much as the Tiv anti-witchcraft movements helped preserve the normal political processes in the society. It is not clear, however, whether the rebellion against the king could be considered an extra-constitutional event, in Bohannan's words, or not, and there are other factors in the system of authority of these southeastern Bantu groups which are not similar to that found among the Tiv.

It has been a commonplace since Durkheim to point out that our own or some other society tolerates or indeed depends for its continued existence upon some institutions which are, though not illegal, felt to be sub rosa. Such institutions as party bosses and political machines are, as it were, extra-constitutional but none the less necessary elements in American social structure. It has been less often pointed out, but it is just

———

[*] Reprinted from *American Anthropologist*, 1958, 60, 1-12, by permission of the author and *American Anthropologist*.

as obviously true, that there are comparable "external" phenomena in the event cycles that form the process of social institutions. The periodic witch hunt in the United States is a case in point. We deplore it, but we do it, and American institutions are relatively little changed by it—in fact, unpleasant though the thought may be, such events may be a necessary part of the functioning of some of our institutions.

Put in another way, we might say that there are certain institutions which are part of the social morphology accepted and approved by the folk of a society; there are others, which may have an important role in maintaining those which are accepted, which themselves are nevertheless not approved. They are considered unfortunate excrescences on the social body, at best necessary evils. Similarly, every people has a notion of the "correct" order of event sequences for the "normal" functioning of an institution: Congress does such and such from the time a new session is called until it adjourns; congregations do this and that in weekly cycles. But there are sometimes events in such a cyclical process which a folk considers "extra-normal," which none the less are, from the analyst's point of view, necessary for the continued recurrence of the "normal events" of the process.

These extra-constitutional institutions and extra-normal processual events also occur in primitive societies, though their description has been relatively neglected for two reasons: (1) the ethnographer must have enough time depth to know what the normal process cycles of his institutions are, and (2) anthropologists have in the last twenty years shown an alarming tendency to blame everything on culture contact, so that these extra-normal events have often been put down as "nativistic movements" simply because they contain some bits of European culture.

Akiga, in his magnificent *Story* of his own people, the Tiv of central Nigeria (Akiga 1939), describes four "movements" or sequences of events of a sort which he and the Tiv consider extra-normal to Tiv society. These movements swept the country in the half century before he wrote. Akiga linked his descriptions with his discussion of *tsav,* usually described by Europeans as "witchcraft." Dr. East, Akiga's translator, dubbed these movements quite correctly as "anti-witchcraft" movements. It is the purpose of this article to provide a more far-reaching analysis of the movements which Akiga describes, and to add the description of another such movement which has occurred since he wrote.

Toward the end of the summer of 1939, all government and in fact almost all major social and economic activity, was at a standstill in Tivland because of a cult which the Tiv called *Nyambua,* or "beef." Special officers were rushed in to restore order, ban the movement, work out famine relief, and reorganize government institutions such as Native Authorities and courts.

Most of the information available today about Nyambua comes

from the working notes and reports of these Government officials. During my field research, Tiv showed no interest in the movement. Those who remembered it would say only, "Oh, that is finished" or "We have forgotten that—it was foolish nonsense." Some informants discussed it briefly but they were not interested in it, for it had no immediacy in Tiv society at the time I studied it.

The notes of the reporting officials show that Tiv were uncertain about the source of the movement. Some officers said that it came from Bamenda, others that it came from various neighbors to the east of the Tiv. One noted similarities between Nyambua and Calibar cults and speculated on a possible connection. I shall discuss here briefly the "origin" report which has the earliest date in the files, and which is typical of the way both Tiv and Europeans thought the movement originated, whether it did or not.

According to this report, Nyambua originated among the Utur, one of the small enclaved fishing groups who live along the major rivers of Tivland. There are about 2000 Utur; they speak a Kwa language closely related to Idoma, and have a religion very like that of the Jukun. An Utur diviner named Shiki, who was said as a boy to "go off in a trance and eat nothing for days on end," and who as an adult suffered from "paralysis agitans of the hand," began to dream and meditate. He became a seer and herbalist and won a considerable reputation among the neighboring Tiv. It was one of these Tiv patients, a man named Kokwa, who became what one might call the "impresario" of Shiki's cult.

According to the files, Kokwa had been "attacked by spirits" (the name of the phenomenon was translated from Hausa, not from Tiv; Tiv cannot translate Hausa notions about spirits, and to translate anything known to Tiv as "spirit" is misleading). Shiki gave him some medicine made from the bark of the *honom* tree, and outlined a ritual in which it was to be ceremonially taken mixed with eggs. Kokwa, apparently on his own, created a sort of shrine with carved figures, gave the cult a liberal sprinkling of Tiv religious and magical traits, and began to make money from it. He claimed that the medicine, properly administered, had granted him protection from the *mbatsav* or "witches" and given him eternal life—the same thing to Tiv. He claimed it would do the same for others.

In order to understand the Tiv view of the "beef" cult, it is necessary to review briefly their notions of tsav. The past literature on the subject has, probably wisely, considered the word untranslatable. One unpublished report by an administrative officer said, more boldly, "Tsav is merely mana." Though unless one is comparing Tiv tsav and Polynesian *mana* this probably gets one nowhere, he was right insofar as tsav deals with ideas which we usually discuss in English in terms of "power." (I am not referring to any of the American Indian situations usually de-cribed by that word.)

John Locke, in an early chapter of the *Essay on Human Under-standing,* says that we sense what we do because of the power in the objects to be sensed.[2] That is, we see a rock because the rock has a "power to be seen." We no longer believe this to be the case: Locke made a subject-object confusion. This particular subject-object confusion, as it refers to the inanimate, would seem to be the basis of the phenomenon which Tylor isolated and called "animism."

But there is power of another sort—the sort which we all experience in social relationships. We know that some people have the power to make other people do what they want them to do. Even today, in our own society, people often have difficulty in distinguishing between this personal power of others and their own psychic states. This is one of the manifestations of the subject-object confusion which is at the basis of belief in witchcraft.

Power, in this latter sense, may be institutionalized, in which case it can be called authority. If it is not institutionalized, there is no need for a special name, and we shall call it merely "power."

Tiv have an especially vivid idiom or metaphor for discussing power relationships: the idiom of tsav. Tsav is a substance which grows on the hearts of some people. It gives its owner control—"power"—over persons and over some things. Although a few domestic and wild animals are sometimes described as having or "growing" (*wa*) tsav, it is essen-tially human. Nothing inanimate is so described—Tiv are not "animists" in Tylor's sense, though they have been casually described as such in the literature and consistently in official reports. A Tiv philosopher would dispute Locke's theory of power just as surely as did Berkeley or White-head.

I have seen tsav on several occasions. At a post-mortem operation, Tiv open the chest of a corpse and examine the heart. Tsav, if it is pres-ent, appears to be blood sacks or clots between layers of pericardium. I have never found a doctor who will commit himself on my description, and I think my wife and I are the only Europeans ever to have seen the operation. Tsav comes in two colors: red and black. Either color alone, especially if it is not large, indicates tsav which is "not dangerous"—that is, legitimate power. But if both colors are found—and worse, if the tsav "grows claws"—it is an indication to Tiv that the person has artificially enlarged or developed his tsav by eating human flesh.

Tsav is considered a natural growth in people whom we might de-scribe as having power: talented people or born leaders. However, it can also be nurtured by cannibalism. A diet of human flesh makes the tsav, and of course the power, grow large. Therefore the most powerful men, no matter how much they are respected or liked, are never fully trusted. They are men of tsav—and who knows?

In Tiv eyes, all persons who have any highly developed skills or abilities have tsav. Those who have power over other people have tsav. Naturally, the men whom the British government found to fill the offices of chief, judge, scribe, policeman, messenger, and tax collector all have tsav. If they did not, they could not carry out their jobs. Old people also grow tsav. By the time a man is old enough, the point is taken for granted and no autopsy is made on his death. If he did not grow tsav, he would not have lived to such an age.

Tiv ascribe all death to tsav. It is incorrect to say that tsav can cause death; rather, it wills the cause of death. "Power," in the form of tsav, is a course of volition. Death, like illness, does not have a single cause, or even a multiple cause in the way Westerners look at multiple causation. Rather, there is a cause and there is also a volition. Tiv tend to assign the same causes to death as we do—old age, accident, disease, and the rest. But knowing the cause is not sufficient for them. They must also know the source of the volition of the death.

Tiv with whom I have discussed the point are doubtful whether God can will death; they are certain that He is indifferent to most deaths, and therefore it is unlikely. Tiv do not have an ancestral cult in the form usually found in African societies (though a few of their fetishes have ancestral relics as part of their emblems, which has led to the mistake of considering it such). Therefore, the volition for death cannot come from ancestors. There is a kind of sprite or being which lurks on hilltops and in forests, called *ijóv*. They bring madness, but far from willing death they were the center of one anti-tsav cult.

Finally there are the fetishes—what Tiv call *akombo*. Fetishes can cause death, but they cannot will it. A man with tsav can kill someone by using as his instrument the disease which is the fetish. Anyone in Tiv-land can learn the ritual by which this might be done, but only a man of tsav would have the volition to make it work. The volition, in other words, is the tsav. It need not be conscious, but it usually is. *Swem,* the great fetish which is itself anti-tsav, kills in the presence of tsav. But again, it is only the cause. The volition comes from the tsav; swem has merely counterdirected it.

Thus we can see the Tiv dilemma: men with tsav—that is, men with power—are natural and necessary. They are the leaders of Tiv society, whether under the indigenous system or the one which the British established while denying that they were making any changes. Being men of tsav, they also have the power to kill. In short, power corrupts. Men attain power by consuming the substance of others.

Tiv believe that persons with tsav form an organization called the *mbatsav*. This group is said to have a division of labor and a loose organization. The mbatsav are said to meet at night, usually for nefarious purposes: they rob graves in order to eat corpses; they bewitch people in order to put corpses into graves which they can rob. There is thought to be a network of "flesh debts" which become established when someone tricks you into eating human flesh and then claims a return in kind: the only thing you can do is to kill your children and your close kinsmen—people over whom you have some sort of power—and finally, because no one can ever win against the organization, you must give yourself to them as a victim because you have no kinsmen left to give. Every Tiv is afraid of being caught out and tricked into eating human flesh, and hence becoming embroiled in a flesh debt. You eat meat, especially pork, only with trusted friends.

However, the word mbatsav is also the usual plural for "men of power." In other words, mbatsav has two meanings: (1) powerful people, and (2) a group of witches who are organized for nefarious and evil purposes. It is just here, in this ambiguity, that Tiv thinking becomes confused—and we are ready to return to the story of the Nyambua movement.

When Kokwa, the "impresario," took over the original medicine from Shiki, the Utur cultist, he assumed the entire set of Tiv beliefs about the mbatsav. The cult became one which offered protection from the mbatsav. It became known to Europeans as an "anti-witchcraft" cult, though as we have seen it is not so simple. Since tsav is the source of all volition and death—that is, no cause of death or illness can be efficient without tsav—the secret of eternal life and health is to be found in some medicine which makes one impervious to tsav.

Nyambua followed the course of most Tiv "fetishes" or akombo. By means of sacrifices, ceremonies, and payment, a specialist in the fetish puts one into contact with it. There are several degrees of such contact. The primary form in the case of Nyambua was what the European observers called initiation. The Tiv called it "repairing Nyambua." This is a difficult phrase because it is used in two meanings: it means (1) that the master ritually puts the novice into contact with the powers of Nyambua, and (2) that the novice has had himself put into contact with those powers. The first meaning of "repair Nyambua" or of "repair" any other fetish is used for all the different ceremonies and grades of contact: that is, no matter what the master does, he can be said to "repair the fetish." However, the novice "repairs" it for himself only at this initiatory rite. For the subsequent rite, he "grasps the fetish." The second rite gives the initiate full mastery of the fetish, so that he can repair it for someone else.

In the specific case of Nyambua, the initial rite gave one protection against tsav in all its forms; it was a simple rite in which one drank medicine, sacrificed a chicken, paid four pence, and ate a ritual meal

There were some very strong purgatives in the medicine. The cult came to the notice of authorities when they began to get reports of deaths caused by the medicines. At an early stage of the movement, one District Officer claimed in writing that this untrustworthy medicine was the only bad thing about it.

In addition to the medicine, sacrifice, and sacrificial meal, one had to give up all of the magic and fetishes which one had acquired previously. This rejection of all one's former magic is an extremely important point, and (since the former medicines might be connected with tsav) it enters into all of the movements of the sort of which Nyambua is representative.

In return for giving up one's magical apparatus, one received the emblems or symbols of Nyambua: a miniature leather-covered wand and a fly whisk. The fly whisk, properly consecrated, was said to allow one to smell out *ijebu*. This word, used throughout Nigeria, means "counterfeit," as of a coin or a pill. Abraham (1940a:90) derives the word from the town of IjebuOde in Yorubaland, which is said once to have been the center of counterfeiting activities. I believe that the word, applied in the Nyambua movement, meant that such a person could tell legitimate or "real" tsav from the illegitimate or "counterfeit" tsav which had been nurtured by cannibalism.

When the "counterfeit" has been located with the fly whisk, then the leather-covered wand could be pointed at the man who was found to be ijebu and his evil thenceforth rebounded upon him. One of the Assistant District Officers noted:

> Indiscriminate use of the fly whisk naturally leads to trouble. To quote a single instance, Ulam, clan spokesman of Ngohor, when on his way to the Central Court meeting at Abinsi met a small band of newly initiated enthusiasts, one of whom smelt him out as *ijebu*. Ulam, however, rose to the occasion and replying that if he was *ijebu,* they had better come and tell the Touring Officer about it, arrested the lot and brought them to Abinsi.

The connection with power and hence with politics has become apparent. Throughout most of Tivland, most of the officials whom the government called "clan spokesmen" at that time, were "against" the new movement. Most of them were declared ijebu—that is, they had false power in Tiv eyes.

When the British set up their administration of Tivland just after World War I, they established an authority system. There had been a system of power relationships—there must be, if there is a social order. But Tiv granted political authority, that is, legitimate institutionalized power, to no one. There were no offices to which authority could adhere. There were no named or achnowledged lineage heads, village heads, judges, or anything else. There were compound heads and there were religious specialists. Compound heads were acknowledged to have authority over the members of their compound. Religious specialists were acknowledged to have authority over varying groups in religious matters. But neither extended to political matters. Political activities took place in terms of a lineage system (Bohannan 1953, 1954). The literature notes that there was a war leader called *kur* (Akiga 1939; Abraham 1940). The statement is correct for the extreme eastern part of Tivland; but the "office" was primarily a religious and not a practical one. Only a few kur ever led wars; usually the kur merely maintained the fetishes to make the wars successful. Into such a situation, the regularizing authority structure of the British administration had been set. Nyambua sought to counter the power of those in authority and so to re-fortify the aspects of Tiv institutions which they considered acceptable.

Nyambua seems to have developed an informal local organization around important cult priests. A man set himself up as head practitioner in the area; an organization tended to follow, apparently growing out of the group of adherents who set out to protect graves from molestation by the mbatsav. Here is the clearest statement in the official reports:

> Nyambuan in Tiv prescribes that corpses shall not be buried in the ordinary way, lest witches devour the vital parts. They must be exposed till they decompose, guarded day and night by friends and relatives who are frequently drawn into the pursuit of imagined witches. When the corpse is sufficiently decayed ashes are poured over it and it is broken up with staves and matchets in order to render it unfit for consumption by witches.

The guards at the graves, together with the head practitioner, apparently formed a fairly stable group. One District Officer describes the group which centered around a practitioner named Jato early in the movement:

> On the 23rd I visited Jato, who did the honors very affably; large crowds of patients and others present. He expounded a good deal of his technique, and appeared to know what he was doing. He showed me the usual heap of cast-off charms, etc.—certainly more unsavoury than those of Nyambua, a staff and a fly-whisk. He proposed burning these. His fees are 4d, a chicken and an egg. Various satisfied patients testified to his treatment, which they preferred to the dispensary's at a penny.
>
> I warned him against peace-breaking, poisoning, etc., and said that we should judge a thing like this "by its fruits" and were still considering what to do about it. Meanwhile he had better urge moderation in his disciples—less running around and shouting by night, respect for elders,

etc. . . . The general air of the party was of calm enthusiasm and conscious virtue: all were very affable.

Sometimes these grave guards found unexplainable phenomena
which led to a witch-hunt. One report describes it this way:

> Enthusiasts were apt to follow the trail of a witch till it leads them
> to the door of some eccentric or unpopular person, who is then denounced
> as a witch and invited to go to the Nyambuan chapel to be cleansed. If he
> refuses, his head is shaved and he is released.

Jato's group detected a "witch" one night with these results:

> A grave was kept open for 5 nights and a very noisy guard kept
> watch over it. On the night of the 18th/19th, there was a scare that a
> witch had come to eat the body; the guard pursued the supposed witch
> for some time; it turned into various shapes, but they always knew it by
> the smell (the characteristic stink of *imborivungu* and similar stuff that
> converts to Nyambua discard). It finished up as a goat on the edge of
> Gboko town: the pursuers were about to catch it when they ran into the
> police.

Nine were arrested, of whom eight were charged with unlawful
assembly. The other was a minor. Here is another case:

> On the night of the 22/23, two youths were at stool outside their
> compound. They were approached by an old man who smelt like a witch
> and hissed at them. They raised a hue and cry which was taken up all
> over the valley, and a man hunt started very noisily and went on till 3 A.M.
> It is said that the "witch" was located at a house to the Southwest. He
> offered to drink sasswood [to prove his innocence] but the pursuers were
> satisfied with identifying and warning him.

The organization continued to grow. The shrines of practitioners
became important meeting centers. In some areas there arose a cluster
of statuses, based on the only authority system which Tiv knew: chiefs,
judges, scribes, messengers, and policemen. Since these new organizations were usually "against" the British-backed officials, the English
considered them dangerous, and in some areas Tiv organized in this
way did establish themselves temporarily. Generally speaking, though
missionaries had to be evacuated from Southwestern areas of Tivland,
the movement was not anti-British; it was anti-authority and particularly
against those men to whom the British had given "legitimate" power.

About the middle of September 1939, matters reached a crisis without changing very greatly in any way. Social life began to disintegrate;
no farming was done; government's authority seemed to dissolve; there

were no effective leaders, and the country was in chaos. European officers, with increased but still small numbers of unarmed Native Authority
policemen, patiently went through the country finding new leaders.
The breakdown of the society led to a complete reorganization of Tiv administration.

If we review the situation in general terms, we can see that anyone
in Tivland who gets too much power obviously grows tsav; so long as
such a person handles his power in what we might call a constitutional
manner, he is acknowledged to have real tsav. But the moment he begins to overstep his power, he becomes what, in the Nyambua movement at least, was called ijebu or counterfeit. Tiv then consider it necessary to take measures against the counterfeit tsav.

Here Akiga's data about "anti-tsav" movements become relevant.
One of these so-called "anti-witchcraft" movements begins every few
years, whenever the power system becomes too rigid. Men who had
acquired too much power or who were careless in the way they exercised
their power were whittled down by means of witchcraft accusations.
Then, with the power of these men at least temporarily broken, a new
power structure was free to emerge. Here is the way Akiga made this
statement.

> When the land has become spoilt owing to so much senseless [dang-dang]
> murder [by tsav], the Tiv have taken strong measures to overcome the
> mbatsav. These big movements [dzege-kwagh, literally "important mat-
> ters"] have taken place over a period extending from the days of the
> ancestors into modern times (Akiga 1939:264, checked against original
> Tiv manuscript).

He then proceeds to describe those which he considers most important:
(1) Budeli, (2) Ijôv, (3) Ivase and (4) Haakaa. They can be summarized briefly.

(1) Budeli was a talisman made of cock's feathers and a gourd,
medicine against witches given to persons who surrendered their evil
magic and underwent a ritual. Akiga says that this movement preceded
the Europeans; its substance was Hausa.

(2) Ijôv. Akiga dates this movement as 1912, a date which checks
with other material in official files. An ijôv is a sort of being of the forest.
At one time, I believe, they were impersonated by masked dancers,
though today it is difficult to be sure of this point. It is impossible to tell
whether they were already present in Tiv culture before this cult, or
whether they entered it then and have stayed on. The rite by which the
ijôv were to counteract the mbatsav was called "drinking the ijôv." These
ceremonies involved some specially brewed beer, said to have the power
to kill those who drank it before full confession and delivery of their
magical equipment. Men would admit to as many as half a dozen kill-

ings, put their magical apparatus into a special basket, and then drink the brew, thereby getting absolution.

I do not know how widespread this cult was; according to Akiga, it was general. In any case, there is good corroborative evidence in a report written in 1913 by a young officer named Auchinleck, about the extreme southeast area of Tivland known as Ikurav Mbashaya. Auchinleck reported the ijôv spirits, and adds these remarks in his report:

> Wainyoru is the most interesting of these spirits. He is believed to take the form of a dwarf and to reside in the hills around *Swem* [an important hill southeast of Tivland, connected with Tiv ritual]. Wainyoru appears at irregular intervals, his last appearance was in the autumn of 1912 (when it was alleged, with no truth, that the Munshis [Tiv] were about to rise against the Administration). There appears to be no reason why or when he should visit the tribe, but the following is believed to be the general manner of his visitation. At some village an old influential man will give out that he has been warned that on a certain night Wainyoru will appear. He then prepares beer and summons all the local elders to meet him. After numerous chickens have been killed, the food and drink partaken of, one man will state in a *falsetto* voice that he has been warned that the message is about to be delivered.
>
> The message is then delivered by some elder, who is believed to be moved by Wainyoru's influence. In 1912 the message was to the effect that the Munshis must go on and prosper: that the *mbatsav* must deliver up their hidden pieces of human flesh, that the world was in course of being handed over to the chosen race—that is, the Munshis.
>
> There appears little doubt that the influence of Wainyoru is all for the good. . . . The moral effect of the message is great as for example those men who believed themselves *mbatsav* after the 1912 message did produce alleged pieces of human flesh, thereby exposing themselves to the scorn and ridicule of their relations and friends.

The common characteristics of these movements are beginning to emerge.

(3) The third cult mentioned by Akiga is Ivase. It consisted of a special rite, said to have been learned from the neighboring Utange people, and performed in a special ivase enclosure. Akiga does not date the cult or give many details about it, and I can find no other mention of it either in the published literature or the administrative records.

There are a good many cults which intervened between the ijôv and the important Haakaa of 1929. One of them was the *Hoyo,* in which age-sets took to beating up and killing elders shown by the divining apparatus to be bewitching their members. Although Akiga describes the hoyo in a completely different context, he notes that it was a cult similar to those he mentioned as "anti-witchcraft" movements (Akiga 1939:329 ff).

(4) The Haakaa (*ha akaa*—throw away things) is a movement dating from 1929 in which the Government itself took the initiative in gathering up the mbatsav paraphernalia from the Tiv. It has been recorded in somewhat greater detail than any of the others before or since, though from very peculiar angles. Captain Abraham mentions it and gives details of one case of alleged murder which sprang from it (Abraham 1940b:52 ff). Akiga mentions it at length (1939:275 ff), but his main object is to show that the magic involved in it was false, and he therefore does not furnish some of the most important data.

Briefly, Haakaa was a movement in which both elders and youngsters denounced their enemies as witches to the administrative officers, who then insisted that the accused hand over their magical equipment and pledge never to use it again. Tiv willingly brought in all that they could find and Akiga says they made a great deal more specifically to turn in. Government officials collected several score decorated skulls of the sort known as "the father's head," a part of the *po'or* fetish; they took up even more *imborivungu,* which is a voice disguiser made from human tibia. These and other items are now to be seen at various Nigerian, British, and South African museums. The Government played exactly the same part in the 1929 movement of Haakaa as the Nyambua cult leader played in the 1939 movement, as the age-set played in Hoyo, and as the self-appointed brewer of beer played in the Ijôv.

So far as I know, there were no movements of any importance during the early 1930's, although there were undoubtedly local ones which did not spread because the political situation did not favor it. Only when a large part of the country is politically upset does such a cult catch on and spread beyond the confines of a small lineage.

Since 1939, a number of cults have arisen. However, Government officials are well aware of the phenomenon by now, and none are allowed to get out of hand. *Garyo* was a cult of the Nyambua type which came up and was quickly squashed in 1948. Its aims, like all the others, were anti-tsav in idiom, with the ultimate purpose of weakening the power system. Another such cult, *Ikumendur,* was illusively present in a part of Tivland during my stay there; however, it was not important in any parts in which I was working.

When we come to a more general analysis of these movements, we must point out two things which they are not. Although some of its manifestations such as counter-government organization and several prophets give it the appearance of a nativistic movement, Nyambua was not actually nativistic. That is to say, it was not a "conscious, organized attempt on the part of a society's members to revive or perpetuate selected aspects of its culture" (Linton 1945:230). Assuming the Tiv idiom for dealing with power, it was a rational if somewhat flamboyant means of changing the power situation.

Neither was Nyambua what Wallace has called a revitalization movement because it was not a "deliberate, organized, conscious effort by members of a society to construct a more satisfying culture" (Wallace, 1956:265), though again there was an element of revitalization present. Revitalization movements seem to me to be new institutions by means of which a people add to their culture. Nyambua, and the other movements like it, were new institutions only in a very special sense. Since they disappeared after their purpose was accomplished (which is to reestablish the fluidity in the power system), they are better considered as "extra-normal" events in the cycle of events which is the "process" of a working institution.

The movements, which obviously all perform the same social function, have taken on many different cultural guises. It was a religious guise in the movement centering around the ijôv spirits. It was a foreign-inspired charm magic in Budeli. Nyambua had foreign elements in it, and enough anti-European flavor to appear at the time as a "nativistic movement"—indeed, I began my analysis of it in these terms. As East has noted (1939:290), there is always a foreign element in these movements, although I read his statement to mean that the idiom in which a movement emerges runs the full gamut of available culture. Because the point is to establish a means of counteracting tsav, and because none of the old methods have worked, it is the fact of newness, and ipso facto, sometimes foreignness, which is important.

Nyambua was one of a regular series of movements to which Tiv political action, with its distrust of power, gives rise so that the greater political institution—the one based on the lineage system and a principle of egalitarianism—can be preserved. Tiv in 1949 considered Nyambua an unfortunate occurrence in their history. Probably many of them did so at the time, though of course we have no record of that. One is reminded forcibly of "movements" affecting power situations and civil rights in the United States.

Nyambua was, further, an "extra-normal" event in the cyclical process of the functioning of Tiv political institutions. The normal, recognized part of the process leads, in Tivland, to a rigidity in power relationships which Tiv find threatening to their constitutional ideas. The "revolt" or counteracting aspect of the event structure is brought into play to regain elasticity. "Revolts" for accomplishing such a purpose may be recognized and "built in" to other systems; elections are a case in point. In such a situation, they are part of the "normal," recognized process. They may, however, take other forms and be considered pathological—witch hunts or paroxysms of war.

Thus, in at least some primitive societies as in our own, both social morphology and social process are marked by institutions and events which are considered to be extraconstitutional, or which we might call extra-processual.

NOTES

[1] Twenty-eight months' field work among the Tiv between 1949-53 was financed by the Social Science Research Council, The Wenner-Gren Foundation, The Colonial Social Science Research Council, and the Government of Nigeria, all of which bodies I wish to thank.

[2] I am particularly indebted for ideas on power to many long talks with J. H. M. Beattie of the Institute of Social Anthropology, Oxford, and to his B.Litt. thesis, Checks on Political Power in African Societies.

REFERENCES CITED

[Starred items are recommended as further readings.]

Akiga (B. Akiga Sai),* 1939, Akiga's Story. London, Oxford University Press for the International African Institute.

Abraham, R. C., 1940a, A dictionary of the Tiv language. London, Crown Agents for the Colonies for the Government of Nigeria.

———, *1940b, The Tiv people (Second Edition). London, Crown Agents for the Colonies for the Government of Nigeria.

Bohannan, Laura and Paul, *1953, The Tiv of Central Nigeria. London, Inter-national African Institute.

Bohannan, Paul, *1954, Tiv farm and settlement. London, Her Majesty's Stationery Office. Colonial Research Studies No. 15.

East, Rupert (translator and annotator of Akiga 1939).

Linton, Ralph, 1945, Nativistic movements. American Anthropologist 47: 230-240.

Wallace, Anthony F. C., *1956, Revitalization movements. American Anthropologist 58:264-281.

FOR FURTHER READING

Bohannan, Paul, Justice and Judgment among the Tiv, London: Oxford University Press for the International African Institute, 1957. An account of the jural system of the Tiv, which serves as a useful complement to this paper.

Gluckman, Max, Custom and Conflict in Africa, Glencoe, Illinois: The Free Press, 1955, Chapter II; and Gluckman, Max, Rituals of Rebellion in South-east Africa, Manchester: Manchester University Press, 1954. These two works analyze the rebellions among the southeastern Bantu mentioned in the introduction to Bohannan's article.

5

Values, Religion, and Aesthetics

AN AFRICAN MORALITY*

Godfrey Wilson

Among the Nyakyusa, as in other societies, an important function of religion is the structuring of interpersonal relations in terms of the ideals of social behavior. Unlike some systems, however, the Nyakyusa sanctions are chiefly the negative ones of punishment of moral offenses, good behavior being assumed as the general rule. The scope of different aspects of Nyakyusa religious belief varies: the ancestor cult deals with the moral behavior between kinsmen, witchcraft is concerned with behavior within the age villages and chiefdom, and magic is used within the local group but may also reach outside the chiefdom.

The solidarity of the age village is reinforced by witchcraft beliefs in which witchcraft is used both legitimately in the interests of the village as a whole in accordance with public opinion, and illegitimately by individuals who take the law into their hands. Both types are based on a power inherent in individuals that can be used constructively or destructively according to the person's will. Here there is a similarity between Nyakyusa witchcraft belief and the Tiv concept of tsav, which gives its owner a power over persons and some things that may be used either for good or evil. How tsav may operate in the maintenance of social order among the Tiv is discussed by Bohannan in the preceding paper in this volume.

Nyakyusa magic, like witchcraft, may be used positively or negatively and is an important force in interpersonal relations. This paper represents one possible combination of the different types of African religious belief, and of the interplay between them, as they relate to the maintenance of order within the society.

This paper is an attempt to introduce the subject of morality for scientific discussion after a new manner. It is inspired throughout by that part of Professor Malinowski's work which relates to Primitive Law, and which he has developed in *Crime and Custom in Savage Society*, in his introduction to Dr. Ian Hogbin's *Law and Order in Polynesia*, and in his oral teaching at the London School of Economics in recent years.

* Abridged from *Africa*, 1936, 9, 75-98, by permission of Monica Wilson and the International African Institute (author's copyright reserved).

In his analysis of law Professor Malinowski finds himself driven to the study of the whole body of sanctioned custom, and of all the various attractions and compulsions that lead men to conform to a social tradition of right behavior. A certain portion of that field is here delimited for separate description, namely morality, which is that part of right custom that is sanctioned by religion.

Custom is not only sanctioned by religion but also by public esteem and disapproval, by the balanced advantages inherent in reciprocal relationships, and by legal compulsion and punishment; and morality, or religiously sanctioned custom, is unintelligible to the mind and could not in life exist except in connection with these other sanctions and the social institutions through which they act.

The main body of custom may be divided up as follows, by distinguishing between the different sources which provide sanctions for conformity to it.

(i) Manners—sanctioned by public approval and disapproval.

(ii) Morality—sanctioned by religion.

(iii) Common Policy—sanctioned by the rewards and punishments which inhere in any reciprocal relationship between individuals or groups and which make "honesty (i.e. conformity with traditional right behavior) the best policy." The working of all social institutions involves such reciprocal relationships.[1]

(iv) Law—sanctioned by institutionalized inquiry, followed by compulsion or punishment.

These divisions, let me repeat, are not separate in life; good manners are usually good morals, good law, and good policy too. There is at times, however, a conflict between them; and in any case to understand how they unite in life we must first see them each distinctly.

The African people whose morality is here described are the Nyakyusa of the Rungwe district of South Tanganyika; the same cultural group extends into Nyasaland under the name Ngonde who are known to linguists and ethnologists by the Europeanized name Konde. All material so far has been collected in Tanganyika.

The Nyakyusa live, some 150,000, under the rule of about sixty traditionally independent chiefs (avanyafyale); of these chiefs the British Government for administrative convenience raised eleven to a superior position, with the introduction of Indirect Rule in 1926. In the traditionally independent chiefdoms (efisu) the adult male population varies from 30 to 3,000 in each; and prior to the arrival of the German Government in 1893, the chiefdoms were generally hostile and frequently at war with one another.

Within the chiefdom the people live in age-villages (efepanga)—local groups of men, all roughly of the same age, living together with their wives and young children. Each age-village has a head, whose title (*olifumu*) is best translated "great commoner," who tries cases in his own age-village and advises the chief, together with his fellow great commoners, in court. In the old days he led his own men to war; and he also has important religious duties in connection with the worship of his chief's dead ancestors, and with the control of witchcraft.

* * *

[A brief summary discussion of the Nyakyusa social system, including material covered in "Nyakyusa Age-Villages," pp. 227-36 in this volume, has here been omitted.]

The religion of the Nyakyusa falls clearly into three parts: i. the cult of dead relatives (ancestor-cult); ii. the belief in witchcraft; iii. the use of "medicines" (magic).

The ancestor-cult provides sanctions for moral behavior only between kinsfolk, but it does not provide them all; witchcraft and magic also exert a moral influence in this sphere; but the most characteristic moral effect of the belief in witchcraft is to sanction the rules of custom between members of the local and political groups (age-village and chiefdom); while only magic is believed to have any power of punishing wrongdoers who are neither kinsmen nor members of the same chiefdom.

The sanctions of custom may take three forms: rewards, punishments, or the reform of individuals. Rewards are given by society to people who attain certain ideals of behavior. In all societies certain ideals of behavior are stated as good; these ideals are always positively stated ("Do this") and often also vaguely and generally stated ("Honor thy father and thy mother"); and the fulfilment of ideals of behavior in the particular society which states them invariably carries with it, or is believed to carry with it, some attractive reward ("—that thy days may be long—"). Punishments, on the other hand, are inflicted by society for the breach of rules of behavior. All social traditions allow people a certain falling short from the ideals of behavior without comment or punishment; but all set more or less rigid limits to their tolerance by stating rules of good manners, of morality, of common sense, of law; beyond which if a man fall short he is considered "no gentleman," "a sinner," "a fool," or "a lawbreaker" by his fellows, and by them or by the gods he is punished. Rules may be framed negatively or positively, but they must be particularly understood, because it is of their essence that a breach of them is at once followed by punishment.

There are also, in all societies, institutions which sanction custom by forming or reforming the character of members of the society; their aim is to implant in men a power of right behavior, or to induce a will to it, which was lacking in them previously. Such institutions often work by the infliction of punishments or the offering of rewards, but they do not always do so. The education of children, religious conversion, the probationary system of treating lawbreakers are of this nature, and they do not always or even generally depend on rewards and punishments.

In this paper the education of children is not dealt with, but only morality among adults.

Among the Nyakyusa the ideals of social behavior are not generally connected with religion; nonetheless they exist; generosity, hospitality, peaceableness, courtesy, affability, loyalty to friends, respect of seniors, care of the old, the sick, the crippled, the half-wits and idiots—all these I have heard praised, and the man who possesses these virtues is an object of social esteem. But their practice is not believed to carry with it any special supernaturally given rewards beyond the general one of the absence of supernatural punishments.

At certain points the tendency of members of this society to fall short of these ideals is checked by rules of morality with religious sanctions. If a man is mean, inhospitable, quarrelsome, rude, sullen, disloyal, disrespectful to elders, and careless of unfortunates beyond a certain point, then frequently he is believed to be punished by ancestors, witchcraft, or magic. But the positive, ideal statement of these virtues is not made in religious terms; the ideals are, according to our definitions, ideals of good manners, not of morality, and the attached reward lies in the esteem and friendship of other men.

In our own societies in Europe many of these same ideals are religiously stated as moral ideals with a supernatural reward, as well as being ideals of good manners; and religious conversion is believed to give men a certain extra power to put them into practice. But the religion of the Nyakyusa, with a few exceptions,[2] takes the ideals of good manners for granted, neither aiding their fulfilment by conversion nor attaching to that fulfilment any supernatural reward. The specifically religious or moral sanctions of custom are believed to be punishments.

These sanctions are actual misfortunes interpreted by the light of faith as the effects of sin; a sin being a breach of a rule of morality.

Whenever a man or his wife, child, or beast falls sick or dies, when his crops fail, or his cows go dry, he usually goes at once to the diviner (*ondagosi*) to confess all his remembered sins and to find out whether any of them is responsible for the misfortune or not. A diviner is often a doctor (*onganga*) as well, but not always, and the two functions are distinct. The most usual method of divination (*obolagosi*) is (i) by the cup and board. This I have seen practiced: the diviner sits on the ground, rubbing an inverted wooden cup over a smooth board, while the victim of the misfortune, or his representative, confesses to him all the sins which he knows of which might, in Nyakyusa belief, be responsible for the trouble; if the cup passes smoothly and continuously over the board his suggestion is refused, if the cup sticks and comes to a halt it is accepted. The suggestions made are not all confessions of sin, for it is believed that disease may sometimes fall on a man, or be inherited from his parents, without any immorality on his or his parents' part, and also that quarrels with neighbors may sometimes lead to trouble with the supernatural powers although no wrong has been done by him; but very many of the accepted causes of disease and misfortune are sins. In this method the diviner's power is believed to be due to a medicine which is pricked into the palms of his hands by another diviner—either his father or elder brother without payment, or by a nonrelative in return for payment. To a skeptical observer it is noticeable that the diviner's hand trembles with effort when the cup sticks, but appears to be slack at other times.

Other methods of divination are (ii) by the examination of a ball of stiff millet porridge, which the diviner previously rolls between his hands; (iii) the rubbing of a small stick with a rounded end on the ground—this is exactly the same as the first method, the cup and board, only with different properties; (iv) knocking on a spear-point; (v) the speaking calabash, which appears to be a form of ventriloquism and is practiced by one doctor only. All these, with the exception of (iv), I have had very fully described to me, but none have I yet seen. The same principle is observed in all: the client makes suggestions to the diviner from which he selects one by his method of divination. All informants agree in this: "Sometimes we do not go to the diviner; if there is only one cause of misfortune known to me then I do not go; but if there are several and I cannot myself decide which is the true one, then I go, or I send my son, to the diviner." Thus in the diagnosis of misfortunes the diviner is assured of the acceptance of his verdict; but he also claims to be able to discover by his divination where a lost cow has strayed, and what has happened to lost or stolen property. And many young men refuse to believe in his power in these directions today; some of them have deliberately tested diviners with questions about lost property and proved them wrong, and such stories of their failures are widely known.

A great part of the misfortunes of life are, then, by the Nyakyusa attributed to sin. It remains to discuss the nature of the faith which so attributes them and to indicate some of their conceptions of sin.

THE ANCESTOR-CULT

The mental basis of the worship of dead relatives (avasyoka) and of the belief in their moral power consists of dreams (enjosi). Dreams of dead kinsmen are common, and they are feared. The elaborate funeral rites of the Nyakyusa have, as their main expressed purpose, "the driving away of the dead person"—"We weep for him at first—then we drive him away—we say to him 'Do not long for our company, do not come to us in dreams.'" The place from which he has to be driven away is the imagination, both sleeping and waking, of those who remain alive.

Lack of space makes a full description of the methods taken "to drive him away" impossible here; one example is enough. An integral part of the funeral ceremonies is the discovery, by divination, of the cause of death. I saw this happen recently on the death of a very old chief; the diviner found, by selection from suggestions made to him, that the cause was just sickness, without sin; and told the men, who were sitting near him, of the decision. Then one of the men got up and spoke across to the women, who were sitting apart and had not heard: "Listen, we have divined; do not say in future that we have hidden things from you, do not whisper and question about Mwangoka's [the dead chief's] death; we tell you that it is disease, no one had a quarrel and used sorcery against him, he wronged no man by taking his cow, it is not because one of his family speared a man, nor because he tied up a relative of his with ropes; he died and we trembled and were afraid, but now we know that it was just disease that killed him, disease which kills us all." This divination was specifically explained to me to be one of the things done "to drive him away."

Very many dreams are believed by the Nyakyusa to be possibly prophetic: "We think that all dreams which we understand the morning after tell us of something; but sometimes we wake up in the morning and cannot understand what we dreamed; then we say: 'It was just a dream, I do not understand it.'" Some of the intelligible dreams are simple and carry an obvious prophecy; I have been told of dreaming of going on a journey, of finding trouble at the end of a journey, of meeting a friend, of being given a shilling by a relative returning from the gold mines, of being given work by a European, and so on. Others are interpreted through the eyes of traditional symbolism, but still others remain, as we have seen, unintelligible. Men's behavior is often guided by dreams, and a man dreaming of meeting trouble on the road does not go on his projected journey; nevertheless it is recognized that only some dreams are true. Dreams are told to husband or wife and to friends in the morning, and if the dream comes true within two or three days, people remark: "He dreamed true." Some people acquire a reputation for true dreaming, and their dreams then may guide other people's behavior than their own.

Some dreams into which dead relatives come are of the simple prophetic kind, and these are not feared unless they come too often. A friend of ours was building a new house and dreamed that his dead father and elder brother came and said to him: "Build it long, with plenty of room for cows." This dream pleased our friend very much; he took it as a promise of luck and did as he was told. But if a man very often dreams of dead relatives he becomes afraid, and his friends fear for him, that he will die. "They have come to take him with them." He then goes to a doctor and gets magic "to drive the spirits away." Some dreams into which the spirits come are symbolically interpreted; people often dream that a dead father or mother comes in a dream and offers the dreamer food—if in the dream it is accepted and eaten, then the dreamer will die, if it is refused he will live.

So we see that a mere meeting with dead relatives in the imaginings of sleep is frequently fearful. And often the spirits come into a man's dreams to reproach him for sin, and to threaten punishment. It is not only actual misfortunes which sanction morality, but also the fear of punishment which rises in a man's sleep speaking with his dead father's voice when he knows he has done wrong. The sins which agitate the Nyakyusa conscience in this particular way, and which are suggested to the diviner as a possible cause of ancestral anger, are all breaches of kinship duty—in particular the failure of the head of a family to use his inherited wealth for the benefit of his juniors and dependents, and the failure of juniors to respect and be submissive to their seniors. "If I inherit my father's cows and do not give marriage-cattle to my junior half brothers whom he left unmarried; or if I neglect to provide food for the children he left young; then my father who has died comes to me in a dream and reproaches me for my wrongdoing; then I wake up in fear, I tell my wife and she fears too that my children will fall sick and die because my father is angry. Then I give my brothers cows, and food to the children. If I neglect to do so my brothers will summon me before the chief and force me to give the cows" (and the mother of neglected children can also sue for maintenance before the chief).

The last sentence reminds us that moral sanctions do not always suffice to secure right behavior; the man who refuses to listen to his conscience or to accept the lessons of misfortune can be legally compelled to conform.

The position of the "father" (i.e. own father or his heir) in each family is morally sanctioned by his power of "muttering" (okwibonesya). In any misfortune of his children, his younger brothers, his junior half brothers, his full and half sisters, if the diviner diagnoses sin, it is he who prays to his dead fathers; and he alone in the family is believed to have the ear of the spirits and to be able to call down trouble. Often the spirits act by themselves, the Nyakyusa say, "for they see all that we do"; but if the "father" is insulted or injured by a child or junior sibling, "he sits over the fire muttering with anger, he does not look at the wrongdoer and no one can catch what he says, his anger makes him incoherent, but the spirits hear, and, if he has a just case, send sickness on the sinner." This power cannot be used wilfully, but only as a moral sanction. "If he just mutters angrily without just cause the spirits do not hear and nothing happens, no, never."

In most of the cases of kinship sin which I have collected, both a change of behavior and a prayer or offering to the spirits was held to be essential to cure the misfortune, and in all the apparent exceptions the sin was a failure of religious duty to the dead, not of everyday morality, and so an offering to the spirits was itself the change of behavior required. Prayer is made by blowing a cloud of water from the mouth and then speaking to the spirits. In one prayer, made, not by a commoner, but by a chief for his country, the prayer went on for twenty minutes. Offerings consist of a bull, a hen, or some beer, in the case of commoners; of a cow in the case of chiefs. The killing of bulls by commoners never now takes place, I think, for no one could tell me of a case since the War. The killing of cows by the chiefs for their immediate ancestors demands an article to itself, for upon this offering the food and health of each chiefdom is believed to depend, together with the fertility of women and cows. But with the worship of dead chiefs, as such, no everyday morality is connected; a general famine is a punishment for failure to kill cows for the spirits, never for moral delinquency; health and plenty are rewards for the fulfilment of religious duty. Offerings are also made to more remote ancestors of chiefs, from whom many of the present-day chiefs are descended; and failure to sacrifice to these remote ancestors is believed to cause famine, disease, and death in the countries of all their direct descendants. Still other offerings are made to a small group of very remote ancestors for rain and health, fertility and food, in whole groups of contiguous chiefdoms to which their holy places give a religious center. Again, however, with this worship no everyday morality appears to be connected.

WITCHCRAFT OR "WAR BY NIGHT" (Obwite pa kelo)

By far the greatest moral influence among the Nyakyusa is the belief that certain people have a supernatural power of causing sickness and death to others by "choking" or "trampling" them, or by "eating them inside." This statement may cause surprise to some who read this paper, and it does not of course imply that the methods of sanctioning morality found in the Nyakyusa culture are the best possible; but the facts are incontestable. A paradox in the belief of Africans with regard to witchcraft, combined with an inadequate knowledge of African languages among Europeans, would seem, at least in this culture, to be jointly responsible for considerable misunderstanding of the subject.

The Nyakyusa have one word ovolosi meaning "aggressive witchcraft" which is bad, and another amanga meaning "defensive witchcraft" which is good, and also a phrase "the breath of men" (*embepo sya vandu*) which means the power of witchcraft used in accordance with general public opinion, and the effect of which is the "curse" (*ekegune*). The paradox is this, that while "the breath of men" is the commonest sanction of morality, and while this "breath" is universally admitted to be nothing but the power of aggressive witchcraft; yet an individual person who is proved an aggressor witch is detested and was, in the old days, either killed or driven from the country and all his cows confiscated by the chief, who gave some to the victim or victims of the believed aggressive witchcraft.

The clue to this paradox seems to be that "the breath of men" is always the general public opinion of a whole group—of an age-village, or a chiefdom, acting supernaturally through the aggressive witchcraft of those of its members who happen to be possessed of it, against a single person; while the individuals proved witches are those believed to have acted by themselves, either against the public opinion of their age-village or chiefdom, or at any rate without securing its support. In both cases the action of the aggressive witchcraft is believed usually to be moral, to be preceded, that is, by a breach of a traditional rule of right behavior; but while in the first case public opinion approves of the moral sanction being called into play, in the second case it does not approve of the method of its calling into play; witchcraft is the chief sanction of morality, but the man or woman who takes the witchcraft into his own hands is a detested criminal. Though to some extent[3] morally justified, he breaks a rule of manners and also of law.

Witchcraft is believed to reside in the stomachs of certain people in the form of pythons, and to be inherited. My information is not yet nearly complete, and I am not yet sure whether witchcraft is or is not believed to be gained by drinking medicines as well; on this point different informants are in conflict. It may be inherited from either father or mother, and the children of mixed marriages may either be witches or not. It is believed also to be gained at times by playing as a child under the care of an older child who is a witch. In children it is entirely dormant, but in adult life it becomes active either as defensive or as aggressive witchcraft. The form it takes depends, as we shall see, on the will of its possessor. The aggressor witches are believed to leave their bodies sleeping and to fly through the air, either singly or in company, to the house of the man against whom they have a grudge, there to enter his body while he sleeps and either "choke," "trample," or "eat" him inside. In the morning, or during the night, the victim wakes up more or less conscious of what has happened to him. If they come often, many nights running, he falls sick and may die, unless he takes steps to defend himself. The defender witches are believed to be able to see and recognize the identity of the aggressor witches and to counter them in two ways: first by turning them back at night, saying: "Where are you going to, to choke your friend? Go back!"; and secondly by reporting to neighbors and the political authorities the next day the names of the people they saw engaged in aggressive witchcraft. An ordinary person can never recognize the witch who attacks him, though he may be conscious that he is being "choked."

The location of these nighttime happenings is in dreams: "the aggressor witches go out in dreams to choke people." "It is in dreams that the defender witches recognize them." Certain dreams, interpreted by a traditional symbolism, are taken as signs of being bewitched: "If I dream that someone comes to fight me, perhaps he beats me with a stick, perhaps he overwhelms me and crushes me down to earth, perhaps he hits me with his fists; then I wake up and tell people: 'Last night they came to choke me.'"—"If I recognize people who come to fight me in my dreams that means I have myself the power of defensive witchcraft; if I do not recognize them then I have not."—"If I dream that I am flying alone through the air high up at night, that means they have come to choke me."—"If I wake up suddenly at night in fear and sweating, even though I do not recollect the dream, I know they have come to choke me." Dreams to the Nyakyusa are the stuff of religious reality.

No one readily admits to the possession of the power of defensive witchcraft; it is a proud and boastful thing to do, and not good manners. One great commoner to whom I put a direct question, knowing from other informants that all great commoners are believed to have it, replied: "I would not so far boast myself, but other people in my village have it." In each age-village of mature and old men the great commoner is believed to have it and often some others are known by name as having it too; besides this there is the general belief that in each such age-village "some people," not specified, have it as well. Young great commoners are chosen by the old ones, and whether it is that the old ones, being themselves defender witches, choose those they know to be also witches, or whether some of the medicines they give them are to induce this power in them, is not yet clear to me.

But what is abundantly clear is that whenever "the breath of men" punishes immorality by sending sickness on men and cows, that "breath" is believed to be the power of all the witches in the age-village; those who are normally defender witches are believed to become aggressors for the time being; and in doing so they act within the law.

A man with whom I have become well acquainted has been mildly sick for a long time; recently he sent to a diviner at a distance to find out the cause of his illness. He is himself convinced it is due to witchcraft, to the "breath of men," but is not certain of the particular cause, the particular sin they are punishing. His first wife is his favorite and he takes no pains to conceal the fact; and one of the suggestions he sent to be put to the diviner was that neglect of his second and third wives was the cause of his illness. He explained his theory like this: "She, my second wife, comes from a bad family, a family of aggressor witches; my third wife is a bad girl but not an aggressor witch (she is a sister of his first wife, and to attribute aggressive witchcraft to her would be an aspersion on his favorite), and these two go round whispering to the neighbors, slandering me, and saying that I do not give them enough good food to eat; and my second wife, I think, also whispers with the aggressor witches in her dreams at night, and shows them where I sleep, bringing them to eat me." ("Does she bring the defender witches too?" I asked him.) "Heavens, yes! If she can persuade them she has a case against me they all come, the 'breath' of the whole age-village comes on to my body and makes me sick."

It is noticeable that here, describing the generally approved and perfectly legal action of the "breath of men," the victim indignantly uses the word "aggressor witch,"until he is asked directly whether the "defender witches" do not join in as well. The word "aggressor witch" is used when the speaker disapproves of the witchcraft, when the witches are his enemies; the word "defender witch" when the witches are his allies, when they defend him against his enemies or "choke" some one for a reason he approves. The speaker here admitted my question in terms of defensive witchcraft, because the people referred to, the great commoner and the pillars of society, are believed never to abuse their power but always to defend people against enemy witches, unless and until the latter can persuade them of the justice of their case. In the example we are considering my friend went on to say: "At first, I think, they, the aggressor witches [he still speaks as a victim and so uses this term of his enemies] refused her, and prevented her 'choking' me, but later she persuaded them to change their minds and come with her."

The only witches generally called aggressor witches are those who are believed to abuse their power by trying to "choke" people or cows without securing the approval of the defender witches, that is of the responsible members of the age-village, for their case. Such people, in the old days before European government, were reported to the chief by the great commoner and put to the final proof of the poison-ordeal. Certain doctors have the knowledge of a medicine called *omwafi* which was used for this; the accused drank it; if he vomited he was held innocent, if he failed to vomit guilty. If thus proved guilty he was killed or driven from the country, and all his cows and other goods taken by the chief and the victims of his aggressive witchcraft. If the accusation of aggressive witchcraft was made by one private individual of another, both were submitted to the ordeal; if both vomited the accuser had to pay two cows to the other for slandering him; if either failed to vomit the punishment was exile (or death) and the loss of all cows and property; and if neither vomited both were thus punished. Men also occasionally died as a direct result of drinking it; and the ordeal is now illegal. I am certain that it very rarely takes place nowadays, although I have a circumstantial story of a case which was settled by it three years ago; and I shall probably never see it. But men generally accused of aggressive witchcraft by a whole age-village still find it best to fly that chiefdom and join another. I am investigating a case of this at the moment of writing.

It is believed that aggressor witches are occasionally able in dreams to get past the defender witches and "choke" men against whom they have a grudge, or their cows, without securing the defenders' approval and cooperation. "The defenders do not go out in dreams to fight the aggressors every night! And an aggressor wanting to 'choke' a man comes night after night." "Nowadays it is much worse than it used to be, since the Europeans prevent us reporting them and getting them stopped; the defenders work hard, but some nights they are all just asleep and the aggressors get past."

My informants all agree that aggressor witches, though they act without public support, seldom act without provocation; some say they occasionally "choke" people just from pride in their power, but no one can tell me of a case of this. The most usual case described is of people whose character makes them to some extent isolated and unpopular, a proud man who treats his neighbors with disdain, a retiring man who always keeps silent in public. Such people are treated with something less of courtesy and hospitality by their neighbors than the traditional ideals of good manners demand. "Perhaps we do not summon him to drink beer or to eat with us; and then when our cows fail to give milk we think: 'Doubtless it is he who is "choking" them!'" The chief characteristic of aggressor witches is always said by pagans to be pride.

The paradox which puzzled us is now explained. Morality we have defined as those rules (or ideals) of right behavior which are sanctioned by religion. Now in so far as witches are believed to send sickness on men and cows in return for a breach of a rule of right behavior, we have a religious sanction acting to punish sinners. The religious power, however, is, in this case, resident in the persons of members of the society; and in consequence their use of it, like any other of their actions, is itself subordinated to traditional rules of right behavior. If they seem to use it wilfully without securing the common assent of their age-village, although their power is believed to be a religious fact, it is none the less wrongly and illegally used. In so far as they themselves have been wronged they are to that extent justified, and their power is a sanction for morality, but if they cannot secure the agreement of their neighbors that they have been gravely wronged, then they must not seem to act alone on the penalty of becoming outlaws. If, however, no individual takes the witchcraft into his own hands, and all are agreed that a certain person has sinned, then any misfortune that may fall on him and be traced to the action of "the breath of men" is perfectly right and legal.

The result of the belief that certain religious or supernatural powers (in this case "witchcraft") are dependent for their action on the will of individuals is that the power itself is in its aggressive form spoken of as an evil one, although its use in the public interest approved by the responsible guardians of law and order (great commoners) is held to be right and necessary. A nonreligious parallel is the usual attitude in our own society to the infliction of pain. We say that to inflict pain wilfully is bad, none the less it is right, subject to legal safeguards, to inflict it on lawbreakers. A further analysis of the effects of belief in the power of individuals to hurt their enemies supernaturally is made in discussing sorcery, the use of destructive medicines.

The "breath of men," as we have seen, is believed to provide a moral sanction for the fair treatment of wives; it also sanctions the performance of any ceremony at which cattle are killed or beer is brewed. If a man fails to kill cattle or provide beer when by custom he ought to do so, then the "breath" of those neighbors who would have eaten and drunk is believed to make his children, or his cows, sick. The everyday customs of eating together are also thus sanctioned—if a man is rich in food and constantly fails to call his neighbors to eat with him, or if at any time he kills a bull "just for eating" and only calls his relatives to eat, then the "breath" of the age-village is thought to make him ill.

The power of witchcraft, be it noted, is never believed to act between relatives, though it may between husband and wife; sickness may be traced to the case of a wronged kinsman supported by the sympathetic and indignant "breath" of the age-village; but he himself is never thought to participate in the "choking." On the other hand, the power of witchcraft is not believed to be able to harm anyone outside the single chiefdom. No religious sanction reaches beyond the groups of kinsfolk and chiefdom but that of sorcery (q.v.).

The power of the spirits and that of the "breath of men" overlap considerably in their support of the moral rules of kinship—the same sins being held to be punished sometimes by the one, sometimes by the other. A young man or woman . . . extends much of the respect due to a father or elder brother to their neighbors in the same age-villages. The "village fathers" and "elder brothers" on the other hand are believed to be, in the person of those of their number who are witches, supernaturally mindful of the rights and obligations obtaining between their friend and his child or junior; and neglect on his part, or insolence on the part of his dependent, is commonly supposed to be punished by their "breath."

The morality of a chief towards his people is sanctioned by his people's "breath," and this fact is a great check on his power; if he abuses it a little, so as gravely to alienate only the sympathy of some, then he can (and does) try to avoid sickness by moving to a friendly age-village, where the defenders of that village will guard him from the aggressors of the others. But if he alienates the sympathy of all age-villages then, they say, he will die.

To alienate the sympathies of one's age-village was more serious in the old days of war; for then, it is believed, the witches of that age-village would fly to another chiefdom, holding traffic with their chief's enemies in dreams, and telling them: "Come and take his cows, he has offended us and we will only seem to fight, we will quickly run away and leave you the victory." This would lead the chief, hearing of it from his younger brothers who, as defenders, saw it happen, to pacify his people with an offering of two cows. When they had eaten they would, I am told, go out again in dreams to the enemy and say: "Go back, we have ourselves taught our chief his lesson, if you come we will fight!"

Permanent recovery from sickness supposed to be caused by the "breath of men" is not, I think, ever believed to be possible without a change of behavior, a moral reform—the neglected wives must be fed; overdue ceremonies must be properly performed; a cow must be paid to an insulted father as a sign of submission; the inhospitable rich man must give a feast to his friends, before he or his children can get well. And in all cases his age-village must be called to eat and drink either by the sinner or (in the case of a sinful son) by his father. At the feast a doctor is present with medicine; the sin which caused the illness is, I am told, openly discussed, the wrongdoer admits it, and the neighbors say: "Yes indeed, it was our sickness, our curse (*ekegune*) which came on you; but now we have eaten and we hope that this medicine will cure you."

"Medicines" against the power of witchcraft exist and are used, but they do not give immunity from its attack. It is believed that while medicines may temporarily cure such a sickness or inoculate a man against it beforehand, their action is not permanently effective; the only real cure is to bring the individual aggressor to trial, or to become reconciled with the angry age-villagers who have sent the curse.

The rules of incest and certain moral rules governing the illegal action of adultery are similarly sanctioned by belief in the "breath of men." But the only moral sanction against adultery in general is provided, at the will of the cuckolded husband, by magic.

MAGIC; THE USE OF "MEDICINES" (emekota)

Magic among the Nyakyusa consists in using "medicines"—leaves, roots, and other material objects which, when collected and manipulated by an expert doctor (*onganga*), are believed to enable the doctor's client to realize some particular desire of the moment. By the scientific observer some few of these "medicines" would be found on investigation to have a biochemical efficiency (e.g. castor oil); while to others, the majority, he would attribute a psychological efficiency. My knowledge does not allow me to distinguish clearly between biochemical and purely psychological efficiency in medicines, so I use the terms "magic" and "medicines" to cover all the materials used by Nyakyusa doctors and called by them *emekota*. No set spells seem to exist, and in most magical ritual words are not an essential factor at all; to some few, however, they are integral; it is, for example, necessary in some forms of sorcery to mention the enemy's name.

Some few "medicines" are generally known to all, but the great majority are known only to the doctors, men and women, and each doctor again knows only some medicines. Doctors acquire their knowledge either from a close relative without payment, or by buying it from non-related doctors. Doctors are usually paid for their services, and only give them free to close kinsmen.

The medicines of the Nyakyusa fall clearly, according to their function, into five divisions: (i) ceremonial magic; (ii) the magic of private ambition; (iii) sorcery, or destructive magic, and its antidotes; (iv) "medicines" for cure of sickness and trouble; (v) magic of appeal.

Ceremonial Magic

Every social ceremony involves the use of medicines as part of it: funeral ceremonies, initiation of girls at puberty, installation of chiefs, ceremonies held after the birth of twins, after the birth of an eldest child, after a man has died of a spear wound gained in a fight, at the eating of certain first fruits—all these ceremonies involve the use of magic. And one at least of these ceremonial medicines has as its object the ensuring of right behavior, which it sanctions, not by reward or punishment, but by conversion. A chief at his installation is given a carefully graded amount of medicine to make him "fierce and impressive." "We do not give him too much or he will go about killing his people afterwards, nor too little or he will lack dignity, men will not respect and obey him." The medicine is supposed to implant in him an extra or supernatural power to act rightly in accordance with his position, to live up to the ideal of a good chief. And informants state that some of the medicines given to a girl at her initiation are to make her "polite and submissive" to her husband's parents and their age-neighbors. But the evidence for this is not yet conclusive.

The Magic of Private Ambition

The magic of private ambition appears to be quite unconnected with morality in any way; it cannot be used to convert people, neither is its successful use a reward of virtue, nor does it in any way punish sinners; and it can be used for flagrantly illegal purposes. Medicines are used by the man desiring a superlative crop from his fields, the woman covetous of the position of favorite wife, the plaintiff eager for success in a lawsuit, the boy wanting a rise of wages from his European master, the girl lacking a wooer, and so on, but also by the adulterer and the thief. Taken as a whole magic is amoral; it can, it seems, nearly always be enlisted by the desire of man whatever his aim may be; it promises him a fulfilment of that desire greater than his own unaided efforts can assure him. The connection of magic with right behavior in this culture is, where it exists, not general but accidental and particular.

Sorcery, Destructive Magic of Aggression and Defense

(a) *Aggressive sorcery or "the snaring of men"* (*ovotege*). So it is believed that a man with a quarrel against another can harm him by buying destructive medicines from a doctor, whether or not he has a legally tenable case against him, whether or not public opinion agrees that he has been wronged. The use of these medicines was always illegal in the old days and punished by the chiefs, because, unlike witchcraft, no previous supernatural control by public opinion was held to be possible. Even if the sorcerer (I use this term of the man with a quarrel, not of the doctor to whom he goes for medicine) had a legally tenable case, I am told that he was punished for contempt of court: "We took him to the chief and if we could prove it the chief said to him: 'What do you mean by using sorcery against your neighbor, instead of coming to me to get your case tried?' and he was punished." European disbelief in the efficacy of these medicines has made such trials now illegal, but has left in the minds, even of educated and Christian Africans, the old fear.

Sorcery of aggression is believed greatly to have increased recently, both because the chiefs are not allowed to punish it any longer, and because with increased travel the import of foreign medicines of sorcery is said to have swelled in volume. Death is believed to result from most of the various types of aggressive sorcery, unless discovery of the cause of sickness and drinking of an antidote quickly intervenes. The putting of medicine on the way (*ekelaso*) must also be accompanied by the saying of the enemy's name to direct the action; pricking of medicine into the enemy's footsteps (also called *eḳelaso*) or putting it into his food or drink (*obwambeḳesye*) act without the name.

I am still, like many other investigators, uncertain how far these medicines are actually used, how far their use is an imagined one. Before the influence of missionaries and Government made itself felt, no stigma attached to a doctor for selling these medicines, for he also had the antidotes and was outside the quarrel. In fact the proof of aggressive sorcery rested with him. "If one of our family died and we went to the diviner and he said: 'It is so and so's aggressive sorcery that has killed him,' then we had no case; if we went and told the chief he would say: 'Where is the doctor?' and refuse to punish the man we had named. But if we could find the doctor who had sold the medicine and if he agreed to tell the chief so, then the man was punished; though he denied it strenuously the chief always took the doctor's word and punished him. The punishment was to be buried head downwards in a hole, alive, and to have a stake driven through." "Yes, doctors would often agree to tell the chief because they wanted to gain. We would pay them a cow afterwards."

Aggressive sorcery is believed to be able to act even against an enemy of another chiefdom, and then it could not be punished in the old days. "It was difficult enough to get any case at all settled before another chief against one of his men, but quite impossible to get a case of sorcery tried at all." Chiefs never held joint court, and beyond the boundaries of the single chiefdom neither public opinion, nor religion, nor law provided any general or effective sanctions for right behavior: public opinion and law (in the person of the defendant's chief) were biased in favor of their own men, while religion in the form of sorcery depended for its action on the individual's judgment of his own case. Morality beyond the home chiefdom, together with manners and law, had only an intermittent existence.

The quarrels (of which I have heard) that the diviners have selected as causes of illness and death due to aggressive sorcery range in type from a girl's refusal of a lover to a case involving a large number of cows, believed by one side to have been unjustly settled by a chief. In very many cases a failure by himself to conform with right custom is believed by the victim of a misfortune to have caused some one to employ aggressive sorcery against him; and when this is so the belief in the action of aggressive sorcery, although a belief in a detested and illegal power, is none the less a sanction of morality. The crime of the sorcerer outweighs, in public opinion, the sin of his victim; none the less, although criminally, he is believed to have punished sin.

But what the fear of sorcery most of all sanctions is a general attempt to avoid quarrels by living up to the ideals of good manners. My informants all agree that the man who does so will not have to fear sorcery, he will have no quarrels with any one at all. This is also true of the fear of aggressive witchcraft. And in this way only are the ideals of good manners generally connected with religion by the Nyakyusa.

Further questions showed me, however, that this connection of aggressive sorcery with right behavior, though very common, is in the last analysis accidental and not universal; what is universal is its connection with personal relations. Quarrels usually come from wrongdoing, but not always; an innocent preeminence may provoke jealousy, refusal of a lover may provoke anger, and anger and jealousy are believed at times to act through aggressive sorcery, even without justification.

(b) *Defensive sorcery.* *"Medicines of Ownership"* (*efelembeko*). Many medicines are used for the defense of chastity and property, and these, although they are supposed to cause a great deal of sickness, were perfectly legal. They are only believed to act against the adulterer, the thief, and the eater of stolen food, and such people only get what they deserve.

A man gives his wives medicines to drink, without their knowledge, and then any lover who sleeps with them will, I am told, contract disease in consequence, though the wives themselves are free. Further, the adulterer will pass the disease on to any women he subsequently sleeps with, including his own wives. . . .

The tracing of these diseases to defensive sorcery (*efelembeko*) directly sanctions morality; and with a single exception the medicines are only held to act against lawbreakers or their friends. The one exception is *akavemba,* which is said to dislocate the knees and thighs of quite innocent men and cows passing through the field, as well as of thieves; as there is no rule of manners or law against trespass, the use of this one medicine was illegal. *Efelembeko* cause disease, never directly death.

'*Protection*' (*elipengo*). Finally, to each form of aggressive sorcery, as we have seen, there exists an antidote (*elipengo*). An antidote if taken in time will always, it is said, save the victim's life; and further, as some forms of aggressive sorcery are believed to attack a whole family, killing off one after another of its members, antidotes are often taken after a death by the surviving relatives, after which they feel safe again. Further, an increased payment to the doctor who gives the antidote will secure an additional medicine to "send the sorcery back again" to the sorcerer, who is believed to die soon after. Such an active antidote was considered legal and its use was not punished. So that we have here an example of a moral sanction against the illegal use of religious power. And this particular moral sanction does extend, it is believed, beyond the single chiefdom.

Magic for Cure of Sickness and Trouble

There are medicines for the cure of wounds and of illness which have no supposed religious cause, and also for troubles like the unwanted presence of dead kinsfolk in dreams. And these medicines have no moral significance whatever. But there are others, already mentioned, which are used to aid the cure of sickness believed to have been sent by the spirits or by the witches; these medicines are believed to act in alleviation of the disease, but to be unable to effect a final cure unless the other methods of moral reform, of prayer or offering to the spirits, reconciliation with the age-village, or expulsion of a single aggressor witch, are also adopted.

Magic of Appeal

Not only was the poison-ordeal (omwafi) appealed to in cases of witchcraft, but also in all cases at law in which lack of evidence made a legal decision impossible. There is also still said to be employed another magical method, the horn (olopembe), to which one of the disputants may appeal when dissatisfied with a legal decision. If his dissatisfaction is justified, they say, members of his opponent's family die one after the other. Neither the poison-ordeal nor the horn is said to bring any harm to the innocent, but only to detect a guilt which legal methods cannot prove.

Readers of this paper will wish to know many details which lack of space, and the present incompleteness of my material, compel me to omit. Such an outline of a moral system, excised from its context of manners, policy and law, must, in any case, be unsatisfying; but, as definition must precede full understanding, it may interest other investigators.

I have throughout used the word "religion," "religious," and "supernatural" without definition to include all the closely related phenomena of the ancestor-cult, of witchcraft and of magic, which have been either hinted at or described. No tenable definition of religion can, I think, be given, which would exclude any of these phenomena, for, taken as a whole, their effect upon the thought and behavior of the Nyakyusa is strictly comparable to the effect of any other religion upon the thought and behavior of the members of the society where it obtains.

On the one hand, these beliefs promise the Nyakyusa, whether in his single person or in company with his relatives, age-neighbors, or fellow citizens, a satisfaction of his desires beyond that which his best effort and skill can assure him, a certain extra happiness which, in whatever shape it is imagined, is the fascination of every faith in the world. Such a happiness we call supernatural and the powers that are believed to give it are those of religion. On the other hand, these beliefs interpret the unhappiness and misfortune of his life in a necessary connection with his sin; that unhappiness and those misfortunes which his best effort and skill are unable to avoid, and which his mind cannot see to be the effects of the ordinary actions of nature or his fellows, they explain as the effect of supernatural causes acting morally. The religion of the Nyakyusa uses sickness, death, hunger, and misfortune as instruments for his education in right behavior within the society to which he belongs; and in this also compares exactly with other faiths, which, in like manner, connect misfortunes supernaturally with sin. Not to the student of religion will that part of Nyakyusa belief which makes even innocent persons fear quarrels with their neighbors, nor that which promises at times a supernatural power of right behavior, appear to be unique.

NOTES

[1] For the close connection of Law and Common Policy and the very great significance of Common Policy in the conserving of custom, cf. B. Malinowski, *Crime and Custom in Savage Society*, esp. pp. 22-49.

[2] *Vide infra,* Section on ceremonial magic.

[3] *Vide infra.*

FOR FURTHER READING

For additional material on the Nyakyusa see Monica Wilson's "Nyakyusa Age-Villages," and the suggested readings following her paper, in this volume.

Wilson, Monica, "Witch Beliefs and Social Structure," *American Journal of Sociology*, 1951, 56, 307-13. A comparative analysis of the forms and functions of belief in witchcraft among the Nyakyusa and a South African group, the Pondo.

Two papers by S. F. Nadel deal with witchcraft beliefs and social control. "Witchcraft and Anti-Witchcraft in Nupe Society," *Africa*, 1935, 8, 423-47, is an account of the place of witchcraft in ordinary Nupe life and measures that arise for controlling it at times of social crisis. "Witchcraft in Four African Societies: An Essay in Comparison," in this volume, is an analysis of witchcraft beliefs among the Nupe and other peoples.

Evans-Pritchard, E. E., *Witchcraft, Oracles and Magic among the Azande,* Oxford: Clarendon Press, 1937, is a basic work on the place of religious belief in the life of the Azande of East Africa.

THE IDEA OF PERSON AMONG THE DOGON*

Marcel Griaule

The Dogon are particularly concerned with questions of their origin and their place in the natural world, with the nature of the individual as a person, and with the reasons for certain rituals. Their religious system contains myths that commonly give explanations of these problems. Dogon mythology is similar to that of other groups in the Niger Bend region in French West Africa. The important rites de passage, *the crucial rituals of everyday life, and the meaning of birth and death are all related to complex mythologies, as are many other social actions and beliefs. The performance of rituals gains meaning for the African through these myths and in turn reinforces belief in them. Unlike some other African groups, the Dogon tend to have a coherent and consistent inner order in their mythology. The myths seem related to each other, not simply separate entities to account for particular social acts or beliefs. Of course, not all Dogon are equally aware of the myths or their symbolism, but certain religious personages, and certain persons who are philosophers in every sense of the word, are familiar with their details.*

Why these people in the Niger Bend should be so vitally interested in these aspects of their culture is difficult to say. It may be that Africanists who have been primarily interested in mythology in terms of structural analysis have simply not explored these aspects of culture as thoroughly as Griaule and his students, Dieterlen and Ganay, who have an obvious interest in religion and mythology, have done. We do know that the extent of the mythology and religion among the Dogon and neighboring peoples is unusual, but how unusual is still not fully understood. In any case, Griaule presents here a rather typical Dogon myth: it is complex, it extends back a considerable time, it is full of symbolism—some of which is obvious and some of which is not—and it ties man and the world of nature into an inseparable whole.

The Dogon, who number over 200,000 persons, are a patrilineal sed-

————

* Reprinted in translation from "Nouvelles recherches sur la notion de personne chez les Dogons (Soudan Français)," *Journal de Psychologie normale et pathologique,* 1947, 40, 425-31, by permission of the *Journal de Psychologie normale et pathologique,* and the Presses Universitaires de France. Translated by C. A. Vaucher.

entary agricultural people who depend mainly on grain crops for their food. They form middle range political groupings.

The article concerning Dogon personality published in the *Journal de Psychologie*[1] presented data collected during several expeditions among the Dogon who live on the elevation of Bandiagara, called Falaise. The idea of person that emerged from the long research pursued among these people was consistent with the beliefs and the everyday popular customs, which first must be considered and observed at length before attempting inquiries concerning more erudite systems.

In the course of an expedition conducted from August to December, 1946—the fifth among the Dogon—a more intricate and subtle concept of person became evident, thanks to the good will of an initiate of high status who consented to reveal to the author a large part of what one could call the Dogon metaphysic.

The Dogon consider that man is composed of a body and of two spiritual principles.

The name that is given to the body and the relation that is felt between it and the earthly surroundings are revealing. The word *gozu* derives from a root, *gozo,* which means "to separate, split." On one hand, the body is the element that started in the form of seed, then became a foetus, then grew and developed limbs. On the other hand, the body of the first man having been created from the soil, a constant relationship exists between the actual human body and the earthly surroundings, a relation whose ritual demonstration is given at the time of circumcision and excision: these operations have a goal, among others, "of paying a tribute to the earth," which is the original matter. Moreover, this matter is not considered inert: the earth, formed directly by Amma, the only god, creator of the primordial things of the universe, was first a lump of clay which, expanding as a foetus, became the body of a being which played the part of the divine wife in the first part of creation.

The human body includes two spiritual principles: the vital force, *nyama,* energy which in fact is formed by elements issuing from various beings in association with the individual concerned (father, ancestor, etc.); and a "conscious shadow," *kikinu say or kindu kindu,* the transcendent part of the person, which knows, thinks, and wills.[2]

The soul is double, as is indicated by its name, *kindu kindu,* which could be translated as "soul soul." It is composed of two spiritual twins created by the water spirit at the time the individual was born. To this end, the spirit draws on the ground twin shadows: the one destined to support the femininity of the individual is laid out first on the ground where parturition takes place. The other, which will receive the masculinity, is sketched over the first. The newborn is then laid face down on the ground, which he touches with his four limbs. He thus takes possession of his souls. If it is a boy, the male principle will dwell entirely in him: the female principle will be harbored on the foreskin. In the case of a girl, the male principle will be placed in the clitoris. For a Dogon doctor, these two principles residing in the individual during all of childhood are equivalent as twins are: neither wins over the other, and the purpose of circumcision and excision is to force the individual to lean definitely toward the one of the two for which his body is the better suited.

The reason for this situation is explained in the myth of the creation of the world.[3] In the beginning, the rule of generation was the production of twins: the ideal unity of the being was formed by a couple.[4] But ever since the first attempt by the god Amma, the rule has not worked. In fact, Amma, the only god, was compelled to create, in order to unite himself with her, a mate, whom he made arise from a lump of clay and who became the earth. The male organ was made of an anthill and the clitoris of a termite hill. From this time, a female principle resided in the first and a male principle in the second. At the moment the god drew near, the termite hill opposed the entrance by asserting her masculinity: Amma was constrained to cut off the obstacle so as to unite himself with the excised earth.

This occurrence influenced the product of the union so that it was born single, in the form of a jackal.[5] Later the god had further relations with the earth that were not disturbed and resulted in the birth of a spirit couple, Nommo, whose body was made of the divine seed, that is to say, water. These two creatures would little by little replace the god in ensuring the progress of the universe.

It is then that the first product [the jackal], whose position was unusual because it could not procreate, committed incest with its mother [the earth], an event that was to upset the course of earthly things. The god Amma, having turned away from his wife, kneaded two clay balls out of which sprang the first human couple, who in turn procreated, giving birth to twins. But after the coming of these two beings the production of twins became a very rare exception. And it is since the birth of this first generation that the spirit couple Nommo, becoming the mentor of the world, minimized the inconvenience of this new situation by creating a double soul for each being, granted through contact with the ground.

However, the first human birth brought about an event of considerable significance. The woman kneaded by Amma had intercourse with the man without having been excised. Becoming pregnant, she gave birth to twins; at that time her pains were directed to her clitoris, which fell off and went away in the shape of a scorpion, whose venom was made of both the water and the blood of parturition.

Previously her mate had been circumcised and his foreskin was transformed into *nay,* a kind of lizard.[6]

These events formed a prototype of the rites of circumcision and excision; they also constituted the preliminaries of the totemic organization.

If the double soul constitutes a remedy for the loss of twin production, it also leads to serious consequences. As long as the child keeps foreskin and clitoris, that is to say, the material expression of the principle of the opposite sex, its femininity has the same value and power as its masculinity. One should not then compare the uncircumcised boy to a woman. He is, like the unexcised girl, both male and female. In theory, nothing allows one to foretell which of the two principles will dominate, and this uncertainty is expressed in the idea of nonfixation of the part of the soul that will definitely play the principal role.

Upon this fixation depends the sexual life of the person involved, who if he were to stay in the state of his first childhood would feel no inclination to procreate. This fixation is the chief purpose of circumcision and excision: the boy is circumcised so as to reduce his femininity, to place him definitely on the male side. A girl is excised to make her a woman.

But the ejected principle is not destroyed by this: as the myth indicates, one of the results is to create for each woman a scorpion that becomes the carrier of her male soul in place of her clitoris, and, for each man, a *nay* which supports the female soul.

Moreover, the eliminated principle does not thoroughly leave its former abode: in the shape of *kindu bummone* (stupid soul), which abides in the shadow, it will remain common both to the one operated on and to the animal created.

We are dealing here with an apparently reduced soul, at least in the part that it plays in the everyday life of the individual.[7] As for the animals thus created, they in some way play the role of twins of the persons concerned.

However, the institution of the scorpion-twin and the *nay*-twin was only a makeshift.

Since man appeared, Amma had created in heaven a pair of forbidden animals corresponding to each of the eight children of the first couple.[8] During their earthly life these eight humans shared their spiritual principles with the heavenly animals. The union—but not confusion—of man and animal, bearers of the same principles, occurred only when man, having transformed himself into the water spirit,[9] reached heaven.

But this favor was granted only to the eight original ancestors. Their descendants remained separated from their heavenly counterparts until the time of the world's reorganization.[10] All the species came down from heaven to earth on their own, classified by categories and earmarked for the eight families From this time on, and up to now, when a man is born, an animal of the forbidden species and of the same sex is also born whose fate is bound to his: it is circumcised and dies at the same time as he. It can be said that man is in a way identified to his family's forbidden animal,[11] whether the same soul (*kindu kindu*) and the same shadow (*kikinu bummone*) go from one to the other, having equal value for each, or the forbidden animal is in possession of his own spiritual principles that are subordinated to those of his counterpart. But this identification should be understood as that of twins.

As a result, to kill the forbidden animal amounts to killing the symbolic twin that represents the species of the person involved. In such a case the *kindu bummone* common to both the man and animal, as well as the animal's *nyama* liberated by death, go to the totemic ancestor, who makes them "dwell" in the culprit so as to exert and apply pressure and sanctions on him until he is purified. When this is effected, the *kindu bummone*, ceasing to act on man, seeks a pregnant female animal, "touches" it, and introduces the victim's *nyama* into the new carrier offered by the foetus.

Now that the principles attached to the symbolical twin have been reintegrated in a body that belongs to the forbidden species, everything is in order again.

In the case in which the forbidden animal is killed by someone who does not belong to the group associated with it, nothing pertaining to this group is included in the proceedings of the *kindu bummone*, which, without going through the medium of the totemic ancestor, directly seeks another carrier. All this occurs outside the group, and no action is taken against any of its members.[12]

It is, however, important to note that each forbidden species itself has a forbidden animal, which has an equal affinity with another animal, and so on, to the exhaustion of the category that bears on the family involved.

All the animals belonging to a category[13] are then linked in theory to a definite family, and each human birth will bring about a series of animal births. One can say, therefore, that each human being is mirrored by a series of twins in the animal kingdom, which itself is considered the most important in nature.[14]

One cannot emphasize enough the importance of the ideas of which only a very brief glimpse is given here. It now appears that the concepts that the Dogon have of the person necessitate a reconsideration of the problems of circumcision and totemism.

Among these people, these important institutions are linked to the loss of twin production, a loss that successive interventions—verbal revelations, redemption—brought about by the heavenly powers, which are substitutes for the god Amma, have tried to mitigate.

Finally let us note that conceptions concerning twin births are not peculiar to the Dogon. The Bambara, who are a more numerous people than the Dogon, have analogous myths, representations, and rites. This is also true of the Bozo of Nigeria, and, within the limits of our knowledge, of the Kouroumba of the Niger Bend.[15]

REFERENCES

[Starred items are recommended as further readings.]

*[1] La personnalité chez les Dogons (Soudan français). *Journal de Psychologie*, Oct.-Dec., 1940-41, pp. 468-475.

[2] *Loc. cit.,* p. 469.

*[3] This myth is expounded in "Mythe de l'organisation du monde chez les Dogons du Soudan," *Psyché,* No. 6, pp. 443-453.

[4] Of the three possibilities: two males, a couple of both sexes, and two females, the last is the height of perfection.

[5] It evidently is *Thos aureus*, an animal which actually plays an important part in divination (information given by the kindness of M. P. Rode, director of the Service national de Muséologie, who identified the animal from a photograph).

[6] This animal has not been identified. It burrows, and its appearance is an omen of bad luck.

[7] It is at the very moment of the operation that the scorpion and *nay* are created, that is, that they are born. The *nay* being uniparous, there is no inconvenience in circumcising an odd number of patients. On the contrary, the scorpion, according to native belief, produces in pairs, so that is necessary to excise girls by twos.

[8] These are the eight original ancestors of the present Dogon.

[9] Concerning this regeneration of the first men, see *Psyché. loc. cit.*

[10] The myths, the numerous representations and rites of this reorganization will be the object of future publications. Here only a brief glimpse is given. [See For Further Reading, below.]

[11] It is necessary to note that the forbidden animal is not the totem. This part is played by one of the eight original ancestors. Concerning this institution see S. de Ganay, "Le Binou Yénébé." *Miscellanea Africana Lebaudy,* 2, Geuthner, 1942.

[12] This is not the place to study the reactions of the principles released by the animal's death, to the detriment of the killer.

[13] In practice, and so as not to hinder the everyday life process, the Dogon consider only the taboos which could be classified as the most important.

[14] Neither vegetables nor insects seem to be considered. However, vegetables and insects were included in the system of the world that the heavenly mentors brought down from heaven.

[15] The Moslem cosmogony includes five twin couples to which the first woman gave birth. The male of the fifth couple having been killed by that of the fourth, there finally remained only four couples and a single woman. These ideas are similar to those that we studied elsewhere.

FOR FURTHER READING

Griaule, Marcel, and Dieterlen, Germaine, "The Dogon," in Forde, Daryll (ed.), *African Worlds: Studies in the Cosmological Ideas and Social Values of African Peoples,* London: Oxford University Press for the International African Institute, 1954, pp. 83-110. An analysis of the relationship of Dogon cosmogony and social organization.

Griaule, Marcel, *Dieu, d'eau: Entretiens avec Ogotemmêli,* Paris: Éditions du Chêne, 1948. The world view and cosmology of a Dogon priest and philosopher.

Dieterlen, Germaine, *Les âmes des dogons,* Paris: Institut d'Ethnologie, Travaux et mémoires, 40, 1941. An account of the idea of the person among the Dogon, as well as considerable data on mythology and the role of the ancestors.

Ganay, Solange de, *Les devises des dogons,* Paris: Institut d'Ethnologie, Travaux et mémoires, 41, 1941. An analysis of salutations or sayings which play an important role in the Dogon religious and social system.

Griaule, Marcel, *Masques dogons,* Paris: Institut d'Ethnologie, Travaux et mémoires, *33,* 1938. A detailed study of the rituals of the Dogon masked societies, and of the symbolism of the masks.

Palau Marti, Montserrat, *Les dogon,* Monographies ethnologiques africaines, 1957. A general survey of the Dogon with a very useful bibliography.

Dieterlen, Germaine, *Essai sur la religion bambara,* Paris: Presses Universitaires de France, 1950. A study of a people with a similar religious system and mythology to that of the Dogon, and who live to the west of them.

Dieterlen, Germaine, "The Mande Creation Myth," *Africa,* 1957, 27, 114-138. An analysis of a myth that is commonly found among many groups in the Western Sudan.

Herskovits, Melville J., *Dahomey: An Ancient West African Kingdom,* New York: Augustin, 1938, 2 vols.; Herskovits, Melville J., and Frances S., *An Outline of Dahomean Religious Belief,* American Anthropological Association, Memoirs, No. 41, 1933; Herskovits, Melville J., and Frances S., *Dahomean Narrative: a Cross-cultural Analysis,* Evanston: Northwestern University Press, African Studies No. 1, 1958. These three works discuss the complex religious beliefs, mythology, and folklore of an African state.

Tempels, Placide, *La philosophie bantoue,* Paris: Éditions Africaines, 1949. A broad and controversial examination of Bantu philosophical concepts, view of the universe, and psychological orientation.

Fortes, Meyer, *Oedipus and Job in West African Religion,* Cambridge: Cambridge University Press, 1959. An examination of the belief in ancestors and in nonancestral spirits among the Tallensi of Northern Ghana, and their relation to the realms of social structure and social interaction.

ANCESTRAL SPIRITS AMONG THE PLATEAU TONGA*

E. Colson

The reflection of a people's ideal social structure in their religious belief and ritual is clearly shown in this discussion of the relations between kinship group members and the spirits of their ancestors among the Plateau Tonga. Here, as in many African societies, such relationships are a projection of those between the living in the kinship system, "existing outside time and space in a perpetual present."

As outlined by Colson in this reading, which is part of a longer paper on Tonga ancestral spirits and social structure, a person receives his initial position in society by his identification with a guardian spirit from his own and one from his father's matrilineal groups, the two bodies of kinsmen who are concerned with his childhood and youth. His personality, aptitudes, and shortcomings are said to be derived from these spirits. As in the parental family, both the father's and the mother's groups play a part in the development of the individual.

After a person matures and takes a position of responsibility within his matrilineal group, he is eligible to become an ancestral spirit when he dies, which spirit is merged with his guardian spirit of his mother's line, while that of his father's line is withdrawn. Since his own ancestral spirit represents the position that he occupied in the community during his lifetime, it is only if he has achieved the expected adult status that he may be recognized as an ancestral spirit after death. The continuity of the matrilineal line is thus emphasized through a number of generations, while the affiliation with the father's maternal line represents an interest for only one lifetime.

In this paper, I am going to describe beliefs held by the Plateau Tonga about the activities of a particular type of spirits, the *mizimu,* and attempt to show how these reflect the ideal organization of Tonga social structure. The term *mizimu* (*muzimu* in the singular) is usually trans-

---

* Reprinted from "Ancestral Spirits and Social Structure among the Plateau Tonga," *International Archives of Ethnography,* 1954, 47, 21-68, by permission of the author and publisher.

lated by anthropologists as "ancestral spirits," but I shall use the native term since this translation does not cover the various ways in which the Tonga use the term and I can find no adequate English equivalent.

I have already published a sketch of Tonga social organization.[1] I need only say here in introduction that the Plateau Tonga are a Bantu-speaking people inhabiting Mazabuka District in the Southern Province of Northern Rhodesia. Their number today has been variously estimated as between 80,000 and 120,000 people. Until British Administration introduced a Native Authority system, they had no large-scale political organization of their own. The basis of their own system was twofold: an organization into a large number of small dispersed groups of matrilineal kinsmen, and an organization into local neighborhoods composed of a few villages with a common rain shrine and cult. Although the rain shrines no longer hold the allegiance of many Tonga, the local neighborhoods continue. To most Tonga they are of greater importance than the chiefdoms or the Plateau Tonga Native Authority which have been imposed upon the old structure. The matrilineal groups are still important units, although their functions have been curtailed with the outlawing of self-help and the institution of courts. They have also been affected by the diminished importance of the cult of the *mizimu* which is an integral element in the organization of such groups.

In this paper, I shall write as though all the Tonga still held to the old beliefs about the *mizimu*. This, of course, is not true. Missions have worked in the area since 1905. Many Tonga are Christians, of eight different sects. Others are skeptics who deny the old beliefs without accepting those introduced by the missionaries. Many claim that they have forgotten the *mizimu,* and that these no longer affect them in any way. There are whole villages where no one makes offerings to the *mizimu* or considers them in any way. On the other hand, there are many Tonga to whom the *mizimu* are a vital part of life. They would claim, along with the old man who heard a woman suggest that the *mizimu* had disappeared since people stopped believing in them: "No, the *mizimu* can never die. They will always be there affecting us."

Little specific information has been published about the Tonga beliefs in the *mizimu,* though many have referred to the cult. I have not attempted to draw this scattered material together and evaluate it. Much of it is contradictory, and from it no coherent picture emerges.[2]

THE *MIZIMU* AND THEIR CULT

The Tonga are constantly making offerings to the *mizimu*. There are the regular offerings made by all adult men and women whether they are involved in any misfortune or not. They have been taught that on certain occasions offerings must be made, and they have learned the names of the *mizimu* which they must call. Changes in the location of a household must be announced to the *mizimu*, by offerings made before leaving the old dwelling and soon after entering into the new one. Changes in status must be announced, as when a household is instituted for the first time, when a man first builds his own cattle kraal, when a man obtains a new gun or plow or other major item of equipment such as a large iron pot. The initiation of some activity and its successful completion—a hunt, a fishing expedition, a journey to work in white country—call for offerings to the *mizimu*. So do the beginning and end of the agricultural year. At planting time, each local community carries out rites to ask for rain and good crops, and these are community rites in which the *mizimu* are not involved. But each family though it contributes beer for the general rite also privately asks its own *mizimu* for assistance. At harvest time, when the community again gathers to offer thanks for the harvest, each family also privately thanks its *mizimu* for help in making the crop. Finally, from time to time, a household should make beer especially for the *mizimu* though there is no special reason for doing so: "Even if everything is going well with me, I should still make an offering for the *mizimu* to tell them that I am all right and that I want to continue to be all right and that they should help me just as they have been doing." Even though beer is brewed primarily for sale, or for gaiety, it is also considered to be made for the *mizimu*, at least among conservative people.

These offerings are concerned with a single household, though large numbers may come to the beer drink which follows later in the day. On two other occasions, large numbers of people gather for offerings to the *mizimu* of their line, and these occasions are not the primary concern of a single household. Offerings to the ancestors form part of the ritual of a girl's puberty ceremony and also of the ritual of the final mourning after a death. But these too are set occasions, when the offerings are made because it is customary to do so.

The *mizimu* are also important in another sphere, as causal explanations evoked to account for illness or other misfortune which has befallen some individual. *Mizimu* are not the only spirit agency which may be involved, and it is necessary to consult a diviner to have the cause of the misfortune identified. If the diviner indicates that the *mizimu* are involved, he will also name some particular *muzimu* and announce that it is angry because it has been neglected. Either it has not been called when offerings have been made, or the offender has been dilatory in making offerings. The remedy is a special offering at which the offended *muzimu* is invoked by name and assured that it will henceforth be remembered.

Besides the *mizimu* and the High God, known as Leza,[3] the Tonga distinguish three other types of spirits which have the power to affect living people. These are the *basangu,* which are effective in affairs of general community interest and which make their demands known through people whom they possess[4]; the *masabe,* which are described as the spirits of animals or of foreigners and which cause illness to those whom they possess until these learn the dances appropriate to the possessing spirit[5]; the *zelo* (*celo* in the singular), which we may call the ghosts of dead people.

If the Tonga are asked to describe these spirits and the *mizimu* and to explain how they differ from one another, they describe each group in terms of its actions. They are not concerned to analyze the nature of the spirits or their ultimate origin, nor are they concerned if the spirits are sometimes said to act in ways which are contrary to the general dogma which relates them to human beings. "We call them all wind (*luwo*) because they are invisible. We do not know what they look like. We know which is affecting us by the way in which it acts." In the great majority of situations where the Tonga are concerned with spirits, it is either on a set occasion for an offering, in which they know the particular spirit involved because this is defined by the situation itself, or because they must deal with an effect which is disturbing to their lives. To remove the effect, they must first identify the causal agency, and this is generally done through the diviner. The identification of the agency defines in broad terms the appropriate actions for dealing with the effects. If the action appears to be successful, this demonstrates that they have also been successful in identifying the agent. This ends their interest in the matter for the time being, and they do not feel that it is relevant to their purpose to enter further into the nature of the spirit agency. Since in general they are concerned with the spirits in moments of personal crisis, they have little reason to see how the belief in the spirits is embedded in their social system nor are they troubled by inconsistencies or contradictions in what they believe. The anthropologist, however, is concerned with the social rather than the personal implications of the beliefs, and it is largely with this aspect that I shall deal in this paper. Radcliffe-Brown has written: "In my own experience it is in ancestor-worship that we can most easily discover and demonstrate the social function of a religious cult." [6] Certainly among the Tonga, social structure and the cult of the *mizimu* are so intertwined that a study of one leads inevitably to the other.

THE NATURE OF THE *MIZIMU*

Mizimu and ghosts (*zelo*) are both thought to be the spirits of former living people, but the two are distinct. A few Tonga have told me that *mizimu* and ghosts are one and the same thing. Others have argued that the ghost exists only for the period between a death and the time when the kinsmen assemble for the final mourning rite and that this transforms the ghost into the *muzimu*. But most maintain that the two are completely different entities, and a study of their actions on different occasions is consistent with this interpretation and not with any identification of ghost and *muzimu*.

When a person dies, therefore, two spirits remain, one the *muzimu* and one the ghost. The ghost is always a newly created spirit, some saying that it originates in the dying breath. Not all people produce a new *muzimu* when they die, and I have never been able to get a clear statement as to how the *muzimu* originates. Indeed, various people have told me: "I have never been able to understand this myself, and I don't think anyone else does either." There is general agreement, however, that only those who have achieved a certain status during their lifetime give rise to a new *muzimu* after death, while others leave behind them only the already existing *muzimu* associated with them since their naming. Once created, moreover, the *mizimu* are not immortal like the ghosts who are independent of the devotion of living people for their continued existence. When the living cease to remember the *mizimu* and no longer call upon them by name, they become nameless spirits wandering at large, who now work only for evil. "They have become like ghosts." Over these the living have no control, for in forgetting the names they have lost the means of summoning or propitiating the spirits.

Over ghosts, the living have no direct control, unless they are sorcerers, and ghosts are presumed to be only evil. They may act against the living of their own volition, or they may be agents of sorcerers who have pressed them into service. A sudden dangerous or mortal illness is therefore usually attributed to ghosts. The *muzimu* is not actively evil in the same way. It may cause injury to the living, but this is not its primary purpose, nor is it free like the ghost to cause injury to anyone with whom it comes in contact. The *muzimu* is dependent upon the living for its own continued existence, and it causes injury to keep its memory alive in the living so that they may provide the offerings on which it depends. If the living refuse to listen to its demands, then it is thought to enlist the aid of the ghosts to inflict more drastic punishment. Some Tonga say that the *muzimu* travels always with the ghost which originated with it on a person's death and which acts as its intermediary with other ghosts.

> The *muzimu* has its own ghost with it when it comes to ask for beer. If it receives nothing, then it becomes angry and says, "What can we do, my ghost? We alone cannot kill this man or make him very ill. We must go to the other ghosts." Then the ghost goes to invite all the ghosts to come and kill the person, and it accompanies them when they come with a rush to kill the man. The *muzimu* does not come that time, but it stands off and waits until the man is dead. Also the ghosts who

actually kill are never those who come from your own kinsmen.[7] Never since we have been born have we known our own ghosts to kill us. It is always strange ghosts we find who have killed.

Here we are already faced with a contradiction in Tonga belief, for the Tonga hold that one type of sorcery is made effective by the owner using it to kill some relative whose ghost then works with him. While it helps its master to obtain fortune and success, it is nevertheless angry at having been killed and it demands the sacrifice of still further relatives in revenge.

Nevertheless, the distinction between ghosts and *mizimu* remains clear, and the *mizimu* are absolved by the Tonga of being the immediate cause of the death of their living kinsmen. Some indeed deny that *mizimu* ever kill. "Long ago perhaps some people died because of the *mizimu,* but today they die only from sorcery, for envy and hatred are very great today."

The *mizimu* are thought to be concerned that they should not be forgotten, and so they send sickness and other misfortune to the living as a reminder that beer and other offerings must be provided. They are anxious that the living should maintain the customs that they practiced when they were alive, and therefore they punish departures from custom. In return they offer to the living some protection against other spirits and against sorcery. They should also assist the living to obtain the good things of life—children, good harvests, herds of cattle, and an orderly existence. These in turn permit the living to procure grain for beer, to marry wives who will brew the beer for offerings, and to perpetuate the names of the *mizimu* through the children whom they beget and who, to some extent, are regarded as the living representatives of the *mizimu*. The living propitiate the spirits to ensure for themselves the good things which they desire; the spirits assist the living to these goods so that they in turn may continue to exist. Each is dependent upon the other, and there is partnership between the living and the *mizimu* in achieving their common ends.

But the *mizimu* are not concerned with all the living, and the living are not concerned with all the *mizimu*. The relationships between them are a projection of those which exist between living persons organized in the kinship system. *Mizimu* and living members of a kinship group are parts of a single whole, and the ties between them transcend the bounds of time and space. Or rather, since the Tonga kinship system is not given a local focus, nor does an ordered genealogical framework or any scheme of historical incidents create a time scale into which the living and the *mizimu* can be fitted, the system exists outside time and space in a perpetual present.

INDIVIDUALS AND THEIR *MIZIMU*

The Tonga maintain that the *mizimu* which are concerned with them, and therefore with which they are concerned, are the spirits of former members of the matrilineal kinship groups of their mothers and fathers, though they also say that the spirits of the matrilineal groups of their two grandfathers may occasionally intervene in their affairs. Nevertheless, it is the affiliation with the two parental groups which is primarily stressed in relation to the *mizimu,* as it is throughout social life. Some of these *mizimu,* however, are of more importance to an individual than are others. When a Tonga speaks of his *mizimu,* or refers to the *mizimu* of someone else, he may be using the term very broadly to include all those spirits which are concerned with him, or more narrowly to refer to particular *mizimu* who stand in a special relationship to him. His meaning is usually clear from the context. For analysis, however, it is necessary to distinguish the different uses of the term, and I shall therefore use the following classification in writing about the role of the *mizimu* in any one individual's life.

1. *Mizimu* as a general term includes all the spirits of former members of the lines of the father and mother, and may even be used still more generally for all the spirits of former members of any group with which a person feels a kinship relationship. If I write of the *mizimu* of a matrilineal group, however, it refers only to the spirits of former members of this group.

2. Guardian *Mizimu* are those associated with the names which each person receives soon after birth. They act as his special guardians throughout life, and from them he is thought to derive his personality.

3. House *Mizimu* are the particular spirits which an adult person installs as the guardians of his household.

4. Inherited *Mizimu* are those which are associated with a person because he has been given the name of someone recently deceased as part of the funeral rites.

5. Own *Muzimu.* This is the new *muzimu* which comes into existence only after a person's death. No living person has his own *muzimu.*

The guardian *mizimu* have a special significance in each person's life. They can be regarded as symbolic representations of the overwhelming importance of the paternal and maternal matrilineal groups in determining the original social status of any individual, and of their responsibility for his wellbeing throughout life. Names are identified with *mizimu,* and the giving of a name implies assumption of social responsibility for a child. A man who begets a child by an unmarried woman may obtain the right to name his child, which is then affiliated to his matrilineal group and comes under the power of its *mizimu* in the same fashion as any child born in wedlock. A man who begets an adulterine child by a married woman has no such right. The woman's husband is the legal father. He names the child, thus bestowing upon it a guardian *muzimu,* and it comes under the protection of the *mizimu* of his line quite as much as do children he has begotten. The names, which thus recognize the existence of the child and give it its initial place in society, are bestowed some months after birth. The first name is given by the father or his relatives, and it is a name belonging to a former member of this line. The second is given by the mother's relatives and is the name of a former member of her line. Each name is associated with a *muzimu.* The Tonga say that the *mizimu* themselves may decide which of their living kin shall receive their names, and thus become their special charges. When a woman is in labor, the midwives call the names of various *mizimu,* saying, "Nangoma, come forth! Mavwali, come forth! Nankambula, come forth! Cimuka, come forth!" The child should be born when they call the appropriate name, and they then know that it is this *muzimu* which has chosen to give its name to the child. They may have no such indication, and may later learn the appropriate name through divination. If the child becomes ill, the diviner may attribute the illness to the desire of a particular *muzimu* to give its name to the child. Even if the child's name has been decided at its birth, the name may still be changed since the guardian *muzimu* has failed in its duty by permitting the illness, or the relatives may decide that henceforth the child shall bear both names and both *mizimu* will be regarded as its guardians and as concerned with its fate. In addition, it will have a name and a guardian *muzimu* from the other parent's side. Occasionally the name is chosen by the relatives without any form of divination. However a name is chosen, it is not identified with the child until the time of the formal naming rite.

The Tonga deny that the guardian *mizimu* associated with its names are incarnate in the child,[8] and at any one time there may be many people who bear the name of the same *muzimu.* One informant said: "We never say that a person has a *muzimu (ulamuzimu)* or that he is entered [*wanjilwa*] by a *muzimu.* We say that the *muzimu* looks after him (*wamulela*) or that it herds him (*wamwembela*)." Some have also told me: "No person while he is living has a *muzimu* which is part of himself. He only becomes a *muzimu* after he dies." Nevertheless, I have heard Tonga speak of a person as having a *muzimu* in the sense of a part of consciousness or personality. Thus, if a man dreams of another, it is said that their two *mizimu* have wandered forth in sleep and met. Some have also said that perhaps animals have *mizimu* because one sometimes dreams of animals, but that perhaps it is only the ghosts (*zelo*) of animals that one sees in dreams. When they are asked to explain the contradictions inherent in this use of the word *muzimu* when they have denied that a living person has a *muzimu* of his own, they do not see that it is a point worth discussing and are willing to permit both statements to stand without attempting to adjust them. They remain positive, however, that guardian *mizimu* are not reincarnated in their ward.

Despite this, a person is closely identified with the two guardian *mizimu* whose names he bears. He may be honored by being addressed by the clan name of the father of either of these *mizimu* just as he is honored by being addressed by the clan name of his own father. The two guardian *mizimu* are thought to determine his character and interests. They react to affairs that concern him as though the incidents were directed against themselves. If a man delays in his marriage payments, the diviner may find that the cause of his wife's barrenness, or the death or illness of her child, is due to the anger of either of her guardian *mizimu*. As one Tonga explained it: "I gave my mother's name to my daughter. Now if my daughter's husband fails to pay his bridewealth, then the *muzimu* will become angry and say, 'Why has this man married me without paying bridewealth? It is not a real marriage at all.' And the *muzimu* will stop her from bearing a child, or if she does bear a child it will always be ill because the *muzimu* is angry."

A person's evil deeds may be attributed to his guardian *muzimu,* as well as any particular skills or abilities or interests which mark him off from others. A man known as a troublemaker killed another during a beer drink. When his maternal relatives were discussing the matter, they said: "Perhaps from his father's side he received a *muzimu* which has caused him to do this. What could he do? A man must work with the *mizimu* that belong to him." Another explained once: "If you name your child after a *muzimu* which is bad, the child will be bad. If you name it after someone who was fierce, the child will be fierce. Now X has killed a man. If X's *muzimu* is given to a child, that child too will grow to kill someone." However, the Tonga might not be prepared to carry this argument to its ultimate conclusion in predestination. As one put it: "Perhaps the *muzimu* whose name they gave to X makes him like that. We think his heart is not all right. Even among you Europeans there are people who are bad, who like to fight, who cannot understand what other people tell them. Such a person has only his own mind and cannot understand what others tell him. That is why we say sometimes that it is due to the *mizimu*. But we don't really know why a person should be like that." Nevertheless, to most Tonga the obvious answer to any type of personal deviance is a reference to the guardian *mizimu.* In one area there was a persistent rumor that an immigrant from the Gwembe District was actually a woman, though "she" dressed as a man, worked at men's occupations, and grew furious at any reference to "her" sex. When I queried why "she" should behave in this fashion, people shrugged their shoulders, expressed disgust, and then remarked that probably the *muzimu* after whom "she" was named had behaved the same way when alive. It makes no difference to this argument that *mizimu* are vague abstractions, save for those who have died so recently that they were known personally to the living, or that the same name is borne by people of varying personalities. The Tonga do not argue that because one who bears a name has a certain nature that all of that name have that nature; nor do they say that the *muzimu* has a certain nature, and therefore those who bear its name will have this nature. They say only that the person's nature is such and therefore the guardian *muzimu* as a person was such.

If a person shows particular aptitudes, these may be attributed to the guardian *muzimu*, or other *mizimu* of the same lines may be thought to have given him the capacity to perform certain skills which they practiced in their lifetime. The particular *muzimu* responsible may be identified through a dream or through divination. The Tonga recognize that even small children show different interests, and they think that these interests persist throughout life. By watching a small boy at play, you can tell whether as a man he will love cattle and acquire wealth, or whether he will be content to be a fisherman or hunter without much chance of growing rich. But it is hopeless to seek to change him, for his interests are determined by the *mizimu*. Diviners, hunters, blacksmiths, craftsmen who make wooden drums or mortars, basket-makers and potters, all are thought to practice their skills under the direction of a *muzimu* which as a living person had had that skill.[9] Success in attaining a prominent position may be attributed to one's guardian *muzimu*, though others may whisper that it is due to sorcery. One man who through his own efforts had acquired wealth and importance as the headman of a large village spoke of his success as due to the guardian *muzimu* whose name he bore: "Ndaba was an important man with many followers. Before I was born, his *muzimu* came and said that I should be called by his name. Now it is easy to see that I am indeed Ndaba, for I too have become an important man with many people who depend upon me." There is no expectation that a *muzimu* will pass on its skills to all who bear its name —it may choose one or pass over all its namesakes to endow a person of another name with its skill. The Tonga do not seek to ensure the character and attributes of their children by the names which they bestow upon them, but as they observe character and attributes unfolding they turn to the *mizimu* as convenient explanations.

As an extension of this belief, a man's successes and failures are not his alone, but belong to the groups which have supplied him with a guardian *muzimu* and share with him a ritual attachment to it. When he dies, the two groups will take the property which he has accumulated. Members of his own matrilineal group will receive the larger portion, but a share is also due to the matrilineal group of his father.[10] While he lives, the two groups share responsibility for his actions. They should help him to pay damages for such offenses as he commits. Both should defend him against the vengeance of others. Both should contribute to the marriage payments for his first wife. Responsibility is accepted the more easily because of the belief that the individual, at least to some extent, is merely the vehicle through which a *muzimu* continues to act— and the *muzimu* is common to them all.

The guardian *mizimu* may thus be viewed as symbols of the identification of a person with his kinship groups. But when as an adult, he establishes his own independent household, he acquires a new social position. His household is one of the units in the local community, and he takes his place within the community as its head. Within the household are joined not only the interests of his own paternal and maternal matrilineal kinship groups, but also of the matrilineal groups of his wife. The importance of his new position is ritually recognized, for he now for the first time becomes capable of making offerings to the *mizimu*. At the same time, the new household is also given a ritual recognition, by the installation of one or more of the husband's *mizimu* as special guardians of the house. Significantly enough, these are rarely the husband's guardian *mizimu,* which stress his identification with his paternal and maternal kinship groups. These remain as his individual guardians, but henceforth his house *mizimu* will hold a dominant position in all that concerns him as his interests are centered in the well-being of his household.

The fact that he has achieved a position of his own is further recognized, for when he dies he himself will become a *muzimu*. Those who die before they set up a household leave behind them only the guardian *mizimu* of their names. I argue that this is because their social personality is still derived from attachment to their matrilineal groups, and their death is of concern only to these two groups. The head of a household is of importance to others besides his own paternal and maternal kinsmen, and his importance to his kinsmen is now at least partially a reflection of the position which he occupies in the community. This is given recognition by attributing to him a *muzimu* of his own when he dies.

At the same time, the primary affiliation of each person to his matrilineal kinsmen is stressed, for the new *muzimu* which he has created bears the name of his guardian *muzimu* from his maternal line, and it has power to affect only those of this line and their offspring. His death breaks the tie which has been created between his own matrilineal group and that of his father by their common interest in him. His father's group have no concern with his own *muzimu,* and it cannot affect them. Part of the funeral rite emphasizes the finality of the break with the father's line in contrast to the continuity with the maternal line. This is embodied in every funeral, whether or not a new *muzimu* is thought to be involved. For, although not every person becomes a *muzimu,* each person once named is associated with his guardian *mizimu.* Formerly, when a child died before it was named, there was no mourning, for no *mizimu* were involved. Even today, the old women will tell the mother to hush her wailing, saying that this is only a ghost (*celo*) or only a person (*muntu*), and the mourning is usually curtailed. But if a person dies after being named, someone must be chosen to inherit the *muzimu* (*kwanga muzimu*). This is the deceased's guardian *muzimu* from his maternal line in the case of one who dies before establishing a household; it is his own *muzimu* otherwise. The father's group come to the mourning, and they are said to take away with them the name which they gave to their child and with it the associated guardian *muzimu.* The name from the maternal side is perpetuated in another member of the group. The person chosen is anointed with oil at the nape of the neck, given tobacco, and as beads are placed about his neck, he is told: "Your name is now such and such." This rite is thought to continue the attachment of the now inherited *muzimu* to the group to which it belongs. If it is a newly created *muzimu,* however, a further rite is performed some months after the death, when the people gather for the final mourning. In the interim, though the *muzimu* has been inherited, it is thought to be wandering disconsolately in the bush. At the final rite, an offering is poured in its name, and it is told to take its place among the other *mizimu* of the line with the assurance that the living will not forget it while it remembers them. Henceforth, it may appear in many different rôles—it may be installed as the guardian of a household, its name may be given to any number of children to whom it will be thought to act as guardian, or it may only be invoked occasionally by a diviner who attributes illness to its anger at being neglected. Its importance will reflect the importance which the person attained in life. Those of little importance to their kinsmen are usually soon forgotten.

The new *muzimu* is a creation of the living, and not an automatic emanation of the dead man. The Tonga believe that the matrilineal group has the right to decide whether or not a dead man's own *muzimu* shall come into existence. They may refuse to mourn for a man or to inherit his *muzimu* if he dies as a leper or if he has been killed as a sorcerer. They may also refuse to inherit the *muzimu* of a suicide. This is in line with their belief that a *muzimu* once in existence can demand the right to act as guardian for new members of the group who would thus be endowed with the unfortunate characteristics of the dead person. They maintain that if no one inherits the spirit, and if no rite is performed to call it to join the other *mizimu,* then the *muzimu* does not exist and therefore it cannot affect them. Its powers and potentialities for evil have been dammed at the source. This happened to one man, who was a leper, and when he died no one inherited his *muzimu*. His kinsmen say that he has never affected them in any way: "He is now only a ghost wandering in the bush." In this belief, again, they are not completely consistent. A diviner may diagnose an illness as due to the anger of a *muzimu* because its mourning rites have not been performed. In 1950, we found the people of a village mourning because the diviner had announced that a man had died while at work in the Union of South Africa and his *muzimu* was sending illness to his kinsmen to announce his death and to ask that the mourning be performed. His relatives had heard nothing from him since he went away to work, and they had had no report of his death. That he should have a *muzimu* which could affect them is contrary to the dogma that only a *muzimu* already recognized by the group has effective power over it, and this is not the only case that belies the dogmas. Nevertheless, it is consistent with our interpretation of the own *muzimu* as a recognition by the community of the place that the dead held in their lives. If for some reason he was so disturbing to them that they wish only to forget him, then they deny to him a *muzimu*. If they are prepared to remember him, then he has a *muzimu* whether or not the rites which are said to establish the new *muzimu* have been performed and these can be performed at some later date.

The one who inherits a *muzimu* does not assume the social personality of the dead, as we shall see below in the discussion on succession. He does, however, stand in a special relation to his inherited *muzimu*. This is true whether he has inherited the guardian *muzimu* of a youth or a dead adult's own *muzimu*. When he makes offerings, he ought to include the inherited *muzimu* among those he calls. He may also be laid under special restrictions which do not apply to those who have never inherited a *muzimu*. Thus, if a girl has inherited a *muzimu*, a special rite should be performed the first time she has sexual intercourse, lest the inherited *muzimu* be angry and send sickness to her, prevent her from bearing children, or harm such children as are born to her. I am told that among the We in the Gwembe Valley, the same rite used to be performed for a boy who had inherited a *muzimu*, but the people of the Plateau deny that they ever had the rite for boys.

It may be of importance that this is one of the few rites involving a *muzimu* that calls for the participation of a large number of matrilineal kinsmen. Usually when a *muzimu* of the matrilineal line is to be propitiated only the person involved, or his guardian if he is still immature, need take part in the rite. Other members of the matrilineal group need not attend. I would argue that the difference is due to the manner in which a person obtains an inherited *muzimu*. The choice of names, and therefore of guardian *mizimu*, for a child is a matter for the immediate relatives, and is not a subject of general discussion among his kinsmen.

If a man installs a *muzimu* of his matrilineal line as a house guardian, he himself decides which *muzimu* it shall be. In either case, the choice may be guided by divination, which is thought to establish that a particular *muzimu* itself has chosen to concern itself in the matter. Other *mizimu* are propitiated when a diviner has announced that they are demanding offerings, and again it is not a matter of general discussion among a group of kinsmen. But the choice of the inheritor of a *muzimu* is made by the assembled group during the funeral without recourse to divination. Moreover, since they are all witnesses to the inheritance of the *muzimu,* they must take part in the rite which propitiates it.

The person who inherits a *muzimu* thus has a recognized obligation in respect to it, but at the same time he retains his own identity, and his guardian *mizimu* continue to be involved in his destiny and are not superseded by the inherited *muzimu*. When he dies, his matrilineal group will have to find someone to take his *muzimu*, which will bear the name given by them at his naming. If his inherited *muzimu* was that of an important man, they will also try to find someone to reinherit it. But so short is the memory of the Tonga for their predecessors that I could not find an instance of a *muzimu* having been inherited more than twice. Most are inherited only once. Nevertheless the people do not feel that a *muzimu* is lost to them when the one who has inherited dies in his turn, for by that time they have given the name to new children and it thus remains within the group.

A *muzimu* in the rôle of guardian *muzimu* may be inherited as often as those who bear its name die before they have reached social maturity when they can produce their own *mizimu;* for when the immature die it is the guardian *muzimu* which is inherited. If ten children receive the name Mwene and all die before establishing a household, someone will be chosen to inherit the name at each funeral though this implies the inheritance over and over again of the same guardian *muzimu*. This seems anomalous in terms of the structure of Tonga belief about the nature of the *mizimu* and the relationship to the matrilineal group, but again it is consistent with our interpretation of the guardian *muzimu* as an acknowledgment of the person's position within the kinship group. Even if he dies before he has achieved a position of his own, his kinsmen recognize their loss and appoint someone to inherit the *muzimu* identified with him.

In summary of the above analysis, each person receives his initial position within society as a member of his own matrilineal group and as a child of his father's matrilineal group. The two groups indicate their acceptance of responsibility for him by giving him a name which is associated with a guardian *muzimu*. During childhood and youth, the person is equally dependent upon his two groups, and their rôle in his life is roughly similar. The two guardian *mizimu,* one from each side, are of equal importance, and both are thought to determine his personality. As an adult, the person acquires a new position of his own as the head of a household. At the same time, he also becomes a responsible member of his matrilineal group upon whom others depend for assistance. Thereafter when he dies his own *muzimu* is thought to come into existence. With this his guardian *muzimu* from the matrilineal group has become merged. The matrilineal group signify their recognition of the position of the person within the group by appointing someone to inherit the *muzimu*. Since the person is not fully identified with his father's group, the guardian *muzimu* from this side does not become identified with his own *muzimu* which represents the position which he has occupied in the community. When he dies, his father's group have no further claims upon the position he has occupied, and they signify that their rights and obligations are at an end by the withdrawal of the guardian *muzimu* with which they have provided him. This is not inherited as it represents an interest for the one lifetime only.

NOTES

[1] See, Colson, 1951a. The material on which this paper is based was gathered during the years, September 1946–September 1947, July 1948–July 1950, when I worked among the Plateau Tonga as a research officer of the Rhodes-Livingstone Institute. Most of the time I lived in villages in the area east of the Northern Rhodesian railway, and my account is therefore most reliable for the eastern people and may not apply to all Tonga. However, I worked in two chiefdoms in the west during my first tour and attempted to check my material with informants drawn from the whole of Tonga country. In 1949, I spent a month in the Gwembe District among the We of the Zambezi Valley. They are closely related to the people on the Plateau. In the course of this paper, I have noted variations in their customs from those described for the Plateau.

My thanks are due to the Trustees of the Rhodes-Livingstone Institute for their support and for permission to use the material. The work was largely financed by a grant from the Colonial Development and Welfare Fund. I also wish to acknowledge the assistance of my clerk, Mr. Benjamin Sipopa; of Mr. Mathias M.

Chona, who verified a number of points for me after I left the field; and of Dr. I. G. Cunnison and Professor M. Gluckman, my former colleagues at the Rhodes-Livingstone Institute and present colleagues at the University of Manchester, who have read and criticized the manuscript.

[2] Myers, 1927, and Hopgood, 1950, are the most lengthy accounts. The latter discusses the *mizimu* with reference to beliefs in God.

[3] See, Hopgood, 1950, pp. 61-67, for an excellent description of Tonga concepts of Leza, who is regarded as the creator and the ultimate cause of all that happens.

[4] For a further discussion, see Colson, 1951a, pp. 152-161.

[5] The *masabe* cult was introduced about 1906, apparently from the Karanga. See, Casset, 1918, p. 104.

[6] Radcliffe-Brown, 1952, p. 163.

[7] I am using *kinsmen* to mean relatives of the matrilineal group, and therefore as an exact translation of the Tonga term, *basimukowa*. Paternal kinsmen will refer to members of the father's matrilineal group, the *bashanaushi*. This usage differs from the standard one, but it is

more convenient than the long "kinsmen of the matrilineal group" and "kinsmen of the father's matrilineal group."

[8] Among the neighboring Ila, according to Smith and Dale, *mizimu* are reincarnated in the living who bear their names. Cf., Smith and Dale, 1920, Vol. II, pp. 152-153.

[9] Cf., Colson, 1949, pp. 15-16.

[10] Cf., Colson, 1950.

BIBLIOGRAPHY

[Starred items are recommended as further readings.]

Casset, A., 1918, "St. Mary's Out Station, Chikuni," *Zambezi Mission Record*, 6 (No. 82), pp. 101-104.

Colson, E., 1949, *Life Among the Cattle-Owning Plateau Tonga*, Livingstone, Rhodes-Livingstone Museum.

————, 1950, "Possible Repercussions of the Right to Make Wills upon the Plateau Tonga of Northern Rhodesia," *Journal of African Administration*, 2, pp. 24-34.

*————, 1951a, "The Plateau Tonga of Northern Rhodesia," in E. Colson and M. Gluckman (editors), *Seven Tribes of British Central Africa*, London, Oxford University Press, for the Rhodes-Livingstone Institute.

————, 1951b, "Residence and Village Stability among the Plateau Tonga," *Human Problems in British Central Africa*, 11, pp. 10-46.

Hopgood, C. R., 1950, "Conceptions of God among the Tonga of Northern Rhodesia," in E. W. Smith (editor), *African Ideas of God*, pp. 61-67, London, Edinburgh House Press.

Myers, J. L., 1927, *Religious Survey of the Batonga, Proceedings of the General Missionary Conference of Northern Rhodesia*.

Radcliffe-Brown, A. R., 1952, *Structure and Function in Primitive Society* (Chapter VIII, originally delivered as the Henry Myers Lecture, 1945), London, Cohen & West.

Richards, A. I., 1934, "Mother-Right among the Central Bantu," in E. E. Evans-Pritchard, R. Firth, B. Malinowski, and I. Schapera (editors), *Essays Presented to C. G. Seligman*, London, Kegan Paul.

————, 1939, *Land, Labour and Diet in Northern Rhodesia*, London, Oxford University Press, for the International African Institute.

* Smith, E. W., and Dale, A. M., 1920, *The Ila-Speaking Peoples of Northern Rhodesia*, London, Macmillan & Co.

Torrend, J., 1931, *An English-Vernacular Dictionary of the Bantu-Botatwe Dialects of Northern Rhodesia*, London, Kegan Paul.

FOR FURTHER READING

Forde, Daryll (ed.), *African Worlds: Studies in the Cosmological Ideas and Social Values of African Peoples*, London: Oxford University Press for the International African Institute, 1954. In this collection of papers, several discuss the role of the ancestors in the belief systems of different African peoples. Of particular interest are: Krige, J. D. and E. J., "The Lovedu of the Transvaal," pp. 55-82; Little, Kenneth, "The Mende in Sierra Leone," pp. 111-37; and Busia, K. A., "The Ashanti," pp. 190-209.

Fortes, Meyer, *Oedipus and Job in West African Religion*, Cambridge: Cambridge University Press, 1959. An analysis of the all-important part the ancestors play in the life of the Tallensi of northern Ghana.

THE SACRIFICIAL ROLE OF CATTLE AMONG THE NUER*

E. E. Evans-Pritchard

For the Nuer, cattle are necessary for survival not only in the economic sense, but also in the symbolic, and their perception of them and attitudes toward them differ on these two levels. In Nuer religious belief, an initiated man is equated with an ox, while the lineage and clan are equated with the ancestral herd of the group, which is thought of as having nurtured and maintained it from its founding, making possible its continuity through the past and in time to come. At initiation a boy's father gives him an ox from which he takes the ox-name that he bears in future years, and at initiation also he becomes a significant adult member of the social group who, with the birth of sons, will help to assure its continued existence. Nuer see initiation in terms of the collective life of the group, as they see the ownership and deployment of cattle as corporate interests. In his analysis, which appears also in revised form in his more comprehensive study, Nuer Religion, *Evans-Pritchard points out that the key to the idea of symbolic equivalence between men and cattle is that ultimately all cattle are reserved for sacrifice, although this does not mean that they are thought of and treated as sacred in everyday life.*

In my two books on the Nuer I gave some account of the importance of cattle in their economy and social life. I scarcely mentioned their role in religion as I did not wish to stray too far from the topics I was then discussing. I summarize very briefly what was said there before discussing their religious significance.

Nuer are very largely dependent on the milk of their herds and, in their harsh environment, they probably could not live without them, any more than the cattle could survive without the care and protection of their owners. Their carcasses also furnish Nuer with meat, tools, ornaments, sleeping-hides, and various other objects of domestic use; and their sun-dried dung provides fuel for the great smouldering smudges

—————

* Abridged from *Africa*, 1953, 23, 181-198, by permission of the author and the International African Institute (author's copyright reserved).

that give protection from mosquitoes to man and beast alike. Women are more interested in the cows, and this is natural for they have charge of milking and dairy work. Men's interest in the cows is rather for their use in obtaining wives, and they are interested in the oxen for the same reason, and also because they provide them with a means of display and, which is the matter I am about to discuss, a means of sacrifice. But for all Nuer—men, women, and children—cattle are their great treasure, a constant source of pride and joy, the occasion also of much foresight, of much anxiety, and of much quarrelling; and they are their intimate companions from birth to death. It is not difficult to understand, therefore, that Nuer give their cattle devoted attention, and it is not surprising that they talk more of cattle than of anything else and have a vast vocabulary relating to them and their needs. Nevertheless, though they are much attached to their beasts, we must beware of putting into Nuer minds a sentimentality about animals so often found among ourselves. In fact, they regard them as rather stupid creatures.

Though I do not repeat all I have earlier said about the value cattle have for Nuer in mundane affairs, particularly in the milk they give and their use as bridewealth, and restrict myself here to a consideration of their religious significance, we must not for a moment forget that their religious significance is bound up with their secular uses. Otherwise the central part cattle play in sacrifice will not be understood. Nevertheless, if cattle were only used for food and obtaining wives, writers about the Nuer, and also writers about other Nilotic peoples, might have been content just to draw attention to the great interest these peoples have in their cattle. But cattle figure so prominently in their lives in ways not directly concerned with their maintenance or their use for practical purposes that European observers have perceived that in the relationship between men and cattle there is something more than can be stated in simple terms of husbandry and exploitation. Some writers even suggest that cattle are venerated. . . . There is, however, no evidence at all that cattle are venerated or in themselves are in any way regarded as guardian spirits, and in so far as it may be true to say that Nuer religion "is centered in the cow" or that their attachment to cattle "may almost be called religious," in so far, that is, as we may legitimately speak, as Marianne Schmidl did in her interesting paper on the subject,[1] of *"die sakrale Stellung des Rindes,"* it is for a different reason.

Another writer about the Nilotic peoples and a very experienced anthropologist, Professor C. G. Seligman, said about Nilotic cattle that "it is difficult to describe their importance to their masters or the love and care the latter have for their beasts, but it is certainly no exaggeration to say that it amounts to what psychologists would call 'identification.'"[2] What seems chiefly to have persuaded Professor Seligman to use this word is the Nilotic custom of taking personal names from their cattle in addition to the personal names they are given soon after birth. I have discussed elsewhere[3] the general social significance of names and other modes of address among the Nuer and here I speak only of their cattle-names and principally of their ox-names, these being of chief importance.

These names are often spoken of in writings about the Nuer as bull-names, but ox-names (using the word "ox" to denote a castrated bull) is a more correct designation.[4] Nuer speak always of such a name as *cot thak,* the name of an ox, and *thak* is a castrated animal in contrast to a *tut,* an entire animal. It is true that when a youth takes his name from a beast it may be entire, but it will be castrated later, for he would not be given it, nor therefore take his name from it, were it intended for stud purposes. Nuer may not castrate a male calf till it is nearly 2 years old, but they do so before it is likely to gender with the cows. It is not from pedantry that I make the distinction: it has a logical, and perhaps psychological, appositeness to the equation of man and ox in sacrifice.

Ox-names are essentially the names of men, males who have passed through the rite of initiation to manhood. Boys may take ox-names in play but only in imitation of their elders. Likewise, maidens may take ox-names, from bulls calved by the cows they milk, but they are mainly used only between girls themselves and in the nature of a game, copying their brothers; and the names are short-lived and have little currency. Married women use cow-names among themselves, but, here again, this is similitude, and it has none of the significance of the ox-names of men. Perhaps also here again the distinction between the copy-names of boys, girls, and women and those taken by men may be important because of its logical relation, which concerns our present discussion, to the fact that men, and not boys or women, are the sacrificial agents. The two sides of the standard equation are the human male and the bovine male, man and ox.

When a boy is initiated to manhood his father gives him in sign of his manhood an ox or, as I have explained, a bull calf which will later be castrated; and this ox, which he describes as *"thak gareda,"* "the ox of my initiation," becomes his *dil thak,* what I have spoken about as his favorite ox . . . though the word *dil* has generally the sense of "pure," "true," "perfect," or "aristocratic." It is the ox of perfection. It is the young man's friend and companion. He plays with it and fondles it. He composes poems about it and sings them to it, and he gets a small boy to lead it round the camp in the morning or evening as he leaps behind it chanting poems. He walks among the cattle at night ringing a cattle-bell and singing of his kin, his loves, and his cattle, and he praises this ox above all other oxen. He makes tassels to hang from one of its horns, and he loves to see it toss the tassel in the air with a sweep of the neck. He acquires an iron bell to hang round its neck, and no music, unless it be the ox's lowing, is sweeter to his ears than its tinkling in the pastures. He goes to the edge of the camp to meet it when it returns from grazing in the evening. He is never tired of describing its points, and as he does so, and also in dancing, he may hold up his arms in imitation of its horns. Should the ox die he is downcast; and should he die it must be sacrificed at his mortuary ceremony.

The youth now also enters through this ox into a new kind of relationship with God [*Kwoth a nhial,* Spirit who is in the sky], the guardian spirits of his family and lineage, and the ghosts of his ancestors. When he has tethered it in the kraal for the night he may pet it, removing ticks from its belly and scrotum and picking out adherent dung from its anus; and he may at the same time rub ashes on its back. Ordinarily, I think he does this simply because the ox, which has suffered from parasites throughout the day, gets pleasure from its back being rubbed, but I was told that he may occasionally utter a prayer or invocation as he does so, speaking to God or to the ghosts. I discuss this point again later. Here I want only to say that while it is not until a man marries and has children and an independent household that he sacrifices animals, dedicates them to spirits, and in other ways makes formal use of them for religious purposes, nevertheless, the ox a father gives his son at initiation provides him, through what Professor Seligman calls "identification" with it, with a direct means of communication with the spiritual world. It is more than a possession, more even than part of his social personality —it is a point of meeting between soul and spirit and has therefore a sacramental character.

From the colors, their distribution, the shape of the horns, and other peculiarities of the ox of his initiation a youth takes, or is given by his companions, his *cot thak,* his ox-name. It may be the same word as that by which the ox's markings are indicated but generally it combines the name for the markings with a prefix descriptive of something connected with the ox. For example, a man whose favorite ox is black and white (*rial*) may call himself *Luthrial* or *Luerial, luth* being a large cattle-bell and *lue* a long tassel attached to one of the horns. At first only his agemates may know his new name, but the older people soon get to know it too, for they hear his mates greet him by it and they also hear him shout it out as he displays himself with the ox in the cattle camps which are formed soon after initiation. Also, young men of about the same age call out their ox-names, with many embellishments, to one another at dances, often after a bout of duelling with clubs, and when in a dance two lines of youths stand opposite each other and shower ox-names on one another preparatory to a spectacular jump into the air in unison.

The calling of a youth by a name the same as, or derived from, that by which his favorite ox is referred to is perhaps the most striking example of, and evidence for, what Professor Seligman speaks of as "identification." Indeed, in listening to Nuer poems one is often in doubt whether it is the ox or the man that is being spoken about. The representations are never quite distinct. Somewhat different, though related and also very striking, is the custom called *thak moc,* the calling out of the (name of the) ox. A man shouts out the name of his favorite ox—the ox's name, not his ox-name which may be an elaboration of the ox's name—when he hurls his spear at an enemy or at his quarry when hunting or fishing; for example, *"ma rial"* "black-and-white (ox)," or *"thakda ma rial,"* "my black-and-white ox." In some of my earlier writings I have translated *moc* by "invocation" and "to invoke," following Driberg's translation of the Lango *gwongo,*[5] but I avoid doing so in an account of Nuer religion partly because I have used these words to translate another Nuer word, *lam,* but also because nothing is in fact invoked, and it is precisely the use of the words in connection with oxen that has led to the erroneous conclusion that a favorite ox is a sort of "tutelary spirit." The ox is not called on, but called out. It is not an invocation but a cry of excitement and triumph as the striker strikes and hits his foe or prey. That the ox is not being called on for aid is conclusively shown by the fact that in the same circumstances a Nuer may shout out instead *"tet cueda"* followed by a kinship term, usually that referring to the mother's sister: *"tet cueda malene,"* "my right hand, my mother's sisters." Nuer are not calling on their mother's sisters for aid but using an emotive ejaculation, in which the ideas of strength (the right hand) and good-will (the mother's sister) are combined; and when they cry out the names of their oxen the ejaculation is a triumphant assertion of the self, for which the ox stands as a symbol. Also a man may cry out the name of his ox on occasions when there is no question of success or failure: as he brandishes his spear as though to strike in dancing, when making spectacular leaps into the air *(rau),* and sometimes in making a sacrificial invocation. It is both self-expression and a drawing of attention to the self.

It should be borne in mind that a man normally retains his ox-name and continues to be called by it and also to shout out the name of the ox from which it is derived long after the ox is no more in his possession. A man may part, though always with regret, with a favorite ox for marriage or sacrifice, or the ox may die. It is then replaced by another favorite, though when a man is older and has a herd of his own he may not identify himself in quite the same way or to the same extent as when he was young with any one particular ox. If another ox takes the place of the first favorite, the ox of initiation, its owner may take, or be given, a new ox-name derived from this second ox; the new name then takes the place of the old or both are used; but most men keep for life the ox-names they acquire at the time of their initiation. It is the name of this ox that a man shouts out in war, hunting, dancing and leaping, and in sacrificial invocations, and by which, in one or other form, he is addressed by his peers; though it has long ago departed. Fundamentally, therefore, it is not the ox of initiation itself with which there is "identification" but ox, the idea of oxen. The ox of initiation is the prototype of the ox-man relationship, and it is a kind of focal point at which the feelings a Nuer has towards cattle converge and run over into demonstration by word and gesture. When the ox is long ago dead the relationship continues because ultimately it is not one between a man and a particular beast, which serves only, as a first favorite or as a replacement, to express, since men's hearts are small, through a particular and personal relationship of possession a general relationship of a human being to cattle which, I am about to suggest, derives from the sacramental equation of man and beast in sacrifice. Any ox will therefore serve the purpose, or, indeed, no ox at all—only the memory, or rather the idea, of an ox.

We may ask why the identification is with oxen and not with bulls. It might be expected that a man, who is himself a *"tut,"* a "bull," not only in the general sense of "male," but also in a common metaphor of speech derived expressly from cattle, would take his name from a bull rather than from an ox. The common sense answer is that Nuer castrate all but a very few of their bulls so that there would not be enough entire animals to go round, and this may be the right explanation. Even if it is not, or is not a sufficient explanation, we must here take it as given that the equation is between man and ox and seek only to show how it is expressed in ritual, and in particular in the sacrificial situation. But it is perhaps necessary to remark that Nuer evaluation of bulls and oxen is not ours. Our representation of an ox, in contrast to a bull, is a docile, inferior, and slightly contemptible beast destined for the slaughterhouse. In the Nuer representation a fat ox is a thing of grandeur and beauty. It is oxen which arouse their admiration. Bulls evoke utilitarian interest rather than emotional and aesthetic attention.

The facts I have related make it understandable that Professor Seligman should have spoken of "identification" of men with their favorite oxen. Had he had either a first-hand or a wider knowledge of the Nuer he would no doubt have elaborated his theme, and especially by drawing on the ceremonies of initiation for illustrations.

A youth takes his cry and his personal name from the markings and other traits of the ox his father gives him at initiation. By the rites of initiation boys are made men, and this means, among other things, a conspicuous change in their relation with the cattle. They now cease to look after the calves and sheep and goats and to perform the more menial services of kraal and byre. Instead they tend the adult cattle. The most marked change is that whereas before initiation they helped the women milk the cows they now altogether cease to milk. But these external and evident changes are accompanied by a deeper, and hidden, transformation, men and oxen being brought into an intimacy of relationship on a different plane from that of mere proximity and association, how-ever close, so that in some way an equation is brought about between man and ox. Such would seem to be the interpretation of certain very peculiar, though outstanding, features of the initiation rites. I have de-scribed these rites and discussed their social significance elsewhere[6]; here I shall only draw attention to those features which have a special rele-vance to our immediate problem.

The rites direct our attention throughout to the relationship between men and cattle. It is the *wut ghok,* the Man of the Cattle, to which he stands in a special ritual relationship, who opens and closes the periods of initiation. During the period of initiation the initiates may not have any contact with the cattle, which are a danger to them till their wounds are completely healed and they formally pass out of seclusion. The pro-hibition extends even to rubbing ashes of cattle-dung over their bodies, a practice common to all Nuer men and boys; though the fact that they drink milk suggests that the taboo really concerns their relation to the oxen rather than to cattle in general, just as the taboo on women drink-ing milk during their periods concerns their relation to cows and not to cattle in general. In the terminal rite of initiation, when the initiates are "loosened" (*lony rar,* the verb *lony* being that used for loosening cattle from their tethering-pegs) they reestablish their contact with the cattle. They are pelted by their seniors with cattle-dung (*buk ka war*). Then they wash in a stream. On their return to the homestead they beat the cattle with wild rice, and afterwards rub themselves with ashes of cattle-dung. They spend the rest of the day leaping and chanting behind the oxen given them by their fathers, and possibly, if they are lucky, by their paternal and maternal uncles also, which are the first oxen they can call their own. The fact that after initiation there is a taboo on men milking also seems to point to an opposition between women and cows on the one side and men and oxen on the other side and to further emphasize the equation of man and ox.

One might perhaps feel that one was attributing to the facts a sym-bolical significance which the evidence does not sustain were it not that further, and very striking, observations push one to the interpretation put forward. Thus, the name of the dances held at the initiation ceremonies is *ruath,* the word for a bull-calf from the time it is weaned, that is to say a bull, normally destined to be an ox, which has broken with its dam in the same way as a youth at initiation cuts, as we would put it, the apron strings which have before tied him to his mother, especially in the matter of food, as some of the symbolism of the rites, which we need not here discuss, indicates. One says *"ba ruath puot,"* "the bull-calf (dance) is held"—or it may be the plural form *ruedh,* "the (dance of the) bull-calves is held." One speaks also of *"bul ruedhni,"* "the dance of the bull-calves," and of the *"bul ruath dholi,"* a phrase which might be rendered as "the dance of the bull-calf boys"; and the lewd songs sung on these occasions are known as *"diit ruadha,"* "bull-calf songs." The metaphor in these expressions seems to be clear: the initiates are equated with the young bulls, though I have never heard Nuer explicitly make the equation. Before initiation a boy is a small calf *(dou)*, during initiation he is a *ruath,* an immature bull, and after initiation he is a *tut,* a bull; and one may speak of an initiated man as either *wut,* man, or *tut,* bull. Further, between the cutting of the marks of manhood on a boy's forehead and his ceremonial emergence from seclusion (or exclusion from the normal life) he is known as *cot,* which appears to be the same word as that used for a hornless cow or ox. That it is probably the same word and that the metaphor is an overt similitude is shown by the remark made to me by a Nuer to explain its use in reference to initiates that "they are like hornless cattle at this time," by which I suppose was meant that they are in the helpless position of a beast without horns. It is remarkable also that Nuer compare the cutting *(ngat)* of one of the horns of a favorite ox (it is an entire animal at the time) so that it will grow against the cut at a fancy angle, generally in a curve across the muzzle *(ma gut)*, to the initiation of youths. . . .

This equation of youths with young bulls in the ceremonies of initiation is made at what is probably the greatest emotional crisis of a Nuer's life. Sheer terror of the ordeal they must pass through—for bravely though they face it " they are all terrified in their hearts"—and the agonies they have to endure before the wounds are healed are succeeded by supreme happiness and elation at having entered the life of manhood so long looked forward to—the life of the herds, the favorite oxen, the spear, leisure, love-making and courtship, and singing and dancing.

Doubtless Professor Seligman's use of the word "identification" could be supported by other examples of what might be interpreted as symbolic behavior. For instance, early in life Nuer remove their lower incisors and their jaws bear therefore a certain resemblance to those of cattle, which lack upper incisors. I have never heard Nuer say that they remove their teeth in order to look like cattle, only that they do not want to look like hyenas; and it might seem fanciful to cite this as a further exemplification of "identification" were it not that the Dinka suggest that they remove their teeth for that reason.[7] If we were to follow Professor Seligman we should, however, have to look below the level of conscious thought for the meaning of this custom, in the symbolic processes of the unconscious in which knocking out teeth stands for castration[8]—a further illustration of "identification" with the favorite ox.

Other examples might be mentioned and the matter might be discussed at great length—would, in fact, require a lengthy discussion were it to be fully treated—but I have given enough information, fringed with some speculation, to show the way Nuer express symbolically their relationship to their cattle. It is true, indeed, that one can easily imagine what is not there. Human thought and expression are inevitably constructed out of man's experience of the world around him, and we do not necessarily have to seek for subliminal explanations for the images he employs. A person may speak of himself or herself as a dog, a bitch, a tortoise, a swine, a rabbit, and so on, without unconsciously, or even partially unconsciously, behaving, or imagining that he is behaving, as if he were one of these creatures. There is nothing that should surprise us in Nuer speaking metaphorically of boys by the same word (*ruath*) as they use for young bulls and for the male young of other animals, and of men by the same word (*tut*) as they use for adult bulls and adult males of other animal species. It is natural—it would be remarkable were it not so—that Nuer use their cattle as symbols in speech and gesture. Nevertheless, the evidence, some of which I have presented, suggests that there is more to it than that. However, I want to cut adrift from any psychological consideration of the matter. Whether Professor Seligman's use of the word "identification" is correct is a question which, being framed in psychological terms, poses a problem that lies outside both my own competence and the scope of this article. We are not concerned with individual psychological processes, which in the literature of psychoanalysis are generally also more or less abnormal, but with a moral identification, a participation imposed on the individual by his culture and inextricably bound up with religious values. When henceforward I speak of identification it is to be understood in this latter sense, and not in any psychological sense.

The strictly social character of the facts I have related does not require demonstration, but, before discussing their religious meaning, I must give a brief account of a symbolic usage which expresses the collective identification of clans and lineages with their herds. We have been discussing hitherto the equation of man with ox. Honorific titles of clans and lineages introduce us to the equation of the idea of a social group with the idea of the continuity of its ancestral herd.

On the day when, by the cutting of lines on his forehead, a boy becomes a man there is much rejoicing on the part of his kinsfolk, and especially of his father and paternal kin, and in talking to Nuer about events on this day they have impressed on me that what is uppermost in the minds of the older men, particularly at the initiation of an eldest son, is that the continuity of the family and lineage is now assured. Initiation is the threshold to marriage and the birth of sons who will remember their forbears, for as soon as the period of healing and seclusion is over the initiates embark on a full sex life leading to courtship, marriage, and begetting. An initiate is part of a lineage and clan and his initiation is seen in terms of its collective life. His new relationship with the cattle is then not only a personal one, important though that is, but the personal relationship is incorporated in a more general lineage one.

Nuer conceive of the ancestor of a clan, and likewise the ancestors of its component lineages, as having possessed a herd, the descendants of which have had, and continue to have, a constant relationship with the descendants of their original owners. This ancestral herd is no doubt a fiction, for the cattle are being constantly dispersed and replaced by others at marriages, but conceptually it is an enduring collectivity. There is ideally a constant attachment, the clan and its herd forming a joint community down the generations, so much so that a common, perhaps the commonest, explanation of a division in the clan is the fighting of the bulls of the ancestors of the divided parts. The social cleavage is represented in tradition as a cleavage in the herd.

* * *

[The unity of clans and lineages is expressed both in the idea of ancestral spears handed down as heirlooms and honorific titles derived from the names of cows symbolizing the ancestral herds; here the idea of the cow stands both for the herd and the lineage of its masters.]

It need not surprise us that it is a cow that is referred to and not an ox or bull. It would be inappropriate to refer to an ox since, as I understand the matter, the whole point of using a symbol from the herds is to express in a single representation the idea of the unity of a lineage and its cattle, the cattle which sustain the lineage by their milk (the cow suckles the ancestor) and by constant calving provide them with bridewealth for marriages, whereby sons are born and the lineage continued, and with a means of maintaining communication with God, both as the universal creative spirit and in the particular refraction or refractions by which he is figured to the lineage and its families, and with the ancestral ghosts. Male animals do not answer to the requirements of the symbolism. The great majority of the bulls are castrated, and, if not later disposed of in marriage, those which survive murrains are sacrificed; and the animals which are left entire are not thought of as being, like the male members of a human lineage, a line of descent. In tracing back the lineage of a beast, which Nuer can sometimes do to several generations, they do so by the points of the dams and not the points of the sires: an ox of certain markings was born of a cow of certain markings, and it of a cow of other markings. Descent in the herd is, so to speak, traced matrilineally; and it is the cows which are seen as the stable element, which calve cow-calves, which calve cow-calves in their turn, and so provide the constant and continuous nexus between herd and lineage. Consequently, if at marriage most of a herd is dispersed and only a core is retained, it is some cows which are kept so that the herd may be built up anew through them. Therefore, it is the cow of the ancestor, and not his bull, which furnishes the symbol of the continuity and solidarity of his descent and which is incorporated in the honorific titles of clans and lineages.

The lineage-herd equation can thus be considered as a structural expression of the man-ox equation. One does not derive from the other but they are parts of a single complex representation, which finds its most logical expression in the rite of sacrifice. The exordial words spoken at sacrifices of the obligatory kind are the spear-names of the clans of the speakers (when I say "clan," "clan or lineage" is to be understood). Thus a man of the Jinaca clan calls out *"mut gwara, mut gham,"* "spear of our fathers, spear of the thigh." The sacrificial spear brandished in invocation represents the spear of the ancestor and hence the clan as a whole. The sacrifice is in the name of the clan, and the animal is speared by a *gwan buthni* (master of ceremonies) who officiates as its representative on behalf of one of its families. But, as we have noted, the name of the ox of the speaker may also be shouted out in sacrificial invocations, as *"thakda ma rol cara,"* "my black ox with the white foreleg." The name of the ox stands for the name of the man, and the name of the spear, which goes together with the cow-name, representing the relation of the clan to its ancestral herd, stands for the clan. The two symbols, ox-name and spear-name, represent two aspects of the sacrificial relationship between men and cattle, the personal and the collective or, as I have put it earlier, the man-ox equation and the lineage-herd equation. One or the other aspect is emphasized according to the nature of the sacrifice.

If this conclusion requires demonstration to be acceptable, the basis of the demonstration will readily be granted: that the facts we have examined—the relationship of men to cattle in the favorite ox situation, in the ritual of initiation, in the cow symbol of clans and lineages, and so forth—show that we are dealing with relations between men and cattle in a complex of thought and experience which includes something that lies outside the uses of cattle for food and bridewealth. This is expressed in the idea of equation or identification, an equivalence between men and cattle; and the only plane of social life on which there is anything that can be called equivalence is that on which men and cattle are things of the same order, so that one can be substituted for the other, namely, in sacrifice. In marriages and in settlements for homicide, in which cattle are paid in compensation for the loss of a daughter or son, they do not stand in the place of the daughter or son. They are rather a means by which replacement is brought about: of a woman (daughter) by a woman (wife) and of a man (the slain) by a man (a son born of a woman married with the cattle of homicide). It is only on the religious plane, in sacrifice, that there is identification, or, in other words, in relation to God. I cannot here discuss the general and particular meanings of Nuer sacrifices, but it can be said that the most common and typical sacrifices, whatever else they may also be, are substitutions of the lives of oxen for the lives of men. This is not only evident in what Nuer say but is indicated also in the rites themselves, and especially in the rite of consecration.

In sacrifice the animal is consecrated with ashes, has an invocation spoken over it, and is speared. What concerns us here is the *buk,* the consecration: the placing, and usually lightly rubbing, of ashes on its back. What is the meaning of this act? It is clear that it is a rite of consecration, the animal's life being thereby devoted to God; but in the most common sacrifices, the piacular ones, it is also sanctified for sacrifice in substitution for the life of a man. It would seem, therefore, that the laying of the right hand on the animal's back identifies the man who lays it, or the person on whose behalf he is acting, with the beast. I must confess that this is not an interpretation that I reached entirely by observation, but one taken over from studies of Hebrew and other sacrifices because it seems to make better sense than any other as an explanation of the Nuer facts. For the Nuer, the right hand stands for the whole person, and by placing it on the animal the officiant identifies himself with it. If this is so, then it is himself that he offers up; or, to put it in another way, in sacrifice the representations of man and ox are fused.

The suggestion that the placing of the hand on the ox in sacrifice is an identification of the officiant with the offering could nevertheless be discarded without vitally affecting the argument, for there is no doubt that in piacular sacrifices at any rate the ox is substituted for the man and that it is therefore possible to speak of a ritual equivalence between man and ox and, in this sense, of identification of man with ox. The interpretation of the laying on of the hand merely strengthens the idea of identification, but it is secondary and the idea by no means depends on it. The particular interpretation is subordinate to an explanation springing from the whole character of the sacrificial act.

It may be asked, however, how the fact that in piacular sacrifice *an* ox is substituted for *a* man affects the general relationship of men to cattle. The answer is that all cattle are reserved for sacrifice. It is not just that in a particular ceremony a particular ox stands for a particular man. The equivalence is a general one between a herd and its lineage of masters, and between men, as men, and cattle, as cattle.

The word used for the killing of a beast in sacrifice is *nak* and this is also the ordinary word for "to kill," there being no special word to denote killing in sacrifice which distinguishes that kind of killing from a killing in different circumstances—the killing of an animal for food or protection or the killing of a man in quarrel or feud. It was largely on account of a similar lack of verbal differentiation that Robertson Smith argued that among the Hebrews all slaughter was sacrifice until the code of Deuteronomy dissociated the two ideas of slaughter for food and killing for sacrifice.[9] In the case of the Nuer I do not think that it is of any great significance that the same word is used both for killing in sacrifice and for other killings. The mere act of killing is adequately covered by the same word, for in a sacrifice it is not the killing in itself which is important but the *kam yang,* the yielding of the animal to God.

Nevertheless, it is a fact that all cattle are reserved for sacrifice. Some caution is necessary here. Nuer are very fond of meat and whether an animal is killed in sacrifice or dies a natural death, its flesh is eaten. All cattle, sheep, and goats eventually go into the pot. Also, it is very noticeable that on ceremonial occasions, which are not also occasions of calamity, most people show more interest in the festal than in other aspects of the ceremonies. People show their desire for meat without reserve and it is the festal character of sacrifices which gives them much of their significance in the life of the Nuer. This is perhaps most noticeable at weddings, when, moreover, those who get the flesh are not those who sacrifice the animal; and also on those occasions when men scramble for meat. Further, Nuer themselves recognize that some men are too eager to sacrifice an ox, sheep, or goat on the slightest excuse, a craving for meat rather than a pressing need for spiritual aid being the incentive for sacrifice. However, the fact that Nuer accuse men of making unnecessary sacrifices to have a feast of meat in itself shows that animals should not be slaughtered except in sacrifice, and there is indeed a very strong feeling, amounting to a moral injunction, that domestic animals—sheep and goats as well as cattle, though it is only cattle I discuss here—must not be slaughtered except in sacrifice and, save in very special circumstances, they are never slaughtered for food, a fact noticed, and noted, by Ernst Marno nearly a century ago.[10] This injunction explains why Nuer are not expected to, and do not, provide meat for guests.

* * *

[The circumstances in which cattle are killed for food are in times of severe famine and in so-called *nak* camps to which youths take oxen for ritual feasting, the significance of which is not yet fully understood.]

Except on those rare occasions when dire necessity or custom compel them to do so, Nuer do not kill cattle except in sacrifice and it is regarded as a fault to kill them otherwise. This is clearly shown, apart from the facts I have already instanced, by the statement that an ox slain simply from desire for meat may *cien* (curse) its slayer, for it has *cuong* (right) in the matter. Maybe the Nuer do not take this very seriously, but that they say it at all is an indication of how they regard the matter, for Nuer greatly fear *cien* and hold that it operates only because God is permissive, seeing that an injustice has been done. The man had no right to take the life of the ox and by doing so he committed a fault. In sacrificial invocations Nuer explain to God why the life of the ox is being taken, and they may also address the ox and tell it why it is being killed; not that they think it understands. They are justifying themselves in taking its life. Consequently I think it possible—I much regret that I did not inquire into the matter—that even when cattle are killed for food in times of famine something may be said to God, and perhaps to the oxen also, to excuse the act; and it may be that they are also consecrated before death. It would perhaps not be permissible to speak of such kill-ings as sacrifice even were this so, for there might be no sacramental in-tention. Here again, further inquiry is required. What can, however, be said on our present knowledge is that, apart from animals devoted by formal acts of dedication or consecration, all cattle, and also sheep and goats, are reserved, or set apart, for sacrifice and their lives should not be taken, except in the special circumstances I have mentioned, for any other purpose; and in that sense we may speak of cattle as being "sacred." If we do so, however, we must note that they are not sacrificed because they are regarded as "sacred" intrinsically, or for reasons extraneous to the sacrificial situation, but, on the contrary, they are regarded as "sacred" only because they are reserved for sacrifice and in the sense defined by that purpose.

Here, two points must be discussed. In sacrifices Nuer speak always of the offering as *yang*. In ordinary usage this word means "cow" in contrast to *tut*, "bull," or *thak*, "ox," but it is also commonly used in a more general sense for any domestic bovine animal of either sex when what is intended is to indicate that it is a bovine beast and not an ovine or any other kind of beast, much as we speak of a "cow" when the ani-mal may in fact be a bull or a bullock. Hence one may speak of a bull as a *yang ma tut*, a male "cow." The word is used in this more general sense in sacrificial invocations. The officiant says to God *"kene yangdu,"* "take thy cow," whether it is a male or female beast. In fact, the animal is normally an ox. Nuer do not, except at mortuary ceremonies for senior persons, kill fertile cows and it is likely that a cow will have died a natural death before it is too old for calving. So generally it is only barren cows which are sacrificed, and they are regarded as equal to males, just as Nuer speak of a barren woman as having become a man. Since Nuer keep very few entire animals and do not kill them in sacrifice, unless they have become old and like oxen, one seldom finds an adult bull being sacrificed; and if a young male calf is required for sacrifice it is castrated before it is killed. One can therefore say—it is difficult other-wise to understand why a bull should be castrated before sacrifice—that the ideal sacrifice is that of an ox, that the sacramental equivalence in sacrifice is man with ox, though "ox" may be regarded as representative of cattle as a whole and the broader meaning as equivalent of men with cattle.

We may therefore ask—and this is the second point to be discussed

—how this conclusion can be accepted in view of the fact that it is more usually a beast of the flocks, a sheep or a goat, than a beast of the herds, an ox or a cow, that is, in practice, sacrificed. However, when goats and sheep are sacrificed they are always regarded as surrogates for cattle. They are not sacrificed in their own right, and a sheep or goat is therefore never referred to in sacrificial contexts as "sheep" or "goat" but always as *"yang,"* "cow" (in the general sense of a bovine animal). In all important sacrifices an ox or cow must be the offering, and though in lesser sacrifices sheep and goats are offered instead, they are offered in the place of cattle, and were a man able to afford it he would offer only cattle. Since sheep and goats are sacrificial surrogates for cattle, they too may not be killed except in sacrifice, but there is this important difference: the sacrificial equivalence is always between *ran* and *yang,* man and cow (bovine beast) and never between man and sheep or goat, even when it is a sheep or goat which is being killed; for even then the ideal equivalence is preserved in speech. The goat or sheep is an "ox" in this context because it takes the place of an ox. God is asked to accept it as an ox. This is also the case even when a fruit, a lump of tobacco, a bead, or some other object is offered in sacrifice. The object is always referred to as a "cow" (bovine beast) in the sacrificial situation and not by the word by which it is otherwise called, for in sacrifice these objects are regarded, like sheep and goats, as surrogates for cattle on occasions of small importance or in conditions of great urgency or poverty.

We may conclude therefore that the observations we have made earlier concerning the relationship of a man with his favorite ox, the ritual of initiation, and so forth, must be viewed in the light of the identification of men with cattle in sacrifices. A Nuer does not look upon his cattle as a stock-breeder or dairy farmer does, for his relationship to his beasts is complicated by their reservation for sacrifice. And it is not simply that he must not kill cattle except in sacrifice because, if he were to slaughter them for meat, he would lower his resources for food, marriage, and religious purposes. It is not merely a negative injunction. It is a positive injunction. It is not "thou must not kill" but "thou must sacrifice." It is not that they must only kill for sacrifice but that they must sacrifice to kill.

We must not be led astray by this conclusion to suppose that in the everyday life of the Nuer they think of and treat their animals in a "religious" manner. If we speak of them as being "sacred" at all it is only in the very special sense of being reserved, or set apart, for sacrifice and not in the sense that they are revered or are thought to have in themselves any spiritual power. Nor do Nuer *thek* (respect) them, not even those dedicated to spirits. Ordinarily, Nuer think of them from the practical point of view of herdsmen who are largely dependent on them for food and are dependent on them entirely for marriage, as valuable and, as I have already said earlier, rather stupid, animals which require their constant attention. They treat those dedicated to spirits no differently from the rest of the herd. Their milk is used, though by members of the family only, like the milk of other cows; and many times I have seen a man slap such a cow on its rump when it was troublesome or slow.

Nor must it lead us to forget that the cattle provide milk, meat, and various other requirements of the practical life, and we are not likely to do so, as we very easily think of cattle in some such way ourselves; nor that they are a means of acquiring wives, validating marriage, and legitimatizing children, and here again it is not difficult to put ourselves to some extent at the standpoint of Nuer once their marriage and family arrangements have been described to us; nor that they confer status and prestige and that a certain kind of friendship and intimacy can obtain between man and beast; and this is also not unfamiliar to us. The Nuer themselves emphasize such uses, when speaking of their cattle, as what gives them value, makes them precious in their eyes, and we are therefore not likely to overlook them. Were we to underestimate their importance, we should fail also to understand one of the elements in sacrifice, to appreciate what it is a Nuer surrenders in sacrifice—the most precious thing he possesses. But even here we are not dealing with something entirely rational. Cows and oxen have not got an economic value, and they and their products are not sold at market. Nor is marriage a purchase. All sorts of personal interests, emotional feelings, social sentiments, and social ties and traditions and customs are involved even on this level.

But it would be no less fatal a mistake to forget the religious significance cattle have for the Nuer. This is easier to do for two reasons. Firstly, because the Nuer are themselves most reticent in speaking of their cattle in this connection. They tend to be reserved in discussing religious matters, and it may even be said that a certain secrecy adheres to them, and those whom a European tends to know best, the younger men, have less awareness of the sacramental role of cattle than the older people. This interest in cattle is less on the surface, less obvious. Secondly, because we have no direct experience of our own which associates animals with anything similar in our culture. We are, therefore, inclined to reason that cattle have a ritual significance because they have a great practical value. If this were really so the cow, and not the ox, would be the object of identification; but, apart from that consideration, an attempt to interpret the religious importance of cattle on this one-way track of reasoning changes the whole character of the relationship between men and cattle. It makes the animals themselves to be in some way the object of religious attention, and nothing could be further from the truth.

The religious significance of cattle is of a very different kind. Cattle are necessary to Nuer not only for food and marriage but also for salvation, for the sanctification of their social undertakings, and for overcoming evil in its twofold character of sickness and sin. As Professor Westermann's text has it, "She [the cow] was ordered [by God] for the deliverance of souls." [11] This soteriological function pertains to cattle as much as do their economic, bridewealth, and other functions. It is not just that, in Nuer sacrifices, something that for other reasons is valuable obtains, through its consecration and sacramental death, a religious significance, which would consequently be secondary and momentarily derived from the immediate sacrificial act. The sacrificial role is always dormant in cattle, which in sacrifice are being used for an ordained purpose for which they are set apart; and their religious significance is therefore intrinsic and primary. This is why the rubbing of ashes on an ox's back while uttering some short prayer or invocation is a rite which can at any time be performed. The animal is already destined for sacrifice. The sacrificial situation is present, as it were, in the act, though no actual sacrifice is made.

I am not suggesting that Nuer have the sacrificial character of their cattle always in mind. They clearly do not. Nor do they have any other bovine function always in mind, their milk or meat value for example. When Nuer look at their cattle they no more think of butter and boiled beef than we do when we look at a herd of grazing cows. But the sacrificial situation is always present in potentiality and intention and it is this which makes all the difference between the mentality of any merely dairy and stock-farming people and the cattle-mentality of the Nuer. Some effort of the imagination is necessary to put ourselves in the place of the Nuer in this respect. All the great social occasions of their lives are occasions of sacrifice, and every grave danger and misfortune which comes their way is met with sacrifice; and in sickness, especially, the lives of their oxen stand between them and death. Their salvation at every crisis depends on the small herd with which they share their home. When, therefore, we seek to estimate what their cattle are to Nuer and how they see them, it would be fatal not to recognize that among other things they are the means by which men can enter into communication with God and obtain by prayer and sacrifice that divine aid without which they are helpless, and especially and on all critical occasions by sacrifice; for, as Father Crazzolara puts it, cattle form "the link between the perceptible and the transcendental" (das Bindemittel zwischen der sinnlichen und übersinnlichen Welt).[12] His cattle, in fulfilling this role, shield a man and his family from disaster, and he conceives of them also collectively as a herd which from the beginning of time has helped his fathers in distress, performing in each generation the same sacrificial service. In the time of the ancestor of his clan the "cow" gave her life for his salvation and so it is with his descendants today and so it will be with their descendants tomorrow. Whence springs the identification of man with ox, of lineage with herd, and of men with cattle.

NOTES

[1] Marianne Schmidl, "Die Grundlagen der Nilotenkultur," *Mitteilungen der Anthropologischen Gesellschaft in Wien,* lxv. Band, Wien, 1935. See also Johannes Weissenborn, *Tierkult in Afrika,* 1904, p. 16.

[2] C. G. and B. Z. Seligman, *Pagan Tribes of the Nilotic Sudan,* 1932, p. 169.

[3] E. E. Evans-Pritchard, "Nuer Modes of Address," *Uganda Journal,* xii, 1948.

[4] Throughout the literature on the Nuer "ox" or "steer" or "bullock" should in most cases be substituted for "bull."

[5] J. H. Driberg, *The Lango,* 1923, pp. 109-10: "One who takes a hostile spear on his shield invokes by name a favorite bull belonging to his father or maternal uncle (*gwongo twon*)."

[6] "The Nuer: Age-sets," *Sudan Notes and Records,* 1936. Since this article was written I have obtained further information which has not been published.

[7] Major G. W. Titherington, "The Raik Dinka of the Bahr el Ghazal Province," *Sudan Notes and Records,* 1927, p. 205: "The suggestion that as one row of front teeth is enough for a cow it ought to suffice a man was probably not serious."

[8] C. G. Seligman, "The Unconscious in Relation to Anthropology," *The British Journal of Psychology,* xviii, 1928, pp. 382-7.

[9] *The Prophets of Israel,* 1902 ed., p. 368.

[10] [*Reisen im Gebiete des blauen Nil,* 1874], p. 348.

[11] "The Neur Language," *Mitt. des Sem. für Orient. Sprachen,* 1912, pp. 116-17.

[12] P. P. Crazzolara, "Die Bedeutung des Rindes bei den Nuer," *Africa,* vii, 1934, p. 320.

REFERENCES

[Starred items are recommended as further readings.]

A résumé of this paper was delivered to the Fourth International Congress for Anthropology and Ethnology held in Vienna in 1952. It forms a section of a general account of Nuer religion, some parts of which have already been, or are about to be, published. They are listed below in logical, not chronological, order.

* "Some Features of Nuer Religion," [*Journal of the Royal Anthropological Institute*], lxxxi, 1951.

"A Note on Nuer Prayers," *Man,* 1952, p. 140.

"The Nuer Spirits of the Air," *Ann. Lateranensi,* [xvii, 1953].

"The Nuer Col Wic," *Man,* 1949, p. 2.

"Nuer Totemism," *Ann. Lateranensi,* xiii, 1949.

* "The Nuer Conception of Spirit in its Relation to the Social Order," *American Anthropologist* [lv, 1953, pp. 201-14].

"Burial and Mortuary Rites of the Nuer," *African Affairs,* 1949.

"Nuer Curses and Ghostly Vengeance," *Africa,* xix, 1949.

"Two Nuer Ritual Concepts," *Man,* 1949, p. 96.

* "Some Features and Forms of Nuer Sacrifices," *Africa,* xxi, 1951.

FOR FURTHER READING

Evans-Pritchard, E. E., "The Meaning of Sacrifice among the Nuer," *Journal of the Royal Anthropological Institute,* 1954, *84,* pp. 21-33. An examination of the two basic types of Nuer sacrifice according to different theories of the meaning of sacrifice.

Evans-Pritchard, E. E., *Nuer Religion,* Oxford: Clarendon Press, 1956. The comprehensive work on Nuer religion.

Evans-Pritchard, E. E., *The Nuer,* Oxford: Clarendon Press, 1940. A general study of the Nuer.

Colson, Elizabeth, "The Role of Cattle among the Plateau Tonga of Mazabuka District," *Human Problems in British Central Africa,* 1951, *11,* pp. 10-46. A general study of the economic, social, and ritual place of cattle in the life of the Tonga under conditions of social change

The Oba (King) of Benin, Bini tribe, Nigeria; bronze, height 11 in.; the Nelson Gallery of Art, Kansas City

[*The first three plates accompanied the article by William Fagg* (*see pp. 458–472*) *in the* Bulletin *of the* Allen Memorial Art Museum, Oberlin, Ohio, Winter *1955–56, and are reproduced by permission of Oberlin College, Mrs. Webster Plass, and Mr. and Mrs. Gustave Schindler.*]

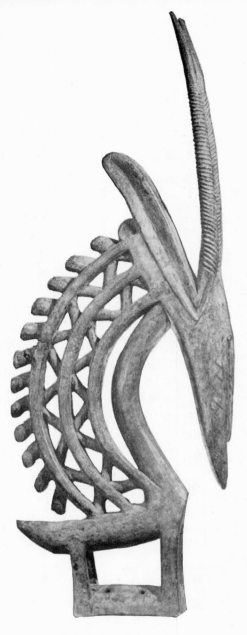

Above: Antelope Headdress, Bambara tribe, French Sudan; wood, height 42¾ in.; owned by Mr. and Mrs. Gustave Schindler, Sands Point, L.I.

Opposite: Dance Mask in form of Horned Antelope Head; Guru tribe, Central Ivory Coast; wood, height 20¾ in.; Webster Plass Collection, British Museum.

Left: Sorcerers in the French Sudan

Right: A Watutsi dancer, Ruanda-Urundi

Below: A *Zébola,* or "possessed" woman, in the Belgian Congo

Top: In the initiation customs of the BaMbuti Pygmies and their Negro neighbors, in the Belgian Congo, the whipping of adults in the Negro village is thought to strengthen the boy initiates for their forthcoming ordeals.

Bottom: Six young Pygmies of the Belgian Congo, after final initiation ceremonies, pose with their fathers in the village of their Negro sponsors.

A member of the Nkumu caste, notables vested with political or spiritual powers, of the Mongo tribes, Belgian Congo

Above: Native Court in session, Usumbura, Ruanda-Urundi

Below: School fees and land taxes are being discussed at a council meeting in the British Cameroons.

The King of the Ashanti State, at a State durbar, surrounded by sword bearers and court officials. On his right, the famous Golden Stool of Ashanti.

Belgian Government Information

Top: The ritual Python Dance, performed by young girls of the Bavenda tribe in the Northern Transvaal, South Africa.

Bottom: In the Belgian Congo, the death of an infant is mourned with ritual lamentations.

This animal, chosen for its distinctive white markings, participates in an age-grade ritual, the "Horn of the ox ceremony," among the Masai hunters of Kenya.

British Information Services

Walangulu Poachers in Kenya dance to celebrate the felling of an elephant, and quickly remove its tusks.

h Information Services

The Paramount Chief of the Dey tribe, in Liberia, dictates a letter to the President of the country, requesting tools with which to build a road connecting his village with the ocean, twenty-two miles away.

At Kabete, Kenya, a Samburu tribesman learns modern breeding methods for his cattle.

British Information Servi

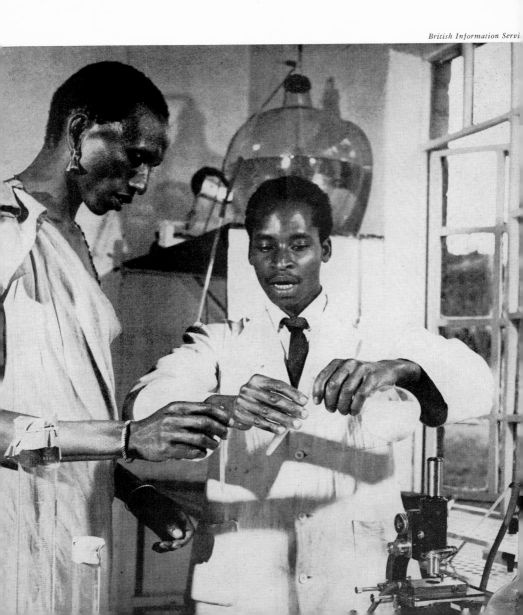

On Sundays, in Johannesburg, the African mine workers put on native costumes and dance for their co-workers.

Above: An Episcopal missionary in Liberia enrolls a new member of the church.

Below: Shanty houses on a street in Sophiatown, Johannesburg

The audience at open-air movies in French Togo

WITCHCRAFT IN FOUR AFRICAN SOCIETIES: AN ESSAY IN COMPARISON*

S. F. Nadel

African witchcraft has long fascinated colonial administrators, mission-aries, and travelers, as well as anthropologists. Anthropologists have car-ried out a great deal of substantive research on witchcraft, and they have made systematic analyses of the reasons why witches are believed to exist in Africa. These have usually emphasized the fact that witchcraft cases involve persons in conflicting social roles or in a state of tension with one another, such as co-wives of a polygynous husband, mother's brother and sister's son in a matrilineal society, elder brother and younger brother in many societies. Witchcraft accusations thus act as a releasing mechanism for tensions inherent in the system of social relations.

Nadel's study is characteristic of his theoretical interest in anthro-pology. He is oriented toward a comparative approach and the examina-tion of variables through which an understanding of causal relations between elements of behavior can be analyzed. As such, this article serves as one sort of model for comparative analysis. Nadel employs the techniques of sociological analysis, and is concerned with the nature of social roles, social groups, and the functioning of society; he also is one of the few anthropologists working in Africa who has tested psychologi-cal concepts as well. In this paper the concepts of child training and of the hostility of the sexes are woven into his sociological analysis.

Nupe is a state on the Niger River in Northern Nigeria. It is pri-marily an agricultural society in which a great deal of trade is carried out. Descent is patrilineal and Islam is the predominant religion. Gwari (Gbari), which is northeast of Nupe and is very similar to it culturally, was formerly a conquered semi-autonomous group within the Nupe state. The Korongo and Mesakin are two of a number of Nuba peoples in the central part of the country, Sudan. They are agriculturalists, being divided into a number of autonomous hill communities, and they are matrilineal in descent.

---

* Reprinted from *American Anthropologist*, 1952, 54, 18-29, by permission of *Ameri-can Anthropologist*.

In this paper[1] it is proposed to present a small-scale model of a comparative analysis, more precisely, of an analysis of "concomitant variations" (to borrow Durkheim's term), such as any inquiry concerned with the explanation of social facts must employ. The facts in question are particular variants of the belief in witchcraft. Indirectly, the study will also refer to a much discussed hypothesis, the assumption that infantile experiences represent a paramount determinant of culture.

The comparison concerns two pairs of societies—the Nupe and Gwari in Northern Nigeria, and the Korongo and Mesakin tribes in the Nuba Mountains of the Central Sudan. Each pair shows wide cultural similarities combined with a few marked divergences, one of these being the diversity in witchcraft beliefs. This discussion will proceed on two assumptions: (1) that any one relevant cultural divergence entails further, concomitant, divergences in the respective cultures; and (2) that witchcraft beliefs are causally related to frustrations, anxieties or other mental stresses precisely as psychopathological symptoms are related to mental disturbances of this nature.

WITCHCRAFT IN NUPE AND GWARI

The two societies are neighbors in an identical environment and also maintain frequent contacts. They speak closely related languages and have an identical kinship system, based on patrilineal succession, patrilocal residence, and localized extended families. Political organization and the regulation of male adolescence are closely similar in both tribes; so is their economy, though marketing and trade are on a much larger scale in Nupe. The religion of Nupe and Gwari is again closely similar (ignoring here the more recent spread of Islam), and the conceptions of life and death, of a body possessed of a double soul ("shadow-" and "life-soul"), or of the reincarnation of ancestral souls, are identical even as regards nomenclature.

Both groups, too, firmly believe in witchcraft; several grave incidents showing the strength of the beliefs occurred even during the period of field work among the two tribes. Both conceive of witchcraft as unequivocally evil, as destroying life, mainly through mysterious wasting diseases, and as implying the power of witches to "eat" the "life-soul" of their victims. Witches are active at night and cannot be seen or discovered by ordinary means. Everything connected with witchcraft takes place in a fantasy realm which is, almost *ex hypothesi*, intangible and beyond empirical verification. This is shown most clearly in the tenet that it is only the "shadow-souls" of witches which roam about and attack victims, while their bodies remain asleep at home, thus deceiving any ordinary attempts at proving, or disproving, these mystic activities.

The two beliefs, however, differ radically in the ascription of sex to the witch. In Nupe witches are always women (called *gáci*, from *egá*, "witchcraft"). They are thought to be organized in a society closely modelled on similar human associations and headed by the woman who is also, in real life, the titled official head of the women traders. It may be noted that this is the only instance of the fantasy world of witchcraft projecting into and becoming tangible in concrete, everyday life. The woman said to preside over the association of witches occupies an exceptional position also in another sense; for she is the only "good" female witch, sometimes a "reformed" witch, and hence a person willing and able to control the sinister activities of her companions.

The men fit into this pattern in an ambiguous way. Certain individuals are said to possess a power similar to witchcraft, which enables them to see and deal with witches. This power is known by a different name (*eshe*) and is essentially good; so that the men possessed of it can control and combat the women witches. At the same time the female witches need the cooperation of the men, for only when the female and male powers are joined does female witchcraft become fully effective, that is, deadly. Here again, the men are said to use their power not to assist, but to restrain the female witches, by withholding the required aid. The ambiguity referred to, then, lies in this: men are necessary for the fullest effect of witchcraft; but as a class, they also stand aloof and are not themselves evil; rather do they attempt to block evil witchcraft. Even so, the fatal effects of female witchcraft are admitted to occur; in which case one argues that a few evil individuals among the men (whom no one can name) have betrayed their own sex and become the helpers of a woman witch. The general picture is that of a sharp sex-antagonism, which assigns the evil intentions to the female, and to the male, a benevolent and ideally decisive—if somewhat utopian—role.

Characteristically, the men are never blamed or accused of witchcraft, and the main collective weapon against witchcraft lies in the activities of a male secret society which, by threats and torture, "cleanses" villages of witchcraft. The same idea that the men alone have the secret power of defeating female witchcraft is expressed in the legends on the origins of witchcraft and antiwitchcraft. The case studies collected add a further twist to this sex-antagonism; for in the majority of cases the alleged witch is a woman, usually an older and domineering female, who would attack a younger man who somehow fell under her dominance; which situation is again pictured in the legends. The men, therefore, though on the utopian or fantasy plane the masters of female witchcraft, are, on the plane of "real" incidents and fears, its main victims.

One case history and one legend may be quoted. The former concerns a young man from a village on the river Niger who one night suddenly disappeared. A body which the police had good reason to believe was his was later fished out of the river; but the people refused to accept this "natural" explanation, maintaining that the young man had been spirited away by a witch. Suspicion at once fell on an elderly wealthy woman whose house the young man had frequently been visiting; he had, in fact, been something like a protégé of that woman or, in Nupe parlance, her *egi kata*—"son of the house"—which term is applied to any individual who seeks the patronage of some influential older person and becomes dependent upon his patron's advice and material help.

The legend tells of a young king "in ancient times," whose mother was an overbearing old woman, constantly interfering with her son's plans and actions. At last the son decided to rid himself of her influence. He consulted a (male) diviner, who told him the secret of a certain cloth mask, which would drop on his mother and remove her from the earth. Thus, it is said, originated the Nupe antiwitchcraft cult *ndakó gboyá*, which is today vested in the male secret society mentioned before and employs the cloth masks as its main paraphernalia.

As regards the Gwari beliefs, a brief outline will suffice. They involve no sex antagonism or sex polarity. Witches and their victims are indiscriminately male and female. Witchcraft is discovered by ordinary divination, practiced by both men and women, and antiwitchcraft measures consist in the main in an annual "cleansing" ritual which embraces the whole community, again irrespective of sex.

So much for the general picture of the two cultures and their divergent conceptions of witchcraft. Turning now to the search for "concomitant" divergences, and taking our lead from psychoanalysis, we might start with infantile experiences and the techniques of child-rearing. Here we meet with one relevant difference only, concerning children of two and over. Until a newborn child has reached the age of two or three the parents in both tribes refrain from cohabitation. Afterwards, when cohabitation is resumed, the Nupe wife visits the husband's hut, the children staying in her sleeping quarters, while in Gwari the husband visits the wife, so that cohabitation takes place in the presence of the young children. The people have no doubt that the children do in fact witness the sexual act. Assuming, with Freudian psychology, that this fact entails deeply unsettling psychological effects, it should foster the oedipus trauma and definite tensions between child (perhaps more specifically son) and father.[2] Assuming further that these tensions, normally repressed or blocked in overt behavior, might find an outlet in the fantasy of witchcraft beliefs, we should expect these to reveal some bias towards sex-antagonism and towards identifying the evil witches either with males (the hated father image) or perhaps, by a more devious transference, with females (the mother avenging herself on all males). In fact, neither assumption is borne out by the evidence, the sex antagonism occurring in the tribe where the traumatic experience is absent.

Certain other cultural divergences, however, concerning adult life, seem to be congruent with the diversity in witchcraft beliefs. They re-volve upon marriage, which, generally speaking, is without serious com-plications and relatively tension-free in Gwari, but full of stress and mutual hostility in Nupe. Two facts may be mentioned. (1) The eco-nomic position of the Nupe wives, many of whom are successful itinerant traders, is generally much better than that of their peasant husbands. Thus husbands are often heavily in debt to their wives, and the latter as-sume many of the financial responsibilities which should rightly belong to the men as fathers and family heads, such as finding bride-price for sons, paying for the children's education, bearing the expenses of family feasts, and the like. This reversal of the institutionalized roles is openly resented by the men, who are, however, helpless and unable to redress the situation. (2) As has been said, many married women become itiner-ant traders. According to the tenets of Nupe morality, this occupation should be reserved for childless women, in whose case one also excuses the moral laxity which, in that society, goes together with this livelihood. But in fact mothers too become itinerant traders, leaving their children once they are four or five years old; more importantly, women also re-fuse to have children, practicing abortion and using alleged contracep-tives, in order to be free to choose this occupation. Again, the men are helpless; they can only brand this voluntary sterility as the gravest pos-sible form of immorality.

In practice, then, the men must submit to the domineering and in-dependent leanings of the women; they resent their own helplessness, and definitely blame the "immorality" of the womenfolk. The wish to see the situation reversed is expressed in nostalgic talk about "the good old days" when all this was unheard of (and which are disproved by all genealogies and concrete records of the past). Equally, it can be ar-gued, the hostility between men and women *plus* this wish-fulfilment are projected into the witchcraft beliefs with their ambivalent expression of sex-antagonism, in which men are the "real" victims but the "utopian" masters of the evil women. A final item of evidence, mentioned before, lies in the identification of the head of the witches with the official head of the women traders. It relates the "projection" in a direct and overt manner to the conscious hostility and the concrete situations evoking it. The psychological "symptom," we might say, and the anxieties and stresses which are its cause are connected by a clear thread of meaning.

WITCHCRAFT IN KORONGO AND MESAKIN

These two tribes are once more neighbors in the same environment; though speaking different languages they know one another and are often bilingual. They share the same economy, political organization, and religious beliefs and practices. Both reckon descent in the mother's line and have the same kinship system and domestic arrangements; more particularly, in both groups children of six or seven are free to leave their father's house, where they were born, for that of their mother's-brother to grow up under his tutelage. A detailed census showed that in each tribe this change of residence and affiliation occurred in about half of all cases. In all other respects, too, child-rearing is identical in the two societies.

So is the regulation of male adolescence, with one exception to be discussed later. It may be pointed out here that male adolescence and, indeed, the whole life cycle of the men, revolve upon a highly formalized division into age classes, each of which is characterized by the right to engage in particular sporting contests, which are exhibitions of virility as well. These sports are light wrestling, wrestling of a more strenuous kind, and fighting with spears. In the first, lowest, age class, before puberty, no sports are practiced. The severe variety of wrestling marks the peak of physical vigor, attained towards the end of adolescence; while spear-fighting, which implies more skill than bodily strength, is considered appropriate to an age of already declining physical vigor. After the spear-fighting stage, the tests or exhibitions of virility cease altogether, the men having become "too old." At the same time the men give up sleeping in the cattle camps out in the bush, which more arduous mode of life is once more regarded as appropriate for youths only. This decline in physical vigor at the end of adolescence is attributed to the cumulative effects of sexual activity, especially to the sex life involved in marriage and procreation. In both groups, finally, the first sporting contest after puberty is celebrated with much ceremony and is made the occasion for an important gift on the part of the boy's mother's-brother. This consists of an animal taken from the mother's-brother's herd, the same herd which the sister's son is in due course bound to inherit. The gift therefore represents something like an "anticipated inheritance," and is in fact known by the term "inheritance," a point which is of crucial importance for the understanding of the witchcraft beliefs.

To turn now to the contrast between the two groups. The Korongo have no witchcraft beliefs at all; the Mesakin are literally obsessed by fears of witchcraft (known as *torogo*) and witchcraft accusations, entailing violent quarrels, assaults, and blood revenge, are frequent. Witchcraft itself is a mysterious, malignant and often deadly power, emanating directly from evil wishes, though it is subject to two significant restrictions. Mesakin witchcraft is believed to operate only between maternal kin, especially between a mother's-brother and sister's son, the older relative assailing the younger. Mesakin witchcraft further operates only if there is a reason, some legitimate cause for resentment or anger; and the latter is almost invariably a quarrel over the "anticipated inheritance" mentioned before. As has been said, both tribes acknowledge this particular duty of the mother's-brother. But in Korongo it is never refused. The gift can be postponed, but is also sometimes made twice, and rarely raises any serious difficulty. In Mesakin the exact opposite is true. The gift is always refused to begin with, and has often to be taken by force, a procedure which is fully sanctioned by public opinion. The gift cannot be postponed, nor is it ever repeated. Quarrels over it between the youth and his mother's-brother are the rule; and if by any chance the former falls ill, dies, or suffers some other misfortune, the older man is invariably suspected of having employed witchcraft.

Practices of child-rearing, being identical in the two tribes, offer no clue either to the sharply divergent attitude towards the anticipated inheritance or to the witchcraft beliefs which, in one of the two groups, come into play in this connection. The clue seems to lie, rather, in certain cultural differences shaping the adult attitudes towards life and, more especially, towards the fate of growing old.

To begin with, the two tribes deal differently with premarital sex relations. Both groups, as will be remembered, firmly believe that regular sexual intercourse is physically weakening for the male, yet also glorify physical vigor and manliness. In both groups, for example, a "born" coward or weakling is called by the name normally given to the male homosexuals (who invariably turn transvestite), is treated with the same contempt, and is often forced to join their ranks. In both groups, too, the men hate growing old, which means, above all, withdrawing from the "manly" pursuits and admitting their physical debility; thus the "old men" will always try to join the sports for which they are supposed to be no longer fit, even at the risk of being ridiculed, or sneak out for a night in the cattle camps to join the company of the younger men. Yet while among the Korongo premarital and highly promiscuous sex relations are fully accepted and openly engaged in, among the Mesakin they are carefully concealed; indeed, the Mesakin insisted that formerly premarital chastity was rigidly observed. In other words, the Korongo accept the "dissipation" of strength through sexual intercourse as something one can do nothing about; the Mesakin at least believe that it should be restricted and postponed, and face the failure of the ideal with all the symptoms of a feeling of guilt.[3]

Furthermore, the two tribes schematize their age classes differently, thus establishing a different correspondence between "social age," as indicated in the age class, and physical age.[4] The Korongo have six age classes, as against three among the Mesakin, so that in the former tribe the various phases of individual life are much more faithfully represented; also, the rights and responsibilities changing with age are more evenly spaced. Above all, the pursuits typical of youth, tribal sports and life in the cattle camps, are discarded gradually, allowance being made for transitional stages. Thus the severe wrestling, indicative of the peak of physical vigor, is assigned to the third age class, of as yet unmarried youths, but lasts into the next grade, when marriage, at the age of 20-22, and regular sexual relations are expected to show their weakening effect. At this stage spear-fighting is the appropriate sport, again lasting into the next higher grade. This, the fifth grade, starts with parenthood and the assumption of the responsibilities of a family head; but the final farewell to sports and life in the cattle camps does not take place until a few years afterwards, at the age of 28-30. The Korongo also specifically name their sixth and last grade the age class of "old men," the criterion now being the visible physical decline of the really old. In short, the Korongo accept a gradual process of growing old, the social "old age" being only one of many steps and congruent with physical age.

The Mesakin, on the other hand, distinguish explicitly only between boys before puberty, youths (unmarried and married) before parenthood, and "men," without further separation of the really old. Wrestling, spear-fighting, and life in the cattle camps all cease together, at the end of the second grade, that is, at the age of about 22-24. The Mesakin, therefore, introduce the indices of social "old age" early in life, and expect men to renounce the cherished privileges of youth abruptly and on purely conventional grounds, which take little account of physical age.

Let us now return to the demand for the anticipated inheritance which figures so prominently in Mesakin witchcraft beliefs. In both tribes the mother's-brother must see in this insistent demand a reminder that he has definitely grown old; not only has he by then probably begotten children (which fact would merely announce his declining youth), but he has now a ward sufficiently old to claim his "inheritance," that is, a gift explicitly anticipating the donor's impending death. Now, among the Korongo the older man is prepared for the gradual decline of age and accepts its onset, which coincides with sex life, with good grace or at least without struggle; furthermore, since among the Korongo the anticipated inheritance can be postponed, the mother's-brother may by then be an older or old man also in the physical sense. Among the Mesakin, who know no such gradual transition to old age and idealize premarital chastity (which would postpone its onset), the "reminder" must find the donor mentally unprepared; and since the gift cannot be postponed it will often be demanded of men still physically young. Hence the violent resentment on the part of the mother's-brother when the demand is made and his invariable first refusal.

The resentment and refusal merely express the older man's envy of youth and virility, the loss of which is brought home to him by the very request for the anticipated inheritance. Clearly, every man in the tribe has gone through this phase or knows about it in the case of others; everybody also knows that the mother's-brother's refusal is bound to be abortive in the end, that he can be forced to yield the gift, and that tribal

1. KORONGO AND MESAKIN AGE CLASSIFICATIONS AND ACTIVITIES

Approx. Age	KORONGO			MESAKIN		
	Age Class	Activities	General Circumstances	Age Class	Activities	General Circumstances
Up to 12–13	1. belad	None	Pre-puberty	1. ngate	None	Pre-puberty
13–16	2. dere	Light wrestling	Post-puberty; first sex-relations	2. kaduma	Light wrestling; severe wrestling; spear-fighting; live in cattle camps	Post-puberty; pre-marital sex relations; later marriage
17–20	3. adere	Severe wrestling; live in cattle camps	Unmarried; premarital sex relations			
21–25	4. adumok	Severe wrestling; later spear-fighting; live in cattle camps part of the time	Married			
26–50	5. asnda-gan	Spear-fighting; visit to cattle camps; both end after 3–4 years	Fathers, family heads	3. mede	None	Fathers, family heads; including physically old men
50–	6. tgif	None	Physically old men			

morality is against him. It is suggested that the belief in the mother's-brother's power to use witchcraft against his would-be heirs arises from this knowledge. The hostility which, one knows, the older man feels but should not feel, and which he has no means of realizing finally and successfully, is accepted as operating in the sphere of secret as well as anti-social aims, that is, in the sphere of witchcraft. Differently expressed, every man projects his own frustrations of this nature into the allegations that others are guilty of witchcraft. In punishing them, the accuser vicariously wipes out his own guilt, unadmitted or admitted.

The picture just drawn is to some extent oversimplified. For the Mesakin believe that witchcraft may also be practiced by a sister's son against his mother's-brother or by full brothers against one another. Here, too, there must be a legitimate motive, which lies again in a grievance over inheritance; but this may be ordinary as well as "anticipated" inheritance. Nor need the alleged witch attack only the kinsman by whom he feels he has been injured; he may equally attack a close relative (patrilineal or matrilineal) of that kinsman or any one of the latter's matrilineal kin, thus venting his anger almost at random. These facts, however, seem significant: the belief in the powers of witchcraft of a sister's-son over his mother's-brother is pure "theory," for which the people themselves can cite no concrete cases; in all the remaining instances, too, including that of brothers bewitching one another, it is invariably the older man who is accused; and finally, even where witchcraft is believed to strike at random, both victim and assailant are always males.[5] If, then, the accusations of witchcraft are not invariably directed against a mother's-brother resentful of his kinship obligations, they are always directed against a person likely to feel the resentment and anxieties that go with mature age; and though the motives imputed to the witch are less single-minded than the previous discussion would suggest, and the occasions thought to provoke them less conspicuously "reminders" of the loss of virility, the witchcraft accusations remain a projection of the hostility of the old towards the young and of the frustrations springing from such envy of youth. This is perhaps borne out most strikingly by the following, admittedly atypical, instance. In one of the witchcraft cases recorded the alleged witch was a transvestite homosexual who had no livestock property, so that the question of inheritance did not arise; he was said to have bewitched his sister's young boy for no reason other than "envy of a true male."

CONCLUSIONS

Before attempting to summarize our findings, some general remarks may be interjected. The correlations suggested in the preceding discussion, between witchcraft beliefs and particular features of the cultures in which they appear (or fail to appear), are not the only ones that can be discovered, even in the few societies here considered. These other correlations have been neglected mainly because they seem to be of lesser relevance; more precisely, they appear to belong only to the background of facilitating or impeding conditions, and not to the core of basic causes and determinants. Two examples may be given.

The Korongo, who have no witchcraft, possess a full and explicit mythology concerned with explaining all the things in the world—the creation of man and animals, the origin of death and disease, the invention of fire, and so forth. The witchcraft-ridden Mesakin, on the other hand, have nothing of the kind. Now it may be argued that an explicit explanatory mythology presents a picture of the universe less obscure and puzzling than does a religion backed by no such intellectual efforts; their absence, therefore, may be taken to foster anxieties and a sense of insecurity, and hence, indirectly, to predispose people toward also accepting the mysterious and malevolent powers of witches. Yet it seems clear that this factor can only have contributory significance since too many instances could be quoted of cultures combining an explicit mythology with belief in witchcraft.

The second example refers to the dualistic nature of the Nupe witchcraft beliefs, which occur in a culture and idea system generally characterized by a marked bias for dichotomous conceptions. Among the Gwari, where the witchcraft beliefs ignore the polarity of the sexes, the idea system is similarly devoid of any dualistic trend. Witchcraft beliefs, then, and that wider orientation hang together logically. Here we are once more dealing merely with predispositions of a general kind—with ways of thinking about the universe and of ordering its phenomena. Nor, in fact, does this last correlation exhibit any causal nexus, however indirect or contributory, but only a general "fit," a logical consistency, linking witchcraft beliefs with a general mode of thought.

Even so, an exhaustive analysis must obviously include these, and further, additional factors also. More generally speaking, in any inquiry like ours, based upon "concomitant variations," we must be prepared to reckon with several concomitants and multiple forms of interdependence, rather than with simple one-to-one correlations. That only studies of this far-reaching order can do justice to the complexity of social situations, need hardly be defended. As regards the present inquiry, this ideal degree of completeness was beyond its scope. Perhaps, too, such completeness will often remain an ideal, unattainable in the present stage of our science.[6]

To turn to the conclusions proper: (1) The witchcraft beliefs here examined are causally as well as conspicuously related to specific anxieties and stresses arising in social life. The word "conspicuously" is relevant because the witchcraft beliefs also indicate the precise nature of the social causes of which they are the symptoms—marriage-relations in Nupe, and the relationship between mother's-brother and sister's son in Mesakin.

(2) The anxieties and stresses need not arise from infantile experiences alone; rather, the present evidence tends to show that adult experi-

ences, too, may be responsible for their emergence, and hence for the emergence also of the particular cultural features indicative of the anxieties and stresses.

(3) The witchcraft beliefs of the Nupe and Mesakin seem to represent two basic potentialities or types. In Nupe, the witch is identified with the person openly and successfully setting aside the social values and thus denying the state of society desired and thought "good"; attacks against witches are thus attacks upon the successful enemies of the ideal society. In Mesakin, the witch is identified with the person who cannot live up to the social values yet cannot openly rebel against them; the attacks upon witches are attacks upon the victims of the ideal society. In the first case one punishes the human agents responsible for the frustrations suffered by the believers in the ideal; in the second, one punishes and tries to obliterate the very fact that submission to the social ideal can give rise to frustration. In both types, then, the imputation of witchcraft serves to uphold the desired, if utopian, state of society by identifying the witch with the transgressor—whether in successful action or in unadmitted, suppressed desire. Gwari witchcraft, so far as the somewhat incomplete data go, seems to stand halfway between these extremes. We may note in passing that if the Mesakin belief in witchcraft wielded by aggrieved brothers and sister's-sons were more than "theory," this would illustrate a third type of witchcraft in which the witch is identified with the victim of the "transgressor" and the act of witchcraft with punitive action—though of a disproportionate and unlawful kind.

(4) It is sometimes said that witchcraft beliefs "canalize" hostility or "deflect" hostile impulses into socially relatively harmless channels, that is, help society to function. Our evidence does not quite bear out this assumption. The witchcraft fears and accusations only accentuate concrete hostilities and in fact give them free rein. The concrete hostilities *are* "canalized," in the sense that they are directed against a few scapegoats rather than against more numerous victims. But every witchcraft accusation or punishment of witches adds to the stresses of the society, through causing a serious disturbance of social life, entailing blood revenge, and the like. The accusations of witchcraft *do* deflect tensions and aggressive impulses; these are deflected, as it were, from the maladjusted institutions which cause them—marriage and the economic system in Nupe, kinship relations and the regulation of adolescence in Mesakin—so that these institutions can continue to operate. But they remain maladjusted and their continued operation only creates further tensions. Each persecution of witches no doubt relieves the tensions and stresses in a cathartic manner; but the relief is itself creative of new difficulties; equally, it is short-lived, for witchcraft cases go on happening all the time.

In brief, the witchcraft beliefs enable a society to go on functioning in a given manner, fraught with conflicts and contradictions which the society is helpless to resolve; the witchcraft beliefs thus absolve the society from a task apparently too difficult for it, namely, some radical readjustment. But from the observer's point of view it is doubtful if this is more than a poor and ineffectual palliative or can be called a solution "less harmful" than open hostility or even the break-up of the existing institutions and relationships.

NOTES

[1] In slightly abridged form and under the title "A Comparative Study of Witchcraft," the paper was presented at the Berkeley meeting of the [American Anthropological Association, December, 1950]. For a fuller account of some of the ethnographical material see the writer, 1942, esp. Chap. IX; 1935, and 1946.

[2] Gwari informants in fact claimed that a marked hostility between father and son was a common feature of their family life. The writer's material on the Gwari, however, is not sufficiently full to permit any more definite statement.

[3] There is an interesting trace of this also among the Korongo; for here the fiancée of a young man will refuse to have premarital relations with him (and with him only), thus avoiding responsibility for the dissipation of strength of her beloved (Nadel, 1946, p. 289).

[4] See chart 1.

[5] Only in one case, said to have occurred "a long time ago," a woman was accused of having bewitched her brother's young son. But the people considered this a most unusual case, which they themselves were at a loss to explain. Nor were they certain of the circumstances.

[6] The methodological issues touched upon above have been treated more fully in Nadel, 1951, pp. 234 and 258 ff.

BIBLIOGRAPHY

[Starred items are recommended as further readings.]

* Nadel, S. F., 1935, "Nupe Witchcraft and Anti-Witchcraft," Africa, Vol. VIII.
*———, 1942, A Black Byzantium, London.
*———, 1946, The Nuba, London.
*———, 1951, The Foundations of Social Anthropology, Free Press, Glencoe, Illinois.

FOR FURTHER READING

For a discussion of concomitant variation see Nadel's Foundations of Social Anthropology, cited above.

Nadel, S. F., Nupe Religion, Glencoe, Illinois: The Free Press, 1954, Chapter VI, contains a further analysis of Nupe witchcraft; and Nadel, S. F., The Nuba, London: Oxford University Press, 1947, contains background data on the Nuba groups.

Gluckman, Max, Custom and Conflict in Africa, Glencoe, Illinois: The Free Press, 1955, Chapter IV; and Mayer, P., Witches, Grahamstown, South Africa: Rhodes University, 1954. Two valuable summaries of theories of witchcraft in Africa.

Evans-Pritchard, E. E., Witchcraft, Oracles and Magic among the Azande, London: Oxford University Press, 1937.

A very fine description and analysis of witchcraft practices in a group in the Northeastern Congo area.

Wilson, Monica, "Witch Beliefs and Social Structure," *American Journal of Sociology*, 1951, *56*, 307-13; and Wilson, Monica, *Good Company: A Study of Nyakyusa Age-Villages*, London: Oxford University Press for the International African Institute, 1951, Chapter V. The first is a comparative analysis of witchcraft among the Pondo of South Africa and the Nyakyusa of Nyasaland; the second a detailed study of Nyakyusa witchcraft.

Three other useful studies are Schapera, Isaac, "Sorcery and Witchcraft in Bechuanaland," *African Affairs*, 1952, *51*, 41-50; Lienhardt, G., "Some Notions of Witchcraft among the Dinka," *Africa*, 1951, *21*, 303-18; and Marwick, M. J., "The Social Context of Cewa Witch Beliefs," *Africa*, 22, 1952, 120-35, 215-33.

Richards, Audrey I., "A Modern Movement of Witch Finders," *Africa*, 1935, *8*, 448-61, and Morton-Williams, P., "The Atinga Cult among the South-Western Yoruba: A Sociological Analysis of a Witch-finding Movement," *Institut Français Afrique Noire, Bulletin*, Series B, 1956, 3/4, 315-34; Ward, Barbara E., "Some Observations on Religious Cults in Ashanti," *Africa*, 1956, 26, 47-61. Three detailed analyses of present-day witchcraft movements in Africa which in some way seem to be reactions to culture change.

For a discussion of witchcraft in relation to political authority see Paul Bohannan's article, "Extra-Processual Events in Tiv Political Institutions," included in this reader.

INITIATION AMONG THE BAMBUTI PYGMIES OF THE CENTRAL ITURI*

Colin M. Turnbull

This paper throws new light on the life and customs of the BaMbuti Pygmies of the Belgian Congo, some of whom have been studied by Schebesta over a period of years. The various groups of BaMbuti use two main hunting techniques: individual tracking with the bow and arrow (and sometimes spear), and communal hunting with nets. The latter is more rewarding than the former but necessitates larger groups and closer cooperation among the Pygmies. In Turnbull's account of initiation practices among a group of Pygmy net hunters in the Epulu region of the Ituri Forest, we have a detailed report of actual occurrences within a specific group at a particular time rather than the generalized "ideal" picture that is sometimes given of ritual belief and practice in African societies.

In the initiation (nkumbi) of Pygmy boys under the sponsorship of a neighboring Negro group, there is considerable disagreement between the Negroes and Pygmies over the procedures involved and over the significance of the rituals. For the Pygmies, their own initiation practices, in which the Negroes do not share, are more important. The picture emerges of two peoples among whom contact is inevitable but whose fundamental difference in values is expressed in their religious beliefs. The symbiotic relationship that has been reported between some Congo Pygmy groups and neighboring Negro villagers is not found, for the BaMbuti described here are a closely integrated group who are not economically dependent on their neighbors and who hold closely to their own traditional values.

The object of this paper is twofold. First, it is to give an account of the initiation (accompanied by circumcision) of Pygmy boys according to the prevailing custom among neighboring Negro tribes. This information is drawn from my own field notes covering part of an initiation which I witnessed in 1951, and an initiation (known locally as *nkumbi*) which I

* Reprinted from *Journal of the Royal Anthropological Institute*, 1957, 87, 191-216, by permission of the author and the publisher.

was able to follow from start to finish in 1954. Secondly, the paper will, it is hoped, throw some new light on the relationship between the Ba-Mbuti Pygmies and their Negro neighbors. To this end I shall use further field observations on initiation among the BaMbuti, including the initiation of Pygmy girls.

My data refer to the Epulu region of the Ituri Forest in the Belgian Congo. Unlike the archers and trackers described by Schebesta (1938-50) the Pygmies in this district are net hunters. Nor do they fall exactly into any of Schebesta's three linguistic divisions, speaking, as they do, Kibira and Kilese (as well as Kinguana) with equal fluency, with a slight preference for Kibira as the camp language. The three Negro tribes with which they have most contact are the BaBira, BaNgwana, and Ba-Ndaka. Their contact with the BaLese at the present day is slight.

Without going into detail here, it should be understood that these BaMbuti are still nomadic hunters and gatherers, and lead a far less settled existence than the Efe BaMbuti described by Schebesta. There is an apparent "official" attachment of individuals to certain Negro "masters." In the eyes of the Negro the Pygmy hunts for him and in return receives products of his master's plantation—mainly plantains. But whereas Schebesta seems to think that the Efe archers and trackers are economically dependent on the Negro plantations, this is not so with the net hunters, except in so far as luxuries tend to become necessities in the course of time. Perhaps it is sufficient here to draw attention to the fact that the Negro "masters," or patrons, in the Epulu district frequently dispute with each other over the affiliation of Pygmy individuals and groups, who come and go much as they please.

Nevertheless there obviously is a relationship between the two people, and the fact that the BaMbuti adopt Negro customs as well as Negro language is often cited as evidence of their subordination to the Negro. One of the most striking instances of this seeming acculturation is the initiation and circumcision of Pygmy boys according to the custom of the local Negro tribes. The 1951 *nkumbi,* only parts of which I witnessed, was in most respects similar to that described by Schebesta, except that there was no evidence of any *kare* pact between individual Pygmy and Negro initiates. The boys are selected without regard to their Pygmy or Negro origin, but simply according to age, those between nine and twelve years old being considered most suitable. They are circumcised together, by the same Negro operator with the same knife, and during the subsequent period of schooling no difference is made between them. They learn the same songs, are taught the same tribal lore, and undergo the same ordeals, privations, and restrictions. They are subject to the same tabus, which they seem to observe with equal respect. In short, apart from the physical difference, it would be impossible to tell a Pygmy initiate from a Negro. All the boys have adult male relatives living in the initiation camp, but all the teaching is done by the Negroes. I did not live in the 1951 camp, and only visited it on a few occasions, which included the final "coming out" preparations and ceremony at the village of the MuBira chief, Effundi Somali. So I can do no more than state that from everything I saw and heard there seemed to be no difference in the attitudes of Pygmies and Negroes to the *nkumbi,* nor in the attitude of the initiation leaders to Negro and Pygmy boys.

The 1954 *nkumbi,* which took place near the village of Camp Putnam, was different in one vital respect. Whereas there were eight BaMbuti boys (from three different hunting groups) of suitable age, there was only one Negro boy. His father had refused to allow his son to enter the previous two *nkumbi,* and insisted that the boy was now too old, and if he was to be circumcised at all it was to be at the nearest hospital by a European doctor. Both Negroes and Pygmies disagreed strongly with the father, but they failed to get his consent. In spite of the knowledge that only Pygmy boys would be initiated, preparations went ahead as usual. Neighboring villages were all informed of the approaching festival, and a date was set for the first cutting. The Negro "patron" of the first five boys to be cut lived at the administrative post of Mambasa, some fifty miles away. The arrangements were all made by the local villagers and Pygmies, and communicated to him for his approval. It was decided that the operator should be a MuNdaka named Andre, from the next village. The reasons for the choice were not clear, but it seemed that it was largely a question of personal choice, the boys' fathers having the most say in the matter. Their "patron," Ngoma, was a MuBira, as were most of the local villagers. Women took no part in the discussions, in which Pygmy and Negro men indulged equally.

The date for the first cutting was set for Sunday July 4 (this being a public holiday), five days ahead. Preparations began immediately. Food and palm wine were brought in to the Negro village and stored; the womenfolk brought out their best dresses and underwent elaborate toilet operations, and some of them prepared the raffia garments to be worn by the operator. Pygmies who were still out in their forest hunting camp came in and occupied a camp at the extreme edge of the village clearing. Dancing, among Negroes, started on the evening of the announcement.

On the evening of the next day, June 30, the first initiation dance took place. This is a type of dance used only for the duration of the *nkumbi* (which occurs once every three years). There were four drummers and about twenty-five dancers, all Negro villagers except for one of the drummers who was a Pygmy. The dancers, following the lead of the soloist, imitated the light, jerky movements of a bird walking along the ground in search of worms. There was no singing, but after certain movements all the dancers would join in a united shout of "Ah! Ah!"

The steps and general pattern of the dance were obviously known to all, and performed together with no little precision. Most of the dancers were BaNdaka. No women were present.

The following day the men continued this dance, up and down the village. The Negro women formed their own dance group, and again used a style seen only during the *nkumbi* festival; the most notable difference between this and their ordinary style of dancing being in the use of small wooden clappers in the place of hand-claps. These are made as soon as the festival is opened, and destroyed by fire on the last day. Their counterpart among the men is the *makata,* a xylophone of eight or nine keys, each of which is carried by a member of the *makata* dance. (These are not made until the day of the first cutting).

In the afternoon, Andre (the operator) suddenly appeared in the village, his body painted all over with white watch dials, the hands pointing to 11 o'clock; this seems to be a variant of the more conventional five- or eight-pointed star. He was wearing raffia arm-bands, a cluster of bells below each knee, a dark hide mask painted with white stars, and a genet's pelt hanging down from the chin. He danced right through the village, pouncing on any uninitiated children and trying alternately to frighten them and to make them laugh. If they failed to keep a poker face, he pressed his thumb hard into the center of their forehead before dancing off. His movements were particularly birdlike, and several BaNdaka referred to him as *ngosa,* which they said was some kind of bird, and, at the same time, a spirit. I could not find out what kind of spirit it was; the belief was shared by BaNdaka and BaBira. The men of the village formed several dancing groups, mostly led by BaNdaka. Many of them dressed for the occasion, either in European clothes or in new cloths which they wore in a special way, between the legs, with a long tail hanging down behind. Short lengths of raffia tied around the legs and stuck into the hair added to the birdlike effect of the dance. The dancing continued in the village up to the day of the first cutting, additional drums being brought in from neighboring villages.

On the day before the cutting, the father of one of the candidates sent word that he had withdrawn his son because, at a BaNdaka initiation six years before, a MuNdaka had killed a MuBira with a knife in a drunken brawl. He evidently chose to regard himself, the other fathers, and the four candidates as BaBira because of their allegiance to the MuBira chief, Ngoma. The uncertainty caused by this announcement— though nobody disputed his right to withdraw his son—was increased by the fact that the *mabondo* tree, cut on the day of the opening of the initiation festival, had suddenly ceased to give palm-wine. This was seized as an excuse by various factions for criticizing the arrangements on various grounds, such as the appointment of a MuNdaka operator, the refusal of the Negro father to allow his son to be circumcised, the lateness of the *nkumbi* (it usually takes place between January and April), and the absence of Ngoma combined with the presence of the white man.

Early on the morning of July 4, the day of the first cutting, disputes broke out all over the village and in the Pygmy camp. Ngoma had arrived the night before, and had insisted that Machine, the Pygmy boy who was withdrawn, should be entered. The boy's father eventually capitulated on the assurance that the BaGanza (members of the initiation camp, i.e. the boys and their male relatives, living with them in the camp) would be well provided for in food, tobacco, and wine. It was Ngoma's responsibility, even though there were no BaBira boys entered. He eventually managed to settle the disputes, pointing out that there could be no question of halting the *nkumbi* at this stage as the drums had been called out for three days, and they could not be called out for nothing. To those who argued that there should be more boys, he said that more could be added later from other villages: further disputes were stopped by the arrival of the *makata,* a set of nine sticks, freshly cut that morning, shaved and cut to give notes of varying pitch when hit with clappers. The sticks were immediately seized and sounded.

It now appeared that an additional operator had been called in, headman of a nearby village. Sobani was sometimes regarded as a MuBira, sometimes as a MuLese, and, as an older and more powerful man than Andre, commanded more respect. It was agreed that while Andre was to do the cutting, and act as leader of the BaGanza, Sobani was to supervise the whole *nkumbi.* The two men dressed up in their raffia skirts and armlets, skin masks and genet pelts, and, their bodies painted with white stars, accompanied the *makata* dancers into the village, where they spent the whole morning. Meanwhile a suitable site was chosen between the village and the river, and a small clearing about thirty feet across was cut. It was approached by two paths from the village, and one from the river. These paths were closed to all women and children for the duration of the *nkumbi,* and for a year following the destruction of the camp. On one side of the camp a house was built in the style of the BaNdaka fishing huts—a windbreak bent over to form a roof covering a floor space of fourteen feet by nine feet, with open ends and front. It was covered with large *phrynium* leaves. The bed for the candidates consisted of a rectangular frame, raised about two and a half feet from the ground, across which a number of split logs were laid, with bundled plantain leaves forming individual pillows at the open end. No provision was made for the men who were also to sleep in the camp. A few paces away from the hut, in between two trees that had been left standing, a trestle was erected with a crossbar three feet from the ground.

This was where the cutting was to take place. Both Andre and Sobani came to check the work, but the details were left to the men to decide for themselves.

In the Pygmy camp, unlike the village, there was no dancing at all. Nor had there been any at any stage of the festival other than normal dancing around the camp fire in the evening. The only abnormal activity on the day of the cutting was the washing of the five candidates, the shaving of their heads by their mothers, and their confinement to their parental huts until midday. At midday they were brought down to the village and placed in the hut of one of the headmen.

Shortly after noon the *makata* were joined by four drums, and to this accompaniment the two masked operators went up and down the village chasing women and children into their huts. Once inside, the doors were firmly closed and barred. The first three boys were then brought in quick succession to the initiation camp and circumcised. Each was carried in on the back of the village headman (a MuBira) and placed on the trestle. The boy put one arm around the headman, and one around his father. Other men, Negroes and Pygmies, crowded around to assist in holding him still. The two operators knelt in front, holding the boys' legs open, and Andre operated with a series of eight or nine steady, deliberate cuts, inspecting the wound carefully after each cut. The actual operation took four minutes in each case. During the operation the boys all maintained silence for the first cut or two, but after that they were smothered by the hands and arms of the onlookers to prevent them from crying. The first boy was given a whistle to blow during the operation, and he was frequently rapped on the head by the onlookers, using their fists or their knuckles.

Immediately after the last cut the wound was washed and wrapped in a leaf containing a medicine prepared from powdered roots and banana skins. Black paste was smeared on the forehead and nose, and each boy was carried to a log on which he was made to sit, legs apart, while the blood dripped into a leaf cup placed on the ground. No sooner had the first boy sat down than he was made to learn his first initiation song. When all three boys had been circumcised and were sitting on the same log, they were painted with white clay. Meanwhile the two remaining candidates were brought down to the Nepussi, near to where it flows into the Epulu, and the operation was conducted there. Instead of being sat on a trestle, the boys were simply held upright by the men, and again, though at a considerable distance from the village, hands were clapped over the boys' mouths to prevent them from crying. The drums and *makata* were beaten loudly all the time to prevent, the men said, the womenfolk from hearing anything that was going on.

As soon as the last two boys had been circumcised and the wounds dressed, they were carried back to the initiation camp, and sat on a log beside their companions, and were also painted white. The series of ordeals that was to last for the next six weeks began almost immediately. Each boy was attacked by a man armed with a stick, made to chase him (despite the wound), seize the stick, and throw it away. Then they were all made to hold out their arms which were lightly whipped with thin sticks. All the time they had to sit with rigid backs, legs apart, arms out in front of them. Any time they wavered or showed signs of flinching they were given an extra whipping and more black was rubbed on their noses. When one of the boys received an extra hard whipping and started to cry, the Negroes began to make fun of him and threatened to whip him harder, at which one of the boy's relatives ran up and put his arms around the boy to protect him. This was the first of many instances of open disagreement between Pygmy and Negro as to the principle and purpose of the *nkumbi*.

The crowds stayed in the camp until nightfall, taking part in the teaching of initiation songs and games, and in the ordeals. As soon as the last boy had been circumcised and brought to the camp, the women in the village came out and resumed their dancing. The few Pygmies that had come in from outside camps returned, but the many Negro visitors, some from as far as fifty miles away, remained until the next day. One uncircumcised Mamvu who was found in the initiation camp was thrown out. Shortly after nightfall the boys had their wounds washed and dressed, the medicine on the leaf apparently causing great pain on contact. They were then lifted on to the bed and placed face downwards, each boy with his head on a leaf pillow, penis hanging between two log slats with a leaf cup below to catch the blood. The foreskins and the leaves used during the operation and dressing were placed in a basket hung on a tree at one end of the hut.

When the boys were all settled for the night, Andre left, and the last of the Negro villagers left with him. Immediately they were gone, the BaMbuti men left in the camp began loudly to criticize the day's events, saying how unnecessarily harsh the Negroes were. They all discussed and agreed on the necessity for toughening the boys during this period, but were unanimous in disapproving of the severity of the Negro method. Throughout the night, every half hour or so, one or another of the fathers would go to inspect the boys, to see that they were comfortable, and to make sure that the blood was being caught in the leaf cups underneath. The men all slept in the open around the camp fire.

Early the next morning, at first light, the boys were wakened, and made to sit on their logs and sing the songs they had learned the day before. They were fed with boiled bananas, which they held on the end of short sticks, and Andre, the operator, gave each of them a drink of water from a leaf cup. After this they were given a leaf cup each. Immediately after the meal a hole was cut about two feet in the ground, and lined with leaves. It was then filled with warm water, and after the boys had been to relieve themselves at a specially prepared place near the camp, their wounds were washed here, and dressed with fresh medicine and leaves. One of the boys was found not to have been properly circumcised, and after some discussion between Andre and the villagers, he was recut without any ceremony, in the camp. The boys were then all put to bed, and seemed to be in pain for over an hour after the application of medicine.

By early afternoon the boys were feeling much better, and were fed again with bananas, which they held on sticks. The number of vine circlets, put over their heads and under each shoulder shortly after circumcision, was increased to about fifteen under each arm. The boys were made to sit erect on their logs while Andre taught them more songs. He presented three (in order of cutting) with an old red label, which he hung around the boy's neck, as a sign that he had been the bravest of all during the actual cutting. The boys were then put through a series of minor ordeals. The one who had to be recut was treated less severely than the others. As soon as the village workday was over, male villagers flooded into the camp, and while some started a *makata* dance, others catechized the boys. This continued for four hours, when the boys were put to bed and the Negro villagers all left the camp. A few BaMbuti visitors remained for the evening meal, then they too left. The BaGanza, or permanent members of the camp, consisted of the boys and their fathers and one or two of their older brothers, averaging two relatives to each boy. During the night a dog came into the camp and was chased out with much laughter. It was explained to me that animals, like women and uncircumcised boys and men, were not allowed anywhere near.

Each subsequent day the routine was much the same. Andre or his assistant instructor, Apimombe, would come into the camp at first light or before, and waken the boys and men. He started his catechism while approaching, and by the time he was in the clearing boys and men would be stirring, a few making the appropriate responses. Boys and men ate separately, but at the same time. After the morning meal Andre inspected the wounds, and treated them as necessary. As soon as the wounds were closed, the boys were allowed to wear small pieces of cloth between their legs, and to dress the penis themselves, using a dry powdered root, until completely healed. As soon as they began wearing cloth they were allowed to use their fingers to eat.

Every day they were rubbed with ashes and white clay; they wore their vine circlets at all times. During the day Andre and Apimombe were in sole charge of the instruction and put the boys through various ordeals. As soon as the village workday finished, villagers joined in the instruction. This was kept up until late at night when the villagers felt in the mood, giving the BaGanza no more than three or four hours sleep.

But if the villagers left early, the Pygmies made no attempt to carry on themselves. As soon as the last Negro left the camp the entire BaGanza relaxed, talked freely about the day's happenings, and made fun of the various initiation practices.

For instance, there was a banana hung from one end of the hut, stuck through with small slivers of wood. Whenever this was touched the boys all stopped whatever they were doing and began chanting. The banana was swung, and they chanted in time to its swinging until it stopped. The banana was treated with great reverence, and during the daytime, in the presence of Negroes, the boys avoided going anywhere near it. At night, however, as soon as they were well enough to move about freely, they would join their elders in making fun of the Negroes, and used to play punchball with the banana saying, "Now where is the chant?"

When the bullroarer made itself first heard, nine days after the first cutting, the boys pretended to be scared, and repeated their catechism about the powerful spirits of the dead. That very evening, when the Ba-Ganza were left alone, one of the boys leapt off the bed and in mime imitated the swinging of a bullroarer while all the men pretended to hear a noise in the forest and take fright.

One of the first things the boys were taught was that if they got wet during the *nkumbi* they would die. This was done by Andre throwing small sticks into the air, saying, as they fell, that it was rain, and more rain, while the boys made suitable exclamations of terror. When, in fact, it did rain, the boys would all huddle together in the initiation hut. But at night, when all the Negroes were gone, if a shower of rain came, the boys were the first to be out in it, washing off the ashes and clay rubbed into their bodies during the day.

Food tabus were treated with similar disrespect. Forbidden foods (mostly certain kinds of meat, salt and pepper) were smuggled into the camp, also palm-wine. The boys in particular are only allowed to eat rice, plantains, and squash, with no seasoning; but when there are Negroes in the camp they share the evening meal with their fathers.

The various ordeals, however, were taken seriously by both boys and their fathers. While the fathers would abuse the Negroes if they were too harsh, and would not hesitate to comfort the boys, they also abused their own sons when they failed to bear the ordeal. They all recognized the openly avowed aim of strengthening the boys in mind and body, but objected to the opportunity given by some of the ordeals for the outlet of individual sadism or cruelty.

The catechisms were difficult to follow owing to the peculiar intonation used, and to the fact that they were sometimes in KiBira, sometimes in KiNdaka, even in Lingala and KiLese. Visitors to the camp from these and other tribes each taught the boys their own particular version, and these were frequently no more than a recitation of the names of

tribal ancestors, totems, and deities, with appropriate adjectives and ejac-
ulations.

At the beginning of the *nkumbi* the BaMbuti men and boys showed
some deference to the Negroes; but by the end of a month there was
open defiance. The half-dozen main instructors at all times maintained
good relations with the BaGanza; the trouble was mostly caused by villagers and visitors who only came to the camp occasionally, often drunk,
for the purpose of having some fun at the expense of the BaGanza.

These are the main observations concerning this particular *nkumbi;*
now it remains briefly to outline the remainder of its course and conclusion.

* * *

[On July 11 a sixth Pygmy boy joins the camp and is circumcised, and,
on July 14, a seventh.]

For the past three days the Pygmy fathers have been making raffia
skirts. These are now tried on all the boys except the last two to be cut,
and the three senior initiates (in order of cutting) are told to keep them
on while the others go back to their log seats. The three senior boys are
then each given a small leaf through which a stick is passed; this gripped
between the teeth forms a mouth mask. In their right hands they hold a
fito whip, about five feet long. Led by one of the villagers, clapping the
bass *makata* stick, the boys venture into the village for the first time since
their circumcision, and go up to the Pygmy camp. There they break up
and run right through the camp lashing out with their whips at any
young girls they can find. The younger girls are frightened and run
away; one or two older ones just laugh at the boys. Then they are
brought back to the camp. The first five initiates also begin to learn the
special dance used for the "coming out" festival at the close of the *nkumbi.*
They are not told when this is to be, and after explaining that one of the
last rites which they have to go through is the presentation of hunting
bows to each boy, bows are produced and handed to them. The boys
take them in a disinterested way and walk to the edge of the clearing and
throw them into the forest.

* * *

[On July 18 a final Pygmy candidate is circumcised. The ordeals continue with increasing severity despite the protests of the Pygmy men.]

By the end of the [third] week all the boys, including the most recently circumcised, have raffia skirts and are being taught the "coming-out"
dance. The Negro instructors call in members of the previous BaGanza
to dress up in the skirts and show the boys how it should be done. In the
evening, when the Negroes have left the camp, some of the older Pygmies
put on the skirts and make a burlesque of the dance, while others imitate
the Negro instructors.

Sex instruction takes place spasmodically, but at no time is it either given or taken seriously. Now that the BaGanza is complete, however, and is entirely Pygmy, the Pygmies say that it is time their sons went hunting. In conversation among themselves this has been agreed on as an opening gambit to get back to the forest. The main body of the hunting group is tired of being camped on the edge of the Negro village and plans to move off in about a week's time. The fathers are not going to be left behind, so they intend to take the rest of the BaGanza with them. To start with, however, they merely suggest that the boys should be taught how to hunt, and fall in with the Negro proposal that they take the boys net-hunting in the forest immediately round the camp, so that they can return in time to shelter if rain threatens. Preparations include a blessing of the nets.

* * *

[Andre performs the ceremony of blessing the nets with seriousness and deliberation, to the amusement of the Pygmy men and boys.]

By this time it is midday, and after a quick meal the six senior boys are dressed in their raffia skirts and leaf mouth-masks, and are armed with *fito* whips. A hunting dog that has been tied up in the camp for the whole morning is cut loose, and the boys are told to go out into the forest and to return when they have caught two animals. The last two initiates, who are still unhealed, remain in camp. Cephu, tapping a *makata* stick, leads the young hunters away, and returns about four hours later having caught no animals at all. (Gloom immediately overcame the entire BaGanza not because the hunting magic had evidently failed, they said, but because they could never hope to persuade the Bantu to let them leave for their hunting camp until the boys had caught at least two animals. And how, they asked, were the boys expected to catch animals armed only with *fito* whips and a *makata* stick and so close to the village? They decided that the only sensible thing to do was for the main body of the hunting group to return to the forest, and to send in a couple of antelope as quickly as possible, and that they would simply tell the Bantu that the boys caught them. The prospect of an early return to the forest revived the good humor of the BaGanza, and all the adults set about making ridiculous clothes out of old pieces of cloth and leaves, saying, "Now we are like the big people." The boys joined in the dancing and miming that followed.)

* * *

[The Negroes reluctantly agree to let the initiates go net hunting, stipulating that only four should be gone at one time. Disregarding this condition, the entire BaGanza prepare to leave.]

Meanwhile, a MuNdaka staying in the hunting camp with the Pygmies has, with their help, made a clearing about a quarter of a mile away, and started building an initiation hut there in the same style as the one near the Negro village. This does not please the Pygmies, who had looked forward to returning to their own beehive-shaped style of hut. On arrival the BaGanza is welcomed by all the men and initiated boys from the hunting camp, and are soon eating a meal of forest roots and fruits. For the first time the boys eat what they want, their fathers saying that now they are in the forest there is no need to pay any attention to what the Negroes say about eating this or not eating that. Asked what restrictions they did observe of their own will, they reply, "We don't eat what our stomach doesn't like." No bed has been made, so leaves are laid on the ground and the men and boys all lie down and sleep together. There is a little singing in the camp, but only when the MuNdaka comes across from the main camp to see how the boys are settling in.

The BaGanza stay in the forest for a week, during which time there are no ordeals, and only singing when the MuNdaka visit them. During the day time they wander off collecting fruits and nuts and roots, or else just laze about the camp. The boys make several sorties into the main camp to find girls to whip, but most of the girls have stayed away saying that the BaGanza are too close for comfort.

In the main camp, however, the young children are all occupied with a new game—playing *nkumbi*. The boys, aged from two to eight years, have formed a miniature BaGanza, and walk about the camp carrying little *fito* whips, or sit round one of the camp fires on logs. By their imitation they show that they know all the ordeals that go on in the initiation camp, the daily routine even down to the inspection of the wound, and the initiation songs. The women, who are meant to be ignorant of everything that goes on in the camp, coach their baby sons and teach them the songs.

At night the path leading up to the BaGanza camp is closed by *fito* whips, brought by the MuNdaka from the original camp, which are stuck in the ground on either side of the path and twined across it. Higher up it is closed more effectively by the Pygmies with tree-stumps and branches. The MuNdaka says that the path is closed against evil spirits of the forest; the Pygmies say that it is closed against the BaNdaka and BaBira, whom they nightly expect to come in pursuit of the vanished BaGanza. On a brief visit back to the village I find the old initiation camp quite deserted, though shortly after my arrival a Pygmy turned up and said that he had been sleeping there every night. Andre, on finding that the entire BaGanza has left, goes on a fishing trip with some other BaNdaka. Apimombe shrugs his shoulders and says that it was a bad *nkumbi*, but what could you expect from BaMbuti? I send word to Andre that the BaGanza intend to return from the forest the following Sunday. (I was asked to do this by the Pygmies when they heard I was going to visit the village.)

On the Sunday morning the BaGanza clean up the camp and leave for the village. One Pygmy stays behind saying that the camp should not be deserted until the *nkumbi* is over. He stays there until a few days later when the MuNdaka leaves the main hunting camp and also returns to the village.

On leaving, the *fito*-whip barrier across the path is closed though normally it is left open during the daytime. Nearby the MuNdaka has placed a stick with a *phrynium* leaf wrapped round it, "to keep the BaGanza dry until they reach the village."

Back at the village the BaGanza go straight to their old camp, and find it deserted. The *makata,* dresses, masks, and other objects that had been hidden under the bed are missing, and the bed itself has been dismantled and the split-logs left lying about on the ground. Shortly after reaching the camp, Andre arrives in a sulky mood, complaining that the Pygmies had no right to remove the BaGanza, and that having done so they should at least have left someone in the camp to look after it. Now, he says, the whole camp is spoiled. It is "not fit for sleeping in." The bed itself was "bad," so he destroys it. After a while he recovers his normal good humor, and starts asking the boys what they did in the forest. They tell him they have been hunting and have caught many animals, and he seems to believe this and be pleased by it. (He then asked me if the BaGanza could use the two-room house I shared in the village with my cousin, who was making a documentary film. . . . The advantage of this house, he said, was that no women had lived in it, and that I was in any case a member of the BaGanza. It was arranged that four boys should sleep in each room, and one father, but in fact all eight fathers came. They spread plantain leaves on the mud floor and slept there.)

The next day a new bed is made for the BaGanza in their old camp, the old logs being used by the men for sitting or sleeping on. Andre and the villagers decide that it is now time to increase the tempo of the *nkumbi,* before the coming-out celebrations in just over a week's time. Every night the boys are kept singing until late, and are wakened up at least once during the night by two or three of the villagers who put them through the catechism and some of the ordeals. The singing starts again before first light. During the daytime the boys are mostly occupied with either learning to play the *makata* or practicing their coming-out dance.

On Friday August 13 the boys are presented with the formal symbol of their manhood, a new bark-cloth and a hunting bow, in spite of the fact that this particular group are net hunters, and not archers.

* * *

[During the final six days of the initiation the catechising and ordeals are continued. When the boys are required to run the gauntlet between lines of Negroes armed with thorn switches, their fathers make further opposition to the brutality of the Negroes. The "coming-out" dance is performed, and the boys receive gifts from the spectators. The initiation hut and paraphernalia are burned. The boys undergo ritual ablution in the Nepussi river, their skirts are hung on trees above the stream, and they are given oiled bark-cloths and beaded belts. On the last day the initiates are tattooed, with vertical cuts being made under each arm and rubbed with black paste.]

The boys return to the Pygmy camp. All are still wearing the oiled bark-cloth and beads used on the final day's celebrations. The last night which they pass in the MuBira's house is that of August 18; after that, apart from the bark-cloth and beads, and the skirts hanging from the trees, it will be impossible to tell that there has been an initiation.

The camp remains tabu to all women until the skirts rot away from the trees on which they hang; this, it is said, takes more than a year. Whereas Negro boys initiated will now be entitled to certain privileges, the Pygmy boys seem to have undergone no change of status. Their relationships with other Pygmies and with Negroes seem to be the same as it was before their initiation, except that now, when in the Negro village, they speak more familiarly with the Negroes and enter their *baraza* more freely. In their own hunting camp they occupy exactly the same position as they did before initiation, take the same subordinate part in hunting activities, and are still barred from taking part in the meetings of the men's religious association, the *lusumba*. Advancement to adult status, for the Pygmy, is entirely dissociated from the initiation ritual just described. This advancement, for men and women, is described in the following section, which also attempts to draw some tentative conclusions from this material as to the nature of the Pygmy-Negro relationship.

The term "initiation" implies, in its broadest sense, admission to some form of exclusive association. It is in this broad sense only that we can talk of initiation among the BaMbuti of the central Ituri. There are two such associations, the Lusumba and the Alima. Neither are "secret" societies, but membership of the Lusumba is exclusively male, and the Alima exclusively female. There is one qualification for entry into either association: maturity. Girls thus enter the Alima when they are between their first and second periods. Boys enter the Lusumba when they have proved themselves as hunters, that is when they have killed an animal considered as "real" meat, i.e. large enough to be worth dividing among the hunting group. There are no exceptions. All adult females are members of the Alima, and all adult males are members of the Lusumba. Without going fully into the function of these associations, for the present paper we have to examine them briefly to see just what constitutes "initiation."

The first thing to be said with regard to the Lusumba is that the *nkumbi* initiation in no way qualifies BaMbuti boys for membership in the Lusumba. As already stated, the *nkumbi* does not affect the status of the boys in their own hunting group. To be a member of the Lusumba one has to be a hunter; to be a hunter one has to kill "real" game, usually antelope; to kill an antelope a boy has to be old enough to be allowed to wander away from his father during the hunt and try his luck at either end of the semicircle of nets, where animals might escape and be shot with bow and arrow, speared, or caught by hand. Entry into the Lusumba, then, depends on a combination of physical growth and prowess. Boys seem to qualify by the time they reach the age of fourteen. Once a member one is a full member; there is no hierarchy within the Lusumba. Like the Alima, it is a religious association without priests. There is no ritual to be performed; and all members play the same part in the meetings of the association with the exception of one who is delegated to play the Lusumba horn. The choice falls invariably on the best performer present, without regard to age or other qualities.

The Lusumba is called out in times of crisis like bad hunting (which is rare), illness, or death. It has the power of communicating with the God of the Forest, who is the source of all good and bad in the Pygmy world. The means of communication is song, special songs sacred to the Lusumba, sung only by initiates, and echoing far into the forest through the use of the Lusumba horn. Participation in meetings of the Lusumba is compulsory for all members. If they are temporarily away from their hunting group, word is sent to them and they have to return. Alternatively if they are visiting another hunting group, they are obliged to take part in the Lusumba if called out there. The songs are not phrased in the form of supplication. They merely call on the God of the Forest by constant and prolonged repetition of his name and recitation of his qualities, they rouse him from an apparent state of detachment, and so bring him to consciousness of their plight. Since the God of the Forest is the source of all good and bad, so long as he is conscious of what is happening the BaMbuti are content. But when he is asleep, then things came to pass which he might have prevented had he been awake.

With the women's religious association, Alima, it is the same. All adult women are members, and participation in meetings of the Alima is compulsory whether in one's own camp or when visiting another. Communication with the forest God is again established by means of songs, which are special and sacred to the Alima. In certain Alima songs, however, the men take part. The Alima is called out on occasions of major concern to the womenfolk—birth, arrival at the age of puberty, marriage, and death. Thus at birth and death—and more particularly death—both the Alima and the Lusumba will be out at the same time. Both hold their meetings in the camp, but out of sight of one another. The Alima always meets in a large hut or cluster of huts, and young children may be present. The Lusumba meets, unless it is raining, round one of the camp fires, when all the women and children have retired inside their huts. The one exception, mentioned above, is when the men take part in the Alima festival of initiation, and sing with them in certain of their songs. Initiation into the Alima appears to be a more formal occasion than initiation into the Lusumba.

When a boy kills his first antelope he is immediately acclaimed as a hunter, and "hunters" are *de facto* members of the Lusumba. I have never witnessed or been told of any formal rite introducing the new hunter to the association, and I have reason to believe that there is none. The boy already knows the Lusumba songs and has probably, for the past year or so, been allowed to sit with the men in the evenings while they sing Lusumba songs, as they do, without reference to any particular need or occasion (and at such times without use of the Lusumba horn). The Lusumba is not called out because a boy has become a hunter; but when it is next called the boy will take his place with the others, as though he had always been a member. The only thing that might be regarded as a formal token of initiation is the cutting of sets of three vertical slits on the forehead—on either side of the eyes, above the eyebrows, or above the nose, or in any combination of these positions. The flesh is gouged out and a black paste rubbed in. The wound heals smoothly, leaving black streaks under the skin. The operation is performed without any formality by one of the "great hunters" (one who has killed an elephant or a forest buffalo) and the "initiate," if he can be called such, becomes the immediate object of interest to the womenfolk, as he is now considered marriageable. But the marks themselves do not qualify the boy for membership in the Lusumba, nor does their absence debar him from taking part. All that seems to be required is public recognition of his having killed "real" game, marked by the kind of feasting and dancing that always follows particularly successful hunts.

Initiation into the Alima is more formal. Schebesta, although he evidently witnessed part of an Alima ceremony, was apparently unaware of the existence of this association among the Ituri Pygmies, and again I must stress that this material only applies, so far as I know, to the central Ituri, in the neighborhood of the Epulu river.

When a number of girls reach puberty, they are secluded in a specially constructed hut, or a hut adapted for the purpose, in the forest hunting camp. They remain there, under care of one of the old women, for about a month, between their first and second periods. While in the Alima hut they are taught all the arts and crafts of womanhood, and learn such of the Alima songs as they do not already know. But, like the boys, they have, in fact, little to learn. During this period the girls may come to the entrance of their hut and sit there, singing certain songs while the men gather around and supply the chorus.

During this period also a girl may invite her lover to visit her. The young man, to accept the invitation, has to fight his way through all the women of the camp, who gather around the hut to protect it. The lover is supported by the menfolk, and a battle is waged, in effect, between the Alima and the Lusumba. Sticks and stones form ammunition, also fruit skins and peelings shot from bows. The women protect themselves with their baskets, and not infrequently worst the men. When the lover finally succeeds in breaking through and entering the Alima hut, he may or may not sleep with the girl, as he pleases. She likewise has the right to refuse to have intercourse with him, but it is generally expected that the two should have intercourse. After the way has been opened, other men, uninvited, can try their luck, and the women redouble their efforts to keep them out. But again the girl can refuse to have intercourse with those who get through, and the men frequently fight their way to the hut merely to prove their valor.

The girls sometimes appear daubed with white clay, and sometimes oiled with a mixture of palm oil and red *nkula* paste. This is possibly in imitation of Negro initiation *nkumbi* practice.

Such is the festival, and it is marked by absence of ceremonial, as is initiation into the Lusumba. The girls are secluded for a month, after which they take their place in meetings of the Alima as women. Yet the Alima, like the Lusumba, is a profoundly religious asssociation. Both are concerned primarily with the supernatural, ordering man's relationship with the spiritual world, dealing with spiritual values. The total lack of ceremonial initiation stands out in sharp contrast to the ritual of the *nkumbi*. What is the significance of this contrast with reference to the relation between the BaMbuti and the Negro tribes, in whose initiations they participate? It indicates a major hiatus, not only between two ways of living, but between two ways of thinking; it shows that we are dealing with two totally different sets of values. Not only is the form of initiation different, but also its accepted purpose. What the *nkumbi* achieves for the Negro boy, from his point of view, bears little resemblance to what initiation into membership of the Lusumba means to the Pygmy. Ceremonial, ritual, and magic are ways of interpreting or influencing the supernatural in terms of the natural and in his forest environment the Pygmy has little need to do either. In the *nkumbi* described we see the Pygmy attitude towards its ceremonial and ritual. This positive attitude is as significant as their own lack of ceremonial.

To the Negroes, the masked dancers represent the *ngosa* bird, indicating the presence of a benevolent spirit; similarly the bullroarer represents the presence of supernatural power. The various tabus applied to the BaGanza express tneir subordination to that power (which was sufficiently strong to prevent the Negroes from staying in the camp through the night, even thougl. this meant losing full control of the BaGanza). The *nkumbi* places the initiates in a definite relationship with the supernatural. But to the Pygmies the masked dancers were Andre and Sobani, and the bullroarer was a piece of wood whirled round on the end of a piece of string. The *ngosa* bird and the voice of the spirit, for the BaMbuti, were neither "real" nor did they represent any reality. They were empty and rather ineffectual theatrical devices, an opinion evidenced by conversation among the BaGanza at night, and by their constant burlesque on all ceremonial performed by the Negro.

If the BaMbuti did not believe themselves to be subject to control by this supernatural power, neither did they expect to be able to control it. The blessing of the nets was for the Negroes a means by which they influenced the natural order of events. For the Pygmies it was as farcical as the rest of the ceremonial and ritual connected with the *nkumbi*. They knew that no amount of spitting and chanting would bring game into the nets if there was no game there. This again was evidenced by their conversation when out of earshot of the Negro, and by the inevitable subsequent pantomime.

It is clear, both from their own lack of ceremonial and by their attitude to that of the Negroes, that the BaMbuti have a quite different concept of the supernatural; and even a superficial acquaintance with their own beliefs associated with the Lusumba and Alima is sufficient to show that they could not do otherwise than regard the *nkumbi* as a farce, at least in its magico-religious context. We are faced then with the question that if this is the case, why do they go through with it, and why do the Negroes, who must be aware of the BaMbuti attitude, admit them as candidates?

To start with, there is the question of initiative. At no time were the Negroes able to exercise any compulsion, even when they tried. Pressure was brought to bear by the BaMbuti on their own people to submit candidates. The Negroes accepted these candidates without query, and on their behalf they organized and carried through the *nkumbi* just as they would have done had all the candidates been Negro. In all discussions concerning the *nkumbi*, Pygmies and Negroes took part without regard to their different origins. It can be assumed that the initiative in opening the *nkumbi* and selecting the candidates is shared equally, but it is plain that as a Negro festival all the work falls on the Negro. Apart from taking part in the discussions the Pygmies assist neither in the preparations nor the preliminary festivities. Whereas the Negro village is a scene of festive turmoil, the Pygmy camp remains unchanged.

The account given shows the extent to which the Negroes were unable to control the BaMbuti, and at the same time the thoroughness with which they attempted to run the *nkumbi*. Despite the fact that the Ba-Ganza were entirely Pygmy, for the Negro the *nkumbi* was none the less sacred; he was interested in the *nkumbi* itself rather than in the individuals undergoing it. Whether or not the Negroes thought that by initiating Pygmies they were subjecting them to tribal and supernatural authority is doubtful, though Schebesta suggests this. The evidence considered here suggests that the Negroes not only lacked control of the Pygmy BaGanza, but were not particularly interested in maintaining it, except in so far as any desecration of the camp or the *nkumbi* itself was concerned. We can assume rather that the Negro was primarily interested in the *nkumbi* as a tribal festival; if subordination of the Pygmies took place, it was incidental.

Similarly with the Pygmies, any subordination was incidental and insignificant, though they lost no opportunities of maintaining their own individuality where their feelings clashed with those of the Negroes. The Pygmies had no interest in the *nkumbi* as such, in contrast to the Negroes. The circumcision itself and the ordeals were regarded as having practical value, but they achieved nothing that the Pygmies could not have achieved by methods of their own. It is not here that we find the reason for their participation in the *nkumbi,* any more than in their often alleged subordination to Negro authority and custom. The fact that the BaMbuti participate in the *nkumbi* yet reject it so completely, and that this is accepted by the Negroes, merely emphasizes the hiatus between the two people.

We seem to be in the presence of an attempt to maintain or establish some kind of common ground between two neighboring peoples who can find no common values, yet who inevitably come into contact with each other. There is, among the forest people, a body of beliefs borne out in legend, in the memory of a few old men, and also in the tales of early travelers. According to this, the original point of contact was the Negro invasion of the BaMbuti's forest, and the use of the BaMbuti, by the Negro, as guides, scouts, spies, and mercenary soldiers in the constant fight against other Negro immigrant tribes. While thus employed by the Negroes the Pygmies were unable to hunt and gather sufficient food for their needs, and came to depend on their Negro patrons for this. Another point of contact was through the ivory trade, but with the control of ivory and the cessation of tribal warfare these relationships came to an end. The Negro no longer had any use for the Pygmy, who in turn was free to return to his nomadic existence. We can suppose that the present relationship between Negro and BaMbuti originated in this way, and not in economic dependence or physical subjection. But whereas it was once a clear patron-client relationship, it now seems to have no such clear basis, economic or political.

There is, among the Epulu Pygmies, a trade relationship with their

Negro neighbors in that meat and honey are provided by the Pygmies in return for products of the Negro plantations. But this is a convenient rather than necessary relationship. The Negroes can and do hunt, though they dislike going far into the forest and are not hunters by nature; and the Pygmies can and do manage without garden food for considerable periods. Except in so far as luxury becomes necessity in the course of time, this trade relationship at present is one of mutual convenience. By itself it is insufficiently stable to provide a satisfactory basis for intergroup relations. The spasmodic nature of contact between the two people complicates the issue further, also the fact that by the nature of their wandering existence the Pygmy hunting groups have to establish a relationship with Negroes in different villages, of different tribes. It seems that this is precisely what their participation in the *nkumbi* achieves, for this is a festival common to the majority of the tribes in this area.

Turning it the other way around, the fact that the BaMbuti simultaneously participate in the *nkumbi* and reject its significance indicates the instability of their relationship with the Negroes. The Negroes would undoubtedly like to assert their superiority, but are unable to exercise effective control over the BaMbuti. The BaMbuti would like to be free from any subordination to the Negroes, yet find it as necessary to submit to initiation in a Negro society as the Negroes find it necessary to accept them. The *nkumbi* undoubtedly gives the Negro an opportunity for driving the first blow in asserting his superiority over the Pygmy, yet it gives the Pygmy a status in Negro society which he requires, and at the same time strengthens his own identity as a Pygmy by enabling him to reject the Negro system of values. (Mime is an important means of expression to the Pygmy, and his rejection of the significance of the *nkumbi* is expressed in mime, among the BaGanza—men and boys; and in the hunting camp we have seen how it is encouraged even among the small children.)

A Pygmy net-hunting group is powerfully integrated, and its contact with alien groups is necessarily unformalized. Less well-knit groups, such as may be found among the Efe archers described by Schebesta, may find it possible to enter into some kind of symbiotic relationship, but not an active, nomadic net-hunting group. The *nkumbi* described, together with the brief account of their own attitude towards initiation, shows the extent to which the central BaMbuti preserve their "in-group" feeling. Some kind of relationship has to be established because of the inevitability of contact between the two people. As the smaller and more powerfully integrated group, the Pygmies have to make the move to fit into the larger, looser group. But there is no question of absorption; the smaller group preserves its identity. The *nkumbi* provides it with an ideal opportunity both for establishing a place in Negro society, and for asserting an independent set of values, emphasizing the opposition between the forest world and the outer world of the Negroes. The antagonism that remains and is even heightened in this way is smoothed over to some extent by the secondary mechanism by which the two groups attempt to formalize their relationship, i.e. mutual trade.

What appeared at first to be a conformity by the BaMbuti to Negro custom has been shown to be no more than a superficial conformity at the best, and one that barely conceals a detachment of two ways of life. By his participation in the *nkumbi* (and, we may suspect, in other Negro institutions), the Pygmy shows his willingness to accept a subordinate position in Negro society, and this is partly responsible for the notion that the Negro-Pygmy relationship is one of master-servant, or patron-client. But his rejection of the inner significance of the *nkumbi* shows not only a superficiality in the process of acculturation and assimilation, but a conscious effort on the part of the Pygmy to keep his two worlds apart: the sacred world of the Forest with one set of values, and the profane world of the Negro with another set of values. The central BaMbuti have as yet assumed the Negro values in name only, and that only for the duration of their contact, outside the forest, where their own values do not apply.

The resulting relationship is highly unstable, and this instability is not alleviated by the irregularity of contact between the two people. The trade relationship, as we have seen, is one stabilizing factor, and may be an initial step in the direction of a symbiosis such as that apparently prevailing among the Efe Pygmies and their Lese neighbors. BaMbuti participation in the *nkumbi,* as described, indicates no more than a willingness on both sides to attempt to formalize an unavoidable relationship due, as much as anything else, to mere territorial propinquity.

In conclusion it might be mentioned that this interpretation of the function of the *nkumbi* initiation ceremony as providing an outer symbol of the association of two neighboring tribes that, for one reason or another, come into contact and cooperate together, is very similar to the interpretation by Dr. J. G. Peristiany of initiation among the Pokot and the Karamojong. On this subject he says (1951, p. 299): "The recognition of a common system of age ranks by these two neighboring peoples permits them to move with ease in each other's society and allows, during peace time, the extension of social bonds and the obliteration of cultural frontiers."

An analysis of the *nkumbi* initiation in the central Ituri along these lines would, I believe, reveal that this is indeed its most important function: the establishment of common values which enable neighboring tribes to move within each other's society. This applies as much to neighboring Negro tribes as to the relationship between Negroes and Pygmies. With regard to the latter I would add that in the material here considered there is strong evidence that this establishment of common values, even with the subsequent subordination of Pygmy to Negro, in no way seems to affect the indigenous BaMbuti system of values which they preserve intact in their forest life.

* * *

[Two appendixes, one a list of ordeals and the other the names of the BaGanza of the *nkumbi* described, have here been omitted.]

REFERENCES

Peristiany, J. G., 1951, "The Age-set System of the Pastoral Pokot," *Africa, 31*, pp. 279-302.

Schebesta, P., 1938-50, *Die Bambuti-Pygmäen vom Ituri.* Brussels.

FOR FURTHER READING

Turnbull, Colin M., "Pygmy Music and Ceremonial," *Man,* 1955, *55,* 23-24. A short paper on the cultural isolation of BaMbuti in close contact with Negroes, as expressed in their music and ceremonials.

Three semipopular works in English by a well-known student of Pygmy life are: Schebesta, Paul, *Among Congo Pygmies,* London: Hutchinson, 1933; *My Pygmy and Negro Hosts,* London: Hutchinson, 1936; and *Revisiting My Pygmy Hosts,* London: Hutchinson, 1936.

Gusinde, Martin, "Pygmies and Pygmoids: Twides of Tropical Africa," *Anthropological Quarterly,* 1955, *28,* 3-61, is a summary paper on the three major groups of Pygmies found in central Africa, and contains a comprehensive bibliography.

NEGRO FOLKLORE*

Melville J. Herskovits

African folklore is less well known to the Western world than African art; yet it is exceedingly rich in variety and in innovation. Like the art, it is difficult to understand when torn from its cultural setting, and although a great deal of African folklore has been collected, there have been few good studies of its uses and functions in a society. Herskovits, an anthropologist with strong interests in religion and aesthetics, classifies the major forms of African folklore and indicates something of their social context. His views on the Old World provenience of much of the folklore strengthen the argument, presented in the introduction to this book, that the isolation of the African continent has been overrated. Herskovits has been a pioneer in the study of African culture in the New World, particularly in the Caribbean, Dutch Guiana, and Brazil, under the varying conditions in which Africans there found themselves. The present article reflects this interest and suggests the value of studying African culture wherever it exists, not only on the African continent.

The forms of Negro folklore are the myth, tale, proverb, and riddle. The area of their distribution is Africa south of the Sahara and those parts of North and South America and the Caribbean where Negroes are found in any number.

Aside from the formal aspects of this body of materials, what strike the student most forcefully are its unity and its vitality. The many plots which, with differing incidents and characters, recur again and again in the myths and tales, demonstrate that despite the kaleidoscopic effect given by these differences, they are but an overlay of variation that masks a basic homogeneity. Vitality is expressed not only in the wide African distribution of these "literary" forms, and of proverbs and riddles as well, but also in the retention of this aspect of aboriginal cultural endowment by peoples of African origin in the Americas.

Struck estimated in 1925 that about 7,000 tales of African tribes had been collected and published. This number is but a fraction of the total,

* Reprinted from Shipley, Joseph T., *Encyclopedia of Literature*, 1946, New York: Philosophical Library, copyright by Joseph T. Shipley, pp. 3-14, by permission of the author and the copyright holder.

which he estimated at between 200,000 and 250,000 stories—a figure which, while arbitrary, does suggest the immensity of the field. The largest bibliography to date, gathered by Klipple in 1938, lists books and papers containing 8,804 stories, though, because of duplications, the author gives 5,000 as "a conservative estimate" of "the number of distinctly individual tales collected in Africa." New World Negro tales, which include most of the incidents and many of the plots recorded in Africa, and which in addition have elements of European derivation and in some regions also reflect borrowings from autochthonous Indian tribes, add many more to the total. The numbers of riddles and proverbs, in both the New World and Africa, are vast. Doke, who collected proverbs among the Lamba of Northern Rhodesia, tells of individual informants who gave him as many as 250 separate items at a single session.

The literature varies greatly in yielding information as to the range of folklore in a given African tribe or in a given New World locality. As far as Africa itself is concerned, while almost every writer who has described native life has also recorded a few tales, collections of sufficient scope to give an adequate representation are not numerous. Fortunately, the larger collections are from tribes widely distributed over the continent. Among them we find the publications of Callaway on Zulu lore, Junod on the Thonga, Doke on the Lamba, Smith and Dale on the Ila, Chatelain on the Angolan Bundu, Weeks on various tribes of the Belgian Congo, Nassau on those of French Equatorial Africa, Gutman on the Chagga, Lindblom on the Kamba, Lederbogen on the Cameroons folk, Frobenius on the Yoruba and other tribes, Rattray on the Ashanti, Schön and Tremearne on the Hausa, Tauxier on the Guro and Gagu of the Ivory Coast, Cronise and Ward on the Sierra Leone tribes, and Equilbecq and Tauxier on various peoples of French West Africa. It is thus possible to obtain working concepts of the range and types of tales over Africa as a whole, especially since the resources of the smaller collections can be used to supplement these larger series.

In the New World, collections of larger numbers of tales from a given region, gathered in accordance with specific plans to illuminate the problem of variation in type, have been the rule; though smaller, incidental series do exist. This is due largely to the influence of Parsons (in the Negro field), and of Boas and others who were concerned with collecting Indian folklore. Their insistence on gathering an adequate representation of the tales of a given people, and on taking down whatever might be offered without *a priori* selection, established a significant methodological tradition. Some of these collections, most of which are to be found in the Memoir series of the American Folklore Society, may be named: those of Parsons from the Sea Islands of Georgia, southern United States, the lesser Antilles. and the Bahamas, of Beckwith from

Jamaica, of Andrade from Santo Domingo, of M. and F. Herskovits from Dutch Guiana. Other substantial series are those of Fortier from Louisiana, Sylvain-Comhaire from Haiti, and Silva Campos from Brazil.

Of the various types of Negro folklore that have been recorded, the animal tales are by far the best known. This is not only because animal tales actually do bulk large in the Negro repertory. It is also due to the popularity of the Bre'r Rabbit stories published by Joel Chandler Harris in the last quarter of the 19th century. These tales are in many cases regarded as the type forms of the Negro animal-trickster tale, and reference is frequently made to them in identifying a given story found in the folklore of various peoples of Africa itself. The result, especially in the case of casual recorders of tales in Africa, but also to some degree as concerns certain serious students, has been that animal-trickster stories have been sought out to the exclusion of other types.

Collectors have also been inhibited from publishing other kinds of tales because of an assumed lack of public interest in them, or because of a feeling that these others are not "truly" Negro. In the New World, the counterpart of this attitude has been to overstress animal stories on the ground that only these are African. It would be unnecessary to indicate the fallaciousness of both these points of view were they not so deeply imbedded in current concepts of Negro folklore. The fact remains, however, that even folklorists do not seem to comprehend the extent to which nonanimal tales are told by Africans and New World Negroes.

When the more complete collections of tales from African and New World groups are read as units, it becomes apparent that in any given tribe or locality the animal-trickster stories comprise one of a number of cycles of tales. This tendency to group stories has not received the attention it merits, for two reasons. In the first place, nonanimal tales were collected in such relatively small numbers that the phenomenon was difficult to recognize. Secondly, collectors of tales in Africa, especially, nonscientific writers, themselves often have had an attitude toward the folklore of natives as something "primitive" and childlike. This stood in the way of serious consideration of how the total literary product of a given people was organized.

It is only necessary, however, to consult the larger collections with the point in mind, e.g., such an early work as Callaway's Zulu collection, where one can page through the various units of the *Tale of Uthlakanyana,* the first of a series of such cycles of stories about kings and commoners, animals and supernatural beings contained in the volume. Tales in manuscript collected by M. and F. Herskovits in Dahomey, West Africa,[1] include animal-trickster cycles centering about Tortoise and Hare, a cycle having as its central character a trickster of gross undisciplined appetite called Yo, a cycle of tales concerning the adventures of twins, another having to do with the precocious child, another of the motherless child, another of the hunter, in addition to the various mythological and "historical" cycles.

In these cycles of African tales, the action centers about a protagonist of outstanding importance. This is not so strikingly the case in the New World as in Africa, but even in the New World, linked tales after the manner of certain connected episodes of the Uncle Remus series appear. Thus a character who has been outwitted will mention an incident in another tale when he explains his motive for seeking revenge; or a situation that brings two stories within the same general framework will be made specific by reference to each.

This grouping of the tales in cycles is no construct of the folklorist. The points that have been made indicate this, but the complete demonstration is had only in the actual telling, where those comments are heard which, given almost as asides, rarely creep into the printed version. "As you remember, Tortoise had come home after winning his race with Deer," the teller will begin a new story, or, "After Spider got out of prison, he thought how to revenge himself on Elephant, who had sent him there."

Despite the existence of these cycles, the problem of classification is no less difficult in the case of Negro folk tales than for any other kind. As always, categories which have validity for one purpose do not serve another, and though the native has his own classifications of the tales he tells, these categories are more useful in affording an understanding of the tales than in furthering systematic treatment of the data, particularly where comparative analysis is the end in view. Animal tales, for example, are divided into various types, while animals and human beings mingle in a considerable number of stories. One widely spread story of this kind recounts how the speech of the animals is revealed to a man on condition that he not tell of his new endowment; which he does, thereupon suffering various penalties. Or there is the tale, of considerable distribution in both Africa and the New World, which recounts man's ingratitude— or sometimes gratitude—to animals who rescue him from danger.

Myths, explanatory tales, tales with the *double entendre,* educational tales with appended morals, are all found in the category of animal stories. Furthermore, sacred tales having the gods as characters in the mythology of one tribe, appear with the same plot and incidents as secular animal tales of one of the several types just mentioned in other tribes, or in the New World. Elements of the familiar racing motif are found in the South African myth of how death came to man, while the most popular story among the Ashanti is that which tells how the Spider Anansi by performing through trickery a series of seemingly impossible feats, "bought" from the Sky-god Nyame the right to have stories called *Anansesem* (Spider stories) rather than *Nyankonsem* (sky-god stories).

There is no doubt in the mind of the native, however, regarding the difference between folk tales and myths, or between certain types of folk tales and myths, or between certain kinds of folk tales themselves. Chatelain gives the native classification of Angolan folklore as follows: 1) all "traditional fictitious stories," including the "fables" wherein animals are personified, termed *mi-soso;* 2) stories reputed true, or "anecdotes," called *maka;* 3) "historical" narratives, the "chronicles of tribes and natives . . . considered state secrets," called *malunda;* 4) proverbs, *ji-sabu;* 5) poetry and music; and 6) riddles, *ji-nongonongo.* Lindblom classifies Kamba stories as 1) tales about animals; 2) tales about ogres, giants, etc.; 3) episodes from the life of the natives; 4) myths and legends, few in number, but including explanatory tales; 5) imported tales. This is not unlike the categories given by Junod for the Thonga: 1) animal tales; 2) stories which illustrate how "human beings, children, the miserable and the despised, triumph over their elders and those who hate them"—what Junod calls "the wisdom of the little ones"; 3) ogre tales; 4) moral tales; 5) stories that "seem based on actual facts"; 6) foreign tales.

In the New World, comparable classifications have been made by only a few collectors. . . .[2]

African concepts of what constitutes a myth, as differentiated from other types of narratives, follow quite closely the folklorist's definition, though of course not phrased in the same manner. That is, any sacred tale that validates belief and ritual is a myth, to be clearly distinguished from the secular tale. Knowledge of the mythology of a given people in Africa varies with the ability of a student to probe their world-view and their conception of the forces in the universe that play upon them; with the extent to which tradition permits those that know such stories to tell them to foreigners, or to tribal members who have not attained a requisite age or are not initiates; with the degree to which the native feels that a given story will cast discredit on his own belief when viewed through European eyes.

Except for West Africa, narrative myth sequences appear only rarely in the literature. There are those who hold, indeed, that in certain parts of the continent, particularly East Africa, the Congo, and those portions inhabited by the Southeastern Bantu there is little or no mythology to be found. That a substantial body of mythology exists among peoples everywhere in Africa has been conclusively demonstrated by Alice Werner, who gives for region after region origin tales and stories of the gods and the country they inhabit, myths that sanction the ancestral-cult, and accounts of natural phenomena, such as lightning or the rainbow, that are regarded as supernatural forces to be propitiated. Yet it is necessary to turn to the discussions of African religion, as Alice Werner did, rather than to studies of African folk literature, to obtain the desired concept of the universe. From the point of view of the student who approaches mythology as a literary phenomenon, what is lacking is the presentation of the narrative sequences, as told by natives, of events in the supernatural world that are believed to have brought about the situations described. It is difficult to understand, to take but one instance, why Junod did not record in this form the myths that, for the Thonga, explain and give meaning to the intricate world-view he describes in considering the tribal religion.

Mythological systems vary with the beliefs of the people—from tribe to tribe in Africa, in the New World in accordance with the degree of acculturation to European religious systems. The sacred tales concern all aspects of cosmology—the creation of the world, the coming of the gods (who are generally conceived as nature-deities), their functions in the world, their relations to each other and to man, the nature of magic, its origin and how the forces controlling it exert their power, and the like. They explain rituals and account for divining practices. In addition, there exists a great body of "family" myths—tales that, recounting the earliest history of a given relationship grouping, validate such totemic beliefs and rites as it may possess, and act to stabilize the social system.

* * *

"Historical" tales, political stories and anecdotes, form another major category of Negro folklore. Except for the fact that the motifs that go into such tales are often found in myths and animal stories, and that this type merges imperceptibly into the former as quasi-supernatural beings such as twins or gifted folk appear in them, little can be said of them as a body. Their functions vary—to amuse, to instruct, to admonish, to recall. They are frequently told by the elders for recreation, in the manner analogous to that in which the animal tales, in large measure, are told by the children.

The animal-trickster tales are highly stable, and in a considerable number of instances stories recur over all the African continent and in the New World as well. Some of the better-known ones may be cited. One is the rope-pulling contest, which in essence recounts how the small trickster wagers a much larger animal that he can match him in a tug-of-war, and wins by repeating the wager with another beast, the size of the first; whereupon the two, out of sight of each other, reach an impasse, each thinking he is pulling against the trickster. This tale has been collected in Senegal, the Ivory Coast, the Sudan, Togoland, Dahomey, Nigeria, Calabar, Gaboon, the Cameroons, the Congo, and South and East Africa; in the New World, it has been reported from the United States, the Bahamas, Haiti, Trinidad, Dutch Guiana and Brazil.

The Tar Baby story, so well known that it needs only its title to identify it, has a similar distribution among Negro peoples, with, however, even more versions on record. Of almost equal fame, and of similar distribution, is the tale where the small trickster humiliates his larger, duller-witted foil by making of him a riding horse; or that in which a slow-moving animal, usually Tortoise, bests another faster animal in a race by posting others of his kind at intervals along the course where each makes his appearance as the swiftly running opponent nears his place of concealment, the last of the series crossing the finish line the winner.

Other widely distributed animal tales are less known. The story in which the animal trickster, posing as doctor or nurse or as a servant, undertakes to care for the children of the larger animal, eating a child each day and deceiving the parent until all are devoured, is one of this kind. It appears in Sierra Leone, in the Sudan, in Dahomey, Nigeria, Gaboon, the Congo, Angola, Uganda, Rhodesia, Portuguese East Africa and South Africa; in the New World it has been recorded in Brazil, Dutch Guiana, Trinidad and Haiti, and in all likelihood is told elsewhere in the Caribbean and perhaps in the United States. In another, trickster wins a loan from a series of animals which habitually prey on each other and arranges the time of repayment of each loan so that as one creditor comes to receive his money he is killed by the next, the last in the series being tricked into cancelling the indebtedness. Still another tells how trickster, finding an object that yields food when the proper formula is pronounced, hides it so others cannot benefit; but when they discover his secret, contrives to obtain a magic whip that punishes the thieves. Over twenty versions of this tale have been reported from West Africa alone, and it is found also in other portions of the continent and among many New World Negro groups.

Whether in Africa or the New World, the trickster is a small animal of high intelligence and facile cunning, quite unscrupulous, with great cupidity and gross appetite. Though in any given cycle he victimizes a series of his fellow creatures, there is generally one animal or sometimes several that are his particular prey. They are inevitably larger and therefore stronger than the trickster, dull of wit, often earnest and hard-working. Despite the many times he bests them—their occasional reluctance to have dealings with him is another indication of how the individual stories are associated in the native's mind—they eventually respond to his suave arguments and alluring promises, and afford him yet another triumph.

The trickster is not always depicted as besting an intended victim. On occasion he not only loses in his enterprise, but in some stories he is shown as anything but clever. This is the case in the Tar Baby tale, where trickster is caught and made to pay for his wrongdoing when he becomes fastened to a figure made of a gummy substance set up for the purpose of trapping him. Another tale of this kind is the Gold Coast story that recounts how Spider, having put all the wisdom of the world in a calabash with the intention of keeping it for himself, decides to hide the container atop a tree. He slings it about his neck to enable him to climb, but because the calabash is over his chest, he can make no progress until his child calls to him to change the position of the gourd; whereupon, in anger, he dashes the calabash to the ground, and wisdom becomes disseminated throughout the world.

In the patterning of these animal tales an element of psychological and sociological significance is found in the relative size of trickster and his opponents. Spider, rabbit, tortoise, chevrotain—all must live by their wits when competing with lion, or elephant, or buffalo, or other large creatures. This element carries over when the animal tales have birds as their characters, the small bird of one widely told story winning a contest for the kingship by concealing himself on the back of Hawk or Eagle so that at the proper time he can continue the ascent and thus appear to fly highest.

Trickster, who must employ his ingenuity to best his more powerful fellows, is to be regarded as a reflection of African thinking in approaching the day-to-day situations a human being must meet and resolve. Such tales, in their New World setting, have been spoken of as a technique developed by Negroes to compensate for their impotence as slaves. Yet the presence of these same tales in Africa itself forces us to regard this as at best only a partial explanation to conclude that we are faced with an adaptation and reinforcement of African ways of thought rather than something devised to fit the new situation in which these people found themselves. Rattray has discussed the phenomenon among the Ashanti in quasi-psychoanalytic terms, though he also assigns political reasons to explain them: "The names of animals, and even that of the Sky-god himself, were substituted for the names of real individuals whom it would have been very impolitic to mention. Later, no doubt, such a mild *exposé* in the guise of a story often came to be related *quâ* story. The original practice is still resorted to, however, to expose someone whom the offended party fears to accuse more openly . . ." (*Akan-Ashanti Folk Tales,* p. xii).

The observtions of Lindblom concerning the reaction of the East African Kamba to the triumphs of the smaller animal over the larger may also be noted: "Presumably this is due to the inclination of the natives as a rule to let the weaker party finally win the victory; and setting the biggest animal they know of against small, harmless creatures and yet letting it be the loser affords them especially great pleasure" (*Kamba Tales of Animals,* p. viii). Junod likewise speaks of "the root idea" of these tales as "the triumph of wisdom over mere brute force," and asks, "Why does this theme of wisdom over strength reappear so frequently and under so many aspects in this popular literature?" His answer is, "because the thought is natural and eminently satisfying to the mind of man," so that the storyteller, "consciously or unconsciously . . . is certainly doing work the philosophical bearing of which is undeniable" (*Life of a South African Tribe,* vol. ii, p. 223). The audience, fully identifying itself with the quick-witted little trickster hero, responds in no uncertain way in acclaiming his triumphs, and in wasting no sympathy on the lumbering beast who is victimized.

Intimately related to the folk-tales are the other two literary forms, the proverbs and riddles. The moralizing aspect of the tales is expressed in the terse statements of proper behavior appended to them, often as the culmination of the action, but sometimes only as an admonition that seems to have but little to do with the sequence of events leading up to it. Riddles, while not a part of the tales, form a prelude to storytelling sessions, where some of them are usually "pulled" before the telling of tales is begun.

Numerous collections of proverbs, from all parts of the continent and the New World, indicate how important an element in Negro folklore this form is. Stylistically, it is terse as all aphorisms are; one interesting consideration is the manner in which it often employs archaic terms, utilizing words no longer heard in current speech. Some proverbs are quite elaborate in form, and occasionally are accompanied by song or are themselves sung. The great number possessed by a given people indicates their place in everyday life, and one hears them continuously quoted. This is true wherever African culture has become rooted; only in certain parts of the United States are Negro groups found whose use of the proverb is relatively slight, this being comparable to the desuetude in which this form has fallen in Europe and among American whites.

The matter of utilizing proverbs brings up the problem of understanding their meaning. This involves an interesting methodological point. For while it is not difficult to record a long series of these short, pithy statements, it is quite different when one attempts to discover their significance. This can be achieved only by employing a careful technique of question and answer, wherein a hypothetical situation that seems to be in accord with the meaning of a given saying is presented to the informant, and then varied until it meets the requirements of an understanding achieved. The problem is, of course, more difficult in Africa than in the New World, where the setting of Negro life and much of its sanction is that of the larger community of which it is a part, and much of the implication of a proverb is therefore patent to the student. How rewarding this approach can be, however, is evident in the studies in which it has been used; those of Travélé for the Bambara, of Herskovits and Tagbwe for the Kru, of Herzog and Blooah for the Jabo.

By the use of this method one sees, above all, the many occasions on which the proverb is employed. It plays an important role in the law courts, where it is cited much as our lawyers cite precedents in building up a case. It is used with great effectiveness as an instrument in achieving the paradox of plain speaking through indirection, that figures so importantly in Negro patterns of argument. It is used to warn, to admonish, to reprove; to guide, to praise, to encourage; its use marks erudition and elegance in speech. It reflects, even more clearly than other forms of folklore, the deepest-set values of a people, showing the drives that motivate behavior and the controls that regularize the relations of an individual to his fellows.

A few examples of Kru proverbs may illustrate the points just made. "The lazy man eats little" is not, as might be thought, a precept of general import; it is used only during a meal to shame one who is eating heartily but who has earlier refused to do a task assigned to him. "A missile quickly thrown misses its mark," on the other hand, is the equivalent of the English saying, "Haste makes waste." "To take out and put back never empties the container," both cautions against too liberal giving and is used to warn a man who is permitting others to take advantage of him. Striking is the case of the proverb, "The sound of the snapping of the trap that has caught me stays in my ears." This saying, which to a European might well be interpreted as meaning "Foresight is better than hindsight," is actually only used in polite conversation when one does not quite understand or hear a remark addressed to him—that is, it is the equivalent of English "I beg your pardon?" Such a saying as "Chicken says, 'The feet of the stranger are small,'" is a rebuke to an outsider who would interfere in the affairs of a group, since the idiom "small feet" signifies lack of power. Ascribing the saying to "chicken" is a stylistic device often encountered in African proverbs, to render the use of a saying the more impersonal when employed as a rebuke. These proverbs enter every phase of life.

Riddles are ordinarily couched in the form of a statement rather than as a question. Examples from Africa and the New World show how widespread this form is. Stayt includes some in his work on the South African Venda that may be cited:

> A chief presided and the people surrounded him.
>> The moon and the stars.
> An old man whose gray hair is inside his belly.
>> (The gray fibres inside) a pumpkin.
> That which does honor to a chief.
>> A slippery place after a rainfall. It makes everyone balance and bow.

The following instances, given by Parsons for the South Carolina Sea Islands, show how the same stylistic device prevails:

> A little man was runnin' off all de time, an' big man was tryin' to ketch him an' couldn'.

Wagon wheels.
Something has one eye and one foot.
Needle.
Two sisters sit in an upstairs winder. Dey kyan't see each oder.
Eyes.

These conundrums are a kind of game—a contest of wits that never fails to attract interested listeners. So common is this situation that it figures in the folk tales themselves, especially in tales concerning human beings, where the point of various stories turns on the ability of a character to "pull" a riddle that has been set for him. In a given African tribe, or a given New World area, the stock of riddles told by the group is fairly stable, and the majority of those in circulation are known to many members of the group. The stability of these riddles under diffusion is striking—such a one from Dutch Guiana as, "Red horse riding a black horse's back," with the answer, "A pot on the fire," is found in various other parts of the New World, and has been recorded several times in West Africa. Children are encouraged to learn riddles, since this is held to sharpen their wits, and riddling is a favorite children's pastime. Riddles often have a type of *double entendre,* the question being posed so that the unwary guesser seeks for an erotic rather than a commonplace answer: "My father took his spade and shot it into my mother's narrow opening.—Key and lock."

Every student that has collected tales among Negro peoples has commented on the dramatic quality of their story-telling sessions. This is in part due to the fact that stories are told only at night. There are various reasons given for not telling them during the daylight hours, but the one most often encountered assigns this feeling to an association of storytelling with rites for the dead. Wakes are the rule in Negro cultures, and folk tales figure prominently among the devices used by the watchers to keep awake. Hence, if told by day, it is felt that the spirits of the dead will wreak vengeance on the teller.

In the main, except for myths and certain "historical" tales, the stories are a primary form of recreation. In the telling, the acting is superb, and from all parts of the areas inhabited by Negroes descriptions have been given of how the antics of the trickster, for instance, are mimicked by alterations in the voice of the teller, accompanied by movements of hands and body. The stories, moreover, involve a degree of participation by the audience that is unheard of in European patterns. One reason for this is the interlarding of tale with song, in which the teller acts as soloist and audience as chorus. Often, too, the audience is questioned by the storyteller when a character must justify the behavior he manifests; and interpolations of assent from the audience as the tale unfolds are regularly heard.

The tales do much more than afford recreation, however. Animal tales which offer explanations of natural phenomena, or account for accepted modes of behavior, or point morals, are regarded by natives themselves as important educational devices. This is why the native African can say to the European, "You have your books, but we teach our children through our stories." Though few reports have been made concerning the types of tales told by various age or status groups, it was apparent in Dahomey at least, that animal tales are regarded as primarily for children, and older informants thought it a slight to their dignity to request such stories of them. For adults there were the "historical" tales, nonesoteric stories of the gods, love stories—which, contrary to general belief, are found in the repertory of the African teller—and risqué stories.

The problem of the origin of African tales has occupied the attention of many students. It is rendered especially difficult by the similarities that are found between stories told in Africa and those recorded elsewhere in the Old World. It has not gone unnoticed that there are many resemblances between African animal-trickster tales, Aesop's fables, the Reynard the Fox cycle, the Panchatantra of India, the Jataka tales of China, and animal stories recorded from the Philippines and Indonesia. Many years ago Bleek, struck by this resemblance, entitled his collection of Hottentot tales *Reynard the Fox in South Africa*. The fact that these complex entities resemble each other so closely and, at the same time, are to be contrasted as a group with the animal tales told by the natives of North and South America, or with Polynesian folklore, gives validity to the assumption of historical connection between the areas where these tales are told. It leads, indeed, to the concept of the Old World as an area wherein a highly consistent body of folklore has been widely though irregularly diffused.

This approach is reinforced by a consideration of the nonanimal tales and motifs. Klipple, who has studied what she terms foreign analogues in African tales, has noted many such correspondences in terms of the tale and motif-index system of Aarne and Thompson. Thus type No. 480, "Spinning-Woman by the Spring," the Frau Holle tale of the Grimm brothers' collection, and also known in Africa under the designation, "The Good Child and the Bad," is indicated by her as having been recorded among the Chaga and Rundi of East Africa, among the Tanga, Bulu, and Mañbettu of the Congo, among the Yoruba and other tribes of Nigeria, among the Popo, in Liberia, and among the Wolof, Bambara, Mossi and Hausa of the subtropical belt of West Africa. Other examples of this diffusion of nonanimal tales over the Old World that can be cited at random are Thompson's type 300, "The Dragon-Slayer," or 403, "The Black and White Bride," for which extensive correspondences in Africa are noted by Klipple.

Does this mean that tales were diffused from Europe into Africa, or in the other direction? The task of unraveling this particular historical skein would seem to be a hopeless one. Those who feel that a tale such as Tar Baby must have originated in India, and have spread from there to Africa and, via Spain, to the New World, can offer but deductions based on present-day incidence to prove their point, rather than furnish the objective historical documentation rigid methodology demands. It would seem more fruitful to accept the underlying unity of Old World folklore as a working hypothesis, and to direct analysis toward an understanding of the manner in which, in their diffusion, the various elements of the tales have been rephrased, reoriented and reinterpreted, than to attempt to reconstruct the historical adventures of a given tale. The most likely conclusion, in this regard, would seem to posit inventiveness in all the area— inventiveness in terms of those conventions of the construction of tales and the ends of telling that mark the region as a whole.

This point of view is strengthened by an analysis of the provenience of New World Negro tales. It will be remembered how, some decades ago, argument was joined on the issue of whether or not the Uncle Remus tales were adaptations of Indian animal stories made by the Negroes after their arrival in the New World. It is today conceded that animal stories found in Negro communities of the United States, the Caribbean, and South America are a part of the heritage brought directly from Africa, some tales even without change of character, such as those which concern Anansi, the Spider. Discussion now turns rather on the stories about human beings, which are held to have been taken over by the Negroes as a result of their contact with whites. That this factor was operative cannot be denied, but it is disconcerting, from the point of view of exclusive European provenience, to find Cinderella tales, Frau Holle stories, Magic Flight sequences, Magic Whip, and other typically European motifs appearing in many collections of folklore from aboriginal African tribes. The phenomenon of syncretism may be held operative here as in other aspects of New World Negro culture, the blending of two cultural streams, both derived from the Old World area, in a manner that has created among the Negroes of the western hemisphere a body of folklore that presents, to those that see its wide range, an harmonious unity.

To analyze Negro folk tales in terms of their stylistic qualities would require the detailed consideration of a number of specific stories. Such an analysis would demonstrate how competently Africans achieve adequacy of characterization, how the situations described attain verisimilitude, how action develops to its climax. Interest is sustained by the inner consistency in the building of a plot, suspense alternates with relief, and devices such as repetition of a phrase to denote intensity, or lengthened time, or distance, are skilfully employed. The dramatic quality of the tale is inevitably diluted when it is written, for the efficacy of the literary devices is heightened by the manner of telling. Yet the wealth of creative imagination that has gone into these tales is apparent in whatever form they may be experienced. This, together with the logic of plot and consistency of action that characterize them, mark them as artistic achievements of no inconsiderable order.

NOTES

[Starred items are recommended as further readings.]

*1 [Dahomean Narrative: A Cross-cultural Analysis, Evanston: Northwestern University Press, 1958, African Studies, No. 1.]

2 [Here and elsewhere discussion of New World Negro folklore has been omitted.]

REFERENCES

M. J. Andrade, Folklore from the Dominican Republic, Mem. Am. F. L. Soc., vol. XXIII, 1930; M. Beckwith, Jamaica Anansi Stories, Mem. Am. F. L. Soc., vol. XVII, 1924; W. H. I. Bleek, Reynard the Fox in South Africa* (London), 1864; Rev. Canon Callaway, Nursery Tales, Traditions and Histories of the Zulus* (Natal), 1868; H. Chatelain, Folk Tales of Angola, Mem. Am. F. L. Soc., vol. I, 1894; F. M. Cronise and H. W. Ward, Cunnie Rabbit, Mr. Spider and the Other Beef (London), 1903; C. M. Doke, Lamba Folk Lore,* Mem. Am. F. L. Soc., vol. XX, 1927; F. V. Equilbecq, Essai sur la Litterature Merveilleuse des Noirs (Paris), 1913; A. Fortier, Louisiana Folk-Tales, Mem. Am. F. L. Soc., vol. II, 1895; L. Frobenius, Atlantis: Volksdichtung und Volksmärchen Afrikas. (Jena), 1921-1928; Bruno Gutman, Volksbuch der Wadschagga (Leipzig), 1914; J. C. Harris, Uncle Remus, His Songs and Sayings (Boston), 1880; Nights with Uncle Remus (Boston), 1883; M. and F. Herskovits, Suriname Folklore* (New York), 1936; M. J. Herskovits and S. Tagbwe, "Kru Proverbs," * Jour. Am. F. L., vol. xliii (1930), pp. 225-293; G. Herzog and C. G. Blooah, Jabo Proverbs from Liberia* (London), 1936; H. A. Junod, Chants et Contes des Ba-Ronga (Lausanne), 1897; The Life of a South Afri-can Tribe* (2nd ed., London), 1927; M. A. Klipple, African Folk Tales with Foreign Analogues, Unpublished doctoral thesis, Indiana University, 1938; W. Lederbogen, Kameruner Märchen (Berlin), 1901; G. Lindblom, Kamba Tales of Animals, Arch. d'Études Orientales, vol. xx, pt. 1 (Uppsala), 1926; B. de Magalhães, O Folklore no Brasil (based on tales collected by J. da Silva-Campos; Rio de Janeiro), 1928; A. H. Nassau, Where Animals Talk (Boston), 1912; E. C. Parsons, Folk tales of Andros Island, Bahamas, Mem. Am. F. L. Soc., vol. XIII, 1918; Folklore of the Sea Islands, South Carolina, Mem. Am. F. L. Soc., Vol. XVI, 1923; Folklore of the Antilles, French and English, Mem. Am. F. L. Soc., vol. XXV, pts. 1-3, 1933-1942; R. S. Rattray, Ashanti Proverbs* (Oxford), 1916; Akan-Ashanti Folk-Tales* (Oxford), 1930; J. Schön, Magana Hausa (London), 1885; E. W. Smith and A. M. Dale, The Ila-Speaking Peoples of Northern Rhodesia* (2 vols., London), 1920; H. A. Stayt, The Bavenda* (London), 1931; S. G. Stoney and G. M. Shelby, Black Genesis (New York), 1930; B. Struck, "Die afrikanischen Märchen," Volkerkunde, Berlin, 1925, p. 35; S. Sylvaine-Comhaire, "Creole Tales from Haiti," Jour. Am. F. L., vol. l (1937), pp. 207-295; vol. li (1938), pp. 219-346; L. Tauxier, Les Noirs du Yatenga

(Paris), 1917; *Nègres Gouro et Gagou* (Paris), 1924; Stith Thompson, *Motif-Index of Folk-Literature,* Indiana Univ. Studies, vol. *XIX-XXIII* (Bloomington), 1932-1936; M. Travélé, *Proverbes et Contes Bambara* (Paris), 1923; A. J. Tremearne, *Hausa Superstitions and Customs* (London), 1913; John H. Weeks, *Jungle Life and Jungle Stories* (London), 1923; A. Werner, "African Mythology" in *Mythology of All Races,* vol. VII, pp. 10-375 (Boston), 1925; *Myths and Legends of the Bantu* (London), 1933.

FOR FURTHER READING

Radin, Paul, and Sweeney, James Johnson, *African Folktales and Sculpture,* New York: Pantheon Books, 1952. Contains a valuable selection of folklore.

Bascom, William R., "The Relationship of Yoruba Folklore to Divining," *Journal of American Folklore,* 1943, *56,* 127-31. An analysis of the use of myths and folktales in divination.

Laurence, Margaret (collector), *A Tree for Poverty: Somali Poetry and Prose,* Nairobi: The Eagle Press, 1954. A compilation with a useful introduction.

Itayemi, Phebean, and Gurrey, P., *Folk Tales and Fables,* London: Penguin Books, 1953. West African folklore showing the influence of westernization.

Tutuola, Amos, *The Palm-wine Drinkard,* London: Faber and Faber, 1952; Tutuola, Amos, *My Life in the Bush of Ghosts,* London: Faber and Faber, 1954; Tutuola, Amos, *Simbi and the Satyr of the Dark Jungle,* London: Faber and Faber, 1955; Tutuola, Amos, *The Brave African Huntress,* London: Faber and Faber, 1958. Fantasies by a Nigerian who uses the style of African folklore with great originality.

Barnes, J. A., "History in a Changing Society," published in this volume of readings, shows the relationship of myth and legend to the form of political organization among the Ngoni of Northern Rhodesia and Nyasaland. See further references at the end of that article.

Griaule, Marcel, "The Idea of Person among the Dogon," published in this volume, is concerned with mythology and cosmogony. See further references at the end of that selection.

THE STUDY OF AFRICAN ART*

William Fagg

African art has long fascinated the Western world. Much of the best work is in museums in Europe and the United States, and is reproduced in numerous publications. These museum pieces often were collected with little understanding of their uses, of their social and cultural setting, or of the localized artistic traditions from which they came, and much mysticism and misunderstanding surrounds their symbolism and functions. For every good book on the subject there are a dozen poor ones. Here Fagg outlines the types of approaches to the study of African art and the general state of development of the field, and he indicates a number of exciting possibilities for further research and analysis.

Three of the plates originally accompanying Fagg's article are reproduced in the present volume in the section of photographs facing page 406.

Let us begin by considering the present condition of the discipline to which we are addressing ourselves. We must first note that we have already begged a very large question by using the word "discipline," for it is hard indeed to detect any quality of discipline when we look at most of the publications and activities in the field of tribal art in the past few years. Much confusion reigns because of the lack of any generally accepted principles of study and criticism and for the more positive reason that the recent and current popularity of African art has been based in large part not on genuine scholarly interest but on fashion—a fashion which may suitably go under the name of *nègrerie*. We may ask ourselves where Oriental studies would be today if they had been as largely based on the ignorant *chinoiserie* and *japonaiserie* of eighteenth-century society. Does my heart swell with Africanist pride when I see in the expensive magazines that So-and-so, the well-known film star, innocent alike of taste and of intellect, has had her home decorated on her behalf in the latest style by Such-and-such, the *avant-garde* interior decorators, and that the necessary note of surrealist incongruity (for the *avant-garde* is always a little behind the times) has been provided by a fake Negro

* Reprinted from *Bulletin* of the Allen Memorial Art Museum, Winter, 1955-56, *12*, 44-61, by permission of the author, of Oberlin College, and of the Dudley Peter Allen Memorial Art Museum, Oberlin, Ohio.

sculpture? No, these gentlemen are applying to the appreciation of African art a kind of hormone weed-killer which could well kill the plant by promoting excessive and weak growth. The activities of "collectors" who are not prepared to become genuine and critical connoisseurs are anything but praiseworthy, especially if they proceed to fix their defective taste upon the community by giving their collections to museums—all or nothing. Fortunately there are a number of collectors who do not deserve such strictures and who must in fact be the spearhead of a true public appreciation of African art.

Whence comes the fashion for uninformed *nègrerie?* It is the fruit, I think, of a fifty-year unbalance between the ethnological and the aesthetic approaches to tribal art. Appreciation of these exotic arts in Europe goes back, of course, much farther than that: about the time when the Spaniards were collecting Montezuma's treasure of turquoise and gold for use as royal gifts, the Portuguese were, somewhere on the west coast of Africa, commissioning beautiful ivory goblets carved by Negro craftsmen in an admittedly hybrid but aesthetically satisfying style, and these likewise found their way into the Royal Cabinets of Arts in the European capitals. The Weickmann collection of Yoruba, Dahomean and other West African works of art at Ulm was formed in the seventeenth century. By the early eighteenth century Sir Hans Sloane, founder of the British Museum, and other collectors were amassing "curios" of tribal craftsmanship along with their classical and Oriental *objets d'art,* and well before 1800 magnificent collections which are still unrivalled for aesthetic and ethnological interest were being made by Cook and other navigators. In the early nineteenth century ethnological science was born, partly on the foundations laid by these travelers and connoisseurs, and ethnographical collections began to be formed on a systematic basis. And if the materialistic philosopher Herbert Spencer could classify African sculpture as "at the lowest stage," museum curators were often more discerning, and the great Sir Augustus Wollaston Franks, Keeper of Antiquities at the British Museum, toured Europe indefatigably in the sixties and seventies seeking out choice specimens of African and Oceanic art with the same exquisite taste which he applied to the arts of the higher civilizations. In such quarters aesthetic appreciation of tribal sculpture was far advanced, and if "presentation" was lacking in the museums of the day, that is only because "presentation" is a peculiarly twentieth-century substitute for appreciation. On the theoretical side, sound foundations had already been laid by the early nineties for the study of the evolution and diffusion of tribal arts, most notably in the works of Haddon and Balfour. These pioneering studies were carried out largely in terms of decorative design, partly for the historical reason that Oceanic art (in which the decorative tends to overshadow the sculptural element) was far better known (no doubt because more accessible to travelers) than that of the African continent, still largely unexplored, but especially because the ethnologists were deeply, and rightly, devoted to the inductive method which is the essential of genuine scientific advance and found that decorative art lent itself more readily to objective analysis. The general principles which they laid down were such only as could be fully supported by observed facts; they made no claim to provide a complete theory of primitive art and in particular they rigorously eschewed value judgments, holding that aesthetics, in an absolute sense (as distinct from the relative study of tribal aesthetic attitudes), were beyond the scope of scientific investigation, at least at that time. Precisely because of this element of discipline, these works have never been superseded and may still be recommended to the up-to-date student more than 60 years later. The methods established in these and similar works in Europe and America were perfectly capable of being developed for the scientific study of sculpture and of making eventually a most valuable contribution to comparative aesthetics.

This was the point at which the study and appreciation of tribal art had arrived early in this century when the Post-Impressionists made the great discovery that tribal art existed. As they were revolutionaries professing to make a fresh start, it is perhaps not surprising that they ignored the knowledge and appreciation of tribal art which already existed and the careful and original work which had been published on it by ethnologists. In their enthusiastic praises of the tribal art which they found in the museums, the artists gave the impression that the explorers and the curators had amassed it quite by mistake; but in fact the artists themselves were often uncritical in their evaluation of tribal sculptures, and there is some reason to believe that the sudden arrival in Europe in 1897 of thousands of bronze-castings from Benin—most of them aesthetically barren —played a great part in preparing them for the appreciation of tribal art in general. (Indeed, some of the worst examples of Benin art have continued ever since to appear in anthologies of Negro sculpture compiled under the influence of the modern art movement.)

These remarks are by no means meant in denigration of the modern artists as such; I am concerned here only with the regrettable effects upon the serious study of tribal art which followed from their incursion into the field and from the way in which, like good revolutionaries, they rewrote the history of its appreciation. What is especially surprising, and especially confusing also, is the extent to which anthropologists nowadays unquestioningly swallow this curious creation myth of the birth of recognition of primitive art fully developed from the brains of Picasso and his friends. The reason for this is presumably that almost all the many volumes illustrating tribal art which have been published during this century have been produced by and for modern artists and their followers and incorporate a pious repetition of the myth, while ethnologists have perforce to use these illustrated volumes as their raw material and must indeed look largely to the same clientèle for the success of any exhibitions or publications upon which they may venture.

But the root of the matter is that whereas the ethnologists had been adhering strictly to the inductive method, proceeding from particular observed and verifiable facts to general conclusions, the artists on the contrary followed the deductive approach, using particular facts and examples as expressions of general truths which they knew or apprehended intuitively. As my friend Leon Underwood, the sculptor, has explained to me, the scientist works his way haltingly, by trial and error, towards what the artist has known with certainty since the beginnings of art and long before the beginnings of science; science is uncertain, only art certain. These are indeed the two essential ways of human thought, and both in their different ways are valid. But we must render to Caesar the things which are Caesar's, and art history, including the analytical study of tribal art, is a matter not of art but of science, that is to say, it must be built up on verified facts. It is in this sense that the usurpation of tribal art studies by the modern artists was unfortunate, especially as the results involved so complete a rejection of the inductive method as to render "art" a concept to be avoided in the eyes of many ethnologists. So the recognition of tribal art by European artists, though in one way belated, was in another way premature: if it had been delayed until the ethnologists had extended their comparative studies over the whole field of tribal sculpture and tribal aesthetics, then a most fruitful collaboration would have been possible between the two approaches and a real, unified discipline might have been created. As it is, ethnologists must bear a large share of blame for allowing themselves to be frightened off by the excesses of the aestheticians and to be deflected from the paths of Haddon and Balfour and Boas.

In the last few years, the spate has continued, and is increasing in volume, of more or less personal anthologies of African and other tribal art in the form of books and exhibitions by people of varying taste; on the whole, it may be said that they reflect prevailing conditions rather than contributing much to their improvement. In the case of books especially, it is a pity that the considerable outlay of money involved cannot be used more often for systematic studies rather than random selections.

* * *

[The major artistic epochs of the world may be divided into industrial or pre-industrial cultures and civilizations according to whether they are based on mensuration. Those of Negro Africa are classified as pre-industrial, and their art, coming from cultures that have traditionally been tribal in character (and generally disappearing with tribal institutions), is referred to as "tribal," rather than "primitive" or "pre-literate."]

What then is the fundamental difference between the pre-industrial and the industrial ways of life and art—for it is obvious enough that there is one? For the answer we must look to anthropology, which has from the beginning been deeply interested in the basic beliefs of primitive peoples. It would seem that tribal life generally is founded on and integrated by a concept or concepts of force, soul stuff, *mana,* or whatever it may be called, which is the ultimate reality. These concepts were formerly misinterpreted as superstitions and later as magical systems, no doubt under the influence of the isolated and disconnected survivals of them which we know in our own culture as folklore; but they seem rather, wherever they have been fully studied, to be coherent philosophical systems, informing the whole tribal life and therefore also the tribal art. Many authorities have termed them "dynamic" or "dynamistic," because of what appears to be a basic difference in ontology, in their conception of the nature of being: for them it seems that the ultimate reality is energy rather than matter, that being is a process rather than a state. In a sense, their world is a four-dimensional one, whereas a three-dimensional world, in which everything can be expressed in terms of measurable states, seems to be a prerequisite for practical purposes of the development of great industrial civilizations—until, that is, science becomes refined enough to probe inside the atom, when energy seems to come into its own again.

It would certainly seem that African philosophy is of the dynamistic kind, and we shall return later to a possible expression of this dynamism in sculptural form. Meanwhile we must be seized of the fact that the difference between African art and the art of the high civilizations is not superficial, like that between "academic" and "modern" art in our own culture, but fundamental. Therefore the successful student of African tribal art must somehow become a "man of two worlds": he cannot and should not entirely put aside the outlook and critical apparatus of our own civilization, but he can and must adopt also the philosophical basis and aesthetic premises of tribal art, in which precise measurements and precisely realistic representations are not only meaningless but inartistic. It may be well before we leave this subject to make it clear that I neither hold African art to be better than European because its ontological basis is dynamic rather than static, nor European better than African because the one is characteristic of "higher" civilization, the other of tribal culture. Nor do I suggest for a moment that the African mind is by nature different from ours; the differences which we have noted are in my view historical, not racial.

HISTORICAL METHODS OF STUDY

Let us now proceed to consider some of the varied methods of study which ought to form part of a discipline of tribal art studies. It will be convenient first to dispose of historical or diachronic studies, and that rather briefly, because I shall have occasion to return to them in more detail in another lecture.

These studies seek to determine dates, relative or absolute, stylistic successions, the origins of art styles and forms, and the outside influences which have contributed to their development. They are pursued chiefly through archaeological means, but unfortunately there has been remarkably little systematic excavation yet in those parts of Africa which have produced sculpture; moreover, stratigraphy—the study of superimposed soil layers and their contents—has proved of little avail in practice owing to the lie of the land and the practices of the inhabitants (who scoop their houses up from the surrounding soil, to which they revert in a very few years). But more excavation may still bring good stratigraphical evidence to light. Absolute dating—in terms of years—may sometimes be achieved by the radiocarbon method developed at Chicago, and we are at present awaiting results from the testing of fossil trees found in association with terracottas of the Nok Culture of Northern Nigeria, which geological evidence puts shortly before Christ, making it the earliest African sculpture yet dated.[1]

We have at present to rely largely on the internal evidence of the antiquities themselves, supported sometimes, as especially at Benin, by evidence from oral traditions. A great deal can be done by these means, but though we can set up reasonably convincing hypothetical successions and stylistic classifications, we cannot yet offer more than the most tentative solutions to such problems as the origins of the naturalistic art of Ife or whether Negro art is of greater antiquity than, say, Egyptian art. We must never forget, too, that most African sculpture is, and probably has always been, in perishable wood. It is, however, of great importance that we should persevere with these studies in the reconstruction of art history, not least for the light which they can throw on the relative importance of traditionalism and individualism in recent art. There is immense scope for archaeological research in West Africa, and we may be sure that as new techniques are developed, and old ones more fully exploited, real and visible progress will be made in the next few years towards the establishment of a coherent history of African art.

PRIMARY OR FIELD STUDIES

Our main purpose now is to survey the ways in which we can usefully study the more recent art of Africa, and this in the main means wood sculpture of the last hundred years, or so. I think that it will be most convenient if we classify these studies into two groups—primary studies, by which I mean direct research carried out in the field, and secondary studies, that is, those which are carried out elsewhere, for example in museums and university departments, using as their raw material the results of primary studies, and the specimens which are to be found in great quantities in museum and private collections throughout the world, some of them well documented, in which case they may be regarded as primary evidence, a much greater part of them undocumented, so that only their internal evidence survives.

The Study of Artists in the Field

All forms of cultural anthropology, including the morphological or technological study of objects of material culture, are in the last resort studies of human behavior. The study of artists is, I suppose, the ultimate purpose of research in African art, and if in field studies we could learn all that there is to know about African artists, then there would be little or no need for other methods of study. But what can still be learnt from the carvers themselves has been redued by time and the advance of civilization to a rather small compass. As with the Sibylline books in early Rome, this shrinking of the source material only enhances the need and urgency of collecting it. There are a good many traditional carvers still working in Africa, though not in all the tribes which were well known in the past for their art. Many of them have been to a greater or less extent affected by contact with western civilization, some having become largely dependent on a European *clientèle* for their livelihood, and of these an excellent example is the famous Yoruba carver Bamgboye, whom I visited at his home at the village of Odo-Owa in northeast Yorubaland; on the evidence of the works of his prime, twenty-five years ago, we must account him a great artist as well as a fine craftsman. The corruption of his style during the late thirties was due not to the crude onslaught of our materialistic civilization but to an enlightened if misguided attempt by British educationalists to harness his genius for the teaching of art in a government school; since then his work has consisted of a long series of barren exercises in technique, and in a direct copy which he made three years ago from one of his finest large works exaggerations of style and finish have wholly supplanted the deep feeling, internal coherence and aesthetic propriety of the original. Only five or six miles away from him at Osi lived until his death last year at the age of about seventy-five another great carver, Arowogun, whose works, in a style quite different from Bamgboye's though within the same framework of conventions, are still to be seen in many villages. He retained his full mastery and unerring boldness of line and form to the end, the major and minor works of his last three years being indistinguishable from those of his early prime.

There is clearly great scope for anthropological and aesthetic research in cases like both of these. But Arowogun is dead, and much of the art history of the Osi school of carvers has undoubtedly died with him. We may still reconstruct it in part with the help of younger carvers and other inhabitants of the village and of the surrounding district; but the collection of such material, if it is to give a true account of the spiritual aspects of the art as well as the material ones, cannot be accomplished in short periods of acquaintance such as are adequate for material-culture studies. Training calculated to draw the full benefit from such field studies hardly yet exists, and there is very little time left to develop it. Africans make less effort than we do to put their aesthetic ideas into words—and in this they are not artistically less advanced but simply more realistic than ourselves; the inquirer who tries to persuade them to do so must have a critical judgment of a high order and considerable experience or understanding of the tribal habits of mind. It is very easy, as I have found to my pain, to come away from an hour's talk with a master carver with an impressive fund of "knowledge" which another hour's talk would almost wholly undo. The capacity to destroy his own work cheerfully is indeed the most important and most neglected qualification of the good field worker.

The Study of Works of Art in the Field

Somewhat less rigorous training is required for the field study of works of art when the artist is not available for direct study, and even the ordinary traveller may with the help of a camera collect valuable information. Good photographs are often hardly less useful to the comparative student than the objects themselves, and since the acquisition of carvings, unless they be freshly made, is generally a lengthy business the field student is probably better employed in expanding and documenting his photographic collection, especially as most of the African territories now rightly restrict the export of their works of art. The photographs must of course be properly documented with the name of the village and of the carver and any other available information about the use, function, age, etc., of the carvings. Patient inquiry will usually elicit such information, for the carvings themselves do not very often outlast the memories of their makers among the present inhabitants. If it were possible to make such documented photographic records of all the millions of traditional carvings still extant in West Africa, I think that it would be possible by reference to them to identify nearly all the thousands of undocumented works in European and American museums and collections, and to assign them not only to their districts but to their carvers. . . .

Tribal Art in Its Relation to Ecology, Economics and Society

Field studies must take account of tribal art and artists not only in themselves but also in relation to their environment in the broadest sense: this will include the geological formation, flora and fauna of the locality, but also the racial and cultural characteristics of the people and their economic and social institutions. All these have or may have their effects, more or less direct, upon the art; and it is essential, if our discipline is to be a sound one, that correlations of this kind should be based on field work and not on *a priori* conjecture of the kind which fills most existing books on African art. The well-known cliché according to which the savannah and the rain forest produce fundamentally different and even opposite kinds of art loses most of its meaning when one seeks to apply it in the field instead of on a small-scale map. The knowledge and use of botany among carvers and the conditioning effects of the size of suitable trees are valuable and neglected lines of study. The economics of carving are of great importance in any study bearing on the survival value of tribal art, and distortion of the economy by European trade or patronage commonly precipitates art's decline. For the importance of social institutions in relation to art, we need only compare the art of the Ashanti, Yoruba and Bushongo on the one hand, with their divine kingship and complex stratified society, and that of the Ibo, the Tiv and the Dan, organized in much smaller units, on the other. The social functions of art are particularly noticeable in the secret societies which occur among so many tribes, and some studies in this field have been carried out by social anthropologists; but it is not very satisfactory to isolate a minor aspect of art in this way, and the resulting conclusions would probably have to be modified in many respects if the art were first studied on a fully comprehensive basis.

The Religious and Philosophical Basis of Tribal Art

Of all forms of field study of African art, the most difficult, the least often attempted, and yet perhaps the most urgent, is that which seeks to define its religious and philosophical basis and content. One obstacle lies in the fact that anthropologists are only gradually progressing beyond the crude concept of animism, a fair enough working theory in the early days of anthropology when primitive religion seemed to be a miscellaneous congeries of superstitious beliefs about things, comparable to the vestigial superstitions fossilized in our own culture; the Victorian doctrine of progress imposed the view of the primitives as groping through a mass of childlike errors towards the light of the rationalistic life, and the idea that these apparently irrational customs were in fact manifestations of an internally coherent and viable philosophy, flourishing as our own was not, would have seemed incomprehensible because of its implication that the primitives had retained something of value which our progressive civilization had lost. The weakness of this philosophy, or these philosophies, was that though they purported to explain the whole universe in terms of force which could be influenced by men through tribal rituals—hostile tribes being regarded as inferior beings of more recent origin and worshipping false and useless gods—they manifestly did not apply to the white man, whose presence and power were thus a living disproof of the tribal belief systems. The consequent disintegration of these probably explains the gradual deterioration of both craftsmanship and artistry which is often to be observed in the works of three generations of a family of African carvers. It is also largely responsible for the difficulties inherent in the scientific study of tribal philosophies; even if he can find an "unspoilt" tribe, the investigator himself necessarily introduces an element of distortion into the system. It is a well-known axiom that ritual outlives belief, and informants commonly give incomplete or conflicting explanations of traditional practices, so that a large element of conjecture is involved in their interpretation. . . .

But we cannot pursue this great subject now. Its difficulty should be a challenge rather than a deterrent to our best field workers, and they may be inspired by the hope that a successful study of the philosophical background of art in a tribal society may contribute usefully to the exploration of such mysteries, neglected enough in all conscience, in our own civilization.

SECONDARY STUDIES

We come now to the consideration of secondary studies—those which consist in the interpretation of data and works of art already collected in what I have called the primary or field studies. The word "secondary" does not of course connote any inferiority; on the contrary, they belong logically to a higher order in the scientific hierarchy, just as ethnology, being concerned with the comparative study of cultures, is higher in the scale than ethnography, the descriptive science from which ethnology inductively proceeds. However, in practice the opportunities of error are clearly greater in secondary studies, and the lack of discipline which I have spoken of has made things easy for those who are encouraged rather than embarrassed by the absence of data by which to test their theories. A common and naive fallacy is the subjective interpretation of supposed expressions observed in the faces of African masks and figures: for example, the soapstone figures found in the Kissi country of French Guinea often seem to be grinning broadly, but there is no evidence whatever that humor is intended, any more than in the "smiling" figures of archaic Greece or Mexico. To take a more serious example, the art critic Sir Herbert Read propounded some years ago a classification of tribal art into two groups, correlating abstract styles with supposedly terroristic religions involving human sacrifice, cannibalism and belief in predominantly hostile spirits, and naturalistic styles with religions of sweetness and light. This thesis, conceived strictly *a priori,* was based on the idea that a cubistic carving of a human head, such as is found among the Ijo of the Niger Delta, was intended to have the same effect on an Ijo which it has on a European brought up on naturalism; but in fact some of the most striking examples are found to represent friendly guardian spirits. And in fact wherever the theory can be tested, it breaks down. Secondary studies should never be thought sufficient in themselves; every opportunity should be sought to check them by primary work, and hypotheses should never be allowed to harden prematurely into dogma. So, though I have here separated primary and secondary studies for convenience of analysis, they must always remain very closely linked if our studies are to become a real discipline.

Stylistic Analysis and Identification

To a museum curator the most obvious aspect of secondary studies is the identification of specimens, at the request of the public or for his own purposes of acquisition or exhibition. This will necessarily involve the more or less conscious analysis of style. Some curators will select particular features of the object in order to compare them with similar features on the works of tribes known to them; others will make an immediate intuitive appraisal, which can later be backed up by stylistic analysis if necessary. In this they of course show much the same variation as the curators of picture galleries and other authorities on painting.

Stylistic analysis has been most seriously and systematically applied to African art by Professor Frans Olbrechts of Belgium and his school, and their work has led to great advances in the study of Congo sculpture. The method is based chiefly on the isolation and comparative study of single features such as the form of the mouth, nose or eyes, the treatment of the spine or the position of the hands, and by using well documented specimens as fixed points they are often able to place an undocumented piece in its proper position on the map by an almost mathematical appraisal of its stylistic relations to surrounding groups. This method has been considerably refined since Professor Olbrechts wrote his excellent work, *Plastiek van Kongo,* in the thirties, but my own feeling is that it does not allow quite enough importance to the peculiarities of the individual carver. It has been my experience, chiefly in Nigeria but to some extent also in the Congo, that stylistic differences between two neighboring carvers of one tribe or subtribe may well be greater than those between that tribe or subtribe and the next—thus paralleling the finding of physical anthropologists that a greater range of anthropometric variation will be found within a people than between the averages of that people and of its neighbors. The Olbrechts method has in my view a slight tendency to exaggerate the degree of uniformity obtaining within a tribe; however, this tendency is readily corrected by study in the field.

The same techniques which are used by curators to make tribal identifications are of course employed also in distinguishing genuine specimens from fakes or forgeries, and from what I call the *demi-monde* of African art, that is, the degenerate works—though they are sometimes of high craftsmanship—produced for sale to European travellers rather than for the traditional purposes within the indigenous community. We need not concern ourselves with these two kinds of spurious works here, except to note that scope for their detection continues to increase in both Europe and America.

Evolutionary Studies

I have already spoken at some length about the study of tribal art from the point of view of the evolution of design, and have explained that such studies have been but little applied to Africa, chiefly for historical reasons. But they are quite readily applicable there and to sculptural as well as decorative design. Owing to the prevalence of the apprenticeship system, the line of development is normally within the family or the workshop, and the material is often present for tracing it through several generations. In the early days of anthropology, evolution meant progress, and it was left to the Diffusionists to draw attention to the part played by stagnation and degeneration in the evolution of design. A master carver of genius may be succeeded by an indifferent artist, who misunderstands and corrupts the master's carving practices, but is in turn succeeded by another good artist, who breathes new life into the corrupt conventions, his work being perhaps as good as but more stylized than that of the first master. The spread of art forms from one tribe to another and their modification in the process are another aspect of evolutionary study for which there is great scope in West Africa.

Technological Study

While the technology of African art is best studied in the field, where the artists can be observed, and perhaps filmed, at work, it can also be studied quite profitably in museum collections, especially in the case of works in which the artist has not been concerned in the finishing process to remove the traces of earlier stages of the work. Thus among the

Bamileke and other Cameroons tribes, the bold marks of the adze are left visible and the length and curvature of the strokes can be determined. Sometimes technological series are available showing progressive states of the blocking-out and detailed carving of a given type of figure or mask. Again, studies can be readily made in museums of the technique of casting metals by the lost-wax process. The study of the relation between the artist's tools and materials on the one hand and the finished work on the other must form an important part of our discipline. And the light of the sun must often be reckoned in, whether it be regarded as a tool or a material, for to the African artist the use of shadow is as important as the use of space to Henry Moore.

Morphology and Anatomy

One of the more instructive aspects of our study is the relation between the morphology of African carvings or castings and the anatomy of the human body. It is easy to form *a priori* judgments here because of our preconceived notions of this relation in our own civilization, whose art is so closely linked with the use of the artist's model—a wholly unafrican concept. Let us first observe that it is misleading to think of the forms of African sculpture as distortions of the body; the carver does not begin from an idea of a natural human body and introduce distortions in the interests of art—and much less, of course, because he does not know any better. It would be much truer to say that he begins from a minimal, germinal concept of the body—the simplest recognizable idea of a body—and that his sculpture is an artistic development from, or series of harmonious variations upon, this concept; he is working outwards from this germ, not inwards from our mortal envelope. His variations are not always purely abstract, but may take as their subject selected minor features of the body, such as the fingers and toes, the kneecap, the shoulder blades, the breasts male and female, and, among human modifications of the body, tribal scarifications and forms of hairdress. My friend Professor Paul Wingert has drawn attention to the possibility of studying African masks according to the emphasis placed by the sculptor on the bony structure, the muscular complex (or parts of it), or the superficial skin. This distinction I consider to be a valuable methodological tool, although the masks certainly do not all fall neatly into three categories, some showing two or all three of these tendencies, others being generalized in a manner to which this classification is apparently irrelevant.

It is probably true to say that the average tribal African has more empirical knowledge of human anatomy than his fellow in our own compartmentalized civilization: quite apart from the recent prevalence of cannibalism for ritual purposes among many tribes, and for more of less normal dietary purposes in some, they have often had more experience than most of us have of treating their own or each other's wounds and ailments themselves, instead of confiding their anaesthetized bodies to surgeons. The human skull especially must have been a commonplace sight in the old days, even for children. Such knowledge is often reflected in art, seldom if ever by direct representation for its own sake, but in artistic stylization which nevertheless implies a deep anatomical insight.

Morphology and Mathematics

I believe that the morphology of African sculpture may be usefully studied from a quite different point of view, namely by reference to mathematics. I do not mean to suggest for a moment that the carver is interested in mathematics as such; but he seems to apprehend certain facts of nature which we define mathematically. The most important of these is perhaps the curve of growth, which we call the exponential or logarithmic or equiangular curve. Curves of this kind such as the horns of rams and of antelopes, the tusks of elephants and the shells of snails, are among the most obvious manifestations of growth or increase in the African world, and that their significance is not lost upon the priests and artists is made perfectly plain by the constant use made of these excrescences in art, either by actual incorporation (as when a horn of a buffalo or of a duiker antelope is inserted in the head of a Basonge figure) or by carved representation, or again by the use of a horn or a tusk as the raw material of a carving. . . .

But it is as an integral element of sculptural design that we are here chiefly concerned with the exponential curve. You may recognize the direct use of curved surfaces approximating to this character in the treatment of the face and the body by the sculptors of many tribes. But exponential curves may also be used far more subtly and fundamentally, though unconsciously, in the form of coordinates by which we may plot the mathematical relation between the natural subject represented and the form of its artistic representation: for example in certain masks for the Gelede Society among the Yoruba, the natural prognathism of one characteristically Yoruba type of physiognomy is exaggerated and "blown up," so to speak, in a way which could be plotted on a set of flaring exponential coordinates, such as may also be used to relate one type of human face, or, for example, one type of fish to another.

The late Sir D'Arcy Thompson, the biologist, says in his great work, *Growth and Form,* which is indispensable to anyone trying to pursue this line of study, that the exponential always involves a time element, and this observation may be useful to us in trying to understand the dynamic character of the best African art.

Clearly all sculptures, except possibly mobiles, may be fully described in terms of three dimensions, that is in terms of length, breadth and depth. But I suggest that many tribal sculptures can be regarded as three-dimensional abstracts from four-dimensional concepts, and their elements as a kind of compromise involving selection from the time as well as the three space dimensions. That the idea of growth should be found to run like a *leitmotiv* through African sculpture is far from surprising in the light of the well-established fact that all, or nearly all, the religious cults of West Africa are concerned with increase, with promoting the enhancement and averting the diminution of the force of the community and of the individual.

NOTE

[Starred items are recommended as further readings.]

¹ [Nok culture seems to have lasted from about 900 B.C. to A.D. 200. See Elisofon, Eliot, and Fagg, William, *The Sculpture of Africa,* New York: Praeger, 1958, p. 58.]

BIBLIOGRAPHICAL NOTE

The soundest introduction to tribal art as a whole is Leonhard Adam, *Primitive Art* (London, third edition, 1953). Among general accounts of African art, the following three books may be read together for their complementary approaches: Margaret Trowell, *Classical African Sculpture* (London, 1954); Paul Wingert, *The Sculpture of Negro Africa* (New York, 1950); and Marcel Griaule, *Arts of the African Natives* (New York, 1950). For a brief and rather impressionistic account of African art, see William Fagg, "On the Nature of African Art," *Memoirs of the Manchester Literary and Philosophical Society,* 1953. As to aesthetics, profound insight is shown in Leon Underwood, *Figures in Wood of West Africa, Masks of West Africa,* and *Bronzes of West Africa* (London, 1947, 1948, 1949), which however are ethnologically somewhat unreliable except in matters of technology. Among general books which are valuable chiefly for their pictures may be mentioned Paul Radin and James Johnson Sweeney, *African Folktales and Sculpture* (New York, 1952) and W.

Schmalenbach, *African Art* (Basel, 1954).

For archaeological aspects of African art see Bernard Fagg, "Some Archaeological Notes from Nothern Nigeria," *Man,* 1946; William Fagg, "L'Art nigèrien avant Jésus-Christ," L'Art *Nègre* (Paris, 1951), and "The Antiquities of Ife," *Magazine of Art* (New York, 1950). The best recorded oral history is Chief J. U. Egharevba, *A Short History of Benin* (Lagos, second edition, 1953).

Hans Himmelheber, *Negerkünstler* (Stuttgart, 1935), is a good "primary" account of African artists (among them the Baule). The best comprehensive account of the art of a single tribe is perhaps Raymond Lecoq, *Les Bamiléké* (Paris, 1953) but an even more thorough study has been carried out, though not yet published, among the Ijo of the Niger Delta by Mr. W. R. G. Horton of Oxford. For summaries (not specially related to the art) of African philosophical systems see Placide Tempels, *La Philosophie Bantoue* (translated from the Flemish, Paris, 1949) and Daryll Forde, editor, *African Worlds* (London, 1954).

The Belgian school of stylistic analysis is best represented by Frans Olbrechts, *Plastiek van Kongo** (Antwerp, 1946), and P. J. L. Vandenhoute, "Classification stylistique du masque dan et guéré de la Côte d'Ivoire Occidentale," *Mededelingen van het Rijksmuseum voor Volkenkunde,* Leiden, 1948. Among the important works of scholarly documentation, valuable as works of reference for the identification of styles, are Carl Kjersmeier, *Centres de Style de la Sculpture Nègre Africaine* (four volumes, Co-penhagen and Paris, 1935-1938); Eckart von Sydow, *Afrikanische Plastik* (Berlin, 1955); William Fagg, *The Webster Plass Collection of African Art** (London, 1953); and for particular areas, F. H. Lem, *Sudanese Sculpture* (Paris, 1949); Marcel Griaule, *Masques Dogons,** Travaux et Mémoires de l'Institut d'Ethnologie (Paris, 1938); William Fagg, "De l'Art des Yoruba," *L'Art Nègre* (Paris, 1951); and the work of Olbrechts already mentioned.

FOR FURTHER READING

Elisofon, Eliot, and Fagg, William, *The Sculpture of Africa,* New York: Praeger, 1958. A very useful survey with magnificent photographs and an annotated bibliography.

Herskovits, Melville J., *The Backgrounds of African Art,* Denver: Denver Art Museum, 1945. A helpful presentation of the cultural background to African art, and an interesting discussion of West African art forms, particularly those of Dahomey.

Bascom, William R., and Gebauer, Paul, *Handbook of West African Art,* Milwaukee: Milwaukee Public Museum, Popular Science Handbook Series, 5, 1953. Written by an anthropologist and a missionary respectively, both of whom have had considerable experience in West Africa. Contains valuable comments on the social aspects of art.

Harley, George W., *Masks as Agents of Social Control in Northeast Liberia,* Cambridge: Harvard University, Peabody Museum Papers, 32, 2, 1950. An analysis of masks in terms of their social uses and their significance to Africans.

There have been many books written on the subject of the cave paintings of South Africa. Among the recent ones, the following are extremely useful: Lowe, C. van Riet, *The Distribution of Prehistoric Rock Engravings and Paintings in South Africa,* Union of South Africa, Department of Education, Arts and Sciences, Archaeological Survey, Archaeological Series, 7, 1952; Bleek, Dorothea F., *Cave Artists of South Africa,* Cape Town: Balkema, 1953; Breuil, Henri, *The White Lady of the Brandberg,* London: Trianon Press, 1955; Willcox, A. R., *Rock Paintings of the Drakensberg, Natal and Griqualand East,* London, M. Parrish, 1956. Among the older works the following are valuable: Burkitt, M. C., *South Africa's Past in Stone and Paint,* Cambridge: Cambridge University Press, 1928; and Stow, G. W., and Bleek, D. F., *Rock-paintings in South Africa from Parts of the Eastern Province and Orange Free State,* London: Methuen, 1931.

6

Culture Contact
and Change

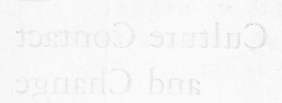

SOME ASPECTS OF NEGRO-MOHAMMEDAN CULTURE-CONTACT AMONG THE HAUSA[*][1]

Joseph H. Greenberg

Something of the general history of the spread of Moslem influence in the Western Sudan has been indicated in Forde's article, "The Cultural Map of West Africa: Successive Adaptations to Tropical Forests and Grasslands," reprinted in this volume. In the present reading, Greenberg is concerned with a specific case of Moslem influence on the Hausa of Northern Nigeria. The impact of Islam in cultures south of the Sahara has taken various forms. The two described here, first the influence of literary works and a specialized literate class among the already con-verted Moslem Hausa, and second the effects of direct culture contact between these Moslemized Hausa and the "pagan" unconverted Hausa, are probably common in the Sudan, though by no means the only type of Islamic influences in Africa. This particular case illustrates how African and Moslem beliefs can become subtly integrated without serious con-flicts and in ways that seem relatively satisfactory to holders of both faiths.

The Hausa-speaking peoples of the central Sudan have been profoundly affected by the impact of Islam over a prolonged period, with the result that at present the vast majority of these folk are practicing Moslems, while the culture of the pagan minority displays an intimate fusion of elements of Negro and Mohammedan origin. The analysis presented here is concerned with the Mohammedanization of the Hausa as this bears on the acculturative processes involved. Although it is believed to be valid in its broad outlines for the Hausa in general, it is only intended to apply in all its details to the inhabitants of Kano Emirate. The data on which these conclusions are based were obtained in Kano itself, an urban center whose population of almost 100,000 is entirely Moslem; in Jigawa and neighboring villages some forty miles west of Kano city in

[*] Reprinted from *American Anthropologist*, 1941, *43*, 51-61, by permission of the author and *American Anthropologist*.

the District of Gwarzo and inhabited predominantly by pagan Hausa; and in 'Dan Zabuwa about thirty miles northwest of Kano city, containing both pagans and Moslems in its vicinity.[2]

In investigating the transformation of Hausa culture effected by Islam, an initial advantage arises from the presence of authentic historical records covering the main incidents of contact. These sources can be classified into three main groups, descriptions of the western Sudan by Arab travelers and geographers (900-1500 A.D.), the works of the celebrated historians who flourished at the Sankore university at Timbuktu during the period of Songhai ascendancy and the subsequent Moroccan conquest (1450-1650 A.D.), and finally local histories written by natives of the Hausa states.[3] Among the latter, the Kano Chronicle deserves special mention, for it goes far beyond the usual bare recounting of names of rulers and lengths of their reign, and thus supplies the indispensable framework for any study of the influence that Islam has exercised in the region of Kano. From these writings, it is clear that the main impulses which converted the bulk of the Hausa to Mohammedanism proceeded, not from Arab traders or elements of the white population of North Africa, but from the Negroes of the central Niger region in the West Sudan. This proselyting activity was carried out, as we shall see, by small parties or single individuals who either departed or became absorbed in the native population.

Because of this absence of prolonged contact with large bodies of other Moslem peoples, the essential acculturative agent has been the books in which Mohammedan teachings are contained. Amalgamation of Mohammedan and aboriginal belief has thus occurred as the end product of a process in which the native learned men, known as Malams, have adapted what they found in sacred texts to the native situation, retaining much of pagan culture at the same time, by fitting it into a Moslem framework. We thus have a situation, in essence acculturative, for which no provision is made in the definition of acculturation advanced by the sub-Committee of the Social Science Research Council wherein only those situations are stated to be acculturative which result when "groups of individuals having different cultures come into continuous first-hand contact." [4]

To understand how this indirect type of contact with Mohammedan doctrines has occurred requires a brief review of the historical data bearing on the question. For the purposes of this exposition it will be convenient to distinguish the main areas of Moslem practice in the North African regions whence Islam underwent its diffusion into the Sudan. There is a western, or Maghrebine area, extending from the Atlantic to the borders of Egypt with its focus in Morocco, and an eastern area, comprising Egypt. It will not be possible here to do more than enumerate a few of the main cultural differences that characterize these areas.

The Maghrib has a Berber ethnic substratum; the "western" style of writing and alphabetical order characterizes its Arabic script; and the dominant legal school is the Malikite. The concept of *baraka*, "blessed-ness," an impersonal force of the *mana* variety has undergone, especially in Morocco, a development so unique and elaborate as to constitute a distinctive cultural feature of the region.[5] The institution of the *'ar*, a conditional curse usually placed upon a saint, the fulfillment of which depends on his failure to carry out a request, is also peculiar to the local area of Morocco.[6] Finally, mention may be made of the peculiar style of decoration known as Moorish, based on the eight-petalled rosette. In Egypt the substratum is Coptic; the oriental form of Arabic script is in use; and the most important legal school is the Shafi'ite. In popular belief an outstanding feature is the role played by spirit possession. This takes two forms, possession by dead saints (*šēḥ*), which is the traditional form, and the *zār* cult, probably imported from Abyssinia within the last century and a half. The belief in the *qarīn*, or soul double, possibly a survival of the ancient Egyptian *ka*,[7] is also peculiar to Egypt.

From these North African regions, three principal routes lead southward across the Sahara to the Sudan. The most westerly requires a relatively short crossing of the Sahara from southern Morocco to the central Niger; the central route goes from Tripoli, in the eastern Maghrib, to Hausa country in the central Sudan; while communication between Egypt and the eastern Sudan is through the Nile valley. The western route was the most important in earlier times (900-1600 A.D.), Islam first reaching the Sudan by this way. The central Niger region, which formed the southern terminus of this route, saw a succession of the great Negro kingdoms of Ghana, Mali, and Songhai, constituting a secondary culture center from which Islamic doctrines, taking the specific and highly characteristic Maghrebine forms received from Morocco, was carried eastward to Kano and the other Hausa centers.

At first this eastward spread of Mohammedanism must have been slow, for it appears not to have reached Hausa country until the fourteenth century when the Mandingo empire of Mali was at the height of its power. Significant information concerning this first contact of Kano with Islam is contained in the Kano Chronicle which describes how Yaji, a ruler of the Kutumbawa dynasty—according to the usual chronology he ruled 1349-1385—was converted by a party of forty men from Mali.[8] This group, never reinforced, became absorbed in the general population of Kano, though its memory has survived in the names of town quarters founded by men in the original party, and the oldest families in these quarters claim descent from them. A far more powerful influence from the same central Niger region was the coming of the Fulani, whose presence in Kano is first recorded during the reign of Yakubu (1452-1463).[9] During their sojourn in Mali, the Fulani had become thoroughly indoctrinated with the teachings of Islam in its Maghrebine form. In Hausa country, they acted as a leaven among the mass of the population, hastening its conversion to Mohammedanism. After their initial appearance, the Fulani came in ever increasing numbers until at the beginning of the nineteenth century they gained political control of the Hausa states.

During the period of Songhai ascendancy in the late fifteenth century and throughout the sixteenth, contact between the Hausa states and the regions to the west continued. The *Tarikh es Sudan* mentions several Songhai notables who, on their return from the pilgrimage to Mecca, settled down in Kano and Katsina to teach for varying lengths of time.[10] Moreover, that the Hausa states owed at least a nominal allegiance to the Songhai rulers for some time appears from the account of Leo Africanus who visited Kano, Katsina, Gobir, and other Hausa cities during the early part of the sixteenth century.[11]

The conquest of Songhai by the army of the Sultan of Morocco at the beginning of the seventeenth century was a turning point in the history of the Sudan. It marked the end of the stable Negro political aggregations in this region and initiated a period of disorder during which trade moved east and the long direct route from Tripoli to the Hausa states came into prominence, producing a marked increase in the prosperity first of Katsina, and later of Kano. Culturally, however, this change involved merely a reinforcement of the Maghrebine influences which had come in earlier times in their more typical Moroccan forms.

The impression drawn from the historical material just reviewed concerning the dominance of cultural currents emanating from the Maghrib, and especially from Morocco, and the relative unimportance of Egypt, finds confirmation in the type of Islam that can be observed in Hausa country today; the Arabic script in use is a variety of the Maghrebine said to have developed at Timbuktu;[12] the Malakite legal school is the only one known to the Hausa; and the popular beliefs of the Hausa more nearly approach those of the Maghrib than of Egypt.

In the rural districts about Kano live a number of Hausa-speaking pagans known as Maguzawa.[13] The process by which Moslem and pagan elements have amalgamated to form pagan Hausa culture involves firsthand contact between these pagans and the Mohammedanized Hausa. It is apparent, therefore, that there are two distinct acculturations proceeding among the Hausa, and in both of them the contributing elements are the aboriginal pagan culture and Mohammedan culture. In the one just cited, the contact is directly between peoples, while among the Moslems, the embodiment of cultural features in literary form and the activities of a specialized literate class has been the acculturative factor. The differences between these two acculturative situations can be illustrated from a consideration of how the Mohammedan belief in a class of spirits called "jinn" has affected the aboriginal cult of spirits of a similar nature, the 'iskoki, with distinct results among the pagan and Moslem Hausa.[14]

The worship of the 'iskoki constitutes the core of pagan Hausa re-ligion, the African character of which has been largely obscured in the literature by a disproportionate emphasis on the Bori or possession cult. For instance, in the list of correspondences between spirits worshipped in various West African cultures listed by Westermann, the Hausa 'iskoki do not figure at all.[15] Krusius' brief, but accurate and well-rounded study, never referred to in the English literature on Bori, places the possession cult in its true perspective as merely one aspect of 'iskoki worship.[16] In this way the affiliations of Maguzawa religion with other forms of West African belief emerge, affiliations clearly demonstrated by the existence of specific correspondences between individual Hausa 'iskoki and the supernatural beings of other West African peoples. Ex-amples of such resemblances include the Hausa Gajimari, conceived as a rainbow serpent, who thus resembles the Yoruban Osumare and the Dahomean Aido Hwedo. Ra, the thunder deity, embodies a conception related to Shango, the Yoruba thunder god, to Xevioso in Dahomey, 'Nyame in Ashanti, and Kenjo among the Jukun. The group of Hausa spirits known as 'Yan Dawa, "children of the forest," have their counter-part in the Dahomey azizā, the Bambara kokolo, and the Yoruba divin-ity Aroni. To the Hausa trickster Nakada, corresponds Legba, the Dahomean god known as Eshu or Elegbara among the neighboring Yo-ruba, and Aku Maga of the Jukun.[17]

The 'iskoki, as conceived by the pagan Hausa, are generally held to be infinite in number, though certain of them are known by name and have definite personalities and powers. Each of these spirits customarily has its favorite type of tree or other specific locale which it visits on oc-casion; and where the proper sacrifices, consisting of sheep, goats, or fowl are offered. These offerings furnish the 'iskoki with the blood which is their sustenance, and placate them so that they will not bring on the diseases they are believed to cause.

The cult of the 'iskoki takes on several forms. Domestic sacrifices are performed semiannually, before the sowing season and after the harvest, at which the head of a Maguzawa compound acts as a family priest. Among some Maguzawa, though not in the region where the field work was carried on, the local headman, known as the Sarkin Noma, "headman of farming," performs rites resembling those carried out by the compound heads, but whose object is the welfare of the whole com-munity. In addition to these rites, anyone may approach the 'iskoki in-dividually by sacrificing to them in his compound, or by always keeping on hand their sacrificial animal. The former method is most often re-sorted to for magical antisocial purposes, the sacrifices being secretly made in order to afflict an enemy with disease.

The most dramatic aspect of 'iskoki worship is the possession cult. In this, the costumes suitable to the spirits who are to be summoned are donned by the initiates and the spirits then come to the sound of appropriate drum rhythms and converse directly with spectators through the mouths of those possessed. A man or woman ordinarily attains membership in the bori cult in one of two ways: by inheritance, when the spirits that possessed a parent come to one of the children, or when illness, determined to have been caused by a spirit, indicates that the victim has been chosen by one of these beings. In this case a cure can only be effected by the performance of an initiation rite lasting fourteen days, during which the initiate is taught how to behave under possession and also learns the medicines to cure the diseases caused by the spirits. Such an initiate may thereafter be consulted by persons suffering from these ailments, and, under possession, will himself reveal the proper remedies, which often utilize the wood of the tree in which a given spirit is held to dwell. The fact that sacrifices to the spirits are performed before a ceremony in exactly the same manner as in the ordinary domestic rites, and that the spirits "called" are the same as those who receive individual and family offerings, demonstrates the relationship of this possession cult to other aspects of 'iskoki worship.

The invasion of this 'iskoki cult among the Maguzawa by Mohammedan patterns is obvious in many details. The integration of cult practices into the Mohammedan week, sacrifices taking place on fixed days, especially Friday and Sunday, the most important of the Moslem weekdays, may serve as an example. This superposition of Moslem influence has been facilitated by the identification of the aboriginal 'iskoki with the jinn, believed in by all Mohammedan peoples. So numerous are the basic resemblances between the cult of the jinn as reported from North Africa and that of the spirits worshipped by West African peoples—the possession of names by these spirits, the prominence of trees as their dwelling place, the causation of disease by them, propitiatory sacrifices consisting of domestic animals, the furnishing of the spirits with blood as the primary purpose of offerings—that this identification could take place with considerable ease.[18] The completeness with which the two concepts have been merged by the Maguzawa is illustrated by the absolute synonymity in native speech of the terms 'aljan (jinn) and 'iska. An important accompaniment of this process has been the application to the 'iskoki of the Mohammedan classification of jinn into "Mohammedan" or white, and "pagan" or black, a division which rests on statements in the Koran that Mohammed converted some of the jinn who thus became Mohammedan, while others refused to listen to his teachings, and remained pagan, or evil.[19] The "Mohammedan" 'iskoki of the Maguzawa are believed to pray and fast in the Moslem manner. Their chief, Malam Alhaji, "Malam, the pilgrim," whose personality may be considered typical of the group, is conceived of as a learned old man, a pilgrim. White, the color of the garments of the pilgrim to Mecca in the state of sanctity known as *'ihrām* is made the keynote of his personality, his clothing all being white while his sacrifice is a white sheep. These "Mohammedan" *'iskoki,* though obviously contact phenomena, are not, as one might assume at first blush, spirits whose cult has been borrowed from Moslem sources, for nowhere among the white jinn of the Mohammedans do we find beings with names and personalities resembling these "Mohammedan" *'iskoki.* In other words, we have here, under the stimulus of Moslem contact, the creation of new spirits; an invention, indeed, in the field of religion.[20]

The free elaboration of Mohammedan elements in accordance with native patterns noted in the above example is characteristic of the Maguzawa treatment of Moslem materials and appears to be a corollary of the conditions under which contact takes place. Pressure from the Malams is only for actual conversion; they show no interest in the incorporation of Mohammedan beliefs into pagan culture. Moreover, the pagan Hausa, living in the rural districts, have their chief contacts with the less educated Malams and with the mass of unlearned Moslems to whom the full significance of Mohammedan practices is generally unknown. Hence the Maguzawa reaction to the Moslems who surround them and with whom they have been in contact for several centuries tends to take the form of spontaneous uncoerced imitation of features of Mohammedan culture and their free reinterpretation and integration with native patterns. As a result of these conditions, in spite of the extent to which the body of Maguzawa culture is ultimately referable to Moslem sources, it remains as truly pagan as, say, Dahomey, where a few elements such as the Mohammedan week days and a system of geomantic divination have penetrated.

The key to the Hausa Malam's attitude toward the *'iskoki* worshipped by the Maguzawa lies in the identification of these spirits with the black or pagan jinn of Mohammedan belief. The Malams conceive of each country as having jinn who practice the same religion as its human inhabitants. It was said, for instance, that there are Gwari jinn in Gwari country, and that when some of the Gwari became converted, some of the jinn embraced Islam at the same time. The casting of spells by incantations called *surkulle,* a practice said to have originated with the cattle Fulani, and still largely confined to them, was revealed by "white" Fulani jinn, the jinn being white because the Fulani are almost entirely Mohammedan. It was only natural for the Malams to conclude, then, that the *'iskoki* were jinn of the Maguzawa, the black jinn native to Hausa country. Hence the cult of the *'iskoki* is assimilated in the minds of the Malams to black magic (Arabic *sihr,* known as *sihiri* to the Hausa), for black magic in Mohammedan countries chiefly involves drawing black jinn into one's service. Therefore, though all phases of *'iskoki* worship are condemned as being *sihiri,* no doubt is thrown on the actual existence of the *'iskoki* or the reality of the effects they produce, such belief being, in fact, a Moslem dogma.[21] Hence, belief in the reality and powers of individual *'iskoki* is retained, particularly their ability to cause disease, for it is held that the jinn of every group causes the diseases suffered by its members. In dealing with the ailments caused by these spirits, the pagan method of offering a sacrificial animal to the *'iska* involved is rejected as *sihiri,* and Mohammedan methods in which some aspects of God's power is utilized to remedy the effects produced by evil spirits, are substituted. For example, the *'iska* Gajere is conceived by the Maguzawa as a dwarf hunter who ranges the forest and shoots his victims, producing a swelling where the arrow penetrates. The treatment suggested by one Malam was the drinking of the ink used in writing chapter 112 of the Koran 33 times.[22] Another method of dealing with this ailment involves the identification of Gajere with the jinn 'Darfaya'ilu. A paper on which a series of nonsense syllables in Arabic, a magic square, and the name of 'Darfaya'ilu is written, is enclosed in a rectangular piece of leather *(laya)* and applied to the part affected by the victim of Gajere before going to sleep. The contents of this same paper are copied on a wooden board *('allo)* and washed off and drunk for seven days in succession.

Such identifications as the one just cited of individual *'iskoki* with jinn mentioned in Arabic words of magic, since they occur in spite of the lack of sharply defined personalities among the jinn, give them a vagueness which stands in striking contrast to the definite characteristics assigned to the *'iskoki.* They thus tend to assume an arbitrary character which is reflected in the marked differences among individual Malams observable in this matter.[23] The Hausa name of the spirit is said to be the "open" one, while the Arabic is the "hidden," or "book," name. This double aspect of things as having an "open" and a "hidden" form recurs in other aspects of the Malams' world-view. The Mohammedan lunar year is said to be the "open" year while the Christian solar years, known especially from works of astrology, is the "hidden" one. There is a "hidden" sun and a "hidden" moon in addition to the generally observable ones, and, according to some, these secret heavenly bodies are visible to white men.

Malams' attitudes toward the "Mohammedan" *'iskoki* of the Maguzawa differ considerably. Some consider them, along with the other *'iskoki* whom the pagans reverence, as black, their cult as *sihiri,* and their attacks to be warded off by the use of Koranic verses. Others accept the Maguzawa evaluation of them as white, or Moslem. Where this attitude is assumed, specific identification with Mohammedan white jinn often occurs and they are assigned a place in the hierarchy of spiritual beings which culminates in God. For, according to the general belief, while the black jinn are free agents of evil, the white jinn are each subordinated to higher beings called *rofanay*,[24] and these in turn are subject to angels, each of whom has access to God through one of His "names," which indicate His separate powers.[25] To work with white jinn is to avail oneself of a particular manifestation of God's omnipotence and is, therefore, not *sihiri* but a legitimate activity.

'Inna, one of the most important of the "white" spirits worshipped by the Maguzawa is envisaged as a Fulani milkmaid. Besides a white ewe, which is her usual sacrifice, a pagan devoted to her first lets a few drops of milk fall on the ground as an offering before he begins milking his cow. She is said to cause *šanyan ƙafa da hannu*, "drinking up (atrophy) of the hand and foot." One Malam identified her with the female jinn Maimuna and described her as dwelling on the *tumpafiya* shrub. As a remedy for atrophy, he recommended the rubbing of the sufferer's body with pulverized *tumpafiya* leaf and the drinking of milk mixed with the ink obtained by washing 'Inna's name from a slate. Thus the native technique of using the plant where a spirit is supposed to dwell is combined with the Mohammedan method of drinking the ink used in writing the spirit's name. Another informant described 'Inna as a Moslem female jinn subordinated to the *rofani* K'amasaya'ilu and the angel Habasaya'ilu. In case a limb atrophied, the procedure was to supplicate her *rofani* and her angel, for by appeasing them, 'Inna herself would be satisfied and cease bothering her victim.

It is clear from what has been said concerning the Mohammedan provenience of much of the *'iskoki* cult among the Maguzawa that the Malams, in rejecting the pagan rites associated with this cult, suppress many elements of ultimate Moslem derivation, while, through their identification of the jinn with *'iskoki,* many aspects of original Hausa belief are retained and incorporated in the synthesis toward which Moslem Hausa culture is tending. Hence the view that the Mohammedanization of the Hausa is a continuous process beginning with the borrowing of Mohammedan elements into the pagan culture, and continuing after conversion to Islam with an ever greater replacement of pagan by Mohammedan features must be rejected as an oversimplification. Conversion is a decisive step involving a shift from the elaboration of patterns of Moslem origin, in native terms characteristic of the influence of Islam on the pagan Hausa, to an acculturation in which the activities of a literate class is the major factor.

NOTES

[Starred items are recommended as further readings.]

[1] Read before the Central Section, American Anthropological Association, Indianapolis, April 26, 1940.

[2] These data were gathered on a field trip carried out during 1938-1939 as a pre-Doctoral Training Fellow of the Social Science Research Council, New York City, under the sponsorship of the Department of Anthropology, Northwestern University.

[3] The only Arab travelers who actually visited the western Sudan were Ibn Hauqal in the 10th century (*The Oriental Geography,* translated by W. Ousely, London, 1800, and *Description de l'Afrique,* translated by Mac Guckin de Slane in the Journal Asiatique, 3 ser., Vol. 13, 1842, pp. 153-196, and 209-258), and Ibn Batutah in the 14th (*Voyages,* translated by Defremery and Sanguinetti, 4 vols., Paris, 1854-1874). Leo Africanus, who passed through the same regions in the 16th century, was a Moor of Granada who wrote in Italian (*The History and Description of Africa done into English by John Pory,* edited by Robert Brown, Hakluyt Society, 3 vols., London, 1896). Arab writers who have left accounts of the Sudan include El Bekri in the 11th century (*Description de l'Afrique septentrionale,* translated by Mac Guckin de Slane, Paris, 1913), El Idrisi in the 12th century (*Description de l'Afrique et de l'Espagne,* translated by R. Dozy and M. J. de Goeje, Leyden, 1866), Yaqut in the 12th century (F. Wüstenfeld, *Jacut's Geographisches Wörterbuch,* Leipzig, 1866-1870), Abulfeda in the 14th century (*Géographie d'Aboulféda,* translated by M. Reinard, 2 vols., Paris, 1848), El Omari in the 14th century (*Masalik el absar fi mamalik el amsar,* translated by Gaudefroy-Demombynes, Bibliothèque des géographes arabes, Vol. 2, Paris, 1927), and Ibn-Klhadun in the 14th century (*Histoire des Berbères et des dynasties musulmanes de l'Afrique septentrionale,* translated by Mac Guckin de Slane, 2 vols., Paris, 1925). The chief surviving works of Sudanese writers are the *Tarikh es Sudan* of Es Sa'di (*Tarikh es Sudan,* translated by O. Houdas, Publications de l'éole des langues orientales vivantes, Vol. 13, Paris, 1898), the *Tarikh el Fettach* of Mahmed Ka'ti (*Tarikh el Fettach,* translated by O. Houdas and M. Delafosse, Publications de l'école des langues orientale vivantes, sér. 5, Vol. 10, Paris, 1913), and the *Tedzkiret en Nisian* of uncertain authorship (*Tedzkiret en Nisian fi Akhbar Molouk es Soudan,* translated by O. Houdas, Publications de l'école des langues *orientales* vivantes, sér. 5, Vol. 20, Paris, 1899-1901). The chief indigenous sources for the history of Air, Bornu and the Hausa states are to be found in H. R. Palmer's *Sudanese Memoirs** (3 vols., Lagos, 1928). Mention may also be made of Al Hadji Said's *Tarikh es Sokoto* published in the same volume as the *Tedzkiret en Nisian.*

[*4] R. Redfield, R. Linton, and M. J. Herskovits, "A Memorandum for the Study of Acculturation (*American Anthropologist,* Vol. 38, 1936), p. 149.

[*5] For an extended treatment of *baraka,* see E. A. Westermarck's *The Moorish Conception of Holiness (baraka)* (Helsingfors, 1916).

[*6] E. A. Westermarck, *Ritual and Belief in Morocco* (London, 1926), Vol. 1, p. 22.

[7] This is the explanation advanced by C. G. Seligman in his essay *Ancient Egyptian Beliefs in Modern Egypt* (Essays and Studies Presented to William Ridgeway, Cambridge, 1913), pp. 448-451.

[8] H. R. Palmer, "The Kano Chronicle" (*Journal Royal Anthropological Institute,* Vol. 38, 1908), p. 76.

[9] *Ibid.*

[10] *Tarikh es Sudan,* translated by O. Houdas, p. 64.

[11] *Leo Afrikanus,* translated by J. Pory, Vol. 3, p. 830.

[12] O. Houdas, *Essai sur l'écriture*

Maghrebine (Publications de l'école des langues orientales vivantes, 2 sér., Vol. 19), pp. 111-112.

13 According to the 1920 decennial census, 5.95% of the Hausa population of Kano province are Maguzawa. C. K. Meek, *Northern Tribes of Nigeria* (2 vols., London, 1925), Vol. 2, p. 250.

14 Of the several terms for spirit current among the Hausa, *'iska* (plural, *'iskoki*), is the most general in application, referring to all aspects of the cult; it is at the same time the expression commonly used by the natives themselves. *Bori* (plural, *borruruka*), is appropriate to the possession by the spirits of their worshippers. *'Aljan, say'dan* and *'ibilis* are of Arabic origin and reflect the identification of the Hausa *'iskoki* with the Mohammedan jinn discussed below.

15 "Gottesvorstellungen in Oberguinea" (*Africa*, Vol. 1, 1928), p. 198.

16 P. Krusius, "Die Maguzawa" (*Archiv für Anthropologie*, Vol. 42, 1915), pp. 228-315. P. G. Harris' failure to mention this article in the bibliography of Bori contained in "Notes on Yauri (Sokoto Province), Nigeria" (*Journal Royal Anthropological Institute*, Vol. 60, 1930), pp. 326-327, is an example of this neglect.

17 The comparative material cited above is drawn from the following sources: Ashanti (R. S. Rattray, *Ashanti,** Oxford, 1923); Bambara (L. Tauxier, *Religion Bambara,** Paris, 1927); Dahomey (M. J. Herskovits, *Dahomey,** New York, 1938); Jukun (C. K. Meek, *A Sudanese Kingdom, An Ethnographic Study of the Jukun-Speaking Peoples of Nigeria,** London, 1931); Yoruba (S. S. Farrow, *Faiths, Fancies and Fetish of Yoruba Paganism*, London, 1924).

18 It is significant to note that this phenomenon of the identification of African spirits with the jinn has occurred at least at two other points widely separated from the Hausa under contact with Islam—among the Bambara of the upper Niger (L. Tauxier, *La Religion Bambara*, Paris, 1927, p. 8), and in East Africa among the Swahili-speaking peoples where the Arabic Shaitān (black jinn)

are merged with the native *mzimu* (H. Kuritschoner, "Ngoma ya Sheitani, an East African Native Treatment for Psychical Disorder," *Journal Royal Anthropological Institute,* Vol. 66, 1936, p. 209). These results, moreover, are quite comparable to those recorded in the New World where Negroes have identified West African deities and Catholic saints. Such identifications are reported from Brazil (A. Ramos, *O Negro Brasileiro,* Rio De Janeiro, 1934); Cuba (F. Ortiz, *Los Negros Brujos,* Madrid, no date); and Haiti (M. J. Herskovits, *Life in a Haitian Valley,* New York, 1937).

19 Koran, vii, 177; lxxii, 1-3.

20 This appears to be an example of what Kroeber has called stimulus diffusion, ". . . the birth of a pattern new to the culture in which it develops, though not completely new in human culture . . ." (A. L. Kroeber, "Stimulus Diffusion," *American Anthropologist,* Vol. 42, 1940, p. 20). In the present instance, the idea of a division of spirits into Moslem and pagan is borrowed from Mohammedan sources, while the manner in which it is carried out involves an invention in Maguzawa culture.

21 Cf. E. Doutté, *Magie et religion dans l'Afrique du Nord* (Algiers, 1909), p. 355.

22 This is one of the two chapters (112 and 114), known as the *mu'awwidhatāni,* "the two warders off (of evil)," used as remedies for a great variety of complaints.

23 The degree of divergence is extraordinary, for though a good number of those identifications were recorded, there was not a single instance in which two Malams identified the same *'iska* with the same jinn.

24 The *rofanay* (Hausa singular *rofani,* from the Arabic *rūhānī,* "spiritual") are, in classical Arabic astrology, the spirits that move the planets (Winkler, *Siegel und Charaktere in der muhammedanischen Zauberei,* Studien zur Geschichte des islamischen Orients, Vol. 7, Berlin, 1930, p. 12). In Morocco the term is commonly used synonymously with jinn

but, according to Westermarck, it is sometimes used to designate only those jinn who live between the earth and the sky (*Ritual and Belief in Morocco,* Vol. I, 262); among the Moslem Hausa the *rofany* are a class of spirits who live in the atmosphere above the earth, transmitting messages from the angels to the white jinn.

[25] The doctrine of the "names of God" is based on the Koran (vii, 179), where the faithful are told that "God's names are the good ones; call on Him thereby . . ." (translation E. H. Palmer, Oxford, 1900, p. 143). The later traditionalists, at Tirmidhi and Ibn Maja (10th century), give divergent lists of 99 epithets of God, while the manipulation of these names and the numbers derived from the letters composing them is at the base of the classical medieval work of al Buni on magic (*Šamsu 'lma'ārifi 'lklnbrā,* printed in Cairo, 1874).

FOR FURTHER READING

Greenberg, Joseph H., *The Influence of Islam on a Sudanese Religion,* New York: Augustin, American Ethnological Society, Monographs, No. 10, 1946; and Greenberg, Joseph H., "Islam and Clan Organization among the Hausa," *Southwestern Journal of Anthropology,* 1947, 3, 193-211. These publications discuss the culture contact situation in detail.

See the article by Daryll Forde, "The Cultural Map of West Africa: Successive Adaptations to Tropical Forests and Grasslands," in this volume, and the suggestion for further reading following it.

Parrinder, Geoffrey, *Religion in an African City,* London: Oxford University Press, 1953. Includes an analysis of Moslem groups in Ibadan, Nigeria.

John Spencer Trimingham has written a number of books on the spread of Islam in Africa from the point of view of a Christian missionary. They include *Islam in Ethiopia,* London: Oxford University Press, 1952; *Islam in the Sudan,* London: Oxford University Press, 1949; *Islam in West Africa,* Oxford: Clarendon Press, 1959.

There are several valuable surveys of the French area, though they are generally based on older material. These include: Gouilly, Alphonse, *L'Islam dans l'Afrique Occidentale Française,* Paris: Larose, 1952; Marty, Paul, *Études sur l'Islam et les tribus maures,* Paris: Leroux, 1921; Marty, Paul, *Études sur l'Islam et les tribus du Soudan,* Paris: Leroux, 1920-1921, 4 vols.; Marty, Paul, *Études sur l'Islam au Sénégal,* Paris: Leroux, 1917, 2 vols.; Marty, Paul, *L'Islam et les tribus dan la colonie du Niger,* Paris: Geuthner, 1932; Marty, Paul, *Études sur l'Islam en Côte d'Ivoire,* Paris: Leroux, 1922; Marty, Paul, *Études sur l'Islam au Dahomey,* Paris: Leroux, 1926.

CHRISTIANITY AND THE TSWANA*

I. Schapera

Anthropologists have seldom studied the impact of Christianity on African peoples in any detail, though they have been very much concerned with the political and economic repercussions of European contact. The precise nature of Christian influence in Africa is hard to distinguish from the influences of Western culture in general. Furthermore, scientific evaluations of the effects of change are difficult to make, and there is much disagreement among social scientists and among missionaries as to the influence of Christianity on African culture.

Schapera's careful argument is based partly on source material and partly on his own experiences of many years as an anthropologist among the Tswana. The Tswana, who number more than 800,000, are a Bantu-speaking people who are divided into a number of tribes and clusters of tribes in Bechuanaland and the neighboring areas of the Union of South Africa. They are agriculturalists and cattle herders, though fair numbers today work as laborers in urban centers. They have had a long history of contact with Europeans.

The scope of the Henry Myers Lectures is defined broadly as the place of religious belief in human development. When invited to give this year's lecture, I was working through the letters and journals that David Livingstone wrote in 1841-52, while stationed in what is now the Bechuanaland Protectorate. In these he mentions repeatedly that almost everywhere he went he was the first European missionary the Natives had seen, and that before his coming to them they had never even heard of the gospel. One of the tribes to whom he preached, in December 1848, were the Kgatla.[1] Just over eighty years later, in 1929, I started field work among them, and soon learned that Christianity is now their official religion. That is also true, I subsequently found, of most Tswana tribes in the Protectorate.[2] Christianity has become well established everywhere, and its adherents usually include the chiefs and many other important people.

* The Henry Myers Lecture, delivered on March 18, 1958. Reprinted from *Journal of the Royal Anthropological Institute*, 1958, *88*, 1-9, by permission of the author and the publisher.

It has recently been claimed by Dr. Emory Ross (1955, p. 168) that "Christianity, in direct and indirect ways, has had probably the most fundamental, widespread, and creative effect of any element entering Africa south of the Sahara in modern time." Other writers say, similarly, that "Missionaries in Africa transformed the lives of the blacks and inculcated the principles of humility, love, obedience, peacefulness, of work and honesty, of cleanliness and sanitation" (Jabavu 1927, p. 113); that "Christian missions have represented the greatest conscious force for change operating upon Bantu life, [and] have deeply affected Bantu thought and culture" (Brookes 1934, p. 153); and that "Missions have intensively contributed to the modern transformation of Africa, and have become a cultural factor in the evolution of the African man which cannot be ignored" (Westermann 1937, p. 1).

Such generalizations are a commonplace in missionary literature. If valid, they show that in Africa at least one form of religious belief has done very much indeed for human development. I propose therefore to examine them, by taking as my theme for today a discussion of how the introduction of Christianity by Livingstone and other missionaries has affected tribal life in Bechuanaland.

It is not quite a century since regular missionary work began in most of the country. Livingstone was with the Kwena from 1845-51, but other tribes first received resident European missionaries during the period 1859-71 or even later. Those missionaries seldom worked in complete isolation from Europeans with interests of other kinds. Livingstone on his travels often came to natives who had never before seen a white man, but sometimes he had been preceded by others, and after his discovery of Lake Ngami in 1849 traders and sportsmen visited Bechuanaland in ever-increasing numbers. By 1885, when the proclamation of the Protectorate brought the tribes under British rule, there were already European trading stores in all the central villages, and many Tswana had already been as migrant laborers to European areas of what is now the Union of South Africa. Several other innovations soon followed, including European government officers, the creation of tribal reserves, and taxation in money. The Protectorate Administration later did much to modernize the indigenous political system, improve agriculture, and develop such social services as education and public health. From the beginning Christian missions thus constituted only one of several European agencies engaged in transforming Tswana life.

Evidence of distinctively Christian influence is however readily apparent. In every tribal capital, a settlement sometimes containing 10,000 or more inhabitants, there is at least one large and impressive church building of European design, and the few European residents[3] invariably include clerical and other mission workers. Churches more modest in size and appearance are found in many other villages. Their presence reflects the fact that nearly 80,000 Africans in Bechuanaland—(27 per cent of the total[4])—are said to be Christians.

Professing Christians differ from fellow-tribesmen in belonging to a church, a form of social grouping previously unknown. The great majority (65 per cent) are Congregationalists (London Missionary Society); the others are chiefly Calvinists (Dutch Reformed Church), (15 per cent), Lutherans (8 per cent), Anglicans (5 per cent), Methodists (3.5 per cent), and Roman Catholics (2 per cent). The two largest denominations accept members after a period of probation and religious instruction extending over three years (L.M.S.) or two (D.R.C.); candidates must be at least sixteen years old, and able to read. The members in every convenient area, say part of a tribal reserve, constitute a separate church governed by a local court of elders and deacons headed by a minister or an evangelist. These offices, unlike traditional positions of leadership and authority, are achieved primarily through special training and moral character, not right of birth, and since some are paid they also provide a new source of income.

Christians worship together in their own building on Sundays and other occasions, the senior officer present usually taking the service. The church officers also conduct or supervise such other routine activities as Sunday School for children, special classes for catechumens, periodical meetings for women, and (in some tribes) "youth movements" for boys and girls; they visit members at home, comfort the sick and afflicted, and bury the dead with Christian rites; and they occasionally organize concerts and similar social gatherings. In these and various other ways people professing Christianity share interests and activities that cut across the traditional pattern of social life and distinguish them as a separate section of the tribe.

In addition, they have to observe special rules of conduct. Some of these are new features in Tswana life. They include, for example, regular attendance at church services (especially communion, of which a record is kept), observance of Sunday as a day of rest, marriage in church, and baptism of infant children. Church members must also pay an annual due (varying usually from five to ten shillings), should purchase and read the Bible and other religious works, and should dress "respectably," i.e. in the European manner. Other rules prohibit certain traditional usages. Applying the moral code to which they themselves were accustomed, missionaries of all denominations condemned as depraved and disgusting various common practices, which they accordingly insisted that converts should abandon. With rare exceptions the prohibitions are still in force. Among the usages affected are *bogwêra* and *bojale* (the initiation rites for boys and girls respectively), polygyny, the levirate and sororate, rainmaking and other forms of magic, and dancing by adults. Most churches also prohibit the giving of *bogadi* (marriage cattle), and some the drinking of alcohol, including the indigenous Kafir beer. Church members everywhere are further expected to refrain from extra-marital sex relations. Violation of such rules is dealt with by the mission authorities, who may, for example, publicly censure or even excommunicate the offender.

But except for their special activities and obligations, Christians are not as a group socially distinct. In ordinary daily life and domestic ceremonies they associate together freely with the pagans, some of whom occasionally even go to church as a pastime or out of curiosity, and there is no obvious means of telling the two sections apart. Elsewhere in Southern Africa Christians and pagans sometimes live in separate villages, or differ in dress, Christians wearing European clothing and pagans the traditional Native costume. In Bechuanaland there is no such residential segregation, and except when in the veld almost everybody but young children wears European clothing of some kind. Superior types of housing and furniture, improved farming methods, and similar signs of material progress, are not necessarily confined to Christians. Even literacy is no longer the monopoly of their class.

Missionary activity, indeed, has in some ways influenced the tribal population generally. The missions introduced and for long were solely responsible for school education; early missionaries also reduced the Tswana language to writing, and helped to create a small but growing body of literature in the vernacular, including several periodicals. It is not merely Christians who have taken to these innovations. More recently mission societies have built and staffed the only hospitals in certain tribal areas; some also give special training in arts and crafts. These services too are available to all.

From the beginning missionaries also acted as secretaries of the chiefs, who relied upon them for guidance in dealing with other Europeans. After the proclamation of the Protectorate they often advised the Administration about local affairs in areas where resident officers had not yet been stationed. With modern developments in the governmental system there is much less need for such services, though on occasion missionaries still intervene in tribal politics. Again, it was partly owing to Livingstone's influence on public opinion in England that the Transvaal Boers were prevented from occupying Bechuanaland. A later L.M.S. missionary, John Mackenzie, was among those chiefly responsible for the proclamation of the British Protectorate. In 1895 the L.M.S. itself, by sponsoring the visit of several chiefs to England, helped to prevent transfer of the administration to Cecil Rhodes's B.S.A. Company. Missionary influence on Tswana life has thus by no means been confined to the field of religion.

The ordinary tribesman was more directly affected when chiefs adopted and enforced certain church laws as tribal laws binding upon pagans as well as Christians. For example, *bogwêra* and *bojale* are now widely prohibited, *bogadi* was abolished among the Ngwato and Tawana, beer-drinking is prohibited among the Ngwato and restricted in several other tribes, leviratic unions are legally invalid among the Ngwato, and polygyny is forbidden among the Ngwaketse without special permission from the chief. But even where still allowed to practice them, many pagans have voluntarily abandoned such marriage customs as polygyny and *bogadi*. Their abstention is obviously not a dictate of church membership. It is nevertheless due at least partly to the spread of missionary influence. That influence is apparent also in generally-accepted changes in the social status of women, who now enjoy marriage and property rights formerly denied to them. Similarly, the marriage and death ceremonies of pagans often include elements borrowed from Christian usage.

Sunday is now universally enforced as a day of rest for Christians and pagans alike. Several tribal courts have punished men for inspanning wagons or ploughing on that day, and in 1939 the Ngwaketse public assembly refused the Seventh Day Adventists permission to build a church, because (speakers said) that denomination "does not honor Sunday, which with us is a great law." Sometimes people have also been obliged to give money or unpaid labor for building churches. In 1903, for example, the Kgatla chief Lentswe imposed a special levy of £5 per head for that purpose upon all members of a certain age-regiment; and the Ngwato chief Kgama, after moving his capital to Serowe in 1902, raised more than £7,000 from his people to meet the cost of a new church, in the actual building of which he also employed the whole of an age-regiment.

Tribal ritual too has been affected. The chief was formerly responsible for organizing certain great public ceremonies, in some of which he personally officiated as priest or magician. Among them were rainmaking and other annual rites connected with the cycle of agricultural activity, the initiation of boys and girls into membership of age-regiments, and the occasional "doctoring" of the army, tribal capital, and tribal boundaries. Almost everywhere they have been either completely abandoned or much modified. In some tribes, for example, rainmaking has been replaced by an annual day for prayer for rain, and the old harvest festival by a special thanksgiving service. These new ceremonies, sometimes held in church, are publicly announced and attended by Christians and pagans alike, and both missionary and chief take part in conducting them. Such other national events as a chief's installation, marriage, or funeral, nowadays usually also include a religious service under church auspices. In effect, the missionary has virtually replaced the chief as tribal priest for both Christians and pagans.

It is more difficult to generalize about religious beliefs. We must assume that members of a church normally subscribe to the Christian faith as taught to them. Pagans are often also familiar with what Christians profess to believe. But, if I may judge from discussions with some of them, they ridicule such Bible stories as the fall of Adam and the virgin birth, and are decidedly sceptical of such doctrines as the second coming and the resurrection of the dead. They seem, however, to have no organized religion of their own. The Christian conception of God, widely and continuously propagated for eighty years or more, has almost completely displaced that of the old supreme deity *Modimo,* whose very name it has usurped. Magicians when at work sometimes pray for success to dead chiefs and their own ancestors, and in cases of illness diviners sometimes prescribe a healing ceremony that includes prayer to the ancestors said to be responsible. With a few such exceptions, ancestor worship too has virtually disappeared; it certainly does not figure at all nowadays in many of the contexts described by early writers on the Tswana.

But the practice of magic still persists strongly. Professional magicians (*dingaka*) continue to flourish everywhere, and despite widely-expressed scepticism of their claims few are the people who do not resort to them on occasion. Almost everybody, whether pagan or Christian, employs protective and fertility magic of various kinds for himself and his family, his huts, cattle, and fields; even at essentially Christian feasts, like those held at the homes of people newly accepted into church membership, steps are sometimes taken to charm both participants and food against sorcery; and magicians delight in telling of church officers who have surreptitiously sought their aid. Court cases show also that deliberate attempts to bewitch other people are still fairly common, and among those convicted have been Christians as well as pagans. Christianity may have provided them with an acceptable substitute for the old religion, but has apparently not been able to convince them that their faith in the efficacy of magic is idle superstition. One obvious reason is that, outside the capital, magicians are usually the only medical practitioners readily available. That alone would be sufficient to ensure that they are still employed in times of need.

Christianity has also affected the cultural homogeneity of the Tswana in general. In some instances it has led to greater uniformity. For example, almost all Christians among the Ngwato, Kwena, Ngwaketse, and Tawana, belong to the L.M.S. Their religious community is enhanced by the occasional transfer of European missionaries and Native ministers or evangelists from one tribe to another; together, moreover, their churches now constitute the Central Regional Council of the L.M.S. in Southern Africa. In contrast, Christians are predominantly Calvinists among the Kgatla, Lutherans among the Malete, and Methodists among the Rolong. Hence, although over 95 per cent of Christians in Bechuanaland are Protestants, they often differ intertribally in details of organization, ritual, and belief. Some tribes have apparently also embraced Christianity more extensively than others. The 1946 census returns show, for example, that Christians comprise 65 per cent of the Kgatla, 38 per cent of the Kwena and Ngwaketse, and only 7 per cent of the Ngwato. But these figures, even if correct, are not a true index of cultural change, since through their chief Kgama (1872-1923) the Ngwato as a tribe were subjected to more Christian reforms than any of the others.

Tribes nowadays sometimes also differ in regard to customs formerly found everywhere. For example, *bogwêra* and *bojale* persist only among the Malete and Tlôkwa, but the Kgatla, unlike others, still have initiation ceremonies retaining much of the old ritual apart from circumcision itself; *bogadi,* completely abandoned by Ngwato and Tawana, is obligatory for Christians among the Kgatla and for everybody among the Ngwaketse, and elsewhere is forbidden to Christians but not pagans; polygyny is legally restricted among the Ngwaketse alone, and only the Ngwato have total prohibition of alcohol. Such differences are due essentially to the policies of the various tribal chiefs, and not of the churches concerned; both Ngwato and Ngwaketse, for example, have long been fields of the L.M.S., yet their laws about *bogadi,* polygyny, and beer, are by no means alike.

The spread of Christian influence among the Tswana has not been the work of the missionaries alone. The Administration for some time subsidized their educational activities and nowadays supports their hospitals; Government legislation, moreover, prohibits the supply of European liquor to Natives, witch-finding and certain other forms of divination, and the forcible subjection of young people to circumcision ceremonies. These measures all contribute to the realization of missionary objectives. The modern cost of maintaining and paying tax for more than one wife has similarly aided in the decline of polygyny, just as the new value cattle have acquired as draught animals and objects of trade makes some men regard *bogadi* as a wasteful practice.

But the missions have not always been able to count on such external assistance. They cannot work in any tribe without its consent, and if that is withheld the Administration will not intervene. The Administration has also taken the control of education out of their hands, and has refused occasional requests from them for the statutory prohibition of *bogwêra* and *bogadi.* In any event, most of them were established in Bechuanaland before it became a Protectorate; consequently they had for many years to work without Government help at all.

However, the early missionaries were usually well received by the Tswana; sometimes they were even specifically invited to come. This was due mainly to the material benefits which they as Europeans were thought able to provide, such as protection from enemies and supplies of firearms and beads; their presence also gave much prestige to any chief with whom they settled. There was little enthusiasm for their message itself. The people objected strongly to their condemnation of polygyny and rainmaking, and saw no good reason for adopting what seemed to be merely the white man's customs, like kneeling in prayer or observing the Sabbath. "To be plain with you," said one of the Kwena to Living-stone, "we should like you much better if you traded with us and then went away, without forever boring us with preaching that word of God of yours" (Chamberlin 1940, p. 105).

Because of this and the other difficulties inevitably confronting them as pioneer settlers, the missionaries at first made little progress. Their early converts did however include some influential men, who believed that learning to read would endow them with the same knowledge and skill as Europeans. That belief, and increasing dependence on missionary help in foreign relations, were among the motives that by the end of the century, and sometimes much sooner, had induced most of the chiefs themselves to embrace Christianity. Their conversion did not mean the mass conversion of their tribe, which indeed was incompatible with the missionary emphasis on individual salvation. But it certainly stimulated others by making profession of Christianity both fashionable and safe. It also meant that from now on the chief gave the mission material as-sistance, as in building churches and schools and encouraging the people to go to them.

Once converted, moreover, he normally excluded other missionary societies from his tribe. The Lutherans, admitted by the Kwena in 1857, several years after Livingstone's departure, were expelled in 1864 to make way for the return of the L.M.S. They were subsequently refused permis-sion to work among the Kgatla, where the Dutch Reformed Church was already established. The Roman Catholics were similarly rebuffed by the Ngwato in 1879 and the Ngwaketse in 1929. Some tribes have fairly recently admitted societies offering services not already given locally, notably medical assistance. Intertribal migration too has led to wide-spread religious diversity. But even now no tribe has more than two different societies stationed in its midst, and in the majority between 80 and 90 percent of the Christians still belong to one denomination.

This restrictive policy long spared the Tswana the spectacle, so com-mon elsewhere in South Africa, of rival Christian churches competing for members. Even so, Christianity has often led to internal dispute. Sometimes, for example, a pagan chief tried to make converts participate in ceremonies forbidden to them, notably circumcision. But on the whole Christians were not widely persecuted, and very few if indeed any suffered actual martyrdom. Much more commonly trouble arose after the chief himself had become a Christian. His people seldom objected violently to his doing so, nor even to his then ordering them to observe the Sabbath, which indeed merely provided the pagans with a new taboo. But most chiefs decided also to abolish ceremonies for which they were personally responsible, such as circumcision and rainmaking. Kgama went further, and prohibited beer-drinking, *bogadi,* and other usages that chiefs elsewhere preferred to leave alone. All such reforms were resented by at least some of the pagans, who both criticized the chief and sometimes defied the prohibition.

Some chiefs, possibly because not truly converted, yielded to public opinion. Among both Kwena and Tawana, for example, they restored circumcision, which however was abolished again by later chiefs. Some sought to compromise. Thus, among the Kgatla, Lentswe instituted an annual churchday of prayer for rain, but in times of drought also resorted to old rainmaking ceremonies; and his successor Isang persuaded the mission authorities to withdraw their objection to *bogadi,* which accordingly is now an essential prerequisite to marriage in church. Other chiefs were more inflexible. Kgama was baptized in 1860, during the lifetime of his pagan father Sekgoma, whom he soon antagonized by refusing to observe certain customs. This ultimately led to civil war. Kgama expelled Sekgoma and made himself chief. He then proceeded to enforce various church laws and other reforms, punishing those who did not obey. But even he never dared to abolish polygyny, and at one time, threatened with wholesale secession, he also rescinded his prohibition of beer-drinking, which he did not renew until many years later. Among the Ngwaketse circumcision was banned in 1902. Successive chiefs rigorously enforced the law, yet in 1940 the present chief still felt obliged to announce that violators would be punished. Many other instances are known of such resistance to prohibitions imposed in the name of Christianity. Even now, though less readily than before, a chief's political opponents can usually gain support by promising to restore old usages that have been abolished.

Conflicts have also developed between Christian chiefs and their missionaries. Some chiefs, jealous of their dignity, claimed the same authority in church affairs as in other aspects of tribal life, and if resisted became decidedly unfriendly. Kgama was an outstanding example. Others objected strongly to being censured for personal misconduct such as adultery or drunkenness. In these and similar cases the Native church officers usually supported the missionary; and when, as sometimes happened, they included prominent aristocrats, the dispute soon spread into the field of tribal politics generally. Both Kwena and Ngwato, for example, were long troubled by serious factional rivalries, in which chiefs were opposed by close relatives ostensibly defending the church, though probably inspired also by personal ambition.

Missionaries themselves have sometimes given offense. Some are remembered with gratitude and affection for what they did to promote tribal welfare, the helpful advice they gave the chief, and the friendliness and sympathy shown in their everyday relations with the people. Others became so disliked owing to autocracy, intolerance, aloofness, and rudeness, that the chief had much public support in insisting upon their removal. Such action was taken, for example, among Ngwato, Ngwaketse, and Malete; and one missionary had to be transferred by his Society from three successive stations because of complaints about his behavior. In other instances it was only through direct intervention from mission headquarters that grievances were settled less drastically.

The personal factor was thus of considerable importance in the local history of Christianity. How the people reacted to the message of the gospel was often determined largely by the character of the man who gave it to them, or by the way in which their chief himself was influenced by the new doctrine.

At least twice, among the Ngwaketse in 1901 and Kgatla in 1937, disciplinary action by an unpopular missionary against a popular Native teacher led to the latter's seceding to form a church of his own. But although at the time a cause of public unrest and political intrigue, such churches soon collapsed or ceased to exist after the founder's death. Separatism in Bechuanaland has never developed to anything like the same extent as in the Union of South Africa, and today there are apparently no separatist churches at all in any tribal area. A few of those in the Union have tried to establish branches locally, but the chiefs concerned have invariably refused to admit them. The reason commonly given was in some such form as the following: "One religion is enough for my people to introduce any others would only cause trouble" (cf. Schapera 1947, p. 63).

At one time there was also widespread dissatisfaction with the educational policy of the missions. Their limited financial resources did not allow them to build many schools or employ proper teachers, and some people objected also to the kind of instruction given, which consisted mainly of religious preparation and the rudiments of literacy in the vernacular. A visiting expert reported in 1906 that the country was "in an exceptionally backward state as regards education" (Sargant 1906, p. 2). In several tribes the chiefs sought to remedy this by special taxation, claiming in return for their help a say on expenditure; occasionally they even established rival schools of their own. Gradually, and with Government support, control of the schools was transferred to tribal committees on which the Administration, missions, and people were all represented. In 1930 the Administration assumed responsibility for educational policy throughout the Protectorate, entrusting each tribe with the management of all schools in its own reserve. This led to rapid improvement. Today missionary societies are still represented on the tribal committees, but out of more than 150 schools in Bechuanaland only four (all outside the reserves) are conducted under purely missionary auspices. One result is that some churches now claim difficulty in finding enough suitable candidates for the ministry and other religious offices.

I mentioned above that a Christian chief's reforms were often opposed by some of his people. Resistance to that aspect of missionary teaching was and is not even now confined to pagans. Many Tswana are evidently devout and honest Christians, sincere in their professions of faith, and seeking to live according to the gospel. But some baptized as children are never confirmed, and some accepted into the church cease to be members. Others maintain their allegiance, but do not always behave as they should. They have illicit love affairs, drink beer, resort to magicians, seldom go to communion, and in various other ways show that they are Christians in name only. To some of the younger people the church is merely a place where they can parade in their best and make assignations; their elders become tired of attending regularly, and comment in disgust that it does not seem to give them greater prosperity than pagans enjoy; and some, not always unjustifiably, criticize church officers as dictatorial, proud, and partial in administering the law. Records of the Dutch Reformed Church in Mochudi (the Kgatla capital) show that by 1926 nearly 30 per cent of some 900 members had relapsed or were continuously under censure, among them even elders and teachers; and in 1931 membership of the L.M.S. in Molepolole (the Kwena capital) was reduced from 600 to 450 "by purging the roll and insisting on a high standard of Church loyalty and discipline" (Shepherd 1947, p. 46). No wonder that pagans sometimes accuse Christians of being hypocrites who pretend to be but are in fact no better than themselves.

Almost everywhere, too, the great majority of church members are women. In some tribes they outnumber men in the proportion of nearly three to one. A church conference among the Kgatla in 1932 noted that 105 girls but only four boys had recently been confirmed, and gloomily visualized a future in which elders, evangelists, and ultimately even the minister, would all be women. "This matter," adds the report, "was discussed a very long time, and with very sore hearts." One reason for the difference is that the economic system compels many men and boys to work abroad and look after cattle in the veld; they are thus unable to attend catechumen classes regularly for the two or three years considered essential. Women stay at home much more continuously, and find the church and its activities a welcome diversion from household routine.

But some men openly object to joining the church because they dislike the restrictions it imposes upon their conduct. It is primarily also weariness of those restrictions, and not loss of faith in the Christian God, that usually makes others abandon or forfeit membership. Particularly irksome is the church code of sexual morality. Some people assert naively its aim is merely to keep down the birth rate. As one magician commented, "The church elders tell us that God said 'Be fruitful and multiply,' yet they preach against fornication and call us unchaste; but how can we be many if we do not use our women?" And violations are common, both before and after marriage. Concubinage is perhaps the main cause of censure, and is a problem that churches throughout Bechuanaland admit to be very difficult.

Another objection sometimes raised, even by Christians, is that Europeans still dominate in church affairs. "Missionaries," Dr. Edwin Smith wrote thirty years ago (1926, p. 281), "are not a permanent factor in the life of Africa—they will one day (the sooner the better) disappear because no longer needed." In this he was stating what is nowadays widely held to be the chief aim of missionary endeavor: the creation of self-supporting, self-propagating, and self-governing churches. In Bechuanaland church buildings are usually considered tribal property; there are now several Native ministers in addition to many evangelists and other religious teachers, all supported from local funds; and the court managing the internal affairs of each church consists predominantly if not exclusively of Native members. But European mission societies still control church policy in every tribe, and European mission workers have actually increased with the provision of medical and other social services.

It may well be, as Dr. Goodall says (1954, p. 283), that owing to "the numerical weakness of the African ministry"—itself, incidentally, a reflection on missionary achievement—the Tswana still lack "capacity for self-government in matters ecclesiastical." There is also reason to believe that some chiefs prefer the present system. They tolerate missionary control of the church, just as they must tolerate the superior powers of the European Administration. But if the church were entirely in the hands of their own people, they would find some of their subjects claiming autonomy in an important sphere of tribal life. That they are not willing to concede. Other Tswana, however, nowadays view the persistence and recent extension of missionary activity merely as additional evidence that Europeans are determined to keep them dependent.

Some even say that Christianity belies its own pretensions. They observe that of Europeans resident in the tribal areas only mission workers habitually attend the same church as themselves. Among the Ngwato, indeed, missionaries were holding separate services for European traders in the capital as far back as the 1870's and a special church for Europeans was built there more than fifty years ago. Some Europeans do not go to church at all, and make no secret of their unbelief. The impression conveyed by such local *apartheid* and indifference is greatly strengthened by labor migration. Tswana working abroad soon learn that many Europeans pay little or no heed to religion, and that Christian ideals of brotherhood and social equality tend to vanish before distinctions of color. They return even more sceptical of missionary aims and professions, and less willing than ever to incur the moral and financial obligations of church membership.

It has been said by Dr. Werner Eiselen, himself the son of a missionary, that "the Christian gospel was, during the nineteenth century, the most powerful agency in the disintegration of South African tribes" (1934, p. 71). Whatever may have happened elsewhere, that is not true of Bechuanaland. Although Christianity did often cause trouble, it never seriously disturbed tribal unity, except perhaps when used to cloak the ambitions of a chief's enemies. Equally inapplicable is another of Eiselen's assertions, that "those natives who became Christians were lost to their tribe" (p. 70). Because chiefs everywhere in Bechuanaland valued the presence of missionaries, and in most tribes themselves joined the church, Christians seldom had to choose between tribal allegiance and devotion to the gospel. They had on the whole less cause for grievance than the pagans, who were often dismayed by a chief's abolition of much-cherished customs. But in general both sections remained loyal to their tribe, and even if resentful of a chief's policy they hardly ever moved away to seek religious freedom elsewhere.

It is rather Christianity itself that seems to have suffered in the process of acceptance by the Tswana. As a faith it appeals, even nominally, to little more than a quarter of the people, a smaller proportion (according to census returns) than in the Union, Basutoland, or even Swaziland with its strongly pagan chieftainship; and many of those calling themselves Christians show by their conduct that they do not really accept the moral code of their church. One reason, as I have indicated, is that the code is widely felt to be too exacting. But that would probably apply also to Christianity elsewhere in Southern Africa. Another reason, I suggest is to be found in the centralized governmental system of the Tswana tribes, whose chiefs even now still have much power. As we have seen, most chiefs fairly early both became Christians themselves and adopted a policy of denominational monopoly. This made conversion to Christianity, for many of their subjects, a matter of fashion instead of genuine and abiding conviction. It gave people no alternative but to belong to the one established church or to none at all. It led to unhealthy and sometimes troublesome dependence of the church upon the personal goodwill and support of the chief. "People are sick of the church," Kgatla told me in 1934; "the church is weakened because the chief does not care for it, so others also have lost interest and stay away." And some chiefs were certainly too zealous and premature in the reforms they attempted, the result of which often was merely to provoke or strengthen resistance.

Christianity has beyond question led to many "fundamental" and "widespread" changes in Tswana life. To that extent we may agree with Emory Ross, even if the evidence suggests that Government activity and labor migration have in some ways also had many far-reaching effects. But I doubt if "creative" is an equally suitable term for a process that, however much of a blessing it may have been to some individuals, has left the great majority of the people either indifferent to religion of any kind or insincere about the one they profess.

NOTES

[1] BaKgatla bagaKgafêla, whose headquarters are now at Mochudi; not to be confused with the BaKgatla-ba-Mmanaana, with whom Livingstone worked at Mabotsa in 1843-5.

[2] My field work was done mainly among the Kgatla, Ngwato, Ngwaketse, Kwena, and Tawana; I also paid brief visits to the Khurutshe, Seleka-Rolong, Malete, Tlôkwa, and Tshidi-Rolong.

[3] The European population of the Protectorate (1946) is approximately 2,400. Most of them live outside the tribal areas, but there are some 500 in the Ngwato Reserve and far fewer (120 or less) in each of the others. The figures include both adults and children.

[4] According to the 1946 census returns (the latest available), the African population of the Protectorate is 292,755, of whom 78,417 are listed as Christians.

REFERENCES

[Starred items are recommended as further readings.]

Much of the material upon which I have drawn consists of my own field notes, periodical publications of the various missionary societies working in Bechuanaland, unpublished documents in missionary archives (L.M.S. London and D.R.C. Mochudi), and unpublished letters and journals of David Livingstone in various collections and private ownership. The following list is restricted to works cited in the text, and a few others of general importance about the history of missionary activity in Bechuanaland.

Brookes, E. H. 1934. The Colour Problems of South Africa. Lovedale and London.

Chamberlin, D. (ed.) 1940. Some Letters from Livingstone, 1840-1872. London.

Du Plessis, J. 1911. A History of Christian Missions in South Africa. London.

* Eiselen, W. M. 1934. Christianity and the Religious Life of the Bantu. In: Western Civilization and the Natives of South Africa, I. Schapera (ed.), pp. 65-82. London.

Goodall, N. 1954. A History of the London Missionary Society, 1895-1945. London.

Groves, C. P. 1954. The Planting of Christianity in Africa. Vol. II; 1840-1878. London.

Haccius, G. 1907-20. Hannoversche Missionsgeschichte. 3 vols. Hermannsburg.

Hepburn, J. D. 1895. Twenty Years in Khama's Country. London.

Jabavu, D. D. T. 1927. Christianity and the Bantu. In: Thinking with Africa, M. Stauffer (ed.), pp. 110-34. New York.

Latourette, K. S. 1943. The Great Century (A History of the Expansion of Christianity, Vol. V). New York and London.

Livingstone, D. 1857. Missionary Travels and Researches in South Africa. London.

Lovett, R. 1899. The History of the

London Missionary Society, 1795-1895. London.

Mackenzie, J. 1871. *Ten Years North of the Orange River.* Edinburgh.

* Ross, E. 1955. "Impact of Christianity in Africa." *Annals Amer. Acad. Polit. Soc. Sci.,* 298, pp. 161-9.

Sargant, E. B., 1906. *Report . . . on Education in Bechuanaland Protectorate 1905.* Unpublished MS.

Sargant, E. B. 1908. *Report on Native Education in South Africa. Part III: Education in the Protectorates.* London.

Schapera, I. 1938. *A Handbook of Tswana Law and Custom.* London. (Revised ed., 1955.)

* Schapera, I. 1940. *Married Life in an African Tribe.* London.

Schapera, I. 1943. *Tribal Legislation among the Tswana.* London.

Schapera, I. 1947. *The Political Annals of a Tswana Tribe.* Cape Town.

* Schapera, I. 1953. *The Tswana.* London. [Ethnographic Survey of Africa. Southern Africa, III. London.]

Shepherd, R. H. W. 1947. *Molepolole: a Missionary Record.* Glasgow.

* Smith, E. W. 1926. *The Golden Stool.* London.

Van der Merwe, W. J. 1936. *The Development of Missionary Attitudes in the Dutch Reformed Church of South Africa.* Cape Town.

Westermann, D. 1937. *Africa and Christianity.* London.

Willoughby, W. C. 1923. *Race Problems in the New Africa.* Oxford.

Willoughby, W. C. 1928. *The Soul of the Bantu.* London.

FOR FURTHER READING

Hutchinson, Bertram, "Some Social Consequences of Nineteenth Century Missionary Activity among the South African Bantu," *Africa,* 1957, 27, 160-75. A complementary study to that of Schapera, but dealing with South Africa in general.

Bascom, William, "African Culture and the Missionary," *Civilisations,* 1953, 3, 491-504. An analysis of the interplay of mission influences and African culture, mainly with reference to West Africa.

Sundkler, Bengt G. M., *Bantu Prophets in South Africa,* London: Lutterworth Press, 1948. A study of nativistic churches and sects.

Parrinder, Geoffrey, *Religion in an African City,* London: Oxford University Press, 1953. Includes a discussion of Christian influences in the city of Ibadan, Nigeria.

Harries, Lyndon, "Christian Marriage in African Society," in Phillips, Arthur (ed.), *Survey of African Marriage and Family Life,* London: Oxford University Press for the International African Institute, 1953. A broad survey with a detailed bibliography.

Groves, Charles Pelham, *The Planting of Christianity in Africa,* London: Lutterworth Press, 1948-1958, 4 vols. The basic source book on the history of African missions.

Oliver, Roland Anthony, *The Missionary Factor in East Africa,* London: Longmans, Green, 1952. A descriptive survey of considerable value.

International Missionary Council, *Survey of the Training of the Ministry in Africa,* London: International Missionary Council, 1950-1954, 3 parts; International Missionary Council, *Survey of the Training of the Ministry in Madagascar,* London: International Missionary Council, 1957. These reports, based on field observations and other data, form an evaluation of the role of Africans in the church.

THE PREDICAMENT OF THE MODERN AFRICAN CHIEF: AN INSTANCE FROM UGANDA[*][1]

Lloyd Fallers

Anthropologists have long wrestled with the problem of developing an adequate frame of reference for the study of social change. In many studies the writer's orientation is vague and is lost in the body of descriptive data. In other cases his frame of reference is not logically consistent and difficulties arise in the analysis of data. Fallers' paper is particularly useful because of the clarity of his approach to social change. Using ideas developed by the theoretical sociologists, Max Weber and Talcott Parsons, he has fused them with his own conceptions and applied them to an African group as a case study. The approach chosen leads directly to the analysis of certain problems of social change.

The Soga political system described by Fallers is that of a small centralized state with a ruling chief. It seems likely that the conflicts and discontinuities that have occurred in the role of leaders in Busoga as a result of culture contact are also found in societies lacking chiefs or considerable centralization of authority. This seems to be particularly so in middle range societies where indirect rule has meant the establishment of Native Authority Councils or some other form of local government councils partially based on traditional patterns of leadership. In this case the conflicts, diffused among a larger body of persons than in the example given by Fallers, may not be so readily observable.

The role of the modern African chief poses difficult problems of analysis because it is a role which is played out in a matrix of diverse and often conflicting institutions. Perhaps it would be better to say that the chief occupies many roles. On the one hand, he has a series of roles in the indigenous institutions of African society. On the other hand, he occupies roles in the imported institutions of colonial government. Of course, in

* Reprinted from *American Anthropologist*, 1955, 57, 290-305, by permission of the author and *American Anthropologist*.

various parts of Africa institutions of African and European origin have met under widely varying circumstances and have interpenetrated in varying degrees, but nearly everywhere the effect is confusing and bizarre. In Uganda, for example, if we were to visit a chief we might find him attending a committee meeting, helping to work out a budget for the coming fiscal year. If we ask for an appointment, we will be received in a modern office equipped with typewriters, telephones, filing cases, and the other apparatus of modern bureaucracy. If by chance we had called on another day, our chief would have been unavailable. He would have been meeting with his clanmates in the thatched hut of his paternal uncle, and the talk would have been of genealogical refinements and the wishes of the ancestors. If we are invited to have tea at the chief's house in the evening, we will be introduced to his several wives, and this may surprise us because we have heard that he is a pillar of the local Anglican parish and a patron of the Boy Scout troop. I have chosen a rather extreme, though not unreal, example. Reading the literature on the various areas of modern Africa, one is impressed by the patchwork character of the chief's social milieu. It appears to be a collection of bits and pieces taken at random from widely different social systems. Modern African society as a whole frequently gives this impression, but in the case of the chief the effect is heightened because his role is so often the meeting point, the point of articulation, between the various elements of the patchwork.

It is perhaps because of this confusing diversity of elements in the chief's social world that relatively few attempts to analyze his role in systematic terms are to be found in the social science literature on Africa. There are, of course, important exceptions, notably the papers by Gluckman and his colleagues of the Rhodes-Livingstone Institute on the village headman in British Central Africa (Barnes 1948; Gluckman, Mitchell and Barnes 1949; Mitchell 1949) and Busia's recent (1951) book on the chief in present-day Ashanti. Probably there are others. Generally, however such published material as is available is of two sorts. First there is the large and growing body of official and semiofficial literature dealing mainly with what might be called the ideal structure of African politics as conceived by colonial governments. Notable here are Lord Hailey's (1950, 1953) five volumes on the British dependencies and much of the content of the *Journal of African Administration*. This is the literature of what is called in British territories "Native Administration," and it is concerned with those institutions which are the result of explicit planning on the part of the administering power. Sometimes these institutions embody many elements of indigenous institutions; sometimes they are wholly, or almost wholly, new. Everywhere they represent attempts by colonial governments to erect intervening institutions, manned by Africans, between themselves and African peoples. Familiarity with this literature on native administration is of course essential to the student of African politics, but by its very nature it seldom reaches deep levels of subtlety in the analysis of political process. It is concerned with formal arrangements, with the ways in which power *ought* to flow, and it treats such arrangements in quite general terms, emphasizing that which is common to native administration over wide areas often containing great diversities of indigenous social structure. It seldom concerns itself with the ways in which such indigenous diversities combine with the formal, official institutions to form the real pattern of politics within a tribal or ethnic area.

The second type of material generally available is that gathered by anthropologists in the course of investigations into the traditional structure of African societies. Such studies are most often concerned with the role of the chief in the *traditional* political structure and tend to treat those features of his role which are the result of modern conditions as peripheral to the main focus of study. If the official literature on native administration looks at the chief as he *ought* to be, or as the District Officer hopes he will be tomorrow, the bulk of the anthropological literature looks at him as he was yesterday. There are reasons for this emphasis. Rightly or wrongly, anthropologists have frequently seen their primary task to be the documentation of the full range of variation in human society. They have therefore devoted themselves to the analysis of precisely those features of African society which existed before contact with Europeans. Modern developments are usually mentioned in monographs but most often only as representing the destruction of the integrated social systems which existed before. Judged by the task which they have set themselves—the analysis of indigenous institutions—the work of anthropologists in Africa has been of a high standard indeed, representing perhaps the richest body of monographic literature possessed by anthropology today. However, such studies do not often yield full analyses of the present-day role of the African chief.

The reason why we have so few adequate studies of the modern chief's role may be found, I think, in certain characteristics of the conceptual schemes commonly applied by students of African societies. African studies have been the home par excellence of structural sociological or social anthropological analysis, a tradition founded by Durkheim, elaborated by Radcliffe-Brown, and more recently applied so brilliantly to empirical research by Fortes and Evans-Pritchard. The virtues of this frame of reference are obvious and familiar to anyone acquainted with the real classics of social science which have been its fruits. Its primary concern is to analyze the ways in which institutions dovetail with one another to form an integrated whole—the ways in which, to put it another way, the institutional demands made upon individuals are harmonized so that the demands of institution X do not run counter to the demands of institution Y, but rather complement and support them. As a result of such studies we now have, for example, excellent detailed analyses of the relationships between political and religious institutions among the Nuer (Evans-Pritchard 1940, 1951, 1953) and the Tallensi (Fortes 1945, 1949).

The difficulty which arises when this point of view is applied to the present-day role of the African chief or, indeed, to many other features of modern African society, is that much of what we observe appears, as I have said before, to be a patchwork of diverse and conflicting elements. Institutions are constantly getting in each others' way, and individuals are constantly being institutionally required to do conflicting things. If our point of departure is a conception of the integrated social system, we can say of such situations only that "society has undergone disorganization" or that "cultures have clashed." We can say relatively little, I think, about why the particular kinds of disorder which we observe occur. Increasingly, however, we want knowledge of precisely this kind.

One key to the escape from this dilemma lies, I think, in a recognition that the notion of "social order" or "social system" can have two referents, both of which are quite valid, but which must be distinguished One consists in order or system in the sense of harmonious integration, the notion which I think structural social anthropology has stressed. Order in this sense exists to the degree that institutions making up a social system mutually reinforce and support one another. The other referent is order in the sense that the phenomena observed may be subjected to systematic analysis leading to greater understanding by the analyst of the connections between events, whether these events relate to harmony or to discord. This meaning corresponds, I think, to the natural scientist's notion of "order in nature," leaving aside the philosophical question of whether the order really exists in nature or only in the scientist's head. In this latter sense, a society which contains major elements of disharmony or conflict may be studied just as fruitfully as one characterized by a high degree of internal integration. It would perhaps be better to say that the *disharmonious elements* of a society may be studied just as fruitfully as the harmonious ones, since presumably no society is ever either completely integrated or completely at odds with itself.

If I am right in thinking that there are these two possible conceptions of order or system in social life, then it follows that the second conception, that of social life as subject to systematic analysis without regard to its harmonious or disharmonious character, is the more fundamental. It is in the nature of a first assumption which we must make if we are to study the disharmonious elements in societies. The first conception then, that of order in the sense of harmony, finds its place in our frame of reference at the next stage and it defines a range of variation. The elements making up a social system will be harmonious or disharmonious in varying degrees and ways, and we will require concepts for talking about these various degrees and types of disharmony.

On the most general level, concepts of this kind are not hard to find. Delineating the elements involved in the *integrated* or *harmoniously functioning* social system has been one of the major preoccupations of social scientists, and lists of such elements may be found in almost any text or theoretical volume. All that is required in order to utilize such a list in the study of relative harmony-disharmony is to treat each of the characteristics of the integrated social system as subject to variation. Perhaps the most generally agreed-upon characteristic of the integrated social system is the sharing of a common system of values by its members. If the actions of the individuals who are members of the system are to be mutually supporting, these actions must be founded upon common conceptions of what is right and proper. Actions which are in accord with the common norm will be rewarded, and those which run counter to it will be punished. Sometimes it is useful to distinguish "means" from "ends" within the general field of common values. Or one may find it useful to distinguish between situations in which value integration requires actual sharing of common values and those in which it requires merely that values held by groups within the system be compatible. Further distinctions under this general rubric might be drawn, but it is clear that integration among the values held by its members is one of the characteristics of the harmoniously functioning social system. It is also clear, however, that in actual social systems the degree to which value systems are integrated is subject to wide variation.

A second general characteristic of the integrated social system is a sharing of belief or a common system of cognition and communication. Persons must share not only a common system of means and ends but also a common system of symbols enabling them to interpret each others' behavior, as well as other events, in a common way. For traffic to flow smoothly on a crowded street, drivers must not only share the common value of obeying the law, but must also interpret red lights and green lights in the same way. Again, however, the sharing of symbols is by no means always complete, and we may expect to find social systems in which malcommunication is a common occurrence.

Again, the integrated social system is one in which the motivations of its component individuals are to a high degree complementary with the shared systems of value and belief. Actually, this is merely the other side of the social coin. To the degree that values and beliefs are actually shared, persons will "want" to do the "right thing" and will believe the "correct thing" and will be responsive to rewards and punishments which nudge them in this direction. The common values and beliefs of the social system will be built into the personalities of its members so that they will be adequately motivated to do the things others expect them to do. Where the system of value and belief is held in common and its parts harmoniously integrated, persons will not be expected to do incompatible things. All this, however, is also clearly subject to wide varia-bility in concrete social systems. Individuals may be insufficiently moti-vated to socially valued behavior, or they may have placed upon them conflicting social demands.

I have been at some pains to spell out a point which may seem obvious to some and irrelevant to others because I believe it has a direct bearing upon the prospects for fruitful research into the role of the chief in modern Africa. In many areas the chief lives in a disordered and conflict-ridden social world, and it is important, if we are to reach some understanding of this chief's position, that we be able to talk about this conflict and disorder, if I may so put it, in an ordered way. In many regions of Africa today, and indeed in many other colonial and semicolo-nial areas, the situation is not simply one of two radically different social systems colliding head on and, as it were, holding each other at bay. Though in some areas something approaching this situation may exist, it is not generally so. More commonly, African and European social sys-tems have interpenetrated with the result that new social systems em-bodying diverse and conflicting elements have come into being. We must therefore be prepared to analyze systematically situations in which in-compatible values and beliefs are widely held by members of the same social system, where individuals are regularly motivated to behavior which in the eyes of others is deviant and where other individuals have conflicting motivations corresponding with discontinuities among the values of the social system. We must be able to think analytically about these elements of relative disharmony and to determine their conse-quences for the functioning of such systems as wholes.

Something of what I have in mind may be illustrated by the situa-tion of the chief today in the Busoga District of Uganda, where I have been engaged in field research under the auspices of the East African In-stitute of Social Research and of the Fulbright Program. Conditions in Busoga, and, indeed, in Uganda as a whole, have provided perhaps the optimum situation for the harmonious mutual adjustment of African and European social systems. The absence of extensive European settlement has meant that there has been little or no competition for land. The suc-cessful importation and cultivation on small peasant holdings of cotton, coffee, and groundnuts have provided a cash crop economy upon which a rising standard of living could be built without detriment to food crop cultivation. Administrative policy has stressed the recognition and grad-ual remolding of indigenous political institutions without sharp breaks with the past. In this situation, European and African institutions have, indeed, merged to a striking degree, but the result remains a social system containing major elements of disharmony and conflict. In large measure, the role of the chief is the focus of this conflict.

Busoga was "discovered" by Europeans in 1862 and came under British administration in 1892; the temporal base line for the analysis of change in the Soga political system therefore lies in the latter part of the nineteenth century. At this time, Busoga was not a political entity. It did have sufficient linguistic and general cultural unity to mark it off from the other Bantu-speaking areas of southern Uganda so that in 1862 John Hanning Speke, the first European explorer of the area, was told that "Usoga" comprised the area bounded by Lake Victoria, Lake Kyoga, the Nile, and the Mpologoma River. These are the boundaries of the present-day Busoga District. (See map.) The inhabitants of the area, the

Peoples of Uganda Protectorate.

Basoga, appear to have numbered some half-million. They were sedentary subsistence cultivators and livestock breeders, relying for staple foods mainly upon their permanent plantain gardens and plots of millet, sweet potatoes, and maize. The country is described by early travelers as being extremely fertile and closely settled, particularly in the south along the Lake Victoria shore.

Politically, Busoga was divided among some fifteen small kingdom-states, which varied widely in size but which shared a fundamental similarity in structure. The elements of this common political structure may be seen in three key institutions: *patrilineal kinship, rulership, and clientship.*

In its fundamentals, Soga kinship followed a pattern common in East Africa. Descent was traced in the patrilineal line, and kinsmen sharing common patrilineal descent formed corporate groups which were important units in the social structure. Kinship terminology was of the Omaha type. The most important unit formed on the basis of patrilineal kinship was the lineage, comprising all those persons within a local area who were able to trace the patrilineal genealogical relationships among themselves. This lineage group was important in landholding, through the rights which it exercised over inheritance and succession by its members. An individual was free to choose his heir from among his sons, but his testament was subject to confirmation or revision by the council of his lineage-mates, which met at his funeral. The lineage played a prominent role also in marriage. Most young men were unable to meet from their own resources the marriage-payment demanded by the bride's kinsmen and so had to depend for aid upon their lineage-mates. Such dependency gave the lineage at least a potential influence over its members' choice of marriage partner and an interest in the stability of marriage. Finally, the importance of the lineage in temporal affairs was matched and complemented by its role in relation to the supernatural. The most prominent feature of Soga religion was the ancestor cult, founded upon the belief that patrilineal ancestors maintained an interest in and influence over the well-being and good behavior of their living descendants. Common descent thus involved a common sacred interest in the ancestors, and this in turn, through the ancestor's graves, which were the focus of the cult, reinforced the lineage members' corporate economic and legal interest in the land.

Units other than the lineage were also formed upon the basis of patrilineal kinship. The individual homestead was located in space by the practice of patrilocal residence, and where extended family homesteads were formed, these took the form of a small lineage group composed of a man and his sons together with their wives and children. Beyond the lineage, groups of lineages which were known to be related patrilineally but which were unable to trace the precise genealogical links among themselves formed clans which were unified by a common clan name, common totemic avoidances, and the rule of exogamy. Patrilineal kinship thus defined a large sector of the individual's life; it controlled inheritance and succession, structured marriage, gave form to religion, and strongly influenced the spatial distribution of homesteads.

Soga society was not, however, a segmentary society in which unilineal kinship constituted the only principle of organization. Through the institution of rulership, members of many patrilineal groups were bound together to form kingdom-states in which membership was defined, not in terms of kinship, but in terms of territorial boundaries and common allegiance to the ruler. In each of the kingdom-states there was a royal clan or lineage (in the case of the royal group, clan and lineage tended to be coterminous because royal genealogies were better remembered), which was set above commoner groups as having higher rank and an inborn fitness to rule. The ruler's position was hereditary within the royal clan. He was the active head of the kingdom and the overlord of all other holders of authority. He was also the chief priest for, as the ancestors of commoner lineages were thought to both assist and control the behavior of their descendants, so the royal ancestors were in a sense *national* ancestors who took a similar interest in the affairs of the nation as a whole. The ruler, being their descendant, was supported and controlled by them in his conduct of national affairs and was the intermediary through whom they might be approached on behalf of the nation. Inherited regalia and a courtly style of living centering around an impressively constructed capital symbolized and enhanced the ruler's political power.

To complete this outline of traditional Soga political structure requires the addition of the third of the institutions noted above—that of clientship. The administrative staff through which the ruler in each of the kingdoms governed was recruited neither through patrilineal kinship in commoner lineages nor through membership in the royal group. The ruler's leading lieutenants—the prime minister and the chiefs of territorial divisions—were commoners bound to the ruler by personal loyalty. Often they were chosen from the many servant boys, sons of ordinary peasants, who were sent to serve in the palace and to seek social advancement. This mode of recruitment to positions of subordinate power was a partial solution to a problem which apparently afflicted most Bantu kingdoms in the Great Lakes region. All members of the royal group shared in some measure the inborn fitness to rule, but within the royal group there was no clear-cut rule of seniority. Throughout the kingdom there were princes—junior members of the royal group—in control of villages or groups of villages, and these persons were a potential threat to the paramount authority of the ruler. When the problem of succession arose, any member of the royal group who could command a measure of support might assert a claim to rulership and fighting not uncommonly broke out. The institution of clientship, through which commoners of administrative and military ability were raised by the ruler to positions of authority and thus were bound to him as personal followers, provided an administrative staff which could be trusted with power. Not sharing the inherited rank of the princes, they were not potential usurpers. At times of succession, the major clients under the previous ruler participated along with members of the royal clan in choosing a new ruler and thus exercised a disinterested and stabilizing influence upon the ambitious princes. They also acted as a check upon the ruler's power, since if he failed to govern within the limits set by custom they might combine in support of a rival prince and drive him from his position.

Traditional Soga society thus took the form of a hierarchy. At the top was the hereditary ruler—the paramount holder of authority and the central symbol of the kingdom's unity. At intermediate levels were the princes administering villages or clusters of villages and, counterbalancing them, the ruler's administrative staff of client-chiefs administering other villages or village clusters in the name of the ruler. Forming the broad base of the society were the communities of commoner agriculturalists organized into corporate patrilineal groups. Commoner and royal, kinsman and kinsman, patron and client, were bound together by highly personal rights and obligations. Subordinates owed superiors economic support through the payment of tribute, military support in war, the recognition of judicial and administrative authority, and personal loyalty. Subordinates in turn received paternalistic protection and aid.

The sixty years which have passed since the establishment of the British Protectorate in Uganda have seen the radical reconstruction of this political system, to a great extent as a consequence of explicit planning by the administration. Innovations were introduced gradually, however, and under circumstances which contributed greatly to the willingness of the Basoga to accept them. During the early years, little was changed in the formal structure of Soga political institutions, though their day-to-day functioning was substantially altered. Initially, the aims of the administration were limited to the establishment of "law and order," which meant an end to warfare, and the creation of a system of revenue and trade. In the pursuit of these limited aims, the indigenous political structure was simply taken over intact, given new tasks, and allowed to continue functioning under the supervision of administrative officers. The rulers of the various kingdoms continued to hold hereditary office and to recruit their administrative staffs through personal clientship. The judicial and administrative powers of rulers and chiefs were recognized, and even enhanced, by Protectorate legislation which made them statutory judges and gave them the authority to issue administrative orders having the force of law. They continued to be supported by tribute paid by the commoner population. In recognition of the authority of the colonial government, they were required to collect taxes, to assist in public works, and to submit their judicial decisions to review by administrative officers. The one major structural innovation was the setting up of a District Council composed of the rulers of the several kingdoms.

Even during this initial period of limited aims, however, important developments were taking place within Soga society. Though the additional functions which were imposed upon the indigenous political structure were minimal, they involved one important change. This was the introduction of literacy. Tax collection involved bookkeeping and administrative supervision over the courts required the keeping of written records of litigation. Every chief or ruler now either had to be literate or required the services of a literate clerk. This development was made possible by, and in turn stimulated, the development of mission education. Soon the sons of important rulers and chiefs, and ultimately the rulers and chiefs themselves, were mission-educated and largely Christian.

The loss of political independence and the innovations which accompanied it were made much more palatable to the rulers and chiefs by the support which they received from the administration and by newly developed sources of wealth. As I have noted above, the position of the ruler or chief in traditional Soga society was not particularly secure. Warfare was more or less endemic and the threat of revolt served as a constant check upon the ruler's exercise of power. Now, not only were the traditional authorities backed by the superior power of the British administration, but they were also able to enhance their economic position. Cotton was introduced at about the time of the first World War and it soon spread rapidly as a peasant cash crop. Tribute could now be collected in cash or in labor upon the rulers' and chiefs' cotton plots. Within a few years there developed a new chiefly style of life, which included imported consumption items such as European-style clothing and houses, automobiles, and, incidentally, mission education, which required the payment of fees.

This early period thus saw the development of a new kind of elite position for the traditional political authorities in Soga society. With greater power and an enhanced wealth differential, they now stood above the common poeple in ways which had not been possible for them in pre-administration times. This situation was very rewarding to them. It goes far to explain, I think, why they were so very ready to accept the supervision of administrative officers and why, later on, they were willing to accept much more profound innovations in the political structure. They had in large measure committed themselves to the new conditions.

The initial period, characterized by limited administrative aims and by the building up of the traditional authorities, came to an end in the nineteen-twenties and -thirties. The new policy of the administration came to be one of remolding the traditional political system in the direction of European-style civil service bureaucracy and electoral democracy. In a series of stages between 1926 and 1936, tribute was abolished and the chiefs and rulers began to be paid fixed salaries from a native administration treasury. The loss of tribute was painful to the chiefs and rulers, not only because it meant a reduction in monetary income, but also because tribute was in itself an important symbol of their power and prestige. Nevertheless, in part for the reasons I have mentioned, the change was accepted. A further fundamental change was introduced which concerned the basis of recruitment to office. Over a period of years, the administration came to insist more and more upon the recruitment of chiefs upon the basis of objective competence, and during the nineteen-forties it became established that not only chiefs but also the rulers themselves, who had previously been hereditary, would be chosen upon this basis.

Since, at first, rulers' and chiefs' sons tended to monopolize the mission schools, "recruitment on the basis of competence" meant, essentially, recruitment of the most competent from this group. With more widespread education, the group from which chiefs were recruited became wider. Again, no serious opposition was encountered. What had previously been a hierarchy of hereditary rulers, princes, and client-chiefs thus became in a strict sense a hierarchy of civil service bureaucrats, recruited upon the basis of competence, increasingly as indicated by formal education; paid fixed salaries out of revenue from general taxation; subject to bureaucratic transfer and promotion; and pensioned upon retirement.

Within recent years, this bureaucracy has tended to proliferate, as the Uganda Government has pushed forward its policy of devolving more and more responsibility upon the native administration, now known as the African Local Government. The hierarchy of civil servant chiefs which replaced the traditional hierarchy of rulers and client-chiefs has been supplemented by specialist officials concerned with taking over from Protectorate Government departments responsibility for matters such as finance, public works, agriculture and forestry, public health, and law enforcement. Concerned that this bureaucracy not become an irresponsible monolith, the Government has also encouraged the growth of elected councils, leading up to a District Council which is responsible for advising the bureaucracy, framing legislation, and preparing an annual budget. The strength of this trend toward devolution of responsibility upon the African Local Government may be seen in the fact that the share of direct taxation allocated to the African Local Government treasury is now four times that collected for the Protectorate Government. In 1952, the African Local Government Budget called for the receipt and expenditure of more than a quarter of a million pounds.

During the period of British administration, Soga political structure has been radically altered by the introduction of new institutional forms, which have achieved widespread acceptance by the Basoga. The new civil servant chiefs are granted great respect and are popularly regarded as legitimate heirs to the former authority of the traditional rulers and client-chiefs. Appointment to the civil service is regarded as a highly desirable goal for the ambitious young man. The acceptance of new institutions does not mean, however, that a harmoniously integrated social system has resulted. In many cases traditional institutions which are in large measure incompatible with the new ones have survived. The result is a social system which shows major deviations from harmonious integration in its value system, in its system of communication and belief, and in the social personalities of its members.

Traditional Soga political institutions emphasized the value of particular personal rights and obligations, a pattern which Parsons (1951) has described by the terms *particularism* and *functional diffuseness*. Relations were particularistic in that they emphasized personal loyalty between individuals who stood in particular status relations with one another, for example, as kinsman to kinsman, patron to client, or royal to commoner. One owed particular loyalty to *one's own* kinsman, to *one's own* patron or client, or to one's ruler *as a person*. Relations were functionally diffuse in that they involved a wide segment of the lives of the persons involved. Kinsmen, for example, were expected to stand together as total persons and to take a legitimate interest in the most intimate aspects of each other's lives. A patron was similarly related to his client, as is indicated by the difficulty of distinguishing a political subordinate from a personal servant and by the common practice of linking client to patron through affinal ties. The basic virtue was personal loyalty between particular individuals.

The value system associated with bureaucratic organization is in most respects in opposition to this pattern. Here the guiding norm is, as Max Weber has expressed it, ". . . straightforward duty without regard to personal considerations. . . . Everyone in the same empirical situation is subject to equality of treatment" (1947:340). Relations in such a system are to be, in Parsons' terms, *universalistic* and *functionally specific* —universalistic in that universally applicable rules, and not particular statuses, are to be the determinants of conduct, and functionally specific in that they relate to specific contexts and not to the whole of individuals' lives. As a civil servant, one ought to treat everyone alike without regard to particular status considerations. One applies general rules and procedures. One's competence is severely limited to what are called "official matters" and one is enjoined not to become involved in, nor even to know about, the personal lives of those with whom one has relations *as a civil servant*. This norm of disinterested service is of course the constant goal of all Western political systems, and it was the aim which led the British administration to introduce the civil service system into Busoga.

In Busoga, these two value systems today exist side by side, and both are represented in major institutions. The patrilineal kinship system is very much a going concern, in large part because its stronghold, the traditional system of landholding, has remained intact. Corporate lineage groups continue to exercise jurisdiction over inheritance and succession and this keeps the ties of kinship alive and strong. The strength of kinship ties is, however, a constant threat to the civil service norm of disinterested-ness. The wide extension of kinship bonds means that a chief is frequently put into the position of having to choose between his obligation to favor particular kinsmen and his official duty to act disinterestedly. He may, for example, be asked to favor a kinsman in a legal case or to exempt him from taxation. Again, the institution of clientship survives and leads a *sub rosa* existence within the civil service. Although formally civil servants are chosen for their objective competence, in fact opportunities may arise for building up personal followings of clients. Senior members of the African Local Government, through their influence with the administration, are able to exercise substantial influence over the appointment and promotion of subordinates and are thus able to build up personal political machines. I want to emphasize that *both* these value systems are institutionalized in Soga society and that both are accepted by most Basoga as, in a sense, legitimate.

The system of belief and communication is also a focus of dis-harmony within the social system. Relatively widespread primary educa-tion and exposure to mass communications media have produced a situa-tion in which at least two sets of symbols and two views of the nature of the world are current in the society. Again, as in the system of values, it is not so much that different individuals interpret events differently as that the same individuals are trying to work with two sets of symbols at the same time. A chief may, for example, read a newspaper and have a good working knowledge of world politics, but he may still not be quite certain that Europeans are not cannibals or that witchcraft does not really work. Again, these disharmonies in the system of belief and communica-tions center upon the chief because it is he who is most simultaneously involved in the two systems through his relations with European officers on the one side and with peasants on the other.

Discontinuities in the systems of value and belief are reflected in inconsistencies in the social personalities of persons playing roles in the system. Since both the civil service norm of disinterestedness and the personal ties of kinship and clientship are institutionalized, both are also internalized in the personalities of individuals. It appears to be the case, though it is somewhat difficult to think about, that chiefs and most other Basoga hold both value systems and both systems of belief at the same time. This results in frequent conflict, both between persons and within persons. In social interaction, an individual is likely to uphold the value or belief which seems advantageous to him in a given situation. The kins-man of a chief is likely to expect preferential treatment in court and to bring the pressure of the lineage group to bear upon the chief if such preferential treatment is not granted. The same individual is outraged, however, if someone else does the same thing. Similarly, a chief is likely to exercise "pull" through a highly placed patron, if he can, in order to secure promotion, but complains bitterly about such behavior on the part of others. A chief who is requested to exercise favoritism on behalf of a kinsman or a friend is put into a literally impossible position. Both his internalized values and the sanctions impinging upon him from society pull him in opposite directions. Whichever way he jumps, he will be punished, both by his own remorse at having contravened values which are part of his personality, and by sanctions applied by others.

One of the consequences of these conflicts and discontinuities is a high casualty rate among chiefs. Where conflicting demands pull him in opposite directions, it becomes very difficult for the chief to avoid falling afoul of sanctions. The administration, of course, strongly upholds the civil service norm. If a chief is caught engaging in nepotism or embezzlement, he is dismissed. But he may also be dismissed for upholding the civil service norm. If he offends a prominent superior by refusing to grant particularistic demands, he may find that charges of corruption have been "framed" against him, and he may be dismissed for the very thing which he has refused on principle to do. The poor communication prevailing between the Basoga and the administration and the consequent dependence of the latter upon senior chiefs for information make it unlikely that such fabrications will be exposed.

Thus, from the point of view of the chief acting in his role, the discontinuities in the Soga social system impose severe burdens. It is possible to view these discontinuities also from the standpoint of their consequences for the system as a whole. From this point of view, it would appear that some of the conflicts noted above act to stabilize the system in a period of radical institutional change. I have stressed the point that these conflicts do not consist primarily in discrete groups of persons holding opposed systems of value and belief; they consist rather in the *same persons,* to a great extent throughout the society, holding two incompatible systems of belief and value. They appear *in action* in the form of conflicts between persons. A chief acts in terms of the civil service norm of disinterestedness and he is punished by others who wish him to act in terms of particularistic obligations. The *persons* in such situations, however, are interchangeable; on another occasion, the same chief may act to fulfill particularistic obligations and may have sanctions brought to bear upon him by the same persons who now, however, wish him to act disinterestedly. This *taking into* the social personalities of individuals of conflicts which might otherwise express themselves in conflicts between discrete groups of persons acts, I suggest, to maintain some unity and stability in the system. Very often—perhaps most often—in societies undergoing rapid change, the latter situation has developed. The society has divided into intransigently opposed factions or parties with the result that consensus can be reestablished only through the defeat, often by violence, of one group by the other. Of course, which of these alternatives one considers "better" depends entirely upon one's value position.

I have described the Soga political system only in outline as an example of the sort of disharmonious situation which I think we must be prepared to study if we are to reach greater understanding of the present-day role of the African chief. The situation is of course much more complex than I have been able to indicate. If there were more time, I should like to say something about what appear to be some of the consequences of the kind of institutional dilemma I have described for the personalities of chiefs. There are indications that for chiefs who do contrive to avoid falling afoul of sanctions, and who remain in office, this success is achieved at considerable psychic cost. The East African Institute of Social Research is currently engaged in a program of research into a number of contemporary East African political systems and we hope, through a combination of institutional and personality analyses, to throw some light upon the reactions of personalities to such situations as well as upon other aspects of political process in these systems.

I should like to add just a word about the situation which I have described in a comparative perspective. This situation, which in its broad outlines is typical, I think, of Uganda as a whole, is probably rather unusual in the broader African picture. In Uganda, there have been few occasions for open conflict between European and African social systems as such. Economic conditions have been beneficent and administrative policy has emphasized gradual and orderly, though steady, change. The result has been a really astonishing degree of African acceptance of things European and a readiness to plunge into radical institutional change. New institutions have been quietly incorporated alongside old ones and conflicts between new and old institutions have been taken into the personalities of individuals who play roles in them. At considerable cost to its component individuals, the social system has come through radical transformation without splitting into opposed factions and without a serious showdown with the European innovators.

Elsewhere in British Africa, two other types of situation appear to be more common. In the classical "indirect rule" territories, such as the Gold Coast and the South African High Commission territories, there was also, as in the early stages in Uganda, a recognition of indigenous political institutions, but it appears that there has been much less emphasis in those territories on remolding such institutions and on devolving new responsibilities upon them. The traditional political systems have been preserved in more nearly their original form so that when new political institutions do develop the traditional ones tend to be bypassed and to remain as centers of conservative opposition. Such a process seems to have occurred in Ashanti where, one gathers, the Youngmen's movement arose as a "progressive" opposition to the "conservative," government-supported chiefs and ultimately contributed substantially to a self-government movement which was even more hostile to traditional political institutions. Another type of situation seems to exist in areas such as the Union of South Africa, parts of Central Africa, and in Kenya, where policy has stressed the rapid adaptation of Africans to the requirements of European settler communities. There again one sees African societies split into conflicting groups: traditional authorities who have had little recognition and who have gradually lost position and influence, government appointees who are often looked upon by others as stooges, and, occasionally, charismatic leaders of radical movements who oppose both the others. Comparisons with French and Belgian Africa should prove illuminating, though I am too little familiar with those territories to attempt such comparisons. One has the impression, however, that the French policy of "assimilation" and the Belgian emphasis upon economic as against political development have produced situations substantially different from those found in British territories (see, for example, Delavignette 1950).

I should like to end with a plea for more empirical studies of contemporary African politics. The great complexity and diversity of political phenomena there provide a fertile field for social scientists of many interests and disciplines.

NOTE

[1] This is a slightly revised version of a paper read before a conference on "Stability and Change in African Societies," jointly sponsored by the Social Science Research Council and the National Research Council, at Princeton, New Jersey, October 14 through 16, 1953.

REFERENCES CITED

[All these references are recommended as further readings.]

Barnes, J. A., 1948, "Some Aspects of Political Development among the Fort Jameson Ngoni." *African Studies* VII: 99-109.

Busia, K. A., 1951, *The Position of the Chief in the Modern Political System of Ashanti*. London, Oxford University Press.

Delavignette, R., 1950, *Freedom and Authority in French West Africa*. London, Oxford University Press.

Evans-Pritchard, E. E., 1940, *The Nuer*. London, Oxford University Press.

——, 1951, *Kinship and Marriage among the Nuer*. London, Oxford University Press.

——, 1953, "The Nuer Conception of the Spirit in its Relation to the Social Order." *American Anthropologist*, 55: 201-14.

Fortes, M., 1945, *The Dynamics of Clanship among the Tallensi*. London, Oxford University Press.

——, 1949, *The Web of Kinship among the Tallensi*. London, Oxford University Press.

Gluckman, M., J. C. Mitchell and J. A. Barnes, 1949, "The Village Headman in

British Central Africa." *Africa* XIX:89-106.

Hailey, Lord, 1950, 1953, *Native Administration in the British African Territories*. London, Her Majesty's Stationery Office.

Mitchell, J. C., 1949, "The Political Organization of the Yao of Southern Nyasaland." *African Studies* VII: 141-59.

Parsons, T., 1951, *The Social System*. Glencoe, Ill., Free Press.

Weber, M., 1947, *The Theory of Social and Economic Organization*, ed. trans. T. Parsons. New York, Oxford University Press.

FOR FURTHER READING

Fallers, Lloyd A., *Bantu Bureaucracy: A Study of Integration and Conflict in the Political Institutions of an East African People*, Cambridge: Heffer, 1956. A more detailed study using the same frame of reference.

Fallers, L. A., "The Politics of Landholding in Busoga," *Economic Development and Cultural Change*, 1955, 3, 260-70. An analysis of problems of land rights in the changing social situation.

Apter, David E., *The Gold Coast in Transition*, Princeton: Princeton University Press, 1955. A study of the development of modern political groupings in Ghana, using a systematic theoretical framework somewhat similar to that of Fallers.

DYNAMICS OF URBANIZATION IN AFRICA*

Daniel F. McCall

Since World War II, there has been much research on African urban communities by anthropologists, sociologists, and other social scientists. Their approaches have been diverse and the data collected often difficult to use in comparative studies of emerging African urban areas. McCall's summary indicates many of the principal factors in urban development and provides a useful outline of the basic stages of the growth of cities in Africa. Though he may underplay the importance of the rural aspects of African society today, his stress on the significance of cities in social change is undeniable. This article should be compared with Hellmann's description of a Johannesburg slum yard and with Bascom's discussion of traditional Yoruba cities, both included in this volume.

Town life, and a constantly increasing movement of people to the expanding towns, is one of the most striking characteristics of present-day Africa. Town life, in itself, is not new to the continent. An early Dutch merchant was surprised at the size and orderliness of Benin City and compared it favorably with the Amsterdam of his time; Diogo Cam was impressed by the efficient organization of the capital of the Bakongo kingdom; Arabic writers testify to an extensive development of urban centers in the medieval Sudanic Empires; and there are the immense ruins of stone towers and walls of Zimbabwe in Central Africa. The Yoruba people are particularly noted for their propensity to build large towns; Ibadan, the third largest town in Africa, has often elicited surprise that it could survive on an essentially indigenous basis.

These old towns, however, were different from modern African towns in several ways: they were different in structure in that they were organized on the basis of kinship, and power and commerce were channeled through that form of organization; they were different in scale [1] in two ways, in actual size and in extent of outside contact; and they were parochial in culture.

---

* Reprinted from *The Annals of the American Academy of Political and Social Science*, 1955, *298*, 151-60, by permission of the publisher and the author.

Many of these older towns have disappeared and those which remain, like Kano, have been modified and are being further transformed. The new cities and towns are the result of contact with the West; one writer says that the cities are a colonial creation,[2] and another, that the city is the creation of the whites and peopled by blacks.[3] The old towns grew out of, and maintained, their distinctive cultures; in the new towns, Africans who are being urbanized are also, to some extent, being westernized. The old towns had trade with some other areas, but the new towns are an integral part of the network of world trade. This paper is concerned only with the new type of town.

The proportion of people living under urban conditions is already significant, but it is not possible to give exact figures for the whole area because of the inadequacy of available statistics. However, in the Union of South Africa, where the process of town growth has gone farthest, approximately 25 per cent of Africans are living in towns,[4] but in some territories, particularly in East Africa, the number may fall below 5 per cent. North and West Africa come next after the Union in the matter of urban growth, and Central Africa has shown a considerable recent growth.

FACTORS IN URBAN DEVELOPMENT

The towns are administrative and commercial centers; they are therefore the nexus between Africa and Europe. As investments increase, urban growth accelerates. Towns are a symbol and an index of economic development. The rate of growth of African towns in this century has been rapid but this pace has accelerated astonishingly during World War II, owing largely to the need of the West for strategic materials and bases. In the postwar period a number of factors, such as the desire of the European powers to meet the threat of anti-colonialism, the acceptance of the doctrine that rich countries should help poor countries, increased knowledge of African economic problems, the generally increased scope of governmental activity in business, and a feeling that the African people should be rewarded for their loyalty during the war, combined to encourage the public sector of investments which it is hoped will stimulate private investment.[5] All of the territories have development plans envisaging extension of transportation and communication systems, education and medical programs, and electrification and industrialization which, if successful, will undoubtedly contribute to urban growth.[6]

The harnessing of hydroelectric power, of which Africa has an enormous potential, is now in varying stages of planning or realization in various parts of the continent. The utilization of this power will necessitate new industries which will require labor, and since the only reservoir of labor is the subsistence sector, more and more people will be drawn out of the tribal villages to build new towns and to enlarge the old ones.[7]

This period has already witnessed the development of some secondary industry which, outside the Union of South Africa, is relatively insignificant in the total economy but is important in regard to urban growth. Some production for the local market has begun. Furniture, cement, bread, beer, and cigarettes are now being made, and textiles are being machine woven from local cotton.

A favorable world market has furthered the increase of cash crops; and finally, in certain areas, there has been a transfer of some capital from Asia. Such developments help to explain the fact that several towns have doubled their populations in the last decade.

It should be recognized that the economy of an African territory is a fragile one. It is an adjunct of the economy of the metropolitan power and would be the first to be affected in the event of a slump. The emphasis on mining, and the tendency toward monoculture with the consequent dependence on a single export, or at best on a small number of exports, make an African economy extremely vulnerable.

A Fragile Economy

The modern African town did not grow out of the needs of, and in service to, its own hinterland; its primary relationship is to Europe. In many cases it has grown beyond the capacity of its hinterland to support it without radical agricultural reform, which has not been achieved anywhere as yet, so that some of the food for townsmen has to be imported from overseas. Even so, some of the towns are a burden upon the land; wood and charcoal are brought to the town, where people can afford higher prices, and fuel becomes scarce in villages at considerable distances from the urban market.[8]

In any economy there is an exodus from the towns when commerce declines, but in Africa a slump not only would mean an abrupt halt in town growth and a dispersal of urbanites but the villages probably could not absorb them. The land under the present methods of farming could not tolerate a return of the urban population to agriculture.

African territories, like other places, cannot hope to achieve autarchy, but an increase in food production and the production of more industrial goods for local consumption would make the economy healthier and the basis of town growth more secure. For the most part, industry means processing for export. The oil from peanuts and palm nuts is being extracted; logs are being sawed into boards; some ores are smelted into ingots of the metal. This reduces the shipping space needed, thereby lowering transport costs, creates more jobs, which require more training for new skills, and increases the amount of money in local circulation; the result is an increase in urban activity but not in economic stability.

THE TOWN AND ITS HINTERLAND

The towns and the countryside are inseparably interrelated; in truth, they are different aspects of the same reality—like the two faces of a coin. The character of the town is determined, among other things, by the nature of the hinterland from which it draws its labor force and for which it acts as emporium. But rural life has been transmuted by the same forces that have given rise to the towns. Money transactions are replacing traditional exchanges of gifts in kind and service. Crops are grown for export now as well as to fill compound storage bins. Much of the money in circulation in the villages has been remitted to rural families by absent members working in the towns, mines, and plantations.[9]

African society has been affected to such an extent by the impact of the West that the tribe is a sick institution even in the rural areas.[10] The superimposition of outside authority, the intrusion of proseletyzing religions which attack the ideological foundations of tribal authority, the values of the market place superseding the values of the kinship system and allowing commoners to become richer than the chief, all contributed to the decline in effectiveness of tribal organization. The necessity of meeting new situations for which there were no tribal precedents, the temporary or permanent loss of much tribal manpower to outside employment, the corruption of chiefs in their role of custodian of land, and the venality of many of them in spending such profits for personal use have further reduced the capacity of tribal organization to function.

The social disorganization of the countryside further contributes to the growth of the towns, which, to a greater extent, are able to provide the basis for the synthesis of a new society.

DIVERSITY AND SIMILARITY OF TOWNS

In a continent as large as Africa, one would expect some regional variation, and, of course, these differences are felt in the structure and life of the towns. National differences among Europeans as well as the diversity of tribal cultures, length of contact, religion, availability of education and the type offered, altitude, latitude, and climate contrive to give different towns different characteristics, but all are undergoing more or less identical processes although the outcome may vary from place to place because of different combinations of such factors.

Given this range of variation, it is difficult to make any generalization on the characteristics of urban centers that would be true of the whole continent. The fact that we are dealing mainly with the process of urbanization allows us to consider some details as irrelevant, but even in the realm of process there are variations. Only the central tendencies can be indicated.

All Africans living in, or moving into, towns find their customs affected by the fact that town relationships are predominately universalistic rather than particularistic;[11] all statuses, except racial, are achieved rather than ascribed; and kinsmen make up only a small part of the people with whom they daily interact. Contacts are numerous but casual; relationships involve segmental roles rather than the whole personality; ethnic and cultural heterogeneity, mobility, the impersonal nature of commercial contracts, and the mere numbers of the community combine to give the individual an anonymity which lessens the effectiveness of approval and derision of others in control of behavior,[12] so that law enforcement agencies become indispensable. The division of labor has antisocial forms and crime is a profession.

The conditions of employment entail the necessity of regularity and punctuality, forcing change from habits based on rural seasonal patterns. Training on the job gives new motor habits and skills. Common experience encourages organization for common interests. A greater variety of goods are available, and new standards of living can be aspired to, even if they are not always reached.

The town is a source of social change because it has its own necessities of organization, arising out of its economic functions and the ethnic diversity of its population, but it is also a transmitter of other forces, such as education and commerce, which also make for a social change. The town is both a response to forces of change and a focus for them, a place where they operate more intensively.

SEQUENCES OF URBAN GROWTH

The following outline of urban growth is an abstraction which applies, within limits, to most African towns. Although only a few have yet completed the process, they generally can be placed somewhere along this line of development.

Before the town is founded, there is a tribal population, probably sparsely settled and living by subsistence farming. A few intruding Europeans select a site suitable for mining, or for a port, a trading station, or a headquarters for regional administration.

There might already have been a village at the spot; in fact, that might have been one of the reasons for choosing the site. A certain amount of labor is needed for the activities which Europeans have begun, and this is hired from the village and the surrounding countryside. As the enterprise expands, labor is drawn from greater distances, and as the number of people increases, it becomes necessary for the supply of food and other necessities to be organized, and for the community to be governed. This, in turn, means additional employment and adds to the growth of the town.

At first tribesmen come into the town to earn money for a specific purpose, such as to pay taxes or to buy a bicycle, and consider their stay in town as a temporary sojourn. They may return when other needs arise; in fact, the desires and necessities for which money is required tend to become recurrent and the habit is formed of spending a certain number of months each year in town.

Some skills as well as muscle power are needed: tallying and keeping records requires schooling, and certain manual operations require training. Clerks and experienced workmen may be brought in from older towns, or even from Europe, but eventually a school is indispensable for the continuance of the commercial and governmental functions of the town. When a school is established, it may be under the auspices of a religious mission and dedicated to other purposes, but most of its graduates will generally find employment as clerks. Manual training is often furnished by the employing company on an apprenticeship basis.

The kinds of tasks performed in the town will multiply; agricultural products that in the beginning were merely collected for export may now be processed first. Even services necessary to the town itself contribute to specialization. As the complexity of labor requirement increases, employers encourage workers to stay on the jobs for which they have been trained. For the employees, a rise in income makes it feasible to keep a family in town.

At this point, the town has a few permanent residents who are outnumbered by the temporary residents, and in addition there are always some visitors who come for various reasons. This majority of temporary residents are semiurban, semirural, spending part of their time in town and part on their farms. Of them, one might say that, in general, the child grows up in the village, the young man comes into the town to earn a living and, when aged, returns to the village. This type of town dweller is tied to his rural relatives and they to him; they send him food from time to time and he sends money home, and they cultivate the fields which will support him in his old age.

There is a great deal of movement back and forth between the country and the town at this stage; relatives may come to visit a man and crowd into his quarters while they sample the excitements of the town or look for work; and he fairly regularly goes home to rest and to display his acquisition of goods and to distribute some of them to kin and relatives by marriage. To the degree that this situation obtains, it minimizes the development of distinctive contrasts in urban and rural traits. As long as these ties last, a villager has somewhere to stay in the town and someone to show him around the pitfalls and through the intricacies of the maze of urban relationships; the villager is abashed at the strangeness and the complexity of the town but does not feel completely solitary and lost. Equally important the townsman avoids making changes in habits that will alienate his rural kinsmen to whom he will return.

During this period, country patterns tend to persist in the town, but town ideas also get disseminated to the villages, and the difference in the rate of change between the two is thus lessened.

The demographic structure of an African town, during this phase, is different from, and inverse to, that of the rural areas. The town has a preponderance of males and youth. There are comparatively few children in the towns and very few of the aged, but between the ages of seventeen and fifty, that is, the employable years, an individual has a greater chance of survival in the town. The number of females, smaller in total than that of the males, shows the same bell-shaped distribution in ages. The newer the town, the greater the unbalance in the demographic structure; the older the town, other things (such as the government's urban policy) being equal, the greater the approach to demographic stability.

Toward Demographic Stability

The subsequent developments in town growth are largely measures tending toward demographic stability, that is, to a lessening of the disproportion in the sex and age ratios. One important prerequisite for stabilization of town populations is housing. African townsmen, primarily, are a labor force, and it is cheaper for employers to provide housing for a single man than for a family. If a married man is hired, he is frequently given the same-sized quarters as a single man; when the married man later wants to visit his family, he may quit his job and hope to find another when he returns. This means high turnover of labor, which in turn contributes to keeping low the level of skill, so that the employer is constrained to offer inducements, at least to his more skilled workers, to remain; better housing is often provided for this reason. Skilled workers tend to change jobs less often than the unskilled.

Another prerequisite for demographic stability of the towns is a larger income for the urban family. In the country, the wife supplements the husband's income by her labor on the farm; in the town there are usually few opportunities for her to contribute to the family income. In the Union of South Africa, an increasing number of urban African women are employed in domestic service and other occupations. Many, however, are dependent on earnings from illicit beer brewing: income from this traffic is curtailed by frequent police raids. In West Africa, women are petty traders who sell food, cloth, cigarettes, and many other things; and some earn more—a few, much more—than their husbands. This economic opportunity, as well as the age of the towns, explains the more nearly normal sex ratio found there.

A further prerequisite for stabilization is a system of social services. Kin groups, due to dispersal, can no longer fulfill their mutual obligations to help an individual in distress. Welfare costs have to be borne by the governments, and this helps to account for administrative ambivalence towards urban stabilization.

In South Africa, a further factor slows down but does not reverse the tendency toward stabilization. The philosophy of *apartheid* designates the African as essentially a rural being, and the town is considered as belonging to the white man. The African can come to the town on sufferance when the purpose is for the service of the white man, but it is thought proper that the African's wife should stay on the reserve and keep a farm; economic development, however, has made this impossible, and cities are building housing for African families despite the contradiction of this action with the prevailing ideology.

In spite of these obstacles, the growth of commerce and industry with its division of labor and specialization and the fight against high rates of labor turnover, constantly force increased stabilization.

As long as an unbalanced sex ratio continues it has serious implications in regard to family life, birth rate, and mobility. Many of the men in the towns are bachelors, but those who are married may keep their wives in the country to cultivate the farms, although a wife sometimes joins her husband in the town. If a man is a polygynist, he is able to achieve both ends of having a wife with him and one tending the distant farm.

The scarcity of women in towns militates against the fidelity of a town wife, who is unceasingly importuned during her husband's absence at work by numerous womanless men. A husband sometimes sends his wife back to the village, where his relatives can guard her chastity, and then, perhaps, he begins to prey upon some other man's wife, or forms a liaison with an unmarried woman, or consorts with prostitutes. Sexual infidelity is a frequent source of friction and a significant factor in the brittleness of urban marriage.

This separation of many of the men in the towns from the women in the villages has a depressing effect upon the birth rate and population growth. In comparison with the rest of the world, Africa appears sparsely populated, and many development plans hinge upon availability of labor supply. Population has increased owing to suppression of warfare, improvement of sanitation and health facilities, and rising levels of living, but a continuation of the unbalanced sex ratio in both towns and rural areas may slow down the rate of increase.

Beginnings of Classes

As the urban population progresses toward stabilization and tends to become distinct from the rural population, further divisions in the urban population take place. An incipient class structure appears. Wealth, education, and occupation set some apart from others less favored or gifted, or perhaps merely newcomers, and doing the less remunerative work.

Differences in fortune, training, and ability in the competitive towns give rise to a number of stations, or statuses, which approximate classes, whose members influence each other in evolving group mores which are a departure from the past.

Several factors hinder the solidification of classes in urban Africa. One such factor is the continuation of kin obligations, which drain the resources of the successful individual to aid his less fortunate relatives. Another is that trade is dominated by European, Asian, and Levantine merchants, and a large, well-to-do African middle class based on commerce is prevented from arising. Discrimination, which varies in degree (and in the rationalization for it) in different territories but is never absent, puts all Africans in one category and all Europeans in another. As long as the European fills the dominant role and is exclusive, the emergent upper group of Africans will feel psychologically bound to the lower group. And frequently housing shortages prevent the rising elite from separating itself residentially from the other elements.[13]

The lesser differentiation of women also retards class formation. Women receive less education than men and although more urban women than rural women are literate, still the number is small. The occupational opportunities for a woman are limited and in some places absent, so that she is less affected by these modifying influences than the man, and because she is not employed, she is free to visit the country relatives and may keep up the contact with her husband's kin as well as with her own. Therefore, the woman, generally, is more conservative, more apt to preserve the traditional customs, and less likely to take up town ways that are glaringly different. To some extent illiterate wives slow the rate of internalization of urban attitudes by the husband and are not able to identify themselves on his level of the class structure.

Children also are often not able to identify with the father's status because of the common practice of sending children to grow up in the country with relatives; accordingly, adjustments to urban and class attitudes have to be made as adults, after rural patterns have been set. Thus men show the marks of class more than their wives and children, a fact which raises the question whether class exists, since class is usually considered as being composed of families. Among the elite especially, where families tend to be stabilized, this less often applies.

Class formation tolls the knell of tribalism in the urban environment. The marks of class are independent of the marks of tribal membership; classes comprise people of various tribes. A European language is not only a means of communication but a symbol of status (like European clothes) for the elite. For other levels, a vernacular lingua franca usually serves the multitribal population. The lines are still fluid and the word "class" should be used with care, but we are not dealing with a static situation and it is necessary to indicate the trend.

Old and New Overlapping

The processes outlined above are operative simultaneously and are interrelated. In the towns we see the old and the new, the contrasts and conflicts of Africa, the past refusing to die and the future struggling to be born. Nowhere has the town completely sloughed off its tribal background; nowhere has the urban synthesis finally jelled; but everywhere change is moving in that direction. It is not implied here that there is a renunciation of all African cultural features but merely of traditional organization.

URBAN SOCIAL STRUCTURE

The feeling of ethnic solidarity carries over into the town and is especially important for new arrivals. Some sections of towns tend toward a tribal or language homogeneity. Even when this is not possible, some form of organization is usually felt necessary for the protection of the members of a common ethnic group in the strange environment of the town. Each "strangers' community" may elect a headman to represent it, and town authorities sometimes find it convenient to deal with certain matters through the several headmen of the various tribal elements. Or a Tribal Union may be formed for mutual aid.

On the other hand, mutual sharing groups in which each contributing member takes the "kitty" in rotation exclude kinsmen, since custom frowns on exactness in exchanges between kinsmen. Other collectivities which have begun to knit the disparate tribal elements into common units are schools, churches, trade unions, political parties, nationalist movements, and public places of recreation such as beer halls and football fields. The more that Africans identify themselves with these groups, the less important tribal affiliation becomes; these associations perform services, or create outlets for emotion and energy, that formerly were found in the tribal organization.

Classes

The upper stratum of African society, which one could logically term a middle class,[14] keeping in mind that the European forms the upper class, includes the most educated, who in some places may be university graduates trained in Europe or America, and in other places locally educated persons of lower level: the upper ranks of government service, which may mean Senior Civil Service, or merely chief clerks; the most responsible employees of commercial firms, which may be managerial staff or only storekeepers or cashiers; perhaps teachers, headmasters of schools, and ministers of religion; and sometimes privately established professional men, or traders successful enough to survive the non-African competition. The actual composition varies with the occupational opportunities in the territory, which in turn depend upon economic, educational, and administrative conditions.

Between the elite and the laborers are an artisan group—tailors, shoemakers, goldsmiths, masons, carpenters, and other skilled workers. Even where the level of skill is low and the craft could be learned in a few months, the apprenticeship is for a number of years, so that ordinarily anyone out of his teens would be discouraged from beginning, but there is nothing actually to prevent anyone from moving from the category of laborer to that of artisan or even to the elite, if he can acquire the education and the income.

Family

The above positions and institutions in the social structure are innovations, but previously existing institutions, such as the family, are modified in the new milieu. An African who ventures into a town is an offshoot of a kin group, and others may follow to the extent that they can be supported; but those who cluster around the man who has gained a foothold in the town are only a fragment of his primary group. The family in the town exists under difficulties and tends to approximate the nuclear family in form, that is, a husband, wife, and children. Other relatives found in the compound of the extended family in the country are found more rarely in town dwellings.

When a crisis arises and the members of the nuclear family want to discuss it with others, being habituated to the extended family of the villages, they call in whatever kinsman, no matter how distant, who happens to be in the town. Proximity in space takes the place of closeness of relationship in the town.

Marriage

In most areas, there are three kinds of marriage which are recognized as legal: civil, church, and customary. The first two are on the Western model and the latter is supposed to be according to tribal customs. In fact, however, customary law cannot operate effectively to attain traditional goals in the towns[15] because a marriage is a contract between families and not merely between individuals, and it often happens that both of the families are not in the town and may even be unknown to each other. Traditional gifts are usually commuted to money, and labor services, if observed, are shortened in time. Furthermore, customary law marriage between members of different tribes is an anomaly unless, as sometimes happens, both agree to accept one of the tribal forms. If a man is an immigrant into a town where one tribe is dominant he may do this. In addition to legal marriage, there are casual unions which break up when either party so desires.

OUTLOOK

The towns and cities will play an increasingly vital part in the life of Africa. The town is the door through which Africa is entering the modern world. Civilization in the twentieth century is an urban civilization. "The influences which cities exert upon the social life of man are greater than the ratio of the urban population would indicate, for the city . . . is the initiating and controlling center of economic, political, and cultural life that has drawn the most remote parts of the world into its orbit and woven diverse areas, peoples, and activities into a cosmos." [16] In Africa cultural groups are beginning to appear in the cities; nationalist movements get rural support but have their headquarters in the towns. Nations are in the process of formation in Africa and the towns are the crucible. The towns today give us an insight into the future. "As the city is, so will the nation be." [17]

NOTES

[Starred items are recommended as further readings.]

*[1] Godfrey and Monica Wilson, *The Analysis of Social Change* (Cambridge, Eng.: Cambridge University Press, 1945), Chap. XI.

[2] Georges Balandier, "Document du travail," presented at the UNESCO Conference in Abidjan, 1954.

[3] J. Dresch, "Ville Congolaise," *Reveue de Geographie Humaine et d'Ethnologie,* Vol. 3 (1949); quoted by Balandier.

[4] Sheila T. Van der Horst, "The Union of South Africa: Economic Problems in a Multiracial Situation," in [*Annals of the American Academy of Political and Social Science*. Vol. 298 (1955), pp. 71-83.]

[5] Cf. Raymond Bertieaux, *Aspects de l'Industrialisation en Afrique Centrale* (Brussels: Institut des Relations Internationales, 1953), p. 24.

[6] Organization for European Economic Cooperation, *Investments in Overseas Territories, in Africa South of the Sahara* (Paris, 1951).

[7] Industrialization based on electricity and automotive transport, unlike that based on steam and railways, need not result in excessive concentration, but it can be assumed that, even with planning for a dispersed development of industry (of which there has been no indication as yet), any increase in industrialization in Africa will contribute somewhat to urban growth. Cf. William F. Ogburn, "Inventions of Local Transportation and the Patterns of Cities," in Paul Hatt and Albert J. Reiss, Jr. (Eds.), *Reader in Urban Sociology* (Glencoe, Ill.: The Free Press, 1951), p. 262.

[8] Similar effects in the competition for water supplies and other goods were pointed out by Lewis Mumford, "The Costs of Costiveness," in his *The Culture of Cities* (New York: Harcourt, Brace and Company, 1938), pp. 240 ff.

[9] United Nations, *Enlargement of the Exchange Economy in Tropical Africa* (New York, 1954), p. 30.

[10] Kofi Abrefa Busia, *The Position of the Chief in the Modern Political System of Ashanti* (London: Oxford University Press for the International African Institute, 1951); Monica Hunter, *Reaction to Conquest: Effects of Contact with Europeans on the Pondo of South Africa* (London: H. Milford, published for the International Institute of African Languages and Cultures by Oxford University Press, 1936); Raymond Leslie Buell, *Liberia: A Century of Survival, 1847-1947* (Philadelphia: University of Pennsylvania Press, 1947), p. 13; Louis S. B. Leakey, *Mau Mau and the Kikuyu* (London: Methuen & Co., 1952).

[11] Marion Levy, Jr., *The Structure of Society* (Princeton: Princeton University Press, 1952), pp. 248 ff.

[12] "Informal means of social control—such as gossip . . . could remain powerless were it not for the fact that they are backed up by economic pressures. . . ." —Svend Riemer, "Villagers in Metropolis," in Edgar A. Schuler *et al.* (Eds.), *Outside Readings in Sociology* (New York: The Thomas Y. Crowell Company, 1952), p. 648.

[13] M. McCulloch, *Survey of Recent and Current Field Studies on the Social Effects of Economic Development in Inter-Tropical Africa* (UNESCO, in preparation).

[14] G. D. H. Cole, "The Conception of the Middle Class," in Schuler *et al.* (Eds.), *op. cit. supra* (note 12), pp. 345 ff.

*[15] A. L. Epstein, *The Administration of Justice and the Urban African: A Study of Urban Native Courts in Northern Rhodesia*, London: Her Majesty's Stationery Office, 1953.

*[16] Louis Wirth, "Urbanism As a Way of Life," in Hatt and Reiss (Eds.), *op. cit. supra* (note 7), p. 32.

[17] William B. Munro, "City," in *Encyclopaedia of the Social Sciences* (New York, 1937), Vol. 3, p. 481.

FOR FURTHER READING

U.N.E.S.C.O., *Social Implications of Industrialization and Urbanization in Africa South of the Sahara,* Paris: U.N.E.S.C.O., 1956. A useful survey with excellent bibliographic aids.

Four recent studies that are thorough in detail and of considerable theoretical importance are Epstein, A. L., *Politics in an Urban African Community,* Manchester: Manchester University Press on behalf of the Rhodes-Livingstone Institute, 1958; Banton, Michael, *West African City: A Study of Tribal Life in Freetown,* London: Oxford University Press for the International African Institute, 1957; Balandier, Georges, *Sociologie actuelle de l'Afrique noire: Dynamique des changements sociaux en Afrique Centrale,* Paris: Presses Universitaires de France, 1955; Sofer, Cyril and Rhona, *Jinja Transformed: A Social Survey of a Multi-racial Township,* Kampala: East African Institute for Social Research, East African Studies No. 4, 1955. The first is a study of a Copperbelt community in Northern Rhodesia; the second, of the major city in Sierra Leone; the third, of Brazzaville in the French Congo, and the fourth, of a Uganda town.

THE UNIFORM OF COLOR
IN SWAZILAND*

Hilda Kuper

There have been many studies of the causes of racial tensions in South Africa and many predictions of future trends. Kuper's analysis, in which she draws on her extensive anthropological fieldwork in Swaziland, presents an important aspect of the caste relationship: the views of Africans held by Whites and those of Whites held by Africans. These attitudes are often found in situations of culture contact between two peoples, particularly peoples of different physical types. In some cases they disappear or are greatly modified with the passage of time, but in southern Africa they have become more and more rigid in recent years. Racial attitudes are reinforced by interaction between groups, and social change has produced an increasing rigidity of relations between White and African.

The Swazi formerly comprised an important African state with highly organized military forces. Today about three-fifths of them live in the British High Commission Territory of Swaziland. There is almost no industry in this small country, which is essentially a reserve from which many Swazi, particularly the men, go to work in South Africa for varying periods of time. Unlike the situation in South Africa, the number of Whites in Swaziland is small, and contacts between African and Whites take place primarily in a rural setting, yet much the same kind of race relations occur in both countries.

Throughout South Africa color has become the primary index of status in all activities. A small self-conscious white community possessed of the technology of a great mechanical age lives in vital dependence on the labor of a black subject people.

To treat Europeans and Non-Europeans as isolated units is legitimate only in sociological analysis. As time goes on, the bonds between the groups increase and even the most prejudiced will have to admit

* Reprinted from *The Uniform of Colour,* Johannesburg: Witwatersrand University Press, 1947, pp. 26-36, by permission of the author and the Witwatersrand University Press.

their interdependence. Even in Swaziland, where Native life has been less affected than in the Union of South Africa, the culture of the Swazi has many features of Western European behavior and belief, interpreted according to traditional Swazi values.

The Swazi, like other nations of the vast Bantu-speaking peoples, appear to possess tremendous strength to resist, to multiply, and even to flourish. Unlike other primitives in Australia and America, they have not disappeared before the White man; they have withstood wars, drought, dispossession, and disease; they have imitated and absorbed new behavior and beliefs. Segregation has become a politician's delusion, denied by the sight of Natives in mines and factories, on European farms and in European homes, denied by the shirt and the blanket in the huts of the Native reserves.

Interdependence does not mean similarity nor equality of the parts which constitute the whole. Nor does it mean harmony between them. In Western European society the culture of the working class is in many ways different from the culture of the professional and leisured upper class. In South Africa difference of class is accentuated by difference of color, culture, and active tradition. And in the tiny Swaziland Territory, where economic classes are scarcely developed, cooperation and conflict are expressed in terms of color.

1. THE COLOR COMPOSITION

The total population of Swaziland in the last census of 1936 [1] numbered 156,715, of whom 2,740 were Europeans, 153,270 were Bantu, and 705 were Colored.

The uniform of color unites each group despite varying degrees of in-group heterogeneity. Within the European group in particular there are marked differences of origin, language, belief, occupation, and interest.

White Swazilanders come from many lands: 1,022, roughly 35% of the population, are second-generation Swazilanders; 1,262, approximately 46%, were born in other British possessions in Africa; 224 come from British possessions in Europe, and the remainder from other parts of Europe, from Asia, America, and Australia. In 1938 Hitlerism drove into the Territory some 70 German-Jewish refugees, the largest number of white immigrants at any one time.

There is no uniformity of language; while English is the official language, 46% of the population speaks English and Afrikaans, 19% speaks English only, 29% Afrikaans only, 1% speaks neither English nor Afrikaans, and the language of the remaining population is unspecified.[2]

They worship in many churches: some 50% of the population belongs to the Nederduitse Gereformeerde Kerk, the Hervormde Kerk, and the Gereformeerde Kerk—the three South African churches that have strong views on the Natives.

They are employed in many occupations: 24% in agriculture, 1% in mining, 3% in industrial pursuits (textile, metal, baking, building, etc.), 7% in "professional service" (administrative, mission, etc.), 5% in commerce, 23% are housewives, and the remainder are engaged in miscellaneous occupations or are junior dependents.

Within the heterogeneous group conflict is frequent. It does not take the direction of class conflict; most of the men are engaged in independent agriculture and the remainder belong to the *petite bourgeoisie* of industry.

The line of cleavage within the White group runs firstly between the two major national units, Boer and British, whose antagonism is rooted in the history of South Africa and persists in the distinction in language, religion, and political loyalty. Secondly, there is occasional friction on economic or political issues between interest groups, farmers sometimes disputing with miners who offer their recruits facilities beyond the limits that agriculture can afford; and settlers criticize the Government for "pro-Native" concessions. Finally, there is latent hostility and competition within the same interest group—between different sects of the church, or different trading companies.

The Natives are predominantly "Protectorate" born. All speak Swazi or Zulu, the official Bantu language, and many have a smattering of English and Afrikaans. The traditional religion, the ancestral cult, is still accepted by over 70%, but the number of converts to one or other of the numerous Christian sects is steadily increasing. While practically every Swazi in the Territory is a peasant in outlook, approximately 40% of adult males are annually absent at work outside the Territory, and a further 15% are employed by Europeans within the Territory. A few teachers, preachers, traders, and artisans are independent of the land for their subsistence.

While in conservative Swazi society the main stratification is by birth, and members of the hereditary aristocracy hold privileged positions in politics, the ancestral cult, and the traditional economy, conflict occurs nowadays between conservative leaders and ambitious subjects, between uneducated and educated, and between converted and orthodox.

The Colored population[3] includes 133 people from other parts of Africa, more particularly from the Cape (26), Natal (34), and the Transvaal (28). Immigration has decreased in recent years, and emigration to the Union, more particularly of lighter skinned Colored individuals, has begun.

On the whole, the Colored section is less heterogeneous than the Black. Over 98% profess Christianity; only 18 Colored individuals belong to the three churches which represent the majority of European Swazilanders. Grades of education and wealth vary considerably: a few Coloreds have passed Standard VI,[4] others are completely illiterate; some speak fluent English or Afrikaans, and others know only a Bantu mother-tongue; a few have learnt trades, serve in shops, or own large farms, but the majority fall into the class of laborers and peasants.

The Coloreds form a less clearly defined community than either Whites or Blacks, and in this chapter I am concerned with them only in so far as they illustrate the grading of people of the two "pure stocks" on the basis of color. A certain amount of "crossing over" takes places from Coloreds to Europeans, but the myth of inequality as well as of difference remains unchallenged. Membership of one color group automatically excludes membership of either of the other color groups. The few Coloreds who "pass" into the White group, aim at assimilating the *mores* of the new group including its exclusiveness.

2. THE WHITE MAN'S MYTH OF THE BLACK MAN

The emphasis on color appears in racial myths. In recent years Nazism has extended, made more formal, more conscious, the nature of race mythology, but the underlying concept has its roots deep in human history, and has led from early times to executions, pogroms, economic starvation, and bloody crusades.[5]

When, in the nineteenth century, Europeans entered Mswati's land, they already held the belief that black men were inferior to white men. The doctrine of racial superiority was drawn from the Bible, and was confirmed and reinforced by the layman's interpretation of Darwin's theory of evolution.

Tales told by white Swazilanders about the black men stress two main features: firstly, their inherent inferiority and inability to acquire the white man's culture and, secondly, their uncontrolled emotional, or barbaric, nature. I collected a number of anecdotes from Europeans of all groups related to me to illustrate Swazi "racial characteristics." "Swazi are just like children" was a favorite opening; I was looked at askance when I asked the Europeans if their own children were like Swazi. The statements are simple and naive: "Natives can imitate but can't think for themselves"; "Natives have such happy natures; nothing worries them." To illustrate the inherent inferiority, stories such as the following were recounted:

(1) "I receive the most ridiculous letters from boys asking me if I can employ them as clerks. Some have passed Standard VI, and yet can hardly write English. They try to be very impressive. One began 'Aged Father,' and another 'Adorable Sir.' Those boys whom I have at present are quite good, but I have to supervise everything they do. They haven't

the brains of Europeans. It will take thousands of years before they reach our level."

(2) "They don't know the meaning of gratitude. I helped Mark whenever he was in trouble, looked after his wife when she was sick, gave him clothes for his children, and then he stole my husband's wallet."

(3) "I think they are pretty stupid. More stupid than we are, at any rate. I suppose it must be baffling to come suddenly into a European house and not know what to do, but they don't seem able to *think*. Lena always puts the cloth on the wrong way, no matter how often I show her, and twice she left the kettle on without any water." Finally, comes envy mixed with patronage: (4) "I think they are a wonderful people, always talking and laughing. They only worry about food, drink, and sex. Of course, they can't think about things as we can."

Stories of the "barbaric" nature of the African are frequent. A leading citizen and member of the Advisory Council stated that "Natives should not be given criminal jurisdiction because they love to see people hurt. That is their nature. It will take hundreds of years to change it. The other day, going to Mbabane, I saw one of the Queen Mother's messengers whipping a young girl. I told him to stop at once, and gave him hell. It seems that the kid had stolen a pumpkin from the Indlovukati's hut."

I was often warned of uncontrollable passions, inexplicable moodiness, and blood-curdling cases were described to me with lurid detail. These need not be repeated; they can be paralleled in the yellow press of any country. Occasional theft with violence, occasional murders, and very occasional rape, were used to characterize the whole nation. I have no figures to show if cases of "brutality" occur more frequently in countries where the inhabitants belong to two distinct cultures than in homogeneous areas. It may well be that if one section is subservient to the other and is not safeguarded and secure and is hostile to the master group, its members will more often take the law into its own hands. This would not be a specific "race" characteristic, but a reaction induced by discrimination and frustration.

It is not unusual to be told a touching story of the noble savage of pioneer days, generous, law-abiding, healthy and happy, and a few minutes later to be harrowed by a tale of his lust and cruelty. The stories are rarely purely descriptive, they point a moral, illustrate a judgment, and, above all, they stress the conviction that the two "races" should be kept distinct, and the desire that the "superior" race be secured in its domination.

Examples could be multiplied indefinitely; they are used to illustrate not the character of a particular individual or the nature of a particular relationship, but the innate psychological characteristics of "the

Native." The citation of an individual case is used to characterize the "race."

Illogicalities and inconsistencies are common to popular thought on controversial issues. A European who loved animals treated his Swazi laborers particularly badly. He was convinced that he was a fine fellow and roundly condemned the Swazi as "cruel savages" because they did not look properly after their animals.

Individual Natives who do not conform to the white man's stereotype of the black man are considered exceptions that do not prove any rule; it is the old story of a few "pet Jews" or tame lions.

But even the exceptions must be controlled, for side by side with the tales of inferiority is the fear, legalized as well as verbalized, that the Natives may acquire the techniques of the white man and oust him from his position of superiority. The white man is not prepared to share with other color groups his monopoly of skill and of knowledge by which he achieved his superiority.

The student is able to watch with scientific detachment the struggles and the hopes and the fears of the settlers, the crimes and blunders perpetrated by them in their fight against social and economic forces stronger than themselves, which threaten to lose for their children the advantages acquired on the basis of an initial cultural, but unproved racial, superiority. Because of this fear there is an outcry against Native development, Native education, and Native equality. The myths of Native inferiority and brutality are the moral supports for oppression and exclusion.[6]

3. THE BLACK MAN'S MYTH OF THE WHITE MAN

The association of inferiority with "race" was a concept introduced among the Swazi by the European. It was not that they had been isolated from contact with other physical types before the Europeans arrived. Swazi describe with a mixture of amusement and contempt the tiny, odd-shaped bodies of the Bushmen (*tiqu*—dwarfs) they found living in parts of the country on their arrival, but they did not associate physical traits with inherent cultural limitations. Bushmen were absorbed by the Bantu, they left their mark in the language and in the culture. Before the Bushmen intermarriage with other peoples had taken place, though in a past that is no longer remembered.

Shades of pigmentation in the nation evoke, in the same way as height and feature, aesthetic appraisal, not social discrimination. The color of the Swazi skin varies from deep brown to the gold of honey, and the features of some Swazi are exquisitely chiseled and delicate, and of others coarse and heavy. Standards of beauty change: since the reign of

Mbandzeni the light-skinned are admired, but I am told that before dark skins were considered more beautiful.

The white men who first entered the country were "a strange species" (*lolunye luhlobo*), and with them came a distinction that overrode the variations within the nation. Color set Swazi apart from European, it was made greater than the similarity of age, sex, belief, or occupation.

Swazi accept domination by the Europeans, but usually reject their myth of "racial superiority." A few Swazi regret their (often idealized) past and try to revive national customs, but most Swazi feel that the European has come to stay, and there is no organized anti-European movement. Hostility exists, however, with the acceptance of domination, and is expressed in isolated situations, but because the situations of contact are numerous and variable, hostility is not consistent nor constantly borne in mind. It may be directed against an administrator, miner, missionary, farmer, or against a specific activity, or even against the traditional Native leaders because of their relationship with the Europeans.

Swazi have developed their own myths to account for racial difference. A very few have taken over the Biblical damnation of the sons of Ham, or recount the following type of tale:—

"The Great, Great Father created the birds of the air and the beasts of the field and saw it was good. 'Now,' he said, 'I must create man.' He made him in the rushing winds, and when he looked he was not pleased with his work. Man was black and he was not beautiful. He then created the second man and he was black, tall and shiny, and the second man loitered by the wayside until he sank down upon the earth. His skin swelled and became wrinkled and then it broke. And when the second man shed his skin, there appeared a new skin, white and shining, and the second man was full of beauty and strength. The Great One said: 'O second man! My work is good! I will give you all power and all wisdom, and you shall be greater than the first man.' So it is then that there are black and white people!"—(W. M. Ntshuntshu).

The majority of stories do not describe the European as "full of beauty and strength," but as a creature different and suspect.

Swazi, like the European, have developed a stereotype, and they react to the stereotype and not to the individual. Swazi often say that all Europeans look alike; a sophisticated informant once remarked, "Even I take some time to learn the appearance of a European. Look. I worked for S. for four years, but when I try to recall him, I only see white faces."

The stereotype is essentially different from themselves; it is more skillful but less kind, more powerful but less generous. In other words, most Swazi acknowledge the superior skills of the European, but not the superior quality of his *ubuntfu* (human kindness). His skill is described as part of the white man, not as the culmination of years of experiment and toil. Just as the average Swazi do not speculate about the origin of the hoe but accept it as their heritage, so they regard cars, "flying machines," electric lights, books, as *imihlolo yabelungu* (white man's wonders). This is why Swazi often express themselves with an accommodating humility. "We are but children and know nothing," "Have patience, Nkosi, we are fools," are common remarks made at meetings with officials. A chief wrote in the *Times of Swaziland* of his people's "lack of logical powers, owing to inferiority of mental capacities." Some of these statements are merely diplomacy, but the tendency is to stress the cleverness of the European in relation to themselves.

Hand in hand with this attitude expressed in terms of admiration mixed with fear, is suspicion of, and sometimes contempt for, the human side of the European. Swazi do not seem to weary of telling of acts of cruelty and cunning, dating from the first years of contact; it is interesting to compare these tales with the European's version of the same period with the stress on Native witchcraft and savagery.

Swazi parents terrify children with stories of the white "bogeyman." Frequently when a baby cried and I was in the hut, it was threatened, "Quiet, or the white one will take you." When I mentioned to Sobhuza how painful it was to me, he replied: "You must expect this. They see you as an *umlungu* (European) until you prove yourself to be an *umuntfu* (person)."

A few stories characterize the Europeans as greedy for cheap workers irrespective of the cost of life and happiness. I heard many legends of Europeans kidnapping little boys and taking them far away to work for them. As a result, when travelers stop their cars in isolated areas to ask herdboys the way, these often scurry off in terror and hide in the grass. The legends have their bases in actual episodes of the pioneering days. From north to south I pursued the elusive Mandatana, the European wizard who was reputed to kill men, and then enslave their shrunken bodies. Other stories tell of European greed, meanness, and lack of hospitality. They describe things experienced and imagined. Facts are often distorted to fit accepted myths. Thus men repeat the statement that European officials shot Native cattle when they strayed into a proclaimed area, and merely impounded the herds of white farmers. But when closely questioned, they were unable to support the allegation. Europeans are accused of victimization, though to an impartial observer they acted with sympathy and justice. A gift, even when it is graciously accepted, is often suspected to be a bribe. Because of the depth of their suspicion, Swazi are slow to adopt new ideas sponsored by the European.

The myth is accentuated and not destroyed by the fact that within the white group Swazi recognize minor subdivisions: a man is a White, then he is an Englishman, Boer, Jew, or German, or he is an official,

farmer, trader or missionary. With these distinctions go emotive generalizations: the English are "people with law"; "the Jews are with
money"; "the Boers hate black people," and so on. But these are not important differences in face of color unity; in fact they serve to stress the
fundamental alliance of color. "White people join together, like a husband who will hit a stranger who tries to help him beat his wife."

A Swazi educated at Lovedale wrote the following rules of black-
white behavior:—

(1) The first thing to remember always is that we do not know the hearts
of Europeans.
(2) Show respect; if necessary, agree to lies.
(3) Never forget to fear the White, for if you fear him, you will be
ready when he deceives you.
(4) Listen carefully to what he says and watch what he does, and you will
learn a lot.
(5) Most Europeans and most Natives deceive, but no European can
feel the pain of a Native.
(6) Europeans hate us and show us no respect.

He ended, "I may be wrong. I agree that I do not understand Europeans." Of course there are exceptions to the type described above; but
on the whole the stereotype is fairly clear.

NOTES

[1] Since these are the most accurate
figures, I use them rather than later estimates. Subsequent figures are also taken
from the census unless otherwise stated.

[2] The census figures do not include
the German-Jewish refugees; they are all
learning English, and some are also learning Afrikaans.

[3] Actually the Colored population is
701, the remaining four are Asiatics, but
in most of the statistics the Asiatics are
included as Coloreds.

[4] [The highest grade of elementary
school in British systems.]

[5] The scientific study of race is the
field of the physical anthropologist and
geneticist, who study the inheritance of
physical characteristics. Their classifications of races are based on recognized
measurements of height, blood tests and
other criteria. Culture is distinct from
race; unfortunately this distinction is

frequently ignored. In this paper I use
the term "race" as a social concept.

[6] The attitude towards a Native attaining higher education was brought
out when Abner Nkosi, a teacher, succeeded, by correspondence courses, in
passing his B.A. and wanted to further
his studies overseas. For this, money was
required, and a committee was formed
to obtain help from various individuals
and organizations. Some considered "his
education was more than enough for a
Swazi"; others asked "what shall we do
with a man so high?" From the majority of Europeans to whom I and others
spoke, there was definite discouragement
on the grounds that "he would get above
himself," that "Kaffirs must not be too
civilized," that "raw Natives are better
workers," that he would put "queer
ideas" in the heads of the people, or
"create trouble." Very few were pre-

pared to assist, and one of them admitted: "Well, it can't do any harm to educate one or two, but we mustn't encourage too many. We must keep them in their place." Finally, largely through the assistance of a high official, the necessary funds were obtained. Abner Nkosi went to Yale, and passed his M.A. He is now headmaster of a large Government school in Ermelo, Transvaal.

FOR FURTHER READING

Kuper has written two general works on Swazi culture: *The Swazi,* London: International African Institute, Ethnographic Survey of Africa, Southern Africa, I, 1952; and *An African Aristocracy: Rank among the Swazi,* London, Oxford University Press for the International African Institute, 1947.

An anthropologist, Hortense Powdermaker, has carried out studies similar in nature to Kuper's but using somewhat different field techniques: "Communication and Social Change Based on a Field Study in Northern Rhodesia," *Transactions of the New York Academy of Sciences,* 1955, *17,* 430-40; "Social Change through Imagery and Values of Teen-age Africans in Northern Rhodesia," *American Anthropologist,* 1956, *58,* 783-813.

Patterson, Sheila, *Colour and Culture in South Africa,* London: Routledge and Kegan Paul, 1953. A study of the problems of the Cape Colored in South Africa.

Hellmann, Ellen, and Abrahams, Leah (eds.), *Handbook on Race Relations in South Africa,* London: Oxford University Press for the South Africa Institute of Race Relations, 1949. A basic source book.

Hoernlé, R. F. Alfred, *South African Native Policy and the Liberal Spirit,* Johannesburg: Witwatersrand University Press, 1945; DeKiewiet, Cornelius W., *The Anatomy of South African Misery,* London: Oxford University Press, 1956; Dvorin, Eugene P., *Racial Separation in South Africa: An Analysis of Apartheid Theory,* Chicago: University of Chicago Press, 1952. Three thoughtful books that present many of the underlying problems involved in South African race relations.

LIFE IN A JOHANNESBURG SLUM YARD*

Ellen Hellmann

This picture of urban Africans living in a crowded yard in a Johannesburg suburb presents graphically the gap between the traditional life of rural South African societies and the anomalous and often confusing setting in which city Africans find themselves. Pressed by social restrictions and the constant struggle for subsistence, many Africans are forced into illegal pursuits for the sake of survival, yet the trend has been increasingly toward urban residence.

The conditions reported here are those of the mid-1930's and slum yards of the type described are now a thing of the past in South African cities. However, in the locations and townships outside urban boundaries, the life of the African is little changed, and the situation is, if anything, compounded.

Although for reasons of a misguided economy a Native Census was not undertaken in 1931 and consequently complete statistics for the African[1] population of South Africa are entirely lacking, the available evidence points to a marked increase in the African urban population.[2] The 1921 census revealed the fact that African women also were settling in town in much larger numbers than had previously been the case, and all indications point to a much greater increase in this section of the urban population since then. This growing inclination of the African to settle his wife and children in the urban center where he earns his livelihood indicates a tendency on his part to divorce himself from his rural bonds and to regard the town as his permanent home and not as the place of his solely temporary employment. The children of these families will, in all likelihood, eventually form a permanent and stable urban population, entirely dissociated from a rural background. Many of them—the potential citizens of a town—have been reared in a slum yard. Such yards represent for many Africans their first, and perhaps only, experience of a home.

---

* Abridged and with the author's revisions from "Native Life in a Johannesburg Slum Yard," *Africa,* 1935, 8, 34-62, by permission of the author and the International African Institute (author's copyright reserved).

Their impressions of Johannesburg, should they return to the Reserves, will be colored by this environment. Should they remain permanently in Johannesburg, even though they change their residence, the influence of their earlier environment must inevitably remain with them. In addition to forming the social setting for the Africans there resident, these yards, the centers of the illicit beer-brewing trade, are also a favored meeting resort for a great number of other Africans during their leisure hours. The Municipality, acting under the direction of the Urban Areas Act of 1923, is pursuing a policy from which it is anticipated that within a period estimated at five years the slum properties constituting these yards will have been demolished and the Africans from them accommodated in the locations and townships on the outskirts of Johannesburg. Despite, however, the transitory nature of the existence of the yards, their importance as a social background is sufficient to merit serious attention.

Rooiyard is typical of many such yards which exist all over those suburbs of Johannesburg where Africans are still permitted to reside. During the course of writing this article, Rooiyard was condemned by the local authorities as insanitary, a demolition order was granted, and the Africans were served with notices of eviction. Rooiyard is therefore no longer in existence. But, except for a difference in locality and slight variations in layout and construction, a description of Rooiyard, its manners and customs, is equally applicable to any other similar yard in Johannesburg, and for this reason I propose to continue using the present tense in my description of it.

Rooiyard, in New Doornfontein, Johannesburg, was chosen as a subject for investigation because it appeared to be typical of yards in general in Johannesburg and especially of yards in New Doornfontein, which is a suburb especially favored by the Africans owing to its central situation. Rooiyard has no special distinguishing marks and it bears a reputation neither more nor less unenviable than other yards which I visited during the course of several tours. Two factors influenced me in my final choice: the accessibility of Rooiyard and its large size, which is above the average and which gave promise of providing contacts with a larger number of families than would have been possible in a smaller yard.

The material for this report was gathered during a period of one year's investigation. I commenced working in Rooiyard in March 1933 and continued till April 1, 1934. During December, January, and February I discontinued daily visits to Rooiyard, but for the rest of the time I spent practically every morning, with the exception of Sunday mornings, in Rooiyard. At the commencement of my investigation I spent both mornings and afternoons there, but soon confined my work, in the main, to the mornings. I found the mornings best because then the women were generally in or about their rooms. In addition, there are far fewer beer customers in the mornings and, as was proved to me time and again, my presence in a room, while beer was being sold, was not welcome. My visits to Rooiyard over the week end were infrequent, and I only paid one night visit there. Initially I was intimidated by the earnest warnings of the police and the health inspectors against visiting Rooiyard during these hours of most active beer-selling. Although it would be an exaggeration to speak of danger—actual or potential—to the investigator in Rooiyard at night or over week ends, the drunken disorder of the yard and the definite hostility to my presence at these times did discourage me. At night, especially, in the gloomy alleyways in which the swaying and stumbling forms of drunken Africans were dimly discernible, I felt compelled to agree that Rooiyard was no place for the field worker.

The material I have been able to collect is by no means as complete as I would have wished it to be, as the difficulties which I encountered in endeavoring to build up a relationship of confidence with my informants were considerable. First and foremost comes the fact that the population of Rooiyard is actually a criminal class. This is an unavoidable result of the beer-brewing activities which, though illegal, are a necessary condition of their economic survival. This continuous conflict with the authorities has made the Africans in the yard, especially the women who are responsible for the making and selling of beer, extremely suspicious of all Europeans. I expended considerable pains and no little eloquence in my attempts to explain the nature of my work. Some women were, after a while, inclined to regard my presence as inoffensive or even to regard me as a friend, but, apart from the open hostility which I was in some cases unable to overcome, the general attitude was one of amused indifference. The men, perhaps owing to their more intimate contact with Europeans during the course of their work, were less hostile, but I did not have occasion to interview them to any considerable extent as they were usually absent from the yard. The shifting nature of the Rooiyard populace was also a hindrance. Several times I succeeded in gaining the confidence of an informant only to find that she was about to leave the yard owing to arrears of rent, a desire to return home, or for the purpose of taking up employment. Often, too, after having trained an informant to keep a daily budget of expenditure—a valuable index of confidence—I found that the more hostile elements in the yard had been at pains to warn my informant of the dire results which must inevitably follow such a reckless committal to paper of her vital statistics. The blame for the increased frequency and thoroughness of police beer-raids in Rooiyard during the last few months was also attributed to me. The language medium presented no difficulty as most of the Africans spoke English or Afrikaans with some measure of fluency.

Rooiyard consists of 107 rooms and covers an area of five stands with a total extent of 1,183 square yards. As a result of the large number of rooms which are built on this confined space, a state of extreme congestion prevails. The yard is roughly triangular in shape. Fifty-seven rooms are built on the boundary and face the yard and 15 rooms, 7 on one side and 8 on the other side of the triangle, face the street. In the center of the yard there is a double line of 35 rooms, built back-to-back and facing the rooms which skirt the yard, thus dividing the yard into two sections with rooms on either side and alleyways, about 15 feet to 20 feet in width, in the center. The 15 outer rooms and 14 of the inner rooms are built of brick and have cement floors, the remainder of the rooms being rickety constructions of old corrugated iron and thin wooden planks. The brick rooms vary in size from 10 feet by 11 feet to 11 feet by 12 feet. The partitioning walls, about 10 feet in height, do not reach the roof, which at its apex is about 15 feet high. The other rooms vary in size from 8 feet by 11 feet to 11 feet square, with a height of from 8 to 10 feet. The flooring boards are, in the majority of these 78 rooms, rotten. Some rooms have no flooring at all and the bare earth forms the floor. The doors of the rooms are badly fitted and have no proper locks, being fastened from the outside by a padlock and from the inside by a bent nail or rough contraption of wire. Each room is fitted with two windows, but as one window often gives access to an adjoining room, it is usually covered with a plate of tin. Cross ventilation is not possible in the 64 rooms which are built back-to-back. In summer the rooms are unbearably hot and in winter the cold winds which enter through the gaps and holes in the walls necessitate the constant burning of large coal-braziers, introducing an element of danger and rendering the atmosphere in the rooms extremely unhealthy. Very few of the roofs are rainproof, windowpanes are often missing, and the level of the floor is in a number of rooms below the level of the yard. In wet weather the rain water flows into the rooms, carrying with it the debris from the yard, and the discomfort of the occupants under these miserable conditions requires very little emphasis. The yard has a narrow entrance. Flanking the entrance inside the yard stand two cement garbage bins which serve the whole yard. The occupants are served by 6 latrines, three for men and three for women, but they are usually in such a bad state of repair and so neglected that the children shun them, as is amply testified by the condition of the alleyways inside the yard and of the pavements surrounding it. There is a "washing room" adjoining the lavatories, consisting of 4 corrugated iron walls with a cement floor and containing two water-taps, one or the other of which is never in working order. This single tap serves all the residents of the yard, and owing to the inevitable congestion a long queue of women waiting to fill their paraffin-tins with water for domestic purposes is a common sight.

The alleyways in the yard and the pavement on to which face the outer rooms are cluttered with an important part of the essential possessions of the Rooiyard Africans. Here stand the motley tins, ranging from one-gallon oil tins to large petrol drums, which are used for the preparation and storage of beer. The cooking-braziers are placed outside the rooms as the smallness of the rooms, which have to serve the needs of the whole family, does not permit of cooking operations being performed inside. Large packing-cases used for firewood occupy much of the available space outside each room. The repeated requests of the Health Inspector that the yard be cemented have remained unheeded, and after rains it is like a quagmire. In dry weather it is usually littered with an assortment of refuse and debris. Six Sotho women have each constructed a *lapa* (courtyard) of clay and cow-dung in front of their rooms, and these little courtyards form oases of cleanliness and order in the midst of the general litter of the yard. The Africans know that they should throw all refuse into the cement bins at the entrance of the yard. But when they see the refuse bins constantly overflowing and only desultory efforts made to keep the yard clean, it is small wonder that they themselves display no vital interest. They are fully aware of the insecurity of their tenure in Rooiyard and have not come to regard the place as their "home." It is merely, owing to the force of circumstances, their temporary refuge. Candles provide the sole means of illumination. At night it is difficult to conceive that Rooiyard, dark and eerie, and lit only by the fitful gleam of candles and the glowing coals in the braziers, is situated in the midst of a progressive city.

The interiors of the greater number of the rooms present a striking contrast to the unsavory disorderliness of the yard. Although the ceilings are often covered with cobwebs, the floors are well scrubbed and the belongings of the family tidily arranged. That this cleanliness is achieved only by the tireless expenditure of energy and labor is conclusively proved by the constant preoccupation of the Rooiyard woman with her washing, scrubbing, polishing, and dusting. It is no mean feat on the part of the African woman to keep the small and congested abode of her family in such good order, for the Rooiyard environment does not offer any stimulus towards greater effort.

The fittings of the rooms reveal the eagerness with which the material culture of Western civilization is being adopted. Every stage of transition is exemplified in the rooms of Rooiyard, from the paucity of furniture of the new arrival from the kraal to the comparative opulence of the fittings of the African who has had several years of urban residence. There are only three rooms which do not boast a bed—invariably the first purchase—and the three families in these rooms are all recent immigrants from rural areas. All the remaining rooms in Rooiyard are furnished with at least one bed, which is always raised on bricks so that the space under the bed may be utilized for the storage of the boxes and trunks containing the possessions of the family. Curtains, usually of cheap chintz, are always hung in front of the bed so that the parents, who occupy the bed, may be ensured some measure of privacy from the prying eyes of their children, who sleep on the floor. Rough, backless benches for the accommodation of beer customers are necessary accessories to every household. The possession of furniture is one of the few criteria of social status in Rooiyard, and the gradual entry of a family into the realms of prosperity synchronizes with its gradual acquisition of new articles of furniture. When a family moves to another room in town or goes home to the country, the furniture, a visible proof of progress, is taken with it.

One of the best furnished rooms contains a bed costing £1, a sideboard costing £13 10s. od., a table and four chairs costing £9, and a gramophone costing £8 15s. od. The walls are tastefully papered with wallpaper instead of being plastered with old newspaper posters as is commonly the case. Linoleum, a much coveted article in Rooiyard, covers the floor. The voluminous curtains in front of the bed and the windows are of silk. Numerous framed pictures, chiefly of film stars, adorn the walls. A rough wooden table accommodates the paraffin cooker and domestic utensils. This table and the inevitable benches are the only articles of native manufacture in the room.

Not many rooms are as completely furnished as this one, some Africans using packing-cases as substitutes for the articles cited above. In other rooms a couch serves the purpose of chairs. One woman is the proud possessor of a second-hand organ which is, however, more valuable as an economic than a cultural asset, as its melodious strains serve to attract beer-customers to this room. Two families have purchased pianos, but as the owners are dependent on casual friends to play them, they are manifestly concessions to a desire for enhancing personal prestige and do not fulfil any practical function.

All these purchases are made possible by the hire-purchase system. The average wage of the Rooiyard man is 18s. 1d. per week. The wife supplements this income mainly through the sale of beer, but nevertheless cash purchases remain an impossibility for practically all Africans. Hence most purchases are made "by time," as is the current expression in Rooiyard. Payments are usually effected at the rate of £1 per month, and it is unusual for Africans to commit themselves to payments for more than one article at a time.

There is very little evidence of the survival of Bantu material culture in Rooiyard. With the exception of a few recently arrived Shangaan women who still wear their tribal costume, consisting of voluminous double-pleated skirts of print lavishly adorned with beads, clothing and personal adornments are predominantly Western. The young girls prefer lipstick and powder to the facial tattooed lines of the older women. Even the time-honored *imbeleko*[3] is giving way to the blanket. Saucepans, pots and pans, and, above all, the ubiquitous tins have ousted domestic utensils of native manufacture. The facilities for the purchase of ready-prepared mealie meal and ready-stamped mealies have rendered the wooden pestle and mortar and winnowing basket nearly obsolete. Some few women still possess these articles and occasionally use them for the more economical preparation of food for a "party." That this absorption of European material culture is not a transient and fluctuating, but a cumulative and permanent process, is not to be doubted. African handicrafts are dying out in the country. In urban areas the art is considered superfluous. The children do not become acquainted with the utensils of native manufacture, nor would they know how to handle them. The persistent endeavors of the African to absorb European material culture are limited only by his poverty. He aspires to possess the amenities which the invading culture has to offer him and a great part of his labor is conditioned by this desire. It is only his utter poverty that restricts and hinders him and gives rise to the malapropisms of culture contact as exemplified by the picture of half-naked children huddling together for warmth under a piano. At present the African is eagerly grasping whatever lies within his economic reach, but the next step will be the sifting of essential from nonessential.

The permanent population of Rooiyard at the beginning of September 1933 consisted of 235 adults and 141 children. These 376 inhabitants were accommodated in 105 rooms, and of the two remaining rooms one was used as a tailoring shop and the other as a church. The average number of occupants per residential room was 3.58. But this low average cannot be accepted at face value, as there is a large shifting population in Rooiyard which cannot be assessed and which consists of relatives and friends who have come to seek refuge while unemployed or to spend a holiday in the city of which they have heard so much. Apart from 11 Indians and 5 Cape Coloreds, the remainder of the population is of Bantu stock, practically every South African Bantu tribe being represented. Of the residents 5 per cent consist of natives of Rhodesia and there are, in addition, one Negro from America and one native of Nyasaland. Of the families 40 per cent are Sotho, 27 per cent are Nguni (including Zulu, Xhosa, Swazi, Fingo, and Ndebele) and 2 per cent are Shangaan. The remaining families are mixed, husband and wife belonging to different tribes. Despite the numerical preponderance of the Sothos, no one single tribe predominates. The Africans of Rooiyard, unlike tribal Africans, are characterized by a pronounced individualism. There are no bonds which integrate the different families in Rooiyard, nor is there any greater cohesion between families of the same tribe. Each family fends for itself and shows but a casual and passing interest in its neighbors.

Temporary friendships, born of common residence and proximity, do exist, but are more frequent between women of the same tribe. This is due more to the facility of intercourse consequent upon speaking the same language, than to a sense of tribal solidarity. But the contacts thus formed are so fleeting that a family will depart from Rooiyard without informing its erstwhile friends either of the day of its departure or of its new address. Possibly the competition which exists between the women as rival beer-sellers is a deterrent to the creation of a greater intimacy and the formation of more permanent bonds. As would be expected, Zulu and Sotho are the two main language media, although it would be a safe generalization to add that length of urban residence and consequent multiplicity of contacts is correlated with a mastery of more Bantu languages.

Although the majority of the inhabitants of Rooiyard have not severed their connection with the country—there is constant going to and fro to relatives in the country for puberty rites, funerals, and conclusions of mourning ceremonies—and hence cannot be considered as a permanently settled urban class, a census of the period of residence in Rooiyard of one hundred families indicates a relatively high degree of permanency of residence. The average period of residence, 17.94 months, points to a greater permanency than obtains among the poorer section of the white population. This high average is in reality maintained by 40 of these families which constitute the more permanently settled section with an average length of residence of 37.27 months. The other 60 families form a relatively shifting population with an average length of residence of 5.05 months.

The rent for rooms in Rooiyard including water varies from 20s. per month each for 4 of the smallest rooms to 40s. per month each for some of the larger brick rooms, the majority of the rooms being let at 30s. per month. A shop, which is situated in the yard and serves as a kind of concession store for Rooiyard, is let at £25 per month. The municipal valuation of Rooiyard is £390 for the ground and £2,030 for the improvements. The valuation of the improvements may assuredly be taken as exaggerated. For the 12 months ending September 1933 the gross rental return based on the municipal valuation was 86 per cent, but since that time rents have been raised for a considerable number of rooms. The net annual return, after deducting £235 13s. 5d. for water, £36 for sanitary charges, £27 for special refuse charges, and £20 3s. 2d. for rates and taxes, is 74 per cent. Even after making allowance for bad debts and the wages of the two Africans in charge of the yard, it is assuredly justifiable to assume that the return on capital outlay is exceedingly high.

The Africans resident in Rooiyard are not blind to the unsatisfactory features of their environment. They complain bitterly of the high rents, which they rightly maintain are out of all proportion to value received. They revolt against the filth and congestion of their surroundings. They inveigh against the appalling state of the sanitary arrangements. But despite its obvious disadvantages, there is an incessant demand for accommodation in Rooiyard. As the number of yards in the central suburbs of Johannesburg decreases as a result of the closure policy of the Municipality, so the demand for rooms in the still existing yards increases. "Skokiaan Yard," the popular designation for yards of which Rooiyard is an example, indicates their nature. They are the centers, *par excellence,* for the brewing and selling of beer. Total prohibition has been enjoined upon the Africans of Johannesburg, but the illegality of beer-brewing only hampers but does not discourage the women brewers from continuing their occupation. It has been estimated that a minimum income of £6 per month is essential to the well-being of a family of 4 in Johannesburg.[4] In Rooiyard the standard of living varies enormously, some childless couples spending £8 per month while a family of 7 managed to subsist, during a month of great hardship and unemployment, on £2 2s. 11d. (excluding rent). The evidence from Rooiyard proves conclusively that the earnings of the male head of the family, averaging 18s. 1d. per week, cannot cover the unavoidable living expenses of a family.[5] Hence it is imperative that the wife supplement her husband's income. Domestic service is becoming increasingly more difficult to obtain and often places the wife under the obligation of residing at her place of employment, consequently separating her almost completely from her family. Among one hundred women in Rooiyard, only 10 per cent earned £1 or more at a legitimate occupation. The remaining women were entirely dependent upon their beer business to augment the family income. The central position of Rooiyard and its accessibility are great attractions to beer customers, and this fact is one of the two most important reasons for the reluctance of the Africans of the yard to move to the locations. "What about my business?" is the common counterquery to questions concerning their unwillingness to leave Rooiyard. Its proximity to the area where the majority of Africans are employed confers one other direct benefit. The Africans are saved considerable expenditure on conveyance. Orlando, the new location to which the Africans are as far as possible being transferred, is 10 miles from the center of Johannesburg. The train fare of 8s. 6d. per month is, according to European standards, not excessive. But it is a great drain on the meager African income. While the distance from the town militates against a beer business, it also increases the obstacles which a woman has to surmount in the pursuance of a legitimate occupation. Some women augment the family income by part-time domestic service. In the intervals they return to Rooiyard and attend to the needs of their children. Such employment would become impracticable were they to reside in a location. Other women take in washing for Europeans. The time and expense involved in fetching washing from Johannesburg, transporting it to the location and returning it again, make this form of occupation unprofitable. These reasons, founded upon economic necessity, actuate the distaste of the African for the locations and their determination to live in a central area.

A more detailed analysis of one hundred families[6] reveals that the breaking up of the family is one of the first results of slum residence. The total number of children born to the hundred wives of these families, many of whom are still of child-bearing age, is 360, of whom 239 still survive. Although accurate figures could not be obtained on this point, the general impression gained was that the majority of deaths occurred in the first year of the child's life. Of these 239 children, 127 are living with their parents in Rooiyard, 104 with relatives in the country, and 8 are either married or are residing at the place of their employment. In the case of 35 families all their children are resident in Rooiyard. There are 34 families in which the children are separated, one or more living in the country with relatives and the remainder living with their parents in Rooiyard. In 23 families all the children are in charge of relatives in the country. The remaining 8 women are childless. This means that in more than half of the families investigated—to be precise 57 per cent—the parents are living in Johannesburg, while some or all of the children are separated for long periods from their parents and from each other.

The two main reasons for this severance of the family are economic necessity and the need for the moral training of the young. The Bantu woman is under tribal conditions an economic asset, and on her work in the fields the family is dependent for its subsistence. Despite the changed nature of her work, the African woman is of no less economic importance in an urban area. But she is no longer able to combine her work with the care of her children. At her home the nature of her work in the fields enabled her to take her children with her, to educate her daughters and to give them the training which would fit them to become, in their turn, the workers of the tribe. In Johannesburg the two means by which a woman can augment the revenue of the family—beer-brewing or a legitimate occupation such as domestic service—are both incompatible with the adequate care of children. Beer-brewing subjects the mother of the family to the constant danger of arrest and imprisonment, with the consequent necessity of leaving the children to the casual and intermittent care of a neighbor. Other employment removes the mother of the family from her home and leaves the children unattended. The uncertainty of regular employment and, in many cases, the desire to shift the burden of the maintenance of the children on to relatives at home are also factors instrumental in effecting a division of the family.

The unhealthiness of Rooiyard surroundings, the lack of playing-fields, and cramped quarters prompt many parents to leave their children at home in healthier surroundings. In addition to these purely utilitarian motives, concern for the moral welfare of their children is also instrumental in determining parents to send their children home to the country. The parents are aware of the inadequacies of such educational facilities as are available to them, as well as of the many harmful influences which will be brought to bear on their children from their earliest years in the Rooiyard surroundings. Daughters especially are not infrequently sent to relatives in the country, there to be secluded after their menses have commenced, and are then not permitted to return, for "here," say some mothers, "the girls only learn washing and ironing and running round with boys. At the kraal the girls learn all jobs and then get married."

Under tribal conditions, though the children do not receive a formal training according to European conceptions, they are gradually instructed, chiefly by their parents, in the performance of such tasks as will be required of them as adult men and women. Slowly and imperceptibly they absorb the precepts of the tribe and reverence for tribal traditions and tribal taboos is inculcated. The sanctions of the tribe become a living force to them. In all this gradual training the parents do not work single-handed. They are largely assisted by their kinspeople and, above all, by tribal institutions which provide for the "gradual initiation of the individual into the various strata of the society." [7] The whole social organization helps to mold the potential tribesman into the requisite social norm. And finally come the initiation rites, impressive in their insistence on and dramatization of tribal discipline and tribal solidarity, and symbolical of the transition from childhood to adulthood with its new duties and new obligations.

* * *

[In Rooiyard parents can spare little time from their economic pursuits to train their children for adult life; the school replaces the informal training that is a part of the tribal environment, but school attendance is lax and is not enforced.]

The parents quite frankly admit that they have no control over recalcitrant children. Their impotence to control their children and their lack of parental authority is a source of dismay to a large number of urban Africans. The individualism which is characteristic of the families of the Rooiyard has already been commented upon. Each family is an isolated unit. There is no framework of a social organization in which each family and each individual may find a rightful place. There is no common body of public opinion against which the individual hesitates to offend. African public opinion has not yet emerged owing to many factors, among the chief of which are mutual distrust between members of different tribes, lack of organized institutions which may cross-sect society and integrate its members, and instability of residence. Hence one extremely valuable method of controlling the members of African society does not, as yet, function. The criminal sanction has been so widely applied to what are, to the Africans, trivial misdemeanors, that conviction and imprisonment carry no social stigma. Offenses in respect of illegal possession of Native liquor, pass laws, and Native taxation,[8] which are treated as criminal offenses, are mainly economic in their implication to the African. The penalty is either the payment of a fine or imprisonment, and the latter, entailing a loss of employment, is an equally severe drain on financial resources. But such offenses, considered to be inspired by the white man and to be an unavoidable concomitant of his régime, do not outrage African public sentiment. In Rooiyard, where there were 65 convictions for illegal possession of Native liquor in a period of twelve months, an offense of this nature is considered merely as an unfortunate but inevitable vicissitude in the career of the beer-brewer. Economic pressure is the one force which permeates and activates the life of the African of Rooiyard. The need for employment and the fear of losing it play an important part in maintaining an equilibrium in African urban society. But the existence of a constant demand for labor, created by European dependence on African labor, has, by widening the scope of activity for the younger Africans, brought about their economic emancipation. Girls and boys of fifteen and onwards feel that they can fend for themselves and are not dependent on their parents for the necessities and, more important still, for the luxuries of life. This demand for African labor also affects the parental control of the rural Africans, for, as was frequently explained, even there a child, either male or female, will often say to its parent, "I can go to town and get better food there than you give me."

Initiation rites, when they take place in an urban area, lack the emphasis which, in tribal life, is placed upon a change of status. Among urban Africans there would seem to be a distinct difference between circumcising and noncircumcising tribes in the treatment of boys who have arrived at the age of puberty. The sons of men of a noncircumcising tribe usually reach maturity without being subjected to any ritual which will mark their emergence as adults. The sons of men of circumcision-practicing tribes are almost invariably sent to the country to take part in the initiation rites. But the main emphasis is on the physical operation and not on the socially valuable educative function of the rite. Despite the paralysis which is creeping over many African customs as a result of contact with a newer and superior culture, the contempt of the circumcised for the uncircumcised African is still plainly evident. The boys who are sent home to partake in the initiation school depart from and return to an environment in whose context the ritual of initiation has no place. It is small wonder, therefore, that these boys place the main emphasis on the physical aspect. In the puberty ritual of girls likewise the main concern is with the physiological change which has taken place. The four girls whose menses commenced while they were resident in Rooiyard were secluded there for periods varying from five days to one month. The main gist of the mother's instructions to her now nubile daughter was to the effect that she must henceforth refrain from any further intimate physical contact with young boys. "You must now know that you are a young girl and not a child. You must keep away from boys and not play with them and do silly things," says the mother to her daughter. And henceforth her vigilance over her daughter, who nevertheless finds many means of escape from it, will increase in an effort to avoid a premarital pregnancy.

But how is this premarital pregnancy to be avoided? The young men demand compliance of the girls as their right, and the young girls, by the absence of a forbidding sanction and by the example of the Rooiyard women to whom adultery is common, do not repulse their admirers. The young girl is importuned by a host of youthful admirers, many of them belonging to the ranks of her mother's beer-customers. Escape from the mother's vigilance is simple. The girl has only to slip outside the yard, and on the pavement, shrouded in darkness by the trees, no one will be sufficiently interested to look twice at her or, if she be recognized, to inform her mother of her whereabouts. Where possible the young man who has seduced a girl and caused her to conceive is mulcted in damages to the extent of £5 if he intends marrying her and £10 if he has no intention of regularizing the union by marriage. But it is easy for a young man to disappear, and furthermore many Africans are handicapped by their ignorance of legal procedure and have no knowledge of the approach to a Native Commissioner's Court where they could obtain redress for their wrongs. The young girls, although in some cases asking that the information be kept secret from their mothers, all admitted that they had had experience of sexual intercourse. And practically all the married women who had worked in an urban area before their marriage stated that their husbands had not been their first lovers. The only two methods of contraception known are coitus interruptus, which alone is known to and practiced by the rural Africans, and the use of condoms, which is being increasingly practiced by the younger urban men. African public opinion no longer demands, with any sincerity, premarital chastity. It accepts premarital pregnancy with a good-humored indifference. When a young girl of barely fourteen years became pregnant, the women of Rooiyard evinced a feeling of shocked amazement, but the girl was everywhere warmly received, and the warmth of her reception was no hypocritical one. Her mother, who prior to that had said, "If my daughter gets a baby before her time, true as God, I'll kill her," said, when her daughter became pregnant, as all mothers say, "What can I do? I can't chase her out." This changed attitude is plainly evident both in the large number of men and women living together in Rooiyard without having entered into any form of marriage at all, and in the total absence of discrimination against them on this account by the other inhabitants of Rooiyard. Of one hundred couples, each of whom occupied a room and constituted a domestic menage, twenty, or one-fifth of the total number, were not married. They were not, however, regarded as differing in any way from the married couples, nor was the illegitimacy of their own estate or of their children made the subject of reproach or abuse.

* * *

[The marriages of the remaining eighty couples were by Native customary union involving the passage of *lobola* (bride wealth, usually in the form of cattle), by Christian religious ceremony, by civil marriage ceremony, or by a combination of two or all of these. Although *lobola* was passed in seventy-seven marriages. its original function of determining the legitimacy of children and guaranteeing the conduct of husband and wife seems to be giving way to economic considerations, with money replacing cattle as the medium of exchange. City women look upon civil contractual marriage, performed by thirty-eight couples, as insurance against the husband's later entering into a civil marriage with a second wife, as he is free to do if he has been married by Native customary law or in a religious ceremony performed by an African minister who is not a recognized marriage officer.]

A responsible and educated African living in a location where 18,000 Africans reside, said, with the exaggeration of bitterness, "You will not find five peaceful homes here." He spoke of the increase of illegitimate children and maintained that in one year twenty girls of 13 to 14 years of age had borne illegitimate children. He commented on this as contributing to domestic quarrels, as the maintenance of an additional child creates a definite additional economic burden. But he dwelt on the alarming prevalence of adultery as constituting the main reason for family dissension. Although it would not be justifiable to attempt statistics of the number of harmonious households in Rooiyard—and there are certainly marriages in which there is evidence of great understanding, harmony, and affection between husband and wife—the abundant evidence of the great prevalence of adultery and prostitution in Rooiyard, and the continuous references to quarrels and fights between husband and wife, point to the disruption of family life. Only a few women admitted that they had one or more *nyatsi* (backdoor husband), but all informants readily and emphatically testified that their neighbors had "sweethearts." Several women were known to have accumulated comparative wealth from the proceeds of prostitution. The common practice of prostitution in Rooiyard is a natural outcome of the poverty of the Africans and of the nature of the main activity of the women. The women are all beer-brewers, and consequently attract to their rooms many men, the majority of whom are either single or far removed from their wives whom they have left in the country. Many women, hard pressed to balance expenditure and revenue and importuned by men in varying stages of intoxication, must be expected to succumb to prostitution as an additional means of supplementing their incomes. Many husbands are kept in ignorance of their wives' infidelity. Some husbands, intent on leading their own lives undisturbed, do not demur. Frequently, however, the husband, on discovering his wife's infidelity, attempts to revenge himself by attacking her lover. The fights, which are such a common feature of Rooiyard life, are practically without exception caused by competition for the favors of a woman or by the desire for revenge on the part of the deceived husband. The statement of a well-tested and reliable informant, a Manyika resident in Rooiyard, an intelligent observer, holding himself aloof from but keenly apprehensive of the prevailing conditions which he describes, states the situation tersely. He says, "All the men in the yard have sweethearts. I can see plenty of people, strange men come to the yard. The women sleep with them. This happens in the daytime when the husbands are away. All the women, only the old not, have men who sleep with them. I could sleep with any of them if I wanted. All the women make a business of it. Nobody tells the husbands. Many women are married by *lobola* only, no court." In an environment where adultery, illegitimacy, and prostitution, even if not completely condoned, are accepted as social norms, and where *lobola* is regarded as payment, the foundations of marriage must inevitably totter. It is a logical conclusion to an unfortunate concatenation of circumstances, in which economic pressure is of great importance, to find extreme disruption in family life.[9]

Economic necessity was the driving force which impelled the Africans of Rooiyard to migrate to Johannesburg. Their lives as seen in Rooiyard bear witness to a continuous struggle to overcome their all too evident poverty. It is a queer paradox that appears in Rooiyard—a combination of Bantu insouciance and of the European enthusiasm for economic gain. The owner of a sewing machine will not lend her machine to a friend but demands the tariff fee of 1s. per day. There is much evidence of a commercialization of Bantu culture. The festivals of tribal life have been converted into the "parties" of urban existence which have become an integral portion of the life of the urban African, largely owing to the fact that, in addition to beer-drinking, they form the whole of the urban African's recreational facilities.

*   *   *

[In such parties, at which the guests contribute money to defray the cost, the emphasis is placed on economic gain, with a loss of the traditional significance of the occasion. Another innovation is taking up a collection from every room in the yard to cover the funeral expenses of a resident who has died.]

Despite the rapid absorption of European material culture, and despite the changes which are being wrought in Bantu institutions as a result of the transition from a subsistence economy to a money economy, little progress has been achieved in loosening the stranglehold which magic has over the Africans. Practically all the Africans have either been converted to Christianity or have been baptized in their childhood. Only six of one hundred women do not belong, nominally at least, to one of the numerous Christian sects which are represented in South Africa. . . . The majority of women find that the time taken up by the domestic tasks and by their beer-selling activities does not leave them sufficient leisure time to attend church services. To judge by the Africans of Rooiyard, Christianity has failed. The minister at the home of these Africans has preached the brotherhood of all men. These Africans come to town and there, where the contrast cannot but fail to make itself felt, they find the white man dominant and the Africans occupying a definitely inferior position. . . . It appears that the inability of the church to alleviate the disabilities from which the Africans suffer has contributed largely to the indifference and apathy which they now manifest towards the white man's religion. Time and again men and women said, "At the kraal I went to church. In Johannesburg I don't go." But skepticism towards Christianity has not, in the case of the Africans of Rooiyard, brought about a reversion to their tribal belief. A few families give proof of the constancy of their faith in the belief of their fathers by invoking the *amadlozi* (dead ancestors) in joy and in distress by propitiating them according to traditional rules, and by offering to them a little of their food before they eat and a gourd of their beer before they drink. A few of the more educated Africans, disillusioned in the white man's religion, advocate a return to their own religion. But the great majority of Rooiyard Africans have tacitly renounced Christianity and have been too long dissociated from tribal religion to find solace in it now. The urban African, cast adrift between two religions, cannot look to religion to help him in the perplexities and difficulties which unavoidably present themselves in the new and unaccustomed conditions of life in an urban center. Magic fulfils this need. In Rooiyard there is a constant demand for the services of the *inyanga* and of his medicines. He fulfils the functions of both lawyer and doctor, for in addition to remedial medicines he gives much practical advice to his patients. In the event of illness most Africans, but not all, prefer the services of the *inyanga* to those of a European medical practitioner. Amongst the most numerous of the diseases for which the *inyanga* is called upon to

render aid are venereal diseases or "sickness from women" as is the parlance of the African.[10] Medicines to ensure that love is requited also feature prominently in the requests of the clientele of an *inyanga*. Very numerous are the demands for protective medicines which will guard the
family from succumbing to the poisons of sorcerers. The belief in *abatha-
kathi* (sorcerers) receives added stimulus in an environment where
neighbors are strangers, mutually distrustful of each other and also com-
petitors in the beer trade. Each tribe believes that another tribe is in possession of more potent medicines than their own, which will make their
beer customers desert them and which will harm their children. Babies,
who in their fragility are believed to be very susceptible to baneful influences, are carefully doctored according to the advice of the *inyanga* by
prudent mothers to render them immune to the attacks of the *abathak
kathi*. One woman, a newcomer to Rooiyard, said, "There is plenty of
beer here, a business yard, and lots of babies, so the *inyanga* must be busy
here."

* * *

[Traditional and new forms of magic are used for purposes such as
finding employment, improving beer trade, or making the magistrate
lenient.]

The aim of this survey, in which only a few of the most salient characteristics of the Rooiyard populace have been discussed, has been to
show that while there is ample evidence of a rapid absorption of Western
material culture, the assimilation of Western spiritual culture is proceeding at a far more leisurely pace. This lag in European cultural assimilation is deplored, not so much because of the inherent superiority of European culture, but because urban contacts between the two cultures
usually result in a shattering of Bantu culture and consequently deprive
the urban African of the supports and restraints which a stable social organization provides. The African is straining onward in an attempt to
satisfy his ever-increasing needs in the way of food, clothing, and furniture. But the low wage level and the resultant inability of the male head
of the family to provide for the needs of the family have caused a disruption of the immediate family. In the drive to town families are separated from their kinsfolk and form isolated units in a town. The restraints of tribal discipline do not affect the urban African, and no
substitute discipline has, as yet, emerged from out of the chaotic welter of
transition. The old sanctions have lost their force and the sanctions
which order European life are not yet applicable to African life. Lest this
picture should appear exaggerated, it may be well to point out that
this survey deals with a people who are living under the most unfavor-
able conditions. These Africans form what is, technically, a criminal

populace whose whole endeavor is to outwit the police, by whom they are continually harassed in the course of their illicit beer-brewing activities. Their contacts with Europeans have been mainly confined to such contacts as occur in the course of employment. They have lost touch with their home missionary, and in urban life they find that the church can do little to relieve their economic distress or to alleviate their social and legal disabilities. From the pedlars and hawkers, both European and Asiatic, who find in these yards a profitable custom, they learn the art of bargaining and the art of swearing. Oftentimes it has been noticed that women, who could not frame a coherent sentence in English, have, during the course of a quarrel, interspersed the argument in their home tongue with a wide selection of abusive and obscene English swear words. This is perhaps symptomatic of the process of contact. The Africans of Rooliyard are really an outcast populace, difficult of approach by the European because of their suspicious antagonism. But the gratitude with which young girls and boys speak of the time spent with their Pathfinder and Wayfarer[11] units reveals that their great need is for European contacts, which are not directed solely towards exploiting them economically or converting them to Christianity. Whether such contacts become available or not, the approximation of the lives of some of the families in Rooiyard, admittedly as yet a small number, to the European model points to the conclusion that out of the chaos and confusion which exists in this transition period, there will emerge a people who will adopt such elements of European culture as may enable them to attain to an ordered and economically secure social life.

NOTES

[Starred items are recommended as further readings.]

[1] [This term is used to denote Negro Africans, as distinguished from those of European descent.]

[2] See *Report of Native Economic Commission,* U.G. 22, 1932, Par. 404-7; and Professor J. W. W. Grosskopf, "The Position of the Native Population in the Economic System of South Africa," *Weltwirtschaftliches Archiv,* vol. xxxviii, No. 2.

[3] Cradle-skin in which children are carried on the back.

[4] *Report of the Native Economic Commission,* U.G., 22, 1932, Par. 232-3.

[5] For further particulars of urban African income and expenditure see my article, "The Importance of Beer-Brewing in an Urban Native Yard," * *Bantu Studies,* vol. viii, no. 1.

[6] Whenever figures are given in the course of this article, they will refer to these 100 families which were selected on account of the readiness with which the women concerned consented to give information on essential points, such as income of husband, number of children, and their whereabouts, etc. These families include the majority of the families with whom I came into contact and may be accepted as representing a typical Rooiyard population.

[7] Mrs. A. W. Hoernlé, "An Outline of the Native Conception of Education in Africa," *Africa,* vol. iv, no. 2.

[8] Convictions for the year 1930: Native taxation, 50,102; Pass Laws, 42,611; Illegal possession of Native liquor, 36,-644. Official Year Book of the Union of South Africa, 1930-1.

[9] For evidence that the disintegration of the family and the modification of sexual morality is not solely confined to urban African life but also applies to the rural African see: Monica Hunter—"Results of Culture Contact on the Pondo and Xosa Family," * South African Journal of Science, 1932. I. Schapera—"Premarital Pregnancy and Native Opin-

ion," * Africa, vol. vi, no. 1.

[10] A series of 42 blood tests of 26 women, 12 men, and 4 children of Rooiyard, kindly taken by Dr. W. Sachs, was submitted to the Wassermann test by the South African Institute for Medical Research. Seventeen (40 per cent) tested positive, 3 doubtful, and 22 negative. Unfortunately these blood tests had to be discontinued owing to the suspicion of our bona fides engendered in the minds of the Africans.

[11] African equivalents of Boy Scout and Girl Guide organizations.

FOR FURTHER READING

Hellmann, Ellen, Rooiyard, a Sociological Survey of an Urban Slum Yard, Cape Town: Oxford University Press for the Rhodes-Livingstone Institute, Rhodes-Livingstone Papers, 13, 1948. A more comprehensive and detailed report of the study on which this paper was based.

Longmore, Laura, The Dispossessed: A Study of the Sex-life of Bantu Women in and around Johannesburg, London: Jonathan Cape, 1959. A recent study which complements Hellmann's work, and which is primarily concerned with marriage and family activities.

Kuper, Leo, Watts, Hilstan, and Davies, Ronald, Durban: A Study in Racial Ecology, New York: Columbia University Press, 1958. A report on problems and policies in residential zoning during the rapid growth of a multiracial South African city and the effects on urban residents.

Hunter, Monica, Reaction to Conquest: Effects of Contacts with Europeans on the Pondo of South Africa, London: Oxford University Press, 1936.

A study of predominantly rural Africans in a culture-contact situation.

Wilson, Godfrey, An Essay on the Economics of Detribalization in Northern Rhodesia, Cape Town: Oxford University Press for the Rhodes-Livingstone Institute, Rhodes-Livingstone Papers, 5 and 6, 1941, 1942. A study of the effects of labor migration on African life.

Hellmann, Ellen, "Urban Areas," in Handbook on Race Relations in South Africa, ed. Ellen Hellmann and Leah Abrahams, London: Oxford University Press for the South African Institute of Race Relations, 1949, pp. 229-74. A general survey of living conditions in South African urban centers.

Sachs, Wulf, Black Hamlet, London: Bles, 1937. The fictionalized case history of an urban African, written by a psychoanalyst.

For references on city life in other parts of Africa, see the suggested readings following McCall's paper on urbanization, pp. 534-5 above.

BIBLIOGRAPHY

JOURNALS AND MONOGRAPH SERIES

Africa, London: International African Institute, 1928—.

Africa, Spain: Consejo superior de investigaciones cientificas, Madrid: Instituto de estudios Africanos, 1943—.

African Abstracts, London: International African Institute, 1950—.

African Affairs (formerly *Journal of the Royal African Society*), London: Royal African Society, 1901—.

African Research Studies, Boston: Boston University, African Research and Studies Program, 1958—.

African Studies (formerly *Bantu Studies*), Johannesburg: University of Witwatersrand, Department of Bantu Studies, 1921—.

African Studies, Evanston: Northwestern University, African Studies Programs, 1958—.

African Studies Bulletin, African Studies Association, 1958—.

Africa und Übersee (formerly *Zeitschrift für Kolonialsprachen,* and then *Zeitschrift für Eingeborenen Sprachen*), Berlin, 1910—.

Archivos, Spain: Consejo superior de investigaciones cientificas, Madrid: Instituto de estudios Africanos, 1947—.

Cuadernos de Estudios Africanos, Madrid: Instituto de Estudio Politicos, 1946—.

Estudos ultramarinos, Lisbon: Escola Superior de Ultramar, 1948—.

Ethnographic Survey of Africa, London: International African Institute.

    Western Africa, 1950—.

    North-eastern Africa, 1955—.

    East Central Africa, 1950—.

    West Central Africa, 1951—.

    Central Africa, Belgian Congo, 1954—.

    Southern Africa, 1952—.

    [French series] *Monographies ethnologiques africaines,* Paris, 1954—.

Harvard African Studies, Cambridge: Harvard University, Peabody Museum, 1-10, 1917-32.

Journal de la Société des Africanistes, Paris: Société des Africanistes, 1931—.

Memorandum, London: International African Institute, 1930—.

Présence Africaine, Paris: 1947—.

Other serials and monographs are listed under the various subject headings.

BIBLIOGRAPHIES

African Bibliography Series: London: International African Institute, 1958—.

"Bibliographie africaniste," in *Journal de la Société des Africanistes.*

"Bibliographie courante," in *Zaïre, revue congolaise.*

"Bibliography of Current Publications," in *Africa,* London.

Great Britain, Colonial Office, *Bibliography of Published Sources Relating to African Land Tenure,* London. H.M. S.O., 1950.

Hambly, W. D., *Source Book for African Anthropology,* Chicago: Field Museum of Natural History, Anthropological Series, 26, 1937, part 2.

565

Hambly, W. D., *Bibliography of African Anthropology, 1937-1949,* Chicago: Chicago Museum of Natural History, Fieldiana, 37, 2, 1952.

Lewin, Evans, *Subject Catalogue of the Library of the Royal Empire Society,* London: Royal Empire Society, Vol. 1, *The British Empire Generally and Africa,* 1930.

Lewin, Evans, *Annotated Bibliography of Recent Publications on Africa South of the Sahara,* London: Royal Empire Society, 1943.

Meek, Charles Kingsley, *Colonial Law: A Bibliography with Special Reference to Native African Systems of Law and Land Tenure,* London: Oxford University Press for Nuffield College, 1948.

Mylius, Norbert, *Afrika Bibliographie, 1943-1951,* Vienna, Verein Freunde der Völkerkunde, 1952.

Porter, Dorothy B. (ed.), *A Catalogue of the African Collection in the Moorland Foundation Library,* Washington, D.C.: Howard University Press, 1958.

Robinson, A. M. L., *A Bibliography of African Bibliographies,* Cape Town: South African Public Library, Grey Bibliographies, 6, 1955, 3rd rev. ed.

Twentieth Century Fund, *Select Annotated Bibliography of Tropical Africa, Compiled by the International African Institute under the Direction of Professor Daryll Forde,* New York: Twentieth Century Fund, 1956.

U.S. Library of Congress, Bibliographic Division, *The British Empire in Africa.* Compiled by Helen F. Conover, Washington, D.C., 1942-43, 4 vols.

U.S. Library of Congress, European Affairs Division, *Introduction to Africa: A Selective Guide to Background Reading.* Prepared by Helen F. Conover, Washington, D.C.: University Press, 1952.

U.S. Library of Congress, General Reference and Bibliographic Division, *Africa South of the Sahara: A Selected Annotated List of Writings, 1951-56.* Compiled by Helen F. Conover, Washington, D.C., 1957.

University of Cape Town, Rondebosch: School of Librarianship, *Bibliographical Series.*

Wieschhoff, H. A., *Anthropological Bibliography of Negro Africa,* New Haven: American Oriental Society, 1948.

For specialized bibliographies see under the various subject headings.

GENERAL AND CULTURE AREAS

Baumann, Hermann, and Westermann, Diedrich, *Les peuples et les civilisations de l'Afrique,* Paris: Payot, 1948.

Frazer, Sir James G., *Anthologia Anthropologia, the Native Races of Africa and Madagascar,* London: P. Lund, Humphries, 1938.

Hambly, W. D., *Ethnology of Africa,* Chicago: Field Museum of Natural History, Department of Anthropology, Guide, Part 3, 1930.

Hambly, W. D., *Source Book for African Anthropology,* Chicago: Field Museum of Natural History, Anthropological Series, 26, 1937, 2 vols.

Herskovits, M. J., *The Backgrounds of African Art,* Denver: Denver Art Museum, 1945.

Herskovits, M. J., "The Culture Areas of Africa," *Africa,* 1930, 3, 59-77.

Hirschberg, Walter, "Die Völker Afrikas," in Bernatzik, Hugo A. (ed.), *Die neue Grosse Völkerkunde,* Frankfort/Main: Herkul, 1954, vol. 1, 279-564.

Hunter, C. Bruce, *Tribal Map of Negro Africa,* New York: American Museum of Natural History, 1956.

Seligman, Charles G., *The Races of Africa,* London: Oxford University Press, 1957, 3rd ed.

COMPARATIVE

Anderson, J. N. D., *Islamic Law in Africa,* London: H.M.S.O., Great Britain, Colonial Office, Colonial Research Publications, *16,* 1954.

Bascom, William R., and Herskovits, Melville J. (eds.), *Continuity and Change in African Cultures,* Chicago: University of Chicago Press, 1959.

Baumann, Hermann, "The Division of Work According to Sex in African Hoe Culture," *Africa,* 1928, *1,* 289-319.

Cline, Walter B., *Mining and Metallurgy in Negro Africa,* General Series in Anthropology, *5,* 1937.

Colson, Elizabeth, and Gluckman, Max (eds.), *Seven Tribes of British Central Africa,* London: Oxford University Press on behalf of the Rhodes-Livingstone Institute, 1951.

Deschamps, Hubert Jules, *Les Religions de l'Afrique noire,* Paris: Presses Universitaires de France, 1954.

Eisenstadt, S. N., "African Age Groups: A Comparative Study," *Africa,* 1954, *24,* 100-112.

Eisenstadt, S. N., "Primitive Political Systems: A Preliminary Analysis," *American Anthropologist,* 1959, *61,* 200-220.

Elias, Taslim O., *The Nature of African Customary Law,* Manchester: Manchester University Press, 1956.

Forde, Daryll (ed.), *African Worlds: Studies in the Cosmological Ideas and Social Values of African Peoples,* London: Oxford University Press for the International African Institute, 1954.

Fortes, M., "The Structure of Unilineal Descent Groups," *American Anthropologist,* 1953, *55,* 17-41.

Fortes, M., and Evans-Pritchard, E. E. (eds.), *African Political Systems,* London: Oxford University Press for the International African Institute, 1940.

Fried, Morton H., "The Classification of Corporate Unilineal Descent Groups," *Journal of the Royal Anthropological Institute,* 1957, *87,* 1-29.

Gluckman, Max, "Kinship and Marriage among the Lozi of Northern Rhodesia and the Zulu of Natal," in Radcliffe-Brown, A. R., and Forde, Daryll, *African Systems of Kinship and Marriage,* London: Oxford University Press of the International African Institute, 1950, pp. 166-206.

Gluckman, Max, *Custom and Conflict in Africa,* Oxford: Blackwell, 1955.

Goody, Jack (ed.), *The Developmental Cycle in Domestic Groups,* Cambridge: Cambridge University Press, Cambridge Papers in Social Anthropology, 1, 1958.

Lukas, J. (ed.), *Afrikanistische Studien Diedrich Westermann zum 80. Geburstag gewidmet,* Berlin: Akademie-Verlag, 1955.

Maquet, Jacques J., *Aide-mémoire d'ethnologie africaine,* Brussels: Institut Royal Colonial Belge, Classe de sciences morales et politiques, Mémoires, Collection in-8°, old series, 38, 2, 1954.

Mayer, Philip, *Witches,* Grahamstown, South Africa: Rhodes University, 1954.

Middleton, John, and Tait, David (eds.), *Tribes without Rulers: Studies in African Segmentary Systems,* London: Routledge, 1958.

Nadel, S. F., "Witchcraft in Four African Societies: An Essay in Comparison," *American Anthropologist,* 1952, *54,* 18-29.

Phillips, Arthur (ed.), *Survey of African Marriage and Family Life,* London: Oxford University Press for the International African Institute, 1953.

Radcliffe-Brown, A. R., and Forde, Daryll (eds.), *African Systems of Kinship and Marriage,* London: Oxford University Press for the International African Institute, 1950.

Richards, Audrey I. (ed.), *Methods of Selection of African Chiefs in Eleven East African Tribes,* Cambridge: Heffer, 1959.

Schapera, Isaac, *Government and Politics in Tribal Societies,* London, Watts, 1956.

Schmidt, Wilhelm, *Der Ursprung der Gottesidee,* Munster: Aschendorffsche,

1922-1955, 12 vols., especially Vol. 4, *Die Religionen der Urvölker Afrikas,* 1933.

Smith, Edwin W., (ed.), *African Ideas of God: A Symposium,* London: Edinburgh House Press, 1950.

Smith, M. G., "Segmentary Lineage Systems," *Journal of the Royal Anthropological Institute,* 1956, *86,* 39-80.

Tempels, Placide, *La philosophie bantoue,* trans. by A. Rubbens, Paris: Editions Africaines, 1949.

Westermann, Diedrich H., *Geschichte Afrikas: Staatenbildungen Südlich der Sahara,* Köln, Graven Verlag, 1952.

Wilson, Monica, "Witch Beliefs and Social Structure," *American Journal of Sociology,* 1951, *56,* 307-13.

GEOGRAPHY

Church, R. J. Harrison, *West Africa,* London: Longmans, Green, 1957.

Fitzgerald, Walter, *Africa: A Social, Economic and Political Geography of Its Major Regions,* London: Methuen, 1955, 8th ed.

Gautier, Emile Felix, *Sahara, The Great Desert,* New York: Columbia University Press, 1935.

Johnston, Bruce F., *The Staple Food Economies of Western Tropical Africa,* Stanford: Stanford University Press, Stanford University, Food Research Institute, 1958.

Kuczynski, Robert René, *Demographic Survey of British Colonial Africa,* London: Oxford University Press, 1948, 1949, 2 vols.

Shantz, H. L., "Agricultural Regions of Africa," *Economic Geography,* 1940, *16,* 1-47, 122-61, 341-89; 1941, *17,* 217-49, 353-79; 1942, *18,* 229-46, 343-62; 1943, *19,* 77-109, 217-69.

Stamp, L. Dudley, *Africa: A Study in Tropical Development,* New York: John Wiley, 1953.

Thewartha, Glenn T., and Zelinsky, Wilbur, "Population Patterns in Tropical Africa," *Annals of the Association of American Geographers,* 1954, *44,* 135-62.

Wellington, John Harold, *Southern Africa: A Geographical Study,* Cambridge: Cambridge University Press, 1955, 2 vols.

PHYSICAL ANTHROPOLOGY AND PREHISTORY

General

Alimen, H., *The Prehistory of Africa,* London: Hutchinson, 1958.

British Museum (Nat. Hist.), London, *Fossil Mammals of Africa,* 1951—.

Hamilton, R. A. (ed.), *History and Archaeology in Africa,* London: University of London, School of Oriental and African Studies, 1955.

Leakey, L. S. B., *Stone Age Africa,* London: Oxford University Press, 1936.

Leakey, L. S. B., *Adam's Ancestors,* London: Methuen, 1953, 4th ed.

Movius, Hallam L., and Jordan, Douglas

F., *A Bibliography of Early Man, Pleistocene Studies and Paleolithic Archaeology in Southern Equatorial and Eastern Africa,* New York: Wenner-Gren Foundation for Anthropological Research, 1954.

Murdock, George Peter, *Africa, Its Peoples and Their Cultural History,* New York: McGraw-Hill, 1959.

Pan-African Congress on Prehistory, Proceedings, 1947—.

Pedrals, Dennis Pierre de, *Archéologie de l'Afrique noire,* Paris: Payot, 1950.

More Specialized Studies

Addison, Frank, and Lacaille, A. D., *The Wellcome Excavations in the Sudan: Jebel Moya,* London: Oxford University Press, 1949-51, 3 vols.

Arkell, A. J., *Early Khartoum,* London: Oxford University Press, 1949.

Arkell, A. J., *The Old Stone Age in the Anglo-Egyptian Sudan,* Khartoum: Sudan Antiquities Service, Occasional Paper, 1, 1949.

Arkell, A. J., *Shaheinab: An Account of the Excavation of a Neolithic Occupation Site,* London: Oxford University Press, 1953.

Arkell, A. J., *A History of the Sudan: From the Earliest Times to 1821,* London: Athlone Press, 1955.

Balout, Lionel, *Préhistoire de l'Afrique du nord, essai de chronologie,* Paris: Arts et Métiers Graphiques, 1955.

Balout, Lionel, *Algérie préhistorique,* Paris: Arts et Métiers Graphiques, 1958.

Briggs, Lloyd C., *The Stone Age Races of Northwest Africa,* Cambridge: Harvard University, American School of Prehistoric Research, Bulletin, 18, 1955.

Broom, Robert, *Swartkrans Ape-Man,* Pretoria: Transvaal Museum Memoir, 6, 1952.

Broom, Robert, *Finding the Missing Link,* London: Watts, 1951, 2nd ed.

Broom, Robert, Robinson, J. T., and Schepers, G. W. H., *Sterkfontein Ape-Man Plesianthropus,* Pretoria: Transvaal Museum Memoir, 4, 1950.

Broom, Robert, and Schepers, G. W. H., *The South-African Fossil Ape-Man: The Australopithecinae,* Pretoria: Transvaal Museum Memoir, 2, 1946.

Burkitt, M. C., *South Africa's Past in Stone and Paint,* Cambridge: Cambridge University Press, 1928.

Caton-Thompson, G., *The Zimbabwe Culture: Ruins and Reactions,* Oxford: Clarendon Press, 1931.

Caton-Thompson, G., and Gardner, E. W., *Kharga Oasis in Prehistory,* London: Athlone Press, 1952.

Clark, John Desmond, *The Stone Age Cultures of Northern Rhodesia,* Claremont, Cape: South African Archaeological Society, 1950.

Clark, John Desmond, *Prehistoric Cultures of the Horn of Africa,* Cambridge: Museum of Archaeology and Ethnology, 1954.

Clark, John Desmond, *The Prehistory of Southern Africa,* Harmondsworth: Pelican Books, 1959.

Cole, Sonia, *The Prehistory of East Africa,* Harmondsworth: Penguin Books, 1954.

Cole, Sonia, *Early Man in East Africa,* London: Macmillan, 1958.

Coon, Carleton, *The Races of Europe,* New York: Macmillan, 1939.

Craig, B., *Rock Paintings and Petroglyphs of South and Central Africa. Bibliography of Prehistoric Art,* Rondebosch: University of Cape Town, School of Librarianship, Bibliographical Series, 1947.

Crawford, Osbert G. S., *The Fung Kingdom of Sennar,* Gloucester: J. Bellow, 1951.

Davies, Oliver, *Archaeology of Natal,* Vol. 1 of *Natal Regional Survey,* Cape Town: Oxford University Press for the University of Natal, 1951.

Field, Henry, *Contributions to the Anthropology of the Faiyum, Sinai, Sudan, Kenya,* Cambridge: Cambridge University Press, 1953.

Fouché, L., *Mapungubwe: Ancient Bantu Civilization on the Limpopo,* Cambridge: Cambridge University Press, 1937.

Goodwin, A. J., *The Bored Stones of South Africa,* Cape Town: South African Museum, Annals, 37, 1947.

Hooten, E. A., *The Ancient Inhabitants of the Canary Islands,* Cambridge: Harvard University, Peabody Museum, Harvard African Studies, 7, 1925.

Jones, Neville, *The Stone Age in Rhodesia,* London: Oxford University Press, 1926.

Jones, Neville, *The Prehistory of Southern Rhodesia,* Cambridge: Cambridge

University Press, National Museum of Southern Rhodesia, Memoir, 2, 1949.

Kirkman, J. S., *The Arab City of Gedi,* London: Oxford University Press, 1953.

Kush, Journal of the Sudan Antiquities Service, Khartoum, 1953—.

Leakey, L. S. B., *The Stone Age Cultures of Kenya Colony,* Cambridge: Cambridge University Press, 1931.

Leakey, L. S. B., *The Stone Age Races of Kenya,* London: Oxford University Press, 1935.

Leakey, L. S. B., *A Contribution to the Study of the Tumbian Culture in East Africa,* Nairobi: Coryndon Museum, Occasional Paper, 1, 1945.

Leakey, L. S. B., *Tentative Study of the Pleistocene Climatic Changes and Stone Age Culture Sequence in N.E. Angola,* Lisbon: Museu do Dundo, Companhia de Diamantes de Angola, Publication Culturais, 4, 1949.

Leakey, L. S. B., *Olduvai Gorge,* Cambridge: Cambridge University Press, 1951.

Leakey, L. S. B., and M. D., *Excavations at the Njoro River Cave,* Oxford: Clarendon Press, 1950.

Livingstone, Frank B., "Anthropological Implications of Sickle Cell Gene Distribution in West Africa," *American Anthropologist,* 1958, 60, 533-62.

Lowe, C. van Riet, *The Distribution of Prehistoric Rock Engravings and Paintings in South Africa,* Union of South Africa, Department of Education, Arts and Sciences, Archaeological Survey, Pretoria, Archaeological Series, 7, 1952.

McBurney, C. B. M., *Prehistory and Pleistocene Geology in Cyranaican Libya,* Cambridge: Cambridge University Press, 1955.

Monod, Theodore, *L'Adrar Ahnet. Contributions à l'étude archéologique d'un district saharien,* Paris: Institut d'Ethnologie, Travaux et mémoires, 19, 1932.

Musée Royal du Congo Belge, Tervuren, *Annales, Sciences de l'homme, Série in-8°.*

Anthropologie, 1951—.

Préhistoire, 1952—.

O'Brien, Terence P., *The Prehistory of the Uganda Protectorate,* Cambridge: Cambridge University Press, 1939.

Oschinsky, L., *The Racial Affinities of the Baganda and other Bantu Tribes of British East Africa,* Cambridge: Cambridge University Press, 1954.

Paver, B., *Zimbabwe Cavalcade,* London: Cassell, 1957, rev. ed.

Pycroft, W. P., and others, *Rhodesian Man and Associated Remains,* London: British Museum (Nat. Hist.), 1928.

Royal Society of South Africa, *Robert Broom Commemorative Album.*

Robinson, K. R., *Khami Ruins,* Cambridge: Cambridge University Press, 1959.

Senyurek, M. S., *Fossil Man in Tangiers,* Cambridge: Harvard University, Peabody Museum Papers, 16, 3, 1940.

Singer, R., "The Sickle Cell Trait in Africa," *American Anthropologist,* 1953, 55, 634-48.

South African Archaeological Society, Claremont, Cape, *Bulletin,* 1945—.

South African Journal of Science, Johannesburg: South African Association for the Advancement of Science, 1909—.

Sudan Antiquities Service, Khartoum, *Museum Pamphlets,* 1953—.

Sudan Antiquities Service, Khartoum, *Occasional Papers,* 1949—.

Summers, Roger, *Inyanga: Prehistoric Settlements in Southern Rhodesia,* Cambridge: Cambridge University Press, 1958.

Union of South Africa, Department of Education, Arts and Sciences, Archaeological Survey, Pretoria, *Archaeological Series,* 1939—.

Vaufrey, Raymond, *Préhistoire de l'Afrique,* Vol. I, *Le Maghreb,* Paris, Masson, 1955.

Wayland, E. J., *Outlines of Prehistory and Stone Age Climatology in the Bechuanaland Protectorate,* Brussels: Institut Royal des Sciences Coloniales, Mémoires, Classe de sciences naturelles et médicales, Collection in-8°, old series, 25, 4, 1954.

Wieschhoff, H. A., *The Zimbabwe-*

Monomotapa Culture in South East Africa, General Series in Anthropology, 8, 1941.

Wulsin, Frederick R., The Prehistoric Archaeology of Northwest Africa,

Cambridge: Harvard University, Peabody Museum Papers, 19, 1946.

For African prehistoric art see the listings under Aesthetics: Art.

HISTORY

Batten, Thomas R., Tropical Africa in World History, London: Oxford University Press, 1953, 2 vols., 2nd ed.

Biobaku, Saburi O., The Egba and Their Neighbours, 1842-1872, Oxford: Clarendon Press, 1957.

Bovill, E. W., Caravans of the Old Sahara, London: Oxford University Press, 1933.

Bovill, E. W., The Golden Trade of the Moors, London: Oxford University Press, 1958.

Burns, A. C., History of Nigeria, London: Allen & Unwin, 1948, 4th ed.

Coupland, R., East Africa and Its Invaders from the Earliest Times to the Death of Seyyid Said in 1856, Oxford: Clarendon Press, 1938.

Coupland, R., The Exploitation of East Africa, 1856-1890: The Slave Trade and the Scramble, London: Faber and Faber, 1939.

DeGraft-Johnson, J. C., African Glory, London: Watts, 1954.

DeKiewiet, Cornelius W., History of South Africa, Social and Economic, London: Oxford University Press, 1941.

Dike, K. O., Trade and Politics in the Niger Delta, 1830-1885, Oxford: Clarendon Press, 1955.

Fage, J. D., Introduction to the History of West Africa, Cambridge: Cambridge University Press, 1955.

Fage, J. D., An Atlas of African History, London: Arnold, 1958.

Forde, Daryll (ed.), Efik Traders of Old Calabar, London: Oxford University Press for the International African Institute, 1956.

Gann, Lewis, "The End of the Slave Trade in British Central Africa, 1889-1912," Human Problems in British Central Africa, 1954, 16, 27-51.

George, Katherine, "The Civilized West

Looks at Primitive Africa: 1400-1800. A Study in Ethnocentrism," Isis, 1958, 49, 62-72.

Groves, Charles Pelham, The Planting of Christianity in Africa, London: Lutterworth Press, 1948-58, 4 vols.

Hamilton, R. A. (ed.), History and Archaeology in Africa, London: University of London, School of Oriental and African Studies, 1955.

Hargreaves, J. D., A Life of Sir Samuel Lewis, London: Oxford University Press, 1958.

Ingrams, William H., Zanzibar, Its History and Its People, London: Witherby, 1931.

Johnston, Harry A., The Opening Up of Africa, London: Oxford University Press, 1911.

Perham, Margery, Lugard: The Years of Adventure, 1858-1898, London: Collins, 1956.

Perham, Margery, and Simmons, J., African Discovery, London: Faber and Faber, 1942.

Reusch, Richard, History of East Africa, Stuttgart: Evang. Missionsverlag, 1954.

Shepperson, George, and Price, Thomas, Independent African: John Chilembwe and the Origins, Setting and Significance of the Nyasaland Native Rising of 1915, Edinburgh: Edinburgh University Press, 1958.

Walker, Eric A., A History of Southern Africa, London: Longmans, Green, 1957, 3rd ed.

Ward, W. E. F., A History of Ghana, London: Allen and Unwin, 1958, 2nd rev. ed.

Woodson, Carter G., The African Background Outlined, or Handbook for the Study of the Negro, Washington, D. C.: Association for the Study of Negro Life and History, 1936.

LINGUISTIC

General

Bulletin of the School of Oriental and African Studies, London: University of London, 1917—.

Greenberg, Joseph H., "Studies in African Linguistic Classification," Southwestern Journal of Anthropology, 1949, 5, 79-100, 190-98, 309-17; 1950, 6, 47-63, 143-60, 223-37, 388-98; 1954, 10, 405-15.

Greenberg, Joseph H., Studies in African Linguistic Classification, New Haven: Compass Publishing Company, 1955.

Handbook of African Languages, London: Oxford University Press for the International African Institute, 1952—.

Homburger, L., The Negro-African Languages, London: Routledge, 1949.

Meinhof, Carl, An Introduction to the Study of African Languages, London: J. M. Dent, 1915.

More Specialized Studies

Basset, André, La langue berbère, London: Oxford University Press for the International African Institute, Handbook of African Languages, 1952.

Bryan, Margaret A., The Distribution of Semitic and Cushitic Languages of Africa, London: Oxford University Press for the International African Institute, 1947.

Bryan, Margaret A., The Distribution of the Nilotic and Nilo-Hamitic Languages of Africa, London: Oxford University Press for the International African Institute, 1948.

Doke, Clement M., Bantu: Modern Grammatical, Phonetical and Lexicographical Studies Since 1860, London: P. Lund, Humphries for the International African Institute, 1945.

Doke, Clement M., The Southern Bantu Languages, London: Oxford University Press for the International African Institute, Handbook of African Languages, 1954.

East African Linguistic Studies, Kampala: East African Institute of Social Research, 1953—.

East African Swahili Committee, Arusha, Journal, 19[?]—. Studies in Swahili Grammar, 1954—.

Guthrie, Malcolm, The Classification of the Bantu Languages, London: Oxford University Press for the International

African Institute, Handbook of African Languages, 1948.

Guthrie, Malcolm, The Bantu Languages of Western Equatorial Africa, London: Oxford University Press for the International African Institute, 1953.

Leslau, Wolf, The Scientific Investigation of the Ethiopic Language, Leiden: E. J. Brill, 1956.

Linguistic Survey of the Northern Bantu Borderland, London: Oxford University Press for the International African Institute, 1956—.

Musée Royal du Congo Belge, Tervuren, Annales, Sciences de l'homme, Série in-8°, Linguistique, 1952—.

Tucker, Archibald N., The Eastern Sudanic Languages, London: Oxford University Press for the International African Institute, 1940.

Tucker, Archibald N., and Bryan, Margaret A., The Non-Bantu Languages of North-eastern Africa; With a Supplement on the Non-Bantu Languages of Southern Africa, by E. O. J. Westphal, London: Oxford University Press for the International African Institute, Handbook of African Languages, 1956.

Ullendorff, Edward, The Semitic Languages of Ethiopia; a Comparative Phonology, London: Taylor's (Foreign) Press, 1955.

Westermann, Diedrich, and Bryan, Margaret A., *The Languages of West Africa*, London: Oxford University Press for the International African Institute, 1952.

Whiteley, W. H., and Gutkind, A. F., *A Linguistic Bibliography of East Africa*, Kampala: East African Swahili Committee and East African Institute of Social Research, 1958, rev. ed.

NORTHERN AFRICA

General

Atiyah, E., *The Arabs*, Harmondsworth: Penguin Books, 1958, rev. ed.

Benedict, Burton, *A Short Annotated Bibliography Relative to the Sociology of the Muslim Peoples*, Montreal: Mc-Gill University, Department of Islamic Studies, 1955.

Brockleman, C., *History of the Islamic Peoples*, New York, 1947.

Conover, Helen F., *North and Northeast Africa: A Selected Annotated List of Writings, 1951-1957*, Washington, D. C.: Library of Congress, 1957.

Coon, Carleton S., *Caravan, the Story of*

the Middle East, London: Jonathan Cape, 1951.

Guillaume, Alfred, *Islam*, Harmondsworth: Penguin Books, 1954.

Hitti, P. K., *History of the Arabs*, London: Macmillan, 1956.

Rivlin, Benjamin, "A Selective Survey of the Literature in the Social Sciences and Related Fields on Modern North Africa," *American Political Science Review*, 1954, *48*, 826-48.

von Grunebaum, G. E., *Medieval Islam*, 1946.

Egypt

Ammar, A. M., *Demographic Survey of an Egyptian Province (Sharqiya)*, London: London School of Economics, Monographs on Social Anthropology, 8, 1942.

Ammar, Hamed, *Growing up in an Egyptian Village*, London: Kegan Paul, 1954.

Awad, Mohamed, "The Assimilation of Nomads in Egypt," *Geographical Review*, 1954, *44*, 240-53.

Ayrout, Henry Habib, *The Fellaheen*, trans. by Hilary Wayment, Cairo: R. Schindler, 1945.

Berque, Jacques, *Histoire sociale d'un village égyptien au XXme siècle*, Paris: Mouton, 1957.

Blackman, Winifred S., *The Fellahin of Upper Egypt*, London: Harrap, 1927.

Harris, George L., *Egypt*, New Haven: Human Relations Area Files, Country Survey Series, 1957.

Kennett, Austin, *Bedouin Justice: Laws and Customs among the Egyptian Bedouin*, Cambridge: Cambridge University Press, 1925.

Lane, E. W., *An Account of the Manners and Customs of the Modern Egyptians*, London: John Murray, 1871, 2 vols.

Leeder, S. H., *Modern Sons of the Pharaohs: The Manners and Customs of the Copts of Egypt*, London: Hodder & Stoughton, 1918.

Murray, G. W., "The Northern Beja," *Journal of the Royal Anthropological Institute*, 1927, *57*, 34-54.

Murray, G. W., *Sons of Ishmael, a Study of the Egyptian Bedouin*, London: Routledge, 1935.

Worrell, William H., *A Short Account of the Copts*, Ann Arbor: University of Michigan Press, 1945.

Northwest Africa and Libya

Berque, Jacques, *Structures sociales du Haut-Atlas*, Paris: Presses Universitaires de France, 1955.

Bousquet, G. H., *Les berbères: histoire et institutions*, Paris: Presses Universitaires de France, 1957.

Cline, Walter B., *Notes on the People of Seqah and El Garah in the Libyan Desert*, General Series in Anthropology, 4, 1936.

Coon, Carleton S., *Tribes of the Rif*, Cambridge: Harvard University, Peabody Museum, Harvard African Studies, 9, 1931.

DesPois, Jean, "Native Life in Tripolitania," *Geographical Review*, 1945, *35*, 352-67.

Evans-Pritchard, E. E., *The Sanusi of Cyrenaica*, Oxford: Clarendon Press, 1949.

Fogg, Walter, "The Organization of a Moroccan Tribal Market," *American Anthropologist*, 1942, *44*, 47-61.

Guadry, Mathea, *La femme Chaouia de l'Aurès: étude de sociologie berbère*, Paris: Geuthner, 1929.

Gautier, E. F., "Nomad and Sedentary Folks of Northern Africa," *Geographical Review*, 1921, *11*, 3-15.

Gautier, E. F., "Native Life in French North Africa," *Geographical Review*, 1923, *13*, 27-39.

Hanoteau, A., and Letourneux, A., *La kabylie et les coutumes kabyles*, Paris: Augustin Challamel, 1893, 3 vols., 2nd ed.

Hill, R. W., *A Bibliography of Libya*, Durham: University of Durham, Department of Geography, Research Papers, 1, 1959.

Letourneau, Roger (ed.), *Initiation à l'Algérie*, Paris: Librarie d'Amérique et d'Orient, 1957.

Montagne, Robert, *Les berbères et le makhzen dans le sud du Maroc: essai sur la transformation politique des berbères sédentaires*, Paris: F. Alcan, 1930.

Westermarck, Edward A., *Marriage Ceremonies in Morocco*, London: Macmillan, 1913.

Westermarck, Edward A., *The Belief in Spirits in Morocco*, Åbo: Akademi Åbo, Acta Academiae Aboensis, Humaniora, 1, 1, 1920.

Westermarck, Edward A., *Ritual and Belief in Morocco*, London: Macmillan, 1926, 2 vols.

Westermarck, Edward A., *Pagan Survivals in Mohammedan Civilisation*, London: Macmillan, 1933.

Wysner, Glora M., *The Kabyle People*, New Haven: the author, 1945.

THE SAHARA

Bovill, E. W., *Caravans of the Old Sahara*, London: Oxford University Press, 1933.

Bovill, E. W., *The Golden Trade of the Moors*, London: Oxford University Press, 1958.

Cline, Walter B., *Teda of Tibesti, Borku and Kawar in the Eastern Sahara*, General Series in Anthropology, 12, 1950.

Lhote, Henri, *Dans les campements touaregs*, Paris: Oeuvres Françaises, 1947.

Montagne, Robert, *La civilisation du désert; nomades d'Orient et d'Afrique*, Paris: Hachette, 1947.

Peel, R. F., "The Tibu Peoples and the Libyan Desert," *Geographical Journal*, 1942, *100*, 73-87.

Rennell, Francis Rennell of Rodd, *People of the Veil*, London: Macmillan, 1926.

THE HORN

Cerulli, E., *Peoples of South-west Ethiopia and Its Borderland,* Ethnographic Survey of Africa, North-eastern Africa, 3, 1956.

Drake-Brockman, Ralph E., *British Somaliland,* London: Hurst & Blackman, 1912.

Duncanson, D. J., "A Native Law Code for Eritrea," *Africa,* 1949, *19,* 141-49.

Eritrea, British Military Administration, *The Races and Tribes of Eritrea* [compiled by S. F. Nadel], Asmara, Eritrea, 1945.

Huntingford, G. W. B., *The Galla of Ethiopia,* Ethnographic Survey of Africa, North-eastern Africa, 2, 1955.

Jones, Ruth, *North-east Africa,* London: International African Institute, Africa Bibliography Series, 1959.

Leslau, Wolf, *Ethiopic Documents: Gurage,* New York: Viking Fund Publications in Anthropology, 14, 1950.

Leslau, Wolf, *Falasha Anthology,* New Haven: Yale University Press, 1951.

Lewis, I. M., *Peoples of the Horn of Africa: Somali Afar and Saho,* Ethnographic Survey of Africa, North-eastern Africa, 1, 1955.

Lifchitz, Déborah, *Textes éthiopiens magico-religieux,* Paris: Institut d'Ethnologie, Travaux et mémoires, 38, 1940.

Nadel, S. F., "Land Tenure on the Eritrean Plateau," *Africa,* 1946, *16,* 1-21, 99-109.

Pankhurst, Estelle, *Ethiopia, a Cultural History,* Essex: Labibela House, 1955.

Prins, A. H. J., *East African Age-Class Systems,* Groningen: Djakarta, 1953.

Trimingham, J. Spencer, *Islam in Ethiopia,* London: Oxford University Press, 1952.

University College, Addis Ababa, *Bulletin of the Ethnological Society,* 1953—.

EASTERN SUDAN AND NILOTIC PEOPLES

General

Butt, Audrey, *The Nilotes of the Anglo-Egyptian Sudan and Uganda,* Ethnographic Survey of Africa, East Central Africa, 4, 1952.

Hill, Richard L., *A Bibliography of the Anglo-Egyptian Sudan from the Earliest Times to 1937,* London: Oxford University Press, 1939.

Jones, Ruth, *North-east Africa,* London: International African Institute, Africa Bibliography Series, 1959.

Seligman, C. G., and B. Z., *Pagan Tribes of the Nilotic Sudan,* London: Routledge, 1932.

Tothill, J. D. (ed.), *Agriculture in the Sudan,* London: Oxford University Press, 1948.

Sudan Notes and Records, Khartoum, 1918—.

Trimingham, John Spencer, *Islam in the Sudan,* London: Oxford University Press, 1949.

More Specialized Studies

Baxter, P. T. W., and Butt, Audrey, *The Azande,* Ethnographic Survey of Africa, East Central Africa, 9, 1953.

Crazzolara, J. P., *The Lwoo,* Verona: Missioni Africane, 1950-54, 3 vols.

de Schlippe, Pierre, *Shifting Agriculture in Africa: The Zande System of Agriculture,* London: Routledge, 1956.

Driberg, J. H., *The Lango: A Nilotic Tribe of Uganda,* London: Fisher Unwin, 1923.

Evans-Pritchard, E. E., "Social Character of Bridewealth with Special Reference to the Azande," *Man,* 1934, *23,* 172-75

Evans-Pritchard, E. E., *Witchcraft, Oracles and Magic among the Azande,* Oxford: Clarendon Press, 1937.

Evans-Pritchard, E. E., "Bibliographic Note on the Ethnology of the Southern Sudan," *Africa,* 1940, *13,* 62-67.

Evans-Pritchard, E. E., *The Neur,* Oxford: Clarendon Press, 1940.

Evans-Pritchard, E. E., *The Political System of the Anuak of the Anglo-Egyptian Sudan,* London: London School of Economics, Monographs on Social Anthropology, 4, 1940.

Evans-Pritchard, E. E., *The Divine Kingship of the Shilluk of the Nilotic Sudan,* Cambridge: Cambridge University Press, 1948.

Evans-Pritchard, E. E., "Luo Tribes and Clans," *Human Problems in British Central Africa,* 1949, *7,* 24-40.

Evans-Pritchard, E. E., *Kinship and Marriage among the Nuer,* Oxford: Clarendon Press, 1951.

Evans-Pritchard, E. E., *Nuer Religion,* Oxford: Clarendon Press, 1956.

Hayley, T. T. S., *The Anatomy of Lango Religion and Groups,* Cambridge: Cambridge University Press, 1947.

Howell, P. P., *A Manual of Nuer Law,* London: Oxford University Press for the International African Institute, 1954.

MacMichael, Harold A., *The Tribes of Northern and Central Kordofán,* Cambridge: Cambridge University Press, 1912.

Nalder, L. F. (ed.), *A Tribal Survey of Mongalla Province . . . ,* London: Oxford University Press for the International African Institute, 1937.

Paul, Andrew, *A History of the Beja Tribes of the Sudan,* Cambridge: Cambridge University Press, 1954.

Schneider, David M., "A Note on Bridewealth and the Stability of Marriage, *Man,* 1953, *53,* 55-57.

Seligman, C. G. and B. Z., *The Kababish, a Sudan African Tribe,* Cambridge: Harvard University, Peabody Museum, Harvard African Studies, 2, 1918.

Southall, Aiden W., *Lineage Formation among the Luo,* London: International African Institute, Memorandum, 26, 1952.

Southall, Aiden W., *Alur Society, a Study in Processes and Types of Domination,* Cambridge: Heffer, 1956.

Westermann, Diedrich, *The Shilluk People: Their Language and Folklore,* Berlin: Dietrich Reimer, 1912.

EAST AFRICA

General

East African Institute of Social Research, Kampala, *Conference Papers,* 1952—.

East African Institute of Social Research, Kampala, *East African Institute of Social Research, 1950-55,* Kampala: Makerere College, 1956.

East African Studies, Kampala: East African Institute of Social Research, 1953—.

Herskovits, Melville J., "The Cattle Complex in East Africa," *American Anthropologist,* 1926, *28,* 230-72, 361-80, 494-528, 633-64.

Prins, A. H. J., *East African Age-Class Systems,* Groningen: Djakarta, 1953.

Schapera, Isaac, *Some Problems of Anthropological Research in Kenya Colony,* London: International African Institute, Memorandum, 23, 1949.

Tanganyika Notes and Records, Dar es Salaam, 1936—.

The Uganda Journal, Kampala: The Uganda Society, 1934—.

Non-Bantu Peoples

Evans-Pritchard, E. E., "The Political Structure of the Nandi-speaking Peoples of Kenya," *Africa*, 1940, *13*, 250-67.

Gulliver, P. H., *A Preliminary Survey of the Turkana*, Cape Town: University of Cape Town, Communications from the School of African Studies, 26, 1951.

Gulliver, P. H., *The Family Herds*, London: Routledge and Kegan Paul, 1955.

Gulliver, Pamela and P. H., *The Central Nilo-Hamites*, Ethnographic Survey of Africa, East Central Africa, 7, 1953.

Hollis, A. C., *The Masai, Their Language and Folklore*, London: Oxford University Press, 1905.

Hollis, A. C., *The Nandi, Their Language and Their Folklore*, Oxford: Clarendon Press, 1909.

Huntingford, G. W. B., *Nandi Work and Culture*, London: H.M.S.O., Great Britain, Colonial Office, Colonial Research Studies, 4, 1950.

Huntingford, G. W. B., *The Southern Nilo-Hamites*, Ethnographic Survey of Africa, East Central Africa, 8, 1953.

Huntingford, G. W. B., *The Northern Nilo-Hamites*, Ethnographic Survey of Africa, East Central Africa, 6, 1953.

Huntingford, G. W. B., *The Nandi of Kenya: Tribal Control in a Pastoral Society*, London: Routledge and Kegan Paul, 1953.

Lawrence, J. C. D., *The Iteso*, London: Oxford University Press, 1957.

Merker, M., *Die Masai*, Berlin: Dietrich Reimer, 1910.

Peristiany, J. G., *The Social Institutions of the Kipsigis*, London: Routledge, 1939.

Peristiany, J. G., "The Age-Set System of the Pastoral Pokot," *Africa*, 1951, *21*, 188-206.

Snell, G. S., *Nandi Customary Law*, London: Macmillan, 1954.

Lacustrine Bantu

Cory, Hans, *Sukuma Law and Custom*, London: Oxford University Press for the International African Institute, 1953.

Cory, Hans, and Hartnoll, M. M., *Customary Law of the Haya Tribe, Tanganyika Territory*, London: P. Lund Humphries for the International African Institute, 1945.

Culwick, A. T. and G. M., *Ubena of the Rivers*, London: Allen and Unwin, 1935.

Edel, May, *The Chiga of Western Uganda*, London: Oxford University Press for the International African Institute, 1957.

Fallers, L. A., "Some Determinants of Marriage Stability in Busoga: A Reformulation of Gluckman's Hypothesis," *Africa*, 1957, *27*, 106-21.

Fontaine, J. S. la, *The Gisu of Uganda*, Ethnographic Survey of Africa, East Central Africa, 10, 1959.

Mair, Lucy P., *An African People in the Twentieth Century*, London: Routledge, 1934.

Mair, Lucy P., *Native Marriage in Buganda*, London: International African Institute, Memorandum, 19, 1940.

Malcolm, D. W., *Sukumaland, an African People and Their Country*, London: Oxford University Press for the International African Institute, 1953.

Maquet, Jacques J., *Le Système des Relations sociales dans le Ruanda ancien*, Tervuren: Musée Royal du Congo Belge, Annales, Sciences de l'homme, Série in-8°, Ethnologie, 1, 1954.

Maquet, Jacques J., "The Kingdom of Ruanda," in Forde, Daryll (ed.), *African Worlds: Studies in the Cosmological Ideas and Social Values of African Peoples*, London: Oxford University Press for the International African Institute, 1954, pp. 164-89.

Maquet, Jacques J., *Ruanda: essai photo-*

graphique sur une société africaine en transition, Brussels: Elsevier, 1957.

Mayer, Philip, The Lineage Principle in Gusii Society, London: International African Institute, Memorandum, 24, 1949.

Nyabongo, Akiki K., The Story of an African Chief, New York: Scribner, 1935.

Oberg, K., "Kinship Organization of the Banyankole," Africa, 1938, 11, 129-58.

Oberg, K., "The Kingdom of Ankole in Uganda," in Fortes, M., and Evans-Pritchard, E. E. (eds.), African Political Systems, London: Oxford University Press for the International African Institute, 1940, pp. 121-62.

Roscoe, John, The Baganda, London: Macmillan, 1911.

Roscoe, John, The Soul of Central Africa: A General Account of the Mackie Ethnological Expedition, London: Cassell, 1922.

Roscoe, John, The Banyankole, Cambridge: Cambridge University Press, 1923.

Roscoe, John, The Bakitara or Banyoro, Cambridge: Cambridge University Press, 1923.

Roscoe, John, The Bagesu and Other Tribes of the Uganda Protectorate, Cambridge: Cambridge University Press, 1923.

Wagner, Günter, The Bantu of North Kavirondo, London: Oxford University Press for the International African Institute, 1949, 1956, 2 vols.

Winter, Edward H., Bwamba: A Structural Functional Analysis of a Patrilineal Society, Cambridge: Heffer, 1956.

Northeastern Bantu

Bernardi, B., The Mugwe, a Failing Prophet. A Study of a Religious and Public Dignitary of the Meru of Kenya, London: Oxford University Press for the International African Institute, 1959.

Bostock, Peter G., The Peoples of Kenya: The Taita, London: Macmillan, 1950.

Driberg, J. H., People of the Small Arrow, London: Routledge, 1930.

Gutmann, Bruno, Das Recht der Dschagga, Munich: Beck, 1926.

Hobley, C. W., Ethnology of the A-Kamba and Other East African Tribes, Cambridge: Cambridge University Press, 1910.

Hobley, C. W., Bantu Beliefs and Magic, with Particular Reference to the Kikuyu and Kamba Tribes of Kenya Colony, London: Witherby, 1938.

Huntingford, G. W. B., "The Social Institutions of the Dorobo," Anthropos, 1951, 46, 1-48.

Kenyatta, J., Facing Mt. Kenya: The Life of the Gikuyu, London: Secker and Warburg, 1938.

Lambert, H. E., Kikuyu Social and Political Institutions, London: Oxford University Press for the International African Institute, 1956.

Lindblom, Gerhard, The Akamba in British East Africa, Upsala: Appelberg, 1920.

Middleton, J., The Kikuyu and Kamba of Kenya, Ethnographic Survey of Africa, East Central Africa, 5, 1953.

Orde Browne, G. St. J., The Vanishing Tribes of Kenya, London: Seeley, Service, 1925.

Prins, A. H. J., "An Outline of the Descent System of the Teita, a Northeastern Bantu Tribe," Africa, 1950, 20, 26-37.

Prins, A. H. J., Coastal Tribes of the North-eastern Bantu, Ethnographic Survey of Africa, East Central Africa, 3, 1952.

Raum, Otto F., Chaga Childhood: A Description of Indigenous Education in an East African Tribe, London: Oxford University Press for the International African Institute, 1940.

Routledge, W. S. and K., With a Prehistoric People, the Akikuyu of British East Africa, London: Arnold, 1910.

SOUTH CENTRAL AFRICA

General

Brelsford, W. V., *The Tribes of Northern Rhodesia,* Lusaka: Government Printer, 1957.

Colson, Elizabeth, and Gluckman, Max (eds.), *Seven Tribes of British Central Africa,* London: Oxford University Press on behalf of the Rhodes-Livingstone Institute, 1951.

Gluckman, Max, Mitchell, J. C., and Barnes, J. A., "The Village Headman in British Central Africa," *Africa,* 1949, *19,* 89-106.

Human Problems in British Central Africa. The Rhodes-Livingstone Institute Journal, Manchester: Manchester University Press for the Rhodes-Livingstone Institute, Lusaka, 1944—.

The Northern Rhodesia Journal, Livingstone: The Northern Rhodesia Society, 1950—.

The Nyasaland Journal, Blantyre: The Nyasaland Society, 1948—.

Rhodes-Livingstone Institute, Lusaka, *Communications,* 1943—.

Rhodes-Livingstone Institute Papers, Manchester: Manchester University Press for the Rhodes-Livingstone Institute, Lusaka, 1938—.

Richards, Audrey I., "Mother-Right in Central Bantu," in Evans-Pritchard, E. E., and others (eds.), *Essays Presented to C. G. Seligman,* London: Kegan Paul, 1934, pp. 267-80.

Richards, Audrey I., "Some Types of Family Structure amongst the Central Bantu," in Radcliffe-Brown, A. R., and Forde, Daryll (eds.), *African Systems of Kinship and Marriage,* London: Oxford University Press for the International African Institute, 1950, pp. 207-51.

More Specialized Studies

Barnes, J. A., "The Fort Jameson Ngoni," in Colson, Elizabeth, and Gluckman, Max (eds.), *Seven Tribes of British Central Africa,* London: Oxford University Press on behalf of the Rhodes-Livingstone Institute, 1951, pp. 194-252.

Barnes, J. A., *Marriage in a Changing Society,* Cape Town: Oxford University Press for the Rhodes-Livingstone Institute, Rhodes-Livingstone Papers, 20, 1951.

Barnes, J. A., *Politics in a Changing Society,* London: Oxford University Press for the Rhodes-Livingstone Institute, 1954.

Blohm, W. A., *Die Nyamwezi,* Hamburg: Friedrichsen, de Gruyter, 1931-33, 3 vols.

Childs, G. M., *Umbundu Kinship and Character,* London: Oxford University Press for the International African Institute, 1949.

Colson, Elizabeth, "The Plateau Tonga of Northern Rhodesia," in Colson, Elizabeth, and Gluckman, Max (eds.), *Seven Tribes of British Central Africa,* London: Oxford University Press on behalf of the Rhodes-Livingstone Institute, 1951, pp. 94-163.

Colson, Elizabeth, *Marriage and the Family among the Plateau Tonga of Northern Rhodesia,* Manchester: Manchester University Press, 1958.

Cunnison, Ian, *History on the Luapula,* Cape Town: Oxford University Press for the Rhodes-Livingstone Institute, The Rhodes-Livingstone Papers, 21, 1951.

Cunnison, Ian, "History and Genealogies in a Conquest State," *American Anthropologist,* 1957, *59,* 20-31.

Doke, C. M., *The Lambas of Northern Rhodesia,* London: Harrap, 1931.

Gibson, Gordon, "Double Descent and Its Correlates among the Herero of Ngamiland," *American Anthropologist,* 1956, *58,* 109-39.

Gluckman, Max, "The Lozi of Barotseland in North-western Rhodesia," in Colson, Elizabeth, and Gluckman, Max (eds.), *Seven Tribes of British Central Africa*, London: Oxford University Press on behalf of the Rhodes-Livingstone Institute, 1951, pp. 1-93.

Gluckman, Max, *The Judicial Process among the Barotse of Northern Rhodesia*, Manchester: Manchester University for the Rhodes-Livingstone Institute, 1955.

Hahn, C. H. L., "The Ovambo," in *The Native Tribes of South West Africa*, Cape Town: Cape Times, 1928, pp. 1-36.

Hambly, W. D., *The Ovimbundu of Angola*, Chicago: Field Museum of Natural History, Anthropological Series, 21, 2, 1934.

Irle, I., *Die Herero*, Gütersloh: Bertelsmann, 1906.

Jaspan, M. A., *The Ila-Tonga Peoples of North-western Rhodesia*, Ethnographic Survey of Africa, West Central Africa, 4, 1953.

McCulloch, Merran, *The Southern Lunda and Related Peoples*, Ethnographic Survey of Africa, West Central Africa, 1, 1951.

McCulloch, Merran, *The Ovimbundo of Angola*, Ethnographic Survey of Africa West Central Africa, 2, 1952.

Mitchell, J. C., "The Yao of Southern Nyasaland," in Colson, Elizabeth, and Gluckman, Max (eds.), *Seven Tribes of British Central Africa*, London: Oxford University Press on behalf of the Rhodes-Livingstone Institute, 1951, pp. 292-353.

Mitchell, J. C., *The Yao Village*, Manchester: Manchester University Press, 1956.

Mitchell, J. C., and Barnes, J. A., *The Lamba Village: Report of a Social Survey*, Cape Town: University of Cape Town, Communications from the African Studies, 24, 1950.

Read, Margaret, *The Ngoni of Nyasaland*, London: Oxford University Press for the International African Institute, 1956.

Richards, Audrey I., *Land, Labour and Diet in Northern Rhodesia*, London: Oxford University Press for the International African Institute, 1939.

Richards, Audrey I., "The Political System of the Bemba of Northern Rhodesia," in Fortes, M., and Evans-Pritchard, E. E. (eds.), *African Political Systems*, London: Oxford University Press for the International African Institute, 1940, pp. 83-120.

Richards, Audrey I., "The Bemba of North-eastern Rhodesia," in Colson, Elizabeth, and Gluckman, Max (eds.), *Seven Tribes of British Central Africa*, London: Oxford University Press on behalf of the Rhodes-Livingstone Institute, 1951, pp. 164-93.

Richards, Audrey I., *Chisungu: A Girls' Initiation Ceremony among the Bemba of Northern Rhodesia*, London: Faber and Faber, 1956.

Smith, Edwin W., and Dale, Andrew M., *The Ila-speaking Peoples of Northern Rhodesia*, London: Macmillan, 1920, 2 vols.

Stannous, N. S., *The Wayao of Nyasaland*, Cambridge: Harvard University, Peabody Museum, Harvard African Studies, 3, 1922.

Tew, Mary, *The Peoples of the Lake Nyasa Region*, Ethnographic Survey of Africa, East Central Africa, 1, 1950.

Turner, V. W., *The Lozi Peoples of North-western Rhodesia*, Ethnographic Survey of Africa, West Central Africa, 3, 1952.

Turner, V. W., *Schism and Continuity in an African Society: A Study of Ndembu Village Life*, Manchester: Manchester University Press on behalf of the Rhodes-Livingstone Institute, 1957.

Vedder, H., "The Herero," in *The Native Tribes of South West Africa*," Cape Town: Cape Times, pp. 153-211.

Whiteley, Wilfred, Stefaniszyn, B., and Slaski, J., *Bemba and Related Peoples of Northern Rhodesia by Wilfred Whiteley, with a Contribution on the Ambo by B. Stefaniszyn, S.J., The Peoples of the Lower Luapula Valley by J. Slaski*, Ethnographic Survey of Africa, East Central Africa, 2, 1951.

Wilson, Godfrey, "The Nyakyusa of South-western Tanganyika," in Colson, Elizabeth, and Gluckman, Max (eds.), *Seven Tribes of British Central Africa*, London: Oxford University Press on behalf of the Rhodes-Livingstone Institute, 1951, pp. 253-91.

Wilson, Monica, *Good Company: A Study of Nyakyusa Age-Villages*, London: Oxford University Press for the International African Institute, 1951.

Wilson, Monica, *Rituals of Kinship among the Nyakyusa*, London: Oxford University Press for the International African Institute, 1957.

Wilson, Monica, *The Peoples of the Nyasa-Tanganyika Corridor*, Cape Town: University of Cape Town, Communications from the School of African Studies, 29, 1958.

Wilson, Monica, *Communal Rituals of the Nyakyusa*, London: Oxford University Press for the International African Institute, 1959.

MADAGASCAR

General

Antananarivo Annual, Tananarive: London Missionary Society, 1875-1900.

Dandouau, André, and Chapus, G. S., *Histoires des populations de Madagascar*, Paris: Larose, 1952.

Decary, Raymond, *Mœurs et coutumes des malgaches*, Paris: Payot, 1951.

Deschamps, H., *Madagascar*, Paris: Berger-Levrault, 1947.

Faublée, Jacques, *Ethnographie de Madagascar*, Paris: La Nouvelle Edition, 1946.

Grandidier, Guillaume, *Bibliographie de Madagascar*, Paris: Société d'Éditions Géographique, Maritimes et Coloniales, 1905, 1935, 2 vols.

Grandidier, Alfred and Guillaume, *Histoire physique, naturelle et politique de Madagascar: ethnographie*, Paris: Hachette, 1908-28, 4 vols.

Gray, Robert F., *Anthropological Problems of Madagascar: A Bibliographical Introduction*, Chicago: University of Chicago, Department of Anthropology, 1954.

Linton, Ralph, "The Culture Areas of Madagascar," *American Anthropologist*, 1928, *30*, 363-90.

Revue de Madagascar, Tananarive, 1933-41.

U.S. Library of Congress, Division of Bibliography, *Madagascar, a Selected List of References*, Washington, D.C., 1942.

More Specialized Studies

Andriamanjato, Richard, *Le tsiny et le tody dans la pensée malgache*, Paris: Présence Africaine, 1957.

Decary, Raymond, *L'antandroy: Monographie régionale*, Paris: Société des Éditions Géographiques, Maritimes et Coloniales, 1930-33, 2 vols.

Deschamps, H., *Les antaisaka*, Tananarive, 1936.

Deschamps, H., and Vianès, S., *Les malgaches du sud-est*, Paris: Presses Universaires de France, Monographies ethnologiques de Madagascar, 1959.

Dubois, H. M., *Monographie des betsileo*, Paris: Institut d'Ethnographie, Travaux et mémoires, 34, 1938.

Faublée, Jacques, *La cohésion de la société bara*, Paris: Presses Universitaires de France, 1954.

Faublée, Jacques, *Les esprits de la vie à Madagascar*, Paris: Presses Universitaires de France, 1954.

Ferrand, Gabriel, *Les musulmans à Madagascar et aux îles Comores*, Paris: Algiers Université, 1891-1902, 3 vols.

Linton, Ralph, *The Tanala, a Hill Tribe of Madagascar*, Chicago: Field Museum of Natural History, Anthropological Series, 22, 1933.

Van Gennep, Arnold, *Tabou et totémisme à Madagascar*, Paris: Leroux, 1904.

SOUTHERN AFRICA

General

Communications from the School of African Studies, Cape Town: University of Cape Town, 1936—.

Mendelssohn, Sidney, Mendelssohn's South African Bibliography, London: Holland Press, 1957, 2 vols.

Nada, Salisbury: The Southern Rhodesia Native Affairs Department, 1923—.

Schapera, Isaac, Government and Politics in Tribal Societies, London: Watts, 1956.

Schapera, Isaac, Select Bibliography of

South African Native Life and Problems, London: Oxford University Press, 1941.

South African Journal of Science, Johannesburg: South African Association for the Advancement of Science, 1909—.

Theal, G. M., Ethnography and Conditions of South Africa before 1505, London: Allen & Unwin, 1910.

Union of South Africa, Department of Native Affairs, Pretoria, Ethnological Publications, 1930—.

SOUTHERN BANTU

General

Duggan-Cronin, A. M., The Bantu Tribes of South Africa: Reproductions of Photographic Studies, with Introductory Articles, Bibliographies, and Descriptive Notes, Cambridge: Deighton Bell, 1928—.

Schapera, Isaac (ed.), The Bantu-speaking Tribes of South Africa, London: Routledge, 1937.

Van Warmelo, N. J., A Preliminary Survey of the Bantu Tribes of South Africa, Pretoria: Union of South Africa, Department of Native Affairs, Ethnological Publications, 5, 1935.

More Specialized Studies

Arnheim, J., Swaziland; a Bibliography, Rondebosch: University of Cape Town, School of Librarianship, Bibliographical Series, 1950.

Ashton, E. H., Medicine, Magic and Sorcery among the Southern Sotho, Cape Town; University of Cape Town, Communications from the School of African Studies, 10, 1943.

Ashton, E. H., The Basuto, London: Oxford University Press for the International African Institute, 1952.

Bryant, Alfred T., Olden Times in Zululand and Natal, London: Longmans, Green, 1929.

Bryant, Alfred T., The Zulu People as They Were before the White Man Came, Pietermaritzburg: Shuter and Shooter, 1949.

Bullock, Charles, The Mashona and the Matabele, Cape Town: Juta, 1950, 2nd ed.

Callaway, H., The Religious System of the AmaZulu, London: Folklore Society, Publications, 15, 1884.

Casalis, Eugene, The Basutos, London: John Nisbet, 1861.

Cook, P. A. W., Social Organization and Ceremonial Institutions of the Bomvana, Cape Town: Juta, 1931.

Earthy, E. Dora, VaLenge Women: The Social and Economic Life of the VaLenge Women of Portuguese East Africa, London: Oxford University Press for the International African Institute, 1933.

Galloway, M., Zululand and the Zulus: A Bibliography, Rondebosch, University of Cape Town, School of Librarianship, Bibliographical Series, 1944.

Gelfand, Michael, *Medicine and Magic among the Mashona,* Cape Town: Juta, 1956.

Gluckman, Max, "The Kingdom of the Zulu of South Africa," in Fortes, M., and Evans-Pritchard, E. E. (eds.), *African Political Systems,* London: Oxford University Press for the International African Institute, 1940, pp. 25-55.

Gluckman, Max, *Rituals of Rebellion in South-east Africa,* Manchester: Manchester University Press, 1954.

Holleman, J. F., "Some Shona Tribes of Southern Rhodesia," in Colson, Elizabeth, and Gluckman, Max (eds.), *Seven Tribes of British Central Africa,* London: Oxford University Press on behalf of the Rhodes-Livingstone Institute, 1951, pp. 354-95.

Holleman, J. F., *Shona Customary Law,* London: Oxford University Press, 1952.

Holleman, J. F., *Accommodating the Spirit amongst Some North-eastern Shona Tribes,* Cape Town: Oxford University Press for the Rhodes-Livingstone Institute, Rhodes Livingstone Papers, 22, 1953.

Junod, H. A., *Life of a South African Tribe,* London: Macmillan, 1927, 2 vols., 2nd ed.

Kidd, Dudley, *Savage Childhood, a Study of Kafir Children,* London: Black, 1906.

Krige, Eileen J., *The Social System of the Zulus,* Pietermaritzburg: Shuter and Shooter, 1936.

Krige, Eileen J., *The Realm of the Rain Queen: A Study of the Pattern of Lovedu Society,* London: Oxford University Press, 1943.

Kuper, Hilda, *An African Aristocracy: Rank among the Swazi,* London: Oxford University Press for the International African Institute, 1947.

Kuper, Hilda, *The Swazi,* Ethnographic Survey of Africa, Southern Africa, 1, 1952.

Kuper, H., Hughes, A. J. B., and Van Velsen, J., *The Shona and Ndebele of*

Southern Rhodesia, Ethnographic Survey of Africa, Southern Africa, 4, 1955.

Lagden, Godfrey, *The Basutos,* London: Hutchinson, 1909, 2 vols.

Laubscher, B. J. F., *Sex and Psychopathology: A Study of South African Natives,* London: Routledge, 1937.

Marwick, B. A., *The Swazi,* Cambridge: Cambridge University Press, 1940.

Mofolo, T., *Chaka, an Historical Romance,* trans. by F. H. Dutton, London: Milford for the International African Institute, 1931.

Reyher, R. H., *Zulu Woman,* New York: Columbia University Press, 1948.

Ritter, E. A., *Shaka Zulu: The Rise of the Zulu Empire,* London: Longmans, 1955.

Sachs, Wulf, *Black Hamlet,* London: Bles, 1947.

Schapera, Isaac, *Married Life in an African Tribe,* London: Faber and Faber, 1940.

Schapera, Isaac, "Political Organization of the Ngwato of Bechuanaland Protectorate," in Fortes, M., and Evans-Pritchard, E. E. (eds.), *African Political Systems,* London: Oxford University Press for the International African Institute, 1940, pp. 36-82.

Schapera, Isaac, *Native Land Tenure in Bechuanaland Protectorate,* Lovedale: Lovedale Press, 1943.

Schapera, Isaac, *The Political Annals of a Tswana Tribe,* Cape Town: University of Cape Town, Communications from the School of African Studies, 18, 1947.

Schapera, Isaac, *The Tswana,* Ethnographic Survey of Africa, Southern Africa, 3, 1953.

Schapera, Isaac, *The Ethnic Composition of Tswana Tribes,* London: London School of Economics, Monographs on Social Anthropology, 11, 1952.

Schapera, Isaac, *A Handbook of Tswana Law and Custom,* London: Oxford University Press for the International African Institute, 1955, 2nd ed.

Sheddick, V. G. J., *The Southern Sotho,* Ethnographic Survey of Africa, Southern Africa, 2, 1953.

Sheddick, V. G. J., *Land Tenure in*

Basutoland, London: H.M.S.O., Great Britain, Colonial Office, Colonial Research Studies, 13, 1954.

Sillery, A., *Sechele, the Story of an African Chief*, Oxford: G. Ronald, 1954.

Soga, J. Henderson, *The South-eastern Bantu (Abe-Nguni, Aba-Mbo, Ama-Lala)*, Johannesburg: University of Witwatersrand Press, 1930.

Soga, J. Henderson, *The Ama-Xosa: Life and Customs*, Lovedale: Mission Press, 1932.

Stayt, Hugh A., *The BaVenda*, London:

Oxford University Press, 1931.

Stevens, Pamela, *Bibliography of Bechuanaland*, Rondebosch: University of Cape Town, School of Librarianship, Bibliographical Series, 1947.

te Groen, Julie, *Bibliography of Basutoland*, Rondebosch: University of Cape Town, School of Librarianship, Bibliographical Series, 1946.

Ziervogel, D., *The Eastern Sotho: A Tribal, Historical and Linguistic Survey*, Pretoria: van Schaik, 1954.

KHOISAN PEOPLES

General

The Native Tribes of South West Africa, Cape Town: Cape Times, 1928.

Schapera, Isaac, *The Khoisan Peoples of South Africa*, London: Routledge, 1930.

More Specialized Studies

Bleek, Dorothea F., *The Naron: A Bushman Tribe of the Central Kalahari*, Cambridge: Cambridge University Press, 1928.

Dunn, Edward J., *The Bushman*, London: Griffin, 1932.

Engelbrecht, Jan A., *The Korana*, Cape Town: Maskew Miller, 1936.

Fourie, L., "Preliminary Notes on Certain Customs of the *Hei-//om* Bushmen," *Journal of the South West Africa Society*, 1925-26, 1, 49-63.

Hahn, T., *Tsuni//Goam, the Supreme Being of the Khoi-Khoi*, London: Trübner, 1881.

Hoernlé, A. W., "The Social Organization of the Nama Hottentots of South-West Africa," *American Anthropologist*, 1925, 27, 1-24.

Jones, J. D. R., and Doke, C. M. (eds.), *Bushmen of the Southern Kalahari*, Johannesburg, University of Witwatersrand Press, 1937.

Schapera, Isaac (ed.), *The Early Cape Hottentots*, Cape Town: Van Riebeeck Society, Publication 14, 1933.

Schapera, Isaac, "A Survey of the Bushman Question," *Race Relations*, 1939, 6, 68-83.

Tobias, Phillip V., "On the Survival of the Bushman," *Africa*, 1956, 26, 174-86.

Vedder, Heinrich, *Die Bergdama*, Hamburg: Friederichsen, 1923, 2 vols.

Vedder, Heinrich, *South-west Africa in Early Times*, trans. by C. G. Hall, London: Oxford University Press, 1938.

THE CONGO AND TROPICAL FOREST AREAS TO THE NORTH

General

Académie Royale des Sciences Coloniales [formerly Institut Royal Colonial Belge], Brussels, Classe de sciences morales et politiques, *Mémoires*.
Collection in-4°, 1938—.
Collection in-8°, old series, 1933-54.

Collection in-8°, new series, 1955—.
Aequatoria, Coquilhatville, Congo: Mission catholique, 1937—.
Collection de Monographies Ethnographiques, edited by C. Van Overbergh, Brussels: Albert de Wit, 1907-13, 11 vols.
DeCleene, N., Introduction à l'ethnographie du Congo Belge et du Ruanda-Burundi, Anvers: Kongo-Overzee Bibliotheek, 1957.
Folia Scientifica Africae Centralis. Informations de l'Institut pour la Recherche Scientifique en Afrique Central (I.R.S.A.C.), Bukavu, Belgian Congo, 1955—.
Institute d'Études Centrafricaines, Brazzaville.
   Bulletin, 1950—.
   Mémoires, 1948—.
Institut Français d'Afrique Noire, Doula, Études camerounaises, 1948—.

Kongo-Overzee, Antwerp, 1934—.
Maes, J., and Boone, O., Les peuplades du Congo Belge, Brussels, Bureau de Documentation Ethnographique, Série 2, Monographies idéologies, 1, 1935.
Musée Royal du Congo Belge, Tervuren, Annales, Sciences de l'homme.
   Ethnologie, 1954—.
   Monographies ethnographiques, 1954—.
Musée Royal du Congo Belge, Tervuren, Bureau de Documentation Ethnographique, Bibliographie ethnographique du Congo Belge et des régions avoisinantes, 1932—.
Problèmes sociaux congolais [formerly Bulletin du CEPSI], Elisabethville: Centre d'Études des Problèmes Sociaux Indigènes, 1946—.
Zaïre, revue congolaise, Brussels, 1947—.

More Specialized Studies

Alexandre, P., and Binet, J., Le group dit pahouin (fang—boulou—beti), Monographies ethnologiques africaines, 1958.
Ardener, Edwin, The Coastal Bantu of the Cameroons, Ethnographic Survey of Africa, Western Africa, 11, 1956.
Bittermieux, L., La société secrète des Bakhimba au Mayombe, Brussels: Institut Royal Colonial Belge, Classe de sciences morales et politiques, Collection in-8°, old series, 5, 3, 1936.
Burssens, H., Les peuplades de l'entre Congo-Ubangi, Ethnographic Survey of Africa, Central Africa, Belgian Congo, 4, 1958.
DeCleene, N., "La famille dans l'organisation sociale du Mayombe," Africa, 1937, 10, 1-15.
Douglas, Mary, "Alternate Generations among the Lele of the Kasai, Southwest Congo," Africa, 1952, 22, 59-65.
Douglas, Mary, "The Lele of Kasai," in Forde, Daryll (ed.), African Worlds: Studies in the Cosmological Ideals and Social Values of African Peoples, London: Oxford University Press for the International African Institute, 1954, pp. 1-26.
Douglas, Mary, "Social and Religious Symbolism of the Lele of the Kasai," Zaïre, 1955, 9, 385-402.
Gusinde, Martin, Die Kongo-pygmäen in Geschichte und Gegenwart, Nova Acta Leopoldina, N. F., 11, 76, 1942.
Gusinde, Martin, "Pygmies and Pygmoids: Twides of Tropical Africa," Anthropological Quarterly, 1955, 28, 3-61.
Gusinde, Martin, Die Twiden, Pygmäen und Pygmoide in Tropische Afrika, Vienna: Archiv für Völkerkunde, Veroffentlichungen, 3, 1956.
Lecoq, Raymond, Les Bamiléké, Paris: Éditions Africaines, 1953.
McCulloch, Merran, Littlewood, Margaret, and Dugast, I., The Peoples of the Central Cameroons, Ethnographic Survey of Africa, Western Africa, 9, 1954.
Schebesta, Paul, My Pygmy and Negro Hosts, London: Hutchinson, 1936.

Schebesta, Paul, *Revisiting My Pygmy Hosts,* London: Hutchinson, 1936.

Schebesta, Paul, *Die Bambuti-Pygmäen vom Ituri,* Brussels: Institut Royal Colonial Belge, Classe de sciences morales et politiques, Mémoires, Collection in-4°, Vol. 1; Vol. 2, No. 1 and 2; Vol. 4, 1938-50.

Schebesta, Paul, *Les pygmées du Congo Belge,* Brussels: Institut Royal Colonial Belge, Classe de sciences morale et politiques, Mémoires, Collection in-8°, old series, 26, 2, 1952.

Soret, Marcel, *Les Kongo nord-occidentaux,* Monographies ethnologiques africaines, 1959.

Tessman, Günter, *Die Pangwe,* Berlin: Wasmuth, 1913, 2 vols.

Torday, E., "The Influence of the Kingdom of the Kongo in Central Africa," *Africa,* 1930, *1,* 157-69.

Van der Kerken, G., *L'ethnie mongo,* Brussels: Institut Royal Colonial Belge, Classe de sciences morales et politiques,

Mémoires, Collection in-8°, old series, 12, 1-2, 1944.

Van Geluwe, H., *Les bira et les peuplades limitrophes,* Ethnographic Survey of Africa, Central Africa, Belgian Congo, 2, 1957.

Van Geluwe, H., *Mamvu-cangutu et balese-mvuba,* Ethnographic Survey of Africa, Central Africa, Belgian Congo, 3, 1957.

Vansina, J., *Les tribus ba-kuba et les peuplades apparentées,* Ethnographic Survey of Africa, Central Africa, Belgian Congo, 1, 1954.

Van Wing, J., *Etudes Bakongo.* Vol. 1, *Histoire et sociologie,* Brussels: Bibliothèque-Congo, 31, 1921; Vol. 2, *Religion et magie,* Brussels: Institut Royal Colonial Belge, Classe de sciences morales et politiques, Mémoires, Collection in-8°, old series, 9, 1, 1938.

Van Wing, J., "La polygamie au Congo Belge," *Africa,* 1947, *17,* 93-102.

WESTERN AFRICA

Brown, Paula, "Patterns of Authority in West Africa," *Africa,* 1951, 21, 261-78.

Butt-Thompson, Frederick W., *West African Secret Societies: Their Organisations, Officials and Teaching,* London: Witherby, 1929.

Forde, Daryll, "The Cultural Map of West Africa: Successive Adaptations to Tropical Forests and Grasslands," *Transactions of the New York Academy of Sciences,* 1953, series 2, 15, 206-19.

Gouilly, Alphonse, *L'Islam dans l'Afrique occidentale française,* Paris: Éditions Larose, 1952.

Historical Society of Nigeria, Ibadan, *Journal,* 1956—.

Institut Français d'Afrique Noire, Dakar, *Bulletin,* Série B, Sciences humaines, 1939—.
Mémoires, 1939—.
Notes africaines, 1939—.

General

Institut Français d'Afrique Noire, *Études dahoméennes,* Porto Novo, Dahomey, 1948—.
Études eburnéennes, Abidjan, Ivory Coast, 1952—.
Études guinéennes, Conakry, Guinea, 1947—.
Études mauritaniennes, Saint-Louis, Senegal, 1948—.
Études nigériennes, Niamey, Niger, 1953—.
Études sénégalaises, Saint-Louis, Senegal, 1949—.
Études soudanaises, Bamako, Soudan, 1953—.

Jones, Ruth, *West Africa,* London, International African Institute, Africa Bibliography Series, 1958.

Nigeria, Lagos: Government of Nigeria, 1934—.

Nigerian Institute of Social and Economic Research [formerly West African Institute of Social and Economic Research], Ibadan, *Annual Conference, Proceedings*, 1952—.

Parrinder, Geoffrey, *West African Religion*, London: Epworth Press, 1949.

Sierra Leone Studies, Freetown, old series, 1918-40; new series, 1953—.

Transactions of the Historical Society of Ghana [formerly *Transactions of the Gold Coast and Togoland Historical Society*], Achimota, 1955—.

Trimingham, John Spencer, *Islam in West Africa*, Oxford: Clarendon Press, 1959.

Guinea Coast

Akindélé, A., and Aguessey, C., *Contribution à l'étude de l'histoire de l'ancien royaume de Porto-Novo*, Dakar: Institut Français d'Afrique Noire, Mémoires, 25, 1953.

Ardener, Edwin, *Coastal Bantu of the Cameroons*, Ethnographic Survey of Africa, Western Africa, 11, 1956.

Bascom, William R., "The Sanctions of Ifa Divination," *Journal of the Royal Anthropological Institute*, 1941, 71, 43-54.

Bascom, William R., "The Principle of Seniority in the Social Structure of the Yoruba," *American Anthropologist*, 1942, 44, 37-46.

Bascom, William R., *The Sociological Role of the Yoruba Cult Group*, American Anthropological Association, Memoir, 63, 1944.

Bohannan, Laura, "Dahomean Marriage: A Revaluation," *Africa*, 1949, 19, 273-87.

Bradbury, R. E., *The Benin Kingdom, Together with a Section on the Itsekiri by P. C. Lloyd*, Ethnographic Survey of Africa, Western Africa, 13, 1957.

Cardinall, Allen W., *A Bibliography of the Gold Coast*, Accra: Government Printer, 1932.

Christensen, James Boyd, *Double Descent Among the Fanti*, New Haven, Human Relations Area Files, Behavior Science Monographs, 4, 1954.

Danquah, Joseph B., *Gold Coast: Akan Laws and Customs and the Akim Abuakwa Constitution*, London: Routledge, 1928.

Danquah, Joseph B., *Cases in Akan Law*, London: Routledge, 1928.

Danquah, Joseph B., *The Akan Doctrine of God, a Fragment of Gold Coast*

Ethics and Religion, London: Lutterworth Press, 1944.

Field, Margaret J., *Religion and Medicine of the Gã People*, London: Oxford University Press, 1937.

Field, Margaret J., *Social Organization of the Gã People*, Accra: Crown Agents for the Colonies, 1940.

Field, Margaret J., *Akim-Kotoku: An Oman of the Gold Coast*, London: Crown Agents for the Gold Coast Government, 1948.

Forde, Daryll, "Land and Labour in a Cross River Village, Southern Nigeria," *Geographical Journal*, 1937, 90, 24-51.

Forde, Daryll, "Government in Umor," *Africa*, 1939, 12, 129-61.

Forde, Daryll, *Marriage and the Family among the Yakö of South-eastern Nigeria*, London: London School of Economics, Monographs on Social Anthropology 5, 1941.

Forde, Daryll, "Double Descent Among the Yakö," in Radcliffe-Brown, A. R., and Forde, Daryll (eds.), *African Systems of Kinship and Marriage*, London: Oxford University Press for the International African Institute, 1950, 285-332.

Forde, Daryll, "Ward Organization among the Yakö," *Africa*, 1950, 20, 267-89.

Forde, Daryll, *The Yoruba-speaking Peoples of South-western Nigeria*, Ethnographic Survey of Africa, Western Africa, 4, 1951.

Forde, Daryll, and Jones, G. I., *The Ibo and Ibibio-speaking Peoples of South-eastern Nigeria*, Ethnographic Survey of Africa 3, 1950.

Fortes, Meyer, "Time and Social Structure: An Ashanti Case Study," in

Fortes, Meyer (ed.), *Social Structure: Studies Presented to A. R. Radcliffe-Brown*, London: Oxford University Press, 1940, pp. 54-84.

Fortes, Meyer, "Kinship and Marriage among the Ashanti," in Radcliffe-Brown, A. R., and Forde, Daryll (eds.), *African Systems of Kinship and Marriage*, London: Oxford University Press for the International African Institute, 1950, pp. 252-84.

Green, Margaret M., *Land Tenure in an Ibo Village*, London: London School of Economics, Monographs on Social Anthropology, 6, 1941.

Green, Margaret M., *Ibo Village Affairs*, London: Sidgwick & Jackson, 1947.

Harley, George W., *Native African Medicine: With Special Reference to Its Practice in the Mano Tribe of Liberia*, Cambridge: Harvard University Press, 1941.

Harley, George W., *Notes on the Poro in Liberia*, Cambridge: Harvard University, Peabody Museum Papers, 19, 2, 1941.

Harley, George W., *Masks as Agents of Social Control in Northeast Liberia*, Cambridge: Harvard University, Peabody Museum Papers, 32, 2, 1950.

Herskovits, Melville J., *Outline of Dahomean Religious Belief*, American Anthropological Association, Memoir, 41, 1933.

Herskovits, Melville J., *Dahomey: an Ancient West African Kingdom*, New York: Augustin, 1938, 2 vols.

Kaberry, Phyllis M., *Women of the Grassfields*, London: H.M.S.O., Great Britain, Colonial Office, Colonial Research Publications, 14, 1952.

Le Coeur, Charles, *Le culte de la génération de l'évolution religieuse et sociale en Guinée*, Paris: Leroux, 1932.

Little, Kenneth L., *The Mende of Sierra Leone*, London: Kegan Paul, 1951.

Lloyd, P. C., "The Traditional Political System of the Yoruba," *Southwestern Journal of Anthropology*, 1954, 10, 366-84.

Lystad, Robert, *The Ashanti: A Proud People*, New Brunswick, N. J.: Rutgers University Press, 1958.

Manoukian, Madeline, *The Akan and Ga-Adangme Peoples of the Gold Coast*, Ethnographic Survey of Africa, Western Africa, 1, 1950.

Manoukian, Madeline, *The Ewe-speaking People of Togoland and the Gold Coast*, Ethnographic Survey of Africa, Western Africa, 6, 1952.

McCulloch, Merran, *The Peoples of Sierra Leone Protectorate*, Ethnographic Survey of Africa, Western Africa, 2, 1950.

McCulloch, Merran, Littlewood, Margaret, and Dugast, I., *The Peoples of the Central Cameroons*, Ethnographic Survey of Africa, Western Africa, 9, 1954.

Mekeel, Scudder, "Social Administration of the Kru," *Africa*, 1937, 10, 75-96; 1939, 12, 460-68.

Meek, C. K., *Law and Authority in a Nigerian Tribe*, London: Oxford University Press, 1937.

Meyerowitz, Eva L. R., *The Sacred State of the Akan*, London: Faber and Faber, 1951.

Nketia, J. H., *Funeral Dirges of the Akan People*, Achimota: University College of the Gold Coast, Department of Sociology, 1955.

Odù, Journal of Yoruba and Related Studies, Ibadan: Ministry of Education, 1955—.

Paulme, Denise, *Les gens du riz: kissi de Haute-Guinée Francaise*, Paris: Plon, 1954.

Rattray, Robert S., *Ashanti*, London: Oxford University Press, 1923, 2nd impression, 1955.

Rattray, Robert S., *Religion and Art in Ashanti*, Oxford: Clarendon Press, 1927.

Rattray, Robert S., *Ashanti Law and Constitution*, London: Oxford University Press for the International African Institute, 1929.

Sarbah, John M., *Fanti Customary Laws*, London: W. Cloves, 1897.

Schwab, George, *Tribes of the Liberian Hinterland*, Cambridge: Harvard University, Peabody Museum Papers, 31, 1947.

Schwab, George, *The Rain Forest People*

of Liberia, Cambridge: Harvard University, Peabody Museum Papers, 30, 1947.

Spieth, Jakob, *Die Religion der Eweer in Süd-Togo,* Leipzig: Dieterich, 1911.

Talbot, D. Amaury, *Woman's Mysteries of a Primitive People: The Ibibios of Southern Nigeria,* London: Cassell, 1915.

Talbot, Percy A., *In the Shadow of the Bush,* London: Heinemann, 1912.

Talbot, Percy A., *The Peoples of Southern Nigeria,* London: Oxford University Press, 1926, 4 vols.

Tauxier, Louis, *Religion, moeurs et coutumes des agnis de la Côte d'Ivoire,* Paris, Geuthner, 1932.

Tessman, Günter, *Die Bubi auf Fernando Poo,* Hagen i. W. und Darmstadt: Folkwang-Verlag, 1923.

Tooth, G., *Studies in Mental Illness in the Gold Coast,* London: H.M.S.O., Great Britain, Colonial Office, Colonial Research Publications, 6, 1950.

Westermann, Diedrich H., *Die Kpelle,* Göttingen: Vandenhoeck & Ruprecht, 1921.

Western Sudan

Abraham, Roy C., *The Tiv People,* London: Crown Agents for the Colonies, 1933.

Armstrong, Robert G., "A West African Inquest," *American Anthropologist,* 1954, 56, 1051-75.

Beraud-Villars, J., *L'empire de Gao, un état soudanais au XVe et XVIe siècles,* Paris: Plon, 1942.

Bohannan, Laura and Paul, *The Tiv of Central Nigeria,* Ethnographic Survey of Africa, Western Africa, 8, 1954.

Bohannan, Paul, *Tiv Farm and Settlement,* London: H.M.S.O., Great Britain, Colonial Office, Colonial Research Studies, 15, 1954.

Bohannan, Paul, *Justice and Judgment among the Tiv,* London: Oxford University Press for the International African Institute, 1957.

Bovill, E. W., *Caravans of the Old Sahara,* London: Oxford University Press, 1933.

Bovill, E. W., *The Golden Trade of the Moors,* London: Oxford University Press, 1958.

Bowen, Elenore Smith (pseud.), *Return to Laughter,* London: Gollancz, 1954.

de Lestrange, Monique, *Les coniagui et les bassari,* Monographies ethnologiques Africaines, 1955.

Desplagnes, Louis, *Le plateau central Nigérien. Une mission archéologique et ethnographique au Soudan français,* Paris: Larose, 1907.

Dieterlen, Germaine, *Les âmes des dogons,* Paris: Institut d'Ethnologie, Travaux et mémoires, 40, 1941.

Dieterlen, Germaine, *Essai sur la religion bambara,* Paris: Presses Universitaires de France, 1951.

East, Rupert (ed. and trans.), *Akiga's Story: The Tiv Tribe as Seen by One of Its Members,* London: Oxford University Press for the International African Institute, 1939.

Forde, Daryll, Brown, Paula, and Armstrong, Robert G., *Peoples of the Niger-Benue Confluence: The Nupe, Igbira, Igala, and Idoma,* Ethnographic Survey of Africa, Western Africa, 10, 1955.

Fortes, Meyer, "The Political System of the Tallensi of the Northern Territories of the Gold Coast," in Fortes M., and Evans-Pritchard, E. E. (eds.), *African Political Systems,* London: Oxford University Press for the International African Institute, 1940, pp. 239-71.

Fortes, Meyer, *The Dynamics of Clanship among the Tallensi,* London: Oxford University Press for the International African Institute, 1945.

Fortes, Meyer, *The Web of Kinship among the Tallensi,* London: Oxford University Press for the International African Institute, 1949.

Fortes, Meyer, *Oedipus and Job in West African Religion,* Cambridge: Cambridge University Press, 1959.

Gamble, David, *The Wolof of Sene-*

gambia, together with Notes on the Lebu and the Serar, Ethnographic Survey of Africa, Western Africa, 14, 1957.

Ganay, Solange de, Les devises des dogons, Paris: Institut d'Ethnologie Travaux et mémoires, 41, 1941.

Goody, Jack R., The Social Organisation of the LoWiili, London: H.M.S.O., Great Britain, Colonial Office, Colonial Research Studies, 9, 1956.

Greenberg, Joseph H., The Influence of Islam on a Sudanese Religion, New York: Augustin, American Ethnological Society, Monograph, 10, 1946.

Greenberg, Joseph H., "The Negro Kingdoms of the Sudan," Transactions of the New York Academy of Sciences, 1949, series 2, 11, 126-35.

Griaule, Marcel, Jeux dogons, Paris: Institut d'Ethnologie, Travaux et mémoires, 32, 1938.

Griaule, Marcel, Masques dogons, Paris: Institut d'Ethnologie, Travaux et mémoires, 33, 1938.

Griaule, Marcel, Dieu d'eau; entretiens avec Ogotemmêli, Paris: Éditions du Chêne, 1948.

Griaule, Marcel, and Dieterlen, Germaine, "The Dogon," in Forde, Daryll (ed.), African Worlds: Studies in the Cosmological Ideas and Social Values of African Peoples, London: Oxford University Press for the International African Institute, 1954, pp. 83-110.

Gunn, Harold D., Peoples of the Plateau Area of Northern Nigeria, Ethnographic Survey of Africa, Western Africa, 7, 1953.

Gunn, Harold D., Pagan Peoples of the Central Area of Northern Nigeria, Ethnographic Survey of Africa, Western Africa, 12, 1956.

Haswell, M. R., Economics of a Savannah Village, London: H.M.S.O., Great Britain, Colonial Office, Colonial Research Studies, 8, 1953.

Heath, Frank (trans.), A Chronicle of Abuja, Ibadan: Ibadan University Press, 1952.

Hogben, S. J., The Muhammadan Emir-ates of Nigeria, London: Oxford University Press, 1930.

Holas, B., Les sénoufo (y compris les minianka), Monographies ethnologiques africaines, 1957.

Hopen, C. Edward, The Pastoral Fulbe Family in Gwandu, London: Oxford University Press for the International African Institute, 1958.

Kirk-Greene, Anthony H. M., Adamawa, Past and Present, London: Oxford University Press, 1958.

Labouret, H., Les tribus du rameau Lobi, Paris: Institut d'Ethnologie, Travaux et mémoires, 15, 1931.

Lebeuf, Jean-Paul, Fort Lamy (Tchad, A.E.F.), Paris: Éditions Union Française, 1951.

Lebeuf, Jean-Paul, and Masson-Detourbet, A., La civilisation du Tchad, Paris: Payot, 1950.

Manoukian, Madeline, Tribes of the Northern Territories of the Gold Coast, Ethnographic Survey of Africa, Western Africa, 5, 1952.

Meek, C. K., The Northern Tribes of Nigeria, London: Oxford University Press, 1925, 2 vols.

Meek, C. K., Tribal Studies in Northern Nigeria, London: Kegan Paul, 1931, 2 vols.

Meek, C. K., A Sudanese Kingdom: An Ethnographical Study of the Jukunspeaking Peoples of Nigeria, London: Kegan Paul, 1931.

Miner, Horace, The Primitive City of Timbuctoo, Princeton: Princeton University Press, 1953.

Monteil, Charles Victor, Une cité soudanaise, Djénné, métropole du delta central du Niger, Paris: Société d'Éditions Géographiques, Maritimes, et Coloniales, 1932.

Nadel, S. F., "The Kede, a Riverain State in Northern Nigeria," in Fortes, M., and Evans-Pritchard, E. E. (eds.), African Political Systems, London, Oxford University Press for the International African Institute, 1940, pp. 164-94.

Nadel, S. F., A Black Byzantium, London: Oxford University Press for the

International African Institute, 1942.
Nadel, S. F., *Nupe Religion,* London: Kegan Paul, 1954.
Palau Marti, Montserrat, *Les dogon,* Monographies ethnologiques africaines, 1957.
Pâques, Viviana, *Les bambara,* Monographies ethnologiques africaines, 1954.
Rattray, Robert S., *The Tribes of the Ashanti; Hinterland,* Oxford: Clarendon Press, 1932, 2 vols.
Rouch, Jean, *Les songhay,* Monographies ethnologiques africaines, 1954.
Smith, Mary F. (ed.), *Baba of Karo: A Woman of the Muslim Hausa,* London: Faber and Faber, 1954.
Smith, Michael G., *The Economy of Hausa Communities of Zaria,* London: H.M.S.O., Great Britain, Colonial Office, Colonial Research Studies, 16, 1955.
Stenning, Derrick J., *Savannah Nomads,* London: Oxford University Press, 1959.
Tait, David, "An Analytical Commentary on the Social Structure of the Dogon," *Africa,* 1950, 20, 175-99.

Tauxier, Louis, *Le noir du Soudan, pays mossi et gourounsi, documents et analyses,* Paris: Larose, 1924.
Tauxier, Louis, *La religion bambara,* Paris: Geuthner, 1927.
Tauxier, Louis, *Mœurs et histoire des peuls,* Paris: Payot, 1937.
Tauxier, Louis, *Histoire des bambara,* Paris: Geuthner, 1942.
Tessman, Günter, *Die Baja,* Stuttgart: Strecker & Strecker, 1934.
Urvoy, Yves, *Histoire des populations du Soudan central (Colonie du Niger),* Paris: Comité d'Études Historiques et Scientifiques de l'Afrique Occidentale Française, Série A, 5, 1936.
Urvoy, Yves, *Histoire de l'empire du Bornou,* Institut Français d'Afrique Noire, Mémoire, 7, 1949.
Worsley, P. M., "The Kinship System of the Tallensi: A Revaluation," *Journal of the Royal Anthropological Institute,* 1956, 86, 37-75.

AESTHETICS

African Music [formerly African Music Society, *Newsletter*], Johannesburg: African Music Society, 1948—.
Jones, A. M., *Studies in African Music,* London: Oxford University Press, 1959, 2 vols.
Kirby, P. R., *Musical Instruments of the Native Races of South Africa,* London: Oxford University Press, 1934.
Kyagambiddwa, J., *African Music from the Source of the Nile,* New York: Praeger, 1955.
Merriam, Alan, P., "African Music," in Bascom, William R., and Herskovits, Melville J. (eds.), *Continuity and Change in African Cultures,* Chicago: University of Chicago Press, 1959, pp. 49-86.
Sachs, Curt, *Les instruments de musique*

Music and Dance

de Madagascar, Paris: Institut d'Ethnologie, Travaux et mémoires, 28, 1938.
Tracey, Hugh, *Chopi Musicians,* London: Oxford University Press for the International African Institute, 1948.
Tracey, Hugh, *Ngoma: An Introduction to Music for Southern Africans,* Cape Town: Longmans, 1948.
Tracey, Hugh, *African Dances of the Witwatersrand Gold Mines,* Johannesburg: African Music Society, 1952.
Tucker, Archibald N., *Primitive Tribal Music and Dancing in the S. Sudan at Social and Ceremonial Gatherings,* London: Reeves, 1933.
Varley, Douglas H., *African Native Music: An Annotated Bibliography,* London: Royal Empire Society, Royal Empire Society Bibliographies, 8, 1936.

Folklore

Barker, W. H., *West African Folk Tales,* London: Harrap, 1917.

Bascom, William R., "The Relationship of Yoruba Folklore to Divining," *Journal of American Folklore,* 1943, 56, 127-31.

Bleek, W. H. I., *Reynard the Fox in South Africa,* London: Trübner, 1864.

Bleek, W. H. I., *Specimens of Bushman Folklore,* London: George Allen, 1911.

Cerulli, E., *Folk Literature of the Galla of Southern Abysinnia,* Cambridge: Harvard University, Peabody Museum, Harvard African Studies, 3, 1922.

Chatelain, H., *Folk-tales of Angola,* American Folklore Society, Memoirs, 1, 1894.

Courlander, Harold, and Leslau, Wolf, *The Fire on the Mountain, and Other Ethiopian Stories,* New York: Holt, 1950.

Doke, C. M., *Lamba Folk-lore,* American Folklore Society, Memoirs, 20, 1927.

Herskovits, Melville J., "Negro Folklore," in Shipley, Joseph T., *Encyclopedia of Literature,* New York: Philosophical Library, 1946.

Herskovits, Melville J. and Frances S., *Dahomean Narrative: A Cross-cultural Analysis,* Evanston: Northwestern University Press, African Studies, 1, 1958.

Herzog, George, and Blooah, Charles G., *Jabo Proverbs from Liberia,* London: Oxford University Press for the International African Institute, 1936.

Itayemi, Phebean, and Gurrey, P., *Folk Tales and Fables,* London: Penguin Books, 1953.

Laurence, Margaret (collector), *A Tree for Poverty: Somali Poetry and Prose,* Nairobi: Eagle Press, 1954.

Lestrade, G. P., *Some Venda Folk-tales,* Cape Town: University of Cape Town, Communications from the School of African Studies, 6, 1942.

Lestrade, G. P., *Some Kgatla Animal Stories,* Cape Town: University of Cape Town, Communications from the School of African Studies, 11, 1944.

Lindblom, K. G., *Kamba Folklore,* Upsala: Appelberg, 1928, 1934, 1935, 3 vols.

Radin, Paul, and Sweeney, James Johnson, *African Folktales and Sculpture,* New York: Pantheon Books, 1952.

Rattray, Robert S., *Hausa Folklore, Customs, Proverbs,* Oxford: Clarendon Press, 1913, 2 vols.

Rattray, Robert S., *Akan-Ashanti Folktales,* Oxford: Clarendon Press, 1930.

Tutuola, Amos, *The Palm-Wine Drinkard,* London: Faber and Faber, 1952.

Tutuola, Amos, *My Life in the Bush of Ghosts,* London: Faber and Faber, 1954.

Tutuola, Amos, *Simbi and the Satyr of the Dark Jungle,* London: Faber and Faber, 1955.

Tutuola, Amos, *The Brave African Huntress,* London: Faber and Faber, 1958.

Art

Bascom, William R., and Gebauer, Paul, *Handbook of West African Art,* Milwaukee: Milwaukee Public Museum, Popular Science Handbook Series, 5, 1953.

Bleek, Dorothea F., *Cave Artists of South Africa,* Cape Town: Balkema, 1953.

Breuil, Henri, *The White Lady of the Brandberg,* London: Trianon Press, 1955.

Brousse, Leopoldville: Les Amis de l'Art Indigène du Congo Belge, 1952—.

Burkitt, M. C., *South Africa's Past in Stone and Paint,* Cambridge: Cambridge University Press, 1928.

Cory, Hans, *African Figurines: Their Use in Puberty Rites in Tanganyika,* London: Faber and Faber, 1956.

Cory, Hans, *Wall-paintings by Snake Charmers in Tanganyika,* London:

Faber and Faber, 1953.

Elisofon, Eliot, and Fagg, William, *The Sculpture of Africa,* New York: Praeger, 1958.

Fagg, William, *The Webster Plass Collection of African Art,* London: British Museum, Department of Antiquities and Ethnography, 1953.

Fagg, William, "The Study of African Art," *Bulletin of the Allen Memorial Art Museum,* Winter, 1955-56, *12,* 44-61.

Gabus, Jean, *Au Sahara: arts et symbols,* Neuchatel: Baconnière, 1958.

Griaule, Marcel, *Masques dogons,* Paris: Institut d'Ethnologie, Travaux et Mémoires, 33, 1938.

Griaule, Marcel, *Folk Art of Black Africa,* New York: 1950.

Herskovits, Melville J., *The Backgrounds of African Art,* Denver: Denver Art Museum, 1945.

Junod, Henri P., and others, *The Art of Africa,* Pietermartizburg: Shuter & Shooter, 1958.

Langlois, P., *Art soudanais, tribus dogons,* Brussels: Marcel Évrier, 1954.

Lowe, C. van Riet, *The Distribution of Prehistoric Rock Engravings and Paintings in South Africa,* Union of South Africa, Department of Education, Arts and Science, Archaeological Survey, Archaeological Series, 7, 1952.

Maes, J., and Lavachery, H., *L'art nègre et l'exposition du Palais des Beaux Arts du 15 novembre au 31 décembre 1950.* Brussels: Librarie Nationale d'Arts et d'Histoire, 1930.

Nigerian Museum, *An Introduction to the Art of Ife,* Lagos: Nigerian Museum, 1955.

Olbrechts, F. M., *Plastiek van Kongo,* Brussels: N. V. Standard-Boekhandel, 1946.

Paulme, Denise, *Les sculpture de l'Afrique noire,* Paris: Presses Universitaires de France, 1956.

Plass, Margaret, *African Tribal Sculpture,* Philadelphia: University of Pennsylvania, University Museum, 1956.

Radin, Paul, and Sweeney, James Johnson, *African Folktales and Sculpture,* New York: Pantheon Books, 1952.

Sadler, Michael E. (ed.), *Arts of West Africa,* London: Oxford University Press for the International African Institute, 1935.

Tong, Raymond, *Figures in Ebony: Past and Present in a West African City,* London: Cassell, 1958.

Trowell, Margaret, *Classical African Sculpture,* London: Faber, 1954.

Trowell, Margaret, and Wachsmann, K. P., *Tribal Crafts of Uganda,* London: Oxford University Press, 1953.

Underwood, Leon, *Figures in Wood of West Africa,* London: Tiranti, 1947.

Underwood, Leon, *Masks of West Africa,* London: Tiranti, 1948.

Underwood, Leon, *Bronzes of West Africa,* London: Tiranti, 1949.

Willcox, A. R., *Rock Paintings of the Drakensberg, Natal and Griqualand East,* London: M. Parrish, 1956.

Wingert, Paul, *The Sculpture of Negro Africa,* New York: Columbia University Press, 1950.

SOCIAL CHANGE AND CONTEMPORARY PROBLEMS

General

Adam, Thomas R., *Government and Politics in Africa South of the Sahara,* New York: Random House, 1959.

Africa from the Point of View of American Negro Scholars, Paris: Présence Africaine, 1958.

Africa South, Cape Town, 1956—.

African Women, London: University of London, Institute of Education, Department of Education in Tropical Areas, 1955—.

L'Afrique et l'Asie, Paris, 1948—.

The American Assembly, *The United States and Africa,* Goldschmidt, Walter (ed.), New York: Columbia University, The American Assembly, 1958.

Bantu, Pretoria: Union of South Africa, Department of Native Affairs, 1954—.

Bascom, William R., and Herskovits, Melville J. (eds.), *Continuity and Change in African Cultures,* Chicago: University of Chicago Press, 1959.

Batten, T. R., *Problems of African Development,* London: Oxford University Press, 1947-48, 2 vols.

Bouchard, Joseph, *L'église en Afrique noire,* Paris: LaPalatine, 1958.

Buell, Raymond, *The Native Problem in Africa,* New York: Macmillan, 1928, 2 vols.

Cohen, Andrew, *British Policy in Changing Africa,* London: Routledge and Kegan Paul, 1959.

Comhaire, J., *Urban Conditions in Africa: Select Reading List on Urban Problems in Africa,* London: Oxford University Press for the Institute of Colonial Studies, 1952.

Comhaire, J., *Aspects of Urban Administration in Tropical and Southern Africa,* Cape Town: University of Cape Town, Communications from the School of African Studies, 27, 1953.

"Contemporary Africa, Trends and Issues," *Annals of the American Academy of Political and Social Science,* 1955, *298,* whole issue.

Drum [formerly *African Drum*], Johannesburg, 1951—.

Forde, Daryll, "Applied Anthropology in Government: British Africa," in Kroeber, A. L. (ed.), *Anthropology Today,* Chicago: University of Chicago Press, 1953, pp. 841-65.

Hailey, William Malcolm, *Native Administration in the British African Territories,* London: H.M.S.O., 1951-55, 6 vols.

Hailey, William Malcolm, *An African Survey,* London: Oxford University Press, 1957, rev. ed.

Haines, Charles C. (ed.), *Africa Today,* Baltimore: Johns Hopkins University Press, 1955.

International Missionary Council: *Survey of the Training of the Ministry in Africa,* London: International Missionary Council, 1950-54, 3 vols.

International Symposium on the Future of Customary Law in Africa, Amsterdam, 1955, Laiden: Universitaire Pers, 1956.

Journal of African Administration, London: H.M.S.O., Great Britain, Colonial Office, African Studies Branch, 1949—.

Journal of African Law, London, 1957—.

MacMillan, W. M., *Africa Emergent,* Harmondsworth: Penguin Books, 1949, rev. ed.

Malinowski, B., *The Dynamics of Culture Change,* New Haven: Yale University Press, 1945.

Methods of Study of Culture Contact in Africa, London: International African Institute, Memorandum, 15, 1938.

Perham, Margery (ed.), *Ten Africans,* London: Faber and Faber, 1936.

Perham, Margery, *Colonial Government: Annotated Reading List . . . ,* London: Oxford University Press for Nuffield College, 1950.

Read, Margaret, *Education and Social Change in Tropical Areas,* London: Nelson, 1954.

Rutherfoord, Peggy, *Darkness and Light: An Anthology of African Writing,* London: Faith Press, 1958.

Smith, Edwin W., *Plans and People! A Dynamic Science of Man in the Service of Africa,* London: Lutterworth Press, 1948.

South African Institute of International Affairs, *Africa South of the Sahara,* London: Oxford University Press, 1951.

Stillman, Calvin (ed.), *Africa in the Modern World,* Chicago: University of Chicago Press, 1955.

UNESCO, *Social Implications of Industrialization and Urbanization in Africa South of the Sahara,* Paris: UNESCO, 1956.

Westermann, Diedrich H., *The African Today and Tomorrow,* London: Oxford University Press for the International African Institute, 1949, 3rd ed.

Wilson, Godfrey and Monica H., *The Analysis of Social Change,* Cambridge: Cambridge University Press, 1945.

More Specialized Studies

Andersson, Efraim, *Messianic Popular Movements in the Lower Congo,* Upsala: Studia Ethnographica Upsaliensia, 14, 1958.

Apter, David E., *The Gold Coast in Transition,* Princeton: Princeton University Press, 1955.

Balandier, Georges, *Sociologie actuelle de l'Afrique noire; dynamique des changements sociaux en Afrique centrale,* Paris: Presses Universitaires de France, 1955.

Banton, Michael, *The Coloured Quarter: Negro Immigrants in an English City,* London: Jonathan Cape, 1955.

Banton, Michael, *West African City: A Study of Tribal Life in Freetown,* London: Oxford University Press for the International African Institute, 1957.

Beckett, W. H., *Akokoaso: A Survey of a Gold Coast Village,* London: London School of Economics, Monographs on Social Anthropology, 10, 1944.

Brown, G. Gordon, and Hutt, A. McG. Bruce, *Anthropology in Action,* London: Oxford University Press for the International African Institute, 1935.

Burrows, Raymond, *Indian Life and Labour in Natal,* Johannesburg: South African Institute of Race Relations, New Africa Pamphlet, 23, 1952.

Busia, Kofi A., *The Position of the Chief in the Modern Political System of the Ashanti,* London: Oxford University Press for the International African Institute, 1951.

Calpin, George H., *Indians in South Africa,* Pietermaritzburg, 1949.

Capelle, E., *La cité indigène de Léopoldville,* Leopoldville: Centre d'Études Sociales Africaines, and Centre d'Études des Problèmes Sociaux Indigènes, 1948.

Carter, Gwendolen M., *The Politics of Inequality: South Africa Since 1948,* London: Thames and Hudson, 1958.

Central African Examiner, Salisbury, 1957—.

Coleman, James S., *Nigeria: Background to Nationalism,* Berkeley: University of California Press, 1958.

Cowan, L. Gray, *Local Government in West Africa,* New York: Columbia University Press, 1958.

Datta, Ansu K., *Tanganyika: A Government in a Plural Society,* Leiden: 1955.

Delavignette, Robert, *Freedom and Authority in French West Africa,* London: Oxford University Press for the International African Institute, 1950.

DeKiewiet, Cornelius W., *The Anatomy of South African Misery,* London: Oxford University Press, 1956.

Duffy, James, *Portuguese Africa,* Cambridge: Harvard University Press, 1959.

Du Plessis, I. D., and Lückhoff, C. A., *The Malay Quarter and Its People,* Cape Town: Balkema, 1953.

Dvorin, Eugene P., *Racial Separation in South Africa: an Analysis of Apartheid Theory,* Chicago: University of Chicago Press, 1952.

Epstein, A. L., *The Administration of Justice and the Urban African: A Study of Urban Native Courts in Northern Rhodesia,* London: H.M.S.O., Great Britain, Colonial Office, Colonial Research Studies, 7, 1953.

Epstein, A. L., *Politics in an Urban African Community,* Manchester: Manchester University Press on behalf of the Rhodes-Livingstone Institute, 1958.

Fallers, Lloyd A., *Bantu Bureaucracy: A Study of Integration and Conflict in the Political Institutions of an East African People,* Cambridge: Heffer, 1956.

Fischer, E., *Die Rehobother Bastards und das Bastardierungs—problem beim Menschen,* Jena: Fischer, 1913.

Fortes, Meyer, "Ashanti Social Survey, a Preliminary Report," *Human Problems in British Central Africa,* 1948, 6, 1-36.

Galletti, R., Baldwin, K. D. S., and Dina, I. O., *Nigerian Cocoa Farmers: An Economic Survey of Yoruba Cocoa*

Farming Families, London: Oxford University Press, 1955.

Ghurye, Govind S., *Race Relations in Negro Africa,* Bombay: Asia Publishing House, 1952.

Gussman, B., "Industrial Efficiency and the Urban African," *Africa,* 1953, 23, 135-44.

Hance, William A., *African Economic Development,* New York: Oxford University Press for the Council of Foreign Relations, 1958.

Hellmann, Ellen, *Rooiyard, a Sociological Survey of an Urban Slum Yard,* Cape Town: Oxford University Press for the Rhodes-Livingstone Institute, Rhodes-Livingstone Papers, 13, 1948.

Hellmann, Ellen, *Sellgoods: A Sociological Survey of an African Commercial Labour Force,* Johannesburg: South African Institute of Race Relations, 1953.

Hellmann, Ellen, and Abrahams, Leah (eds.), *Handbook on Race Relations in South Africa,* London: Oxford University Press for the South African Institute of Race Relations, 1949.

Herskovits, Melville J., *The Myth of the Negro Past,* New York: Harper, 1941.

Hill, Polly, *The Gold Coast Cocoa Farmer, a Preliminary Survey,* London: Oxford University Press, 1956.

Hoernlé, R. F. Alfred, *South African Native Policy and the Liberal Spirit,* Johannesburg: Witwatersrand University Press, 1945.

Holden A., and Jacoby A., *Supplement to Select Bibliography of South African Native Life and Problems: Modern Status and Conditions,* Rondebosch: University of Cape Town, School of Librarianship, Bibliographical Series, 1950.

Hunter, Monica, *Reaction to Conquest: Effects of Contact with Europeans on the Pondo of South Africa,* London: Oxford University Press, 1936.

Hutchinson, Bertram, "Some Social Consequences of Nineteenth Century Missionary Activity among the South African Bantu," *Africa,* 1957, 26, 160-75.

International Missionary Council, *Survey of the Training of the Ministry in Madagascar,* London: International Missionary Council, 1957.

Issawi, Charles, *Egypt at Mid-Century,* 1954.

Jones, G. I., *Basutoland Medicine Murder: A Report on the Recent Outbreak of "Diretlo" Murders,* London: H.M.S.O., 1957.

Keiskammahoek Rural Survey, Pietermaritzburg: Shuter and Shooter, 1952, 4 vols.

Kuper, Hilda, *The Uniform of Colour,* Johannesburg: Witwatersrand University Press, 1947.

Kuper, Leo, Watts, Hilstan, and Davies, Ronald, *Durban: A Study in Racial Ecology,* New York: Columbia University Press, 1958.

Laye, Camara, *The African Child: Memories of a West African Childhood,* trans. from the French by James Kirkup, London: Collins, 1959.

Leakey, L. S. B., *Mau Mau and the Kikuyu,* London: Methuen, 1952.

Levin, R., *Marriage in Langa Native Location,* Cape Town: University of Cape Town, Communications from the School of African Studies, 17, 1947.

Lewin, Julius, *Studies in African Native Law,* Philadelphia; University of Pennsylvania Press, 1947.

Lewis, Roy, *Sierra Leone,* London: H.M.S.O., 1954.

Longmore, Laura, *The Dispossessed: A Study of the Sex-Life of Bantu Women in and around Johannesburg,* London: Jonathan Cape, 1959.

MacMichael, Harold A., *The Sudan,* New York: Praeger, 1954.

Mair, Lucy P., *Native Administration in Central Nyasaland,* London: H.M.S.O., Great Britain, Colonial Office, Colonial Research Studies, 5, 1952.

Mannoni, O., *Prospero and Caliban: The Psychology of Colonization,* trans. by Powesland, Pamela, London: Methuen, 1956.

Marquard, Leo, *The Peoples and Policies of South Africa,* London: Oxford University Press, 1952.

Marquard, Leo, and Standing, T. G., *The Southern Bantu*, London: Oxford University Press, 1939.

Meek, C. K., *Land Law and Custom in the Colonies*, London: Oxford University Press, 1946.

Murray, A. Victor, *The School in the Bush*, London: Longmans, Green, 1938, 2nd ed.

Natal Regional Survey, Cape Town: Oxford University Press for the University of Natal, 1951—.

Notcutt, L. A., and Latham, G. C., *The African and the Cinema*, London: Edinburgh House Press, 1937.

Oliver, Ronald Anthony, *The Missionary Factor in East Africa*, London: Longmans, Green, 1952.

Orde Browne, G. St. J., *The African Labourer*, London: Oxford University Press for the International African Institute, 1933.

Parrinder, Geoffrey, *Religion in an African City*, London: Oxford University Press, 1953.

Patterson, Sheila, *Colour and Culture in South Africa*, London: Routledge and Kegan Paul, 1953.

Perham, Margery (ed.), *The Economics of a Tropical Dependency*, Vol. 1, *The Native Economies of Nigeria*, ed. by Forde, Daryll, and Scott, Richenda, London: Faber and Faber, 1946.

Perham, Margery, *Native Administration in Nigeria*, London: Oxford University Press, 1937.

Phillips, Ray E., *The Bantu in the City*, Lovedale: Lovedale Press, 1938.

Powdermaker, Hortense, "Communication and Social Change Based on a Field Study in Northern Rhodesia," *Transactions of the New York Academy of Sciences*, 1955, Series 2, 17, 430-40.

Powdermaker, Hortense, "Social Change through Imagery and Values of Teenage Africans in Northern Rhodesia," *American Anthropologist*, 1956, 58, 783-813.

Richards, Audrey I., *Bemba Marriage and Present Economic Conditions*, Cape Town: Oxford University Press for the Rhodes-Livingstone Institute, Rhodes-Livingstone Papers, 4, 1940.

Richards, Audrey I. (ed.), *Economic Development and Tribal Change*, Cambridge: Heffer, 1954.

Schapera, Isaac (ed.), *Western Civilisation and the Natives of South Africa*, London: Routledge, 1934.

Schapera, Isaac, *Select Bibliography of South African Native Life and Problems*, London: Oxford University Press, 1941.

Schapera, Isaac, *Migrant Labour and Tribal Life*, London: Oxford University Press, 1947.

Shepherd, Robert H. W., *Bantu Literature and Life*, Lovedale: Lovedale Press, 1955.

Silberman, Leo, "Social Survey of the Old Town of Mombasa," *Journal of African Administration*, 2, 14-21.

Sillery, A., *The Bechuanaland Protectorate*, London: Oxford University Press, 1952.

Smith, Edwin W., *The Golden Stool*, London: Holborn Publishing House, 1927, 3rd ed.

Sofer, Cyril and Rhona, *Jinja Transformed: A Social Survey of a Multi-racial Township*, Kampala: East African Institute of Social Research, East African Studies, 4, 1955.

South African Institute of Race Relations, Johannesburg.
  Monograph Series, 1938—.
  New Africa Pamphlets, 1942—.
  Race Relations, Official Journal of the South African Institute of Race Relations, 1933—.

Southall, Aiden W., and Gutkind, Peter C. W., *Townsmen in the Making*, Kampala: East African Institute of Social Research, East African Studies, 9, 1956.

Talbot, David A., *Contemporary Ethiopia*, New York: Philosophical Library, 1952.

Taylor, John Vernon, *The Growth of the Church in Buganda*, London: S.C.M. Press, 1958.

Thompson, Virginia, and Adloff, Richard, *French West Africa*, Stanford:

Stanford University Press, 1958.

Thurnwald, Richard C., *Black and White in East Africa,* London: Routledge, 1935.

Van der Post, L., *The Lost World of the Kalahari,* London: Hogarth, 1958.

Villard, Henry S., *Libya: The New Arab Kingdom in North Africa,* Ithaca: Cornell University Press, 1956.

Wagner, Günter, *The Changing Family among the Bantu Kavirondo,* London: International African Institute, Memorandum, 18, 1939.

Wilson, Godfrey, *An Essay on the Economics of Detribalization in Northern Rhodesia,* Cape Town: Oxford University Press for the Rhodes-Livingstone Institute, Rhodes-Livingstone Papers, 5 and 6, 1941, 1942.

THE CONTRIBUTORS

J. A. BARNES, Head, Department of Anthropology and Sociology, The Australian National University, was trained at Cambridge, has been a Research Officer of the Rhodes-Livingstone Institute, and has taught at the University of London and the University of Sydney. He carried out field research among the Lamba of Northern Rhodesia in 1946, and among the Fort Jameson Ngoni between 1946 and 1949 while on the staff of the Rhodes-Livingstone Institute. More recently he has conducted research in the Norwegian parish of Bremnes. He is the author of numerous articles and the book, *Politics in a Changing Society,* and is coauthor of *The Lamba Village* (with J. C. Mitchell).

WILLIAM R. BASCOM, Director, Museum of Anthropology, University of California, Berkeley, was trained at the University of Wisconsin and at Northwestern University and has taught at Northwestern University. His field experience includes research among the Yoruba of Nigeria in 1937-38 and 1950-51, and he has also worked among the Kiowa of Oklahoma, the Gullah of Georgia and South Carolina, in Ponape in the Caroline Islands, and in Cuba. He has published *The Sociological Role of the Yoruba Cult-Group,* and is coeditor, with Melville J. Herskovits, of *Continuity and Change in African Cultures.* In addition, he has written a number of articles on folklore and on Africanisms in the New World.

PAUL BOHANNAN, Program of African Studies and Department of Anthropology, Northwestern University. Trained at the University of Oxford, he has taught there and also at Princeton University. He carried out twenty-eight months' research among the Tiv between 1949 and 1953 with his wife, Laura Bohannan, who is also an anthropologist. His works include *Justice and Judgment among the Tiv, Tiv Farm and Settlement,* and, with his wife, *The Tiv of Central Nigeria.*

ELIZABETH COLSON, Chairman, Department of Anthropology, Brandeis University, was formerly Director of the Rhodes-Livingstone Institute and has taught at Boston University in the African Research and Studies Program and at the University of Manchester. Trained at the University of Minnesota and at Radcliffe College, she has carried out field work among the Pomo and Makah Indians and extensive research among the Plateau Tonga of Northern Rhodesia. She is author of *The Makah Indians, Marriage and the Family among the Plateau Tonga of Northern Rhodesia,* and is coeditor (with Max Gluckman) of *Seven Tribes of British Central Africa.*

IAN G. CUNNISON, Department of Social Anthropology, University of Manchester. Trained at Cambridge and Oxford Universities, he has carried out field work in the Luapula Valley in 1948-51 as Research Officer of the Rhodes-Livingstone Institute, and among the Humr tribe of Baggara Arabs in 1952-55 as Anthropologist to the Sudan Government. He is author of *Kinship and Local Organization on the Luapula* and *History on the Luapula.*

MARY TEW DOUGLAS, Department of Social Anthropology, University of London, received her graduate training at Oxford University and carried out field research among the Lele of the Congo in 1949-50 and 1953. Her publications include *The Peoples of the Lake Nyasa Region* and numerous articles on the Lele.

E. E. EVANS-PRITCHARD, Head, Institute of Social Anthropology, Oxford University, received his graduate training at Oxford University and the University of London, and has taught at the London School of Economics, The Egyptian University at Cairo, the University of Cambridge, and the University of Chicago. He has also been a Fellow of the Center for Advanced Studies in the Behavioral Sciences, Stanford, California. His research includes work among the Azande, Nuer, Anuak, Luo, and other Nilotic groups in the Sudan area, and among the Sanusi of Cyrenaica. One of the most prolific of anthropologists, he has published *Witchcraft, Oracles and Magic among the Azande, The Nuer, Nuer Religion, Kinship and Marriage among the Nuer,* and the *Sanusi of Cyrenaica.* He is also the author of a general work, *Social Anthropology,* and co-editor (with Meyer Fortes) of *African Political Systems.* He has trained a generation of students at Oxford.

WILLIAM B. FAGG, Deputy Keeper of the Department of Ethnography, British Museum, was trained at Cambridge University, has been the editor of *Man,* and has carried out research in West Africa, particularly in Nigeria. Coauthor, with Eliot Elisofon, of *The Sculpture of Africa,* he has written numerous articles, especially on the art of Benin and Ife but also on African art in general.

LLOYD A. FALLERS, Department of Anthropology, University of Chicago, was trained at the University of Chicago and has taught at Princeton University and at the University of California, Berkeley. In addition, he has been a Fellow of the Center for Advanced Studies in the Behavioral Sciences, Stanford, California. He carried out field research among the Busoga in 1950-52, was subsequently Director of the East African Institute of Social Research, and has also worked in Buganda. He is the author of *Bantu*

Bureaucracy and a number of articles on the Busoga.

DARYLL FORDE, Director, International African Institute and Head of the Department of Anthropology, University of London, received his graduate training at the University of London and has taught at the University of Wales and at the University of California, Berkeley, California. He is editor of *Africa, African Abstracts,* and the *Ethnographic Survey of Africa.* His field investigations include work among the Yakö of southeastern Nigeria in 1935 and 1939. He has published numerous papers on the Yakö and a monograph, *Marriage and the Family among the Yakö of South-eastern Nigeria.* He is author of *Habitat, Economy and Society,* and he has also published papers on broad aspects of African culture and society and on social anthropology. He edited *African Worlds, Efik Traders of Old Calabar,* and is coeditor (with A. R. Radcliffe-Brown) of *African Systems of Kinship and Marriage.*

MEYER FORTES, William Wyse Professor of Social Anthropology in the University of Cambridge, was trained as a psychologist but later studied under Malinowski and Seligman. He has taught at the London School of Economics, the University of Oxford, and the University of Chicago as well as at Cambridge, and he has been a Fellow of the Center for Advanced Studies in the Behavioral Sciences, Stanford, California. He carried out field work among the Tallensi of Northern Ghana for nearly two and a half years between 1934 and 1937 and among the Ashanti of Southern Ghana in 1945-46. He has written two major works on the Tallensi, *The Web of Kinship among the Tallensi* and *The Dynamics of Clanship among the Tallensi,* and he has also published a number of important articles on the Ashanti, as well as on general social anthropology. He is coeditor (with E. E. Evans-Pritchard) of *African Political Systems,* and he has recently published *Oedipus and*

Job in West African Religion. He has pioneered in the study of African kinship and descent systems and political organization.

L. FOURIE. Formerly Medical Officer for the Government of South West Africa, he wrote two short but valuable papers based on his personal experiences, "Preliminary Note on Certain Customs of the *Hei-//om* Bushmen," and "The Bushmen of South West Africa."

MARCEL GRIAULE (1898-1956). Professor of Ethnology, University of Paris, and Consultative Director, International African Institute. Griaule carried out field work in Abysinnia in 1928-29, and from 1931 until his death he engaged in a series of field studies in the Western Sudan, particularly among the Dogon. He published numerous articles and a number of monographs on the Dogon, including *Masque dogons, Jeux dogons,* and *Dieu d'eau.* He had broad ethnological interests but his best-known studies are of Dogon cosmology.

JOSEPH H. GREENBERG, Department of Anthropology, Columbia University, has also taught at the University of Minnesota and Northwestern University, and he has been a Fellow of the Center for Advanced Studies in the Behavioral Sciences, Stanford, California. He carried out ethnographic field work among the Hausa of Northern Nigeria in 1938-39, on which he published a monograph, *The Influence of Islam on a Sudanese Religion,* and several articles. More recently he has conducted linguistic research in the Plateau area of Northern Nigeria, and he has developed a new classification of African languages, first published in a series of articles in the *Southwestern Journal of Anthropology* and later in a book, *Studies in African Linguistic Classification.* He has also written a number of important papers in theoretical linguistics.

P. H. GULLIVER, African Research and Studies Program, Boston University, took his graduate training at the London School of Economics and the University of London, and he has taught at the London School of Economics and at Harvard University. He has served as Government Sociologist in Tanganyika, Uganda, and Kenya. He has carried out lengthy research among the Turkana of Kenya and the Jie of Northern Kenya and of Uganda and has also studied labor migration in Tanganyika. He is the author of a general work on the Jie and Turkana, *The Family Herds,* as well as *The Central Nilo-Hamites* (with his wife, Pamela Gulliver) and *A Preliminary Survey of the Turkana.*

ELLEN HELLMANN received her graduate training at the University of Witwatersrand, and has carried out research in Johannesburg over many years. Active in the South African Institute of Race Relations for a long period of time, she has written extensively on racial and social problems of the Bantu in South Africa. In addition to her monograph, *Rooiyard, a Sociological Survey of an Urban Slum Yard,* she has written *Sellgoods: A Sociological Survey of an African Commercial Labour Force,* and edited (with Leah Abrahams) *Handbook on Race Relations in South Africa.*

MELVILLE J. HERSKOVITS, Director of Program of African Studies and Professor of Anthropology at Northwestern University, has taught at Columbia University, Howard University, and the University of Illinois, and he is past president of the American Folklore Society and former editor of the *American Anthropologist.* He conducted field research in Dahomey in 1931, and he has visited Africa a number of times since then. His research includes work in Dutch Guiana, Haiti, Trinidad, and Brazil. He is author of *Dahomey, An Outline of Dahomean Religious Belief, Dahomean Narrative* (with his wife, Frances S. Herskovits), and *Backgrounds of African Art,* and he is coeditor (with William R. Bascom) of *Continuity and Change in African Cultures.* In addition he has published extensively on Afro-American culture, primitive economics, acculturation, and general anthropology. As one of the pioneers of African studies in America he has been particularly concerned with religion and aesthetics and with culture change.

G. W. B. HUNTINGFORD, School of Oriental and African Studies, University of London, and editor of the *Journal of the Royal Anthropological Institute*. An administrative official in Tanganyika for a number of years, he has carried out extensive research among the Nandi and Dorobo and is the author of *The Nandi* and *Nandi Work and Culture*. His wide interests in East African anthropology and linguistics is indicated by his numerous publications, including *The Galla of Ethiopia, The Northern Nilo-Hamites,* and *The Southern Nilo-Hamites*.

HILDA KUPER received graduate training at London School of Economics, studying for two years under Malinowski, and has taught at the University of Witwatersrand and the University of North Carolina. She carried out research in Swaziland for six months beginning in October, 1934, and for eight months beginning in September, 1956, and she has made frequent trips to the Swazi since then. In addition she has conducted research in Johannesburg. She is author of *The Uniform of Colour, The Swazi, An African Aristocracy,* and a number of articles on the Swazi.

RALPH LINTON (1893-1953). Formerly Sterling Professor of Anthropology at Yale University, he also taught at the University of Winconsin and at Columbia University, and he was an Associate Curator of Anthropology at the Field Museum of Natural History, Chicago, where he was in charge of the North American Indian Collection. He received his doctorate at Harvard University and was sent to Marquesas in 1920-22 by the Bernice P. Bishop Museum as an archaeologist. Here he developed an interest in living Marquesans that was the turning point in his career. From 1925 to 1927 he carried out field research in Madagascar, mainly among the Tanala, and he also studied various American Indian groups. He published a major monograph on the Tanala, *The Tanala, a Hill Tribe of Madagascar,* and his general anthropological work, *The Study of Man,* was a major landmark in the development of American anthropology.

KENNETH L. LITTLE, Head, Department of Social Anthropology, University of Edinburgh, was trained at Cambridge University and the University of London, and he has taught at the London School of Economics, Fisk University , and the University of California, Los Angeles. He carried out field research in Sierra Leone in 1945 and 1946, in the Gambia in 1948, and he has also done research in Cardiff, Wales. He is the author of *The Mende of Sierra Leone, Race and Society,* and *Negroes in Britain*.

DANIEL F. McCALL, African Research and Studies Program, Boston University. Trained at Columbia University, he carried out field research in Koforidua, Ghana, in 1951-52 as a Fellow of the Social Science Research Council, New York. He has taught at the University of Liberia and has visited Africa several times since his original field research. He is the author of a number of articles on social change in Africa.

JACQUES J. MAQUET, Université Officielle du Congo Belge et du Ruanda-Urundi, Elisabethville, Belgian Congo. He studied at the University of Louvain, the University of London, and Harvard University, and he was formerly Director of the Centre de Recherches Scientifiques de l'Institut pour la Recherche Scientifique en Afrique Centrale (I.R.S.A.C.) at Astrida. Much of his basic field research in Ruanda was carried out between 1949 and 1951. He is author of *Le Système des Relations sociales dans le Ruanda ancien*, and of *The Sociology of Knowledge*, a critical study of Mannheim and Sorokin.

SIEGFRIED F. S. NADEL (1903-1956). Head of the Department of Anthropology and Sociology at the Australian National University at the time of his death, he also had taught at the London School of Economics, Durham University, and at Northwestern University. He had an early interest and training in music and then in psychology and philosophy, which he studied at the University of Vienna. He worked under Malinowski in England for two years beginning in 1932, and then entered upon a long research career, conducting field work among the Nupe and related groups in Nigeria between 1934 and 1936 and among the Nuba of the Anglo-Egyptian Sudan between 1938 and 1940. During the Second World War he served in the British Military Administration in Eritrea and Tripolitania. Nadel wrote two major works on the Nupe, *A Black Byzantium* and *Nupe Religion*, and also published *The Nuba, Land Tenure in the Eritrean Plateau,* and *The Races and Tribes of Eritrea*. In addition to his research activities he had a strong interest in problems of theory and method, and he wrote two general works, *The Foundations of Social Anthropology*, and *The Theory of Social Structure*. His interest in applied anthropology was reflected in his research, and in his essay, *Anthropology and Modern Life*.

ROBERT S. RATTRAY (1881-1938). He first went to Africa as a trooper in the South African War and afterward served the African Lakes Corporation in Nyasaland, where he collected folklore and stories in the Nyanja language. He went to the Gold Coast in the Customs Service in 1907, became an Assistant District Commissioner in 1911, a District Commissioner in 1915, and acting Senior Assistant Colonial Secretary and Clerk to the Legislative Council in 1920. Dur-

ing his leaves from duty in the Gold Coast he studied law and was admitted to the bar. He also received training in anthropology at Oxford under Marett. In 1921 he became the first head of the new Anthropology Department in the Gold Coast, having studied various groups in this country in preceding years. He investigated the Ashanti kingdom and the nature of the Golden Stool and published *Ashanti, Religion and Art in Ashanti, Ashanti Law and Constitution,* and *Tribes of the Ashanti Hinterland*. He also wrote *Hausa Folklore and Customs, An Elementary Mole Grammar, Akan-Ashanti Folk-tales*, and a novel, *The Leopard Princess*. After retirement he taught for the Colonial Service at the University of Oxford. He was an aviation enthusiast and had flown his own plane to the Gold Coast. After his retirement he took up the sport of gliding, and it was in a gliding accident that he met his death.

AUDREY I. RICHARDS, Newnham College, University of Cambridge, formerly Director of the East African Institute of Social Research. She took her graduate training at the University of Cambridge and the University of London and has taught at the University of London, London School of Economics, and the University of Witwatersrand. She has carried out extensive research among the Bemba in Northern Rhodesia and has worked also with the Kgatla of the Transvaal. Her broad anthropological interests are reflected in her publications, which include *Land, Labour and Diet in Northern Rhodesia, Bemba Marriage and Present Economic Conditions,* and *Chisungu: A Girls' Initiation Ceremony among the Bemba of Northern Rhodesia*. She edited *Economic Development and Tribal Change* and has written important papers on the kinship system of the matrilineal groups of South Central Africa.

ISAAC SCHAPERA, Department of Social Anthropology, London School of

Economics, took his graduate work at this school and has taught at the University of Witwatersrand, the University of Cape Town, and the University of Chicago. Between 1929 and 1935 he carried out extensive research among the Tswana, and he returned in subsequent years for further field work. In 1947 he carried out a survey of research needs in Kenya. He is the author of numerous works on the Tswana, including *Married Life in an African Tribe, A Handbook of Tswana Law and Custom,* and *Tribal Legislation among the Tswana.* He has been interested in the various African groups of South Africa, having published *The Khoisan Peoples of South Africa, Select Bibliography of South African Native Life and Problems,* and *Government and Politics in Tribal Societies,* and edited *The Bantu-speaking Tribes of South Africa* and *Western Civilization and the Natives of South Africa.*

DERRICK J. STENNING, Faculty of Archaeology and Anthropology, University of Cambridge, took his graduate training at Cambridge and has taught at the University of London. He carried out research among the Fulani of Northern Nigeria in 1951-53, and has published a book, *Savannah Nomads,* on these people. More recently he has been engaged in research on the Ankole under the auspices of the East African Institute of Social Research.

DAVID TAIT was Lecturer in Social Anthropology in the Department of Sociology at the University College of the Gold Coast at the time of his death in a motor accident in March, 1955. He received his graduate training at the University of London, and he carried out his major research among the Konkomba of Northern Togoland in 1950-52. He wrote numerous articles on this group and also published on the Dagomba and the Dogon. He is coeditor (with J. Middleton) of *Tribes without Rulers.*

COLIN M. TURNBULL is Assistant Curator, American Museum of Natural History, New York City, where he is in charge of the African Collection. He was trained at the Institute of Social Anthropology, Oxford, and has carried out field work in the Eastern Province of the Belgian Congo in 1954 and again in 1957-58.

GODFREY WILSON (1908-1944). He studied under Malinowski at the London School of Economics as a Fellow of the International African Institute. He married Monica Hunter in 1935, and they carried out field work together among the Nyakyusa and Ngonde people in 1935-38. Appointed the first Director of the Rhodes-Livingstone Institute of Northern Rhodesia in 1938, he established research standards and policies that have been followed by other African research institutes since that time. He had strong interests in the practical applications of anthropology, in primitive law and morality, and in economic change. He is the author of *Land Rights of Individuals among the Nyakyusa, Essay on the Economics of Detribalization in Northern Rhodesia,* and, with Monica Wilson, *The Analysis of Social Change.*

MONICA HUNTER WILSON, School of African Studies, University of Cape Town. She studied at the University of Cambridge and the London School of Economics, and she has taught at Fort Hare College and at Rhodes University College. She carried out field research among the Pondo of South Africa in 1931-32, and with her husband she worked among the Nyakyusa and Ngonde for a number of years. She wrote one of the first systematic studies of culture change in Africa, *Reaction to Conquest,* and with her husband published another major work in this field, *The Analysis of Social Change.* Her extensive publications on the Nyakyusa include *Good Company: An Analysis of Nyakyusa Age-Villages, Rituals of Kinship among the Nyakyusa,* and *Communal Rituals among the Nyakyusa.*

THE EDITORS

SIMON OTTENBERG received his B.A. from the University of Wisconsin in 1948 and his Ph.D. from Northwestern University in 1957. His doctoral thesis was "The System of Authority of the Afikpo Ibo of Southeastern Nigeria." He has taught at the University of Chicago, Washington State University, and at the University of Washington, where he is now an Associate Professor of Anthropology. From December 1951 to February 1953, he was in Nigeria as an Area Research Fellow for the Social Science Research Council, studying the system of authority and leadership in a group of 26 villages. His other field research includes a community study made in a small Negro fishing village near Savannah, Georgia.

Mr. Ottenberg has published articles on the Ibo in *Africa, African Studies,* the *Journal of African Administration,* and the *Southwestern Journal of Anthropology,* and in the book *Continuity and Change in African Cultures* (William R. Bascom and Melville J. Herskovits, eds.). His article "Leadership and Change in a Coastal Georgia Negro Community" appeared in the Spring 1959 issue of *Phylon.*

In August 1959, Mr. Ottenberg returned to Nigeria on a thirteen-month grant from the National Science Foundation, in order to continue his work among the Afikpo Ibo, especially to study social change and urban influences in the area.

PHOEBE VESTAL OTTENBERG was graduated from the University of Illinois in 1943 and received her Ph.D. from Northwestern University in 1958. She taught at the University of Washington, and then accompanied her husband on his return trip to Nigeria in 1959. On her first field trip to Nigeria in 1951-53, as an Area Research Fellow for the Social Science Research Council, she made a study of marriage and co-wife relations in the polygynous family. In addition to her doctoral thesis, "Marriage in the Double-Descent System of the Afikpo Ibo of Southeastern Nigeria," she is the author of "The Economic Position of Women Among the Afikpo Ibo," in *Continuity and Change in African Cultures* (William R. Bascom and Melville J. Herskovitz, eds.).

INDEX

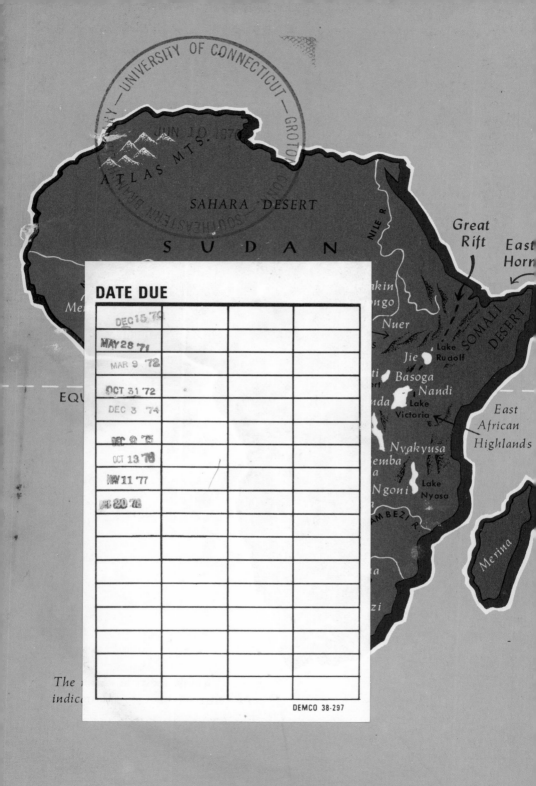

ATLAS MTS.

SAHARA DESERT

S U D A N

NILE R.

Great
Rift

East
Horn

akin
ongo

Nuer

SOMALI DESERT

Jie
Lake
Rudolf

Mer

Basoga
Nandi

EQU

Lake
Victoria

East
African
Highlands

DEC 3 '74

Nyakyusa

emba

Ngoni
Lake
Nyasa

ZAMBEZI R.

Merina

zi

The
indic